LUSITANIA

ALSO BY DIANA PRESTON

The Road to Culloden Moor:
Bonnie Prince Charlie and the '45 Rebellion

A First Rate Tragedy:
Robert Falcon Scott and the Race to the South Pole

The Boxer Rebellion:
The Dramatic Story of China's War on Foreigners
That Shook the World in the Summer of 1900

LUSITANIA

AN EPIC TRAGEDY

Diana Preston

WALKER & COMPANY, NEW YORK

First published in the United States of America in 2002
by Walker Publishing Company, Inc.

Every effort has been made to locate and contact all the holders of
copyright to material reproduced in this book.

For information about permission to reproduce selections
from this book, write to Permissions, Walker & Company,
435 Hudson Street, New York, New York 10014

Library of Congress Cataloging-in-Publication Data

Preston, Diana, 1952–
     Lusitania : an epic tragedy / Diana Preston.
         p.   cm.
     Includes bibliographical references and index.
     ISBN 0-8027-1375-0 (alk. paper)
     1. Lusitania (Steamship)   2. World War, 1914–1918—Naval operations, German.
3. World War, 1914–1918—Naval operations—Submarine.   4. Shipwrecks—
History—20th century.   5. World War, 1914–1918—Great Britain.
6. World War, 1914–1918—United States.   I. Title.

D592.L8 P74   2002
940.4'51343—dc21

                                                              2001056767

BOOK DESIGN BY RALPH L. FOWLER

Visit Walker & Company's Web site at www.walkerbooks.com

Printed in the United States of America

2 4 6 8 10 9 7 5 3 1

TO MY HUSBAND, MICHAEL

CONTENTS

Contents

LUSITANIA

Prologue

OWARD SUNSET on 7 May 1915, an alert member of a lifeboat crew spotted an intermittent flash of light from a dark shape bobbing on the gentle swell of the Irish Sea. The crew rowed closer, carefully avoiding the drifting debris of RMS *Lusitania*, the British luxury liner sunk by a German U-boat a few hours earlier. As they finally drew near, they found that the flashes were not the desperate signals of a last, despairing survivor. They came from a handsome diamond ring sparkling in the evening light on the well-manicured hand of a female corpse.

All that evening "a ghastly procession of rescue ships" drew alongside the quay at Queenstown, some twelve miles north of the disaster, on the southern coast of Ireland. Under flaring gas torches, they landed the living and the dead. Most survivors were in shock, wrapped in blankets and staring silently ahead. Many were injured; at least two quick amputations without any anesthetic took place aboard the rescue fleet. Adult corpses were lifted ashore on stretchers to be stacked "like cordwood . . . among the paint-kegs and coils of rope on the shadowy old wharves." Sailors gently carried dead children and babies in their arms to an improvised mortuary in an empty Cunard freight shed.

Waiting journalists recorded how one woman, a baby in her arms and a rough blanket donated by a sailor around her shoulders, refused to leave the quay. She waited, the very emblem of forlornness, "until the last survivor had passed, searching each face as it went by in the vain hope of finding her husband, from whom she had been separated in the last terrible scene on the liner's deck."

As one American survivor hobbled ashore, he put his hand in the pocket of his soaking Norfolk jacket to retrieve his spectacles. He found them wrapped in a scrap of newsprint that had almost turned to pulp. He put them on and inspected the paper more closely. On it was printed the warning inserted by the German embassy in the American press the day that the *Lusitania* had pulled away from New York's Pier 54 into the Hudson River for the last time. Under the headline "Notice !" it read: "Travellers intending to embark on the Atlantic voyage are reminded that a state of war exists between Germany and her allies and Great Britain and her allies; that the zone of war includes the waters adjacent to the British Isles; that, in accordance with formal notice given by the Imperial German Government, vessels flying the flag of Great Britain, or of any of her allies, are liable to destruction in those waters and that travellers sailing in the war zone on ships of Great Britain or her allies do so at their own risk." It was signed by the imperial German embassy, Washington, D.C.

Over the next few days a collective howl of outrage arose from the American and British press. "German Pirates Sink the Lusitania," proclaimed the *Daily Sketch*. "What Women and Children Endured When Murderers Sent the Lusitania to Her Doom" was the headline in the *Daily Mirror*. The *New York Nation* called the sinking "A Deed for Which a Hun Would Blush, a Turk Be Ashamed, and a Barbary Pirate Apologize." The papers told their shocked readers that some 1,200 passengers and crew, including more than 100 Americans, were dead or missing, among them the millionaire Alfred Vanderbilt. The U.S. ambassador to London telegraphed Washington that "the United States must declare war or forfeit European respect." America's entry into the conflict was expected to be only a matter of time.

In Germany the press hailed the sinking as a triumph of courage, seamanship, and superior technology. The *Kölnische Volkszeitung* declared it "a success of our submarines which must be placed beside the greatest achievement of this naval war." The commander in chief of the German High Seas Fleet sent an unprecedented message of congratulation to the U-boat commander Walther Schwieger and his crew. Crown Prince Wilhelm telegraphed his father, the kaiser, to report the "great joy" the news had caused among the German troops in France.

The day after the sinking, the local Irish coroner opened an inquest into the sinking in the town of Kinsale, near Queenstown. The main witness was the *Lusitania*'s captain, William Turner, now clad in an ill-fitting borrowed suit rather than the resplendent dark blue uniform in which he had been washed off the bridge of his ship. He described how the liner had been torpedoed without warning. She had immediately taken a heavy list to starboard, and he had been unable to stop his engines. These factors had made it difficult and dangerous to launch the lifeboats in the eighteen terrible minutes before the ship sank. At the end of his evidence Captain Turner bowed his head and burst into tears. The coroner and his jury took little time to reach their verdict. It was "wilful and wholesale murder" by the officers of the submarine and "the Emperor and Government of Germany under whose orders they acted."

Everything seemed clear-cut. But within minutes of the verdict came a message from the British Admiralty, belatedly trying to stop the inquest and prevent the captain from giving evidence about his secret instructions. Germany had already begun to issue claims that the *Lusitania* had been carrying Canadian troops to Britain; that she had been armed and that contraband ammunition, loaded in New York with the connivance of the American authorities, had exploded as a result of the torpedo strike, dramatically hastening her end; that Winston Churchill, the first lord of the Admiralty, had deliberately exposed the ship with a view to bringing America into the war. The *Lusitania*'s unsuspecting passengers—the German government alleged—had been mere human shields for hypocritical and self-serving British and American interests.

Britain retaliated with a successful propaganda campaign portraying the Germans, and the kaiser in particular, as ravening, barbaric "Huns" rejoicing in dead babies and "the latest achievements of German frightfulness at sea." The British and American press linked the sinking to the German army's first use, just a few days earlier on the Western Front, of a new "scientific torture"—poison gas. The German government began to imply that the sinking of the *Lusitania* had been a matter of chance and that the U-boat commander had not even identified his target when he unleashed his torpedo. The kaiser was deeply wounded by anti German comment in the world's press. Under pressure from America and from his own civilian ministers he ordered a cessation in Germany's campaign of unrestricted submarine warfare. Admiral Alfred von Tirpitz, the father of the German navy, complained that by abandoning his cherished campaign Germany had lost her best chance of winning the war,

British poster memorializing the sinking of the Lusitania.

and submitted his resignation. The United States remained neutral, and the kaiser now told the American ambassador that he would not have permitted the torpedoing had he known about it in advance. "No gentleman," he said, "would kill so many women and children."

Official hearings into the sinking were held in Britain, and later in America, after she entered the war in 1917 following Germany's resumption of unrestricted submarine warfare. Both governments worried that the finger of accusation might point in directions other than Germany's. Therefore they steered the hearings away from sensitive issues. As a result many questions were not fully answered. Why was a tragedy so clearly signaled and widely anticipated allowed to happen? Why did the British navy not provide the *Lusitania* with an escort? Why was the ship going so slowly on a dead straight course after receiving warnings about the presence of enemy submarines? What was really in her cargo hold? What were Captain Turner's "secret" orders? Why did the ship sink so quickly? Who were the mysterious stowaways who went down with the ship, and what were their links with the network of German spies and saboteurs operating in New York?

The *Lusitania* continued to cast a long shadow. The patriotic press reported how in late 1917 American doughboys advanced into battle with the cry "Remember the *Lusitania*!" In the summer of 1918 the kaiser, believing the war lost, ordered a review of the implications of the *Lusitania* sinking for an armistice and peace negotiations. He feared that the Allies might press war crimes charges. In 1937, with a second conflict with Germany approaching, Winston Churchill wrote of the importance of the sinking for the Allied cause: "In spite of all its horror, we must regard the sinking of the *Lusitania* as an event most important and favourable to the Allies. . . . the poor babies who perished in the ocean struck a blow at German power more deadly than could have been achieved by the sacrifice of a hundred thousand fighting men."

Over the years since, dives to the wreck and searches through mysteriously incomplete British and American archives have produced many, often conflicting, explanations and theories about what happened, but no conclusive answers to the questions so deliberately left unanswered.

The story of the *Lusitania* is, above all, about people—whether British, German, or American, whether afloat on the liner, submerged in the submarine, or enmeshed in the various government machines ashore. Many who lived through the extraordinary events were deeply affected by their experiences, not only the survivors waking night after night "in a sweat of terror" but also the politicians and officials whose careers and causes prospered or faltered as a result of the sinking. Based on personal accounts and on archives, including those in Germany, which have often been overlooked, this book tells the story of all those involved, wherever possible in their own words.

But their stories and this new material also provide a fresh perspective on why some acted as they did and how their actions and decisions influenced not only the fate of the *Lusitania* but, as a consequence, the outcome of the First World War and the conduct of warfare in general. They allow us to reconsider that charge of "wilful murder" made in the coroner's court in Kinsale on a warm May day in 1915. Was it really justified? And, if so, against whom?

PART ONE

Troubled Waters

CHAPTER ONE

A Scrap of Paper

A T THE OUTSET of the First World War, German chancellor Theobald von Bethmann Hollweg handed the Allies the moral high ground and an unassailable propaganda advantage. At 3 P.M. on 3 August 1914, the day Germany declared war on France and two days after she declared war on Russia, he rose to address a packed and expectant Reichstag. He informed his fellow countrymen that German troops, advancing on France, had occupied Luxembourg and were "already in Belgium." Then, in a moment of candor he would almost immediately regret, he added: "Our invasion of Belgium is contrary to international law but the wrong—I speak openly—that we are committing we will make good as soon as our military goal has been reached."

The next day the British ambassador to Berlin, Sir Edward Goschen, called on Bethmann Hollweg to present the British ultimatum: Quit Belgium or face Britain's entry into the war. Germany had until midnight to decide. Goschen found the chancellor "excited" and "very agitated"; he complained that Britain was committing an "unthinkable" act, "like striking a man from behind while he was fighting for his life against two assailants." Britain, the chancellor said, would be responsible for all the dreadful events that must follow, and it was all "just for a word—'neutrality,' a word which in war time had so often been disregarded"—all just "for a scrap of paper that Great Britain was going to make war on a kindred nation." This "scrap of paper" was the Treaty of London, signed by the European powers, including Prussia, in 1839 and guaranteeing Bel-

EUROPE
on the Eve of World War I

0 Miles — 300
0 Kilometers — 300

NORWAY

North Sea

Glasgow

Dublin

IRELAND

Liverpool

GREAT BRITAIN

THE NETHERLANDS

Brem

AMSTERDAM

Queenstown
(Cobh)

Thames R.

LONDON

BRUXELLES

BELGIUM

Rhine R.

LUX.

Atlantic Ocean

Brest

Seine R.

PARIS

Nancy

Basel

Loire R.

FRANCE

SWITZERLAN

Bay
of Biscay

Lyon

Milan

Garonne R.

Rhône R.

Toulouse

Duoro R.

Marseille

PORTUGAL

MADRID

Ebro

CORSICA

LISBON

Barcelona

S P A I N

SARDINIA

Guadalquivir R.

Mediterranean Sea

© 2002 Jeffrey L. Ward

OSLO

Gulf of Bothnia

FINLAND

6°

St. Petersburg

• STOCKHOLM

SWEDEN

55°

MOSCOW

DENMARK

• COPENHAGEN

Baltic Sea

Dvina

• Königsberg

Hamburg

Elbe R.

BERLIN

RUSSIAN EMPIRE

50°

Vistula R.

• Warsaw

GERMANY

Weser R.

Leipzig

Dresden

Oder R.

Frankfurt

• Prague

Cracow

Dniester R.

Danube R.

Munich

AUSTRO-HUNGARIAN

VIENNA

• Budapest

Odessa

45°

EMPIRE

Danube R.

BUCHAREST

Venice

ROMANIA

Danube R.

Black Sea

• BELGRADE

SERBIA

BULGARIA

ITALY

MONTENEGRO

• Sofia

Adriatic Sea

Tiber R.

CONSTANTINOPLE

Bosphorus

• ROME

40°

ALBANIA

Gallipoli

Dardanelles

Tyrrhenian Sea

GREECE

Aegean Sea

OTTOMAN EMPIRE

Ionian Sea

ATHENS

SICILY

35°

CRETE

Mediterranean Sea

Theobald von Bethmann Hollweg

gian neutrality. Goschen replied that if it was strategically a matter of life or death for Germany to advance through Belgium, it was equally a matter of life or death for Britain to keep her solemn compact.

It was still some hours before midnight and the expiry of the ultimatum when Goschen left to find newspaper billboards in the streets already proclaiming Britain's entry into the war. According to one of the diplomats within, a mob "of quite well-dressed individuals, including a number of women," gathered to stone the British embassy, smashing many of the windows. The crowd, stirred by the accusations of propagandists and the press, "seemed mad with rage and was howling 'Death to the English pedlar nation!'" that was guilty of *Rassen-verrat!*—race treason—against Germany, which, unlike Britain's allies, France and Russia, shared her origins. As the British diplomats prepared to depart, the embassy's three German servants, who had been paid off with a month's wages, "took off their liveries, spat and trampled on them and refused to help carry the trunks down to the taxi cabs."

In his unfortunate comments, Bethmann Hollweg had raised two issues that would be hotly debated throughout the Great War, issues of respect for international law and the balance between expediency and the rights of neutrals. In so doing he had placed Germany at such a disadvantage in the battle for the minds of neutral countries that she would never fully recover. Goschen duly reported to the foreign office in London what Bethmann Hollweg later claimed to have been a privileged and personal conversation, including the disparaging reference to the "scrap of paper." Goschen perhaps disingenuously said he had little idea of how the phrase would resonate. For his part, Bethmann Hollweg later commented: "My blood boiled at his hypocritical harping on Belgian neutrality, which was not the thing that had driven England into the war." Anglo-Saxon hypocrisy would soon become a familiar German charge against both Britain and America.

Many argued at the time, and many have argued since, that world war was not the inevitable consequence of the assassination in Sarajevo of Archduke Franz Ferdinand, heir to the throne of the Austro-Hungarian Empire, and of the empire's subsequent declaration of war on Serbia. David Lloyd George, then British chancellor of the Exchequer, later suggested that there was a general slide to a war that no nation really wanted. Others have argued that military mobilization, once begun, achieved a momentum of its own, even that summer holidays and consequent unfortunate delays in communication played a part in provoking war that summer of 1914 when tensions between the powers seemed, if anything, to have eased. A British battleship squadron was paying a courtesy visit to the Kiel Week regatta—a celebration of the imperial navy. The German officers were entertaining their guests with great bonhomie when news of the Sarajevo assassination reached both parties courtesy of the kaiser. He had learned of it himself while competing in one of the races aboard his yacht, the *Meteor*.

Other contemporaries and historians believed that war could not have been long delayed. There was tension between Austria and Serbia over borders; Russia, Germany, and Austria were at loggerheads over Slav rights; France was aching for revenge for her defeat by Prussia in the war of 1870–71 and to regain her lost provinces of Alsace and Lorraine; Germany was feeling hemmed in and deprived of the colonies and international status to which she felt her commercial and military strength entitled her. Her conservative leaders saw expansion abroad as a useful damper on liberal and socialist reforming aspirations at home. In seeking such expansion Germany was bound eventually to challenge Britain, either directly, by taking a portion of the Flanders coast (which was one of her later declared war aims), or indirectly, by challenging Britain's command of the seas and preeminence in maritime trade.

—∞∞—

By 1914, the naval rivalry between Britain and Germany was well established. Since the turn of the century their dramatically increasing expenditure had accelerated technical development and exacerbated international tensions. Strong, charismatic personalities dominated the Admiralties of both nations. The sixty-five-year-old secretary of state for the imperial German navy, Alfred von Tirpitz, had been born plain Alfred Tirpitz, son of a lawyer and a physician's daughter. He joined the navy not out of enthusiasm but because he was "very mediocre" at school. Hearing that a friend was to join, he decided that "it might mean a certain relief for [his] parents" if he too "were to take up the idea." During his early years at sea he came into close contact with the British navy and admired its methods. While a gunnery officer in 1877, he reported enthusiastically on a visit to the Whitehead Torpedo Company in Fiume and was immediately put in charge of torpedo development for the German navy. He tried to render the wildly unstable torpedoes more reliable. "I worked on them," he later recalled, like "a tinker with my own hands."

Tirpitz's success was rewarded by appointment as chief of staff of the Baltic Squadron in 1890. A few months later he attended a dinner at Kiel Castle with the army chief of staff, General Helmuth von Moltke, along with several admirals and generals. Their host, the kaiser, was seeking advice on the future of the navy. Tirpitz kept silent throughout a long, desultory, and inconclusive discussion but eventually, at a sign from his senior officer, gave a spirited exposition of his vision of a stronger navy, one equipped with battleships rather than the cruisers currently deployed. His views coincided exactly with the kaiser's aspirations.

As a result, Tirpitz was soon in Berlin as chief of staff to the navy high command, where, at the kaiser's personal behest, he was to devise a strategy for a German high seas fleet. His forthright views, bluntly expressed, brought him into conflict with much of the naval establishment. In particular he irked the secretary of state for the navy, Admiral

Admiral Alfred von Tirpitz

Friedrich Hollmann, whom Tirpitz wrote off as a "high-minded man who was never quite clear as to the direction to be followed!"

For a time Tirpitz seemed likely to lose out in this power struggle, but in January 1896 his memorandum calling for a German fleet of seventeen battleships reached the kaiser. It was excellent timing. The kaiser was bitterly regretting his impotence to influence events in South Africa following the Jameson raid precisely because of his lack of a high seas fleet. Hollmann did not last long thereafter. On 6 June 1897 Tirpitz replaced him as secretary of state for the navy, the post he still held in August 1914. Just nine days after his appointment he presented a 2,500-word top-secret memorandum claiming that "for Germany at the moment the most dangerous naval enemy is England. . . . the strategy against England demands battleships in as great a number as possible." He went on to argue for nineteen such vessels. By March 1898 a naval bill had passed through the Reichstag but only after Tirpitz had secured the support of former chancellor Otto von Bismarck, the armaments magnate Gustav Krupp, and Albert Ballin, president of the Hamburg-Amerika Line, whose ships were becoming a force on the transatlantic route. A second naval bill followed in 1900, at the height of the Anglo-Boer War. The kaiser awarded Tirpitz his ennobling "von," and Britain began to worry that Germany might rival her naval supremacy.

Prime among those doing the worrying was Admiral "Jackie" Fisher. In the spring of 1902 his successful three-year tour of duty in command of Britain's Mediterranean Fleet was coming to an end, and his future looked uncertain. He felt he had been "tabooed" by the Admiralty for his radical ideas and that, at sixty-one, he had no further chance of advancement. This did not prevent him from arguing to everyone who would listen that "the Germans are our natural enemies everywhere. We ought to unite with France and Russia."

John Arbuthnot Fisher in some ways resembled Tirpitz. Both men combined passionate beliefs with a facility for winning converts to them. Fisher was born in January 1841 in Sri Lanka; his father was an ex–army officer and failed coffee planter, his mother the daughter of a failed wine merchant. He was brought up from the age of six in London by his maternal grandfather and never lost the sense of being abandoned by his parents. He later claimed, not entirely accurately, that when he joined the navy he was "penniless, friendless and forlorn." He was more correct in describing the arcane entrance tests of the time: "I wrote out the Lord's Prayer and the doctor made me jump over a chair naked and I was given a glass of sherry."

Once in, he made swift progress. He became a great advocate of torpedoes. Upon his promotion to captain at age thirty-three, he became commander of the newly established torpedo school at Portsmouth. After that his rise was even faster, interrupted only by periodic bouts of dysentery and malaria. The latter left him with a sallow, yellow complexion that his enemies, imbued with the racist sentiments of their day, maliciously attributed to Malay or Singhalese blood—a charge which wounded Fisher and which he took pains to refute in his memoirs.

To his credit, Fisher was at least as good at making friends as enemies. He was a man of great charisma, intelligence, frankness, and humor. He was also a superb dancer. The czar's sister, Grand Duchess Olga, wrote to him: "I believe, dear Admiral, that I would walk to England to have another waltz with you." He made other eminent conquests, including Queen Victoria, and through her won the ear of the Prince of Wales. Fisher lectured him ebulliently and forcefully about the right way to run a navy. His plan was simple: less bureaucracy, less ship painting, and far fewer time-wasting drills; far more training, far better gunnery, heavier armaments, a broader officer-recruitment base, and a new emphasis on torpedoes and defenses against them.

Admiral Lord John Arbuthnot "Jackie" Fisher

Once, when he was in full flow, the Prince of Wales asked plaintively, "Would you kindly leave off shaking your fist in my face?"

Fisher's language was exaggerated and colorful. He signed letters "Yours till hell freezes" and "Yours till charcoal sprouts." He was often tactless and execrated his enemies in the vilest terms. The existence of politicians had "deepened his faith in Providence. How else could one explain Britain's continued existence as a nation?" His temperament was mercurial, his laughter infectious, but his anger quiveringly awesome. He wrote as he spoke—impetuously—and never revised his words. His large, bold scrawl was peppered with exclamation marks, double and triple underlinings, and frequent admonitions to the reader to burn his letters after a quick scan to protect his confidences. Fortunately for the historian, few followed his advice.

If Fisher's good characteristics, his decisiveness and ability to command, grew more pronounced with age and increased power, then so did his bad ones, particularly his lack of patience and restraint. In May 1899 he was appointed a member of the British delegation to the first Hague Peace Conference, called by the czar to try to limit arms, to define a code to mitigate the horrors of war, and to develop a system of arbitration that would solve international disputes and thus render war obsolete.

Fisher charmed his fellow delegates and "danced down everyone else in the ballroom." His influence on the conference was mostly exercised through informal conversations. At every opportunity he derided the objective of humanizing war as naive: "The humanising of war? You might as well talk about humanising Hell! The essence of war is violence! Moderation in war is imbecility! . . . I am not for war, I am for peace. That is why I am for a supreme Navy. The supremacy of the British Navy is the best security for the peace of the world. . . . If you rub it in both at home and abroad that you are ready for instant war . . . and intend to be first in and hit your enemy in the belly and kick him when he is down and boil your prisoners in oil (if you take any) . . . and torture his women and children, then people will keep clear of you." An enemy's realization of the horrors of war, coupled with conviction about Britain's readiness to fight, was the best deterrent. It was his duty, Fisher said, to see that his country, and in particular her navy, was prepared.

Fisher was equally impatient with the delegates' debate about the theoretical rights of "neutral shipping" carrying supplies to the enemy: "Suppose that war breaks out, and I am expecting to fight a new Trafalgar on the morrow. Some neutral colliers try to steam past us into the enemy's waters. If the enemy gets their coal into his bunkers, it may make all the difference in the coming fight. You tell me I must not seize these colliers. I tell you that nothing that you, or any power on earth, can say will stop me from sending them to the bottom, if I can in no other way keep their coal out of the enemy's hands; for to-morrow I am to fight the battle which will save or wreck the Empire. If I win it, I shall be far too big a man to be affected about protests about the neutral colliers; if I lose it, I shall go down with my ship into the deep and then protests will affect me still less."

Fisher's next posting, and the one which in 1902 he had believed would be his last, was to command the Mediterranean Fleet. But then, much to his surprise, he was offered the post of second sea lord at the Admiralty. He so excelled that he was soon made commander in chief, Portsmouth. Fisher now argued ever more passionately in favor of submarines, promoting them against opposition from what he called reactionary "fossil" admirals. He predicted "these invisible demons" would have an awesome effect on troop transports, whose frightened human cargoes would confront the prospect of "Death near—momentarily—sudden—awful—invisible—unavoidable!"

On 21 October 1904, Trafalgar Day, Fisher became first sea lord, the professional head of the Royal Navy. Now he was in a position to implement all his plans. He went at it with a will and with little regard for the enemies he made within the navy. He scrapped ninety obsolete ships, useful only for showing the flag and providing a comfortable billet for elderly admirals on foreign stations. Other ships were transferred unmanned to the reserve. In accordance with his belief that the enemy was Germany, he concentrated the fleet in home waters. He ordered submarines. Above all he built the world's first all-big-gun battleship, HMS *Dreadnought*, which rendered all others obsolete at a stroke. She took only fourteen months from the laying of her keel to her acceptance into the Royal Navy in December 1906. Among her many advanced features were steam turbines, like those incorporated in the *Lusitania*, also launched in that year.

Tirpitz and the German navy responded by announcing both an increased battleship building program and plans to enlarge the Kiel Canal to allow their new battleships to make their way easily and swiftly from the Baltic to the North Sea. Fisher accurately predicted both the cost and timetable for the canal widening and that Germany would go to war after bringing in the harvest in the year of its completion: 1914.

Fisher by now had many opponents in the British navy, chief among them Admiral Lord Charles Beresford, a generally amiable but obstinate, rich, aristocratic Anglo-Irish officer. He was rumored to have been the lover of the murdered Empress Elizabeth of Austria. He shared her passion for riding to hounds, surpassing it to the extent of having a hunting scene tattooed across his buttocks with the fox disappearing into the cleft. In naval matters he had a high opinion of his own abilities and a low one of Fisher's. He considered Fisher's very existence a threat to his own prospects for promotion. He opposed anything Fisher advocated, whether it was submarines, emphasis on gunnery, or concentration of forces, and he made unrestrained use of press and political contacts. Such was the support for Beresford's opinions that Fisher rushed ever more quickly at his reforms with ever less concern for the feelings of others, so that he could complete them quickly in case Beresford ousted him.

Eventually, Beresford's insubordination became both so blatant and so well publicized that in March 1909, following a confrontation with Fisher's ally Rear Admiral Sir Percy Scott, he was forced to retire. Their argument was over the relative merits of gunnery practice, about which Scott was fanatical, and Beresford's alleged preference for preserving pristine paintwork. It was an unseemly and very public squabble. As it turned out, Scott also had to retire, and, not long after, so too did Fisher, despite an inquiry into the conduct of naval affairs that broadly exonerated him.

The navy's wounds needed time to heal away from the public spotlight. Fisher was not a conciliator; nor was he at his best when not playing to an audience, preferably an appreciative one. He was now raised to the peerage as Lord Fisher of Kilverstone, with the apposite motto Fear God and Dread Nought. Lord Charles Beresford became a Conservative member of Parliament and a thorn in the flesh of whoever was responsible for the Admiralty.

Meanwhile, the naval race between Britain and Germany had been accelerating. In 1912, Tirpitz secured an additional 15,000 men for what was now a very substantial German navy. Britain adjusted her own plans and encouraged the Russians' ambitions to augment their Baltic Fleet. Since October 1911, Britain's Liberal government had had a new first lord of the Admiralty: Winston Churchill.

It is difficult to view Churchill in 1911 free of hindsight about what he became in 1940. He was then a young man in a hurry who had already been home secretary. He was born in November 1874 to Randolph Churchill, the duke of Marlborough's second son, and his wife, the beautiful twenty-year-old American Jennie Jerome, a Wall Street heiress. Randolph soon discovered symptoms of syphilis and no longer slept with his wife but concentrated on politics while she discreetly took lovers. Neither of them showed any interest in their son and never visited him during his wretchedly unsuccessful school days, despite his pleadings and pathetic attempts to attract their attention. His father died when Churchill was twenty-one. So too did his nanny, to whom he was devoted as the only consistent source of affection during his childhood.

After Sandhurst, Churchill went both as an army officer and a successful reporter wherever the military action was: Cuba, the northwest frontier in India, the last-ever cavalry charge of the British army at Omdurman in the Sudan, and, of course, South Africa, where he was captured in a Boer attack on an armored train. His spectacular escape, and his thrilling first-person account of it for the *Morning Post*, made him a national hero, and for the first time his mother took notice and promoted his career. In September 1900 he was elected a member of Parliament, which he was to remain, almost uninterrupted, until just before his death sixty-five years later. "Restless, egotistical, bumptious, shallow-minded and reactionary but with a certain personal magnetism, great pluck and some originality"—that is how the socialist Beatrice Webb described him during his early years in Parliament. Originally a Conservative, he crossed the floor to join the Liberals, serving as trade secretary before being appointed home secretary and then first lord.

The first lord was the cabinet minister responsible for the navy. The first sea lord, as the senior professional sailor, was directly answerable to him. In theory there was a clear distinction between the professional role of naval strategy, tactics, and operations and the political one. In practice Fisher had often ignored the bounds, crossing into the political sphere just as Churchill now crossed into strictly naval matters. The German naval attaché in London, Captain Erich von Müller, reported to the kaiser that "the sea-officers of the British Navy are often enraged against Mr. Churchill in spite of their unlimited appreciation of his merits in Navy politics, for the youthful civilian Churchill . . . puts on the air of a military superior. Through his curt behaviour he offends the older officers in their feeling of rank and personal pride. And thus . . . through his lack of tact he injures discipline by his ambition for popularity with the lower ranks, especially the 'Lower Deck.' " The kaiser noted against this paragraph: "Thus, even in England civilians and the military don't get along!"

Churchill had settled in quickly at the Admiralty and adopted a reforming program. This was at least in part due to the advice he had wisely sought from Fisher and which the admiral had given in great quantity. Lord Charles Beresford was predictably as fierce a critic of Churchill as he had been of Fisher. Churchill brushed his labored parliamentary questions and rambling interventions aside, once saying of Beresford's performance as an M.P. that before he got up to speak he did not know what he was going to say, that when he was on his feet he did not know what he was saying, and that when he sat down he did not know what he had said.

Despite the British and German ordering and counterordering of new ships, both Churchill and the German administration were conscious of the cost and the potential threat to world peace. They held

Winston Churchill

inconclusive discussions in 1911 and 1912 about a pause in the naval race. In June 1913, Churchill tried again through private conversations with Captain Müller. Müller, who disliked the British, sought advice direct from Tirpitz rather than from his ambassador. Tirpitz suggested he make a brief report through his formal diplomatic reporting chain to the German foreign office noting Churchill's proposal but suggesting that it was a mere ploy to delay Germany's naval plans. He did so, and the initiative foundered.

Müller's actions in consulting Tirpitz about how best to manipulate the foreign office were symptomatic of the conflict between the kaiser's civilian ministers and his immensely influential professional military and naval advisers. This conflict was crucial both to the slide to war and to the conduct of naval and in particular submarine operations thereafter. Put simply, the tall, imposing, chain-smoking chancellor, Theobald von Bethmann Hollweg, and the diminutive foreign minister, Gottlieb von Jagow, were more inclined to caution and to acquiring a better appreciation of the likely reactions of other nations than the military and naval staff who advocated confrontation and, later, unrestrained action. Unfortunately for

Germany, the key battleground for these sparring factions was the uncertain, troubled, and shifting ground of the kaiser's mind.

—❧—

The kaiser, formally Wilhelm II, emperor of Germany and king of Prussia, was born on 27 January 1859, the first grandchild of Queen Victoria, then only thirty-nine herself. His mother was Queen Victoria's eldest daughter, Victoria, whose nickname was Vicky, and his father the Prussian heir Frederick, known to the British royal family as Fritz. To Queen Victoria he was "our darling grandchild . . . a fine fat child with beautiful white soft skin, very fine shoulders and limbs." In fact, he had a damaged left arm due to a birth injury for which his mother felt responsible. It was Princess Victoria's aim to make her son a liberal, constitutional ruler. When he was only twelve she wrote home with surprising candor: "He is not possessed of brilliant abilities, nor of any strength of character or talents, but he is a dear boy and I hope and trust will grow up a useful man . . . there is little of his Papa or the family of Prussia about him."

Kaiser Wilhelm II

Over time, following his marriage to Princess Auguste Viktoria of Schleswig-Holstein, known to her family as Dona, and under the growing influence of his grandfather Kaiser Wilhelm I and the Bismarcks, the young Wilhelm began to grow away from his parents and their liberal views. In 1886 his father objected to his involvement in foreign office business: "Considering the unripeness and inexperience of my eldest son, together with his leaning towards vanity and presumption, and his overweening estimate of himself, I must frankly express my opinion that it is dangerous as yet to bring him into touch with foreign affairs." Wilhelm became almost totally estranged from his parents. Then, in March 1888, his grandfather died. His father, terminally ill with cancer of the throat, ruled for only three months. Wilhelm became emperor on 15 June 1888, when he was just twenty-nine. Within two years he had dropped his pilot Bismarck. He wrote triumphantly: "The position of officer of the watch on the ship of state has fallen to me. The course remains the same. Full steam ahead!"

Wilhelm loved ships in fact as well as in metaphor, and it was for this reason, as well as for political and commercial considerations, that Tirpitz's naval vision and Albert Ballin's Hamburg-Amerika ocean liners captured his imagination. He was always bombarding Tirpitz with suggestions for new ship designs following any discussion he had aboard ship with naval officers. Tirpitz wrote: "I could never discover how to ward off the frequent interference of the Emperor whose imagination, once it had fixed on shipbuilding, was fed by all manner of impressions. . . . Suggestions are cheap in the Navy and change like a kaleidoscope."

Wilhelm was a complex and contradictory character. Bismarck had convinced him that it was the emperor's prerogative to rule. Ministers were responsible to him and not the Reichstag, and he could dismiss them at will. Furthermore, the Reichstag could exercise only limited budgetary powers. The kaiser was also head of the armed forces, with the title "supreme warlord." He involved himself in military and naval decisions at all levels, although he could play only a limited part in exercises since his staff took the view that "as Kaiser he cannot be beaten by one of his generals." He was disdainful of democracy and, in consequence, failed to understand both the power of public opinion in Britain and America and how to manipulate it—a failing that severely damaged his country's relations with both those powers.

The young kaiser had, however, been deeply devoted to his British grandmother. He rushed to Victoria's bedside when she was dying in 1901 and is said to have held her in his arms as she passed away. He believed that good relations between ruling monarchs meant that they could between them arbitrate the destiny of the world. On the very eve of war, in late July 1914, he placed great credence in an account from his brother Henry, then yachting in England at Cowes, of a conversation with King George V in which the latter said that Britain would remain neutral. He told a skeptical Tirpitz: "I have the word of a King and that is good enough for me." When Britain declared war, he complained, childishly and pathetically, "George [George V of England] and Nicky [the czar] have played me false! If my grandmother had been alive she would never have allowed it."

The kaiser's relationship with Britain was his most ambivalent. He admired not only his grandmother but much else about the country, especially its might, but felt this was not reciprocated. At a personal level he complained that his uncle Edward VII, whom he loathed, while only Prince of Wales had treated him, already an emperor, too lightly. He formally requested Edward to call him "Your Imperial Highness" rather than "nephew." Edward wondered privately whether his nephew was a little deranged. Similarly, Wilhelm believed that Britain treated Germany too lightly and that she should recognize Germany's new position in the world and share power with the country that shared her race. Together they could order the world.

Initially rebuffed, Wilhelm misread the British character. He thought that building a powerful rival navy would compel Britain to concede some of her power and that she would at least remain aloof while Germany "sorted out" Europe. Bismarck had shared his view of the British, writing: "I have had all through my life sympathy for England and its inhabitants but these people do not want to let themselves be liked by us." Tirpitz also was something of an Anglophile; he spoke fluent English, read English books, sent his daughters to Cheltenham Ladies College, and admired the British navy wholeheartedly. But he too had come to feel patronized, complaining at the outbreak of war that "the English think they can treat us like Portugal." Nevertheless, when a distressed and weary Bethmann Hollweg told the German cabinet on 3 August that Britain's entry into the war was inevitable, Tirpitz is said to have cried, "All is then lost!" James Gerard, American ambassador to Berlin, described just what a terrible blow it was: "The army and all Germany believed . . . that Great Britain would remain neutral, and that Germany would consequently become, if not the actual owner, at least dictator of the world."

Resentment of years of being patronized, mingled with feelings of inferiority and "race betrayal," focused German hatred on Britain more than on any other belligerent nation. But as the early months of the war progressed and the German push through Belgium into France was halted at the Marne River and before Paris, German bitterness grew toward neutral America as well. The United States not only was seen as linked to Britain through culture, language, and history but was fast becoming the Allies' armory. Ambassador Gerard described the hostility he encountered even in the opening phases of the war as he was driven through an angry crowd and was "assailed by the peculiar hissing word that the Germans use when they are especially angry, and which is supposed to convey the utmost contempt. This word is 'Pfui,' and has a peculiar effect when hissed out from thousands of Teutonic throats."

<hr />

Back home across the Atlantic, the American press had tended to favor the Serbs in the crisis that followed Franz Ferdinand's assassination but had not seen events in Europe as likely to affect the United States. The *North Dakota Daily Herald* said of the assassination, "One archduke more or less makes little difference." The *Philadelphia Public Ledger* caught this semidetached mood in its punning piece of 28 July 1914 addressed to Austro-Hungary: "If the Serbs defeat you it will 'Servia right'!" There was also a view that the Europeans were sensible enough and cost-conscious enough to pull back. One columnist considered that the great safeguard "against the armies and navies Europe has gathered for war is that Europe is not rich enough to use them and is too human and humane to want to use them." These views reflected a consciousness on Americans' part of their rapidly increasing wealth compared with Europe's but also a misplaced and sentimental trust in the mature wisdom and civilized values of their "mother countries."

War, when it came, was a shock to the American public. Most had forgotten about the Serb assassination. However, as Count Johann von Bernstorff, the German ambassador to Washington, noted, Germany's invasion of Belgium turned sympathy toward the Allies. The same columnist previously quoted wrote that "the invasion of Belgium changed the

Woodrow Wilson

whole face of affairs. As if by a lightening flash the issue was made plain; the issue of the sacredness of law; the rule of the soldier or the rule of the citizen; the rule of fear or of law."

Such emphasis on the rule of law chimed well with the views of Woodrow Wilson's administration, then in the second year of its first term. Many of its members, including the president himself and William Jennings Bryan, his secretary of state, were lawyers. They believed in the application of reason and the use of mediation to solve international disputes and saw the United States as well able "to reap a permanent glory" by restoring peace.

Woodrow Wilson was born in December 1856, of Scottish descent, the son of a Presbyterian minister. He was a sickly child and could not read before the age of twelve, when he at last went to school. He soon made up ground, studying law at Princeton, where he founded a new society, the Liberal Debating Club, modeled on the British Parliament. He became an ardent enthusiast for cabinet government, mulling over the speeches of Britain's Liberal prime minister William Gladstone.

Following further legal studies, Wilson practiced law for a year but soon returned to academia. In 1890 he was back at Princeton as professor of jurisprudence and political economy. By 1902 he was president of the university, which he set out to reform to produce principled young men dedicated to serving the state. He introduced a tutorial system based on Oxford and Cambridge Universities. Both his views and his ability to express them began to attract attention beyond academic circles. In 1907, after temporarily losing the sight of one of his eyes, attributed by one doctor to hardening of the arteries, he was told to rest and took a cottage in England's Lake District for the summer. He enjoyed it, becoming even fonder of William Wordsworth. His health also appeared to recover completely, but in fact over the years ahead he was to suffer periodic bouts of exhaustion.

Wilson now grew disenchanted with college life and turned to politics. He ran successfully for governor of New Jersey in 1910. One of his key campaign advisers was a young Irish-American, Joe Tumulty. In 1912, still with Tumulty as his aide, he won a closely fought contest to become the Democratic candidate for president. In the election the Republican vote was split by Theodore Roosevelt, who was running as a Progressive. Wilson beat Roosevelt by 2 million votes and the Republican incumbent, William Howard Taft, by nearly 3 million. Their combined votes were 1 million more than his. Wilson moved into the White House. Tumulty was installed in his outer officer as his private secretary and acted as a buffer between the somewhat reserved, patrician, constitutionally delicate president and the demands of officials, press, public, and politicians.

Wilson's secretary of state, William Jennings Bryan, was thrice a candidate for the presidency himself, and his support had been crucial to Wilson's success at the Democratic Convention. Bryan was born in 1860 in Salem, Illinois. He was a lifelong fundamentalist Christian and teetotaler. After earning a law degree and getting married at a young age, he moved out to Nebraska. One evening he stood in for an absent speaker at a Democratic Party rally and was so well received that he rushed home, woke his wife, and told her: "I found I had power over the audience. I found I could move them as I chose. . . . God grant that I may use it wisely." Then he knelt by the bed and prayed. He was swiftly elected to Congress and then, at the age of just thirty-six, was chosen as the Democratic Party's presidential candidate in 1896. He was only narrowly defeated by William McKinley. The Democrats chose him again

William Jennings Bryan

in 1900, but he lost again to McKinley, and in 1908, when he lost to Taft. On each occasion, though, he won over 6 million votes—more than Wilson secured when winning against divided opposition in 1912. He remained a powerful force on the left of the Democratic Party for whom a post had to be found in government.

At home, Bryan's politics were to support labor rights against Wall Street big business. Abroad, he had always been a champion of the Hague treaties and of arbitration, seeing the United States as a "republic . . . becoming the supreme moral factor in disputes." Propounding the benefits of peace and arbitration at home and abroad occupied much of his time both before and after he became secretary of state. He supplemented his income as a congressman by frequent performances on the lecture circuit. His audiences' response convinced him they shared his love of peace, but many American commentators doubted whether Bryan's intellect and political acumen matched his eloquence and undoubted sincerity.

One of his first actions on taking office as secretary of state in 1913 was to persuade most of the major powers—Great Britain and France among them, but not Germany—to sign treaties committing themselves, to some extent at least, to the use of cooling-off periods and arbitration to settle international disputes. At the signing ceremony Bryan presented the diplomats with paperweights in the symbolic form of plowshares, cast from old swords from the Washington Naval Yard. On one side was engraved the phrase "Nothing is final between friends," while on the other was the biblical quote from Isaiah about the beating of swords into plowshares.

Britain and America had been drawing closer over the preceding years. As Rudyard Kipling expressed it, Britain was beginning to look consciously to the United States to "take up the white man's burden" of policing and arbitrating the world's affairs. Together they had devised a solution to border problems in Venezuela. Britain had given moral support to the United States during the Spanish-American War. The two countries had cooperated both in suppressing the Boxer Rebellion in China and in pursuing an open-door policy in that country, allowing free trade for all, rather than the colonization favored by Russia and Germany.

Britain had also supported the United States when, despite Bryan's pacifist principles, she had intervened militarily in Mexico in April 1914. American forces had seized Vera Cruz in an attempt to prevent a German Hamburg-Amerika Line ship, the *Ypiranga*, from delivering German arms to the Mexican dictator Victoriano Huerta for use against internal rebels. Within days Bryan had apologized to Germany for exceeding international law, and the *Ypiranga* had slipped away to deliver her cargo lower down the Mexican coast. The crisis was smoothed over. However, as a result of a loss of prestige, Huerta's regime fell to the rebels in July 1914. A German cruiser bore the embittered dictator into exile. Key to Germany's support of the dictator was the desire to disrupt the supply of Mexican oil to the British navy and to divert American attention from events in Europe. Germany would persist in both these objectives.

A further token of the rapprochement between Britain and America was that the British Admiralty had left the American navy out of the equation when making her "two power naval strength" calculation. The purpose of the calculation was to ensure that Britain had a navy strong enough to defeat the next two strongest naval powers in the event they formed an alliance against her. The grounds for excluding America were that war with the United States was inconceivable.

The political situation, the ties of language and culture, and the president's own personal affinity with Britain all meant that in August

1914 there was no chance of the United States allying herself with Britain's enemies. However, this was far from implying that America would actually join Britain and the Allies. George Washington's advice to avoid foreign wars and entangling alliances and the Monroe Doctrine's renunciation of involvement in Europe's affairs remained potent. A poll of newspaper editors in late 1914 showed that 105 favored the Allies, 20 the Germans, but 242 thought themselves neutral. Even among those leaning toward the Allies, there was virtually no support for any precipitate action by the United States. In their turn, the Allies were content to rely on benevolent neutrality and the munitions with which America supplied them. After all, if America joined the war, she would want to join them in dictating the peace.

In the days immediately leading up to the outbreak of war, Wilson himself was preoccupied with domestic tragedy. He and his wife, Ellen, were a devoted couple—he referred to them as "wedded sweethearts." Now she was dying of kidney disease. Wilson, when he first heard of Austro-Hungary's declaration of war on Serbia, put his hands to his face and said, "I can think of nothing, nothing when my dear one is suffering." Ellen died on 6 August. Just three days earlier Wilson had made his first public pronouncement on the war at a press conference. He told the eager newsmen that America "stood ready" to help the rest of the world resolve their differences peacefully. On 18 August he asked his people to be "neutral in fact as well as in name . . . impartial in thought as well as in action" so that the United States could "speak the counsels of peace" and "play the impartial mediator."

Yet over the next few months Wilson and his government were to find their principles of neutrality and impartiality and adherence to the tenets of international law challenged and buffeted on all sides. They would have to contend with the demands of American commerce and British and German declarations of blockade and counterblockade. Above all, they would have to respond to Germany's relentless use of a new weapon, the submarine, which would not only disrupt the transatlantic trade and passenger routes but also challenge the accepted rules of war.

CHAPTER TWO

The Weapon of the Weaker Nation

*T*HE RAPID PACE of submarine development in the years immediately preceding the First World War owed much to the naval race between Germany and Britain, although in both countries the idea of an underwater vessel as a serious offensive weapon was initially derided.

The concept of underwater warfare was nothing new. In classical times Thucydides described how divers were used as underwater saboteurs at the Siege of Syracuse in 413 B.C. In the Middle Ages Arab historians related how some kind of underwater apparatus was used to get a message into Acre while the crusaders besieged it. Leonardo da Vinci sketched a form of diving suit but refused to disclose his detailed plans because he feared such equipment might be used to attack ships.

In 1578 William Bourne, an English scientist and mathematician, designed a submersible that could rise and sink by filling or emptying ballast tanks on either side—a key characteristic of modern submarines. Early in the next century Dutchman Cornelius Van Drebbel is said to have demonstrated a vessel based on Bourne's design on the River Thames. But it was not until over a century later, during the War of Independence, that the Americans produced the first documented precursor of the modern submarine when, in what George Washington described as an "effort of genius," former Yale student David Bushnell launched his submersible *Turtle* against HMS *Eagle* in New York Harbor on 6 September 1776.

The egg-shaped *Turtle* was a one-man vessel, seven feet high and four feet wide. She was made of oak and equipped with four portholes, three

The Turtle

sleeved armholes, and an access hatch on top. She was propelled by two hand-operated screws—a vertical one to propel her up and down and a horizontal one to move her backward and forward. A foot-operated valve in the bottom let water flow in to help her descend, while a foot pump pushed it out again to enable her to rise. Bushnell's plan was for the *Turtle* to attach an underwater bomb with a time-delayed detonator to the *Eagle*. This involved manipulating a giant corkscrewlike device to drill into the *Eagle*'s hull, fasten the bomb by a chain, and then pull away smartly before it exploded. However, the attack failed. The *Turtle*'s operator, Sergeant Ezra Lee—a last-minute stand-in for the inventor's brother Ezra Bushnell, who had been struck down by fever—was unlucky. The section of the *Eagle*'s hull into which he was trying to drill was reinforced with a metal plate. After several futile attempts and with his air supply running out, Lee surfaced and fled. As dawn broke, the British spotted the *Turtle* and gave chase. Lee released his bomb, which exploded in the water to the consternation of his pursuers, and reached safety.

Another American, Robert Fulton, an amateur engineer from Pennsylvania, followed up Bushnell's work. Fulton believed that navies (and the British navy in particular) were instruments of oppression and thus a threat to his ideals of universal peace. In 1797, when Britain was at war with France, the thirty-two-year-old Fulton arrived in Paris and began experimenting with floating mines on the River Seine. Before long he approached the French revolutionary government with plans to construct a "mechanical machine," the *Nautilus*, for "the annihilation" of the British fleet. When the British *Naval Chronicle* got wind of the project, it denounced the inventor as "a crafty, murderous ruffian."

Fulton launched the copper-skinned *Nautilus* in May 1801. She was the first submarine to be built of metal. Her barrel-like shape resembled Bushnell's *Turtle*. Despite an initially favorable reception, the low speed and limited range of the *Nautilus* convinced Napoleon that she was, after all, useless, and he dismissed Fulton as a crank. Abandoning his anti-British stance, Fulton retired in a huff across the Channel to try to interest the British. However, with Britain's victory over France at the Battle of Trafalgar, there was little practical need of Fulton's metal barrel, and in any case his plans seemed distasteful.

Admiral Horatio Nelson, the hero of Trafalgar, had called submarines "burglarious . . . sneak dodges down below." The *Naval Chronicle* stigmatized them as "revolting to every noble principle" and deplored the idea of Britain's "hardy, dauntless tars" becoming "submarine assassins." Nelson's old commander, Admiral Earl St. Vincent, summed up the general view: "Don't look at [the submarine], and don't touch it. If we take it up, other nations will; and it will be the greatest blow at our supremacy on the sea that can be imagined." Rebuffed, Fulton returned to America, where he perfected the steam-powered paddle wheeler and, come the War of 1812, built the first steam-powered warship.

Some half a century later, the USS *Housatonic*—a new 1,264-ton frigate—became the first ship to be sunk by a submarine. In early 1864, the third year of the Civil War, the *Housatonic* was serving with the Yankee squadron blockading the Confederate port of Charleston. On a clear, cold, moonlit February night, the CSS *Hunley*, a slender submersible about forty feet long but just forty-two inches in diameter and built of three-eighths-inch boilerplate, slunk out of Charleston Harbor. The *Hunley* had an unfortunate past. During trials she had been swamped while sailing on the surface and sunk and recovered three times at a cost of twenty-three lives. Now, gallantly commanded by Lieutenant George E. Dixon of the Alabama Light Infantry, she crept semisubmerged toward the Union fleet. The eight-man crew labored over the hand crank, which, connected to the propeller, drove the *Hunley* forward at a meager four knots. Dixon was standing up since the only way he could navigate was by peering out of the forward hatch.

Just before 8:45 P.M., Acting Master F. K. Crosby of the *Housatonic* saw something resembling a piece of driftwood making straight for the ship. Realizing that no current or tide could cause this, he desperately tried to take evasive action but was too late. Dixon brought the *Hunley* alongside and detonated the 143 pounds of gunpowder supported on her projecting spar. The result was dramatic and instantaneous: the *Housatonic* was flung into the air, settled back, and slowly sank. The *Hunley*'s crew were also lost, probably sucked into the gash they had blasted in the frigate's side.

The sinking of the *Housatonic* impressed an Irish engineer and patriot, John P. Holland, who had emigrated to the United States in 1873 at the age of thirty-one. Convinced that underwater warfare was an ideal way to strike at Britain's oppressive rule of Ireland, he threw in his lot with the Fenian Brotherhood, an Irish nationalist organization that could provide the necessary funds. In spring 1878 he launched his first submarine in the Passaic River. A cynical observer commented sourly that Holland had built a coffin for himself. Sure enough, the fourteen-and-a-half-foot boat sank immediately—Holland had miscalculated the boat's displacement—but no one was on board and she was quickly retrieved. He rectified the errors, and subsequent trials showed that Holland had achieved major improvements in buoyancy and stability.

Meanwhile, a Manchester clergyman, the Reverend George William Garrett, had become convinced that Britain needed a cordon of submarines to protect her islands from attack. Unlike Holland, Garrett believed their role to be purely defensive, particularly to guard harbor mouths. This debate on the submarine's role—offense or defense—would continue until the beginning of World War I. Garrett built an experimental boat, which, with characteristic optimism, he named the *Resurgam*—"I will rise again." The Reverend Norman McLeod, chaplain to Queen Victoria, endorsed Garrett's company's prospectus, reassuring potential investors with arguments that sound familiar today: "As to the inventions being for murdering people—this is all nonsense. Every contribution made by science to improve instruments of war makes war shorter and, in the end, less terrible to human life and to human progress."

Garrett's prototype was successful, and a new thirty-ton vessel powered by steam, the *Resurgam 2*, followed in 1879. However, she was lost the following year while being towed along the Welsh coast.

Back in America, Holland was building a new boat to be deployed against the British. Funding again came from the Fenian Brotherhood, and Holland's work proceeded in secrecy. Blakely Hall, a dogged reporter from the *New York Sun*, discovered enough to call the boat a "Fenian Ram"—a name that stuck. Powered by a gasoline engine, the three-man *Ram* had the streamlined porpoise shape characteristic of all Holland's creations and their modern descendants. Capable of some eight or nine knots on the surface, she did not ascend or descend by her own weight but dived by tilting her hydroplanes and propelling herself by her own engine power. In 1883 the *Ram* dived for the first time, and Holland described his excitement: "Everything grew dark and we were entirely submerged, and nothing could be seen through the ports except a dark green blur." The trials showed that this boat was well ahead of any rivals.

However, the *Ram* was soon sacrificed to internal Irish nationalist politics. The Fenians had been squabbling among themselves, and one faction decided to seize the boat. Forging Holland's name on a pass, they towed the *Ram* up Long Island Sound to New Haven, where their inept handling caused an exasperated harbormaster to declare the vessel a menace to navigation. Her kidnappers promptly beached the *Ram* and then tried unsuccessfully to sell her to the Russians. An angry, disillusioned Holland refused to help, declaring, "I'll let her rot on their hands."

After severing his Fenian links, Holland was persuaded by the U.S. Army to design a submarine from which a new "dynamite gun" could be fired. The wooden fifty-foot craft crashed into piles at her launch off the Brooklyn shore in September 1885, and a frustrated Holland began exploring the possibilities of mechanical flight. Yet his true passion remained underwater warfare. In his article "Can New York Be Bombarded?" he argued that the United States must have submarines to protect her fleet and her coastal defenses.

The idea that America could be so vulnerable touched a nerve. The U.S. Navy Department announced a design competition for a submarine, and Holland won. His satisfaction was, however, short-lived because a change of administration saw the money for his project reallocated to surface vessels. Holland now took a job in a friend's dredging company at a meager four dollars a day, but after the reelection of the pro-submarine president S. Grover Cleveland he won some powerful and passionate advocates within the U.S. Navy. Lieutenant Commander William Kimball told a somewhat astonished Senate Committee on

The Holland VI *submarine, designed by John P. Holland.*

Naval Affairs that if he were given six Holland boats he would "pledge [his] life to stand off the entire British Squadron ten miles off Sandy Hook without any aid from a fleet."

Holland's fifth boat, the impractical, steam-powered *Plunger*, was launched in 1897. Dissatisfied, he immediately began work on the famous *Holland VI*, which, unlike the compromised *Plunger*, was built to his preferred design. Constructed in New Jersey, the *Holland VI* was nearly fifty-four feet long, large enough for a crew of fifteen. Powered by a forty-five-horsepower gasoline engine for surface cruising and a fifty-horsepower electric motor when submerged, she could be controlled beneath the surface at any speed. Her main weapon was a single eighteen-inch torpedo tube, and she could carry two reload torpedoes. She made her first successful dive off Staten Island on St. Patrick's Day, 17 March 1898, and her formal trials ten days later were so impressive that Assistant Secretary of the Navy Theodore Roosevelt recommended that the Holland submarine be purchased, writing, "I don't think . . . we can afford to let her slip." On 11 April 1900 *Holland VI* became the USS *Holland (SS-1)*, and in October 1900 she was formally commissioned. The American press greeted the boat with such headlines as "Uncle Sam's Devil of the Deep" and "The Monster War Fish." The modern submarine had arrived.

———— ⚭ ————

In Britain a powerful and contemptuous lobby within the Admiralty had long dismissed submersibles as "not our concern." There was a comfortable perception that submarines were simply not needed. After all, British naval supremacy had not been seriously challenged since the days of Napoleon. In April 1900 Lord Goschen, first lord of the Admiralty, assured the House of Commons that "submarines were a weapon for Maritime Powers on the defensive" and that, whatever the case, "we know all about them." His parliamentary secretary, Hugh Oakeley Arnold-Foster, was yet more categorical, stating that "the Admiralty are not prepared to take any steps in regard to submarines because this vessel is only the weapon of the weaker nation."

There was also a more emotional objection. Many still considered that there was something dishonorable, sneaky, and unfair about underwater warfare. Rear Admiral Sir Arthur Wilson, controller of the Royal Navy, said: "Underwater weapons, they call 'em. I call them underhand, unfair and damned un-English. They'll never be any use in war and I'll tell you why: I'm going to get the First Lord to announce that we intend to treat all submarines as pirate vessels in wartime and that we'll hang all the crews."

It was only with the success of the Holland boats in the United States and the worrisome evidence of the interest in submarines of potential European rivals, particularly France, that the Admiralty stopped dismissing underwater vessels outright. Their most vocal advocate was Admiral Fisher, who believed passionately in "the immense impending revolution which the submarines will effect as offensive weapons of war," and who succeeded in convincing his friend the Prince of Wales. In 1901, one year after the U.S. Navy purchased its first submarine, the British Admiralty ordered five Holland boats. Even skeptics accepted that this would at least enable the Royal Navy to assess the extent to which the boats might be a threat in enemy hands. An approving *Times* wrote: "We must not be caught napping, and when a particular weapon has found favour with a nation shrewd as the Americans and as ingenious as the French, it behooves us not to neglect it ourselves."

The boats were to be built in England by Vickers Sons and Maxim Ltd. under license from the Holland Torpedo Boat Company. Captain Reginald Bacon was appointed "inspecting captain of submarine boats." The Royal Navy's first submarine was launched at Barrow in Furness on 2 October 1901 and began her trials. The crew spent the night in the craft to test whether this would cause them breathing difficulties. So little was known that some had even warned that it was "by no means certain that human bodies in close confinement did not give off poisonous exhalations!" As it turned out, the most trying aspect was not the bad air but the noise: One elderly member of the team, an American sent over by the Holland Torpedo Boat Company, insisted on playing his flute through the night. Captain Bacon wrote that the boat's crew "all looked upon flutes thereafter with a personal measure of animosity."

The trials continued with surface runs, then the first dives and submerged sea trials. Bacon claimed to be the first to introduce the periscope to the submarine—certainly, the U.S. Holland boats had had to bob up and down so that men could look through the glass ports in the side of the conning tower. By the end of 1902 the Royal Navy had its first submarine flotilla when all five of the Holland boats reported to Portsmouth Harbor. They were berthed alongside prison hulks and quarantine vessels in a remote part of the port—a reminder that they were still unloved parvenus. Submariners were soon to earn the name "unwashed chauffeurs" from their snottier surface colleagues.

It was vital to keep the engines well ventilated and to protect the crew from being poisoned. Two ventilation tubes supplied air to the boat, while a third was intended to siphon away engine fumes. In case the latter failed, three white mice—preferred to brown because they were believed to be tamer—were on board to sound the alarm. Picture postcards informed a fascinated public that the mice could be relied on to squeak at the slightest escape of gas. They were apparently so comatose with the food lavished on them by a sentimental crew that their reactions may well have been blunted. In any case, like canaries in mines, it was by dying, not squeaking, that they were supposed to alert the crew to a buildup of noxious fumes.

Good progress was made in solving the Holland boats' technical problems, and from 1906 Britain spent some 5 percent of her shipbuilding budget on submarines. By 1914 she had the world's largest underwater fleet, with seventy-five boats ready for service. Twenty were diesel powered and truly oceangoing. Another twenty-eight were under construction.

—⚬⚬⚬—

By August 1914 Germany had twenty-eight submarines in service and another twenty-five vessels under construction. Her fleet was only the fourth largest in the world, but it was the newest and most technically advanced. Germany had been experimenting with underwater craft for some time. In 1851 a Bavarian artillery NCO, Corporal Wilhelm Bauer, had demonstrated, albeit none too successfully, a submarine designed to defeat the Danish blockade of the northern German coast. These and subsequent experiments prompted considerable skepticism in official circles. In 1901 Tirpitz declared that "Germany has no need of submarines." In the spring of 1904 he was still lecturing the Reichstag about his contempt for submarine warfare. But in July he announced his intention to build a submarine. Germany's decision, just as Britain's had been earlier, was primarily reactive: Britain was now pressing ahead with a submarine program, so Germany must have one too. The construction of the German navy's first *Unterseeboot*—the *U-1*—began at Krupps's *Germaniawerft* plant in Kiel. She was completed in 1906 and underwent her trials the following year.

The *U-1* was followed by a succession of U-boat classes, each surpassing its predecessor in design and performance. German engineers achieved a breakthrough with the introduction of improved diesel engines. Beginning with the Danzig-built *U-19* class, all German submarines were henceforth diesel powered. They were a great advance on Germany's earlier gasoline- or paraffin-fueled U-boats, which, when running on the surface, had been "almost as visible as a smoke-belching steamer." Also, diesel has a lower flash point and was therefore much safer. However, the real significance was the reliability and endurance of these large, powerful diesel engines. Designed by MAN of Augsburg, they changed the character of submarines. Now, they no longer needed to be deployed primarily defensively and tactically but could be exploited as independent, offensive, strategic weapons. On the eve of the war Germany had twelve newly built oceangoing diesel-powered craft. These boats had the best range and depth performance in the world, and each was capable of traveling some 5,000 miles.

As yet, however, few even in Germany realized the new potential. On 2 August 1914, when the U-boats were sent out from Heligoland (an island off the coast of Germany in the North Sea) with instructions to moor at allotted stations and keep watch, they were given an escort; the German navy would not trust them out of sight of land without a mothering convoy of surface ships. A young German submarine officer wrote that little was expected of the U-boats at this time "because they had not been tried out and developed, while in some of the foreign navies many accidents had occurred." H. G. Wells's acid comment that it was hard to imagine a submarine doing anything other than "suffocate its crew" rang disturbingly true in these prewar years. If seawater came into contact with sulfuric acid leaching from the batteries, this produced lethal chlorine gas. Discharging batteries generated volatile hydrogen gas, which a single spark could ignite. Between 1901 and August 1914, there were sixty-eight serious submarine accidents, including twenty-three collisions, seven battery explosions, and twelve fuel explosions.

Submarines were also worryingly susceptible to human error; thirteen sank because hull openings had not been closed tight. In Britain the *A-1* sank in March 1904, with the loss of eleven men. While concentrating on a mock attack on the cruiser HMS *Juno*, the *A-1* was rammed by the Castle Line steamer *Berwick Castle*, thus becoming the United Kingdom's first submarine casualty. The captain of a Japanese submarine that sank after an operational mishap in Hiroshima Bay in 1910 spent his last moments composing a farewell letter later recovered with his body. It makes harrowing reading. After explaining in careful detail what had gone wrong and the sad condition of his comrades, he concluded: "Atmospheric pressure is increasing, and I feel as if my eardrums were breaking. At 12.30 o'clock respiration is extraordinarily difficult. I am breathing gasoline. I am intoxicated with gasoline."

But if questions of design, safety, and power plagued the creators of the early submarines, so did the question of how best to arm them. Torpedoes, named after the crampfish, or electric ray, were the natural weapon of the submarine but were at first erratic and unreliable. Their development owed much to British engineer Robert Whitehead, born in Bolton in 1823. While working in Austria for a company supplying the Austro-Hungarian navy, he developed in strict secrecy, with the assistance of only his twelve-year-old son and one trusted workman, an "automobile device," driven by compressed air, that could travel at some seven or eight knots and carry dynamite. He soon after perfected a mechanism to control its depth. The Royal Navy invited him home to demonstrate the new weapon and after exhaustive trials in 1870 concluded that "any maritime nation failing to provide itself with submarine locomotive torpedoes would be neglecting a great source of power both for offence and defence." The Royal Navy paid £15,000 for the right to manufacture Whitehead's torpedoes, and France, Italy, and Germany quickly followed suit.

The first torpedoes were designed to be fired from surface vessels. Soon all sizes of warships were being fitted with torpedo tubes. Admiral Fisher was delighted. He had been one of the first and very few officers to recognize the torpedo's potential as a weapon of sudden destruction. Early in 1868, two years before Whitehead's invention had even been seen in Britain, his "Short Treatise on Electricity and the Management of Torpedoes" predicted that the weapon "would play a most important part in future wars" since ships as currently constructed were powerless against them and "the constant dread of sudden destruction" would demoralize seamen. Yet other senior naval men remained dubious, even hostile. In one sense the detractors were right. Torpedoes needed considerable further development to improve their accuracy and dependability. However, by 1904 the British Holland boats had a one-in-two chance of hitting a destroyer from a range of 300 to 400 feet with a torpedo set to run at a depth of six feet.

If submarine weaponry was still an uncertain science, so were anti-submarine tactics. By 1914 minefields, nets, and destroyer patrols were the principal methods of keeping submarines at bay—effective anti-submarine devices like the depth charge had yet to be developed. The best response a ship could make to a submarine running on the surface was to fire at it, if the ship was suitably armed, or to try and ram or outrun it. Imaginative if impractical British suggestions included sabotaging periscopes by spraying their lenses with a sticky substance, training seagulls to defecate on them, or using a very long boat hook to hang explosives on them.

A submerged submarine was even harder to deal with. First of all, how could a ship even know that it was there? The British Admiralty was bombarded with suggestions, not all of them helpful. Someone suggested the use of psychic mediums. Others thought that it would be worth studying the reactions of sea lions to underwater noises. A British clergyman, believing, probably correctly, that it was easier to spot submerged objects from high above, suggested that ships should carry balloons for aerial reconnaissance.

Hydrophones—listening devices to enable a ship to pick up the tell-tale thuds of a submarine's propellers—were as yet very crude and understanding of underwater acoustics was limited. The only way a ship's captain could hope to hear anything was to take the highly dangerous course of stopping his engines. Even then it was hard to decipher the sounds of the sea. In a precarious experiment Sir Richard Roget was suspended by his legs over the side of a ship. While a submarine circled round he tried to capture in his head the pitch and frequency of the submarine's propellers so that he could later make a note of it. It was not until 1916 that the first successful attack on a U-boat using a hydrophone took place.

—◦◦◦—

In 1914 almost every aspect of the submarine—equipment, tactics, and weaponry—was still evolving. In both Britain and Germany many still saw submarines as mere "tin fish" going into battle against the best-built and most sophisticated vessels the world had yet seen. In Britain naval men considered the U-boat menace a chimera and politicians ignored the predictions of Fisher and his ally retired admiral Sir Percy Scott, who conducted a pro-submarine campaign in the pages of the *Times*. Scott irritated his opponents with his assertion that "submarines and aeroplanes have entirely revolutionised naval warfare." In the last few days of peace he wrote passionate warnings that the submarine was a deadly new weapon. "Will feelings of humanity restrain our enemy from using it?" he asked, only to be accused of midsummer madness. Sir Arthur Conan Doyle joined the pro-submarine lobby, arguing that Britain must build submarines and cautioning that, while "England has often been stupid, but has got off scot-free . . . you can't expect luck to be your saviour always."

Yet many members of the establishment such as Lord Charles Beresford continued to find such fears laughable. Beresford was exchanging chatty notes with the kaiser on the very eve of war, assuring him that Sir Percy Scott was a scaremonger, that he personally had "shown up the hollowness of the scare" and "been supported by our sober-minded naval opinion." "Underwater warfare," he concluded, "cannot at present drive surface vessels from the sea."

Beresford's complacency was punished by Germany's U-boat men within weeks of the outbreak of war. Admittedly, the first German submarine assault on a British naval ship in early August failed when the *U-15* was sliced in half by the cruiser *Birmingham*. However, on 5 September 1914 the 3,200-ton cruiser HMS *Pathfinder* was torpedoed by the *U-21* in the Firth of Forth. The cruiser sank in under four minutes, with the loss of more than half her crew of 360. Worse followed on 22 September 1914. Otto Weddigen, captain of the *U-9* patrolling off the Dutch coast, spotted three four-funneled British cruisers steaming line abreast straight toward him at a modest ten knots. They were the obsolescent cruiser HMS *Cressy* and her two sister ships, the *Aboukir* and the *Hogue*. This seemed an opportunity to avenge the loss of the *U-15*, and Weddigen immediately launched a torpedo attack. The *Aboukir* was hit by a single torpedo and listed immediately as water flowed into the longitudinal coal bunkers, which ran the length of the ship. The bunkers had been designed to protect against shells, not torpedoes. Within twenty-five minutes the *Aboukir* had capsized, leaving her crew struggling in the freezing water. The *Hogue*, believing a mine to have caused the explosion, approached to pick up survivors, only to be hit by two torpedoes and to sink in ten minutes. The surviving *Cressy* also tried to rescue the drowning and was similarly attacked, sinking in fifteen minutes.

Within barely an hour the almost unthinkable had happened: Three ships—36,000 tons in total—had been destroyed by an unseen enemy. Fourteen hundred fifty-nine men were killed, two-thirds more than the number Nelson had lost at Trafalgar. It was an astonishing event and provoked serious thought both in Britain and Germany. Yet even now, in September 1914, neither country fully appreciated how submarines might be deployed against maritime commerce and the pivotal role they would play in the war within a very few months.

—⊶⊷∞⊶⊷—

CHAPTER THREE

More Beautiful than Solomon's Temple

HE *Lusitania* was the pride of Britain's commercial fleet. When, in September 1907, she sailed into New York Harbor on her maiden voyage from Liverpool, she received a celebrity's welcome. From the roof of the world's tallest skyscraper—the 557-foot-high Singer Building, where a gigantic sixteen-foot American flag flapped in the wind—a greeting was flashed to the world's largest ship. One hundred detectives had been specially brought in to watch for pickpockets among the thousands crowding the shore, eager for their first glimpse of the *Lusitania*. As she cruised up the Hudson, the first liner to enter New York through the newly dredged Ambrose Channel, hysteria grew. As she approached the Cunard Line's Pier 54, people fought at the dock gates. Women fainted in the crush.

The 30,395-ton, four-funnel, 785-foot vessel looked to the admiring crowds like "a skyscraper adrift." She had crossed the Atlantic at an average speed of just over twenty-three knots. Excited sightseers up from the country told journalists, "No one will believe us when we go back and tell them about this ship." The newspapers raved about the speed, strength, and safety of the liner, a ship "as beautiful as she was big, as graceful as she was swift." She was the loveliest of all "that have made memorable crossings from the carvels of Columbus."

Headlines like "Gorgeous in Apartments" and "A Marvel of Speed and Luxury" whetted the American reader's appetite for the "wonders" inside. Underlying the popular excitement was "the thrill of man's pride in himself and his achievements." Keyed up by the media coverage, the visitors swarmed aboard the *Lusitania* to find her "more beautiful than Solomon's Temple and big enough to hold all his wives." The ship was certainly big. She could accommodate 540 first-class, 460 second-class, and 1,200 third-class passengers and a crew of 850. A stroll around her Promenade Deck was over a quarter of a mile. En route to New York, passengers and crew had eaten their way through 40,000 eggs, 4,000 pounds of fresh fish, two tons of bacon and ham, 4,000 pounds of coffee, 1,000 pineapples, 500 pounds of grapes, 1,000 lemons, 25,000 pounds of meat, nearly 3,000 gallons of milk, over 500 gallons of cream, and 30,000 loaves of bread. The ship's galleys could prepare 10,000 meals a day.

In Britain, *Engineering*, a publication not usually noted for emotional outpourings, devoted some fifty pages to a celebration of the *Lusitania*'s aesthetic as well as technical qualities. It described the lavishly fitted first-class suites and cabins, which were well located amidships, the

most comfortable part of the vessel where the ship's movement was felt the least. It detailed the domed, double-tiered first-class dining room, decorated in white and gilt in the style of Louis XVI, and the first-class smoking room, also in eighteenth-century style, paneled with Italian walnut and furnished with "dignity and elegance" under a stained-glass barrel-vaulted dome. It lingered over the Adam-style writing room and library, whose walls were hung "in delicate grey and cream silk brocade" and whose etched windows were curtained with Rose du Barri silk taboret copied from an old design discovered at Milton Abbey.

The second-class accommodation, situated toward the stern, was also a source of wonder. Cunard claimed justifiably that, though it was "more chaste" in style than the *Lusitania*'s first-class quarters, it was as luxurious as first class on any other ship. Cabins were spacious and well appointed, with washbasins in mahogany stands and soft woolen hangings that could be pulled around the berths for privacy. The public rooms were elegant and charming, with gleaming mahogany paneling, well-upholstered furniture, and intricate stained glass ceilings. They were

The Lusitania *steams into New York Harbor on her maiden voyage, September 1907.*

First-class cabin, with gilding and marble basin.

located in a deck-island at the stern, separated by a walkway and gate from the first-class section farther forward.

Third-class passengers were accommodated toward the ship's bows, where the motion was most pronounced. The cabins were utilitarian but well designed, better fitted and less cramped than on other ships. Also, unlike many other ships, the *Lusitania* had public rooms for third-class passengers. This was in recognition of the fact that they were the most important to Cunard financially. Once known as "steerage" passengers because their accommodation had often been right astern near the steering gear, they traveled in huge numbers in the final years before the First World War and were the bread and butter of all steamship companies, providing the bulk of their profit. The very year that the *Lusitania* made her first crossing—1907—was the high point, with 1.2 million immigrants admitted to the United States.

Engineering understandably reserved its greatest plaudits for the *Lusitania*'s technical characteristics, concluding that "the vessel represents the greatest step that has ever been taken either in size or power in

The double-tiered first-class dining room.

a merchant ship." She was half the size again of any vessel yet built, and three-quarters more powerful. She was also the first ship to incorporate high-tensile steel in her hull for additional strength. Novel features included electric controls for steering, for closing her 175 watertight compartments, and for detecting fire. Her four giant steam-turbine engines, fitted for the first time to a large merchant ship, were far more efficient than the old reciprocating pistons. When the *Lusitania* was under full steam, her turbine blades produced 68,000 horsepower, and her quadruple screws gave a top speed of twenty-five knots.

———

The social prestige of sailing on the *Lusitania* was tremendous. The *Philadelphia Inquirer* was in no doubt that "just now, the man who came over in the *Lusitania* takes precedence of the one whose ancestors came over in the *Mayflower*." To other papers, the *Lusitania* epitomized progress. They were right; by 1907, passengers could travel across the

First-class elevator.

Atlantic comfortably, safely, quickly, and with relative certainty about when they would arrive.

It had taken a long time to reach this stage. Behind a ship like the *Lusitania* lay the transition from wooden to iron and then steel-hulled ships, from sail to steam propulsion, from paddle wheels to screw propellers. This technological change had been driven by fierce rivalry among shipping companies competing for dominance of the lucrative transatlantic trade and, particularly in later years, for the rich profits from transporting increasing numbers of emigrants. Nations raced to produce the largest, fastest, most luxurious and prestigious ships afloat as symbols of national power and pride.

American sailing ships of the early 1800s were the first to adopt fixed schedules. Previously, ships had simply sailed once their cargo holds were full, whenever this might be. Passengers were left to cool their heels or find another vessel. The concept of a *liner*, which left port at a specific and previously advertised time and sailed in a straight line to its destination, revolutionized transatlantic travel. Nevertheless, there was still a great deal of uncertainty. Who could say how long a sailing ship would take to make the passage? Journey times varied by days, even weeks, depending on the conditions.

American Moses Rogers pioneered more predictable steam propulsion. In 1809 he coaxed the river paddle steamer *Phoenix* from Hoboken to Philadelphia in a precarious two-week sea voyage. A decade later he captained another paddle steamer, the *Savannah*, across the Atlantic to Liverpool. The voyage lasted twenty-seven days and eleven hours, during which the *Savannah* used steam power for only some eighty-five hours and sail for the rest. Rogers attempted to use steam and sail combined, but the ship keeled over. One paddle plowed too deep into the water; the other was left impotently beating the air—so that the *Savannah* went around in circles like a one-legged duck.

The first ship to steam continuously across the Atlantic was the British *Sirius* in 1838. A wooden ship of about 700 tons with a mongrel dog for her figurehead, she was fitted with the recently invented

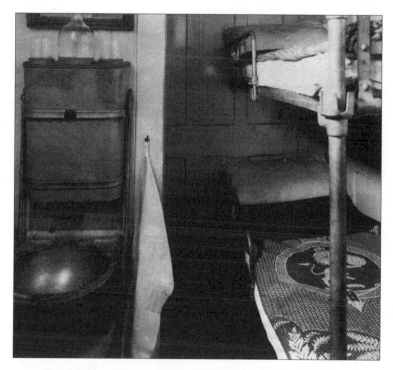

Third-class two-berth cabin, with Cunard logo on the bedspreads.

Spacious third-class dining room of polished pine could accommodate 350 at one sitting.

marine surface condensers, which prevented her boilers from becoming clogged with salt. The ship arrived in New York with forty delighted passengers to an enthusiastic reception followed by a weeklong celebration.

Samuel Cunard noted these developments with interest. His family were Shropshire Quakers who had emigrated to Philadelphia in the seventeenth century. After the American Declaration of Independence they, like many other loyalists, moved to Canada, where Samuel was born in Halifax in 1787. He became a successful and respected businessman with a wide portfolio of interests from banking, whaling, and lumber to fire insurance. In 1838, the same year that the *Sirius* made her remarkable crossing, the British government invited tenders to carry transatlantic mail by steamer.

Samuel hurried to London, where he offered to take the mail to and from the United States twice a month for a fee of £55,000. He won the contract and immediately ordered a fleet of four wooden paddleboats capable of nine knots an hour to be built on the River Clyde in Scotland.

His instructions were simple: "I want a plain and comfortable boat, not the least unnecessary expense for show." His orders to his captains were equally blunt: "Your ship is loaded, take her; speed is nothing, follow your own road, deliver her safe, bring her back safe—safety is all that is required."

On 4 July 1840, the first of Cunard's fleet, the *Britannia*, made her maiden voyage from Liverpool, reaching Boston in fourteen days. Her single stack was painted in the soon-to-be famous company colors: orange-red between two black bands. The vivid, distinctive red was the result of an old trick used by crews of coastal steamers, who mixed buttermilk and ochre to produce a species of heat-resistant emulsion. The 2,000 guests at the celebratory banquet recognized that, though by no means the largest or the fastest ship of her day, the *Britannia* had established an important communication link and source of prosperity.

These early steamers were, nevertheless, profoundly uncomfortable. The cumbersome paddle wheels, one port, one starboard, took up most of the room amidships, while their vibrations shook the whole ship. Passengers were squeezed into the cramped spaces fore and aft. Charles Dickens never forgot sailing on the *Britannia* on his first trip to the United States in 1842. He was shocked by the tiny proportions of his stateroom, which he derided as "an utterly impracticable, thoroughly hopeless, and profoundly preposterous box." He grumbled that the only thing conceivably smaller for sleeping in would be a coffin and that the flat quilt that covered him was "like a surgical plaster." Furthermore, there was as much chance of accommodating his wife's luggage as of persuading a giraffe into a flowerpot. Bad weather forced him to spend a great deal of time in the unsatisfactory cabin, and he felt seasick. "Read in bed (but to this hour I don't know what) . . . and reeled on deck a little; drank cold brandy and water with unspeakable disgust and ate hard biscuits perseveringly," he wrote. "Not ill, but going to be."

Dickens decided that the much-vaunted dining room, enticingly described by Cunard as "in a style of more than Eastern splendour," more accurately resembled "a gigantic hearse with windows." The lunches of "pig's faces, cold ham, salt beef" disgusted him. On arrival in Nova Scotia, the *Britannia* ran aground in a mud shoal. She was freed and sailed into Halifax, where some of her relieved passengers celebrated with over-generous quantities of oysters and champagne and were found "lying insensible on their backs in unfrequented streets." When the ship finally reached Boston, Dickens made determined arrangements to return in a slower but more spaciously appointed sailing ship.

Yet despite cramped sleeping cabins and dubious plumbing, the steamships had one unassailable advantage over sail: reliability. Samuel Cunard's steamers could be trusted to make the crossing from Liverpool to Halifax in a little over twelve days. Sailing craft, dependent on the weather, could take anywhere from twenty-two to thirty-eight days.

The first real challenge to Cunard's dominance came from the American Edward Knight Collins, who had started the profitable and successful Dramatic line of sailing ships. By 1846 his fortune was estimated to be over $100,000. Yet suddenly, at the age of forty-four, he chose to sell all his vessels and place his faith in steam and in the prospect of a government subsidy. He had noted a statement in the *Congressional Record* that American shipowners should be encouraged "to proceed with the absolute conquest of this man Cunard."

Collins's offer to build a fleet of wooden paddle steamers was accepted, and the first of these, the comfortable 2,800-ton *Atlantic* and *Pacific*, were launched on 1 February 1849. For a while Collins prospered. Within two years his ships were carrying 50 percent more first-class travelers than Cunard. In 1851 he claimed the prestigious Blue Riband for the fastest crossing from Cunard. In the following year, the *Pacific* became the first ship to cross the Atlantic in under ten days. Collins wooed his passengers with comfort and elegance as well as with speed. His interiors were inspired by the sumptuous American river steamers and offered steam heating and thick carpets, although the latter were prudently rolled up once the ship was at sea. The Cunard ships, by contrast, seemed austere and utilitarian. The Quaker Samuel Cunard set no store by what he regarded as fripperies.

Yet despite the prestige and a hefty subsidy, Collins lost $2.5 million. Then came two awful disasters. In 1854 the *Arctic* sank after colliding with the French steamship *Vesta* in thick fog off the Grand Banks. Collins's wife, son, and daughter were among the victims. In 1856 the *Pacific* simply vanished; the only traces ever found were some ornamental doors floating among the ice floes. Collins lost his subsidy from Congress and was forced to sell his remaining three ships to pay off his creditors. He left New York for landlocked Ohio and turned his attention to iron and coal.

Meanwhile, one of the most inspired engineers of the Victorian period, Isambard Kingdom Brunel, had been trying his hand at steamship design, as well as at railways and bridges. After two smaller ships, the *Great Britain* and the *Great Western*, his *Great Eastern* was launched in 1858. She had soaring clifflike sides, five funnels, and an iron hull with 3 million rivets. She had a double bottom as well as transverse and longitudinal bulkheads. At 22,500 tons she was *six* times the size of the next-largest ship in the world. Ultimately, she was a commercial failure as a passenger vessel, consistently losing money for a series of owners. Yet she had proved that very large ships with iron hulls would not disintegrate in bad weather.

Cunard's next serious rival was Englishman William Inman, a partner in Richardson Brothers. This Liverpool company transported emigrants to Philadelphia by sailing ship but by the mid–nineteenth century was losing out to the larger, newer American sailing packets, which were taking their immigrant cargoes to the more popular port of New York. Inman therefore persuaded his partners to buy the Clyde steamer *City of Glasgow*. She was popular because she reduced the journey time by one half compared to the sailing ships, and also because Inman provided decent food for his emigrants. Thus they reached their destination in better condition and were less likely to be quarantined or rejected by the American authorities. Inman became converted to screw propulsion when he bought the *City of Brussels*, powered by a screw propeller. The orthodox view was that the screw was a slower form of propulsion than the paddle wheel, but Inman found it both faster and more economical. In 1866 his *City of Paris* crossed the Atlantic at thirteen and a half knots to take the Blue Riband.

T. H. Ismay's White Star Line was another rival. Working with the Belfast shipbuilders Harland and Wolff, Ismay developed a style of ship that paved the way for the floating palaces to come. His ships were the first to win plaudits for offering all the comforts and amenities of a good Swiss hotel, with smoking rooms hailed as "narcotic paradises." Ismay placed his first-class passengers in the more stable and therefore more comfortable midships portion of the ship. He also built dining rooms that were the full width of the ship and provided far larger cabins than the "coffins" that had so affronted Dickens. Millionaires such as William Henry Vanderbilt and John Pierpont Morgan clashed over securing the best suites.

Yet despite their advances in passenger comforts, neither Inman nor Ismay could match Cunard for safety. Inman lost five ships within three decades, while, in 1873, the White Star's *Atlantic* sank within sight of land with the loss of over 500 lives. Discovering that there was insufficient coal in her bunkers to reach her destination of New York, the captain had made for Halifax but foundered in the heavy seas. A witness recorded a truly harrowing scene: "Then I saw the first and awful sight. . . . a large mass of something drifted past the ship on the top of the waves, and then it was lost to view in the trough of the sea. As it passed by a moan—it must have been a shriek but the tempest dulled the sound—seemed to surge up from the mass, which extended over fifty yards of water: it was the women. The sea swept them out of the steerage, and with their children, to the number of 200 or 300, they drifted thus to eternity."

Crossing the Atlantic, whether by steam or sail, remained a relatively hazardous business, even by the later nineteenth century. The sailing packets were nicknamed "coffin brigs," and one in six ran aground or sank. In 1878 Katherine Ledoux, author of *Ocean Notes for Ladies*, advised her readers to dress with due care and attention: "I have always felt that a body washed ashore in good clothes would receive more respect and kinder care than if dressed in those only fit for the rag bag." Her advice on bidding farewell to loved ones on the quayside was equally depressing: "Do not sadden others who are trying hard to be brave. . . . Leave yourself and them in God's hands, for he will be with you and them though the trackless deep lies between."

Cunard was the only major line able to claim the distinction of never having lost a passenger. Nevertheless, the austerity of Cunard's ships meant that it was losing ground. The company responded in the 1880s with the single-screw *Umbria* and *Etruria*, intended as the epitome of comfort and grace and the most powerful ships then afloat. Their hulls, funnels, and superstructure defined the style of liner to which Cunard's *Lusitania* would belong. Cunard lured first-class passengers with the promise of ten snacks and meals a day, from fruit before breakfast, when passengers could toy with grapes and melons, through midmorning bouillon to a late-evening supper. For those more interested in romance than food, ever more seductive advertisements promised romantic interludes on moonlit decks.

The shipping lines vied to produce ever-faster, larger, more advanced, and more opulent liners. In 1888 the Inman Line's *City of Paris* and *City of New York*, completed after Inman's death, were greeted with astonishment. Their baronial dining rooms were lit by glass roofs more than fifty feet long. Their smoking rooms were paneled in black walnut and furnished with scarlet leather couches. Their oak-wainscoted libraries held some 800 books and were flooded with purple light through delicately stained glass windows inscribed with poems of the sea. The following year, the White Star Line's *Teutonic* and *Majestic* roused similar excitement. All four of these ships could run at twenty knots. Not to be outdone, Cunard built the even larger and faster *Campania*, fitted throughout with electric light, and the sumptuous *Lucania*.

The chief rivalry was still between British and American companies. Inman's line had passed to American ownership. Initially a technicality forbade his ships to fly the Stars and Stripes because they were British, not American, built. The problem was overcome when the owners agreed with Congress to change the company name to the American Line and to build two new liners in American yards. In return the company won the right to carry European mail for four dollars a mile and to sail under Old Glory. On 22 February 1893, Washington's Birthday, the American flag was raised on the *City of Paris*. The American Line's *St. Louis* and *St. Paul* were the first liners to be built in the United States for thirty-eight years. It would, in fact, be another thirty-seven years before any more such ships were built there. Nevertheless, by 1896 the line was the second-largest carrier of cabin passengers to New York. Cunard was carrying 18,000, the American Line 14,000, and White Star 12,000 per annum.

Yet the days of Anglo-American dominance were ending. In 1889 the Prince of Wales had taken his nephew, the German kaiser, to a naval review. The emperor proved to be less interested in the torpedo boats and warships than in the White Star's new liner *Teutonic*, taking part in the review as an auxiliary cruiser before departing on her maiden voyage to New York. Her beautifully appointed saloons inspired him to remark, "We must have some of these."

The Germans did already have "some of these." However, their fleets of liners had not been built either for the transatlantic trade or for the luxurious end of the market. North German Lloyd and Hamburg-Amerika, founded in the mid–nineteenth century, specialized in shipping emigrants worldwide in vessels that were well regarded for speed, good food, and plenty of music—only musicians were employed as second-class stewards, and they gave concerts every morning. Now, however, Germany sought to challenge Anglo-American dominance of the so-called Atlantic Ferry.

In 1897—the year of Queen Victoria's Diamond Jubilee, a significance not lost on the British—North German Lloyd introduced the huge *Kaiser Wilhelm der Grosse*. The company had issued an unusual ultimatum to the Vulkan shipyard in Stettin: If Vulkan could build the fastest ship in the world, North German Lloyd would buy her. If not, the shipyard would have to keep her. In fact, the huge ship took the Blue Riband from the Cunarder *Lucania* on her maiden voyage, and it was to be ten years before the *Lusitania* regained it for Britain. Not only was *Kaiser Wilhelm der Grosse* the fastest ship in the world, with a top speed of twenty-two and a half knots; she was also the largest on the Atlantic, with a tonnage of 14,350 tons.

She carried four funnels, although three would have been adequate. This was for effect and set a fashion that the builders of the *Lusitania* and others would emulate. Indeed some shipbuilders would even go to the lengths of fitting a dummy fourth funnel—as on the *Titanic*—because of the public perception that four funnels were synonymous with luxury and speed. The interiors of *Kaiser Wilhelm der Grosse* were on a monumental scale. "Late North German Lloyd" became a recognized style, causing one American to comment waspishly that it meant "two of everything but the kitchen range, and then gilded." She was also the first European ship to be equipped with wireless as a convenience to passengers, rather than for use by the crew. However, her top-heaviness meant she was not the most comfortable of ships and earned her the nickname *Rolling Billy.*

In 1900 the *Kaiser Wilhelm der Grosse* narrowly escaped a catastrophic fire when bales of cotton ignited while being loaded at the North German Lloyd piers in New York. She still had steam up, and her crew managed to back her hastily out into the Hudson. Three other North German Lloyd ships were less fortunate. The flames spread to them. Their rope hawsers burned through. Despite frantic efforts by firemen and longshoremen, the burning vessels drifted out with the tide. One ran aground on mudflats north of Ellis Island as fire blazed from her stem to her stern. Many crewmen were trapped belowdecks, and commuters on a passing ferry were appalled to see a line of white faces pressed desperately against portholes less than a foot in diameter. Rescuers fought to cut through the steel deck plates to reach them, but in vain. Thereafter marine architects designed portholes that were significantly larger to allow escape. A disaster always seemed necessary to bring about safety improvements.

The challenge to North German Lloyd, when it came, was not British or American but from another German company, Ballin's Hamburg-Amerika, which in 1900 launched the *Deutschland*. This was another gargantuan vessel. It vibrated horribly but could achieve twenty-two and three-quarter knots. North German Lloyd hit back with a fleet of liners named for the German imperial family: the *Kaiser Wilhelm II*, in honor of the kaiser himself, which took the Blue Riband in 1903; the *Kronprinz Wilhelm* and *Kronprinzessin Cecilie*, named for his son and daughter-in-law; and the *Augusta Viktoria*, built in tribute to his wife, the empress. The Empress's name was actually Auguste Viktoria, but the error, perhaps strangely, remained uncorrected for a decade.

By 1903, Germany owned the four fastest ships crossing the Atlantic. Although they were only a knot or so swifter, they were new and their magnificence caught the popular imagination. North German Lloyd quickly captured a quarter of the Atlantic passenger trade and was carrying more first-class travelers than Cunard, which had no new ships with which to hit back. The Hamburg-Amerika Line's *Amerika* scaled new heights, offering wealthy travelers sumptuous interiors designed by architect Charles Mewes, responsible for the decor of the Paris Ritz and London Carlton Hotel, and a restaurant under the exclusive supervision of Ritz-Carlton staff. The staff were trained by Cesar Ritz himself.

White Star had responded in 1899 with the *Oceanic*—the first ship to be longer than Brunel's *Great Eastern* and, for a short time, the largest ship afloat. Her marble lavatories attracted excited comment, and she was compared to London's smartest hotel, the Cecil. But in 1902 the American banker John Pierpoint Morgan bought up White Star for $25 million in gold for his new shipping conglomerate International Mercantile Marine (IMM). J. P. Morgan was a formidable predator. He was so rich that in 1896 he lent the American government $62 million in gold to bolster the U.S. Treasury Reserve, while his company U.S. Steel was the world's first billion-dollar enterprise. He was also a man who enjoyed traveling, kept suites in the best European hotels, and took a lively personal interest in transatlantic voyaging.

The commercial possibilities caught his eye, and he decided to try to unite the North Atlantic steamship companies so that they ran at a monopolistic profit rather than in fruitless competition. After forming IMM he bought up a number of lines, of which White Star was by far the most prestigious. His next step was to negotiate a working alliance with Hamburg-Amerika and North German Lloyd. These maneuvers were an obvious threat to Cunard, which was also in Morgan's sights. He approached the company, whose directors were, at first, not unattracted by his offer for their shares of 80 percent above the market value.

Public and political reactions in Britain to Morgan's monopolistic aspirations were rather different. Posters appeared offering "a licence to stay on the earth," signed by J. P. Morgan, price one penny. The press railed against the "Morganisation of the Atlantic" and warned of the consequences of losing "the great north Atlantic trade, the only trade which can support ships of great speed and tonnage so essential as cruisers in time of war." The British government was worried that Germany would shortly possess a fleet of some nine liners, all of which could outstrip the fastest British steamers. The stark choice lay between the acquisition of Cunard by IMM or rescuing Cunard "for the nation" through a large government subsidy. While the debate ebbed and flowed, one now-aging Cunard liner, the *Etruria*, broke down in the middle of the Atlantic and had to be towed to the Azores by an IMM tramp steamer. The press seized on the disturbing symbolism.

In July 1903 an embarrassed British government, under Conservative prime minister Arthur Balfour, agreed to lend Cunard £2.6 million to build two new ships that, with a top speed of at least twenty-four and a half knots, could outstrip the upstart German liners and whose specifications would be approved by the Admiralty. It also agreed to continue to pay Cunard an annual subsidy of £150,000 for maintaining both vessels in a state of war readiness, together with £68,000 for carrying the mail. In return, the Admiralty had the right to commandeer the ships for use as auxiliary merchant cruisers, troopships, or hospital ships. The agreement stipulated that all "certificated officers," apart from the engineers, and not less than half the crew must be members of the Royal Naval Reserve. Cunard also had to guarantee to remain a purely British concern.

This was the genesis of the *Lusitania* and her sister the *Mauretania*—the largest, most powerful, and fastest transatlantic liners of their day. *Lusitania*'s designer, naval architect Leonard Peskett, worked hard to reconcile the Admiralty's wishes with those of Cunard, drawing up plans

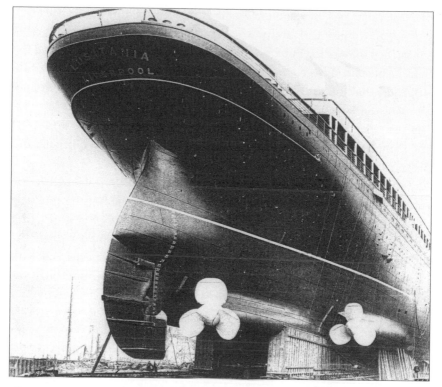

The Lusitania *under construction in the shipyards of John Brown on the Clyde, in Scotland.*

for high, slender ships with six decks above the waterline. The *Lusitania* was built by John Brown on the River Clyde in Scotland, and both the Admiralty's specifications and the design drawings included space for emplacements for twelve six-inch quick-firing guns—to be constructed, if required. For additional safety, the *Lusitania* was subdivided into twelve watertight compartments by eleven transverse bulkheads extending up to the main deck, each of which had a watertight door. Two longitudinal bulkheads extending some 400 feet against either side of the ship, similar to those in the *Aboukir*-class cruisers, were used to store coal.

The British press whipped up huge patriotic interest in the *Lusitania* and her sister as the last word in naval architecture. "Great will be the rejoicing of the British Race when the turbined Cunarders win back the Blue Riband of the Atlantic," predicted the *Daily Mail*. There was a protracted but enthusiastic debate about what the two ships should be called. At one stage a bewildered Cunard board sat down to consider a list of 461 proposed names. The problem was eventually solved by Professor G. G. Ramsay of Glasgow University, who reminded Cunard that the attractive, evocative names of the ancient Roman provinces had already inspired the naming of such ships as the *Umbria*, *Etruria*, *Campania*, and *Lucania*. He suggested that the names of the old western provinces might be suitable. Many of the latter had five rather than four syllables, but he felt that "these new monsters deserve an extra syllable." The Cunard board agreed and named their newest daughters *Mauretania* after Roman Morocco and Algeria and *Lusitania* after Roman Portugal.

The *Lusitania* fulfilled every expectation. On only her second Atlantic run she averaged just under twenty-four knots, reducing the crossing time to four days, nineteen hours, and fifty-two minutes. It was the first time the crossing had been achieved in under five days, and it brought the highly symbolic Blue Riband home again to Britain. Newspapers with headlines like "First 4-Day Liner" described how the firemen had labored in searing temperatures to keep the boilers going, buoyed up by a promised reward of £175 from the passengers. The strain was apparently too much for one man, who, overcome by heat and physical strain, went insane: "He attacked his fellows with his shovel and for a time it seemed as though the staff of firemen would be reduced through the cracking of the skulls of several good men. But he was finally overpowered and taken to the ship's hospital."

During her sea trials the *Lusitania* suffered serious vibration in the second-class accommodation in her stern. The public rooms were stripped, and the structure was stiffened with steel ribs. This lessened but by no means cured the vibrations that afflicted the *Lusitania* throughout her short life. Efforts to camouflage the structural changes with pillars and arches somewhat spoiled the decor. The *Lusitania*'s only other teething problem was minor: Steam escaped through the third-class drinking fountains.

Cunard could reflect with quiet satisfaction that in the *Lusitania* and the *Mauretania* it possessed the largest, fastest, most technologically advanced and sumptuous liners afloat. They were also the safest: In over half a century's operations, Cunard had never lost a passenger. Yet safety was being taken rather too much for granted as the new century advanced. Man's ability to create ever larger, more marvelous floating cities suggested that he had also managed to conquer nature. In 1911 a giant liner, the first to surpass the *Lusitania* and the *Mauretania* in size, was greeted with huge enthusiasm. The White Star Line's *Titanic* was, so it was claimed, unsinkable. When she struck an iceberg during her maiden voyage the following year, the world was deeply shocked.

The subsequent inquiry revealed a ludicrous and terrible overconfidence. The *Titanic* had been carrying insufficient lifeboats for her 2,201 passengers and crew on the grounds that, as a company executive sheepishly explained: "These steamers were considered tremendous lifeboats in themselves." The inquiry revealed a further disturbing feature. There had been little equity in the frantic scramble for the lifeboats. First-class passengers had a higher survival rate than second-class passengers, who in total had fared better than those in steerage. Thirty-four percent of first-class men had been saved, compared with only 12 percent of steerage men. Ninety-seven percent of first-class women survived, compared with 55 percent in steerage. All the children in first class and second class were saved, but only 30 percent of the steerage children were rescued.

The disaster did not, however, lessen the passion for ever-larger ships. In 1912 Hamburg-Amerika launched the 52,000 ton *Imperator* while the *Titanic* inquiry was still under way, though it did festoon its new ship with an ostentatious number of red lifeboats and mounted an impressive-looking searchlight under her crow's nest to scan for icebergs. Had the *Titanic* survived, she would have been the world's largest ship only for a bare month more. In fact, the race was now in danger of degenerating into farce. Cunard promptly announced that its new ship, the *Aquitania*, would, at 901 feet, be a foot longer than the *Imperator*. Hamburg-Amerika responded that it had made a mistake; if the figurehead of a huge bronze eagle bearing the company motto, *Mein Feld is die Welt* (loosely, "The world is my oyster"), was included, the ship's length was 917 feet.

The boastful eagle later lost its wings in a gale, but sailing on the *Imperator* was clearly an impressive experience. The American ambassador to the German imperial court, James Gerard, thought her "a marvelous ship," adding that "at times it is hard to believe that one is on the sea. In addition to the regular dining saloon there is a grill-room and Ritz restaurant, with its palm garden, and, of course, an Hungarian band.

There is also a gymnasium and swimming pool, and nightly, in the enormous ballroom dances are given, the women dressing in their best, just as they do on shore." The *Imperator* was followed within two years by the *Vaterland*—"designed to look as much like a sumptuous hotel and as little like a ship as human imagination can do it." Then, on the brink of the First World War, the vast *Bismarck* was launched.

As soon as the conflict began, British and German ships were requisitioned and converted for war duties. Cunard had some twenty-six major vessels afloat. The British government reminded the company of its obligation to hand over the *Lusitania* and the *Mauretania*, but the Admiralty decided neither was suitable as an auxiliary cruiser—they simply consumed too much coal. The *Mauretania* was repainted to camouflage her for her new role as a troop transporter and hospital ship. During a lengthy refit in 1913, four six-inch gun rings had been fitted to the *Lusitania*'s deck to allow guns to be mounted quickly in time of war. However, she was now left with Cunard to continue the transatlantic run, but under the close eye of the Admiralty. The Admiralty would inform her master of the course she was to follow; any contact between Cunard and the ship, while at sea, had to be through the Admiralty; her cargo space had to be at the Admiralty's disposal.

It was a source of national pride that the swift and beautiful *Lusitania* would continue the transatlantic run. Her great speed could outpace most warships, and she could run twice as fast as any German U-boat yet built. There seemed little risk to a ship with such credentials. In the words of one admirer, she was "as unsinkable as a ship can be."

CHAPTER FOUR

Gott Strafe England!

*B*Y THE END OF 1914 a line of trenches over 450 miles long ran from Switzerland to the North Sea. Over 300,000 Frenchmen and nearly a quarter-million Germans were dead. Britain had lost some 30,000 men, nearly one-fifth of her small regular army. The war of movement on the Western Front was over. Stalemate had begun. In the east, too, stalemate was approaching. The Austro-Hungarian army had lost over 1.25 million men, and the Russians 1.5 million. Morale in both these armies was low, particularly among conscript troops from subjugated nations. Both needed to be shored up by their respective allies, who, in turn, were each looking for ways to achieve an early end to the impasse and a speedy victory.

In January 1915 the British war cabinet, with Winston Churchill playing a prominent role, saw the solution in a naval expedition to the Eastern Mediterranean and began to plan accordingly. The aim would be to force the Dardanelles, the heavily guarded strait between the Aegean and the Black Seas, so that, at a minimum, supplies could be got through to Russia and, at best, Turkey, which had joined the Austro-German alliance on 31 October 1914, could be forced quickly out of the war. Vigorous Allied action might perhaps draw Greece, and maybe even Bulgaria and Romania, into the Allied camp. Churchill believed that "at the summit true politics and strategy are one. The manoeuvre which brings an ally into the field is as serviceable as the one which wins a great battle." To that end, the British and the French were also strongly wooing the Italians to join their cause.

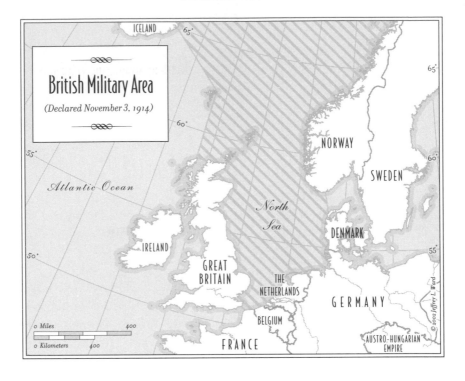

British Military Area

(Declared November 3, 1914)

ICELAND

NORWAY

SWEDEN

Atlantic Ocean

North Sea

DENMARK

IRELAND

GREAT BRITAIN

THE NETHERLANDS

GERMANY

BELGIUM

FRANCE

AUSTRO-HUNGARIAN EMPIRE

0 Miles 400
0 Kilometers 400

© 2002 Jeffrey L. Ward

Perhaps surprisingly for a nation whose power was historically land based, Germany was looking to the sea and to the submarine to break the deadlock. The actions of a U-boat captain on 20 October 1914 had first wakened the German navy to the U-boat's potential as a commerce raider. Captain Feldkirchner of the *U-17* forced the British merchant ship *Glitra* to stop in waters off the coast of Norway. He briefly searched her cargo of whiskey and sewing machines and ordered her crew to hand over their papers and take to their lifeboats. The *U-17* then sank the *Glitra* but obligingly towed her laden lifeboats for a quarter of an hour toward the shore. The *Glitra* was the first merchant ship to fall prey to a U-boat, and, as he sailed home to Germany, Feldkirchner was anxious about how his superiors would react. According to fellow U-boatman Johann Spiess, his action was "entirely unexpected. Attacks on commercial steamers had not been foreseen. The possibilities of that kind of warfare had not been anticipated." Feldkirchner need not have worried. He was commended, not censured, for his attack on the enemy's supply line.

From the first days of the war, each side had attempted to cut off the other's maritime commerce. On 5 August Germany mined the approaches to British North Sea ports. Britain responded with a long-range blockade of Germany. She stationed her cruisers to stop and search ships, neutral or not, destined for enemy ports. The Royal Navy then impounded "contraband" cargoes designed to help Germany's war efforts. In November Britain mined the North Sea and warned neutral shipping to stay clear. Like the German mining of the North Sea ports, these actions, in particular an elastic definition of what constituted *contraband* to include food, were of dubious legality.

Now, incensed at the British blockade and heartened by the attack on the *Glitra*, German submariners began to pressure the High Seas Fleet command for an all-out unrestricted trade war. "As England completely disregards international law, there is not the least reason why we should exercise any restraint," they argued. "We must make use of this weapon, and do so in the way most suitable to its peculiarities. A U-boat cannot spare the crews of steamers but must send them to the bottom with their ships. The shipping world can be warned . . . and all shipping trade with England should cease within a short time."

The high command agreed to this new initiative. On 4 February 1915, Germany announced a campaign of unrestricted submarine warfare. From 18 February, the waters around Great Britain, except for a designated route north of Scotland, would be a war zone in which all enemy ships "would be destroyed even if it is not possible to avoid thereby the dangers which threaten the crews and passengers." The announcement continued: "It may not always be possible to prevent the attacks meant for hostile ships from being directed against neutral ships." In a telegram to the German embassy in Washington, Berlin was even more specific, advising that "neutral vessels will not in most cases be recognizable as such in the war zone and will therefore be destroyed without more ado." The embassy should use the press to warn American vessels to keep clear of the war zone "to avoid dangerous complications."

U-boats were now to be equipped with machine guns, grenades, and formal instructions about contraband. Copies of the British-produced *Lloyd's Register*, listing every ship in the world, were a highly prized aid to identifying targets, but, as Johann Spiess wrote with regret, they "could not be obtained in Germany in sufficient quantities . . . and for the while we had to dispense with these."

U-boat men were euphoric: "We are, indeed, the masters of the sea," wrote one submariner. "U-boat after U-boat . . . like a girdle round our enemies, in defiance of them and their unscrupulous blockade." The Germans struck medals to celebrate this new phase of the naval war. One was shown to the American ambassador to Berlin, James Gerard. Tirpitz, with his domed bald head and long white forked beard, gazed sternly from one side. On the other a terse legend—*Gott Strafe England!*—expressed the hope that God would smite the enemy. Behind this motto Neptune, assisted by a submarine, rose dripping from the sea to blockade the distant English coast.

The German declaration was a personal victory for Admiral Tirpitz, who was convinced that the submarine was Germany's "most effective weapon" against British commerce. According to his postwar memoirs, he had personally favored a more limited blockade of the Thames on the grounds that Germany did not yet have sufficient submarines to effectively stop all traffic to British ports. He knew that to have any semblance of legality a blockade had to be "effective"—that is, there must be a reasonable chance of stopping any ship trying to break it. However, as one admiring young naval officer wrote, Tirpitz had "fought, with a doggedness which can hardly be described, for the employment of submarines and for the inauguration of intensified U-boat warfare." He had had to overcome opposition from Chancellor Bethmann Hollweg, Foreign Secretary Jagow, and the army high command, all of whom had been nervous that an unfettered U-boat campaign would provoke neutral countries.

But in early 1915 the British were not yet taking the U-boat threat to commercial traffic seriously. A year earlier Admiral Fisher, Churchill's unofficial adviser, had warned that U-boats were "a truly terrible threat for British commerce." Churchill's response had been that no "civilised power" would ever launch such a submarine campaign. He had continued to believe so, even after reappointing the seventy-three-year-old Fisher, officially over the age limit, as first sea lord at the end of October 1914. The returning Fisher succeeded Prince Louis of Battenberg, father of the future Lord Mountbatten, who had retired, despite his royal connections, at least partly due to suspicion of his German name and antecedents. Lord Charles Beresford proclaimed that "he is a German—he has German property and German servants and should not therefore occupy his present position."

Fisher strode back into the Admiralty demanding improvements to his office suite. "Lord Fisher can only think on a Turkish rug," commented a colleague acerbically. Fisher began firing off a series of his scrawled, heavily underlined memos in green ink, calculated to shake up the deepest recesses of the Royal Navy. He wrote cheerfully to a friend: "I'm *exceeding* busy! I've just told Garvin that war is 'Great conceptions' and 'Quick Decisions'! 'Think in Oceans,' 'Shoot at Sight.' I'm stirring up accordingly." Even so, British merchant ships continued to operate largely as normal, sailing unarmed and unescorted. The cream of the British navy's destroyers—the vessels best suited for defending vessels against U-boats—were otherwise engaged protecting Fisher's beloved Grand Fleet at Scapa Flow. It was a good time for Germany to strike.

By declaring unrestricted submarine warfare, the Germans were abandoning established international maritime law and custom. Indeed, the unfolding conflict was seeing laws reinterpreted, even reinvented, by both sides with great rapidity. A cartoon in the *Chicago Tribune* summed up the situation. Titled "An Overgrown Guest, or, The God of War Restricted by Old Rules," it showed Mars lying uncomfortably on the tiny procrustean bed of "international law," knees forced under his chin and shoulders against the headboard. "How do they expect a man to be comfortable in this?" he asks.

The convention that the Germans were now challenging was the ancient and chivalrous "Cruiser Rules," based on a code of conduct written in 1512 in the reign of King Henry VIII. They stated that an unarmed merchant ship could not simply be attacked on sight. She must be stopped and searched to establish her identity and the nature of her cargo. If neutral, she must be allowed to continue on her way after any contraband had been impounded. If hostile, the ship and her cargo could be seized as prizes or, if far from land, destroyed. Whatever the case, proper provision had to be made for the safety of passengers and crew.

These rules had largely been observed during the opening phase of the war, including by the British in their blockade of Germany, but they hardly fitted the evolving character of submarine warfare. To conform with Cruiser Rules, submarines had to surface—as the *U-17* had done to challenge the *Glitra*—but this made them highly vulnerable to attack. Furthermore, a submarine was too small either to spare a crew to take over the captured ship and sail her into port or to take on board the passengers and crew of a vessel it intended to sink.

The German U-boat service had been finding these archaic conventions of the sea increasingly unacceptable, complex, and risky. Johann Spiess, commanding the *U-9*, recalled a close shave during a U-boat raid on the British fishing fleet off the Dogger Bank. Sighting the trawler *Merry Islington*, he surfaced and fired a warning shot across her bow as required by the Cruiser Rules. The fishing crew lost no time and "nearly jumped out of their so'westers in clambering into their boats." Nevertheless, it still took too long—a British destroyer was making straight for the scene. The *U-9* had no time to dive—she needed seventy-five seconds to submerge the necessary fifty feet to reach safety—and only narrowly escaped by hiding behind the trawler in the gathering fog as the destroyer plowed past oblivious.

Another U-boat commander complained that it was often impossible to distinguish between enemy and neutral merchant shipping. This was not only because of poor visibility but because the British Admiralty had been vigorously encouraging merchant shipping to adopt what Churchill called "the well-known *ruse de guerre* of hoisting false [neutral] colours in order . . . to baffle and confuse the enemy." The Germans regarded this as illegal and began assiduously collecting evidence. Even a faint handwritten letter by a British sailor, noting casually that his ship had raised a neutral flag, found its way into the files of the German high command.

The Germans were particularly angered by one recent such incident involving Colonel Edward Mandell House, President Wilson's laconic Anglophile adviser. House was a Texan some eighteen months younger than Wilson. He was the son of an English emigrant who had made his money running the federal maritime blockade during the Civil War. He became a prominent adviser in Texas Democratic circles. When he first met Bryan, he described him as "impracticable . . . he feels his ideas are God-given" and the most opinionated man he had ever met. On the other hand, when he first met Wilson at the Gotham Hotel, New York City, in November 1911, a year before the presidential election and just as the latter was beginning his run for the presidential nomination, each recognized in the other a sympathetic soul mate and political ally. Soon afterward, House asked Wilson whether it was not strange that two men who had not known each other before should be so alike. Wilson replied, "My dear friend, we have known one another always." House delivered the Texan delegation to Wilson.

As a man who seems to have enjoyed bad health, House always refused office, taking pleasure both in proximity to power and in his ability to take time off when he wished or felt his health demanded it. In Britain the *Daily Mirror* attributed his lack of personal ambition to being "very wealthy and not a partisan." Wilson and House became even closer after Ellen Wilson's death as the president struggled both with consequent depression and the early months of the war.

In early 1915 Wilson recognized that the stalemate in the war offered one of the best opportunities for the United States to mediate a peace settlement before casualties rose too high and both troops and political positions became too entrenched to allow concessions on either side. He therefore sent House abroad on a secret mission to investigate the prospects for a brokered peace. Somewhat surprisingly, given his neutral status, House chose to sail on 30 January 1915 not on board an American ship but on the British Cunarder *Lusitania*.

As the liner neared the Irish coast after a rough crossing—during which, House recalled, "the *Lusitania* big as she is tossed about like a cork in the rapids"—her captain, David Dow, flew the American flag. As House wrote in his diary, this "created much excitement, and comment and speculation ranged in every direction." A fellow passenger and relation of Lord Charles Beresford told him that the captain "had been greatly alarmed the night before" and had asked the passenger, given his naval connections, to remain on the bridge with him because he "expected to be torpedoed, and that was the reason for raising the American Flag. . . . The alarm of the Captain for the safety of his boat caused him to map out a complete program for saving of the passengers, the launching of lifeboats." He told the passenger that "if the boilers were not struck by the torpedoes, the boat could remain afloat for at least an hour, and in that time he would endeavor to save the passengers."

House was pursued by the press as soon as he landed and gave a subtly evasive and thus suitably diplomatic response, recording in his diary: "Every newspaper in London has asked me about it, but fortunately, I was not an eye witness to it and have been able to say that I only knew it from hearsay." He foresaw "many possible complications arising from this incident," and he was right. The incident caused fury in Germany, which insisted that it was illegal for British shipping to hide behind neutral flags. In the United States the British action roused fears that U-boats would start attacking American vessels on suspicion of their being enemy ships in disguise. President Wilson protested formally to London on 10 February 1915 that the use of neutral flags would create intolerable risks for neutral countries while failing to protect British vessels. The British government responded blandly that the flag had been flown at the request of the *Lusitania*'s American passengers to indicate that there were neutral Americans on board. Furthermore, Germany's declaration that she would sink any British merchant ships on sight clearly made such actions legitimate. An American journalist wrote wryly that Britannia not only ruled the waves but waived the rules.

Scarcely a week after Germany declared her intention to launch unrestricted U-boat warfare, the British Admiralty issued secret guidance to merchant captains. If they sighted a hostile submarine, they should do their "utmost to escape," but if attacked head-on, they were to steer straight for the submarine at "utmost speed" and force her to dive. In other words, they should attempt to ram her, although the word *ram* was studiously avoided in the text. By 15 February the German government had learned of this unwelcome development from a copy of the guidance discovered on a captured British vessel. Anxious memos passed between the various German government departments reporting their interpretation of the document that "merchant ships are ordered to sail in convoy and to ram German submarines seeking to search them." The former was not true. The latter essentially was.

Germany complained to America, alleging that the British had offered a large reward for the destruction of the first U-boat rammed by a merchantman. The Germans also claimed that this "right to ram" changed the status of merchant ships from peaceful vessels, entitled to be given warning, to that of warships, which often used ramming as a mode of attack. They warned that any merchant captain who attacked in this way would be treated not as a serviceman but as a criminal. In March 1915 Captain Charles Fryatt saved his merchant ship the *Brussels* by attempting to ram a U-boat. When the Germans caught him ten months later, they shot him.

The Germans were also well aware that a number of British merchantmen were defensively armed. This was in line with precedent established during the age of sail that possession of one or two modest guns, usually mounted on the stern to hold off an attacker while fleeing, did not turn a merchantman into a naval vessel. The existence of these armaments was no secret. Winston Churchill had spoken of them openly to Parliament on several occasions well before the war, arguing that "if the British ships had no armament, they would be at the mercy of any foreign liner carrying one effective gun and a few rounds of ammunition." In March 1914 he had told Parliament specifically that forty merchant ships had been equipped with two 4.7-inch guns apiece and that by 31 March 1915, seventy merchant ships would be so armed. The original intention of arming merchant ships was to protect them against surface raiders. But on 25 February 1915 the Admiralty advised that if a defensively armed merchantman was being pursued by a U-boat with obviously hostile intentions, the captain should "open fire in self-defence" even if the submarine had not yet fired a gun or launched a torpedo.

Britain's actions were denounced by Germany in an increasingly angry war of words during which each side accused the other of illegality and the British taxed the Germans with "pure piracy." Churchill ordered that in future any captured U-boat crewmen should not be treated as ordinary prisoners of war but should be segregated for possible trial as pirates. In retaliation, the indignant Germans selected thirty-seven captured British officers, "picking those whom they supposed related to the most prominent families in Great Britain," and placed them in solitary confinement. An enraged British press demanded that any special privileges given to Tirpitz's son, a naval officer captured earlier in the war, should be removed.

In the United States, the German declaration of unrestricted submarine warfare drew a swift response. On 10 February President Wilson declared that Germany's action violated the rights of neutral countries and that she would be held to "strict accountability" for any consequent loss of American life. Those two words would achieve great significance in the months ahead. Yet he still hoped that this latest escalation could be curbed. On 20 February he sent a conciliatory note to both Germany and Britain suggesting that submarines should not attack merchant vessels of any nationality. He also proposed that food should be allowed to reach the civilian population of Germany through agencies in Germany designated by the United States. But such hopes were disappointed. Walter Hines Page, U.S. ambassador to Britain, reported the impasse: "I do not see a ray of hope for any agreement between Germany and England whereby England will permit food to enter Germany under any condition. Since Germany has declared her intention to prevent anything from abroad entering England, it is practically certain that England will prevent everything from entering Germany."

Woodrow Wilson had appointed his friend Page as ambassador despite his lack of diplomatic experience as a reward for his loyal support. Their friendship went back to the time when Page, a publisher and editor, had published Wilson's books. It continued during his election campaign, in which Page played a prominent role. Page had, at first, been slightly reluctant to serve, worrying that he might not have enough money to keep up the position and that his attractive daughter Katherine would have so much contact with foreigners she might marry one. House advised him to keep her in the United States but noted privately, "I did not tell him so but I thought the fact that he was a man of very small means would protect her more than anything else."

Gott Strafe England!

Once arrived in London in spring 1913, the fifty-eight-year-old Page quickly began to enjoy his new position. Like House, he maintained good relations with the long-serving British foreign secretary, Sir Edward Grey. When war came, Grey took particular care to spend time with both men, listening and carefully setting out the Allied position. Page was soon unreservedly pro-British, seeing the conflict as one between British democracy and German autocracy. In September 1914 he wrote that the British were not militarists, but that the nation had "a quality that is invincible." He also noted, "I thank Heaven I'm of their race and blood." His wholehearted advocacy of the British cause slowly lost him Wilson's trust. It may also have inhibited clear understanding of the two governments' respective positions.

America's threat to hold Germany to account was tested when, on 28 March 1915, the *U-28* sank the SS *Falaba*, an unarmed British passenger-cargo ship of 5,000 tons, in the recently declared war zone off the southern Irish coast. Over 100 lives were lost, including that of one American, mining engineer Leon Thresher, bound for the Gold Coast. The *Falaba* was one day out of Liverpool on her voyage to West Africa and was given some warning by the *U-28*'s commander, Baron Forstner, who had surfaced. However, he did not allow many minutes for evacuation before firing a single torpedo—twenty-three minutes according to the U-boat war diary, seven according to British accounts.

The *Falaba* was hit in the engine room, and it seems likely that one of her boilers exploded. She sank in eight minutes. The British set up an inquiry under Lord Mersey, who had chaired the inquiry into the loss of the *Titanic*. The Germans claimed that the *Falaba* had been sending wireless messages and firing distress rockets, hence the short time allowed for abandoning ship. They also maintained that some of the rifle cartridges she was carrying among her general cargo exploded, hastening the sinking. There was a furious outcry in the American press, which called the sinking "massacre" and "piracy," but the president did not invoke the doctrine of "strict accountability" or react formally in any way.

Meanwhile, Churchill was not unduly perturbed by the U-boat campaign, which initially was having little impact. By the end of its first week, only 11 ships had been attacked and 7 sunk out of 1,381 vessels arriving at or departing from British ports. During the second week, out of 1,474 arrivals and departures, only 3 ships were attacked and all escaped. By April 1915, the British press was rejoicing that inward and outward sailings were now running at over 1,500 a week. On the surface it was business as usual. Churchill even believed that there might be certain political advantages in the new situation. On 12 February, just a week before the German declaration came into force, he had written to the president of the Board of Trade, Walter Runciman, that it was "most important to attract neutral shipping to our shores, in the hope especially of embroiling the United States with Germany. . . . For our part we want the traffic—the more the better; and if some of it gets into trouble, better still." He was disappointed by President Wilson's reaction to the *Falaba* sinking but could hope that U-boats might attack an American vessel within the war zone.

The British press might have been less complacent had they known that in early March the *U-27* had been lying submerged on the approaches to Liverpool in wait for the *Lusitania.* In his war diary for 2 March, her commander, Kapitänleutnant Bernhard Wegener, recorded how several large steamers passed temptingly close but he let them go. He was reluctant to reveal his position because, thanks to briefing from Fregattenkapitän Hermann Bauer, commander of the Third U-boat Half-Flotilla, he knew there was the prospect of a far more glittering prize. "The *Lusitania* was expected to arrive in English waters on 4 March and in my present position I believed I had a good chance of attacking her," he wrote in his war diary. But his wait was in vain. On 5 March he turned reluctantly homeward.

Wegener had missed the *Lusitania* by less than a day. Furthermore, Admiralty attempts to provide the ship with an escort had degenerated into farce. The episode had begun at 10 A.M. on Friday 5 March when the Cunard office in Liverpool received a telephone call from Holyhead from "someone enquiring where the *Lusitania* was." The Cunard official asked repeatedly who the caller was. Then over the crackling lines he thought he made out a voice saying that he was the commanding officer of HMS *Liffey*, although the line was so bad he could not be sure. By now thoroughly suspicious, he told the inquirer to apply to the Admiralty and terminated the call. The company at once alerted Captain Richard Webb, who, as director of the Admiralty's Trade Division, was responsible for providing guidance to merchant shipping.

Several hours later came another land telephone call to Cunard. This time the line was clearer, and the caller identified himself as the officer in command of HMS *Louis*. He demanded to know "when I may expect the *Lusitania* off the South Stack as I have orders to escort her into Liverpool." The Cunard official again replied that he was not in a position to give out such information and again referred the caller to the Admiralty.

That night Captain Dow, on board the *Lusitania*, was astonished to receive a wireless message en clair asking when he expected to be off the Stack. Using Britain's Merchant Vessel (MV) code, he inquired who was asking. The reply came back: "I HAVE NO M.V. CODE. WHAT OTHER CODES HAVE YOU? *LAVEROCK* AND *LOUIS* ARE DETAILED TO ESCORT YOU." Dow asked where these ships were, and learning that they were some distance away, he decided he would be better off sailing straight to Liverpool. He also refused to reveal his position in spite of a further pleading message: "YOU ARE QUITE RIGHT NOT TO SIGNAL YOUR POSITION 'EN CLAIR' BUT TRY AND GIVE ME SOME HINT SO AS TO SAVE WASTING YOUR ESCORT'S TIME AND FUEL." The *Lusitania* crossed the Liverpool Bar without incident in the early hours of Saturday, 6 March.

A subsequent Admiralty inquiry into the fiasco revealed that no one had bothered to inform Cunard that the *Lusitania* was to be escorted; that the two ships detailed to protect the liner had "no idea at what time she might be expected"; that the officer commanding the escort first tried telephoning the coast guard for help, and when that failed, he contacted Cunard. He then had the idea of contacting the *Lusitania* direct, only to be thwarted by his lack of the MV code. After patrolling fruitlessly, he at last recalled both vessels back to Milford. His report to his senior officer ended apologetically: "I did everything I could think of to find the *Lusitania*. But I regret that I did not think of communicating with the Senior Naval Officer at Liverpool."

The Admiralty inquiry concluded that the inducements to the *Lusitania* to "hint" at her position were "extraordinary" and that "had this hint been received by a submarine she might have made use of it." But it also concluded that no further action should be taken.

CHAPTER FIVE

The American Armory

G ERMANY MEANWHILE was growing increasingly anxious about the huge quantities of armaments being shipped from America to the Allies. The United States had half a dozen large powder and explosive factories and numerous other industrial enterprises that had readily adapted themselves to production of war materials. At the outset of the war Britain, France, and Russia had agreed to "cash and carry" contracts whereby they undertook to receive at the factories whatever war matériel was available, to pay for it on the spot, and to accept the whole risk of transporting it.

In August 1914 the French government had attempted to raise loans to finance its purchases through J. P. Morgan and Company. However, Secretary of State Bryan believed money to be "the worst of contrabands. . . . it commands all other things." He convinced President Wilson that it would be "inconsistent with the true spirit of neutrality" for American bankers to make loans to governments at war. J. P. Morgan Jr., known as Jack, the head of the company following his father's death in 1913, determined to overturn this ruling by an administration that he despised. In his view, "a greater lot of perfectly incompetent and apparently thoroughly crooked people has never, as far as I know, run or attempted to run a first-class country."

Jack Morgan approached Robert Lansing, a fifty-year-old New York lawyer, who had been appointed counselor to the State Department in March 1914. Lansing was an Anglophile and an ambitious right-wing Democrat often to be found wearing British tweeds. One of his colleagues unkindly described him as "meticulous, metallic and mousy." Lansing was out of sympathy with the secretary of state's radical, antiestablishment ideas. Both temperamentally and professionally he inclined to interpret the detail of existing legislation to justify his preferred policy stance. Nevertheless, he took much of the burden of day-to-day administration from Bryan, who had never been happy with detail. In any case, it distracted Bryan from the lucrative lecturing which the president had specifically agreed he could continue. Wilson and Lansing were drawn into frequent contact, short-circuiting Bryan. Lansing's butler later recalled that messages and calls to Lansing's home came often from the White House but only infrequently from Bryan.

Morgan and a fellow New York banker, Samuel McRoberts of National City Bank, soon persuaded Lansing about the benefits to U.S. commerce of a more flexible approach toward the financing of Allied purchases. On 23 October 1914 McRoberts provided Lansing with a helpful memorandum on the subject. Profiting from Bryan's absence from Washington, Lansing quickly copied the phraseology of the letter verbatim, pausing only to insert a few first-person pronouns to claim the ideas as his own. He rushed over to the White House at 8:30 the same evening with his memo and easily secured Wilson's approval. Henceforth, American banks would not make loans to warring governments; they would *extend them credit*.

The hairsplitting distinction between credits and loans could only have come from lawyers such as Wilson and Lansing. According to the formal note of their conversation, which Lansing wrote later that night, they concluded that "an arrangement as to credits has to do with a commercial debt rather than with a loan of money" and therefore was not a matter for government. Lansing's stock rose with both Wilson and Wall Street. Bryan's views can be imagined. The Allies hastened to arrange large credits with American bankers, who in turn eagerly advanced money to fund contracts with American manufacturers. J. P. Morgan and Company was soon playing a pivotal and highly profitable role in keeping Britain and her allies supplied with American munitions.

George Booth, deputy director-general of the Ministry of Munitions and a cousin of Sir Alfred Booth, the chairman of Cunard, had quickly identified Britain's need for a central purchasing and financial agency in New York and suggested Morgan's. He believed not only that Morgan's firm would do the job competently but also that this would bind the powerful banking house still closer to the Allied cause. The arrangement worked well. In the first year of the war Morgan's "credit department" purchased war matériel worth $1,100,453,950, assisted by British Treasury staff and naval and military ordnance officers dressed as civilians and attached to the British consulate in New York. After inspection, the purchased goods were passed to the British Admiralty's forwarding agents, G. K. Sheldon, amid strict security to prevent enemy agents from discovering the names of shippers and manufacturers.

Germany observed these activities with anger and alarm. Feelings against the United States ran high in all levels of society. When Ambassador Gerard sought an audience with the kaiser in March 1915, the uncompromising reply was "I have nothing against Mr. Gerard personally, but I will not see the Ambassador of a country which furnishes arms and ammunition to the enemies of Germany." Indeed, the kaiser's refusal to receive Gerard would last until 25 September 1915. The ambassador was taken aback by the strength of feeling. He was surprised to find an article in a Cologne newspaper which said, "quite seriously," that "Germany had done everything possible to win the favor of America, that Roosevelt had been offered a review of German troops, that the Emperor had invited Americans who came to Kiel on their yachts to dine with him, and that he had even sat through the lectures given by American exchange professors!"

The United States responded that under international law private individuals and corporations had the right to sell arms and munitions to any country they chose and that the 1907 Hague Convention had expressly endorsed this right. In theory there was no reason why Germany, too, could not import munitions from America, but she knew there was little chance of getting them through the British blockade. In April the German ambassador, Count Johann von Bernstorff, delivered a note from his government complaining, with some justice, that "in reality the United States is supplying only Germany's enemies, a fact which is not in any way modified by the theoretical willingness to furnish Germany as well." However, in making his protest Bernstorff conveniently forgot that during the Boer War German manufacturers had sold arms to Britain, claiming that if the Boers could also transport them from Germany they could also make purchases. He overlooked, too, Germany's supply of arms to Mexican dictator Huerta despite the informal American blockade.

Germany also saw evidence of America's partisan stance in the fact that when war broke out the United States had interned German liners berthed in American ports on the grounds that they were effectively auxiliary cruisers of the German navy. Yet no such criteria had been applied to British ships like the *Lusitania* and the *Mauretania*, which were classed as Royal Naval Reserved Merchant Cruisers and liable to be called up at the Admiralty's pleasure.

The German government tried to pressure the Wilson administration, arguing that the level of exports from America to the Allies had reached unacceptable proportions. Official German communiqués contained such pointed references as "heavy artillery fire in certain sections of the Western front, mostly with American ammunition" and "captured French artillery officers say that they have great stores of American ammunition." The U.S. government remained unresponsive, but Germany was already pursuing another method of redressing what she perceived to be an unfair balance—namely, sabotage. A German foreign office telegram dispatched to the German military attaché in Washington on 25 January 1915 said bluntly: "The sabotage in the United States can extend to all kinds of factories for war material deliveries" and named several contacts who could suggest the names of "suitable people for sabotage." Such activities were, of course, both illegal and undiplomatic and could only lead to a worsening of relations if revealed.

―――∞∞∞―――

By early 1915, New York, and particularly the hectic docksides from which 80 percent of ships bound from the United States to Great Britain departed, had been infiltrated by Allied and German spies. The latter included Captain Franz von Rintelen, a tall, well-dressed German naval officer with greenish gray eyes and hair cut *en brosse*. He was well connected and knew Tirpitz as a family friend. On 22 March the thirty-six-year-old Rintelen had boarded the Norwegian SS *Kristianiafjord* for the United States. He was traveling under a false Swiss passport under the alias Emile Victor Gaché. New initials had been sewn onto his linen, which had then been laundered so it would not look brand-new.

He reached New York safely on 3 April 1915. He had two main objectives on which to spend the considerable official German funds at his disposal. The first was to bring about General Huerta's return to Mexico, and to power, thereby embroiling the United States in Mexico again. If successful, this stratagem would both distract America from goings-on in Europe and prompt the diversion of weapons from export to the Allies to use by America's own forces. Rintelen's second and more general mission was to sabotage the shipping of war matériel from the United States to Germany's enemies.

According to his memoirs, he had a very specific task in this regard. A member of the German Reichstag, Herr Erzberger, had made contact with an American named Malvin Rice, who claimed close connections with the American Du Pont de Nemours Powder Company, believed to be supplying the Allies with various explosives, including pyroxiline, commonly known as "gun cotton." Rice said that the company was holding a large stock of explosives, and Rintelen hoped that Germany "might, with his help, make large purchases of that product . . . sufficient in fact to jeopardize, for some time at least, the delivery of munitions for the Allies." He summarized his task with cheerful directness: "I'll buy up what I can, and blow up what I can't!"

When Malvin Rice failed to make contact, Rintelen bided his time. He called on the monocled German military and naval attachés, Franz von Papen and Karl Boy-Ed, who stayed at the German Club when they were in New York. "I cannot say that they were very glad to see me," he later wrote. But he was not perturbed, dismissing von Papen as a crude, stupid man who had married for money and whose only claims to be military attaché were "good horses, good address, and similar social amenities."

For their part, the two attachés had their own schemes in New York. They resented an interloper, however enthusiastic, over whose activities and funds they had little control. The mood was little different when Rintelen was summoned to meet Count Bernstorff, the suave, elegantly dressed German ambassador with a well-deserved reputation as a lady-killer. Over drinks at the Ritz-Carlton, Bernstorff coolly and directly asked Rintelen, "What is the object of your presence in America?"

Rintelen's arrival threatened to disrupt Germany's carefully oiled, if somewhat crude, intelligence and propaganda machine in New York City. At its head was George Viereck, a "rather decadent poet" whose works had overtones of Oscar Wilde and Algernon Charles Swinburne, but who, as editor of the *Fatherland*, the chief newspaper for German-Americans, was an eminent pro-German publicist. He had set up a "propaganda cabinet" of ten men, including Bernhard Dernburg, erstwhile colonial secretary of the Reich who was also heavily involved in espionage, and Heinrich Albert, commercial councillor at the German embassy, who would later distinguish himself by leaving a briefcase full of spying secrets in a New York streetcar. Their aim was to influence American public opinion in favor of the German cause. They also tried to woo influential public figures. Viereck managed to engineer a meeting with former president Teddy Roosevelt in February 1915, only to be told that Germany was "a nation without a sense of international morality."

The propaganda cabinet worked closely with the German ambassador and the naval and military attachés, and their efforts sometimes lacked subtlety. The *Times* correspondent in Washington reported that "the story is revived that Mr. Schwab and the Bethlehem Steel Works are evading Mr. Bryan's prohibition of the export of submarines to the Allies by despatching to England and Canada parts of submarines packed and disguised as machinery. This story is regarded as the product of the band of propagandists who, under the auspices of Captain Boy-Ed, the German Naval Attaché, were apparently responsible for other canards which have been exposed."

Boy-Ed and von Papen were also embroiled in harebrained schemes of which the ambassador chose to be unaware. As Bernstorff later wrote, "each received independent instructions from Berlin" from their military and naval superiors. Indeed, he went on to describe their activities as "crimes." They had close links with the Austro-Hungarian ambassador Constantin Dumba, another enthusiastic intriguer. Boy-Ed had encouraged Richard Stegler, a German naval reservist, to obtain a false American passport so that he could travel to England as a spy. Stegler was arrested by federal Secret Service agents and put on trial but managed not to implicate Boy-Ed, whose involvement was so well known that the press reported the case under such headlines as "Stegler Keeps Boy-Ed Out of Passport Case."

Von Papen's activities were inhibited by his scarcely concealed contempt for his hosts, whom he considered "idiotic Yankees." He had recently and unsuccessfully incited a German, Werner Horn, to blow up one of the railway bridges connecting Maine and Canada. It was one of several such plots. A witness later gave evidence that in early 1915 von Papen had "financed to the extent of over $3,500 . . . an outfit of sleigh and horses, dynamite, fuse, food, etc, etc, in Tacoma for the purpose of going through the Rockies and dynamiting a bridge." Like Rintelen, von Papen was anxious to frustrate British purchases of munitions. His tactics were to uncover the names of Britain's suppliers and to place huge

Franz Von Papen

orders to delay the filling of British ones. He also invented fake companies with reassuringly English-sounding names that offered nonexistent products to the Allies and wasted their time and sometimes even secured substantial prepayments. However, J. P. Morgan and Company's coordination of purchasing for the British largely put an end to this. With Boy-Ed, von Papen was keeping a close watch on the docks and sending regular reports to Berlin of shipping schedules and cargoes. In spring 1915 both were taking a keen interest in the *Lusitania*.

<hr />

The British were well aware of such activity through their naval attaché at their Washington embassy, Captain Guy Gaunt, who coordinated intelligence reports from Allied agents and informants. Gaunt had been born in Australia and was a likable, outgoing man. He was also a fine horseman and yachtsman. Among his key contacts in the American administration was Robert Lansing, with whom he lunched frequently and discreetly and with whom he soon formed a close friendship. Both their careers and their countries benefited from the confidences exchanged. Unsubstantiated gossip suggested that Lansing also benefited financially due to his exploitation on Wall Street of insider information on forthcoming British arms contracts with American companies. It was

not the first time that Lansing had been accused of using insider knowledge and official position to his own commercial benefit. Similar
charges had been made ten years earlier, but when reexamined at President Wilson's request prior to Lansing's appointment in spring 1914,
they were found to be unproven.

To provide intelligence on the activities of the German and Austro-
Hungarian embassies, Gaunt had the good luck to secure the services of
a Czech patriot named Emmanuel Viktor Voska. Voska saw the Austro-
Hungarian Empire's defeat as key to his country's independence. He
managed to secure intelligence for Gaunt from Czechs already employed
at the Austro-Hungarian embassy such as the mail clerk. He also infiltrated compatriots into the two embassies, including, he claimed, a
young woman as Countess Bernstorff's personal maid and a young man
as one of the German embassy's chauffeurs. Among the intelligence provided in due course by the chauffeur was news of former Mexican dictator Huerta's return to the United States in April 1915 and his contacts
with Rintelen, von Papen, and Boy-Ed. Guy Gaunt kept such valuable
information largely to himself but occasionally traded it with Robert
Lansing over their confidential lunches. He leaked much of the low-level
but discreditable material, including details of Ambassador Bernstorff's
affairs with American beauties, to friendly American newspapers to
assist the British propaganda campaign.

Gaunt also worked closely with Britain's consul general in New York,
Sir Courtenay Bennett, who was responsible for civilian counterintelli-
gence. Gaunt was irritated by "the excessive stupidity and gullibility of the
Consul-General," who had "an unfortunate knack of believing any story
no matter what its source." However, he shared Bennett's alarm at the
poor security and potential for sabotage in the docks, which were a melting pot of different nationalities. Sir Courtenay Bennett had long been
sending agitated reports to the British foreign office: "There is no doubt
whatever that every vessel of the Cunard Company, whilst in the port of
New York, is kept under the closest possible observation by German
agents from the time she arrives to the moment she sails. . . . men of
unmistakable German appearance have been on the docks at different
times, whilst steamers including the *Lusitania* have been tied up." Gaunt
and Bennett knew that the Germans were targeting not only German-
Americans but also supporters of the Irish nationalist cause and crew
members of German ships interned at the start of the war. These men

were cooling their heels with little to occupy them and could mingle easily among the dockworkers. As a result, Gaunt and Bennett were employing detective agencies such as Pinkerton's to keep watch on the docks and
photograph anything suspicious.

As early as December 1914, Cunard had alerted the captains of the
Lusitania and the *Mauretania* to Admiralty concern over "the question of
enemy aliens working in connection with loading and discharging cargo
or bunkers on board British ships." In reality, though, the ships' officers
had as much chance of vetting dockworkers as the U.S. Customs' Neutrality Squad had of ensuring there was no contraband aboard departing
ships. Bennett also warned Cunard that attempts might be made to
smuggle bombs on board the company's ships, but Cunard's general
manager in New York, Bostonian Charles Sumner, was dismissive.

Sumner's attitude confirmed Bennett's long-held belief that Cunard's
New York offices had been infiltrated at the senior level. He had previously
complained to British intelligence in London about Sumner's attitude and
behavior, which he considered disloyal, offensive, and rude. Gaunt's reaction was more measured. When he first met Sumner, he concluded that he
was "undoubtedly hostile to the British Government" but wondered "how
far this negative attitude had been brought on by a stupid Consul-General
and how far it had existed before."

Meanwhile, Rintelen, who had moved into the "modest but good"
Great Northern Hotel on Fifty-seventh Street, was pursuing his own
schemes. He had soon discovered that his plan to buy up large quantities
of explosives was a pipe dream. America's manufacturing capacity was so
great that "if I had bought up the market on Tuesday, there would still
have been an enormous fresh supply on Wednesday." Instead, he too
began to frequent the docks and saw "numerous English, French and
Russian transports waiting to take munitions on board." He systematically studied conditions on the docks, looking for potential saboteurs.
He noted the "large number of German sailors, mates, and captains . . .
hanging about the harbor with nothing to do" and the many Irish dock-
ers "who were far from friendly to England or those allied to her."

Rintelen reestablished contact with a man he had known previously
who seemed to be trusted by both Germans and Irish alike. Dr. Bunz
had formerly been German consul in New York but was now the representative there of the Hamburg-Amerika Line. He asked Rintelen to
help him lay his hands on some detonators to enable him to sabotage

Allied shipping leaving New York. Rintelen eagerly agreed and set up a spurious import-export company—E. V. Gibbons, Inc.—in a two-room office on Cedar Street in New York's financial district. One day, a German chemist, Walther Scheele—whose Hoboken laboratory was already funded by von Papen—called on him, bringing along a curious device "as big as a cigar" and the same shape. It was made of hollow lead with a circular disk of copper dividing it into two chambers. One chamber was filled with picric acid, the other with sulfuric. Wax plugs at either end ensured that it was airtight. Scheele explained the simple principle behind his surprisingly effective invention. The two acids would gradually eat their way through the copper disk. When they came into contact, an intensely hot flame some eight to twelve inches long would shoot out of both ends and the lead tube would melt away. The device was, in fact, a time-delayed firebomb. He described to the fascinated Rintelen how, by precisely controlling the thickness of the copper disk, one could also control the timing of the explosion.

Rintelen immediately saw the possibilities and paid the chemist for the right to use the device however he wished. He then set about finding dedicated saboteurs to smuggle them on board ships carrying munitions to the Allies. His plan was to make the copper disk sufficiently thick to delay the moment of ignition until the ships were well beyond U.S. territorial waters. But he faced a problem. Where could these incendiary bombs safely be manufactured? The New York Police Bomb Squad was keeping a rigorous lookout for exactly such activities. The most secure place Rintelen could think of was on board one of the German liners interned in New York Harbor. If his scheme was discovered, at least Germany could not be accused of making bombs on American soil. Rintelen chose the liner *Friedrich der Grosse* and manufactured five bombs in this "great dark ship," which now became the scene of "ghostly activity." The bombs were designed to explode in fifteen days.

Meanwhile, stories were reaching the German embassy that the *Lusitania*, due to sail from New York on 1 May, was carrying small-arms ammunition concealed in barrels of flour and that heavy guns were mounted on her deck. Captain Boy-Ed was instructed to find out whether the *Lusitania* was indeed armed. He approached Paul König, originally an auditor for the Hamburg-Amerika Line but since 1912 a species of special investigator and now security chief in charge of the interned German liners at Hoboken. He was also a spymaster and saboteur with close links with Boy-Ed, von Papen, and Rintelen. Upon the outbreak of war, he had organized a network of agents and maintained discreet links with the German embassy, instructing the attachés in such elementary espionage techniques as how to avoid being shadowed. This quiet, tall, powerfully built man used many aliases, and his agents knew him as Stemler. Evidence suggests that he had a number of New York detectives on his payroll and that he had even infiltrated agents into the police as cadets.

König was particularly interested in the movements of enemy ships, their cargoes and routes. In early 1915 he sent a man named William McCulley to Britain to obtain "information as to certain ships" that would be useful to German U-boats. In New York he paid his spies three dollars a day for intelligence. One of them was a poor German reservist, Gustav Stahl, who had arrived in America in August 1914 after, it was rumored, a fight with a policeman whom he had pushed off a Frankfurt bridge into the River Main. Stahl, always desperate for money, agreed to investigate whether the *Lusitania* was carrying guns and report back. There was a long-standing suspicion that she was. Two years previously, in May 1913, when she had entered dry dock in Liverpool for repairs, the *New York Tribune* reported dockside gossip that she was to be equipped with "high-power naval rifles in conformity with England's new policy of arming passenger ships."

Members of the German propaganda cabinet were also worried about the *Lusitania*, but their concerns were rather different. Sensitive to American public opinion, they were becoming increasingly anxious about what might happen if a large number of Americans were killed in a U-boat attack. As George Viereck remarked, "Sooner or later some big passenger boat with Americans on board will be sunk by a submarine, then there will be hell to pay."

PART TWO

Final
Crossing

※

CHAPTER SIX

The Warning

> **NOTICE!**
> TRAVELLERS intending to
> embark on the Atlantic voyage
> are reminded that a state of
> war exists between Germany
> and her allies and GreatBritian
> and her allies; that the zone of
> war includes the waters adja-
> cent to the British Isles; that,
> in accordance with formal no-
> tice given by the Imperial Ger-
> man Government, vessels fly-
> ing the flag of Great Britian, or
> of any of her allies, are liable to
> destruction in those waters and
> that travellers sailing in the
> war zone on ships of Great
> Britian or her allies do so at
> their own risk.
> **IMPERIAL GERMAN EMBASSY,**
> WASHINGTON, D. C., APRIL 22, 1915.

*A*s New York's docks stirred into life early on Saturday, 1 May 1915, the *Lusitania*'s sailing day, a rumor began to spread from pier to pier. Workers left their stations and hurried through the light drizzle to find a paper and read the startling news for themselves. In more than half a dozen New York newspapers, sometimes on the very page where Cunard was advertising its transatlantic schedules, was a stark warning framed in black.

Such a warning was unprecedented, and, of course, it caused a sensation. Ambassador Bernstorff told the reporters who now swooped on him in Washington that the notice was no more than a general friendly warning. However, he later confided to a well-known American newspaper editor that Berlin had sent him the notice two months previously. He had kept it in his desk until Berlin peremptorily ordered him to publish it. George Viereck would tell a different story, claiming in his memoirs that he and the German propaganda cabinet had drafted the warning and urged it on the ambassador, who had in turn consulted Berlin before approving it.

The British ambassador, Sir Cecil Spring-Rice, was also besieged by newspapermen, which he probably disliked as much as did Bernstorff. Bearded, bespectacled, balding, with a preference for baggy suits whose pockets he stuffed with documents, he was a nervous man whose health had broken down soon after his arrival in 1912. Although only in his midfifties, he was by now a semi-invalid, accounting for his sometimes peevish manner.

Spring-Rice had received warning of the notice on 29 April, when an anonymous caller left a proof at the embassy, together with a terse handwritten note:

> *Above notice will appear in a local paper Saturday, May 1 and in about 40 other papers the same day and two ensuing Saturdays. The information may have no value but am sending it because I wish Allies to win. No signature because it might cost me my job.*
>
> *signed 'patriotically' 1776*

Spring-Rice had dismissed it as a hoax or a bluff. It was only now, on 1 May, that he cabled the news to London.

The Warning

To the *Lusitania*'s passengers, some of whom were already converging on Cunard's Pier 54 at the west end of Fourteenth Street, the warning was a shock. Although the notice did not specifically mention the *Lusitania*, the threat seemed clear enough. Charles Sumner hurried to the pier as the Cunard Company's spokesman. He assured anxious passengers that there was no risk whatsoever and briefed reporters with equal confidence: "The Germans have been trying to spoil our trade for some time, but never until to-day have they manifested such an actively unfriendly desire to put us out of business. . . . The fact is that the *Lusitania* . . . is too fast for any submarine. No German vessel of war can get near her."

Sumner did not mention that the ship would be sailing under reduced power. Cunard had closed down one of the ship's four boiler rooms at the beginning of the war as an economy measure—at top speed the liner consumed 1,000 tons of coal a day. As a result, the *Lusitania*'s top speed was reduced from twenty-five knots to twenty-one. But although speed was commonly agreed to be the best protection against U-boat attack, such a small reduction seemed insignificant. No ship doing more than fourteen knots had yet been torpedoed. Sumner's staff adopted the tactic, when asked, of giving passengers an "indication" that the *Lusitania* would arrive "on the sixth day" while being vague about the precise arrival time. Meanwhile, another Cunard official was telling a *Tribune* reporter that not only was the liner fast, but the British Admiralty would take "mighty good care of the *Lusitania*." There was "absolutely nothing to fear."

Despite such reassurances, arriving passengers were disconcerted by press attention that smacked of hysteria. Photographers seemed more assiduous than usual. And they were not exclusively interested in celebrities. One remarked ghoulishly to a young man, "Well, if anything happens, we've got your picture!" Olive Hanson, who had been visiting her sister in Canada and was now sailing home, was chilled to notice that some photographers were taking pictures of the ship while announcing blatantly, "Last Voyage of the *Lusitania*." Other passengers were disturbed that, as far as they could see, no special precautions were being taken. Friends and relations were allowed to accompany them on board without challenge, and at least one first-class passenger fretted that "no officer or any one else questioned me or asked me about my baggage." Captain Gaunt shared their concern about security. He knew, through British decoding of messages from the German embassy, that Rintelen and von Papen had met with the chemist Scheele. Possibly suspecting they were manufacturing incendiaries to be smuggled on board ship, he had asked Consul General Bennett to insist that only bona fide passengers be allowed on board the *Lusitania* the day she was due to sail.

Some efforts were indeed being made by Cunard and the federal authorities. U.S. immigration officials were moving among the throng on the pier, while private detectives "were all about the ship to make sure that no explosives were smuggled aboard." Secret Service men also mingled with the excited crowds. They watched while passengers handed over their tickets and were then escorted by uniformed Cunard clerks to their baggage, which was marked in chalk before being loaded onto a wide conveyor belt. But it was no easy task to keep track of everyone and everything, given the commotion and piles of constantly arriving baggage. One male first-class passenger alone arrived with one large steamer trunk, two dress suitcases, one umbrella bag, one silver-mounted rosewood cane, one silk American flag, one silk Irish flag, and a package containing some eleven pounds of Old Rover tobacco and 300 cigars. Under the circumstances total security could not be guaranteed, and within hours of the ship's sailing would come evidence that at least three "suspicious characters" had slipped aboard in the confusion.

As the morning unfolded with more than the usual bustle and chaos, Charles Sumner could at least congratulate himself that the German warning had had little practical effect. On that warm spring day five liners were scheduled to sail from New York carrying 2,500 passengers—the largest number to depart on a single day so far that year. Few of *Lusitania*'s passengers had opted to transfer. Officially, the company vigorously denied that anyone had canceled, but this was not strictly true. A sprinkling had switched to other ships or abandoned plans to travel because of the notice or because of more general unease. These included two friends who had been prevented only by luck from sailing on the *Titanic*. Others retained their bookings but were sufficiently apprehensive to write letters to loved ones in Europe, which they posted in New York so that this mail would follow on other vessels.

Most passengers, however, placed their faith in the qualities of the *Lusitania*. Oliver Bernard, a British theatrical designer, read the Ger-

man warning over breakfast in the Knickerbocker Hotel. For this rather
waspish young Englishman, it would be his twelfth transatlantic voyage.
Though now well-accustomed to America, he had never forgotten the
impact on his artistic senses of his first arrival in New York with its
"mighty stronghold ascending sheer out of the sea; towers of burnished
brass welded into cliffs of bronze, smoldering above massive shadows
descending far below where hoards of electric jewels glittered." The
sirens of the ferryboats "were as the sound of many times seven rams'
horns before the ark of a new empire, their signals blended in a sym-
phony of acclaim before the walls of new Jerusalem."

Bernard's primary motive for returning home was patriotic: He was
going to make a final attempt to enlist. His earlier efforts had been frustrated by "deafness and discriminating methods of muddled recruit-
ing." He was also motivated by a nagging disillusion with his profession.
He had once relished New York's exuberant energy and the company of
chorus girls, whose careers had become "a matter of sinister, not to say
succulent report" in their hometowns. He had even met Oscar Hammer-
stein on a shoeshine stand at the corner of Broadway and Forty-second
Street. But he had begun to feel embarrassed by being "poor" in a city
where poverty was regarded "as infamy." He had moved to Boston, where
he became resident technician at the newly built Opera House.

But Boston was not New York, his job failed to satisfy his creativity,
and he soon developed a love-hate relationship with America, commut-
ing restlessly between England and the United States in search of fulfill-
ment. The final straw had been a commission from William Lindsey—"by
occupation a millionaire, by inclination a successor of minstrels in
Provence"—to design the set for "a deplorable play which he had written
round medieval Picardy" that proved a box-office flop. Bernard had not
yet severed his connection with Lindsey, who had made his fortune manufacturing military equipment. The aspiring playwright's daughter, Lesley, and her husband, Stewart Mason, were also sailing on the *Lusitania*
on their honeymoon trip. Lindsey's parting words to Bernard were "Keep
an eye on my little girl, please!"

Bernard was not unduly worried by the German warning, dismissing
it as a bluff to annoy the American government and cause consternation
in England. Like many other passengers, he believed that the speed of
the fastest liner on the Atlantic would "reduce possibilities of submarine
attack to zero." He began his final packing with only momentary regret

Charles Frohman

for what he was leaving behind in America: "the biggest hotels, the finest theatres, the handsomest apartments, the most luxurious clubs, the most gigantic office buildings," and, best of all, "the most up-to-date plumbing."

In his yet more handsome permanent suite in the Knickerbocker, Charles Frohman was also preparing for the transatlantic voyage. This renowned impresario and theater manager, the producer of more than 500 plays on both sides of the Atlantic, traveled every year to England, his cabin filled with the sweets for which he had a boyish passion, to find the cream of London's plays to bring to the United States. Frohman was a quiet, humorous, mildly eccentric man, a square dealer with kind but blunt views. He once sparred with the redoubtable Mrs. Patrick Campbell. When she rejected his criticisms of her acting on the grounds that she was an *artiste*, he replied, "Madam, your secret is safe with me." He worried what would become of the American stage, foreseeing a future of "popular drama, bloody, murderous, ousting drawing-room comedy. Crook plays, shop-girl plays, slangy American farces, nude women invading the auditorium as in Paris." He predicted chaos but told a friend, "Fortunately you and I won't live to see it."

When Frohman announced that he would make his annual visit to the London stage, despite the war, his friends protested, particularly when he decided to sail on a British ship. He derided their fears but took the precaution of dictating his entire program for the next season before he sailed, something he had never done before. The day before the *Lusitania* was to depart, Frohman's friend Al Hayman made one final attempt to dissuade him. He pointed out that Frohman could just as well travel on the American Line's *New York*. She was scheduled to sail under her neutral American flag just two hours later, at noon, and would arrive in Liverpool just a day later than the *Lusitania*. The actress Ellen Terry, Isadora Duncan and her dance troupe, and many of his friends would be on board. Frohman brushed him off with: "Well, Al, if you want to write to me, just address the letter care of the German Submarine U-4." He told another friend, "When you consider all the stars I have managed, mere submarines make me smile." As he made his way slowly along the dock supported by his stick, another friend, the composer Paul Potter, who had come to see him off, asked curiously, "Aren't you afraid of the U-boats, C.F.?" Frohman replied, "No, I am only afraid of the I.O.U.'s."

Frohman's friend the actress Rita Jolivet was similarly dismissive of the danger of sailing on a British ship. She decided at eight o'clock that morning to book a cabin on the *Lusitania* and ignore the suggestion of her friend Ellen Terry that she join her on the *New York*. Of French parentage, she had a sudden impulse to get to Europe to see her brother, who was going to the Front. She was delighted to encounter not only her brother-in-law, thirty-eight-year-old George Vernon, but also another of Frohman's set, the playwright Charles Klein. After an unsuccessful stint as an actor—his small size and nervousness restricted him to minor character parts—he had turned to writing plays and also to reading scripts for Frohman. Asked about the German warning as he walked toward the companionway, he told a reporter that he was going to devote his time on board to thinking about his new play, *Potash and Perlmutter in Society*. He would not have time "to worry about trifles."

Reporters also quickly spotted the striking figure of Elbert Hubbard, best-selling writer and founder of the Roycrofters, a semicommunal and commercially successful "brotherhood of craftsmen" in East Aurora, New York. Hubbard's quirky costume, like Mark Twain's white suit, was a kind of personal and literary trademark: wide-brimmed Stetson hat, long coat, baggy corduroys, floppy "aesthetic"-style silk cravat done up in a bow at his throat. It also perfectly conveyed his homegrown ideology, which married American rugged individualism to an Arts and Crafts foppishness. An unabashed partisan of the Allies, Hubbard regarded the

German warning not as a threat but as a personal challenge. In his mind, and in those of his readers, he was traveling to Europe to do battle with the kaiser.

In a supplement to the October 1914 issue of the *Philistine*, his plain-spoken, prettily printed "periodical of protest," Hubbard had written an uncompromising indictment of the emperor under the title "Who Lifted the Lid off Hell?" It depicted him as a monster lusting for blood: " 'Bill Kaiser' has a withered hand and a running ear. Also he has a shrunken soul, and a mind that reeks with egomania. He is a mastoid degenerate of a noble grandmother [Queen Victoria]. In degree he has her power, but not her love. He has her persistence, but not her prescience. He is swollen, like a drowned pup, with a pride that stinks. . . . Caligula, the royal pagan pervert, was kind compared with the kaiser." While praising "the Germany of invention, science, music, education, skill," Hubbard reminded his readers that Germany had resorted to cannibalism during the Thirty Years War and suggested she might do so again under the malign leadership of "the crazy kaiser." He had packed copies of his essay to distribute to fellow passengers.

Before he could sail, Hubbard had been obliged to take the unusual step of seeking the president's pardon in order to regain his rights as a U.S. citizen and secure an American passport. In 1913 he had pleaded guilty in Buffalo, New York, to misusing the mail by sending "filthy" materials and been fined $100. One of the counts related to a joke in his magazine about a "whirling-spray affair" birth-control device. The conviction automatically deprived him of his rights of citizenship. At first President Wilson denied Hubbard a pardon on the grounds that his application was premature. However, after the outbreak of war Hubbard called at the White House and made a passionate appeal to Wilson's private secretary, Joe Tumulty, that he must go to Europe to write about the conflict. President Wilson at once signed a pardon.

Now, standing on deck surrounded by newspapermen and munching an apple, Hubbard said: "Speaking from a strictly personal point of view, I would not mind if they did sink the ship. It might be a good thing for me. I would drown with her, and that's about the only way I could succeed in my ambition to get into the Hall of Fame. I'd be a regular hero and go right to the bottom."

As the *Lusitania*'s sailing time drew closer, the crowds grew. The photographers and reporters flitted among the passengers, friends, relations, and curious sightseers and the stacks of trunks and suitcases. The arrival of the lean, tall, and elegant Alfred Gwynne Vanderbilt prompted a scramble. He had inherited the bulk of the fabulous Vanderbilt fortune and moved in a society of unimaginable opulence. His socialite friends gave dinners during which their dogs were fed pâté de foie gras by footmen and for which the famous restaurateur Delmonico, goaded to produce ever more impossibly extravagant dishes, invented truffled ice cream.

Alfred Vanderbilt, though, was personally modest and unpretentious. He had followed the family tradition of theoretically beginning at the bottom of the ladder by working for a while as a clerk in the family business. But his weakness was women, as the reporters buzzing around him very well knew. His first marriage, to the rich, "tall and divinely fair," and well-connected Elsie French, had ended in divorce in 1908 because of his adultery aboard his private railroad car the *Wayfarer* with Agnes O'Brien Ruiz, wife of Cuba's attaché in Washington. The settlement was reputed to have cost Vanderbilt $10 million. Not

Alfred Gwynne Vanderbilt

long afterward Agnes Ruiz, duly divorced by her husband, had killed herself in a London hotel, and the story had been hushed up. It was rumored that the only two journalists present at the "mysterious inquest" had been bought off for a spectacular sum.

Vanderbilt himself would never discuss the matter. In 1911 he had married Margaret Emerson McKim, heiress to the vast Bromo-Seltzer fortune. Her doctor husband, whom she divorced on grounds of drunkenness and cruelty, had earlier threatened to sue Vanderbilt for alienation of affection but settled with his enormously rich rival out of court. The rumor was that Vanderbilt's bride price was sufficiently high to soothe McKim's injured pride. Margaret shared Vanderbilt's passion for horses, which he coached at his farm in Newport, Rhode Island, equipped with the largest private riding ring in the world. While he sailed to Europe, she had chosen to remain in New York with their two young sons at the Vanderbilt Hotel, which her husband had bui.   Park Avenue. As a director of the International Horse Show Association, Vanderbilt was eager to attend a board meeting in London in May. He also wanted to offer a fleet of vehicles to the British Red Cross. The night before sailing, he and his wife went to see Charles Frohman's and David Belasco's coproduction on Broadway, *A Celebrated Case*. That morning, they both laughed at the news of the German warning.

Jack Lawrence was one of the reporters to descend en masse on James McCubbin, the stout, white-bearded, fifty-year-old chief Purser. The accommodating McCubbin, who was planning to retire after this voyage to farm in Golders Green, then a leafy rural area on the fringes of northwest London, told them which celebrities were aboard. Lawrence tracked Vanderbilt down in his suite on the starboard side of the Boat Deck. His valet, Ronald Denyer, was busy unpacking, so Vanderbilt opened the door himself, his "inevitable pink carnation" in the buttonhole of his charcoal-gray pinstripe suit. According to the journalist, he was holding a telegram in his hand. The message was brief and signed "MORTE." It read: "THE *LUSITANIA* IS DOOMED. DO NOT SAIL ON HER." Vanderbilt shrugged it off on the grounds that it was "somebody trying to have a little fun at my expense." In 1912 he had booked passage on the *Titanic* but had changed his mind several days before she sailed, and he believed in fate.

Charles Lauriat, a distinguished Boston bookseller, who had been crossing the Atlantic for the past twelve years, though never before on the *Lusitania*, was one of those who did feel uneasy. When purchasing his ticket at Cunard's Boston office, he had asked whether the ship would be convoyed through the war zone and was told: "Oh yes! Every precaution will be taken." When he read the German notice, he tried to reassure himself with the thought that no "human being with a drop of red blood in his veins, called a man, could issue an order to sink a passenger steamer without at least giving the women and children a chance to get away." Ogden Hammond, a former member of the New York legislature with interests in the insurance business, and planning to travel with his wife, was similarly cautious. He sought advice from the Cunard office and was told that the ship was "perfectly safe; safer than the trolley cars in New York."

Many read the warning only after they had boarded the *Lusitania*. Businessman Oscar Grab and his wife were driving through Central Park on their way to the ship when Grab's brother-in-law, who was coming to see them off, asked, "Do you feel nervous about that article in the paper this morning?" Grab noticed his mother-in-law nudge him to keep quiet and decided not to pursue it, but as soon as he was on board he went to find the chief purser. McCubbin showed him the advertisement but reassured him that the ship was too fast to be caught. Theodore and Belle Naish, an affluent couple from Kansas City, read the warning only once the *Lusitania* was heading out to sea. Theodore Naish decided to ignore it, believing that if it were official, "each American passenger would have had warning sent and delivered before boarding the vessel."

Many of the British passengers saw it as their duty to sail on a British vessel whatever their fears. One of the most prominent was fifty-nine-year-old David Thomas, the Welsh coal magnate and former Liberal member of Parliament who had been in the United States on a business trip to discuss his wide-ranging business interests there. These extended from coal-mining ventures in Pennsylvania to plans for railways across northern Canada and a new barge service on the Mississippi River. This unpretentious man, said to have "the income of a duke and the tastes of a peasant," was now sailing home with his daughter, Lady Margaret Mackworth, in her early thirties, after an enjoyable stay at the Waldorf-Astoria. In the days leading up to the ship's departure, Lady Mackworth had become aware of "much gossip of submarines. It was freely stated and generally believed that a special effort was to be made to sink the great Cunarder, so as to inspire the world with terror." However, this strong-minded former militant suffragette tried to dismiss such thoughts.

Also eager to return home were Ian Holbourn, laird of the Shetland Isle of Foula, and an art and architecture historian, who had just completed a lecture tour of the United States; Matt Freeman, amateur lightweight boxing champion of England; and Commander J. Foster Stackhouse, who was returning to England to be reunited with his wife and twelve-year-old daughter. This Quaker explorer was planning to lead the British Antarctic and Oceanographical Expedition to survey as much of the Antarctic coastline as possible. He had put down £1,000 as a deposit on Captain Robert Falcon Scott's old ship, the *Discovery*, which he hoped to purchase from the Hudson's Bay Company, and had been in the United States raising funds. There were also rumors that Stackhouse was a British agent.

Art expert, collector, and director of the National Gallery of Ireland, Sir Hugh Lane had been in New York to advise an insurance company on a claim relating to a shipment of valuable pictures damaged by fire. Knighted for his services to art in 1909, this frail, greyhound-thin Anglo-Irishman had just offered to donate £10,000 to the Red Cross for a portrait to be painted by John Singer Sargent. He had not yet chosen the sitter. Famed for his discovery of a fine painting by George Romney beneath a layer of early-Victorian paint, his most passionate ambition was to build a modern art gallery in Dublin to house his collection of paintings by French, Italian, and British contemporary artists. On 1 May the forty-year-old Sir Hugh was more preoccupied with the safe stowing in the hold of a collection of paintings he was bringing back from New York than with any submarine threat, which he dismissed as "too absurd for discussion." The canvases, reputedly including works by Rembrandt, Monet, and Rubens (whose paintings were considered too fleshy for New York tastes), were rolled up and sealed into lead tubes packed in a crate. Sir Hugh was shipping them to Ireland on behalf of a fellow art dealer for inspection by the National Gallery of Ireland. He was said to have insured them for $4 million shortly before sailing.

———— ∞∞ ————

As the time before departure ticked away, Charles Sumner realized that the *Lusitania* would actually be carrying her biggest eastbound complement since the start of the war. According to Cunard's official list, 1,257 passengers would be aboard. They were predominantly British and Canadian but included nearly 200 Americans. Many passengers were traveling precisely because of the war. There were businessmen, like the millionaire Frederick Stark Pearson, one of the leading consulting engineers of his day, and munitions and equipment manufacturers, like Isaac Lehmann, who was furnishing supplies to the Allies and hoping for further contracts. Some were in the shipping business, like Charles Bowring, of Bowring's Shipowners and Agents, and Fred Gauntlett, of the Newport News Ship Building and Dry Dock Company, who was traveling to the United Kingdom "to make arrangements with builders of a certain submarine, with a view to building them in this country." He hoped that his company might thereby "assist in overcoming" the submarine menace facing Britain. Another passenger claimed to have developed a formula for the manufacture of poisonous gases, which he intended to offer the British government as a means of retaliating against German chemical warfare. A Chicago manufacturer, Charles Plamondon, fearing prohibition was imminent in the United States, was traveling with his wife, Mary, in the hope of finding European markets for his brewing equipment. He was particularly hopeful of concluding a deal with Guinness in Dublin.

There were convalescent soldiers like Captain Fred Lassetter, an officer in a Scottish regiment who had been wounded early in the war and was now returning home with his mother, Elizabeth. He was pleased that his friend from Oxford days, twenty-three-year-old Harold Boulton, was also on board. After receiving a medical discharge from the British army in 1912, Boulton had been working for the American Creosote Company, but he was anxious to persuade the army to allow him to reenlist.

A lieutenant in the Sixtieth Rifles of Canada, Robert Matthews of Moose Jaw, Saskatchewan, was also hoping for a fresh start. In his midthirties, he was accompanied by a woman named Annie, ten years his junior. She was traveling as his wife, which she was not. Matthews had left England for Canada in 1904. He had run a labor bureau, married, and had two daughters. In 1913 he was given a commission in the Sixtieth Rifles. However, his marriage was breaking up, and in 1914 he had abandoned his commission and spent the winter on a farm in northern Manitoba with Annie. After failing to obtain another commission in the Forty-sixth

Battalion of the Canadian Expeditionary Force, he had decided to return to England and booked passage for himself and Annie on the *Lusitania*.

There were other young Canadians who were also hoping to join up and Canadian families traveling to Europe to be closer to their men, who had already enlisted. A young woman from Toronto was sailing to England to attend to the affairs of three brothers who had all been killed in action. George Smith, a thirty-two-year-old Scottish-born Canadian, was, like many others, going back to Britain to seek work. He was a ship's carpenter and knew that "men were needed for war work" in the docks and the pay was good. There were Americans planning to volunteer as ambulance drivers with the Red Cross or, like Dorothy Conner and her brother-in-law, Dr. Howard Fisher, brother of a former U.S. secretary of the interior, intending to help set up hospitals. A party of Persians from Chicago were on a sad mission to visit the sites of recent Turkish massacres to discover the fate of their relations.

Surgeon Major Warren Pearl was taking his young family to London, where he had been instructed to report to the American embassy. He had served as a surgeon in the U.S. Army during the Spanish-American War. The previous year he had been arrested by the Germans in Lübeck on suspicion of being an English spy. Now his chief concern was to settle his family and their two nannies into one of the Regal Suites and adjacent cabins.

Marie de Page, special envoy in the United States of the king and queen of Belgium and wife of the surgeon general of the Belgian army, was also on board. During her time in the United States she had raised over $100,000 for the Belgian Red Cross, but now family ties were bringing her back to Europe. A few days earlier she had received a message that her seventeen-year-old son, Lucien, had joined the Belgian army and would soon be in the trenches. Marie was only on the *Lusitania* by chance. She had intended to sail the previous day on another ship but had delayed her departure to address one more fund-raising meeting. She was accompanied by an American doctor, James Houghton, who was going to assist at her hospital at La Panne. She hoped that British nurse Edith Cavell, well-known for her work in Brussels, would join him there.

In addition, there was the usual miscellany of people to be found on board a transatlantic liner in war or peace. Newlyweds, like the imposingly tall Reverend Gwyer and his wife, Margaret, and the youthful Harold and Lucy Taylor, were on their honeymoons. The Taylors had been planning to travel on another ship, but a maiden aunt had paid the difference for them to travel on the *Lusitania* "as a wedding gift." Nineteen-year-old Lucy was so shy that she didn't want people to know she was newly wed, but confetti dropping from their clothes as they came on board betrayed them.

Margaret Cox, a lively and resourceful Irish woman living in Winnipeg, was homesick and thought it would do both her and her infant son, Desmond, just recovering from whooping cough, good to see the "old country." Julia and Flor Sullivan were returning home to Ireland to take over the Sullivan family farm in Kerry. Their feelings were mixed. Flor was leaving a job he enjoyed as a New York bartender. Julia had worked for a long time for a kindly, generous old couple on Long Island, of whom she had grown very fond but who had recently died. Shortly afterward, a letter from Flor's father had begged them to return home; then he too had died. The Sullivans knew that if they did not go back to Ireland, they would lose the farm.

Doris Lawlor was traveling with her father, a Canadian book dealer. He was taking some valuable manuscripts to England and had decided to bring his twenty-one year-old daughter, who was about to be married, with him as a treat. On the dockside she was amazed by the "huge wide escalator" carrying the passengers' luggage on board and by the ship herself, which, "so big and beautiful," was beyond anything she had imagined. In their first-class staterooms they found piles of books sent by New York publishing friends, five-pound boxes of Hardy's Candies, and bouquets of sweet-scented roses. Doris felt on the verge of "something so new in my life."

Edwin Friend, a thirty-five-year-old graduate of Harvard and a former official of the American Society for Psychical Research, was traveling to England with Theodate Pope, an architect, interior designer, and progressive thinker fifteen years his senior from Farmington, Connecticut. This tall, imposing woman was also a keen psychical researcher who was planning to induce the English counterpart of the American society to organize a new body in the States. While in England she was to be the guest of Britain's leading spiritualist, Sir Oliver Lodge.

Sixty-six-year-old Father Basil Maturin, Roman Catholic chaplain at Oxford University who had been Lenten preacher at the Church of Our Lady of Lourdes in New York, was returning to his pastoral duties. While in the United States, Maturin had carefully canvassed the views of Americans, and particularly the Irish-Americans with whom he chiefly mixed, about the war. He had been a little apprehensive but was gratified to discover: "The whole tone in regard to the war is all that we could wish. . . . I can't imagine where we got the idea in England that they are pro-German." He was particularly anxious to sail on the swift *Lusitania* because he was impatient to return to Oxford.

William Mounsey of Chicago was also hoping for a swift passage. He was sailing to Liverpool with his daughter, Sarah Lund, and her husband, Charles, in the hope of a poignant reunion with the wife he had believed to be dead. The family had thought that Mrs. Mounsey had been lost on the *Empress of Ireland*, which had sunk the previous year with the loss of over 1,000 lives after colliding with a freighter in thick fog in the St. Lawrence River. However, her body had never been recovered, and they had recently received news of a mysterious "Kate Fitzgerald" who answered her description and had been found sheltering "in a Liverpool asylum under a mental cloud." Not surprisingly, the family were so overjoyed at the thought that, however mentally confused, she had been "rescued from the dead," that, like many passengers that warm spring day, they paid no heed at all to the German notice.

CHAPTER SEVEN

᳁

Leaving Harbor

NEWS OF THE GERMAN warning spread quickly among the *Lusitania*'s crew. Firemen and trimmers came up from the bowels of the ship sweaty and grimy from their shift to see what was going on. Coaling had been completed by nine o'clock the previous night, with coal shoveled by hand from the barges onto elevators that carried it up to the loading bays in the ship's sides. From there it had been spread evenly between the longitudinal bunkers stretching down each side of the ship. The *Lusitania* had taken on some 5,690 tons of Berwick's Standard Eureka coal—it took twenty two trains to deliver it for a single transatlantic passage—and her bunkers now held some 6,010 tons. For eighteen hours before she could sail, her firemen and trimmers had been working to raise steam. The trimmers had been bringing coal from the bunkers and piling it ready for the firemen to shovel into the furnaces. Now, leaning curiously over the rail, they saw people they believed to be German agents "giving pamphlets out to various people all round especially the passengers that were coming aboard . . . and sticking these things on the wall—don't go on this ship . . . she won't reach Liverpool, all that kind of business."

A fifteen-year-old bellboy, William Burrows, returning to the ship in the early hours, had been greeted by a policeman on the dock gate who said with grim humor: "You're not going to get back this time, sonny. They're going to get you this time."

Some of the crew did feel the tension. Passenger Lucy Taylor was amazed when a sailor grabbed her hat off her head and hurled it into the water. She had bought it for her trousseau and was particularly proud of the lavish peacock feathers adorning the crown, but the sailor told her firmly that peacock feathers always brought bad luck. Some crewmen also took it as a bad omen that the ship's cat and stoker's mascot, black, four-year-old Dowie, had run away the night before.

Yet most of the crew going about their duties that morning shrugged off thoughts of danger. It seemed unreal. As one later recalled, "We had no idea about what would happen if we got belted but . . . we knew no submarine could chase us and catch us." Another remembered, "Quite a lot of passengers backed out, but we the crew we took no notice at all—you don't if you're a member of a crew of a ship—you've got a different outlook, it's work whereas the other people they've nothing much to think about—they're liable to get a bit jittery." Together with an inherent confidence in the *Lusitania*'s performance was a quiet belief that "they daren't sink her."

This confidence was echoed by their captain, fifty-eight-year-old "Bowler Bill" Turner, who told a reporter in his broad Liverpudlian accent, "It's the best joke I've heard in many days, this talk of torpedoing the *Lusitania*." He had some experience of submarines. In January, while captaining the Cunarder *Transylvania*, he had successfully eluded a pursuing U-boat, and on the recent outbound voyage from Liverpool on the *Lusitania* he had outrun what he believed to be a submarine while clearing Irish waters. Known to his friends as Will, this short, stocky man was popular with his crew, "up to a point," but was hardly "the picture-postcard commodore of an Atlantic fleet." He struck his passengers as an "ordinary type of 'old man,' who wore, rather than carried, his gold braid, as if conscious of his Sunday best." He was certainly taciturn. He disliked idle chitchat with passengers, whom he was prone to describe as "bloody monkeys," and gratefully left the social side to his more "clubbable" staff captain, forty-nine-year-old John Anderson.

William Thomas Turner was born in 1856 to a Liverpool sea captain, Charles Turner, and his wife, the daughter of a cotton mill owner. His parents wanted him to be "respectable" and enter the church. This led to violent scenes in which Will Turner stubbornly refused to become "a devil-dodger." When he was just thirteen years old, he found a berth on the small barque *Grasmere*, only to be shipwrecked off the northern Irish coast and forced to swim ashore. He next ran off as a deck boy on the sailing ship *White Star*, plying from the Mersey River to Aden around the

Captain William Thomas Turner

Cape of Good Hope, and was clearly quick-witted and resourceful. One day, while scrubbing out one of the cabins, he was unable to resist helping himself to a slice of bread and butter. Realizing that the captain was coming, he slapped the piece of bread on the underside of a table and so escaped detection.

Turner was appointed a junior officer by Cunard but left after discovering that it was impossible to captain a ship of this most prestigious of lines without having held a command elsewhere. He duly became captain of a sailing ship and, after several successful voyages, rejoined Cunard in 1883. At the age of forty-seven, he was appointed master of one of the company's small steamships, the cargo boat *Aleppo,* trading in the Mediterranean. Thereafter promotions came quickly, and he commanded the *Carpathia, Ivernia, Caronia,* and others on the transatlantic run. The company regarded him not only as a safe pair of hands but as one of their most skillful navigators and the most speedy of all their captains at docking large liners to meet tight schedules. He deserved his high salary of £1,000 a year. Turner was also a man of considerable personal courage and an excellent swimmer. In 1883, the year he returned to Cunard, he jumped into the freezing waters of Liverpool's Alexandra Dock to rescue a drowning boy and received the Shipwreck and Humane Society's medal for bravery.

Turner briefly commanded the *Lusitania* before being given command of the *Mauretania* and becoming commodore captain of the Cunard Line. In August 1913 he was appointed an honorary commander in the Royal Naval Reserve by King George V, which was the closest he came to formal contact with the Royal Navy. In May 1914 he took command of the mammoth *Aquitania* on her maiden voyage to New York, but, after the outbreak of war, she was commandeered by the Admiralty. Turner was given various commands before again commanding the *Lusitania* when her captain, David Dow, became "tired and really ill" in early 1915, possibly because of the stresses of the February voyage and the American flag incident.

Turner was married, with two grown sons. The elder, Percy, was "very big and strong and never happy unless mixed up in a fight." He had gone to sea but gave it up and went to Mexico, where he became "mixed up in Huerta's rebellion . . . and narrowly escaped being shot against a brick wall." For whatever reason, Turner's relationship with his wife had become increasingly strained. They lived largely apart, and he now employed a lively young woman, Mabel Every, as housekeeper. Austere in many respects, Turner was nonetheless a connoisseur of good food and wine, "with a preference for German restaurants and cooking," and he enjoyed smoking a pipe. The night before the *Lusitania* sailed from New York, he dined at his favorite New York hostelry, the Nibelungen Room at Lüchow's Restaurant on Fourteenth Street. The proprietor, August Lüchow, had emigrated from Hanover thirty years earlier and offered his guests hearty German cooking to the accompaniment of an eight-piece Viennese orchestra.

Earlier in the day, Turner had given evidence as an expert witness in the case before Judge Julius Mayer to determine the White Star Line's financial liability over the loss of the *Titanic*. Asked what he knew about the construction of ships, he had answered, "I don't bother about their construction as long as they float. If they sink, I get out." Pressed about what lessons he had learned from the *Titanic* disaster, his bleak response was that he had not learned the slightest thing and that "it will happen again."

Afterward Turner had called at the customhouse, where, before Deputy Collector John Farrell, he swore that the single-page manifest he was presenting was a full and truthful list of all goods and merchandise on board the *Lusitania*. Under the heading "Shipper's Manifest—Part of Cargo," it listed thirty-five miscellaneous consignments, from tongues, bacon, beef, pork, lard, and 205 barrels of Connecticut oysters to shoelaces, cloth, furs, machine parts, and tobacco samples. Neither Farrell nor Turner noticed that the paperwork had actually been completed in the name of the *Lusitania*'s previous captain, David Dow.

The *Lusitania* had already been searched in the days prior to departure by the U.S. Neutrality Squad, which had strict orders to look for guns or for evidence of attempts to mount guns. Turner knew that the next morning Dudley Field Malone, collector of customs for the Port of New York and Farrell's boss, would come on board to inspect the ship. However, as all parties recognized, this was little more than a formality. As Malone, a former Treasury Department lawyer appointed collector by President-Elect Wilson in 1912, later wrote after the adequacy of his inspections had been queried, it was "entirely impracticable to make a physical examination of each package or case going into the cargo of an outgoing ship."

As he returned to his ship, Turner's greatest concern was probably over the number and caliber of his crew. He would have been affronted to learn that Captain Boy-Ed shared his view. The German naval attaché had reported to Berlin on 27 April that "the crew of the *Lusitania* is in a very depressed mood and hopes this will be the last Atlantic crossing during the war. . . . The *Lusitania* crew is incomplete. It is difficult to service the engines adequately." In addition to Staff Captain Anderson, Turner had six other deck officers and a total crew of 702. Of these, seventy-seven were seamen in the Deck Department, but their quality, compared with "the old-fashioned sailor" of prewar days, gave him little satisfaction. Many were relatively untrained replacements for the men of the Royal Naval Reserve and the Royal Fleet Reserve who had been called up for war service, but Cunard had little choice but to employ any likely young men who presented themselves.

On the forthcoming voyage these would include two brothers, Leslie and John Morton. They had just completed "a particularly vicious passage from Liverpool" of sixty-three days on the sailing ship *Naiad*, with Leslie serving as second mate and his brother completing his indentures. Faced with the prospect of a yearlong voyage taking oil to Australia and grain back to England, they had appealed to their father for help, and he had cabled them the money to enable them to sail home on the *Lusitania* in second class. Leslie was keen to qualify as a full mate, and both brothers were anxious to see something of the war, which, they believed, was likely to be "over and done with in a matter of months."

Together with some similarly disillusioned shipmates from the *Naiad*, they went to look at the *Lusitania* lying in her berth "as large as a mountain" and were persuaded to sign on as deckhands by an officer who complained: "We have had ten of our deckhands run away this trip in New York" because of "the threat of conscription coming at home. They don't like the idea." The Mortons and their friends readily agreed, and that night recruited some further escapees. They put on "as many clothes as we could possibly, wearing singlets, shirts, jersey, oilskins, in fact we must have looked like . . . supermen from another world as we waddled up the wharf from the *Naiad*. We could not for obvious reasons take our trunks with us, and we had £37 10s. 0d in our pocket." Later they went on a tremendous spree with the now unneeded money from the Mortons' father, drinking Manhattan cocktails with cherries on sticks. It was only the second time in his life that Leslie Morton had tasted alcohol, and he passed out on Broadway. But by 8:30 A.M. on Friday, 30 April, the soreheaded and bleary-eyed young seamen went up the crew's gangway to report to Chief Officer Piper and sign on.

Another new crew member was Neal Leach, a slightly built Englishman of middle height with dark brown hair and a thin smooth face. He had only recently arrived in New York and had spent the days prior to sailing living in a boardinghouse on West Sixteenth Street, where he had made numerous German acquaintances. Leach, who was in his early twenties, was the son of a magistrate in Jamaica. He had studied to be an attorney but, failing to pass his final exams, had gone to Germany to be tutor to the son of a winegrower at Steeg. Upon the outbreak of war, he was interned but was subsequently released, according to his own account through the help of his employer and a Jesuit priest, apparently on the promise that he would return to the West Indies and not become a combatant.

Leach sailed via Holland to the United States, but on 24 February 1915, before he had even embarked, the German foreign office sent a coded message to its Washington embassy: "PLEASE INFORM DERNBERG

THAT NEIL [SIC] LEACH HAS RECEIVED PERMISSION TO LEAVE FOR AMER-
ICA." This is the only such notification of a departure to be found in any
surviving German messages intercepted by the British. During the voyage Leach met Paul König's agent Gustav Stahl. On their arrival in New
York, Stahl took him to his lodgings. Through his uncle, who had friends
in Cunard, Leach had managed to secure a position on the *Lusitania* as a
steward.

———— ⬤⬤⬤ ————

As both crew and passengers prepared for departure in the curious circumstances of 1 May 1915, the tension on board the *Lusitania* was heightened by an unexpected delay. At the expected cry of "all ashore," friends
and relations had made their last farewells. Oliver Bernard, feeling a
frisson of excitement that "the voyage might rank as an event in the war
itself," noticed how "a sense of importance rather than apprehension"
pervaded these partings. As friends and relations clustered along the
pier, the excitement was palpable. But the departure time of 10 A.M.
came and went, and news spread that the sailing had been delayed to
allow forty-one first- and second-class passengers and crew who should
have sailed on the Anchor Line's *Cameronia* to be transferred. The
Cameronia had been requisitioned by the Admiralty as a troop transporter. Trucks and taxis were dispatched to the Anchor Line pier at the
foot of West Twenty-fourth Street to bring the passengers down to the
Cunard pier at the foot of West Fourteenth Street, but it took time to
ferry them and their bags.

Captain Turner had received his operational instructions from
Cunard's general manager, Mr. Mearns, before leaving Liverpool, but,
like other captains of merchant vessels, he had effectively been under
Admiralty control since the war began. The government had set up the
Liverpool and London War Risk Association whereby the government
indemnified merchant ships subject to their obeying Admiralty guidance and instructions issued without reference to the ship's owners. If
the ship failed to follow guidance without good reason and was lost, her
owners forfeited their rights to insurance payment. In recent months
Turner had received a stream of general Admiralty guidance about how
to counter the risk from submarines and what route to follow across the
Atlantic. Among the advice was to avoid headlands where submarines

were said to lurk, to pass harbors at full speed, to steer a midchannel course, and to approach ports at a time when there was no need to linger outside the harbor. Specific instructions were "regarded as confidential" and forwarded unread by the company to its captains. Turner's personal view was that there was far too much paperwork. However, his recollection of and adherence to such guidance would be scrutinized in the light of subsequent events.

The all-ashore gongs finally sounded on the *Lusitania* shortly after 11:30 A.M., the last visitors reluctantly disembarked, and the gangplank was raised. But the departure of the *Lusitania* was delayed yet further when Captain Turner suddenly appeared at the top of the gangway with his actress niece, Mercedes Desmore. He had visited her backstage the night before, at the New Amsterdam Theater where she was appearing in Henry Arthur Jones's *The Lie*, and she had come on board to say good-bye. Turner called angrily for the gangplank to be relowered. It was. She went ashore. It was raised again. The hawsers were loosed from the bollards on the quayside. Finally, to the gentle thrumming of her four steam turbines,

the *Lusitania* backed into the Hudson River just after 12:20 P.M., nudged by three tugs. She gave three earsplitting blasts of her horn, while on the quayside people waved hats, handkerchiefs, and flags and flung fistfuls of confetti into the air. At one end of the Boat Deck the ship's band played "Tipperary," while at the other the Royal Gwent Male Voice Singers from Wales, who had been touring the United States and Canada, sang "The Star-Spangled Banner." Their famous tenor Parry Jones was in particularly good voice. He had heard the warnings but had been told that even if she were attacked, "a great ship like this wouldn't sink for five or six hours so there would be plenty of time to get everybody off."

The rain had cleared, and the great vessel sailed away in brilliant sunlight, caught on cinefilm for one last time by a film crew on the pier. Although her name and port of registry had been painted over as a precaution, she looked both festive and magnificent with streamers of alphabet flags fluttering from the fore and aft masts and thick black smoke pouring from her stacks. She passed the German liners, laid up alongside their piers at Hoboken, scene of the gruesome fire in 1900. The

The Lusitania *glides down the Hudson River past the New York City skyline.*

Gazing out from the deck of the Lusitania, *these women are possibly American nurses departing for the Western Front.*

old American Line's ship *New York* was just ahead and managed to beat her glamorous rival past the harbor bar. In the increasingly salty air the *Lusitania* nosed past Sandy Hook, the pilot departed, and the expanse of the Atlantic began to open out before her. Passengers crowded the rails to see the three camouflage-painted British warships keeping watch from outside American territorial waters on shipping entering and leaving New York. They included the Cunard liner *Caronia*, converted into an auxiliary cruiser and looking as if she were now "armed with teeth." Twelve of her seamen rowed a cutter into the swell to sling sacks of mail aboard the liner. A photographer on the deck of the *Caronia* took one of the last pictures of the *Lusitania*.

The passengers now thronging the *Lusitania*'s decks were pinning their faith on the ship's speed, great size, and special construction—especially her honeycomb of watertight compartments. Many naval experts believed that if she were hit, these compartments would keep her afloat long enough for the lifeboats to be launched. Passengers also reminded each other, as many had eagerly told reporters, that the Admiralty would send an armed escort when the *Lusitania* reached the war zone. They would have been disturbed to learn that just five days earlier a top-secret intelligence report had been prepared in Berlin and passed to German ministers and military and naval heads of staff for distribution to their subordinates. It detailed the movements of enemy merchant ships. A brief entry under "steamer departures from New York" read: "1. Mai: D. *Lusitania* (Cunard), englisch, 30,396 R.T., nach Liverpool, an etwa 8 Mai." Translation: 1 May: *Lusitania* (Cunard), English, 30,396 tons, on passage to Liverpool, [arrival] around 8 May.

CHAPTER EIGHT

The Ostrich Club

*D*ESPITE THE LOVELY spring weather, seasoned trans-atlantic travelers quickly noticed that the mood was more subdued than usual. Spiritualist Theodate Pope decided that her companions "were a very quiet shipload of passengers." Some were still unnerved by the German warning: One young woman had barely boarded the ship before she "looked about and mentally decided upon the place to make for in the event of any incident." Others were inevitably reflective because the *Lusitania* was bringing them closer to the conflict. British leaflets placed strategically around the ship informed passengers about "the origin and issues of the present war." Cunard management had issued instructions to all captains to have these placed "wherever possible in the hands of passengers of neutral nationality." Red Cross collecting boxes and appeal notices were also prominently placed.

Yet the routine of ship life soon asserted itself. The ship's doctor, J. F. McDermott, was worrying about the "epidemic outbreak of typhus fever" in New York, of which he had been warned, and wondering whether any passenger was infected. Chief Purser McCubbin, under instructions to ensure that the ship's music program was "not calculated to cause offence," particularly on a Sunday, was scrutinizing the band's playlist in his office, which faced the main first-class staircase. Standing behind decorative metalwork grilles resembling the tellers' cages of fashionable shops, his staff were carefully issuing receipts for valuables from wealthy passengers such as Theodore and Belle Naish, who wanted to deposit $390 in gold.

In normal times, the purser's office also served as a telegraph office, sending passengers' messages on to the radio room for transmission. Transatlantic passengers could wire other ships at sixteen cents a word, although wiring the United Kingdom or the United States was much more expensive—a short telegram could cost a manual worker a week's pay. But in May 1915 this was academic. Bob Leith and David McCormick, the two experienced telegraphists in the radio room in the Marconi house high up on the Hurricane Deck under its mass of wire aerials, were working six-hour shifts to keep up a continuous service. However, Captain Turner had instructed that "no passengers' messages must be sent from the ship whatever." His own instructions from Cunard were to use his wireless "as little as possible and send us no messages." The only radio contact with the ship would be controlled by the Admiralty. The ship could, however, receive messages, and a number of passengers, including Frohman and Vanderbilt, received fond farewells. An affectionate message to Frohman ended: "GOD BLESS YOU DEAR FRIEND."

The purser's staff were also kept busy explaining the layout of the enormous ship to bewildered and inexperienced passengers. Some were confused that the six decks where passengers' cabins and the public rooms were located had names but were also known by designated letters. The Boat Deck, beneath the Hurricane Deck and where the lifeboats were hanging, was also known as A Deck, the Promenade Deck, immediately beneath, was known as B Deck, the Shelter Deck as C Deck, the Upper Deck as D Deck, the Main Deck as E Deck, and the Lower Deck as F Deck. (Lower still were the Orlop and Lower Orlop Decks used for cargo and crew purposes.)

The staff had to deal with passengers' complaints about their accommodation. Actress Rita Jolivet was disappointed with her first-class stateroom, an inside cabin on the Upper Deck. Theodate Pope found the noise made by the "very noisy family" next door intolerable and changed her stateroom for one on the Boat Deck. This presented no problems since there were only 290 passengers in the first-class section in the comfortable center section of the ship, compared with the 540 it had been designed to carry. Their staterooms, with cabin-to-cabin telephones connected through a central switchboard, were nearly all on the Boat, Promenade, and Upper Decks. The two-tiered dining room was accessible from both the Upper and Shelter Decks, while the main lounges, libraries, and smoking rooms were all high up on the Boat Deck.

The third-class section, situated in the forward third of the ship,

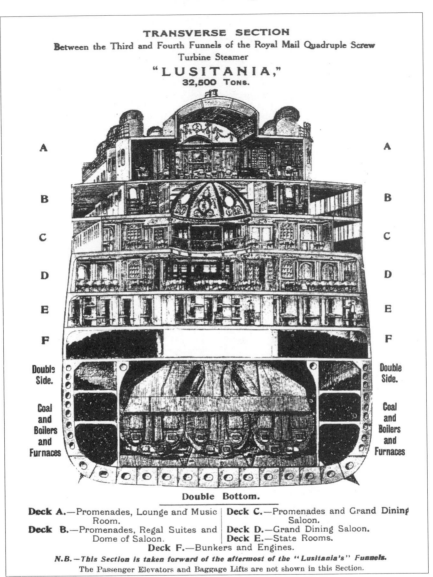

TRANSVERSE SECTION
Between the Third and Fourth Funnels of the Royal Mail Quadruple Screw
Turbine Steamer
"LUSITANIA,"
32,500 Tons.

Double Bottom.

Deck A.—Promenades, Lounge and Music Room. **Deck C.**—Promenades and Grand Dining Saloon.
Deck B.—Promenades, Regal Suites and Dome of Saloon. **Deck D.**—Grand Dining Saloon. **Deck E.**—State Rooms.
Deck F.—Bunkers and Engines.
N.B.—This Section is taken forward of the aftermost of the "Lusitania's" Funnels.
The Passenger Elevators and Baggage Lifts are not shown in this Section.

was also relatively empty, with 367 occupying accommodation on the Lower and Main Decks designed for a capacity of 1,200. Although this part of the ship was the least comfortable when the ship was pitching, the third-class cabins were thoughtfully though plainly fitted out. Passengers were gratified to find the two- to eight-berth cabins clean and comfortable and, somewhat to their surprise, equipped with crisply laundered sheets. Six months earlier, the chief steward of third class had reported that "quite a number of the third-class passengers who were of a very superior type had enquired for sheets for the beds." A Cunard study established that it would cost only £358 to equip the *Lusitania* with bedding and quilts, and it had promptly been done. To discourage pilfering, the bedclothes were embossed with the company emblem: a lion gripping the Western Hemisphere between its paws. The *Lusitania*'s designers, fearing third-class passengers might not have seen flushing lavatories and might not understand the principles, had taken the innovative step of installing toilets that flushed automatically.

Among those now settling in were Elizabeth Duckworth, a fifty-two-year-old twice-widowed weaver in a Taftville, Connecticut, cotton mill. She was returning to her native Lancashire simply because she was homesick. Her companions in third class included the friendly Hook family. George Hook and his children, Frank and Elsie, had originally planned to travel in second class but, on learning that their former housekeeper, her husband, and the couple's baby boy were returning to England and would be traveling in third, had good-naturedly decided to join them. The Hooks had quickly befriended young New York engineer Jack Welsh, who was already much smitten by a milliner, Gerda Nielson, whom he met on deck. Also in third class was Annie Williams, whose husband, John, had deserted her and their six children immediately on their arrival as immigrants in the United States. She was returning to England with her offspring, ranging from nine-year-old Edith to four-month-old David, in the desperate hope of tracking down her runaway spouse.

They could get some air by promenading along the third-class portion of the Shelter Deck. They also had the benefit of clean and comfortable public rooms on that deck, including a smoking room, and the best dining room for steerage passengers on the Atlantic on the deck below. The long tables were arranged in rows, with steel-legged, wooden-backed chairs ten to a side, but the room was well lit and the austerity was softened by Doric columns whose purpose was structural as well as artistic. Women had their own sitting room. Although it was uncarpeted and furnished with unupholstered wooden benches, it was spacious and airy and offered a welcome degree of privacy. Poorer passengers also appreciated the fact that medical care was free, with a twenty-four-bed hospital—an incentive, or so it was said, for pregnant women to time their voyage with the date on which they expected to give birth. An isolation ward in the stern of the ship dealt with passengers with highly infectious diseases. The *Lusitania*'s usual doctor was laid up with rheumatism, and his place had been taken by the younger, thirty-eight-year-old McDermott.

Second-class passengers, whose accommodation was in the third of the ship toward the stern, and whose open decks were separated from those of first class by a gangway, were less content. Some 600 had been crammed into quarters designed for 460; consequently there were two sittings for meals instead of one. The reason for the congestion was, quite simply, value and price. Second class on the *Lusitania* was considered as good as first class on many other ships: The sixty-foot-long dining room on the Upper Deck, with delicately carved panels under a graceful open well, was in the Georgian style, as was the handsome, barrel-vaulted smoking room on the Promenade Deck; the adjacent ladies' drawing room had deep prettily curtained windows and slender fluted columns; the Louis XVI saloon, a lounge up on the Boat Deck, was in soft gray and rose, set off by gold-hued satinwood furniture. What's more, Cunard had discounted the second-class tickets from seventy dollars to fifty dollars. One man found himself sharing an inside cabin with three other men on the Shelter Deck, but, as he later reported, "we joked about it and slept with the doors open, and we got on fairly well." Some passengers who had wished to travel in second class had been forced to take cabins in third.

For many passengers new to the *Lusitania* or to transatlantic travel, there was the charm of novelty. They were fascinated by the ship, gazing up at her four great funnels rearing seventy-five feet above the Boat Deck and secured by thick guy wires to prevent their keeling over in high seas. They hungrily absorbed snippets of information from the crew, like the fact that 4 million rivets weighing some 500 tons had gone into the ship's construction. One steward who was quite lyrical about the *Lusitania* assured his passengers that "the personality of the ship was perfect, she had no high-speed roll, and was a very comfortable ship to sail in." Experienced sailors, like Florence Padley from Vancouver, knew better. She had sailed on the *Lusitania* before and recalled that the ship had a "wonderful roll in the calmest of seas!!"

Passengers learned that, as with most ships of that period, the *Lusitania*'s bow was delicately flared so that she cut deep into the sea rather than pushing it aside, throwing up great sheets of water almost vertically.

She was therefore regarded as a "wet ship," where seawater regularly sprayed the passenger decks. In consequence, her deck had an eighteen-inch camber to allow water to drain off.

But the *Lusitania* was quieter than she might have been, thanks to her powerful steam-turbine engines. The marine steam turbine was the product of the buccaneering talents of a British engineer, the Honorable Charles Parsons. In 1897 he had launched the world's first turbine-driven vessel, the elegant little *Turbinia*, driven by nine propellers divided between three shafts, each connected to a turbine. Parsons had chosen a spectacular occasion to reveal her to the world: the naval review at Spithead in honor of Queen Victoria's Diamond Jubilee. The Prince of Wales, wearing the magnificent regalia of a Fleet Admiral, was surveying the assembled fleet when the *Turbinia* suddenly dashed out in the wake of the royal yacht. Only 100 feet long, a mere nine feet wide, and with a twenty-foot flame leaping from her stack, she gave a dazzling display of speed, reaching around forty miles per hour while dodging between lines of battleships and narrowly avoiding collisions with pursuing naval craft. No other ship could catch her, and Parsons had made his point. Within a very short time the Royal Navy was building ships powered by Parsons's turbines, and Cunard installed them in the *Lusitania*.

On the first full day at sea Captain Turner conducted the Sunday service but, as usual, showed little inclination for socializing with his passengers. He hated answering their ignorant questions and had a particular distaste for the pushier among them. On one occasion when the wife of a prominent passenger tried to pressure him into letting her onto the bridge while the liner sailed down the River Mersey, he told her that only those responsible for the ship's navigation were allowed there while the *Lusitania* was negotiating narrow waters. She asked what his reaction would be if a lady were to insist. His acid response was "Madam, do you think that would be a lady?" Burly Staff Captain John Anderson, urbane and charming, supplied the deficiency. He chatted easily with passengers and initiated them into the mysteries of how a ship was run.

— ∞∞∞ —

Passengers quickly discovered that the ship was a highly organized, stratified world with different officers in charge of different departments. The Stewarding Department, under Chief Steward John Jones, made the most immediate impact on passengers' comfort. His staff numbered 306 and included a large body of stewards, twenty-one stewardesses (lodged well away from male employees, who were liable to be sacked if caught making nocturnal visits), cooks and scullions, the five-man orchestra, and a trio of barbers including the popular and heavily booked Lott Gadd. Many were related to one another, like sixteen-year-old assistant cook George Wynne, who had managed to secure a job as a scullion for his semi-invalid father, Joseph. It was hard work preparing mountains of

vegetables in the pantries, even harder toiling in the steaming galleys, where in high seas cooking vessels could easily jump the guardrails around the stove and spill their boiling contents. Dressed in the traditional cook's garb of check trousers and white undershirts, the Wynnes worked fourteen-hour days, but conditions and pay were reckoned to be far better than anything to be had ashore. George earned three pounds, fifteen shillings a week, of which he sent ten shillings to his mother in Liverpool. The young bellboys like William Burrows also worked hard—

The Lusitania *at high speed.*

sometimes sixteen hours at a stretch—racing around the ship in their brass-buttoned uniforms. But the tips made it all worthwhile; a successful bellboy could earn enough to set himself up ashore in a trade.

The 314 men of the Engineering Department worked under Archibald Bryce, a powerful, leather-skinned Scot with a walrus mustache. Bryce, a fit and youthful fifty-four, had the boiler room in his blood; his father had been chief engineer of one of Cunard's old paddle steamers, and he himself had worked belowdecks all his life, much of the time under Captain Turner, whom he could truthfully call his friend. He managed a "black gang" of trimmers, firemen, oilers, and wipers, who fed and maintained the *Lusitania*'s immense boilers. Steam from the boilers—exerting 195 pounds of pressure per square inch—drove the massive turbines, which required 65,000 gallons of water per minute to stay cool. The turbine rooms were in the stern section, but the four boiler rooms housing the ship's twenty-five boilers extended toward the bows. Beyond them was a small hold and the trim tanks. The engine and boiler rooms, rudder, and steering equipment were sited as far below the waterline as practical to protect them against enemy fire, whereas the huge coal stores were located within the longitudinal bunkers to give additional protection to the boilers. The engine room communicated with each of the four boiler rooms—and with the bridge, seven decks above and 400 feet forward—using a system of engine telegraphs.

The trimmers and firemen—including many Liverpool Irishmen like John O'Connell, who at nineteen was the youngest—worked two four-hour shifts in each twenty-four-hour cycle in the "stokeholes," as they called the boiler rooms. Their dormitories and washing facilities were located close by the engine-room hatches. The driving hum of the ship's engines was for them ever present.

The trimmers were at the very bottom of the boiler-room pecking order. Their job was to shovel away inside the coal bunkers themselves, shifting the coal to the doors so that a ready supply could be barrowed across to the firemen at the furnaces. Stripped to the waist and wearing clogs to protect their feet from the showers of hot ash, the firemen had a precision task. They usually worked the furnaces in twenty-one-minute bursts: seven minutes to clear the fire grate with a ten-foot skewer, the slice bar, sending ash to the pit below and raising the white-hot "clinkers," fused lumps of impurities, to the top of the coals; seven minutes to rake them over; and seven minutes to load the coal into the roaring furnaces and ensure that it was levelly spread over the glowing bed to a depth of some four inches. After a brief pause the indicator gong sounded, and the exhausting cycle began again.

It was noisy, scorching, choking work in air that was thick with acrid noxious gases and coal dust, and soft bituminous American coal had a particularly high dust content. In high seas it was even more hazardous. The firemen struggled to keep their footing on the coal-covered floor as the ship heaved and pitched, bows sometimes rearing sixty feet before plunging back again into the waves. The firemen tried to stoke as the bow went down, slamming the furnace door shut as soon as the ship began to rise to avoid being showered with burning coals. The work was also stressful mentally—a man knew that to slow up meant dropping behind his comrades and appearing weak. It was not surprising that firemen and trimmers—wisely denied access to alcohol on board—went on gargantuan drinking binges ashore and had a bad reputation. Tales were still told of the men of the stokehold on the Cunarder *Ultonia*, who went on a rampage and broke into the wine stores before being corralled. A gruesome story circulated about an engineering officer who unwisely intervened in a fight between stokers; he was felled with a shovel and incinerated in a furnace. Passengers on the *Lusitania* who caught sight of the "black gang" thought them "a wild lot."

Passengers found the activities of the deckhands more appealing. The Morton brothers' daily routine consisted of washing down the decks, the paintwork, and the lifeboats and doing "a great deal of sailoring" like repairing and maintaining the ship's mooring ropes, lifeboat tackle, and davits. They frequently had an audience. Leslie Morton, a newcomer to liners, found himself "putting an eye splice in an eight-stranded wire hawser on the fore deck, with a crowd of admiring passengers watching me, which called forth all my latent histrionic abilities." He added gratuitous flourishes to what was usually a simple activity and was amused by the oohs, aahs, and gasps of admiration.

At first the Mortons found the *Lusitania* disconcertingly different from their former vessel, the *Naiad*. The vast ship was confusing, with "innumerable people, noise, passengers"; the forecastle three decks down, where many of the crew had their bunks, was "more like a workhouse dormitory." But the sheer wonder of the great ship soon gripped them. There was a porthole by Leslie Morton's bunk, and he wrote of "the thrill of looking through . . . watching the water cutting away like magic as *Lusitania* went through the seas."

As mere deckhands, they had virtually no contact with Captain Turner; nor did they desire any. Turner had a reputation for conscientious efficiency but also for aloofness. One of the *Lusitania*'s young quartermasters recalled that "as far as the quartermasters or the seamen or anybody else in the crew is concerned—the captain doesn't know anything about them as long as they are all doing their job."

Turner certainly set great store by old-fashioned seamanship. One evening, as four of his officers were sitting down to the newfangled game of bridge, he sent them a four-stranded Turk's Head knot with a message: "Captain's compliments, and he says he wants another of these made." The card game was reluctantly abandoned while the exasperated young men tried to remember how to tie this extremely complicated knot. As one wrote, "It was Turner's idea of humour."

One of Leslie Morton's tasks was to paint the lifeboats on the Boat Deck with the gray paint known as "crab fat." He was lying flat on his back beneath one of the boats when he heard the patter of feet followed by slower, rather heavier footsteps. Glancing from under the boat, he saw two girls with their nanny. They made a deep impression: "I could not help thinking what lovely children they were and how beautifully dressed." The eldest was wearing a white pleated skirt and a sailor blouse. They stopped and quizzed him about what he was doing, then asked whether they could help. Morton sensibly replied that it was too messy a job, but the elder girl seized the piece of rag he was using to apply the paint and "dabbed it on the boat and also all over her beautiful clothes." Fearing both the furious nanny and "the irate bosun," Morton slid over the side and down to the next deck.

There were in fact an unusually large number of children on board. According to one stewardess, "It was a record number of youngsters for the *Lusitania*," with fifty-one boys, thirty-nine girls, and thirty-nine infants. The children of first-class passengers, like the six young Cromptons, whose father was a business associate of Cunard chairman Sir Alfred Booth, could be left to play in a nursery on the Shelter Deck under the watchful eye of stewardesses. They also had a special dining room, where the decoration was in the style of Louis XVI but "advisedly simpler." In second class a section of the dining room was used as a children's play area when meals were not being served. Some of the children were so strikingly beautiful that there was talk of organizing a baby contest, but the idea was wisely abandoned for fear that "many mothers might be up in arms if somebody else's child won." The youngsters included twelve-year-old Avis Dolphin, on her way to school in England. Her parents had emigrated to Canada, but her father had died within a year from tuberculosis contracted while fighting in the Boer War. Avis's mother had set up a nursing home in Ontario but was now sending her home in the care of two nurses, Hilda Ellis and Sarah Smith, in second class.

The *Lusitania* was an amazing sight to the young girl, "a wonderful ship . . . like a floating palace," but early in the voyage Avis had begun to feel homesick and seasick. She was also lonely, realizing that the nurses supposed to be looking after her "had other interests on board." She was lying rather miserably on a deck chair when the writer and laird of the Isle of Foula, Professor Holbourn, also traveling in second class, noticed her. Missing his own little boys back home in Scotland, the professor was glad to befriend a child and took Avis under his wing. Together they roamed the ship, and, as he was a keen yachtsman, she found him very knowledgeable. He showed her the small observation corridor forward on the Promenade Deck, which gave first-class passengers a spectacular view over the bows, and, like all the children, she was fascinated by the two first-class elevators. These had intricate grilles with gilded rosettes and medallions, and each was operated by a uniformed elevator attendant.

As they rambled, Holbourn told Avis how, in August 1914, the terrible news of the outbreak of war had taken time to reach the Isle of Foula because the weekly mail boat had been delayed. The husband of the island's schoolmistress had thrust a copy of the *Scotsman* at Holbourn, exclaiming, "There is war!" To Holbourn, it had been so totally unexpected that it seemed incredible. "I sat down on the grass dazed and stupefied," he recalled, "and watched the islanders quietly unloading sacks of flour and meal, and talking calmly about things in general."

He told Avis all about his beloved island—just three and a half miles long and half a mile wide and so remote that it took four days to reach from Edinburgh. He described its heart-stopping beauty, with the changing colors of the hills ranging from "a pale jewelled green to deep purple." Holbourn was strongly made, athletic with deep-set, penetrat-

Avis Dolphin

ing eyes. He had an extraordinary talent for storytelling, and he made the shy, homesick child laugh with his quirky tales of the Foula bogey-man, who lived in an old, wrecked herring boat and was swept out to sea one day, to the great satisfaction of a small boy who, looking on, remarked, "The Bogey-man will be getting his feet wet." He also told her about the giant of Foula, who became so enraged that he hurled a large boulder from the island across the twenty-mile stretch of sea to the mainland.

Holbourn, who was a cautious, sensible man as well as a kind one, "thought that everyone should know how to put their lifebelts on and suggested this to a number of passengers." Soon a deputation came to him asking him not to talk about the possibility of trouble "because it was upsetting the women passengers." He named them "the Ostrich Club." Professor Holbourn was "angry with the captain because he refused to order a lifeboat drill. The captain gave as his reason for refusing that he feared that such a drill might cause panic or worry." Although he promised to discuss the matter with the first officer, nothing resulted. Perhaps Captain Turner feared that some passengers would refuse to be drilled. As one later recalled, "We should not have stood it at that time." Holbourn also noted that although there was a list of designated boat stations for the crew, nothing had been done to assign pas-

Ian Holbourn

sengers to specific boats—a practice suggested after the *Titanic* disaster but rejected by Cunard as "impracticable."

Some shared his concern that the ship's safety arrangements seemed complacent and amateurish. The daily crew boat drills seemed particularly pointless. At the sounding of the ship's siren, eight crew members would line up in front of either lifeboat thirteen on the starboard side or lifeboat fourteen on the port side, depending on the wind direction. After being inspected by the third officer, the men "climbed up the davits into the boat; they then stood for a moment in the boat with oars dressed, and immediately sat down ready for the boat to be launched." At a further command, they jumped back on deck to be dismissed. One passenger described the performance as "pitiable." Another suggested to an officer that "unless they changed their boat, they would wear the boat out." "Would you like to take your chances with that crowd in case we are torpedoed?" a third remarked sourly.

Theatrical designer Oliver Bernard noticed that during the drills at sea the boat was not lowered or even brought to the ship's deck level, so that there was "no actual practice of launching the boat." What, he wondered, would happen if the boats had to be lowered fully loaded and in difficult conditions? He comforted himself and fellow passengers with the thought that the crew's casual approach must mean that "the possi-

bilities of submarine attack were to be regarded as extremely remote."
He would have been alarmed to know that some of the crew shared his
misgivings. One of the firemen, John O'Connell, grumbled that all the
crew were required to do at boat drill was "give your name in and that's
the lot." They had "no idea of how to get the boat away, lower the boats, or
. . . who's going to pull the oars or any damn thing."

There were, however, plenty of life preservers—big, bulky Boddy's
Patent Jackets filled with fiber. They made their wearers look like "a
padded football player, especially around the shoulders." The *Lusitania*
carried life jackets for all 1,959 aboard, with 1,228 to spare and 175 for
children. Knowing they would soon be sailing into the war zone and conscious of the terrible lessons of the *Titanic* disaster, passengers quizzed
the crew about the provision of lifeboats. As a result of the *Titanic*
inquiry, Cunard had doubled the number of lifeboats on the *Lusitania*.
She was carrying twenty-two open wooden lifeboats capable of carrying
1,322 people and twenty-six collapsible boats that could hold another
1,283. The collapsibles were boats with shallow, rigid wooden keels and
folding canvas sides that could be raised and held in position by wooden
pins and iron or steel stays. The action of raising the sides also pulled the
seats into position.

Most of the collapsibles were stowed in cradles under the main
lifeboats so that they could be slung from the same davits once the
wooden boats had been launched. Alternatively, if time was running out,
they could simply be released from the deck by slip hooks and allowed to
float away. While the *Lusitania* had been berthed in New York, Ship's
Carpenter Neil Robertson had checked the wooden lifeboats' condition
and equipment and tested them for possible leaks by "sounding the
boat." He had also examined the six-foot-long snubbing chains, two of
which were fastened to each wooden boat and secured to the deck. Their
purpose was to prevent the wooden lifeboats from swinging back and
forth too much and crashing against the sides of the collapsibles when
the *Lusitania* rolled. Before the wooden boats could be launched, the peg
holding the snubbing chain had to be knocked out with the wooden mal-
let stored in each boat.

Significantly, Cunard had not followed the *Titanic* inquiry's recom-
mendation that high-sided liners should use a type of davit that would
allow lifeboats to be swung out effectively, even if the ship was listing.
Nor did Cunard act on a suggestion that a form of geared davit be used in

First class passengers strolling along the wide Boat Deck outside the Verandah Café.

preference to a manual system of blocks and pulleys. Instead, the *Lusitania*'s boats remained slung from metal brackets at either end of the lifeboat. These davits were worked by simple block and tackle. They were also independent of each other, so that, if the ship was down either at the bow or at the stern, it would require great expertise from the men using each block and tackle to lower the boats evenly.

———✸———

After the recent reports in the newspapers, passengers debated whether the ship was armed and what was in her cargo. Michael Byrne, a first-class passenger, decided to make a search for guns. Setting off briskly at 7 A.M. on the first day at sea, he checked from bow to stern and inspected every deck above the waterline. He found no traces. Passengers could not, of course, check the hold; the *Lusitania*'s relatively limited cargo space was located near the bows, on the Orlop and Lower Decks. It was accessible only to the crew. A group of bellboys had spent the night before sailing electrocuting rats down there. One described the procedure with relish:

"We got some electric wires, we took off the insulation and we laid there while the rats ran across [them]. . . . That was our pastime."

Crew members told curious passengers that the ship was carrying "general cargo." That was certainly true, according to the one-page manifest sworn by Captain Turner the day before sailing. However, four days after the *Lusitania* had left New York, a twenty-four-page handwritten "Supplemental Manifest" was submitted to the New York customs authorities. The list of some eighty consignments included further enormous quantities of cheese, beef, lard, bacon, and furs, together with 655 packages of confectionery, bales of leather, automobile parts, dental goods, crates of books, sewing machines, wool, beeswax, and the case of oil paintings belonging to Sir Hugh Lane.

The cargo list also disclosed munitions: 4,200 cases of Remington rifle cartridges, packed 1,000 to a box; 1,250 cases of shrapnel shells and eighteen cases of fuses from the Bethlehem Steel Company; a large amount of aluminum and fifty cases of bronze powder. In monetary terms, over half the *Lusitania*'s cargo consisted of material being shipped for the Allies' war effort. In the words of a U.S. Treasury official, "Practically all of her cargo was contraband of some kind" because if the ship had been stopped by a German vessel and boarded, most of the goods in her hold would have been impounded and destroyed. Transporting both small-arms ammunition and empty shell cases, as these shrapnel shells were stated by their manufacturers to be, was, however, legal under U.S. law. In May 1911, the Department of Commerce and Labor had issued revised orders allowing small-arms ammunition to be carried on passenger ships. The cases of small-arms ammunition and fuses now in the *Lusitania*'s hold were all stamped "non-explosive in bulk."

Passengers of course knew nothing of the ship's diverse cargo of goods as the *Lusitania* steamed onward. Nor did they know that the war had taken the hideous direction some had been predicting. The first reports were coming in of "a new phase" in the war: the use in the trenches of "a very barbarous form of attack . . . asphyxiating gases." In Britain horrified people were scanning accounts of how "by means of poisonous gases" German troops had finally succeeded in taking a hill near Ypres.

Passengers were also unaware that, on the day that the *Lusitania* had sailed from her berth in New York, a German U-boat had torpedoed the American oil tanker *Gulflight* off the Scilly Isles near the southern entrance to the Irish Channel, close to the site of the recent attack on the *Falaba* and in the very waters for which the *Lusitania* was now making. Two members of the *Gulflight*'s crew, terrified that the cargo would ignite, jumped overboard and drowned, while her captain, Alfred Gunter, died of a heart attack induced by the shock. In London, Colonel House was worrying that "a more serious breach may at any time occur, for they [the Germans] seem to have no regard for consequences." The British press were demanding to know whether, following the *Falaba* sinking, President Wilson would "make good his words of February; and hold the German government to 'strict accountability.'"

Nevertheless, the outside world was continuing to treat the German warning to transatlantic shipping with complacency, even derision. Cunard chairman Sir Alfred Booth had only learned of the threat on 2 May when he opened his newspaper. His New York agent, Charles Sumner, had not even bothered to cable a report to the company's Liverpool headquarters. Booth pondered the significance of the warning but decided there was no reason to think that "the ship was in any serious danger of being sunk." In mid-April Cunard had briefed its captains on the submarine menace, ordering that, while in the danger zone, watertight doors were to be closed, boats swung out, portholes closed, and the ship darkened. Ships bound for Liverpool were not to stop at the Mersey Bar for a pilot but make straight for home port and safety. Booth believed that if there were any specific risk to the *Lusitania*, the Admiralty would advise her captain and send an escort.

Booth's confidence reflected the general reaction to the German warning. On 3 May the *Daily Telegraph* called it "Berlin's latest bluff" and maintained that it had been "ridiculed in America." The *Times* carried an article under the headline: "The Ineffective Blockade—New Tricks to Frighten Americans—Lusitania Warned." It further declared that "the manoeuvre is simply an ill-timed and excessively impertinent effort, begotten probably of the failure of the submarine blockade, to advertise German frightfulness." The *American Tribune* of 2 May commented ironically, "No big passenger steamer has yet been sunk."

Wesley Frost, U.S. consul in Queenstown on the southeast coast of Ireland, learned of the German warning from the Irish press on 2 May. The *Lusitania* had in the past called in at Queenstown, and he knew that she was already eastward bound out of New York. But he, too, wasn't worried about the people on board, particularly the Americans: "The reference to the *Lusitania* was obvious enough," he later wrote, "but personally it never entered my mind for a moment that the Germans would actually perpetrate an attack upon her. The culpability of such an act seemed too blatant and raw. . . . in addition, I did not believe that the submarines had yet shown any striking power equal to the task of attacking and destroying a ship as huge, well-built and fast as the *Lusitania*."

Passengers on the *Lusitania* reassured each other with many of the same arguments during the early days of the voyage. Theodate Pope told Edwin Friend of her conviction that "they intend to get us" but comforted herself with the thought that "we would surely be convoyed when we reached the war zone." An additional frisson was provided by reports, confirmed by Staff Captain Anderson, that three stowaways had slipped on board. They were discovered hiding in a steward's pantry near the Grand Entrance on the Shelter Deck during a routine check for stowaways. Detective-Inspector William Pierpoint, a fifty-one-year-old Liverpool policeman and erstwhile clerk and ship's steward, questioned them through the ship's interpreter, Adolph Pederson. Pierpoint had also been on the *Lusitania*'s outbound voyage, was traveling first class, and was said to be assigned to protect the vessel. He now ordered the men, who were found to be German-speaking, to be locked in the *Lusitania*'s comfortable cells below the waterline where they could do no harm. They could be questioned properly upon arrival in Liverpool. The strong rumor was that they were not simple stowaways but German spies or saboteurs. After all, why else would Germans wish to travel to the country with whom they were at war?

CHAPTER NINE

Fellow Passengers

*D*ESPITE SOME underlying unease, time ebbed away pleasantly for most passengers on the *Lusitania*. Some read and wrote letters or simply relaxed in the comfortable Georgian-style first-class lounge with its veneered, inlaid mahogany paneling, satinwood furniture, and wood-burning fireplaces. They could recline comfortably on "double-stuffed settees and large easy chairs" and gaze up at a stained-glass ceiling depicting the twelve months of the year. Alternatively, there was the plant-filled Verandah Café at the aft end of the Boat Deck. Open on one side to the deck, it re-created the ambience of an elegant pavement café from which the fashionable could watch their friends stroll by. Cunard had recently refurbished it, adding deep wicker chairs and hiring large numbers of plants from a florist to create an impression of relaxing greenery.

Some, like wealthy New York wine merchant George Kessler, known as the "Champagne King," held lavish private parties. He had a reputation as an extravagant host and had once re-created a Venetian lagoon by flooding the courtyard of London's Savoy Hotel and serving his guests dinner in shimmering white gondolas. This imposing man, with a thick, bushy black beard, was traveling with $2 million in cash and securities.

Harold Boulton, the young Briton traveling home in the hope of re-enlisting, was enjoying the sight of glamorous, fashionably dressed women like actresses Rita Jolivet and Josephine Brandell drifting elegantly around the ship. Rita was well-known for her appearances as the heroine in such plays as *Oh, I Say!* and *When Knights Were Bold*, and

Josephine had been leading lady in the London Opera House's production of *Come Over Here* in 1914. Boulton was hoping for the opportunity to dance with one of them.

After dinner the ship's small orchestra, whose number included the splendidly named Handel Hawkins, played for first-class passengers wishing to indulge in such new crazes as the One Step, the Bunnie Hug, and perhaps the Turkey Trot, which was so deplored by the kaiser for its lack of dignity and decorum that he banned his officers from taking part. Tables and chairs were unbolted from the deck, and the dancers neatly sidestepped the metal fastenings.

Evening concerts were held in the first- and second-class lounges. Third-class passengers were invited to entertainments in the second-class lounge. Dedicated bridge players like the Reverend Gwyer and a young Scottish structural engineer named Archie Donald, like Boulton on his way to enlist, quickly found soul mates in the second-class lounge. Bridge was fast eclipsing whist in fashionable circles; nevertheless, keenly fought whist drives were organized even in first class. Those who enjoyed playing cards for serious money made discreet arrangements. There was a rule against gambling on the ship, but it was not enforced. Games could easily be arranged in private rooms and suites away from the public gaze.

Chief Purser McCubbin was keeping a watchful eye in case any professional cardsharps had managed to get aboard. A six-day crossing was an ideal length of time for an experienced sharper to find his prey, win his confidence, then shake him down before fading from the scene. The cardsharps operated all kinds of scams. A favorite ploy was to steal the wallet of a wealthy passenger and then to hand it in to the purser with some spurious message about having found it and being anxious to return it to its owner. When the grateful passenger went down to his benefactor's first-class cabin to thank him, he would find him smoking a cigar and engaged in a lively game of cards, in which the passenger would be courteously invited to join. The passenger would initially win, but on the last day, or perhaps even on the boat train to London, he would suddenly lose heavily.

The cardsharps were seemingly charming, cultivated, sophisticated people—women as well as men—who blended easily into first class. One gambler named Jay Yates went down like a true gentleman with the *Titanic* after sending a poignant farewell letter to his family in Ohio via a lifeboat crammed with women. Oliver Bernard had had his first experience of these con artists in his naive younger days. Boarding the *Umbria*, he had been gratified by the number of extremely sociable people eager to make his acquaintance, only to be warned against being too friendly with so many strangers. One of these indeed turned out to be one of "those card-sharping scoundrels" who made their living traveling in style and fleecing the rich. On her last voyage the *Lusitania* was certainly not immune. Julia and Flor Sullivan were taken by a friend to watch card games in the first-class smoking room, and there they saw an argument break out between a passenger and a well-dressed cardsharper. Staff Captain Anderson was summoned to adjudicate, and the incident was smoothed over.

Pursers on ships like the *Lusitania* kept lists of notorious gamblers and posted warnings on the walls of the smoking rooms. Sometimes victims would suspect they had been cheated and shamefacedly seek the purser's help, but there was little he could do after the fact. Sometimes the tricksters worked in pairs and operated other kinds of confidence tricks. In some cases the female of the pair would seduce one of the many rich men traveling alone on business. As soon as they were in her cabin and in a sufficiently compromising state of undress, an angry pistol-brandishing "husband" would burst in. Calming down slightly in response to his "wife's" distraught pleas, he would eventually settle for money in recompense for his lost honor. The "Girl with the Waxen Arm"—a siren with a withered limb who brought many naive men to their ruin—achieved almost legendary status on the transatlantic run.

As the *Lusitania* sailed on, bright sunshine, a calm ocean, and the occasional sighting of porpoises lured many outside. Belle Naish was delighted that "the vessel pitched only slightly at times" and that "the sky was clouded only enough to make the light easier for the eyes than the brilliant sun would have been. The wind was not strong. . . . it was most delightfully warm all the way across, and the few whitecaps looked not over six inches high. I marveled that the Atlantic could be so smooth—it was like Detroit River on the finest afternoon." Women took their children outside for regular airings. People played deck games with gusto, in particular deck quoits and that long-established maritime favorite, shuffleboard. Throwing the heavy medicine ball was a more energetic game, as were the hotly contested sack, egg-and-spoon, and potato races. A runner-up in one of the latter was the woman passengers knew as Annie Matthews, wife of Lieutenant Robert Matthews. She was awarded a badge of the *Lusitania*, which she delightedly slipped into Robert's pocket.

Physical activity did something to offset the meals. Eating was a great pastime in all classes. Even in third class the food was more abundant and varied than many passengers' normal diets. Breakfast there usually began with oatmeal porridge and milk or syrup, followed by a variety of savory dishes from boiled eggs and Irish stew to fried fish or steak and onions, all served with plenty of "best quality" bread, jam, and marmalade. The midday "dinner" was a substantial affair of roasts, pies, and puddings. It was followed by an afternoon "tea" offering such dishes as mutton chops, sausages, and fish cakes with yet more fresh bread and butter. Gruel was served at 8 P.M. to anyone still hungry. Invalids could order a range of nourishing broths and easily digestible jellies. There were even live plants on the long tables, although not as numerous or fine as those in first and second class.

In second class, the food was elaborate as well as generous. Breakfast offered haddock or Yarmouth bloaters, omelettes cooked to order, broiled Wiltshire bacon, American hash, sautéed liver, grilled steak or lamb chops, fried potatoes, and hominy cakes with golden syrup. Diners could choose from different types of rolls, breads, and scones. A typical lunch included hors d'oeuvres, soup, a fish course, a choice of salmis of game, boiled mutton, pork cutlets, or cold meats with salad, sago pudding, apricot tart, and cheese. Dinner was as bountiful but more sophisticated, offering such dishes as fillet of plaice in white wine, braised Cumberland ham with Madeira sauce, and roast gosling Normande, rounded off with puddings, ices, cheese, nuts, and fruit.

In the double-tiered first-class dining room, the food was luxurious, even sumptuous, with mounds of glistening caviar, served with wafer-thin slivers of toast and finely minced hard-boiled eggs, and dishes of juicy oysters nestling on beds of crushed ice. Passengers could choose to dine off the table d'hôte in the marble-columned restaurant or à la carte in the elegant and intimate salon overhead. They soon discovered that the war had influenced the range of drinks. American lager had been substituted for German, and stewards informed passengers that

"Austrian claret and enemy mineral water" had been embargoed. The war had also pushed up the price of champagne: A bottle of 1906 Lanson could be had for 15 shillings and a bottle of Perrier Jouet for 12 shillings and 6 pence. Nevertheless, the *Lusitania* took in nearly eight times as much money from the sale of wine and liquor (£1,150) as the charitable donations from all classes from the ships' concerts (£175).

Oliver Bernard, eating in the main first-class restaurant, was outraged to find that an "abominably supercilious" steward, "the autocrat of the *Lusitania*'s dining-table arrangements," had given his table to a more important passenger, no doubt in return for a large tip. On the first night of a voyage there was ruthless jockeying for the best tables. On the plus side, Bernard was relieved that the newly married Masons seemed to be ignoring him. He had no need to keep an eye on his former patron's "little girl." Jilted not long before by a sultry Italian opera diva, he was not disposed to look kindly on young love and especially not the gushingly sentimental outpourings of this privileged young couple. His own early years had been bleak. His parents, a theatrical couple, had taken little interest in him as a child, leaving him with an aunt in case he "encumbered them on their travels." He overheard his nurse telling another woman that his mother's first words on seeing him were "very nice, but please take him away."

Bernard disliked most of the well-heeled passengers with whom he shared first class, writing acidly about "that guy Vanderbilt" with "nothing better to do than driving a four-in-hand to Brighton and coming three thousand miles to do it." He concluded that "even America was lousy with idle rich who commissioned the best architects to fake homes like royal brothels, steam yachts like harems . . . a conglomeration of tawdry dwellings like Coney Island for the rich when they're not prancing around the Pyramids or . . . Paris."

Unaware of the bitter gaze of his critic, Vanderbilt, dining at the captain's table with, among others, the Hubbards, Rita Jolivet, and George Kessler, was gregarious and pleasant to all. Few knew that on the second day of the voyage he had been distressed to receive a radio message from his wife that his great college friend, Fred Davies, had died. He was inevitably a focus of gossip and speculation about everything from his marriages to his four yachts, racehorses stabled under nameplates of solid gold, $30,000 ninety-horsepower Fiat automobile, and passion for driving horse-drawn carriages which so irritated Bernard. But the true source of people's fascination was his vast fortune. His elder brother, Cornelius Vanderbilt Jr., who should have been the heir, had been virtually disinherited by his father following a family breach over his marriage to "queenly" Grace Wilson, whose family moved in circles similar to the Vanderbilts', but who had a reputation for being "fast."

The full extent of the Vanderbilts' disapproval had become clear three years later when Cornelius Vanderbilt Sr. unexpectedly died at the age of just fifty-six. The grieving but expectant family gathered for the reading of the will in the walnut and leather–paneled library of the family house in Newport, Rhode Island, to learn that Cornelius Senior had left the bulk of the $72-million Vanderbilt fortune (around $1 billion in today's values) to Alfred. His inheritance symbolically included the gold Congressional Medal awarded to the founder of the family's fortunes, Commodore Cornelius Vanderbilt, for his gift of the SS *Vanderbilt* to the Union government during the Civil War.

Alfred tried to make amends to his brother by giving him a further $6 million and thereby making his share equal to the sum received by the other Vanderbilt siblings. This, however, led to arguments, eagerly reported in the press, about whether far from committing an act of unprecedented generosity Alfred was reneging on a private compact that Cornelius should receive not less than $10 million. The once-affectionate brothers were still unreconciled by the time Alfred sailed for England. Indeed, as Cornelius's son later sadly described, they were "as far apart as the planets."

Vanderbilt often called on Charles Frohman, who largely kept to his suite with its open fireplaces and curtained windows in place of portholes. The *Lusitania*'s famed suites, which came in every style from English and Colonial Adam, Georgian, William and Mary to Empire, were fitted out in beautifully grained satinwood, mahogany, sycamore, and walnut. The pièces de résistance were the two Regal Suites. The suite on the port side had a private dining room with moldings of burnished gold, paneled ceilings in white and gold, and a Fleur-de-Pêche marble fireplace modeled on the interior of Marie Antoinette's Petit Trianon at Versailles. The suite's drawing room was modeled on Fontainebleau.

The impresario enjoyed both the comfort and the privacy. He had bought a portable gramophone, which he placed next to his bed so that he could listen to his favorite song, "Alexander's Ragtime Band." Just three years earlier he had tripped on the porch of his house in White Plains and become almost crippled. What had at first appeared to be only a bad bruise on his right knee seemed to have prompted articular rheumatism. When he did occasionally venture out on deck or to the smoking room—a short, squat figure in a dark, double-breasted suit, stiff collar, and felt hat—he moved stiffly, even painfully. He needed the support of the stick he ironically called "his wife," though people whispered that he was secretly married to his protégée, the boyish actress Maude Adams, who had made her fortune when he cast her as Peter Pan.

In his last letter, sent with the departing ship's pilot, Frohman had sketched a submarine attacking a transatlantic liner. What he called "the horror, the tragedy, the wantonness" of the war obsessed him. He had even produced a play, *The Hyphen*, written by forty-one-year-old author Justus Miles Forman, who was also on board, which expressed this inner anguish. The word *hyphen* referred to the nickname "hyphenated Americans" by which German-Americans, or U.S. citizens of German origin, were known. But the play was not in keeping with the mood of the public, and it had flopped. Forman was one of the many who now paid court in the impresario's wonderfully appointed suite. Depressed at the failure of his play, Forman had decided to try his hand as a war correspondent.

The flamboyant figure of Elbert Hubbard stalked the decks telling anyone who would listen that "if Teddy Roosevelt and his rough riders went over there they could clean up the Germans in a couple of days!" To many of his fellow passengers, Hubbard's boyish good cheer and his raw American boosterism must have seemed slightly ridiculous, as inappropriate to a man nearing sixty as his graying Buster Brown haircut. Ridiculous or not, the man was sincere. "I believe in sunshine, fresh air, spinach, applesauce, laughter, buttermilk, babies, bombazine and chiffon," Hubbard wrote in his well-known business credo. "I believe in myself . . . I believe in the goods I sell . . . [and] I believe in American business methods . . . always remembering that the greatest word in the English language is 'Sufficiency.' "

Hubbard's happiness was self-made; his beginnings had been quite sober. He was born in 1856, in Bloomington, Illinois, the only surviving son of a struggling country doctor who eked out a living by farming. In 1875 he became junior partner in a soap manufacturing company, where his innovative approach to direct-mail marketing brought him sufficient money to sell out and transform himself. An admirer of William Morris and the English Arts and Crafts movement, he launched his own

Elbert Hubbard

publishing house, the Roycroft Press, in East Aurora, New York, leading to other creative ventures in furniture, metalwork, stained glass, and leather goods.

Hubbard's community of East Aurora became a perfect example of self-sufficiency, and tourists flocked to see it. Still not content, Hubbard launched himself as a popular philosopher and champion of self-help and self-education. He styled himself simultaneously an anarchist, a socialist, and a defender of big business. He advocated fresh air, hard work, individuality, and positive thinking and disparaged formal education, lawyers, and doctors. His ten-page pamphlet *A Message to Garcia*, a pro-employer polemic about U.S. labor relations, first published in 1899, sold some 45 million copies. He also argued keenly for feminism, women's rights, and liberal divorce laws. The latter was partly a result of personal experience. He had become bored with his first wife, Bertha Crawford, whose banality and preoccupation with potted plants got on his nerves. The opening sentence of one of his novels read "Great men often marry commonplace women," and this was a recurring theme in his writing. Modest, Hubbard was not.

Poor "commonplace" Bertha divorced him in 1903 after a considerable scandal, which split the local community. The cause was his long-standing affair with Alice Moore, a graduate of Emerson College, Boston, who taught in the East Aurora Academy and had boarded with the Hubbards. This forthright feminist rode in bloomers and exemplified the "New Woman." Their affair produced a daughter, Miriam, in 1894. They were finally married in 1904, and Alice was now accompanying Elbert to Europe on his crusade.

Margaret Mackworth, the Hubbards' fellow passenger in first class, was something of a kindred spirit. She was still feeling exhilarated by her experience of "open-hearted American hospitality" in a city whose dazzle and sparkle contrasted agreeably with "the heavy cloud of war at home." For the first time in her life she had felt able to shed the "annihilating shyness" that had plagued her ever since she was a girl. She had never forgotten the young Englishman who had urged champagne on her in the hope that "it might make you talk!"

In fact she had plenty to say. This energetic, intelligent, strong-jawed young woman had unconventional views and little time for the idleness of "drawing-room life" despite her privileged upbringing. She was a feminist who believed that it was wrong to treat prostitutes as untouchables because they performed sex for money. She was also a convinced suffragette. Her most militant act had been to attempt to set fire to a letterbox—an act of sabotage and gesture of suffragette defiance against authority—using tubes of combustible substances. It had taken far more courage than she had supposed, and she had paced to and fro several times before finally stuffing the vials into the red pillar box. Returning home, she had buried the rest of her sabotage kit under some black-currant bushes. A week later she was arrested and put in a cell reeking of vomit and urine. Her husband, Sir Humphrey Mackworth, who disapproved of her methods but was fond of his wife, helped her get bail. He also stood by her when she insisted on going to prison, rather than paying a fine, and when she went on a hunger strike.

Margaret Mackworth and her industrialist father, David Thomas, made friends with their table neighbors Dorothy Conner and her brother-in-law, Dr. Howard Fisher, and learned of their plans to set up Allied hospitals. Dorothy confessed in a lighter moment, "I can't help hoping that we get some sort of thrill going up the Channel." They also chatted with Lady Allan, wife of Canadian shipping magnate Sir Montagu Allan and mother of the two pretty girls Anna and Gwen who had sabotaged Leslie Morton's attempt to paint lifeboats. Theodate Pope, however, remained an imposing and somewhat unapproachable presence in the first-class salon, talking to practically no one except Edwin Friend and pretty Madame de Page.

Sir Hugh Lane

The more gregarious Boston bookseller Charles Lauriat was enjoying "roaming about the boat exceedingly, as I had never before taken passage on one of the 'greyhounds', although it was my twenty-third crossing." He preferred smaller and slower boats, but this year had wanted to keep his business trip as brief as possible by sailing on the fastest ship. He was an enthusiastic participant when, each evening in the smoking room, the pool for the following day's run was auctioned. Passengers estimated how many sea miles the ship was likely to make and bid for the particular number they favored. The money that they staked was pooled, hence the name, and then paid out to the winner. The pool was so enthusiastically supported that the proceeds averaged £105 a day.

However, like other observant passengers, Lauriat quickly realized that the ship was not making the speed he had expected. Oliver Bernard was chagrined to discover on the very first day that "the *Lusitania* was making no effort to maintain her reputation as the record holder of the Atlantic." He reckoned that they were averaging no more than eighteen knots despite the calm weather and the most tranquil seas he could recall. Another disappointed passenger, equipment manufacturer Isaac Lehmann, asked First Officer Jones, with whom he strolled most evenings, the reason: "Jones told me that they were not working all of the boilers, and that the crew was picked up here and there as they could get them, and they were very scarce over in Liverpool at that time."

Passengers now became aware of the fact kept from them at the time they had booked: Boiler room number four with its six boilers had been closed down as an economy measure. As the *Lusitania* began to near the war zone on 5 May, this fact began to dominate the conversation. After all, the ship's speed was supposed to be her greatest protection against submarine attack. Lauriat, confident that Turner would put on a burst of speed when the Irish coast was sighted, "bought the high number in the pool" for three pounds. It was to prove a poor investment.

CHAPTER TEN

Inside the *U-20*

AT 6 A.M. ON FRIDAY, 30 April 1915, the engines of the *U-20* began to revolve, and the submarine quivered in her moorings. The narrow gangway was yanked ashore, the ropes were cast off, and words of command rang from the conning tower. The slim gray *U-20* glided slowly between the cork fenders of the dock toward the harbor mouth and out of Emden, the German naval base on the North Sea west of Wilhelmshaven. Her thirty-year-old commander, Kapitänleutnant Walther Schwieger, had briefed his crew on the official object of their voyage. His general orders from his commanding officer, Fregattenkapitän Hermann Bauer, read: "Large English troop transports expected starting from Liverpool, Bristol Channel, Dartmouth. . . . Get to stations on fastest possible route around Scotland. Hold as long as supplies permit. . . . U-boats to attack transport ships, merchant ships and warships."

Schwieger's mission was part of a concerted action to be undertaken by the Third U-boat Half-Flotilla, comprising the *U-20*, the *U-27*, and the *U-30*. The *U-20* was to make for the approaches to Liverpool, the *U-27*, due to sail several days later, was to go to the Bristol Channel, while the *U-30*, which had already sailed and received her orders by radio, was to make for Dartmouth. Schwieger had also received further oral orders, but he did not record them or divulge them to his crew.

Walther Schwieger was an urbane, cheerful man from an old, established Berlin family. Photographs show a sharply chiseled, square-jawed face and close-cropped blond hair. Tall and broad-shouldered, he had a confident, easy manner and a reputation for being good with his men. They, in turn, respected him, and this was critical to their safety. As another U-boat captain wrote, "The commander must possess the absolute confidence of his crew, for their lives are in his hands." Schwieger was not afraid to exercise his own judgment even when it conflicted with orders. Indeed he considered it his duty to make operational decisions at sea as he saw fit. He would have agreed with the German admiral who later wrote, "The submarine commanders had to be given freedom of action as the authorities back home were never in a position to ascertain accurately what military and nautical conditions the submarines would encounter in their field of activities."

Hermann Bauer encouraged such initiative. As commander of the Third U-boat Half-Flotilla, he had little patience with the nervousness of the civil government about the possible consequences of U-boat warfare. On the very eve of the unrestricted U-boat campaign, a worried Bethmann Hollweg had insisted that U-boat captains be ordered not to attack neutral and hospital ships. Since then, Bauer felt that the U-boat service had been subjected to a flood of confusing, contradictory instructions, which he found increasingly frustrating. He was determined that his U-boats should not be put at risk because of political wavering and that his captains must have some freedom to act. He also agreed with the naval chief of staff, Gustav Bachmann, who had been lobbying the kaiser for "yet harsher measures" against Britain and her allies.

Walther Schwieger had entered the imperial navy as a sea cadet at the age of eighteen and gained rapid promotion. He joined the U-boat branch in 1911, winning command of his first U-boat, the gasoline-driven *U-14*, the following year at the age of only twenty-seven. He was appointed to the *U-20* in December 1914 as a successful U-boat commander with a proven track record. He was also by now a recognized expert on submarine matters—one of the few commanders consulted by Admiral Tirpitz and on whose advice Tirpitz relied.

Schwieger was proud of the *U-20*, with her beautifully fitted optics, instruments, and equipment, built by the Kaiserliche Werft shipyard in

Danzig. She was the second of the first class of four diesel submarines to be commissioned in 1913 and was powered by two eight-cylinder engines. She had a displacement of 650 tons, a length of 210 feet, while the width between her ribs was just twenty feet. She mounted one 3.5-inch gun and seven torpedoes of two types: the old-fashioned bronze torpedoes and the newer gyro torpedoes, which were in short supply at this stage of the war. The latter carried a charge of 350 pounds of a new TNT-type explosive called trotyl. The *U-20* had four eighteen-inch torpedo tubes, two forward and two aft. She could make over fifteen knots on the surface and over nine knots beneath it. In October 1914, her previous commander, Dröscher, using a school atlas to navigate, had circled the British Isles in the *U-20*, becoming the first man to take a U-boat west of Ireland and the British mainland.

The *U-20* was carrying her wartime complement of four officers and thirty-one men. Among them were Schwieger's young torpedo officer, Oberleutnant Raimund Weisbach, who had joined the navy two years after his commander; a radio operator, Otto Rikowsky; and an ex-merchant navy mariner, Lanz, on whom Schwieger relied for his encyclopedic knowledge of British shipping and who would act as pilot. Lanz was

adept at identifying ships from their silhouettes, smokestacks, and masts, knowing "all English ships from their structure" and "at what speed they usually run." The rank and file of the U-boatmen were largely "good-humored, solid seamen." They included twenty-year-old Hermann Lepper from Bochum, and Charles Voegele, a young electrician from Alsace conscripted at the start of the war. Electricians, machinists, and other technical personnel were needed to man the constantly evolving and technically challenging U-boats.

As the *U-20* slipped out to sea, the barking of dogs mingled with the thudding sound of the engines. Schwieger had adopted a dachshund that his men had plucked from the water after they had sunk a Portuguese sailing ship. She had later given birth to a litter of puppies, which helped give some sense of normality to an otherwise very abnormal world. The U-boat crews worked under difficult and stressful conditions. Every spare inch of the *U-20* was crammed with supplies, from butter under the bunks to sausages next to the grenades. A young officer wrote a heartfelt description of "the poor living conditions" on board a U-boat: "In order to live at all in the wardroom, a certain degree of 'finesse' was required. The Watch Officer's bunk was too small to per-

The U-20.

mit him to lie on his back. He was forced to lie on one side and then, being wedged in between the dripping bulkhead to the right and the clothes cupboard to the left, to hold fast against the movements of the boat. . . . The occupant of the berth could not sleep with his feet aft as there was an electric fuse box in the way. At times the cover of this box jumped open and it was all too easy to cause an electrical short circuit by touching it with one's feet."

The ordinary crewmen were even more cramped. Their quarters were farther aft so they felt the motion of the submarine even more acutely. Only a few had bunks, and the rest had to sleep in hammocks. There was not even enough space for the torpedoes, those "gleaming, red-tipped, death-dealing, precious 'eels'" to which they gave such names as Yellow Mary and Bertha. One U-boatman recalled: "I had a strange bedfellow aboard the *U-20*. We were short of room and when the boat was fully loaded there was one torpedo more than there was place for. I accommodated it in my bunk. I slept beside it. I had it lashed in place at the outside of the narrow bunk, and it kept me from falling out of bed when the boat did some of its fancy rolling. At first I was kept awake a bit by the thought of having so much TNT in bed with me. Then I got used to it, and it really made quite a comfortable 'Dutch wife.'"

Schwieger knew that in the days ahead all his crew, officers and sea-men alike, would be living cheek by jowl in a physically and mentally taxing world of foul air—"enough to give you a headache that you would never get over"—foul breath, slopping bilge water, and fluctuating tem-peratures. Water for washing was scarce, and men stank of sweat and oil fumes. Lack of fresh food, fresh air, and exercise would wear them down, and nerves would begin to fray. Constipation was an occupational hazard, and officers doled out castor oil to sufferers who then had to negotiate the unpredictable sanitary system. If anything exemplified the sheer nastiness of life on board a submarine it was the lavatory arrangements. The toilets, or "internal heads," operated on a compli-cated system of valves and levers that blew the contents back in the user's face if he made a mistake. Submariners called it "getting your own back." They could not flush the lavatories while their U-boat was submerged in enemy waters during daylight because the frothy release of air bubbles from the compressed air used to discharge the contents could betray her presence. Lavatory pans frequently overflowed as a consequence. A German U-boat officer advised colleagues likely to be at sea for more than twelve hours to take a little opium, not for its hallu-cinatory properties but for its binding qualities.

There were other discomforts. Since the internal temperature of a U-boat was greater than that of the seawater outside, "the moisture in the air condensed on the steel plates and formed drops which had a very disconcerting way of dripping on the face of a sleeper." The crew tried to protect themselves with waterproof clothing or rubber sheets, but the fact remained "it was really like living in a damp cellar." Men woke up choking and congested "with considerable mucus in the nose and frequently a so called 'oil head.' " U boatmen wore the same leather clothes, day in, day out, sometimes for weeks on end. They hardly shaved, becoming, in the words of one, as bearded and shaggy haired as "the real pirates of old days."

Some of the crew, like the men in charge of the lateral and depth steering or handling the torpedo tubes, had to perform hard physical work in the confined space. While off duty the crewmen were expected to be as inactive as possible to save air in a submerged submarine. One U-boat captain noted that sleeping men used up less air: "A well-drilled crew, off duty, is therefore expected to sleep at once, undisturbed by the noise around them, and their efficiency is all the greater when the time comes to relieve their weary comrades." He added approvingly that his wireless operator, whose duties ceased after submersion, "had so well perfected the art of sleeping that he never cost us more than fifteen liters of air, hourly, underseas."

Yet the harsh conditions were balanced by moments of exhilara-tion. Submarines offered new and exciting experiences, sights, and sounds. Claus Bergen, a German war artist assigned to the U-boat ser-vice, described what happened on the order to dive, "Alarm! *Tauchen!*" In an instant the deck of the U-boat emptied as men jumped, climbed, or swung down the open hatchway and the smooth iron ladder, careful their fingers were not crushed by the great seaman's boots of the man above. Each crewman dashed to his position, dodging the hazards of "this iron tube, plastered with iron plates, levers, screws, and wheels and now crammed with scrambling men." In the conning tower the captain stood at the periscope as the heavy hatch was swung shut over his head.

A bell signaled shrilly that the hatch was sealed. Levers spun, and seawater poured hissing into the diving tanks. Gently the floor began to sink, and the boat tipped forward. The interior took on a spectral quality. "In the dim glow of the electric light, a mystic modulation of various shades of gray, stands a figure enclosed in a narrow iron space, surrounded by all manner of levers and wheels, on a sort of pedestal, connected with the periscope that can be raised and lowered like a lift . . . the commander." Oily water, trickling through the crevices round the periscope, dripped down onto the commander's cap as he kept watch.

Faces pressed against the glass of a small side porthole saw "foaming masses of water crashing over our bows. . . . Then a confusion of bright foam and clear water, inaudible, fantastic, outside the glass: light gray, dark gray, the deep water grows ever darker and more calm." There was an enchantment in "the magical green light," the air bubbles sparkling over the hull and a nervous thrill in the knowledge that the "greased and glittering" periscope was the only link with the brighter world above. As a U-boat came to rest on the ocean floor, shoals of fish, ordinarily frightened away by the noise of the propellers, were lured by the electric lights and would "come and stare . . . with goggling eyes close to the windows in the turret."

Later, at the order "Surface stations," the chief engineer blew out the diving tanks with compressed air. The boat began to rise to an "infernal din of hissing, roaring water." The bow and the gun rose first from the water. Soon the whole deck was clear. Men swallowed to relieve the pressure in their ears. They opened the conning-tower hatch again. Fresh sea air streamed in. With the sea slapping against the hull, the diesel engines began to hum once more. The conning tower and deck dripped with seawater. Fragments of jellyfish and strips of golden yellow seaweed dangled from the steel hawsers. It was a relief to surface, but it was also essential. The batteries that powered a submerged U-boat's electric motors needed frequent recharging—an exercise that could be carried out only on the surface.

A U-boatman never forgot the "peculiar thrill and nervous sensation" of standing for the first time in the conning tower and looking through the glass ports cut into the sides at a stream of silver bubbles as the deck submerged. Or the tension of hours spent wondering whether all the valves and hatches had been properly closed, whether the steel body could resist the pressure, and when the next attack would come. He and his comrades would shuffle a pack of cards to predict the outcome, feeling that the boat around them had become "a gigantic mouse-trap."

If a submarine were rammed or struck a mine, death would be almost inevitable and very unpleasant.

A shaken German submariner described what it was like opening a U-boat that had been salvaged after hitting a mine: "A burst of choking poisonous air poured out, and the sight of the corpses was terrible. . . . What scenes of horror and madness had been enacted in that narrow cabin! The scratches on the steel walls, the corpses' torn finger-nails, the blood-stains on their clothes and on the walls, bore all too dreadful witness." The sight brought home that "death in a plunging submarine was as evil a fate as the imagination could conjure."

Schwieger and the *U-20* had had a narrow escape just a few months earlier. Sailing submerged off the Scottish coast, the *U-20* had become enmeshed in a giant metal antisubmarine net suspended between two buoys. Schwieger and his terrified crew heard a rasping sound, "as if huge chains were banging against the boat and were being dragged over it." The men at the diving rudders found that the submarine was out of control and wondered what to do as "the boat turned this way and that, lurching and staggering drunkenly" as she quickly sank, thudding help-lessly against the bottom. "Each man thought of his home in Germany and how he would never see it again." A desperate Schwieger ordered the engines to reverse, and the *U-20* painfully tore herself free with "a rip-ping and rending." He was lucky that the net had not been "hung with bombs, like tomatoes on a vine," as would soon become the practice. But British destroyers were waiting patiently above, like cats by a mouse hole, and the *U-20* had to run blindly through deep water to evade "those persistent hounds that were on our trail."

The lack of visibility under water was very stressful. As one U-boatman wrote: "Light objects, and even the stem and stern of our own boat, are invisible from the turret. We are unaware, therefore, of advancing ships, derelicts, or projecting rocks, and no lookout can preserve us from these dangers. The crew is entirely ignorant of their surroundings. Only the commander in his turret surveys through the periscope now and then a small sector of the horizon; and in turning round the periscope he grad-ually perceives the entire horizon." But it was grueling, nerve-racking work: "The periscopes erected through the upper cover of the turret must not be too easily turned in their sockets, and the latter are very tightly screwed in, for otherwise they would not be able to resist the water pressure at a great depth. The effort of simply turning the periscope is so exhausting that casual observations of the horizon are made by the officer of the watch; but during naval maneuvers or in time of war, the commander alone manipulates the periscope. It is essential in this case that the periscope should not arise needlessly above water and betray the presence of the U-boat."

Captains knew that it was good for crew morale to allow their men to look though the periscope: "It is their highest ambition, and the result is excellent, for it reassures them and they feel more confident as to their own safety after the granting of this small favor." Even so, knowledge of their own vulnerability was inescapable and difficult to live with. Schwieger understood this and the critical importance of maintaining morale. As 1914 drew to its close, he had been determined that his crew should enjoy Christmas even though they were on patrol. He ordered the U-20 to dive and "found a snug resting place on the muddy floor of the North Sea."

The tiny mess room was decorated with a green wreath in place of a Christmas tree. There were no candles because naked flames would have been too risky in the reeking, oil-laden interior of a submarine, but the tables were loaded with food. Fresh food had run out long ago, and it all came "out of cans, but we didn't mind that," wrote one feaster. Men and officers, dressed in their creaking leather submarine suits, ate together, washing the meal down with tea laced with rum. After dinner there was an impromptu concert based on a violin, a mandolin, "and the inevitable nautical accordion" played by a gnomelike red-haired crew member from the Engineering Department. Schwieger found his own relaxation in classical music; one of his greatest pleasures was to listen to the gramophone he had inherited from the U-20's previous commander, Dröscher.

Of all the crew, the captain most needed some form of release. As one of Schwieger's fellow commanders wrote bleakly but stoically: "The commander, himself, is on duty during the whole of the expedition in time of war, and he seldom gets a chance for rest in his tiny little cabin. Day and night, if there is the slightest suspicion of the approach of the enemy, he watches on the exposed bridge on top of the turret; for a few seconds' delay in submerging might forfeit the taking of a much-coveted prize. So he learns to do without sleep, or to catch a few brief seconds of repose by lying down in his wet clothes, and he is at once ready to respond to the alarm signal of the officer of the watch." The captain knew

Kapitänleutnant Walther Schwieger

that if a ship were sighted, he had to make his observations in a few seconds. It was all too easy for a sailor perched high in the crow's nest "to detect the slender stem of a periscope, although the hull of the boat is scarcely visible on the face of the waters."

Schwieger clearly merited the respect his crew accorded him. He combined concern over their safety with coolness and daring. He was an ambitious, often ruthless submariner, calm under pressure, and unsentimental about the outcome of his actions. On 30 January, before the proclamation of unrestricted warfare, he sank three British merchant ships outside Le Havre without giving warning. In February 1915, he fired a torpedo at the British hospital ship *Asturias*, painted white with red crosses on her sides. He missed, probably because of torpedo malfunction. He later claimed that he believed her to be an enemy merchant vessel, probably a troop transport ship. The *Asturias* was outward bound from Britain. She could not have had wounded on board.

Now, on this 30 April 1915, Schwieger must have wondered what his journey would bring. Although ordered to reach his station as quickly as possible, the route ahead was necessarily circuitous. He would have to negotiate his way around northern Scotland into the Irish Sea. Earlier in the war, U-boats had been able to take the shorter, swifter route to the Irish Sea via the Dover Straits, but now a combination of British mines, wire nets, and frequent naval patrols made this route too dangerous. Schwieger would need to decide whether to take the North Channel between Britain and Ireland, which was "the fastest possible route" albeit the more hazardous, or to go west of Ireland, the longer but safer passage. On the eve of his departure, his commanding officer, Hermann Bauer, had instructed that, "in view of the great distances, all detours on the way to the field of operation must be avoided unless necessary for the safety of the ship."

As the *U-20* passed the Borkum Reef Lightship, she tested her radio by signaling to the Borkum station and to the *Arcona*, an old German cruiser in the North Sea. Schwieger noted cheerfully, "Signals good at both ends." Schwieger could congratulate himself on the excellent quality of German transmitters as he proceeded to report his progress some fourteen times during the first twenty-four hours of his journey. He knew that if atmospheric conditions allowed, he could remain in contact for up to 500 miles. He would have been appalled to learn that every single one of his messages had been intercepted and decoded by the British.

CHAPTER ELEVEN

———— ∞∞∞ ————

"The Miraculous
Draught of Fishes"

*A*LL COMMUNICATIONS to and from the *U-20* were
being carefully studied by a small team working in
absolute secrecy in a room in the Admiralty's Old Building in London. Known simply as Room 40, the unit owed its existence to
a haphazard sequence of events early in the war. On 5 August 1914, the
British had severed the first of Germany's five overseas cable lines running from Emden to France, Spain, Africa, and the United States. By
early 1915 Germany's remaining cable links had also been cut, so that
Germany could only send cablegrams to a few adjoining neutral or allied
countries and none beyond. Instead she was forced to communicate
either by letter—a slow and risky process since the mail could easily be
intercepted—or by wireless, where transmissions had to be encoded.

At first Britain did little to monitor the growing stream of German
wireless traffic. The messages were passed to the director of the Admiralty's Intelligence Division, Rear Admiral Henry Oliver, who realized
their significance but had no infrastructure or code-breaking capability for dealing with them. He asked an old friend, Sir Alfred Ewing,
director of naval education, to set up a code-breaking organization.
Ewing was a distinguished engineer with a predilection for mauve
shirts and dark blue bow ties with white polka dots. He now spent many
hours combing the dusty shelves of the British Museum to educate
himself about codes. He also began to seek out suitable volunteers for

Room 40. The criteria were discretion and a good knowledge of both German and mathematics.

Room 40's focus sharpened when, through an astonishing run of good luck, Britain acquired the German navy's three principal codes. It all happened within just four months. On 11 August 1914, men of the Royal Australian Navy disguised as quarantine inspectors boarded the German-Australian steamship *Hobart* off Melbourne. In the early hours they caught the German captain in the act of retrieving his confidential papers from behind a secret panel in his cabin and forced him at pistol point to hand them over. Among them was the *Handelsverkehrsbuch* (HVB), the merchant shipping codebook. This code was originally intended to help warships and merchant vessels to communicate with one another, but it was also used within the German High Seas Fleet, including the U-boats.

By the time the HVB code reached London, Room 40 had acquired a second and even more important German naval code—the *Signalbuch der kaiserlichen Marine* (SKM), the signal book of the imperial navy—courtesy of their Russian allies. In late August in deep fog a German light cruiser, the *Magdeburg,* had run aground on an island off the Estonian coast. An accompanying German destroyer, the *V.26,* came to her aid, but it soon became clear she could not be refloated. Orders were hastily given for her crew to board the destroyer with the cruiser's confidential papers and for the *Magdeburg* to be blown up. However, before the sailors could do this, two Russian cruisers loomed out of the mist and attacked. In the confusion the Germans detonated their explosive charges on the *Magdeburg* too soon, injuring some of the *Magdeburg*'s crew.

According to Winston Churchill, the German petty officer responsible for the SKM codebook was blown overboard. Next day the Russians retrieved his corpse and discovered the code and its key—"priceless sea-stained documents," as Churchill called them. This story may be romantic elaboration. The codebook can be seen in the Public Record Office in London. It is some twelve inches by eight inches, with thick pages, examples of Morse code with neatly written amendments and updates, and illustrations of signal flags in red, blue, yellow, and green. It shows no sign of water damage. According to other accounts, the Russians found the code in the ship's charthouse, but whatever the case, it was a fortunate find.

Then, less than three weeks later, and through a piece of almost outrageous good fortune, the British gained possession of the third impe-

Zahlen-Signal	Buchstaben-Signal	Bedeutung	Zahlen-Signal	Buchstaben-Signal	Bedeutung
686 89	T N L	Torpedoheizer	687 45	T Ö J	Torpedosteuermann
686 90	T N M	Torpedohilfszielapparat	46	T Ö K	Torpedotransport
91	T N O	Torpedohilfszielstelle	47	T Ö L	Torpedoübernahme
92	T N Ö	Torpedoingenieur	48	T Ö M	Torpedoübernahmestelle
93	T N P	Torpedoingenieurkorps	49	T Ö N	Torpedoverbindungsstelle
94	T N Q	Torpedokampf	687 50	T Ö O	Torpedoversuchskommando
95	T N R	Torpedokessel	51	T Ö P	Torpedoversuchsschiff
96	T N S	Torpedokopf	52	T Ö Q	Torpedowaffe
97	T N U	scharfer Torpedokopf	53	T Ö R	Torpedowaffe außer Gefecht
98	T N Ü	Torpedolehrgang	54	T Ö S	Torpedoweitschuß
99	T N V	Torpedololsleitung	55	T Ö U	Torpedowerkstatt
687 00	T N W	fliegende Torpedololsleitung	56	T Ö Ü	Torpedowesen [s. Inspekteur]
01	T N X	Torpedoluftpumpe	57	T Ö V	Torpedowinkeleinstellung soll sein (n) Grad achterlicher als querab
02	T N Y	Torpedoluftpumpe ist unklar			
03	T N Z	Torpedomaschinist	687 58	T Ö W	Torpedowinkeleinstellung soll sein (n) Grad vorlicher als querab
04	T N a	Torpedomaschinistenanwärter			
05	T N γ	Torpedomaschinistenmaat	4 8 12	Y M	mit Torpedowinkeleinstellung schießen
06	T O A	Torpedomatrose	687 59	T Ö X	Torpedowinkelschuß
07	T O Ä	Torpedomunitionsraum	687 60	T Ö Y	Torpedozielapparat
08	T O B	Torpedonachtzielstelle	61	T Ö Z	Torpedozielschiff
687 09	T O C	Torpedonahkampf	62	T Ö α	Torpedozielschlitz
4809	Y J	Torpedonahkampf suchen	63	T Ö γ	Torpedozielstelle
687 10	T O D	Torpedonahschuß	64	T P A	tot, Toter [s. Punkt]
11	T O E	Torpedonetzschere	65	T P Ä	keine Toten
12	T O F	Torpedonetzscheren aufsetzen	66	T P B	wieviel Tote?
13	T O G	Torpedonetzscherenpistole	67	T P C	total -ität
14	T O H	Torpedooberingenieur	68	T P D	töten -ung
15	T O I	Torpedooberstabsingenieur	69	T P E	Totenliste
16	T O J	Torpedooffizier [s. Flotten-, Geschwader-, Sitzung]	687 70	T P F	Totenschein
17	T O K	Torpedopersonal	71	T P G	Totschlag
18	T O L	Torpedoreserveschütze	72	T P H	trachten (nach)
19	T O M	Torpedoreservezielstelle	73	T P I	Tradition -ell
687 20	T O N	Torpedoschaltbrett	74	T P J	Tragbahre
21	T O Ö	Torpedoscheibe	75	T P K	tragbar -keit
22	T O P	Torpedoschießen	76	T P L	träge, trägheit
23	T O Q	Torpedoschießen abhalten (bei, in)	77	T P M	tragen, Trag-
24	T O R	Torpedoschießen fällt aus (wegen)	78	T P N	Träger
25	T O S	Torpedoschießprämie	79	T P O	tragfähig -keit
26	T O U	Torpedoschuß	687 80	T P Ö	Trägheitsmoment
27	T O Ü	durch einen Torpedoschuß	81	T P Q	Tragweite
28	T O V	auf Torpedoschuß manövrieren	82	T P R	Train (Bataillon Nr. n)
29	T O W	Torpedoschußweite [s. Nahgefecht, Passiergefecht]	83	T P S	Trainkolonne
			84	T P U	Trajekt, Trajekt-
			85	T P Ü	Trall
687 30	T O X	auf Torpedoschußweite herangehen	86	T P V	Trall ausbringen
4810	Y K	außerhalb Torpedoschußweite (passieren)	87	T P W	Trall vorausschleppen
4811	Y L	innerhalb Torpedoschußweite (passieren)	88	T P X	Trank
687 31	T O Y	Torpedoschutznetz [s. Feind]	89	T P Y	transatlantisch
32	T O Z	Torpedoschutznetze bergen	687 90	T P Z	Transformator -isch
33	T O a	Torpedoschutznetze setzen	91	T P α	Transit-
34	T O γ	Torpedoschutznetze sind gesetzt	92	T P γ	Transport, Transport-
35	T Ö A	Torpedoschutznetze sind nicht gesetzt	93	T Q A	auf dem Transport (von — nach)
36	T Ö Ä	sind Torpedoschutznetze gesetzt?	94	T Q Ä	mit dem Transport gehen
37	T Ö B	Torpedoschutznetzmanöver	95	T Q B	Transportarzt
38	T Ö C	Torpedoschutznetzspier	96	T Q C	Transportdampfer
39	T Ö D	Torpedostabsingenieur	97	T Q D	transportfähig
687 40	T Ö E	Torpedolaufbahn	98	T Q E	Transportflotte
41	T Ö F	Torpedoraum	99	T Q F	Torpedotreffer
42	T Ö G		688 00	T Q G	..... (T. Boot)
43	T Ö H		01	T Q H	----- (U Boot)
687 44	T Ö I		688 02	T Q I	Torpedowerft

A page from the Signalbuch der kaiserlichen Marine (the signal book of the German Imperial Navy).

rial German naval codebook—the *Verkehrsbuch* (VB), the so-called traffic book—used to communicate with overseas naval attachés and warships. On 30 November, a British trawler fishing off the Dutch coast winched up a lead-lined chest. Upon opening it, the British found that it contained a collection of vital German documents, including the VB, the last piece of the jigsaw. The captain of the German destroyer *S.119* had jettisoned the chest in desperation while under attack from British ships. Room 40's personnel called this last discovery "The Miraculous Draught of Fishes."

With the SKM, HVB, and VB codes all safely in Room 40, the staff could now decode most intercepted wireless signals sent by the German navy. They could follow movements of the German fleet and knew the total strength of the U-boat fleet, which submarines were in port or at sea, and which had failed to return home. They also knew which areas were most at risk from U-boat activity. By February 1915 the Marconi Company had perfected a technique of radio direction finding. This was particularly timely since the Germans had discovered that U-boats could receive and send wireless messages at far greater distances than previously thought. U-boats now tested their communication systems by reporting their positions frequently, sometimes every two to three hours, during the first two days of their missions. These often unnecessarily chatty messages provided Room 40 with specific information about their course and speed. Once U-boats were far out into the Atlantic, the huge area of the sea, weather conditions, and decisions of individual U-boat officers prevented Room 40 from pinpointing positions—but they made informed guesses.

The Room 40 team was responsible to Oliver, now chief of the naval war staff, who was personally briefed by Churchill on how to run the unit and to preserve absolute secrecy. Within the Admiralty, circulation of the decodes was limited to only a privileged few, including, of course, both Fisher and Churchill. Even some members of the cabinet do not seem to have been permitted to know either of Room 40 or of the material it produced, although Prime Minister Herbert Asquith seems to have often discussed it with his mistress, twenty-seven-year old Venetia Stanley, a cousin of Churchill's wife. At the Admiralty the man best placed to exploit the information flooding into Room 40 was the newly appointed director of naval intelligence, Captain William Reginald Hall, known as "Blinker" within the navy because of his habit of constantly blinking his eyes. Hall's father had been the first director of naval intelligence, and it had been his life's ambition one day to succeed him.

Hall now learned from the intercepted messages that the *U-20* and the *U-27* would be operating off the Fastnet Rock, the landfall off the southern coast of Ireland, within just a few days. He was in fact himself partially responsible for their missions, which had been prompted by a careful campaign of misinformation. The reason for Hall's campaign was that the British were planning to go ahead with amphibious landings in Gallipoli, advocated strenuously by Winston Churchill. They were doing so despite the failure of purely naval attempts to force the Dardanelles and against the opposition of Admiral Fisher, who insisted that any seaborne invasion should be in the Baltic and a direct threat to Germany herself.

In April 1915 Hall had begun working with the British secret service on a scheme to trick the Germans into believing that the Allies were, as Fisher wanted, planning an early invasion of Schleswig-Holstein. The main aim was to convince the Germans that the massive shipping of Allied troops to the Dardanelles—the first landings in Gallipoli were planned for 25 April—would not cause any reduction in the number of British troops in northwestern Europe. On 24 April the Germans received false reports, planted by Hall, of heavy sailings of transports from Britain's western and southern coastal ports. As a result, they immediately instructed their U-boats to hunt these transports down. As well as the task given to the *U-20*, *U-27*, and *U-30* by Hermann Bauer, the *U-35*, *U-36*, *U-39*, and *U-41* had all been ordered out on 29 April.

✦

Schwieger, of course, knew nothing of this as he set a course north toward Peterhead on the northeast coast of Scotland that would eventually see the *U-20* threading a careful path between the Orkneys Islands and the Shetlands, watching out for patrols of British destroyers protecting the Grand Fleet in its Scapa Flow home and avoiding areas mined by the Allies. In this first stage of her journey the *U-20* was running on the surface. It was pleasant to be outside on the deck in the fresh air and the spray. He and his men had become accustomed to the various "square holes in the deck that catch one's boot-heels," although some still stumbled around clutching the rails. His men were still laughing about an encounter with a German fishing trawler that had sold them fresh herrings. One of Schwieger's officers signed a bill to the German Admiralty. He responded to the fishermen's cry of "Good Hunting" with a cordial *"Gott strafe England!"*

Schwieger was certainly hoping for some good hunting. Although sixty-six merchant vessels had been sunk since the declaration of unrestricted submarine warfare, April had been an unsatisfactory month.

Only seventeen merchant ships (eleven British and six neutral) had been attacked, of which six had escaped. He badly wanted to add to the tally. There was a strong element of competition among the U-boat commanders, and the German government had begun to publish a record of the tonnage sunk each month, including neutral vessels "in the service of the enemy."

Like other U-boat commanders, Schwieger believed there would be huge kudos in sinking a liner. After the declaration of unrestricted U-boat warfare, war artist Claus Bergen wrote of a trip he made aboard a U-boat: "We are now outside the entrance of the North Channel to the Irish Sea, a highway of the great Transatlantic steamers. An alarm soon followed, and we dived ahead of a gigantic creature, guarded by two destroyers, coming in from the Atlantic. Their speed was far too great to give us any possibility of maneuvering into a position for attack. And regretfully we watched the 24,000-ton Cunarder make her escape. It would have been a good catch."

However, on 1 May Schwieger was worried to find thick fog in the North Sea and a growing swell. He was forced to submerge until midmorning, but even then visibility in the light drizzle was poor. By 4 P.M. the *U-20* was again under water because she was now in the steamer lane to the Firth of Forth. A small steamer passed by, heading east, but Schwieger could not attack because of the poor weather.

On 2 May came real danger. Now some forty miles off Peterhead, the *U-20* was forced to dive to avoid patrolling British destroyers. At 3:20 A.M. Schwieger spotted a group of at least six coming directly toward him "in a broad searching line." After his initial order it took an agonizing seventy-five seconds for the *U-20* to plunge the necessary *fifty* feet. The watch officer and his lookouts jumped down the hatchway in the conning tower, scrabbling for a purchase on the narrow steel ladder. The last man slammed the upper hatch behind them, then secured it with two levers, and snapped the lower hatch shut. Inside there was desperate activity as the earsplitting Klaxon summoned the crew to open the diving valves to flood the tanks.

That evening, Schwieger ordered the *U-20* up to periscope depth. His batteries badly needed recharging, and he was in danger of being pulled off course by the strong currents round the Orkneys. To his relief, he saw no further signs of enemy vessels and ordered the tanks to be blown so that the *U-20* could surface and run on her oil-burning diesel engines. He recorded that if any destroyers had still been around, "our situation would have been critical as our battery was pretty nearly gone."

On 3 May the *U-20* reached the North Atlantic in "very beautiful weather." Schwieger sighted a number of ships, including a Danish freighter off Ronaldsay and, later, "a large neutral steamer, its name lit-up, which had apparently passed Ronaldsay and was now sailing to North America [probably a Danish passenger steamer from Copenhagen to Montreal]." German intelligence reports had noted that British ships often used Danish flags to disguise themselves as neutrals. The steamer was moving too quickly for him to attack, he wrote in his diary. It seems he would have gone for her, if he could, without warning despite doubts as to her nationality.

Then, in the hazy early-evening light the *U-20* encountered another small steamer. Lanz told him it was an English vessel from Leith, although she was flying a Danish flag. Schwieger ordered a torpedo attack. If all went according to plan, the torpedo's compressed air motor would launch it from the tube, and the twin propellers rotating in opposite directions would hold it on course. As it hurtled toward its target, the small propeller on its nose should spin down a threaded rod, arming the torpedo. But the firing lock jammed, and the bronze torpedo stuck in its tube. This was a frustrating but common problem; between February and September 1915 some 60 percent of German torpedo launches failed because of faulty triggers, dud warheads, and faulty steering mechanisms. It was nerve-racking for the crew, who knew that a torpedo that failed to eject might explode in its tube. Further attempts to attack steamers that night, including an English ship that fled past without lights, were similarly unsuccessful. Schwieger wrote reflectively that "in twilight and under water it is easy to underestimate a target."

Careful and cautious as ever, Schwieger decided not to risk the North Channel route but to go west of Ireland. The next day, 4 May, he sighted the northwestern point of Ireland. Black Rock Light was clearly visible despite a hazy horizon. Spotting a steamer coming toward him, Schwieger dived and prepared to fire a "clean bow shot," but she passed too close. He recorded that "the steamer was Swedish. *Hibernia* with neutral markings, no flag."

On 5 May Schwieger rounded the southern tip of Ireland and entered the Irish Channel to run into thick fog. The *U-20* was now in the lanes of the great passenger steamers. They could easily smash his fragile craft, so he decided to submerge until conditions improved. At 8:25 A.M. Schwieger brought his submarine to the surface again but spent a disappointing time: "During the entire afternoon no steamer sighted in spite of the clearing weather, although we were within one of the main shipping lanes." Toward evening, still on the surface and approaching the Old Head of Kinsale, he at last spotted a small three-masted 132-ton schooner, the *Earl of Lathom*, coming out of the mist. She was too small to be any threat, so he challenged her, shouting through a megaphone that her crew should abandon ship and surrender her papers. With twelve shells from his deck gun Schwieger sank the old vessel, with her cargo of Irish bacon, eggs, and potatoes bound for Liverpool, while her crew rowed frantically for the Irish shore some ten miles distant.

Later that evening, while the *U-20* was still on the surface, a 3,000-ton steamer loomed out of the fog, passing perilously close. She was "Norwegian with neutral markings," but these looked "unusually high" and were "probably painted on tarpaulins." Suspecting she was a British ship in disguise, Schwieger maneuvered for a torpedo attack, calculating his target's course, speed, and range. One U-boat officer described the principle as being like that of duck shooting: firing ahead of the target in the expectation that it would fly into the shot. Schwieger attacked, loosing "a clean bow shot" with one of his bronze torpedoes at his target some 300 yards away. The torpedo just missed, leaving a telltale trail of bubbles. Schwieger hastily veered "around hard and ran away to avoid the danger of being fired upon." As fog and darkness increased, he dived to avoid being rammed by other vessels in the shipping lane.

Schwieger had been at sea for five days. His early radio messages had been intercepted by the Room 40 team, and he had now given ample evidence of the *U-20*'s location. The attack on the *Earl of Lathom* had been clearly heard on the Irish coast. At 10 P.M. that night, a worried Vice Admiral Sir Charles Coke, the naval area commander based in Queenstown, informed the Admiralty in London of the menace. At 10:30 he began broadcasting a warning message at regular intervals to all ships. It told them that a U-boat was active off the southern Irish coast.

CHAPTER TWELVE

Into the War Zone

O N 6 M A Y Theodate Pope was awakened in her Boat Deck state-room at around 5:30 A.M. by "shouts and the scuffling of feet" and the sound of the ship's bugler, Vernon Livermore. She looked out of her porthole to see "the crew loosening the ship's boats and swinging them clear of the railing." This noisy task was being under-taken by a mixed bag of cooks, stewards, sailors, and, according to one of the officers, "any other men that we could raise." All twenty-two wooden lifeboats, suspended eight feet above the Boat Deck, were made ready for lowering and their ropes, the "falls," brought down. The boats' equip-ment—matches, sea anchor, oil for their storm lamps, provisions, drink-ing water—was checked as well.

Belle Naish also heard the commotion and jumped up, saying, "Oh, what can it be?" "Keep cool," her husband told her, "don't worry, just take a look." He had been seasick all the way and lacked the energy to go and see for himself. Belle went out to discover what was happening and was not reassured, returning to tell her suffering husband that if trouble came, "our only hope lay in our life preservers, as the boats seemed very small and the passengers were by hundreds." Another passenger, Mrs. J. McFarquhar, was also "rather uneasy" and wondered why the boats had not been swung out earlier and why they were being so now. Another noticed that "they did not tear off the cover of canvas on the collapsible boats, which were piled on the aft saloon decks in groups of three."

There was a growing sense of expectation as the *Lusitania* neared the danger zone. Passengers speculated about the real chances of an attack and when an escort from the Royal Navy might be expected to appear. The discussion gave some a not unpleasurable frisson. To those sitting comfortably in the walnut-paneled first-class smoking room, the threat seemed reassuringly remote, even academic. But others were not so sure. They noticed that at sunset that night the crew extinguished all outboard lights, placed covers over cabin skylights, drew curtains in the salons, and closed and darkened portholes. One passenger berthed on the Promenade Deck found "a blotter placed over my skylight that night to obscure the light." The Admiralty had not yet banned all lights on merchant ships, believing that a U-boat might assume a partially lit vessel was neutral, whereas any blacked-out ship would be marked down at once as an enemy. Nevertheless, even these precautions brought home the reality that the *Lusitania* would shortly enter the war zone. The betting among passengers was now "that the attempt would be made in the Irish Sea during our last night."

That evening, some passengers felt sufficiently nervous to form a committee to instruct everyone, including the children, how to put on their life jackets. Notices about use of the life jackets were displayed on cabin walls and posted around the ship, but few had bothered to read them. Captain Turner was asked to sanction the idea. He gave approval in principle but cautioned the committee to take care not to cause panic. There should be no suggestion that this safety measure was at all urgent. Turner might have felt differently had he known that during the six days that the *Lusitania* had been at sea twenty-three merchant vessels had been torpedoed in the waters his ship was now entering.

Some of these vessels had, of course, fallen victim to the *U-20*. The sixth of May had been a particularly rewarding day for Walther Schwieger and his crew. Early in the morning, despite thick, drifting fog and poor visibility, the *U-20* sighted a large steamer some thirteen miles southeast of the dark-green Coningbeg Lightship off the Waterford coast. Her name had been painted out, and she was flying no flag. Schwieger had to decide quickly whether she was a neutral or an enemy vessel. His interpretation of his orders was "if in doubt, attack."

Schwieger would have had little sympathy with the letter sent that very day by Chancellor Bethmann Hollweg to the naval chief of staff, Gustav Bachmann, complaining about the large number of neutral ships that had been attacked in recent days and demanding a guarantee that U-boats would not destroy neutral ships. Bachmann had been urging the kaiser to be less squeamish about neutral vessels, insisting that the only way to damage Britain's economy was by waging a vigorous campaign "without regard to the special rights of ships under neutral flags."

Bethmann Hollweg and Foreign Minister Jagow were also trying to ease tension with neutral countries through diplomatic channels. In particular, they were anxious to appease American public opinion. On 6 May a senior official at the German foreign office in Berlin told an American diplomat that although Germany would do everything in her power to destroy British merchant shipping, she had never had any wish to interfere with neutral shipping unless it was carrying contraband. While the occasional destruction of a neutral ship was unavoidable given the British practice of arming their merchant vessels and disguising them under other flags, submarine commanders had been given special instructions "to use the utmost care consistent with their own safety to avoid attacks on neutral vessels." If a neutral ship were accidentally destroyed, Germany would immediately make a formal apology and pay an indemnity. Any reports of the destruction by German vessels of a neutral ship would be immediately investigated by both the German foreign office and the German Admiralty, and, if necessary, the case would be settled by a commission composed of representatives of both nations with a neutral arbiter whose decision would be final.

Untroubled by this political sparring behind the scenes in Berlin, Schwieger launched a surface attack, firing on his target with his deck gun. He was confident that in the poor visibility "there was little danger of our boat being rammed or fired upon." In fact, the steamer tried to make a run for it as soon as she saw the submarine, but the *U-20* gave chase, firing on her. The fleeing vessel "continued at top speed" even after she had received two hits, and disappeared into the fog banks. However, they failed to blanket her completely. As soon as she became visible again, Schwieger continued the assault, and the steamer stopped at last. Her frightened crew, including her sweating coal-streaked firemen, abandoned ship, tumbling into four overcrowded lifeboats, one of which was swamped as soon as she hit the water. They were later picked up by a naval trawler and landed at Milford Haven.

Schwieger launched a bronze torpedo that smashed into the steamer's engine room, but still she would not sink. Finally, he ordered his helmsman to steer in closer and told his gun crew to fire at her waterline. Schwieger identified his victim correctly in his war diary as the *Candidate*.

The 6,000-ton Liverpool steamer had been en route to Jamaica with a cargo of groceries and hardware. News of the sinking of the *Candidate* would not reach the Admiralty until the early hours of 7 May. Vice Admiral Coke in Queenstown would not learn of it until over twenty-four hours after the attack.

Within an hour of disposing of the *Candidate*, Schwieger was doing his best to sink without warning a 16,000-ton passenger steamer, again with no visible markings, which he sighted on the port beam and identified correctly as a liner of the White Star Line. She was keeping a straight course and not zigzagging. Schwieger was hopeful, but this time his target, the *Arabic*, was too quick. Schwieger was still maneuvering for his favorite "clean bow shot" when she sped past some 10,000 feet away and vanished into the fog banks. The *Arabic*'s luck was not to hold. She would be torpedoed just three months later by the *U-24* off the Irish coast and would sink within minutes.

Finding the fog had become "thicker again," Schwieger dived to 72 feet. An hour later, rising to 36 feet, he was pleased to find it had "cleared a little" and that there was just a gentle swell. In the early afternoon Schwieger was excited to see another steamer "heave in sight," smoke spiraling from her stack. Once again he prepared to attack without warning, launching a gyro torpedo from 300 yards away and hitting the ship near the bridge. The ship began to sink by the bow almost immediately, and her crew abandoned her, pulling away frantically in the lifeboats. Schwieger loosed a bronze torpedo to complete his task. The air split with the sound of the explosion, and air hissed from the stricken hull. Schwieger did not wait to watch her sink but was "as good as certain" of his kill, recording that he had sunk a ship of some 6,000 tons whose name was again concealed and which flew no flag. He also recorded that she was English. She was in fact the *Centurion*, sister ship to the *Candidate* of the British Harrison Line. She had been en route to Durban.

According to the *U-20*'s official war diary, Walther Schwieger now ordered the *U-20* to dive and head out to sea while he reviewed his options. His position was some twenty miles due south of the Coningbeg Lightship, and his orders were to head north to his assigned station off Liverpool. He still had three torpedoes left, but he was under standing orders to save at least two for the return voyage. The war diary records a momentous decision in considerable detail. Schwieger would not sail on to his "true field of operations" because the thick fog of the past two days would probably not clear, the poor visibility would put his U-boat at risk in the busy shipping lanes, and he would have to sail submerged. It would be hard in these conditions to attack troop transports, which would be likely to slip out at night under cover of the fog and would perhaps be escorted by destroyers. Also, if he went on to Liverpool, he would not have enough fuel left to enable him to return to Germany around the south of Ireland. He would be forced instead to take the dangerous North Channel between England and Ireland. The *U-20* would therefore remain in the Irish Channel, south of the entrance to the Bristol Channel, and attack steamers until she had used up 40 percent of her fuel. Then she would begin her journey home, retracing her outbound route. That night, the *U-20* made for the open sea to recharge her batteries at a safe distance from enemy lightships and bide her time till dawn.

At 7:52 P.M. bellboy Ben Holton handed Turner a plain-language wireless message from Coke sent via the Valentia station. It read "SUB-MARINES ACTIVE OFF SOUTH COAST OF IRELAND" and was one of the general messages that Coke had begun transmitting the previous evening. This was the first warning the *Lusitania* had received. A perturbed Turner dashed off a response asking for the message to be repeated. It was so brief that he feared some of it might have been lost in transmission. By 7:56 P.M. one of the Marconi operators was tapping out the request in Morse. A few minutes later Turner had his answer—the message was identical with the first. At 8:30 P.M. came a further general message from the Admiralty, this time in code: "TO ALL BRITISH SHIPS 0005: TAKE LIVERPOOL PILOT AT BAR AND AVOID HEADLANDS. PASS HARBOURS AT FULL SPEED. STEER MID-CHANNEL COURSE. SUBMARINES OFF FASTNET." Turner knew that the *Lusitania* was now some 370 miles, or eighteen hours steaming, from the Fastnet landfall.

Earlier that year, while commanding the *Transylvania* off the Irish coast, Turner had received an order to divert to Queenstown because German U-boats had sunk three British ships off Liverpool the day before. He had tried to dismiss the fears of his passengers and had finally reached his destination with the comment "I fooled them that time." Now he must have wondered whether a similar sequence of events was about to unfold and whether he could fool the U-boats again.

Under the circumstances, a preoccupied and anxious Turner was in no mood for socializing with his passengers. Still, he had no choice but to attend the traditional passengers' talent concert—a fund-raiser for the Seamens' Charities—due to take place that night in the first-class saloon. It was the last important social event of the voyage and an excuse for extravagant party giving. George Kessler was once again urging cocktails on his guests, including Fred Gauntlett, Charles Lauriat, the formidable Theodate Pope, and the more sociable Staff Captain Anderson. Charles Frohman's suite was jammed with the theatrical set. Alfred Vanderbilt was also there, buoyed up by an affectionate wireless message from a woman in Britain named May Barwell: "HOPE YOU HAVE A SAFE CROSSING. LOOK FORWARD VERY MUCH TO SEEING YOU SOON." The democratic Frohman had also invited the gregarious ship's barber, Lott Gadd. Charles and Mary Plamondon were celebrating their thirty-sixth wedding anniversary in quieter style with a bottle of champagne in their cabin nearby.

Taking his place for the concert, Oliver Bernard noticed how polarized people were, "split up into dismal twos and threes . . . not on speaking terms with anybody." He reflected darkly that "a submarine would have at least socialized the audience." He watched Alfred Vanderbilt insist on paying a young Canadian woman, Charlotte Pye, five dollars for one of the ten-cent, gold-embossed programs she was selling. The event was a good-natured success, raising £123 10s. 7d. compared with the £6 15s. 4d. collected at the separate third-class event. The Welsh choir and Parry Jones sang, a pianist played Irving Berlin's "I Love a Piano," and passengers tried their hand with greater or lesser success at telling jokes, performing magic tricks, singing such popular songs as "Indian Love Lyrics," and reciting poems. Some crew members took part, though not Chief Purser McCubbin. He had once been famed for his flute playing while purser of the *Saxonia*, until some wag put flour inside his instrument prior to a concert. At the first note both he and the imposing Bostonian matron accompanying him were enveloped in a white cloud. He refused to perform in public ever again.

There was an expectant hush as Turner stepped forward to address his passengers during the intermission. He explained that there had been a submarine warning but assured them that "on entering the war zone tomorrow we shall be securely in the care of the Royal Navy" and that "of course there is no need for alarm." He added that the next day he

First class lounge.

would steam at full speed so as to arrive at Liverpool in good time. Finally, he warned male passengers not to light their cigarettes on deck that night.

The concert went on, but many, distracted by news of the warning, found it difficult to concentrate on their fellow guests' artistic efforts. As soon as the ship's orchestra had wound up with "God Save the King" and "America," an anxious murmur broke out. Isaac Lehmann was so perturbed that he decided not to go to bed but to remain "dressed all night" in his stateroom on the Upper Deck. Some passengers were too nervous to spend the night in their cabins at all and opted to sleep in the public rooms. Stewards and stewardesses bustled backward and forward with blankets and pillows. Other passengers walked on deck to calm their nerves. When they saw a thick pall of fog beginning to descend, they wondered whether this would protect the ship as she neared the war zone.

Professor Holbourn was simply hoping for the voyage to end quickly so that he could be reunited with his family. That night, Marion, his wife, had a bizarre experience that she would later describe as "a waking vision." She had read of the German warning but had been reassured by the attitude of the British press, which depicted the threat "as an impudent joke—like a small boy putting out his tongue at the headmaster." She had dismissed it from her mind. Now, on the night of 6 May, she retired to bed about eleven. She was not yet asleep when she saw: "a large vessel sinking with a big list from side to side and also from stem to stern. There was a crush of frightened people, some of them slipping and sliding down the sloping decks. I thought it strange that I could be seeing this while I was wide awake, and I stretched my arms out of bed and clenched and unclenched my fingers to make sure that I was not dreaming!"

Marion was not the only one to have presentiments. Captain Turner later recalled that both Staff Captain Anderson and Chief Purser McCubbin had premonitions of death.

Meanwhile, across the Atlantic, telephones were ringing in New York's newspaper offices. Perplexed and irritated editors were assailed by a barrage of mysterious callers, many from suburbs in Long Island, New Jersey, and Connecticut. Had the *Lusitania* arrived in England? Was she in any danger? Had she actually been torpedoed? Editors dismissed the individual anonymous calls as a hoax perpetrated by cranks. Only later, when they compared notes, did some begin to see the concerted episode in a different light.

CHAPTER THIRTEEN

"Suppose They Should Sink the *Lusitania*?"

WHILE PASSENGERS SLEPT fitfully, seamen worked through the night. Lookouts were replaced every two hours, but it was stressful, eye-straining work. Leslie Morton, on watch between 2 and 4 A.M., felt drained from peering anxiously into the darkness and starting at shadows. Others were preparing for the *Lusitania*'s arrival in Liverpool in twenty-four hours' time. Able Seaman Thomas O'Mahoney and his colleagues on the 4-to-8-A.M. watch sweated to bring up the mailbags from the mail hatch. O'Mahoney's height and long arms made him particularly adept at reaching into the cavernous hatch, and he was told to stay there and take his turn as lookout at midday. The mail was always the first cargo to be unloaded. The deckhands knew they would be expected to spend most of their watches that day in the mail and luggage rooms, to which the only access was by electric elevator.

The early hours of 7 May were fresh and clear, but at around 6 A.M. a heavy fog closed in again. Julia and Flor Sullivan, who had risen early for their first sight of their native Ireland, were disappointed. Flor had been intending to recite a poem to mark their homecoming. The master-at-arms called for two able seamen to go to the forecastle as extra lookouts. The fog was so dense that by the time Captain Turner arrived on the bridge he was worried about his precise position and the depth of water beneath his keel. He ordered depth soundings to be taken, then went to his usual breakfast of porridge, kippers, and a boiled egg.

At around 8 A.M., as those passengers who had chosen to sleep in the public rooms were picking up their pillows and blankets and returning to their cabins to dress, Turner telegraphed the engine room to reduce speed from twenty-one to eighteen knots. A little while later he ordered the duty engineer to lower it yet further to fifteen knots—the same speed that the *U-20* could travel on the surface in a calm sea. He also ordered the foghorn to be sounded every minute. Its mournful tone woke some passengers. It also alarmed them. Theodore Naish remarked to his wife: "I do not like this; it is too much like calling for trouble." David Thomas was also anxious, complaining to his daughter, "That wretched foghorn gives our whereabouts away."

The continued sounds of the *Lusitania*'s siren spoiled the flavor of Oliver Bernard's breakfast. "Now that they were so near the danger zone," he later recalled, "I could not understand the policy of announcing a liner's whereabouts to friend and foe alike." For some, the fact that the captain felt sufficiently confident to do this restored their sense of equilibrium, but others were becoming increasingly tense and planning what to do if the worst should happen. One group of men agreed that, "in view of the number of women and children on board," it would be impossible for any men to get away honorably by lifeboat. These should be left to the women. In an emergency they would meet at the stern below the Boat Deck to see how best they could save themselves.

A clergyman, all too aware that his wife suffered bitterly from the cold, decided that a place in a boat would be her only chance of survival. She would die if in the water for any length of time. He must ensure she reached a lifeboat. Surgeon Major Warren Pearl, traveling with his extensive young family, ensured that his wife and their nurses, Alice Lines and Greta Lorenson, "had been drilled as to what to do in an emergency." Henry Adams, a London merchant who had been reluctant to travel on the *Lusitania* but had been persuaded by his wife of four weeks, "a confirmed Cunarder," to book passage on her, insisted on getting their life jackets down from the top of their wardrobe and trying them on. Then he stowed them carefully under their berths, where they would be more accessible if needed in a hurry.

Around 10 A.M. the spring sun began to burn off the fog. Soon the lookouts aloft could make out "the loom of the land through the haze." By midday the visibility was good, the sun shone, glinting on a pancake-smooth, deep-navy sea. Captain Turner sighted familiar landmarks along the Irish coast. Relieved, he brought the speed back up to eighteen knots. The sight of the southeast coast of Ireland "in the sunshine of an ideal early summer day" reassured some passengers but not Charles Lauriat.

Lauriat had woken to the sound of the ship's foghorn. He decided to take a bath and then returned to his warm berth for a few hours' "extra snooze . . . for there was no use in getting up if it was foggy and disagreeable weather." His steward roused him at noon. He told him that Cape Clear had been "picked up" by the lookouts. Lauriat decided to take a stroll around the deck before lunch. He found it was now a beautiful day with "light wind, a smooth sea, and bright sunshine" but reflected that "if a German submarine really meant business," the conditions could not be more ideal. On the port side he could clearly see "the good old Irish Coast." As a transatlantic veteran, he noticed that Captain Turner was taking "the good old beaten track that ocean liners have taken for the last fifty years." He was surprised that Turner was keeping the ship "the same distance off" as on previous voyages and that it "went in there, so near shore."

Joseph Myers, another seasoned transatlantic traveler, shared his concern. To his recollection, the only time he had ever sailed closer to land was one occasion when the ship "went inside Fastnet," the solitary rock at the southwest tip of Ireland. Myers felt particularly nervous. He could not banish for long the disturbing memories of a recent Channel crossing when a U-boat had chased his ferry.

Passengers were puzzled by the ship's continuing slow speed. Mabel Henshaw, who had settled in Saskatoon and was taking her baby, Constance, to England so that her sick father, an honorary director of Dr. Barnado's Homes for Orphans, could see his only granddaughter, felt it was as if the *Lusitania* were saying to the enemy, "Here I am, do your darndest." Oliver Bernard agreed. He thought that Turner was calling the bluff of the Germans' newspaper warnings "more heavily than healthily." He noted how "the general feeling . . . that morning was . . . patient expectation, that when the fog lifted the *Lusitania* would at last give some demonstration of speed to meet the potential danger she now faced." But that did not happen.

As an enthusiastic participant in the daily pool, Lauriat had a sharp eye for such things. He checked the notice in the smoking room announcing the previous day's run to find that the *Lusitania* had sailed just 462 miles during the past twenty-four hours and "wondered at our loafing along at this gentle pace." He thought it particularly strange given Turner's comments at the previous evening's concert that he intended to make full speed. Another passenger later recalled: "You could hear [the comment] whenever you passed a group of passengers: 'Well, why are we not making full speed . . . as Captain Turner told us[?]' "

Harold Boulton asked a crewman why the ship was traveling at a snail's pace and was told: "It's not only the fog, sir. We're saving coal and keeping reserve steam up so that if we spot a submarine we can muster enough speed to get us out of danger." Belle Naish thought it would be worth running the ship faster through the fog. Any increased risk would be balanced by lower risk of submarine attack.

In fact, Turner had another reason for reducing speed, apart from the fog. He was planning to steam through the final stretch of the Irish Sea in darkness, timing his arrival at the Mersey Bar to catch the tide in the early hours. He then intended to sail straight over the bar without waiting for a pilot, to avoid delaying in waters known to be infested with submarines. High tide at the Mersey Bar was 6:53 A.M., giving him a window of opportunity of some five hours.

Others attributed the ship's "curiously cautious" progress to the fact that the captain must be "waiting for something to happen, perhaps for an escort." They anxiously debated the whereabouts of the British warships expected to see the *Lusitania* safely home. Now that she was in the war zone, where were they? The Naishes recalled how at the concert Turner had promised that on entering the war zone they would be safely in the care of the Royal Navy. The empty seas puzzled and worried them: "We had been told that we were protected all the way by warships, wireless and that submarine destroyers would escort us in the channel."

⚬⚬⚬

In fact the *Lusitania* had received a fresh warning about U-boat activity. At 11:02 A.M. the Valentia station had relayed a message from the Naval Centre in Queenstown in the Admiralty's Merchant Vessel (MV) code. It read simply "QUESTOR," meaning "Which edition of the M.V. code do you have?" The *Lusitania* replied "WESTRONA," meaning "I have the first edition of the M.V. code." Having established this, the Valentia station quickly transmitted a coded warning. The *Lusitania* received it while she was off the Fastnet. It read: "SUBMARINES ACTIVE IN SOUTHERN PART IRISH CHANNEL; LAST HEARD OF TWENTY MILES SOUTH OF CONINGBEG LIGHTSHIP." The Valentia station had been instructed to "make certain *Lusitania* gets this."

Turner, as he entered the war zone, had already taken precautions. In accordance with Admiralty guidance, he had ordered portholes to be closed, together with all watertight doors not necessary for the operation of the ship. The hydraulically operated doors in the engine rooms had to be left open to allow the ship to function but could be quickly closed from the bridge in an emergency. Staff Captain Anderson assured Turner that he was satisfied that all ports and bulkheads were closed on the Main and Lower Decks, but Turner did not order a spot inspection. The majority of portholes on both decks were in any case dummies that could not be opened while the Lower Deck was closed up and not in use. As also suggested by the Admiralty, Captain Turner had doubled the look-outs at dawn and posted two quartermasters on either side of the bridge "to look out for submarines." In addition, he had instructed the engine room to be ready "to give . . . full speed" and "to keep the highest steam they could possibly get" on the nineteen operational boilers. But he did not order the boilers in the fourth engine room to be fired. Senior Third Engineer George Little, coming on duty at midday, found the engines

The enclosed bridge of the Lusitania.

working at some 120 revolutions, sufficient to give a speed of eighteen knots. He was handed a written instruction from the chief engineer that "in the event of any emergency arising the telegraph would ring" and that he must "keep a good head of steam . . . to give exceptional speed" if suddenly required.

As the morning drew on, "everybody was tense" on the bridge. Quartermaster Hugh Johnston, coming on duty to take the wheel at midday, overheard worried officers discussing the danger: "You could catch words about the submarines and they were in the vicinity and all this stuff you know. . . . Oh we knew there were submarines around." Neil Robertson, the ship's carpenter, noticed how the off-duty chief engineer spent much of the morning looking out to sea through his binoculars, "watching for ships or anything like that in the water."

Cunard's senior staff in Liverpool were also tense. That morning, company chairman Sir Alfred Booth learned for the first time of the sinking of the Harrison Line's *Candidate* and *Centurion* off the Irish coast. Up to this point he had "preferred to trust to the Admiralty and to Captain Turner's discretion," but now, "knowing that the *Lusitania* was likely to be coming along that afternoon or sometime before very long," he felt compelled to do something, if only for his own peace of mind. His membership on the Committee of the War Risks Association had made him particularly aware of the danger to ships approaching the port of Liverpool. Turner had to be warned that "submarines were on his track." Since the Admiralty would not allow Cunard to communicate directly with the *Lusitania*, Booth asked the senior naval officer in Liverpool, Admiral Stileman, to send a wireless message to the ship. Stileman promised to see what he could do, and a relieved Booth returned to his office.

U.S. consul Wesley Frost was busily at work in his office in Queenstown. Frost had arrived a year earlier in this little town whose serene beauty had captivated him from the first: "The landing was like an arrival into paradise. A rose madder daybreak in the east and a pale gold moon setting in the west threw an unneeded glamour over the romantic fortresses of Carlisle, Camden and Templebreedy, and over the estuaries and inlets of the most beautiful harbour in the world." Now, on this lovely spring day, Frost would have found it inconceivable that in just a few hours Queenstown would become known to the world as "the port of horrors."

Queenstown was a gateway for emigration to the United States. Nearly 3 million Irish people had already left for America from the port. Frost's duties were quite time-consuming: "The inspection of emigrants, the invoicing of Irish whiskey, mackerel and tweeds, and the issuance of bills of health to the passenger liners . . . provided a substantial office routine." The outbreak of war made him even busier as he found himself dealing with a stream of anxious American nationals. "Judges and policemen, ladies' maids and chauffeurs, clerics and liquor-vendors all poured in and out of the Consulate in quite a continuous stream; often merely to learn in what way the war was likely to affect their personal plans, and also to apply for gratuitous transportation or loans." Occasionally Frost was induced to loan money, including to a stranded and bemused "aggregation of Irish-American motion-picture artists who had been staging scenes in the Black Valley."

Following the declaration of war and the severance of diplomatic relations between Britain and Germany, the United States had agreed to represent German interests in Britain. Frost therefore also assisted German sailors from captured ships on their way to internment and helped support the dependents of those German nationals who had been interned from funds lodged with Ambassador Page in London. If the *Lusitania* were to call at Queenstown with her large complement of American passengers, there could well be further demands on his limited time.

First Lord of the Admiralty Winston Spencer Churchill had other matters on his mind. He had left the country on 5 May. He was staying incognito in Paris at the Ritz Hotel under the name Spencer and was participating in negotiations with Italy, which had broken off diplomatic relations with Germany and Austro-Hungary on 4 May, about her possible entry into the war. He was then intending to travel to the headquarters of Sir John French, commander of the British Expeditionary Force to France, on the weekend. Here, near to the front lines, the two men would hold discussions and witness an attack to be launched at daybreak on Sunday, 9 May.

Churchill had left First Sea Lord Admiral Jackie Fisher in charge in London. The relationship between the two had become increasingly difficult as their disagreement over the wisdom and conduct of the Dardanelles campaign came to a head. As early as 2 April, Fisher had written that the Dardanelles entirely exhausted his time. He resented the heavier and heavier calls it was making on his naval resources, particularly in the buildup to the first amphibious landings on the Turkish coast, which had taken place none too successfully on 25 April. He also feared the consequences of diverting forces to the Mediterranean away from the Home Fleet. He thought that any decisive naval action could only be fought in the North Sea and that the British Home Fleet's margin of superiority over the German High Seas Fleet was already dangerously narrow.

By early May Fisher was generally worn out and in a high state of nervous tension. The seventy-four-year-old admiral was rising at around 4:30 A.M., working until 8 A.M., then usually attending service at Westminster Abbey before returning to the Admiralty and working until 7 P.M., going to bed only an hour or so later. His hours, like his views on the Dardanelles, were completely out of harmony with those of the forty-year-old Churchill, who rose late and worked late and who, according to Reginald Hall, was usurping executive functions that were properly Fisher's.

Hall could see that Fisher was no longer his old self: "In his place was a sorely harassed and disillusioned man who was overtaxing his strength in the attempt to carry on. He might still on occasion show the old flashes of brilliance, but, beneath the surface, all was far from being well. In these critical days he could display a nervous tension which only remained hidden from those outside owing to the tireless efforts of his naval secretary. At any moment, we felt, the breaking-point would come."

However, the *Lusitania* was being discussed in the highest diplomatic circles in London. At 10 A.M. on 7 May, Colonel House called on Foreign Secretary Sir Edward Grey. The two men had been planning a pleasant morning together at Kew Gardens, but House had been invited to see the king at 11:30, which meant their visit to the botanical gardens must be brief. As they drove through London's western suburbs toward Kew, House and Grey discussed the ways in which the United States could best aid the Allies were she to enter the war. They also "spoke of the probability of an ocean liner being sunk," and House told Grey, "If this were done, a flame of indignation would sweep across America, which would, in itself, probably carry us into the war." Later that morning, in his study on the second floor of Buckingham Palace overlooking the gardens, the king greeted House cordially, then they "fell to talking, strangely enough, of the probability of Germany sinking a trans-Atlantic liner and of the consequences of that act." House repeated many of his earlier comments to Grey, and the king said thoughtfully, "Suppose they should sink the *Lusitania* with American passengers aboard?"

∞∞∞

Meanwhile, on board the *Lusitania*, passengers were quietly going about their normal activities, trying to push their fears aside and taking comfort from the proximity of land. Julia and Flor Sullivan gazed delightedly at the light green coastline of their native land, dotted with fishermen's cottages, through binoculars lent them by Chief Purser McCubbin. Art collector Sir Hugh Lane was also watching the sharpening outline of his homeland. A press photographer was busily taking pictures of life on the ship. He hoped that by capturing the atmosphere of this controversial voyage he would get a good price for his work. A woman had just completed a letter, to be posted in Liverpool, with the closing lines: "We can see Ireland quite well now. Thank God for a safe journey."

Some were reading the Cunard *Daily Bulletin*, scanning it for news of the war. The banner headline, set in bold type, read "Reports of German Victory a Hoax." The *Bulletin* claimed that the French had made a string of gains in Belgium and reported that the Germans had made "lavish use of gases against British." Tactfully, there was no mention of submarines. Submarine sinkings had been covered in the *Bulletin* during the outward voyage, but it was thought that any mention of them in the wake of the German warning would only agitate passengers. Others were already packing in preparation for the morrow's arrival in Liverpool, wondering what the weather would be like and what clothes to wear. Many first- and second-class passengers had sent their young children to the nurseries to be kept amused by stewardesses. Avid bridge players like Archie Donald were playing their customary game. Poker players like Martin Mannion were wondering whether they would have the opportunity to recoup losses or make fresh profits during the few remaining hours of the voyage.

Avis Dolphin had taken another enjoyable walk with Professor Holbourn, who pointed out the coast of Ireland to her. Like many children on board, she understood why so many of the adults seemed anxious and preoccupied. One small boy had even got into the habit of adding to his nightly prayers an additional plea: "Please, God, do keep the nasty submarines away." Holbourn reflected how the children had "been the life and charm of the voyage." The previous day, a little girl

[183]

of eight, Ailsa Booth-Jones, had proudly shown him and Avis the four prizes she had won in the various sports and games organized for their amusement. They included a small, mock-gold brooch in the shape of the ship.

Just before noon, a hazy smudge of land appeared off the port bow. Captain Turner decided it must be Brow Head, a promontory almost on the western tip of Ireland and fifteen miles northwest of the Fastnet Rock, which he had been unable to see through the fog, though some passengers thought they had glimpsed it. He was surprised; by his calculations, the *Lusitania* should have passed Fastnet well to seaward and should now be running up the coast toward Queenstown.

At around 12:40 P.M. Turner was handed a further coded warning: "SUBMARINES FIVE MILES SOUTH OF CAPE CLEAR PROCEEDING WEST WHEN SIGHTED AT TEN A.M." Turner hastily assessed the position. Devoid of modern techniques like radar, and unable to make radio contact, he had to rely on his navigational skills and the judgment born of many years at sea. He also made his decisions alone. In his view, that was a captain's duty and responsibility, although it made his position all the lonelier and more stressful.

Turner reasoned that if the land spotted at noon had indeed been Brow Head, the *Lusitania* must be well past the U-boat, which should now be many miles astern, probably on a southwesterly course. Bearing in mind the earlier warning of other U-boats ahead of him, twenty miles south of the Coningbeg Lightship, Turner decided it would be safer to move in toward land.

He altered his course to 67° east. Soon after 1 P.M. the watch on the bridge picked up a landfall that Turner assumed must be Galley Head. But Galley Head was forty miles from Brow Head. The *Lusitania* could not possibly have covered that distance since just before noon when Turner had sighted what he believed to be Brow Head. He had therefore identified one of the two landmarks wrongly. He comforted himself that the U-boat spotted off Cape Clear must by now be far away.

Turner was hugely relieved when, around 1:40 P.M., the familiar landmark of the Old Head of Kinsale—rising 256 feet out of the water and extending three miles seaward from the mainland—and with its lighthouse quite unmistakable, came into view. At last Turner knew where he was and reverted to his original course of 87° east, ordering his helmsman to starboard. Passengers felt the ship change course "very quickly."

The Lusitania *steaming past the Old Head of Kinsale on a 1911 voyage.*

They wondered for a moment what was happening before resuming their lunches or their conversations.

Turner decided to make for the Coningbeg Lightship and to take a four-point bearing on the Old Head of Kinsale, on the port side, to fix his exact position. Precise navigator that he was, he wanted the best possible fix in case the weather deteriorated again. Taking the bearing would occupy some forty minutes and require him to hold his ship on a rigorously straight course at a completely constant speed while he and officers made the necessary calculations. With the ship running on a steady course some twelve miles from land at a speed of eighteen knots, Turner ordered Junior Third Officer Albert Bestic, now on duty with Second Officer Percy Hefford, to make the calculations. Turner went briefly below to his day cabin, probably to use the lavatory.

At 1:50 P.M. Bestic began to take the bearing on the tower of the lighthouse on the Old Head of Kinsale, from which he would be able to calculate the distance once it came abeam. Ten minutes later another officer relieved him, and Bestic climbed down the bridge ladder to his cabin. On the way he met the senior Marconi operator Bob Leith, who told him he had heard that one submarine had been reported at 10 A.M. off Cape Clear, now astern of them, and that another had been spotted ahead of them a few miles south of the Coningbeg Lightship.

Bestic did some quick mental arithmetic. The Coningbeg Lightship was still some four hours' steaming from the Old Head. In that time any lurking submarine would probably have moved off into the Bristol Channel. Reassured, he continued on to his cabin, planning to write up the log and then rest before going back on watch. Within moments came a knock on the door. Crank, the baggage master, told him that as the weather was fine, orders had been given to bring the luggage and mail right up on deck. The rules required the presence of an officer. The weary young man promised to get down to the baggage room as soon as he had changed from his clean uniform, just purchased in New York, into an old one. His decision to change would save his life.

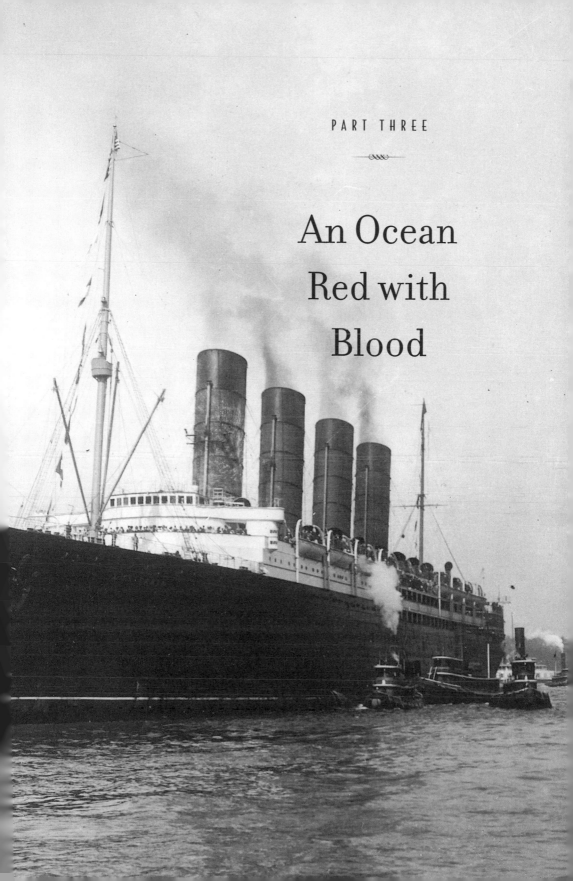

PART THREE

An Ocean Red with Blood

CHAPTER FOURTEEN

"My God, We Are Lost"

ALL MORNING, unknown to Turner and his crew, the gap between the *Lusitania* and the *U-20* had been closing steadily. Also unknown to them, the U-boatmen had been closely watching the ship's latest maneuvers. The decision Turner had just made to alter course had played almost uncannily into Walther Schwieger's hands. He had turned the *Lusitania* directly toward the *U-20*, now some eleven miles away and racing to get into position for an attack.

According to his war diary, Schwieger had surfaced at 5 A.M. to find the same thick fog that was dogging the *Lusitania*. It was dangerous running on the surface, but at least he could recharge the *U-20*'s wet-cell storage batteries while he ran on diesel power. He could also renew the air below, expelling the mingling odors of oil fumes and close-confined human bodies. By 10 A.M., with the liner and the submarine now less than 100 miles apart, visibility was good enough for the *U-20*'s lookouts to spot a small trawler approaching slowly from the coast. Fearing that it might be a naval patrol boat, Schwieger dived to 79 feet. At 11:50 the U-boatmen heard the thudding of a vessel with powerful engines passing overhead. Rising cautiously to 36 feet, Pilot Lanz identified her as an older English warship, possibly a small cruiser of the *Pelorus* class. She was in fact the elderly cruiser *Juno*, hurrying back into Queenstown after receiving warnings sent at 7:45 A.M. that U-boats were active in these waters. Schwieger decided to pursue her in case there was an opportunity to attack, but she was running at full speed, zigzagging as she went to avoid giving a submarine time to aim a torpedo on target. She soon vanished toward Queenstown. A disappointed Schwieger swore in exasperation and took solace in a lunch of sausage-and-potato soup.

The *Juno* was a sister ship to the *Aboukir*, *Cressy*, and *Hogue*. Like these ill-fated vessels and the *Lusitania*, she had longitudinal coal bunkers, which were highly vulnerable to torpedo strike. *Juno* had therefore been relegated to the small fleet of some forty ships commanded by Vice Admiral Coke from his headquarters in Queenstown. Coke's job was to ensure that some 285 miles of the south coast of Ireland were adequately patrolled. He was assisted by Vice Admiral Horace Hood, recently transferred in semidisgrace to Queenstown from command of the Dover Patrol after incurring the wrath of Admiral Fisher. The volatile first sea lord had blamed him for the fact that U-boats had begun to appear in the Irish Sea, assuming wrongly that they must have slipped through the Dover defenses.

Any regrets over the lost prize of the *Juno* quickly faded on board the *U-20*, which had now resurfaced. At 1:20 P.M., in "very beautiful weather," an excited petty officer summoned Schwieger. Schwieger later told his friend Max Valentiner that when he looked through his binoculars, he saw "a forest of masts and stacks." At first he thought "they must belong to several ships. Then I saw it was a great steamer coming over the horizon." As he and his men watched in excitement Schwieger's war diary records how they made out the four funnels of a large passenger steamer dead ahead. Schwieger gave the order "diving stations," and the men in the conning tower flung themselves down the steel ladder. Quick, efficient hands spun the wheels opening the vents and allowing the *U-20*'s tanks to flood while the boat's pumps expelled the air from them.

The U-boat slid under the water, leveling off at the periscope depth of 36 feet. Powered by her quiet electric motors, the *U-20* began a stealthy approach at nine knots as the *Lusitania* sailed closer. Schwieger watched through the periscope's lens. According to Max Valentiner, at first Schwieger feared his efforts would be futile: "When the steamer was two miles away it changed its course. I had no hope now, even if we hurried at our best speed, of getting near enough to attack her." A disappointed Schwieger called to his pilot to take a look at the ship through the periscope, but "at that instant . . . I saw the steamer change her course again. She was coming directly at us. She could not have steered a more perfect course if she had deliberately tried to give us a dead shot. A short fast run and we waited."

With his target just some 2,300 feet away, Schwieger ordered his torpedo officer, Raimund Weisbach, to prepare to fire a G-torpedo, the fifth of his original seven torpedoes. Weisbach checked the position of the hydroplanes and the rudder and set the depth at ten feet. Aware that the target was a passenger ship, Charles Voegele, the young conscript electrician from Alsace, protested against attacking a ship carrying women and children. He was ignored.

At 2:10 P.M. Schwieger gave the order to fire. With a shudder and a hiss, the heavy missile went singing through the water from a bow torpedo tube, unleashing a trail of bubbles.

Many of the *Lusitania*'s passengers had just finished eating. Others were lingering over what they knew would be the last lunch before Liverpool. For two-thirds of those on board, it would be the last lunch of their lives. The orchestra was playing the perky strains of "The Blue Danube."

Oliver Bernard noted that "the anticipative animation which breaks out on board a liner nearing port" had asserted itself at lunchtime, in spite of everything, "in the usual manners which are characteristic of different nations." American passengers "became quietly and alertly interested in the landbreak of the old world." Several asked him "why there were no warships about." The British, who were in the majority in first class, "woke up, as it were, and put on those authoritative habiliments of mind which distinguish British passengers as such." That attitude, he surmised sourly, "would be almost torpedo-proof; England had been ruled by an authoritative class that had always agreed to agree" that they could not ever be "in the wrong about anything."

Bernard was amused that people at last took the trouble to become acquainted as the voyage was about to end. "The dining-saloon was transformed by the invasion of a spirit of animated, intimate, spontaneously confidential sociability which had been conspicuously absent during the past week of the voyage. Even those marine ambulances, otherwise deckchairs, gave up their dead to join the party." Bernard found himself being chaffed by the wife of an American ambassador "about her choice of lifeboat in case anything happened later." He told her he would prefer to be on a raft.

Looking around the magnificent room with its sparkling glass, shining silver, and lavish flower arrangements, he saw his bête noire, Alfred Vanderbilt, laughing with Staff Captain Anderson at the captain's table. An animated Charles Frohman sat surrounded by his theatrical friends at another table. Josephine Brandell was making her way gracefully between the tables, collecting for the members of the orchestra. Detective-Inspector William Pierpoint was, as usual, lunching alone.

While he ate, Charles Lauriat noticed that the portholes were open, allowing warm spring sunshine and sea air to flood the first-class dining room. In fact, there was such a draft that Lauriat asked the steward to switch off the electric fan directly above his chair.

Theodate Pope and Edwin Friend were lunching with a young Englishman, who looked mock-ruefully at some particularly tempting ice cream and remarked that "he would hate to have a torpedo get him before he ate it." They laughed and talked about how slowly the ship seemed to be running. So slowly, in fact, that they "thought the engines had stopped."

In the second-class dining room Margaret Cox was at the second sitting and about to eat a bread-crumbed pork chop that her steward had ordered especially for her. She was looking forward to a pudding of pears and blancmange. By her side was her five-month-old baby, Desmond. The steward had tried to persuade her to come to the first sitting when the food would be hotter and the table linen cleaner. "Some of these people don't know how to eat," he said, but she had declined. She felt thankful that her journey was nearly over and that Desmond would soon be safe on dry land. As soon as she had finished eating, she planned to put her baby son down for his afternoon nap and then, perhaps, go to sleep herself.

Medical student Dick Prichard was teasing Grace French, the young woman sitting opposite him, that she had a double on board. As soon as they finished eating, they went, "laughing and joking," out on deck to search for the woman.

In third class, passengers like the Hook family, Elizabeth Duckworth, and the lovers Jack Welsh and Gerda Nielson were enjoying the generous and hearty fare laid out on the long banks of tables. Some were reflecting that once the voyage was over they would be unlikely to eat so well for a long time.

Meanwhile, the *Lusitania*'s lookouts were keeping their vigil. They had been ordered to "report *anything* that appeared suspicious," even if it was just "a broom handle in the water." At about 1:50 P.M. they had spotted "an object 2 points on the starboard bow, conical in shape," which caused "a little commotion on the bridge" but turned out to be only a buoy.

Just before 2 P.M. Leslie Morton came up on deck to recover his sweater and other gear to get ready for lookout duty. As he explained, "My place was extra look-out, right up in the eyes of the ship on deck; my responsibility being the starboard side of the bow from ahead to the beam." His old friend Jo Eliott, who had joined with him from the *Naiad*, was another extra lookout on the port side. The two friends were supplementing Able Seamen Frank Hennessy and Tom Quinn, watching out from the crow's nest. In the clear fine weather they could see some twelve to thirteen miles without the aid of binoculars.

Suddenly Morton, on the starboard side, "saw a turmoil, and what looked like a bubble on a large scale in the water, breaking surface some 800 to 1,000 yards away." A few seconds later he "saw two white streaks running along the top of the water like an invisible hand with a piece of chalk on a blackboard. They were heading straight across to intercept the course of *Lusitania*. I grabbed the megaphone which was provided for the look-outs use and yelled towards the bridge: 'Torpedoes coming on the starboard side, Sir!'" His immediate thought was to find his brother John, resting down below. He left his position to dive down the scuttle to the forecastle.

Up in the crow's nest, Hennessy heard a shout as Tom Quinn, the starboard lookout, yelled, "Here's a torpedo coming, Frank!" The two men leaped for the rigging and began scrambling down, shouting warnings as they went. Hearing Quinn's cries, Second Officer Percy Hefford grabbed his binoculars and saw the telltale traces in the water. Within seconds he gave the order for the closure of all watertight doors. Albert Bestic, coming out of his cabin and onto the deck and still buttoning up his old uniform, also heard the warnings. He could see a lengthening streak of white bubbling foam heading straight for the ship. His one thought was "This is the approach of death."

Turner heard Hefford call out, "There's a torpedo!" Running from his cabin up the narrow stairs to the bridge, he was in time to see the stream of bubbles from the missile's wake speed toward his vessel. It was too late to take evasive action. He heard a sound "like the banging of a door on a windy day" followed by "a kind of a rumble." He thought the ship had been struck between the second and third funnels. Quarter-master Johnston, hanging desperately to the wheel and choking in coal dust so thick "we couldn't see each other for quite a while," thought she had been hit "very close behind the bridge" and that "she was going straight over."

⸺⸱⸱∞⸱⸱⸺

Many passengers returning from lunch had been drawn by the lovely weather to go out on deck just as Schwieger was positioning the *U-20* for the attack. Oliver Bernard, strolling aft to the Verandah Café, gazed at a sea that pleased his artistic eye and soothed his irritation with the ship's slow speed and the vagaries of his fellow passengers. He saw "a sunlit expanse of perfectly smooth water; the sea was like an opaque sheet of polished indigo, absolutely still." Suddenly he saw on the starboard what at first seemed to be "the tail of a fish." He was convinced it was a submarine periscope. As he stared fascinated, he saw "the fast-lengthening track of a newly-launched torpedo, itself a streak of froth." Although he and his fellow passengers had "all been thinking, dreaming, sleeping, and eating submarines" from the hour they left New York, he could hardly believe the evidence of his own eyes now that the *Lusitania* was under attack. An American woman rushed up to him for reassurance, exclaiming, "This isn't a torpedo, is it?" Bernard, spellbound and "absolutely sick," could not answer.

A broad-shouldered American, whom he was never to see again, said, "By heavens, they've done it." Then the torpedo hit. Bernard felt "a slight shock through the deck" and then "a terrific explosion." A column of white water rose high in the air followed by an eruption of debris. A moment later came "a sullen rumble in the bowels of the liner." A huge column of water seemed to shoot upward and tons of debris to rain down on the deck. "Water seemed to be cascading everywhere."

Theodate Pope and her companion Edwin Friend had been leaning over the railing on deck and looking at a sea of "a marvelous blue" and so "dazzling in the sunlight" that Miss Pope remarked, "How could the officers ever *see* a periscope there?" Within seconds they felt the impact of the torpedo. The sound was "like that of an arrow entering the canvas and straw of a target, magnified a thousand times, and I imagined I heard a dull explosion follow."

*Oliver Bernard's eyewitness sketch of the moment the torpedo exploded
against the side of the* Lusitania.

Michael Byrne, walking on the Boat Deck, had halted just beneath
the bridge when he saw "what I thought was a porpoise, but not seeing
the usual jump of the fish I knew it was a submarine." It disappeared,
and about two minutes later he saw a torpedo. "In an instant it hit the
ship. . . . It made a noise like a million-ton hammer hitting a steel boiler,
a hundred feet high and a hundred yards in length. Then came that awful
explosion, the expansion of which lifted the bows of the ship out of the
water."

Joseph Myers also saw the periscope, remarking with horror to his
friend Frank Kellett: "My God, Frank, there is a periscope. . . . My God,
Frank, they have put off a torpedo. My God, Frank, we are lost." As the
two men stared paralyzed, they saw it "cutting through the water like a
razor describing a distinct arc rising from the submarine." It seemed to
hit with "a flash like lightning accompanied by a peal of thunder." They
watched in horror as "clouds of debris, bits of wood, iron and cinders
were blown up through funnels and fell down" on the roof of the Verandah Café.

Charles Lauriat, ready for "a real walk," had gone to his stateroom to
put on a sweater under the coat of his knickerbocker suit. As he came up

the main companionway and stepped out onto the port side of the Boat Deck, he saw the Hubbards standing by the rail. Elbert Hubbard, who was about to play a game of medicine ball, was in a cheerful mood, remarking that he was unlikely to be "a welcome traveler to Germany" because of his vitriolic essay "Who Lifted the Lid Off Hell?" He had barely finished speaking when they felt the shock of the impact. It sounded heavy and muffled, and, Lauriat later remembered, "the good ship trembled for a moment under the force of the blow." They looked in the direction of the sound to see "smoke and cinders flying up in the air on the starboard side." A second explosion followed quickly, but it sounded different to Lauriat.

James Brooks was talking with his friends the Grants on the Marconi Deck. They were planning to play a game of shuffleboard and waiting for a fourth to join them when he saw the torpedo approaching on the starboard side. Brooks stood mesmerized as "a solid shock went through the ship, as if it had struck an immovable object, and instantly up through the decks went coal, debris of all kinds . . . in a cloud, up in the air and mushroomed up 150 feet above the Marconi wires." This was closely followed by "a volume of water thrown with violent force" that knocked him to the ground.

Brooks got shakily to his feet and heard his friend Mrs. Montague Grant call weakly to her husband, "Oh, Monty." Brooks then ran to their aid, finding them lying by the side of the Marconi house, between the second and third funnels, on the starboard side. Suddenly he felt "a slight second shock," and clouds of hot, dense steam enveloped everything, making it hard to breathe. When it cleared, his friends had disappeared.

Grace French was on deck with Dick Prichard when "the awful crash came." She looked around for her companion, "so sunburned and full of life and ambition," but he was gone.

Charles Hill, hurrying to an appointment with the ship's stenographer, stopped on the starboard side of the Promenade Deck for a quick word with Chief Steward Jones. The steward was at the railing, intent on something moving in the water. As Hill stepped up to him, Jones turned and whispered, "Good God, Mr. Hill, here comes a torpedo." Hill followed Jones's arm and made out the periscope of a U-boat. He also saw the wake of the torpedo and the line of disturbance in the water. Hoping the torpedo would cross the ship's bows, the two men leaned over the rail and "saw something strike the side of the ship" accompanied by "a noise

Lady Margaret Mackworth

like that made by the slamming of a door" immediately followed by "a dull, heavy, muffled explosion."

As the torpedo struck, those inside the ship had little doubt what had happened. Isaac Lehmann was smoking in the Verandah Café when he heard a noise "like a blast in the subway or a cannon." The ship "shook like a leaf," and the café's hanging baskets and plants came crashing down around them. Fred Gauntlett was still in the first-class dining room when he "heard the sound and felt the jar" of an explosion. For a moment he was stunned. Then he left his coffee and nuts, rose from the table, and shouted to the stewards to close the ports.

Actress Josephine Brandell, having just finished taking her collection for the musicians, was lunching with her friend Mrs. Crighton when they heard the explosion. They jumped up, and Mrs. Crighton exclaimed, "They have done it!" To Charles Bowring, lunching at the purser's table, the torpedo sounded like a "damnable concentrated thud." He found himself sitting in a shower of glass and water. Margaret Cox, still at lunch in the second-class dining room, felt a "thud and a shiver in the ship." Archie Donald heard "a shattering of glass" as if somebody was falling through a glasshouse.

Margaret Mackworth and her father, David Thomas, were strolling into the elevator when Thomas decided to go out on deck and take the

David Alfred Thomas

air. The mine owner had just been telling his daughter that they might be wise to sleep up on deck that night. Before his daughter could reply, "there was a dull, thud-like, not very loud but unmistakable explosion," which seemed to come from below them. Margaret's correct instinct was to step out of the elevator immediately; "somehow, the stairs seemed safer." David Thomas rushed to look out of a porthole.

The Sullivans were still watching the coastline in quiet content-ment when "the most dreadful explosion the world has ever heard" shook the liner, lifting Julia up and then "throwing her down and rolling her from side to side." Half stunned, the young woman grabbed her husband.

Harold Boulton was in the Verandah Café drinking coffee and talk-ing to Commander Stackhouse. The commander "was busy explaining to me how the *Lusitania* could never be torpedoed, that the watches had been doubled, and the people were looking out, and they'd see the periscope of the submarine a mile away. . . . And in the middle of his try-ing to prove to me that the *Lusitania* could not be torpedoed," there were two "almost simultaneous crashes." Water and debris came crashing through the roof, and the two startled men rushed outside.

Oscar Grab had been planning a quiet afternoon finishing a book up on the Boat Deck. He paused to talk to two fellow passengers on the star-board side when one of them pointed out to sea and asked, "What is that over there?" Grab noticed something like "a stick out of the water," then he saw "this torpedo coming straight towards us. . . . I followed it very carefully and slowly because it could be very plainly seen. . . . It was like when you sit in the rear of a motorboat and you see the white foam." He leaned over the rail, and as he watched, it hit the ship. Involuntarily he yelled out loud, "I knew it would happen!" In that moment he perhaps recalled his brother-in-law's remark about the German warning as they rode through Central Park on the way to the ship: "Do you feel nervous about that article in the paper this morning?"

Norah Bretherton, who had just put her little boy, Paul, to sleep in her second-class cabin on the Upper Deck and taken her little girl, Betty, up to the nursery on the Shelter Deck, was on the stairs midway between the two decks when she heard the explosion. Paralyzed with panic, she could not decide which way to run first. Passengers packing or resting in their staterooms felt the impact and wondered what it could be. One woman looked up from her cases to see "what looked like splinters of wood falling from the port hole." Rita Jolivet, who had had a bad night and had just got up, "felt a great big shock." She was "thrown about a great deal." Feeling trapped and isolated in her inside cabin, she looked out into the corridor to see a woman putting on a life jacket.

Among the crew, Acting Senior Third Officer John Lewis was just finishing lunch with First Officer Arthur Jones when they heard a sound "just like a report of a heavy gun about two or three miles away." It was followed within seconds by a further "heavy report" and "a rumbling noise like a clap of thunder." Realizing what had happened, the two men looked at each other aghast before jumping to their feet. Senior Third Engineer Robert Duncan was walking on the Shelter Deck, looking across to the land calculating how long it would be before the ship arrived in Liverpool, when he heard two successive crashes and felt the ship "give such a shudder."

Radio Officer Bob Leith was lunching when the torpedo struck, and rushed immediately up to the Marconi room. Men preparing luggage for disembarkation in the hold heard the thud and made for the electric elevator, their only means of escape. Cornelius Horrigan, a steward in the first-class dining room, heard the explosion and, knowing exactly what it meant, dropped the plates of pudding he was carrying and ran outside.

Bellboy Robert Clark was sitting on his bunk in the crew's quarters, when he felt "this terrific explosion." It was as if "two gigantic hands lifted the vessel out of the water and shook it and put it back again." He was thrown to the deck from his top bunk.

Fireman John O'Connell was off duty and had just been complaining that there was no jam left for his lunch. A fellow stoker promised him a tin of jam provided he read aloud the ship's news bulletin, which was the only source of news afloat. About half his colleagues were illiterate, and he collected a crowd of some forty around him as he read out the highlights. Disgusted that the tin of jam had not materialized after all, O'Connell went up on deck. He was just observing the wash of the ship when he heard "this dull thud." It took him a moment to realize what it was. "I was surprised and stood and looked . . . wondering what happened."

Down in the galley young cook George Wynne had wearily begun preparations for that evening's dinner. He had fallen behind and was not looking forward to tackling "asparagus and Jerusalem artichokes, which was one of the worst jobs." He and seven others were hard at work in the vegetable locker when he heard "a kind of thud." Running into the galley, he saw his heavy pots and pans shooting over the guardrails to the floor. Bellboy Holton was just rounding off his lunch in the pantry with a "sweet boiled apple pudding" when he heard "a shattering roar."

At 2:12 P.M. Turner ordered Johnston to steer "hard-a-starboard the helm," intending to make for the shore. Johnston wrenched the wheel thirty-five degrees to starboard and shouted the stock response, "helm hard-a-starboard." The captain shouted to him to hold the ship steady and "keep her head into Kinsale." Johnston tried to steady the helm but found he could not. Turner repeated the order "hard-a-starboard." Johnson turned the wheel again, but this time the ship would not respond. The steering mechanism had locked.

A despairing Turner tried to check the *Lusitania*'s speed by reversing the engines and gave the order "full speed astern." Down in the engine room Senior Third Engineer George Little heard the bell ring with the order, but there was nothing he could do. Second Engineer Smith was shouting to him in despair that the steam pressure had plunged from 195 pounds to 50. The engines were out of commission.

The *Lusitania* was out of control, arcing helplessly into the wide blue sea.

CHAPTER FIFTEEN

———∞∞∞———

"Come at Once!"

*T*HE *Lusitania* plowed onward at what seemed a frightening
speed. Quartermaster Hugh Johnston was still reporting
"ship not answering the helm" as he tried desperately to
steer her. Turner told him tersely to "keep trying." Second Officer Hefford, scanning the list indicator beneath the compass, told Turner that
the ship was listing fifteen degrees to starboard. Johnston heard him
mutter, "My God."

Turner immediately ordered all boats "to be lowered to the rail" and
sent Staff Captain Anderson to superintend, with the instruction that it
must be "all women and children into the boats first." With the exception of Hefford, and of Chief Officer Piper, who had gone forward to
close a hatch in the bow, he dispatched the remaining officers to their
boat stations. First Officer Arthur Jones, hurrying to the Boat Deck, met
the carpenter's yeoman, who assured him that all the doors below had
been closed.

In the wireless room Bob Leith had relieved his assistant David
McCormick and was frantically tapping out an SOS message—"COME AT
ONCE, BIG LIST OFF SOUTH HEAD, OLD KINSALE"—over and over again. He
was thankful to be able to report that the *Lusitania*'s distress call was
picked up almost at once by a coastal wireless station. An officer then
told him the ship's precise position, "10 miles south of the Old Head of
Kinsale." He at once transmitted this further information, and it was
again acknowledged, but he knew that the ship's electrical power was

weakening. He hoped his emergency dynamo would work as he continued repeating the message to make doubly sure help was on its way.

On deck officers tried to keep order and give instructions. Bellboy
Ben Holton later recalled, "There were no loud speakers or public address
[system] or anything like that, it had to be done by word of mouth." With
the roar from "the steam escaping from the engine room and up the
exhausts and black smoke from the funnel and the startling list to starboard, it wasn't conducive to running a well-organised exercise."

In those first moments passengers felt bewildered, dazed, uncertain
what to do. Michael Byrne noticed that "most of the people seemed
transfixed where they stood." George Kessler, the New York champagne
magnate, found the Boat Deck "crowded with passengers milling about
and wondering what was the matter." Had they really been torpedoed?
Some had glimpsed the telltale traces in the water and even seen what
they took to be the point of impact, but most had seen nothing and could
only guess. A rumor spread that the Lusitania had not been torpedoed at
all but had merely hit a small mine. Scrambling for a footing on the sliding deck, passengers peered anxiously out to sea, scanning the glinting
dark blue waters for conning towers and periscopes. The danger was
brought home to one man only when "a large flowerpot standing on the
port side fell over, and threw its water on to the linoleum." He said, "I
noticed that because, unfortunately, I slipped on it and fell."

Some remained oblivious. Martin Mannion of St. Louis was so
absorbed in his poker hand in the second-class smoking lounge that he
did not realize his companions had deserted him till he looked up to
find an empty room. Unperturbed, he suggested to the bartender that
they might as well "die game anyway." The bartender told him to go to
hell and raced out on deck while Mannion salvaged a bottle of beer and
settled down to enjoy it. A third-class passenger, Canadian Soren
Sorenson, well primed with whiskey, was also deep in a card game. With
"a pair of kings back to back," he stood to make twenty-five dollars and
"played for ten minutes after the hit" before his wiser friend dragged
him away. Fellow Canadian Harold Day was playing solitaire when he
heard "a tremendous bang." He strolled into the lounge in search of a
cigar, only to be told by the amazed bartender that "you'd better get out
of here, she's going to sink." The list was now so great that the ship's
cash registers had tipped forward, opening and spewing their contents
across the floor.

After initial hesitation, the reaction of many was to get to their cabins and their life jackets or out on deck as fast as possible. Passengers rose in a body in the second-class dining room, where for a moment it had seemed "as if the whole dining room, all the china, came in on top of us." Margaret Cox was clutching her baby, Desmond, trying to protect him in the crush as she picked her way through the broken crockery. Spotting her friendly steward, Margaret pushed through the crowd and begged him, "Tell me what to do. Whatever you say I'll do it." "Get up the stairs. Get up as quickly as you can," he replied. It was easier said than done. Margaret found that "everyone was just beating everybody." A frantic man jabbed her baby in the mouth with his elbow, and she "caught his hair and shook his head," shocked to find how primitive she could be "when it comes to life and death." A young man put his arm around her and said, "Think of the one above and hold on." She was amazed and touched to receive such advice from "a gay young card player."

Archie Donald and the Reverend Gwyer both rushed to the door and yelled at the top of their voices "that everything would be all right, and that there would be no need of hurrying." A woman just ahead of Donald fainted, "but luckily her husband was with her, so he took her head and I took her feet, and we managed to get her up the stairs." Harold Taylor, dressed only in shirt and trousers, and his young bride, Lucy, with a seal coat thrown around her shoulders and no shoes, forced their way up. They stepped over the mess of strewn earth and broken remains of the magnificent potted palms that had stood at the top of the stairs.

Passengers from third class came surging up from the Main Deck. Elsie Hook, standing on the stairway leading down to the third-class dining room, ran in search of her father and brother. Elizabeth Duckworth was walking with her friend Alice Scott and Mrs. Scott's young son, Arthur, when she felt the ship shake "from stem to stern" and found herself showered with what felt like hot cinders. Elizabeth grabbed the little boy and began to climb up the rigging of the forward mast until coaxed by an officer to climb down and go in search of a lifeboat.

Chief First-Class Steward Robert Barnes joined the swarm heading for the main staircase. He quickly saw how the initial calm was dissolving, and he felt a cold fear in the pit of his stomach. "I had taken hold of the banister with one hand, whilst keeping a woman up with the other," he later recollected. "It took us quite a few minutes to get up the stairs, there was such a lot of people pushing and pulling their way up. I was calling out all the time 'Take your time, she's not going down,' but to tell the truth I really thought different. I felt that her inside had been blown out, it was such a heavy explosion."

The list seemed terrifying to the frightened and confused throng. For a moment or two the ship seemed to right herself "in a rocking motion." But almost at once came the sensation that she was again listing "heavily to starboard" and going "over and over and over." As people came pouring out onto the Boat Deck, officers were yelling, "Keep the Boat Deck clear," to allow the lifeboats to be lowered. Another officer kept shouting, "It is all right now," but few were listening. Some, like Michael Byrne, had already realized with a chill that "our power was entirely cut off" and that "the captain had no control."

Passengers were now crowding the stairways, particularly to the upper decks. Officers tried to order passengers down to the Promenade Deck as the lifeboats were hanging at that level, but few took any notice. Ian Holbourn and Avis Dolphin were among the crowd. Knowing that Avis would be at the second sitting of lunch in the second-class dining room, Holbourn had waited "till the worst rush was over" and had then gone to find her. He led her to his cabin to find life jackets, but the list was so steep that they found it hard to get up the staircase. When at last they reached his cabin, just off the main staircase, he and a fellow passenger fastened a life jacket on Avis. Holbourn then gathered a few of his most valuable manuscripts, including his text "The Theory of Beauty," and carrying his own life jacket managed to find the two nurses traveling with Avis. Nurse Hilda Ellis already had a life jacket, but Sarah Smith refused the professor's offer. "She felt he should have it as he had a wife and three children." They compromised. If he could place her in a boat, he would keep the jacket. Then he led his small party out on deck to see what he could do to save them.

Charles Frohman seemed curiously unconcerned by the drama. He had been on deck talking to Rita Jolivet's brother-in-law, George Vernon, and the English captain Alick Scott when Schwieger attacked. Frohman continued smoking a cigar, but Scott insisted on going belowdecks in search of life jackets. He returned with two and began to put one of them on Frohman, who accepted only with great reluctance and soon gave it away to a woman. He kept on smoking and remarked conversationally, "I didn't think they would do it." A frightened Rita Jolivet, carrying her life jacket, came out on deck to join the group. Vernon helped her on with it,

Rita Jolivet

while Scott went belowdecks a second time, returning with more life jackets, which he also gave away. They all offered Scott their jackets, but, according to one passenger, he said "No, he could swim better than any of us, and if we had to die we had to die; why worry?" The little group agreed to stick together. As the ship lurched, Frohman advised Rita Jolivet to hang on to the rail "to save her strength" as calmly as if he were giving her stage directions.

Theodate Pope and Edwin Friend had arranged to meet friends on the Boat Deck if the worst should happen. Miss Pope thought that "the deck suddenly looked very strange, crowded with people." She saw two women "crying in a pitifully weak way." Even the normally resolute Miss Pope now hesitated, uncertain what to do.

Charles Lauriat turned to the Hubbards and suggested that they go to their cabin on the port side of the Promenade Deck to fetch their life jackets. He knew that Alice Hubbard could not swim. He was surprised that "Mr. Hubbard stayed by the rail affectionately holding his arm around his wife's waist" and that "both seemed unable to act." Another passenger heard Hubbard remark, "What is to be, is to be." Hubbard had always expressed admiration for the quiet courage of Mr. and Mrs. Isidor Straus, passengers on the *Titanic*, who, unwilling to be parted after decades of married life, had simply returned to their cabin, lain down side by side, and awaited death together. Writing of the *Titanic* victims, Hubbard had said: "One thing's sure, there are just two respectable ways to die. One is of old age, and the other is by accident. All disease is indecent."

Spurred to action by the sights around him, Lauriat hurried to his own cabin on the starboard side, tied on a life jacket, and grabbed the others in the room, thinking that he could give two to the Hubbards. He also picked up a small leather case containing his business papers and went back up on deck to the spot where he had left his friends, but to his distress "they had gone." He waited a few moments, hoping they would return, but there was no sign. He distributed the spare jackets to several frightened women who had none and helped them put them on. The list seemed about the same, but he noticed "the pitch by the head had increased a good deal"—an ominous sign.

Moments later, a family of Italians—an elderly grandmother, a mother, and three children who had found their way up from third class—surrounded Lauriat, beseeching him unintelligibly "in their native tongue." He put life jackets on the two women and found another for the oldest child. The family then sat down on one of the collapsible lifeboats "quietly awaiting instructions as to what to do next." The sight of that frightened group, uncomprehending and sitting so patiently on the deck, would haunt Lauriat as "one of the most pathetic things" he saw that terrible afternoon.

Lauriat now looked around to see who else needed life jackets. He noticed that among the crowds now pouring out on deck, "about everybody who passed me wearing a life jacket had it on incorrectly." In his panic one man had thrust one arm through an armhole and his head through the other. Others rushed past wearing them upside down. No one had read the "neat little signs" around the ship telling people how to put them on. Lauriat tried to help, but some thought he was trying to take their life jackets from them and fled in terror.

Other passengers were also trying to help. New York importer Charles Hardwick noticed that the distraught Joseph Myers had put on his life jacket incorrectly, and helped him adjust it, saying, "This will never save you." He tied it tightly and added, "Good luck to you." Josephine Brandell had joined the stream of passengers heading for the Boat Deck but was "simply horrified with fright" and unable to think logically. As one man tried to calm her, she recalled that another passenger, Bond Street art dealer Mr. Gorer, "put a life jacket on me . . . and told me to be brave." Harold Day, who had acted upon the lounge bartender's sage advice to "get out of here," gave his jacket away to a frightened girl who was holding a little boy. Conscious of the odium heaped on male survivors of the *Titanic,* it struck him that it might not be "a very good thing to be saved" and live to be accused of cowardice.

David Thomas tried to reach his cabin on the Promenade Deck but was beaten back by the sheer weight of people on his first attempt. He attributed some of the confusion to the "noxious fumes which suffocated and stupefied many passengers." His coolheaded daughter, who had wisely decided not to get in the elevator, was also trying to get to her cabin. Margaret Mackworth had to fight the instinct to make straight for the Boat Deck, finding it "a horrible feeling to stay under cover even for a few moments in a boat that may be sinking." As she ran upstairs to the Promenade Deck, "the boat was already heeling over" and she knew she was "beginning to get frightened." At the back of her mind was her morbid fear of water. She knew she could swim no more than 100 yards; moreover, she said, "having my head under water terrified me so much that I had never dared to learn to dive." Running along and clutching the rail on the lower side of the passage to steady herself, she collided with a stewardess. They wasted a minute "making polite apologies to each other" before realizing how ludicrous this was. Margaret hurriedly retrieved her life jacket and then ran into her father's cabin to fetch one for him.

Back on the Boat Deck, she looked around for her father, but there was no sign of him. Instead she found the American doctor Howard Fisher and his sister-in-law, Dorothy Conner. She asked whether she might stay with them until they found David Thomas. As they stood there she saw "a stream of steerage passengers" come "rushing up from below. . . . They were white-faced and terrified; I think they were shrieking; there was no kind of order." They were fighting their way toward the boats. It seemed to her that "the strongest got there first, the weak were pushed aside. Here and there a man had his arm around a woman's waist and bore her along with him." She was struck that "there were no children to be seen." She thought it just as well since "no children could have lived in that throng." She turned to Dorothy Conner and remarked tautly, "I always thought a shipwreck was a well-organised affair." The American girl replied, "So did I, but I've learnt a devil of a lot in the last five minutes." An officer came along the deck and told them, "Don't worry. The ship will right itself." Dr. Fisher doubted it. The officer had hardly moved on before the ship "turned sideways and seemed to plunge head foremost into the sea."

Some were still concerned about their possessions, wondering whether they dared risk going back to their cabins. But for most, fear now far outweighed material considerations. Captain Fred Lassetter's mother Elizabeth's "first thought was to get to her cabin to collect her jewellery," but she quickly recognized that it was impossible. Another woman, who had obsessively carried her jewels with her everywhere since the day the *Lusitania* sailed, was so shocked and bemused that she left them sitting on the dining-room table—"the first time during the whole voyage she forgot them."

The Naishes were by now up on the Boat Deck. Belle Naish, sent outside by her husband just before the attack to admire "the land, . . . the green, the trees, the lighthouse," had been soaked by water thrown up by the torpedo explosion and then trapped in the surging crowd. As she fought to get back to her husband, she feared "the force of the crush would carry many through the rail into the water." Regaining their cabin, she found her husband untying the three sets of knots on their life jackets at the neck, chest, and waist. They put them on and tied each other in, then struggled to the Boat Deck. Clinging to the rail, they heard people cry, "She's all right, she will float for an hour."

The Naishes were unconvinced. Theodore whispered to his wife: "It is not true, we are sinking rapidly. . . . It cannot be long." Like Lauriat and others, they kept their heads and tried to help others with their life jackets, "shouting to dozens" to tie the fastenings more tightly. "One woman we helped out of her life jacket and fur coat and put the jacket on again; another had her two-year-old tied inside and had on a heavy wool coat with large fur collar. Mr. Naish said 'Madam, if you wish to save your child take him out and hold him up; you will both go down that way, and you must take off that coat.'" He advised her to tie the child into a chair, "which would float easily." Another woman stubbornly refused to jettison her hat with its long floating blue veil, despite the Naishes' best efforts.

Oliver Bernard noticed that by now "there was on all hands a pell-mell scurry below to obtain life jackets." Every second, people were reappearing singly, in pairs, or in groups with jackets in their hands or with them "inadequately strapped on." Others seemed to have forgotten all

about jackets and were frantically hunting for friends and family. His former patron's "little girl," Lesley Mason, rushed up to Bernard, shrieking,
"Have you seen my husband?" Realizing she was hysterical, Bernard
"took her by the shoulders and shook her violently, saying at the same
time, 'Pull yourself together and listen to what I'm saying now.' " He told
her not to move from this spot on the port side of the deck and that her
husband would be bound to look for her here since this was the side from
which they would be lowering the boats. He asked her whether she understood, and she nodded. He then promised to go and find some life jackets.

Hurrying through the crowd on the port Promenade Deck, he saw
men attempting to lower some of the boats. Several passengers trying to
climb in were repelled by an ax-wielding seaman. Someone shouted,
"Nobody in the boats yet, keep back everybody!" Reaching the entrance
to the first-class saloon, Bernard nearly collided with Alfred Vanderbilt,
smartly dressed in a gray suit and jaunty polka-dot tie, who grinned at
him. He was holding what looked like a large purple jewel case, "doubtless for a lady who was powdering her nose before going ashore."
Another passenger heard the millionaire remark quietly, "Well, they got
us this time, all right."

Harold Boulton, hurrying down to his cabin in search of a life
jacket, was shocked to discover that "somebody had taken it in the very
short time." He stumbled out into the corridor again, but the ship's list
was so pronounced that he found himself walking with one foot on the
wall and one on the floor. At the end of the passage by the stairs he saw a
steward who was handing out life jackets. He took one and put it on.
Then he tried to go up the stairs but tripped and collapsed at the feet
of "a very attractive woman" and her daughter. He asked "in a hurry
and rather nervously" whether he could help, but the woman admon-
ished him: "We've been told by the captain that the ship can't sink, so
we're not going to get excited." Boulton clambered up the stairs to the
Boat Deck to look for his friend Fred Lassetter and Lassetter's mother,
Elizabeth.

At 2:14 P.M., four minutes after the torpedo hit, the ship's electricity
failed completely. In the Marconi house the two operators switched to
their emergency dynamo powered by storage batteries. Elsewhere in the
ship darkness added to the terror. Oliver Bernard felt his way downstairs, crashing painfully at the bottom. The passage was eerily deserted.
He tripped again, finding "the angle of side inclination down that pas-

sage" to be "horribly magnified by the darkness." His cabin was at the far end. Climbing on his berth, he felt in the gloom for his life jacket and dragged it off the top of the tilting wardrobe. He remembered there was another way back onto the deck via stairs just by his cabin. He made for them in a panic, suddenly terrified that he was "going to be drowned like a rat in the dark."

Regaining the deck, he found the emotional Lesley Mason gone. Before he could decide what to do, another woman rushed at him screaming, "Where did you get that, where did you get it?" and snatched the life jacket from him. The port deck was now clogged with frantic people. Bernard was appalled to see a stoker "reeling about as if drunk, his face a black and scarlet smear, the crown of his head torn open like a spongy, bloody pudding."

The electricity failure had trapped some members of the crew down below. In the baggage room Boatswain's Mate Florence Sikking had jumped into the elevator with four or five other men of the watch the moment they heard an explosion. They were fortunate enough to make it abovedecks. Just as he was about to go back down and tell the remaining men to come on up, the generators failed. The electric elevator was their only means of escape, leaving many trained seamen trapped and helpless below with dire consequences not only for themselves but for the efficient lowering of the lifeboats.

Some butchers, working three decks beneath the galleys, rushed for the elevator used to bring meat up and down, only to be trapped as it jammed between decks. Bellboy Clark was horrified: "We could hear their screams coming up—they knew they were trapped." Young George Wynne, who had abandoned his asparagus and artichokes, could hear the sickening sound of the butchers hammering and screaming. Thoroughly frightened, George found his father, Joseph, in a confused crowd of some forty men, including stewards, cooks, butchers, and bakers. They hurried up to the Boat Deck, wondering what they should do amid "the big panic" they found there.

Passenger James Leary, already unnerved by the fact that "everybody was running around and screaming and looking for a jacket," made a horrible discovery. He realized that the passenger elevators, too, were stuck between floors "and filled with passengers screaming. . . . evidently they could not go up or down, because the boat was on such a list." They were futilely beating on the elegant metal grilles. The horrible spectacle of shrieking men and women trapped like vermin strengthened his own resolve to save himself.

The loss of electrical power and light made the situation in the engine and boiler rooms yet more confusing. Andrew Cockburn, senior second engineer, was on the Shelter Deck when the ship was struck. After checking that the bulkhead doors on the Lower Deck were closed, he put on a life jacket and went below to the multilevel engine room. He found the place in acrid, smoky darkness and that "nothing was working whatever. . . . No steam. All the steam had gone." Chief Engineer Archibald Bryce asked him what could be done. Cockburn replied bleakly, "Absolutely nothing." The men stood in the dark listening and heard water pouring into the engine room. Senior Third Engineer Robert Duncan spent some minutes assisting passengers before he too made for the engine room. He met the chief engineer coming out. Bryce told him bluntly, "You can do nothing. Look after yourself."

Like other terrified trimmers and firemen from the number-one boiler room, Thomas Madden groped his way through choking dust and blinding steam to the most obvious exit, the watertight bulkhead door amidships, only to find it shut. The hydraulic machinery that opened and closed the bulkheads between the boiler rooms had failed. He could not open it manually. The force of the rapidly rising water knocked Madden down, but he managed to grab a floating coal barrow and use it to help him reach the narrow-runged escape ladder in the port-side ventilator. Close behind him was trimmer Frederick Davis, who had heard "a loud bang" and seen "objects blowing about" before the lights went out in the number-one boiler room.

Ian McDermott, a trimmer in the number-two boiler room, was also knocked off his feet by "a rush of water," which left him "struggling for two or three minutes" before washing him "out through the bottom of the ventilation shaft." He was to be the only survivor from that boiler room. Leading Fireman Evans was in the center of the number-three section stokehold when he heard a big crash. The stokehold "filled with dust," and he scrambled out for his life. Passengers who saw the "wounded and bleeding" and soot-stained firemen and trimmers escaping onto the decks through the ventilators thought they looked like creatures ascending from hell.

Probably no one gave a thought to the three German stowaways incarcerated by Detective-Inspector Pierpoint in the darkness below.

They must have heard the explosions, the shouts, the people crashing about, and as these noises died away the ever-approaching sound of rushing water. They must have wondered frantically and despairingly whether anyone would remember they were there. Even if they did, no one reached them.

―⚭―

In the mounting panic distraught parents were trying to gather up their children. Surgeon Major Warren Pearl rushed on deck to find one of the family's nurses and three of his children missing. He made three separate attempts to find them on the crowded decks, but in vain. Meanwhile the Pearls' young nurse, Alice Lines, down below on the Main Deck when the ship was struck and separated from her employers, rushed for baby Audrey, whom she tied in a shawl around her neck, and the toddler Stuart, also in her charge, "and took them up on deck as quick as possible." The slight young girl found it hard struggling with "a baby in her arms and a little boy of five hanging to her skirt."

Despairing mothers tried to give their children to strangers in the hope they could save them. Florence Padley was on deck when "one lady asked me to take her baby in arms. . . . I told her I did not have a life jacket, she could look after it better. I felt awful about it." Norah Bretherton, at first mesmerized with shock at the moment of attack and buffeted by the crowds surging past her on the stairs, rushed up to the Shelter Deck "and got baby from her play-pen." She then hurried up to the Boat Deck clutching her little girl in her arms. Recognizing a man who had often played with her son, Paul, she pleaded with him to go to her cabin and fetch him. The man ignored her as if she did not exist. In desperation she "forced baby into some man's arms" and ran back downstairs to her cabin, thrown from side to side in the gloom as the ship listed. She seized her son and made for the crowded stairs again. As she struggled out on deck, she was horrified by the callousness of her fellow passengers: "Not one of the men who rushed by offered to help me and I saw a woman with a little baby fall and slide along the deck but saw no one help her. . . . It was every man for himself."

Mabel Henshaw was shaking, and her "knees were kind of like jelly." She had just laid her eight-month-old baby, Constance, down to sleep and was on her way up the stairs when "this awful thing happened." She rushed back down, hastily dressed the infant in her coat and bonnet so that, if anything should happen, "she would at least be warm," and made for the stairs again. Then she remembered that the woman in the next-door cabin had an eighteen-month-old toddler who was probably asleep in there. She could see no sign of the mother and felt "it would be terrible if he was left in there." But he was a big child. "I had my baby in my arms and I tried to pick him up . . . but I couldn't do it and I had to leave him." His face would haunt her for the rest of her life.

Paul Crompton and his wife were desperately seeking to gather up their six children, ranging from five-month-old baby Peter to fourteen-year-old Catherine. Annie Williams of New Jersey, traveling with her six children, was in a similar plight, not knowing which way to turn. While parents ran frantically around the decks, lost children screamed for their parents. Baby carriages, some empty, others not, rolled wildly down the tilting deck.

Helen Smith, just six years old, had become separated from her parents and was at risk of being trampled. She appealed for help to newspaperman Ernest Cowper—whose half-written profile of the Hubbards was in his pocket—"to save her." He tried to find her parents, but without success.

Chief Steward John Jones and his staff were doing what they could to calm people. He was hurrying from deck to deck "telling everybody, stewards and passengers, to get their life jackets on and come on deck." Stewardess Marian Bird told the anguished women in her care "to keep calm, get their life jackets as quickly as they could, and get on deck." She made sure "not one person was left" in her section of third class before she went above. The lights failed while she was still below, rushing from cabin to cabin. Another third-class stewardess, Fannie Morecroft, ran along her section looking in all the rooms to make sure they were empty, then went up to the Shelter Deck to see whom she could round up, urging passengers to get to the higher decks as quickly as possible. Many were running around "like a bunch of wild mice." Charles Hill, who had spent precious minutes searching in vain belowdecks for his friend Mrs. Witherbee and her four-year-old son, was thankful to run into his steward, Percy Penny, who helped him into a life jacket "although he had none on himself."

John Griffith, chief third-class steward, went immediately to his Shelter Deck cabin to fetch his life jacket. He also grabbed his automatic pistol "to get hold of it in case it was wanted." He found that his inside cabin on the starboard side was "full of a kind of brown smoke." This smoke was very dense and quite unlike anything he had experienced on board ship. It seemed to be coming through the cabin's two internal windows, which opened into the casing of the number-two funnel and which he always kept open. Still puzzled, he ran into the corridor and went to direct his passengers from the lower decks to the Boat Deck. He later went down to the Main Deck to check that no one had been left there but was appalled to see "one green mass of water" surging toward him. He turned and ran, just reaching the stairs before the "wall of water" caught up with him. In the dining rooms "silver and flowers and dishes" were now afloat.

Despite the best efforts of some stewards and other crew members, many passengers were still without life jackets. They either were too afraid to go below or found when they did that their jackets had been stolen from their cabins. Now they could find none on the open decks either. Ogden Hammond and his wife searched in vain. When Hammond said he would go down to their cabin to fetch some, his wife begged him not to leave her. For a while they joined white-faced Lady Allan and her two daughters, who also had no life jackets. Lady Allan had been thrown against the rail by the force of the explosion and feared her arm was broken. One of her maids appeared with two life jackets, while another man donated his to one of the Allan girls. The Hammonds, still without jackets, walked anxiously along the deck. Any thoughts Hammond might still have harbored about going below to their cabin were banished by a young man who told him that he had been to the Upper Deck to find "a rush of water" in the dark corridor.

James Leary, too, was still without a life jacket. He saw a man wearing a blue uniform, whom he assumed to be an officer, carrying a life jacket in his hand. Leary demanded he hand it over. The man replied, "You will have to go and get one for yourself; this is mine." Leary said, "I thought, according to law, passengers came first." "Passengers be damned," the man replied coolly. "Save yourself first." A now hysterical Leary tore the life jacket from him, shouting, "If you want this one you will have to kill me to get it." In his agitation Leary put the jacket on upside down. A calmer passenger told him, "If you got in the water that way you would be feet up" and helped him put it on correctly.

Other passengers and crew were becoming violent. Frightened bellboy Ben Holton was just coming out of his cabin when he was assaulted by a man who grabbed his life jacket from him and pushed him back into his cabin. The boy struggled back on deck, where Archibald Bryce, the Scottish chief engineer, tried to calm him, saying reassuringly, " 'They'll no sink a Scots-built ship,' showing his belief in all things Scots." Holton thought Bryce was talking through his hat and took comfort from the fact that he himself had been captain of the school swimming team.

The lovely weather and the proximity to land made the unfolding catastrophe seem surreal. "The Atlantic giant might have been peacefully at anchor in the glorious sunshine off Kinsale," Oliver Bernard later recalled. There was also an incongruity about the man seen by one passenger with two camera cases on his back taking photographs as he made his way forward, capturing the excited and terrified men and women as they ran shouting about the decks and converged on the lifeboats. Many were crowding on the high port side.

Charles Bowring, an imposing figure with his powerful shoulders and thick white hair, had been watching the first attempts to lower boats on the port side with foreboding. This experienced shipowner and witness at the *Titanic* inquiry saw the difficulties all too clearly. Unlike the *Titanic*, the *Lusitania* had no shortage of lifeboats; the twenty-two wooden clinker-built boats suspended from davits and the twenty-six wooden-and-canvas collapsible boats mostly stowed beneath them were more than adequate for the numbers on board. The problem was that the *Lusitania* was still making "considerable headway" and was by now listing by some thirty degrees to starboard. Bowring knew it would be "almost impossible to get the boats safely into the water" in such conditions. Detective-Inspector Pierpoint was also gloomily convinced that "they would have great difficulty in lowering them if they could lower them at all on account of the list." Nevertheless, frightened passengers were swarming hopefully around the boats, trying to scramble in.

Harold Boulton and Fred Lassetter helped Elizabeth Lassetter into a lifeboat on the port side. They were just congratulating each other that the boat was about to be lowered when they saw Captain Turner appear on the bridge. He shouted in a loud, clear voice: "Don't lower the boats. Don't lower the boats. The ship can't sink. She's all right. The ship can't sink." He paused, then added: "Will the gentlemen kindly assist me in getting the women and children out of the boats and off the upper deck?" Lassetter and Boulton dutifully did as they were asked and handed Elizabeth Lassetter back out of the boat. Glancing down the deck, Boulton was shocked to see "the bow just beginning to submerge."

Joseph Myers and his friend Frank Kellett had helped a woman and her son into a port-side lifeboat and climbed in after her. After a couple of minutes "the bath-room steward that had given me a bath in the morning came aft, a great big fat fellow with a life jacket on, and he called out, 'Everybody out of the lifeboats. We are hard aground and we are not going to sink.'" Myers and Kellett climbed out again and waited. A woman called out to Turner, "What do you wish us to do?" He replied, "Stay right where you are, Madam. She's all right." When she asked, "Where do you get your information?" he replied in a severe voice, "From the engine room, Madam."

To some, the captain's reassurances came as a relief. Mrs. Henry Adams was trying to care for her "dazed and almost unconscious" husband. Now that the event he had dreaded had happened, he seemed incapable of action. Relief flooded through her, and she sat her husband down on a collapsible boat and waited patiently. The nervous James Leary felt sufficiently reassured to return to his stateroom. It was "quite a struggle" because of the ship's list, but as he slithered along he met Purser McCubbin, who had locked all Leary's money in the safe. Leary said, "How about my valuables?" The purser replied, "Young man, if we get to port you will get them, and if we sink you won't need them." Leary continued to his cabin to retrieve a little flask of brandy and his overcoat and hat.

Others heard the captain's order in frank disbelief. James Brooks, who had seen Captain Turner standing on the bridge "in full uniform with a life preserver put on properly," hand raised, and ordering the launching to stop, looked down the forward starboard deck and saw that it was nearly awash. He could only keep his footing by clinging to some chairs. Charles Lauriat looked over the side and was horrified to see the degree to which the ship was listing. A mere ten minutes after she had been hit, the incredible truth was that the *Lusitania* was sinking rapidly.

Walther Schwieger, observing closely through his periscope, agreed. His official war diary recorded: "Clean bow shot. . . . Torpedo hits starboard side right behind the bridge. An unusually strong explosion takes place. . . . The explosion of the torpedo must have been accompanied by a second one (boiler or coal or powder?). The superstructure right above the point of the impact and the bridge are torn asunder, fire breaks out and smoke envelops the high bridge. . . . The ship stops immediately and heels over to starboard very quickly, immersing simultaneously at the bow. It looks as if the ship is going to capsize very shortly by the bow."

According to German accounts, published after the war, his pilot Lanz was beside him, and Schwieger ordered him to take a look. "He put his eye to the periscope and after a brief scrutiny yelled: 'My God, it's the *Lusitania!*'," implying that neither he nor his captain had realized this previously. Schwieger resumed his place at the periscope and took it in turns with his men to watch what Radio Officer Otto Rikowsky described as the "ghastly drama" of which they were the authors.

CHAPTER SIXTEEN

A Bizarre Orchestra of Death

*J*UST TEN MINUTES after the attack Captain Turner knew he could do nothing to save his ship. With water lapping over the bows, he told Staff Captain Anderson to lower the boats into the water as soon as the ship had slowed sufficiently for this to be done safely. Anderson, working feverishly among the boats in his shirt-sleeves, must have known that no lifeboats could yet be lowered safely because of the speed with which the ship was still moving. Nevertheless, and in the confusion, some crew and passengers persisted in the attempt.

The list to starboard made it virtually impossible to launch boats from the port side since they were "all swinging into the ship's side." Seamen and passengers struggled to push them out over the rail, but as they were lowered the sixty feet or so to the water they bumped down the ship's side, where the protruding rivets, nearly two inches long, snagged and damaged them. At each bump and jolt people spilled like rag dolls into the water below. Ship's Carpenter Neil Robertson described how it was "just like drawing a crate of unpacked china along a dock road. . . . if you started to lower the boats you would be dragging them down the rough side of the ship on . . . snap-head rivets; they stand about an inch from the shell of the ship, so you would be dragging the whole side of the ship away if you tried to lower the boats with a 15 degree list."

Conversely, those lifeboats on the starboard side that had been released from their snubbing chain were swinging crazily out. Some of the more agile passengers jumped seven or eight feet to get into the starboard boats. Others had to be helped, but many were too frightened to launch themselves across the gulf between deck and lifeboat. Third Officer John Lewis saw many women going "to the ship's side all right, but when they saw the distance down to the water they seemed to be frightened of getting into the boat."

Crewmen came rushing to their boat stations on both sides of the deck—each of them had been issued a badge earlier in the voyage denoting to which lifeboat they should report in case of emergency—but frantic passengers obstructed them. Charles Bowring watched people "rushing and trying to get in the boats and all the people passing back and forth and rushing around." They hindered the crew from lowering the lifeboat ropes, or falls, used to hoist and lower the boats, from the Hurricane Deck. The ropes "had been coiled up there and when they started coming down the people were walking past and naturally getting in the way." One man even got a rope "twisted around his leg."

Fear rose with the water. The veneer of order very soon wore thin. There was confusion over Captain Turner's commands, and as one survivor recalled, they were "not generally acted upon." There was no public address system. The officers shouted out orders but could barely be heard over the din of wood scraping against metal, the banging to release the boats, and the cries and shouts of frightened passengers. James Brooks, walking along the Boat Deck toward the bows and wondering which lifeboat to make for, was challenged by a "young fellow" with a revolver, whom he took to be an officer, and who yelled, "You cannot get in that boat." "Who in hell is trying to?" Brooks snapped back.

Passengers made instinctively for the boats on the higher port side of the listing ship, even though these were more difficult to launch. Crewmen like Able Seaman Leo Thompson and Boatswain John Davies, a nonswimmer in his sixties, could not even reach their assigned port-side boats because of the crush. Instead they pushed their way over to the starboard side. Davies was formally responsible for piping the crewmen to their stations in an emergency, but under the circumstances there seemed to him little point in doing so. Everyone was only too aware of the necessity of abandoning ship.

Desperate efforts to get the port-side boats away produced catastrophic results. Third Officer Albert Bestic was in charge of some of these boats. He managed to stop parties of men from climbing in, so he could give priority to women and children, but with so many seamen trapped belowdecks there were not enough experienced sailors to help. Bestic appealed at the top of his voice to several men in the crowd pressing around him to assist him in heaving the No. 2 boat, loaded with women and children, over the side. Hard as they tried, they did not have the strength to shift the weight of over two tons. Among the passengers who attempted to help was one Mr. McConnel, who later recalled, "By that time there was so much list that a boat on the port side was obviously grinding against the side" and swinging in over the ship's rail. "I saw that the only thing I could do to help anybody was to use my not very considerable strength in shoving to get the boat past . . . because each of the planks of the boat caught on the ledge of the balustrade."

Bestic watched helplessly as the laden boat slammed violently inward against the superstructure, crushing people as it went. At that moment No. 4 crashed to the deck and came careering down the tilting and already blood-spattered deck, smashing into people as they tried to jump from its path. An increasingly desperate Bestic decided to try swinging empty and thus lighter boats over the port rail and fill them later.

Meanwhile a group of passengers trying independently to push the No. 8 boat over the edge of the port deck were nearly crushed between the lifeboat and the side of the first-class smoking room. Realizing the great difficulty of trying to launch boats from a severely listing ship, Staff Captain Anderson ordered Bestic "to go to the bridge and tell them there to trim the ship with the port tanks." Anderson hoped that flooding the tanks on the port side would correct the list somewhat and ease the problems of launching the boats. Bestic managed to get near enough to shout the request up to Second Officer Hefford on the bridge, but the answer came back that "it was impossible."

As No. 12 was being lowered, the excited passengers got in the way of the rope falls and the boat began to dip by the bows. Charles Bowring watched as an officer tried to correct the angle, ordering, "Let her go a little faster by the stern," but the man in charge of the falls "evidently could not let go quick enough . . . and the stern absolutely lost control and the boat went right down stern first. . . . I looked over the side and saw the passengers being spilled into the water." No. 14 was successfully lowered about halfway down, but then "they evidently lost control of her . . . and she went down straight on an even keel right down on the people that were in the water out of the first boat."

Margaret Mackworth saw the struggling, shrieking people and

turned away: "It was not safe to look at horrible things just then." She decided not to try to get in a boat herself: "Even at that moment death would have seemed better than to become part of that terror-infected crowd." The "white-faced stream" of people milling about reminded her "of a swarm of bees who do not know where the queen has gone."

The No. 16 boat also broke away from the falls to plunge battered and splintered into the sea. Charles Hill was one of the passengers inside. He had tried to get into another boat, but a hysterical woman had cried out, "Please don't come in here—we are overcrowded now," even though the boat was far from full. His lifeboat now smacked into the water with such force that it sprang a leak. The occupants, craning instinctively around to watch the last moments of the *Lusitania*, overbalanced the already waterlogged craft and capsized it, spilling everyone into the water.

The Hammonds, still without life jackets, were among the frightened group huddling inside another port-side boat. They had been seeking sanctuary on the port side, as high above the water as possible, when a petty officer told Mrs. Hammond to get in. She refused to be parted from her husband, and the couple hung back. Eventually, seeing that there was space for them both, they climbed in. According to Ogden Hammond, "The boat was about half filled, about 35 people in it. They started to lower the boat, and the men at the bow let the tackle slip." Hammond, perched in the bow of the boat, grabbed at the speeding rope falls, losing "all the skin off my right hand." The bow dropped but "the stern tackle held, and everybody fell out of that boat from the top deck" some sixty feet above the water. The boat then broke free, crashing on top of the people struggling in the water below. Hammond never saw his beloved wife again. James Brooks also witnessed screaming passengers slide to the end of the almost vertical boat and "spill into the ocean."

Isaac Lehmann was so sickened and frightened that he returned to his cabin on the Upper Deck, determined to find a life jacket, only to find that someone had taken it. Then, "I don't know whatever possessed me, but I looked in my dress suitcase and got hold of my revolver, as I figured this would come in handy in case of any body not doing the proper thing." Meanwhile his steadfast steward, Robert Barnes, had found him a life jacket. By now water was running along the passageway on the starboard side and "coming in volumes up C deck [Shelter Deck]." Finally reaching the Promenade Deck, the sodden Lehmann ran into the ship's doctor and Chief Purser McCubbin, who to his disbelief "were walking up and down deck smoking a cigarette." He demanded to know why they were not at their positions. They replied that "there was not a chance for the boat to go down, that I should remain calm, and said I was very foolish to have my life jacket on." Lehmann told them tersely that "it was better to be prepared" and hurried back onto the port side of the Boat Deck.

He saw some forty women and children sitting inside the No. 18 boat. A crewman was standing by, ax in hand. Lehmann demanded to know why he was not chopping through "the block and fall . . . that would release the boat from the davit to let it down." The man replied, "It is the captain's orders not to launch any boats." An infuriated Lehmann drew his revolver and replied: "To hell with the Captain. Don't you see the boat is sinking? And the first man that disobeys my orders to launch the boat I shoot to kill." In the ensuing panic the boat swung on its davits up against the superstructure, "smashing the passengers who were standing there." Lehmann fell on the deck, his right leg severely injured. As he lay dazed and in pain, the next thing he knew was that "the water commenced coming over the smoke-stack . . . in fearful volumes." It swept him "right off the deck into the ocean."

The crew managed to get sufficient temporary control of boat No. 18 to make it descend jerkily toward the water below. An irate male passenger who had jumped in stood up in the swaying boat to yell at the top of his lungs to those sweating at the falls, "Don't you drop this boat!" But, perhaps distracted by his call, according to him, "just at that time they did, and we were all dumped into the water."

In the end, only one port-side boat got safely away without capsizing or becoming waterlogged. A trembling Alice Lines, with baby Audrey tied tightly in a shawl around her neck and five-year-old Stuart clinging to her skirts, tried to climb in. A crewman lifted the little boy in, but when Alice tried to follow, the sailor told her the boat was full. As the boat was lowered, the distraught girl decided all she could do was jump. She landed in the water beside the boat and for a moment had "a terrible sensation of being sucked under the ship." But then she felt someone grab her long auburn hair and pull her on board still clutching the baby. Alice Lines later said, "My hair saved our lives."

First Officer Arthur Jones and Third Officer John Lewis were superintending the starboard boats. When Lewis arrived at his station, the first thing he saw was that the forward fall of the No. 1 boat "had been

A drawing published in The Sphere *showing desperate people struggling in the water.*

lowered too much and in consequence the boat was beam on to the way the ship was travelling and the bow was out." He at once gave orders for the after fall to be lowered to straighten it up. The two officers then tried to persuade passengers to climb into the boats, but they were frightened of jumping across the large gap between the deck and the boats produced by the list. Many "refused point blank."

Able Seaman Leslie Morton, reaching his station on the starboard side, found "great excitement" on the heavily listing Boat Deck, with passengers and crew of all departments rushing here and there. Again and again he caught the anxious comment "surely she cannot sink." But he knew, however, with true seaman's instinct that the buoyancy that would keep the *Lusitania* afloat had gone. The lifeboat was quickly filled. The more able-bodied leaped the seven- or eight-foot gap. Others were helped across. At the order "lower away," Morton grabbed the after boat fall, while another seaman operated the forward fall. They succeeded in lowering the boat almost to the water, but the *Lusitania* was still plowing through the sea. With one final effort they managed to drop the boat into the water, but because of the ship's speed it immediately fell behind by the length of one boat, coming up alongside the listing ship directly beneath the next lifeboat. Morton, whose job it would have been to slide down the falls and try to get his lifeboat away from the sinking ship, did not have time to act. Instead he had to watch aghast as the other boat full of people dropped twenty-five or thirty feet fairly and squarely onto it.

The agonized shouts and screams of the crushed and injured, the sight of bodies maimed and thrashing about in pain or spread-eagled motionless in the water, brought home to Morton the reality of what was happening. "The turmoil of passengers and life jackets, many people losing their hold on the deck and slipping down and over the side, and a gradual crescendo of noise building up as the hundreds and hundreds of people began to realize that, not only was she going down very fast but in all probability too fast for them all to get away"—all of this created "a horrible and bizarre orchestra of death in the background." Charles Lauriat felt "it only added horror to the whole situation to put people into a boat that you knew . . . would go down with the steamer." It would be better to leave them to cling to a piece of wreckage.

Professor Holbourn had tried to put Avis and the two nurses into a boat on the port side but, confronted with crushed and bleeding bodies littering the deck, decided their best chance was on the starboard side. He forced a way through the crowd swarming over the sloping deck. No one could stand up without hanging on to the rail. The eighteen-inch camber of the *Lusitania*'s deck made the list even worse. Terrified people clutched at the rail and each other to stop themselves from falling into the water. One young girl fell and "rolled the full length of the deck" before being picked up by a steward. Another female passenger found the list so strong that "we had to sort of rush down, clinging to the railing, which at that time was nearly under water . . . and sort of tumble into the boat, assisted by passengers and seamen."

Professor Holbourn managed to reach a starboard boat. Using his strong physique, he braced himself against the crowd and helped Avis and the two women across the gap into the swaying boat. As he did so, he kissed the little girl. He was afraid he would not survive, and so, calmly and gently, he asked her "to find his wife and children and kiss them goodbye from him" when she reached Britain. Gathering himself together now that they were safely in the boat, he looked down at his watch to see that it was a mere twelve to fifteen minutes since the *Lusitania* had been struck. Shocked by how low the ship was in the water, he put on the life jacket he was still carrying and tucked his manuscripts into it. He went forward a little to find a clear section of rail to jump from. As he leaped into the blue-green waters below, "he had the horrible shock of seeing the child's boat swamp and capsize." However hard he tried, he could not reach Avis through the mass of wreckage and people gasping for breath around him. As he struggled to do so, he saw her pulled under by the suction of the waters swirling against the ship's side.

James Brooks had also slithered down to the starboard side. Unnerved by what he had seen, especially the people who had tumbled out of the boats "bobbing for a mile back, as long as they lasted," he had begun running down the deck. Then he asked himself, "What am I running for?" and stopped. Seeing that the water was almost up to the Boat Deck, he helped some twenty or thirty women clinging to the rail into a boat and jumped in after them. The tackle, fall, and snubbing chain were still attached, and he looked around desperately for a hammer or some other implement to release the boat. Finding none, he and a crewman "both used our fists" but could make no impression on the imprisoning equipment. He heard "a crushing sound of wood" and saw that "the boat would never get away." He and the sailor "both jumped . . . and swam."

Leslie Morton went to help his brother, who was struggling to lower the No. 1 boat. They managed to get it into the water, then tried to push off from the side with boat hooks, but "many of the passengers were hanging on to bits of rope from the side of the ship and the rails, which were now level with the water, in some mistaken belief that they would be safer hanging on to the big ship rather than entrusting their lives in the small lifeboat." Fearing that the boat was about to be dragged under, the two brothers dived overboard. As he hit the water, Leslie remembered his brother had never learned to swim.

An Ocean Red with Blood

Boatswain's mate Florence Sikking reported to the No. 5 boat on the starboard side but found it was missing. He assumed it had been blown to pieces by the explosion. He tried to help passengers into another boat, but the numbers of people packed inside destabilized it: "The bows of it got underneath the boat deck" as the *Lusitania* sank, and it flipped over.

Looking down the starboard deck, Charles Lauriat saw that "wild confusion had broken loose." Boat No. 7, "well filled with people, principally women and children," was still attached to the ship. After what he had seen of people spilling from boats as they were lowered, he had no desire to get into one. Nevertheless, he felt impelled to act. He jumped in and tried to free the after falls. At the forward falls a steward was "bravely cutting away at the thick ropes with a pocket knife." Lauriat grimly wished the man had an ax. He tried to go to his aid, "but it was impossible to climb through that boatload of people, mixed up as they were with oars, boat hooks, kegs of water, rope ladders, sails, and God knows what." Looking up at "the tremendous smokestack" hanging out over them as the ship listed even further only added to the terror of all around. Lauriat pleaded with the boat's occupants to jump, "but truly they were petrified." Only a handful of men and women would listen. Lauriat gave up and jumped himself. Once in the water, he tried to help any who had obeyed his call to get clear by pushing them ahead of him. Looking back, he saw the lifeboat dragged under. He heard the choking cries of its occupants as the waters closed over them.

Seeing that the starboard Boat Deck was now no more than "eight or ten feet from the water," Charles Bowring methodically tucked his glasses into a pocket of his Norfolk jacket. Then he climbed over the rail, jumped the short distance into the heaving water, and struck out. His aim was to get clear before the *Lusitania* went under. Glancing back, he saw the dreadful spectacle of a crowded lifeboat being dragged under the waves by the mother ship.

The highly strung James Leary had the terrifying experience of being in such a boat. Already further traumatized by a fellow passenger's tale of how an ax-wielding seaman had deliberately chopped off the fingers of a man scrambling and clawing to board a lifeboat, he had completely lost his head. "Through some insane idea" he jumped into a lifeboat still attached to the ship. As it sank with the *Lusitania*, he went down too. One of the lifeboat's oars trapped his leg, "and it seemed to me I went as far as the ship did, because there was a terrible drag from this thing holding me."

Another boat, filled with women and children, was safely lowered to the water. As a relieved Officer Lewis watched, a female passenger called up to him, "For God's sake, jump." He looked at her and replied, "Good-bye and good luck. I will meet you in Queenstown." As the sailors took up their oars, Lewis cried, "Row for your lives." Another woman in the boat took one quick glance, unable to believe the *Lusitania* was truly sinking, then looked away again. The sight was "too terrible to see."

Able Seaman Leo Thompson helped Chief Steward John Jones try to launch boat No. 17. Despite "a great crowd of people" surging around the boat, they managed to fill it and began to lower away. But Thompson had great difficulty lowering the after fall because of "the list of the ship and the people crowding on top of me. I was in danger of being pushed over the side by the crowd behind me." He braced himself by putting his feet against the davit and his back against a collapsible boat and lowered away in that position. He was prevented by "the many people between me and the forward davit" from communicating with the man handling the forward fall. When the bow of the boat suddenly dipped, he hastily let go of the after fall "in an effort to equalize the boat." The effort failed, and the boat "dived into the water bow first" and capsized.

First Officer Jones loaded over eighty people into the No. 15 boat, also helped by Leo Thompson, who threw some fifteen to twenty children in. After successfully lowering it—a tricky task given the weight—both men slid down the falls and jumped in. As the boat hit the water, it became entangled in the ship's Marconi wires, which caught the boat's gunwale. Thompson got out of the way while someone else cut the boat free. The No. 19 boat was also launched successfully, even though it was "full of people" and some fell in the sea. Number 21 reached the water safely too, with some seventy frightened people aboard. Diminutive fifteen-year-old bellboy William Burrows, who was regretting that in his panic he had left his "little bellboy's jacket" hanging in the bathroom three decks down, was in one of the lifeboats that got away. As it was lowered he noticed "all the water rushing in through the portholes."

David Thomas, separated from his daughter, managed to find a boat on the starboard side that was only three-quarters full. Two women and a small boy were standing hesitantly and timidly beside it. One woman and the child decided to climb in. Thomas, seeing that "the A deck then was level with the water" and that the other woman was by now "too hysterical" to enter the boat, grabbed hold of her and "rather forcibly" pushed her in, then followed.

Detective-Inspector Pierpoint also helped load people into one of the starboard lifeboats. Realizing that the *Lusitania* was sinking fast, he jumped into the bows of the boat as it was being lowered. To his despair, he found that the boat was still firmly anchored to the ship: "One of the crew shouted out and asked had anybody got a knife to cut the fall . . . and before we could do anything the ship was on top of us and the davits pulled the boat over and threw every one of us into the water." Florence Padley, still without a life jacket, was one of those "dumped" into the water. She had already lost her shoes in the scramble to get on deck. Josephine Brandell was also tossed into the sea and managed to grab a floating deck chair.

Oscar Grab watched what was happening on the starboard side. He saw boats handled by crewmen in such a way that "they couldn't hold on to the ropes or they slipped through their hands. . . . the boats fell down and one end struck the water first and dropped everybody into the water." He watched one boat turn over, "and everybody screamed. It was such a horrible sight to see these poor people drowned like rats." He decided he would be far better off jumping over and swimming away.

Julia Sullivan agreed. She refused to get into a lifeboat even though her husband, Flor, had found places for them both. Although Flor could not swim, she was a strong swimmer and was convinced she could save them both. Her less-confident husband gave her their money to tuck into her bodice, saying, "You'll need this by and by." Telling him not to be absurd, she selected a place to jump and told him to hold on tight to her. George Hook also persuaded his two children, Frank and Elsie, to stay away from the boats and jump with him.

Joseph Myers was also unimpressed with the seamen's efforts to launch the boats. Watching them swing out the boats the day before, he had thought that "they looked more like day laborers than seamen." The deck was so crowded that he climbed glumly back into the lifeboat he and Frank Kellett had been ordered to vacate. Then he waited for the ship to tip over, thinking that the lifeboat "would be the safest place to be thrown from." He reflected that the scenes around him were disgraceful—indeed, the "worst discipline I ever saw."

Nevertheless, many passengers acted bravely, from Professor Holbourn, whose first thought had been to find Avis Dolphin, to Alice Lines, who against the odds had saved the two children in her care, to the Naishes, calmly helping others into their life jackets, to Charles Lauriat, trying selflessly to save a group of passengers petrified with fear from being dragged under in a lifeboat still attached to the ship. The usually cynical Oliver Bernard was particularly struck by one bedroom steward—"a little, stunted man, the kind on whom men of big physique are accustomed to look down with mingled pity and contempt" but "with the heart of a lion"—who struggled ferociously and selflessly to free the boats.

Now there was little time left for heroics. A passenger "saw a man from a great height throw himself into the water and come down what seemed to me to be a fearful smash." Shuddering, he made for the starboard side to try his luck there. He tried to get into one boat, but a woman clutching a child screamed at him "not to jump." He found another boat and climbed in, only to find "two of the funnels were hanging over that side and threatening to smash the boats up." Those in the boat "were so tightly packed that it was impossible to move the oars at first," and the cowering people were convinced the stacks would come crashing down on them.

Two stewardesses, Marian Bird and Fannie Morecroft, had found seats in a lifeboat. After throwing all the life jackets she could find in the darkened cabins into a pile on the open deck, Marian climbed into "the last boat that was leaving." Fannie was with her, after braving the list "which made us slide right across on to the rail." The anxious people huddling in the boat as the *Lusitania* loomed over them thought that they would surely be dragged down with her. The trailing Marconi wires fouled one of the oars, but with a burst of effort the frantic oarsmen just managed to get the boat clear.

Many thought that their salvation might lie with the twenty-six collapsible boats piled on deck or stowed under the open lifeboats. The collapsibles were designed to float free if the ship should sink before they could be hoisted over, but many were bolted down or seemed glued fast to the deck by paint. Captain Turner had decided against loosening them when the ship reached the war zone because of the risk of them sliding across the deck. Now crew and passengers made often futile efforts to free them. One passenger watched stokers "trying to release these . . . with the hope that they would more or less float when the steamer went down, and they worked there very hard . . . but they were too heavy." Passengers also tried, but as one anguished man discovered, the boats were "tied down so tight that I couldn't do it." The metal frames of other collapsibles, which did finally float free, were so rusted their canvas sides could not be rigged. It was hopeless.

CHAPTER SEVENTEEN

Wave upon Wave

*A*s THE SHIP'S LIST increased, so did the despair of those still trapped on board. Fireman O'Connell, running along the deck, saw two women crying and instinctively put his arms around them. The older woman insisted on going into one of the salons and sat down helplessly in a wicker chair, water lapping at her ankles and the detritus of the once elegant room floating past her.

Many women refused to be parted from their men. Lucy and Harold Taylor were standing at the rail, near a lifeboat loaded with women. " 'I won't go, I won't!' Lucy Taylor was screaming. Her husband extricated himself from her desperate embrace, kissed her, and dropped her into the boat." As the boat pulled away she could see him waving to her and she "waved back as he went down with the boat." Jack Welsh insisted that his new love Gerda Nielson should get into a lifeboat. When he saw her flung from it, he dived in to try and save her. In the last moments some women were bundled willy-nilly over the rail into the boats—one determined man recalled that he "shoved this woman over—all I saw was her feet." Another who had fallen on her back on the wet decks and thought her spine was broken was in danger of being trampled to death. A crewman seized her and pushed her into a boat. The dazed woman heard a steward shouting, "Passengers be calm, the boat will not sink."

Many threw propriety to the winds and stripped down, believing their chances of survival would be better if they were wearing fewer clothes. Mr. Stroud, an American veteran of the Mexican war, ripped the clothes off his wife so that "all she had on was her stockings and her life jacket." Mrs. Stroud was already numb with shock. She was one of the many mothers unable to find their children in the general confusion. Harold Boulton realized that the ship was sinking and told the Lassetters that "the only thing to do is to jump." He instructed a shaken Elizabeth Lassetter to remove her skirt and to clasp hands with her son and himself. The three then jumped some ninety feet into the water below. One man wearing only his underwear dived from the rail.

Seeing that the ship's screw propellers and rudders were now above the water, those still on board knew that their situation was desperate. Some tried to slide down wires and ropes, including the log line that trailed astern to record the ship's run. After the first six feet of rope, the line was made of wire. The sharp metal line flayed the skin from people's hands and feet as the speed of their descent increased. Many survivors were scarred for life. Red Cross volunteer Lorna Pavey, who mere minutes earlier had been quietly eating a grapefruit in the second-class dining room, slid bloodily and painfully down one wire. Her "skirt seemed to make a balloon in the water when she dropped."

Archie Donald had helped keep men back while "all the women in sight" and any children were loaded into a boat, only to see it "hang perpendicularly" and throw out all the passengers. Now he looked around him in anguish to see that many passengers were "crawling up on a rope netting on the lower deck, climbing higher as the water reached them." Knowing that the ship "was going very quickly down" and that the water was rushing toward him, he asked a steward to adjust his life jacket, and then set about stuffing his money—some eight pounds—into his sock. He was just starting to undo his shoes when he realized there was no more time. He jumped the remaining twelve feet into the water.

Michael Byrne decided to leap after making sure his life jacket was properly fastened. He asked a passing officer, "Are we badly damaged?" to which the man replied that they intended to beach the ship. Byrne then said scornfully, "How can you when your engines have gone dead?" As the water reached the tops of his shoes, he dived off the rail and struck out, terrified of being pulled under by the suction.

Father Basil Maturin, pale and without a life jacket, but perfectly calm, was giving final absolution to several passengers on the plunging deck. He handed a tiny child into one of the last boats with the quiet injunction "Find its mother." Assistant Purser W. Harkless gathered little Barbara Anderson, standing lost and alone, clinging to a rail, into his arms and leaped with her into a lifeboat. Francis Luker, a British postal clerk returning to enlist, was startled to find two babies "snuggled in the shelter of a deck house." As the ship neared her final plunge, he tucked one baby under each arm and took a flying leap into a lifeboat below. Women in desperation thrust their children into the arms of strangers. In the ship's dying moments children were being thrown from the decks to be caught by men in the lifeboats; such a drastic measure required considerable nerve, but there was no alternative or time for reflection.

Charlotte Pye had grabbed her baby, Marjorie, and come running onto the deck. She saw "women shouting and screaming and praying to be saved." Again and again she was thrown off her feet by the list. A man came up to her and said, "Don't cry. It's quite all right," to which the distraught mother replied, "No, it isn't." He promised to find her a life jacket, but failing to locate one, he gave her his own. As he tied it on her, Charlotte recognized him as the man who had paid her five dollars for a concert program: Alfred Vanderbilt. He strapped her baby to her, then helped her toward a boat. Seeing how steeply the ship was now listing, he advised her to untie the baby again and carry it in her arms. The crew helped her climb over two oars into the boat, then handed the child to her. Looking up, Charlotte thought that the *Lusitania* was "just about ready to roll on top of us." She had "the terrible feeling that I'd have to get up and push her back."

Vanderbilt turned away to continue his heroic efforts. According to ship's barber Lott Gadd, Vanderbilt was "trying to put life jackets on women and children. The ship was going down fast. When the sea reached them, they were washed away. I never saw Vanderbilt after that. All I saw in the water was children—children everywhere." Canadian Mrs. Lines saw Vanderbilt with his valet, Ronald Denyer, by his side. She heard him say, "Find all the kiddies you can, boy." The man rushed off immediately to collect the children, and as he brought them to Vanderbilt, the millionaire "dashed to the boats with two little ones in his arms at a time." He looked as composed as if waiting for a train.

Norah Bretherton would have been glad of his help. She was dragging her little son, Paul, whom she had rescued from her cabin, over the sloping deck while gripping her baby, Betty, in her other arm. She begged several passing men for assistance, but no one stopped. The terrified mother managed to find a place in one of the last lifeboats to pull away from the ship.

Margaret Cox, slithering down the deck to look for a space in the boat, lost hold of her infant, Desmond, as water came "dashing up" over the liner's deck, but somehow she managed to catch him. Someone called to her from a boat, "Throw in the baby." She went to the edge and tossed the baby to the waiting hands. Above her she saw "these big funnels coming over me . . . and I thought oh God, if I've got to die, let me die in the water." It was the first and last time she prayed that afternoon. As she stood petrified, she felt someone grab her and fling her facedown into a lifeboat.

Oliver Bernard, having abandoned his search for Lesley Mason, had been horrified by the scenes in the lifeboats. Now he gazed hopelessly out to sea. Unlike Margaret Cox, he could take no comfort in prayer. He did not believe in an afterlife but rather that "the end of all life lay in the dust." But at this moment his sometimes despairing attitude only enhanced his will to survive. Some distance away he saw a man "swimming on his back, stripped naked and paddling gently, looking up at the ship with a smile, waiting for a boat to come and pick him up." Encouraged by his example, Bernard began to strip off his clothes. Force of habit made him methodically fold coat, vest, collar, and tie, which he laid at the base of the third funnel "as on an altar." Mechanically he put his tiepin in his pocket "as if about to have a wash." Thoughts were pouring through his mind "like a stream of light through a kaleidoscope screen."

Untying his bootlaces high up on the Hurricane Deck, Bernard heard a voice. He glanced around to see Chief Electrician George Hutchinson talking to Radio Operator Bob Leith. Leith was still sitting in the Marconi house determinedly tapping out his SOS message using his fading emergency power. When Bernard confessed that he could not swim, Leith jumped up and offered him his wooden swivel chair to hang on to. Bernard declined, and somehow the men found themselves laughing with grim humor as the chair careered wildly down the sloping deck to crash against the rails. Leith took some quick photographs of the scene, then the three men, as if by common consent, together made for the starboard rail, "half-sliding into a run down the slope." Bernard dropped onto the Boat Deck below, his unlaced rubber-soled boots gripping the sloping deck as he tried to steady himself. The edge of the Boat Deck was nearly awash, and he was carried over, clinging as best he could to some davits. Leith leaped "into a boat that was full of water"—he had no idea which one.

Robert Leith

Margaret Mackworth was sucked into the water off the Boat Deck. After the horror of watching attempts to launch the port-side lifeboats, Dr. Howard Fisher had gone to hunt for life jackets for himself and Dorothy Conner. While he was gone, the ship had seemed to right herself a little. Word went round that the danger was over, and Margaret and Dorothy had laughed and shaken hands while Margaret remarked, "Well, you've had your thrill all right." But almost at once it had become clear that the danger was far from over. Fisher returned with news that he had had to wade through deep water to reach the life jackets below. Margaret unhooked her skirt so that the heavy folds would not impede her, and the three prepared to jump. He and Dorothy stepped forward, but Margaret hesitated, "feeling frightened at the idea of jumping so far"—at least sixty feet. Her fear of water also held her back. Then she saw that water was seeping over the deck and that "we were already under the sea." In a moment she was up to her knees in green water and was gone.

Theodate Pope and Edwin Friend decided to jump. He would not get in a lifeboat while women and children were still on board, and she would not leave him. Also "the ship was sinking so quickly we feared she would fall on and capsize the small boats." They went to look for a good place to leap, and "turned to make our way up again through the crush of people." Walking close together, arms around each other's waist, they passed Marie de Page. The Belgian woman had just been bandaging boxing champion Matt Freeman's hand, which he had injured while helping crewmen try to lower the lifeboats. Madame de Page's eyes were "wide and startled but brave." Theodate saw that she had a man on either side of her who she assumed were her friends and "so I did not speak. It was no time for words unless one could offer help." Moments later, Madame de Page and one of the men, Dr. James Houghton, leaped into the sea in each other's arms.

Theodate Pope and Edwin Friend eventually reached the port side and pushed their way toward the stern, "which was now uphill work." Theodate's maid, Emily Robinson, joined them, "her habitual smile" seemingly frozen on her face. Friend found life jackets for them all. They "could now see the grey hull and knew it was time to jump." Theodate begged him to go first, which he did. He surfaced, and she saw "a pleasant smile of encouragement on his face." Theodate stepped forward, slipped, but then found a foothold on a roll of canvas. With a patrician instruction to her maid—"Come, Robinson"—she pushed off from the canvas and leaped into the sea.

Elizabeth Duckworth had climbed out of a lifeboat because of the difficulties in lowering it, only to watch in horror as it plummeted into the sea, tossing out its occupants, including her friend Alice Scott and Alice's little son, Arthur. She decided to await her fate and began to pray. Nearby she heard three Irish girls singing "There Is a Green Hill Not Far Away" in thin, frightened voices, twisting the words of the hymn to reassure themselves that land was near.

As water lapped over the Boat Deck, Fred Gauntlett lost his footing. He slid down the starboard side and collided painfully with a boat davit. Recovering, he put his left foot up onto the wooden rail, grabbed some rope lifeboat falls, and heaved himself over onto an unreleased lifeboat. He intended to use the ropes to swing himself across the boat and then leap into the sea since he "didn't want to get caught between the boat and the *Lusitania*." But as he made the attempt he heard from below a cry of "For God's sake, help me." Jumping down into the boat, he saw a woman struggling in the water between the boat and the ship. He grabbed her and pulled her in. Then he saw a man in the water holding a baby in his arms and managed to haul him up too, but "by that time the davits came down on the boat and carried her under." Gauntlett found himself "in the water practically up to my neck." Looking around, he "saw one of the funnels apparently coming right down on top of me" and swam for his life from under the shadow of the ship, only to become entangled in the ship's wireless antennae.

Commander Stackhouse, who had refused a seat in a lifeboat and given his life jacket to a little girl, was seen "standing, erect and smiling, without a life jacket on the boat deck." Journalist Ernest Cowper, who had helped little Helen Smith find a place in a lifeboat, flung himself into the sea.

Surgeon Major Warren Pearl abandoned his vain search for his missing children and nurse Alice Lines. He felt the ship make a sudden plunge and saw foaming water come rushing in over the forecastle. He just had time to grab several wooden planks to serve as support for his wife, remaining children, and other nurse when the sea overwhelmed them and sucked them beneath the greasy water.

Belle Naish and her husband, Theodore, were standing quietly on deck watching the rising water and discussing their options when "there seemed to be a great rush, a great roar and splintering sound, then the lifeboats or something swung over our heads." Belle threw up her left hand "to ward off a blow, then the water was up to my waist; it was dreadfully cold on my back below my shoulders; something seemed to push my feet upwards, and I felt as though I were shot upwards and forward, but saw and heard nothing."

Rita Jolivet had seen the fiasco of the lifeboats with women and children "thrown out" and decided to stay with Charles Frohman, Captain Alick Scott, and her brother-in-law, George Vernon. As the *Lusitania* lurched and rolled, Charles Frohman was still calmly philosophical. Seconds before the water engulfed them, he quoted a line from one of his greatest theatrical successes, *Peter Pan*: "Why fear death? It is the most beautiful adventure that life gives us." Rita Jolivet did not tell him that she was so terrified of drowning that she was carrying a little pearl-handled pistol with which to shoot herself in the water. As the little group huddled together and clasped hands, "a mighty green cliff of water came rushing up, bearing its tide of dead and debris." The water tore Rita Jolivet from her companions with such force that her buttoned boots were swept off her feet. The terrified woman felt herself sink, then rise, only to sink again.

Mrs. Henry Adams, who had sat her petrified husband on a collapsible boat while they awaited further orders from the captain, saw "a great wave come over the bow" and was similarly engulfed. Her husband was gone from her side forever. She found herself struggling for breath in pitch blackness deep beneath the surface.

Up in the wheelhouse Hugh Johnston saw that "the starboard wing of the bridge was level with the sea and it was coming over the rail." Some minutes earlier he had reported that the list to starboard had reached twenty-five degrees. He had received no response. He was now wondering whether Captain Turner, going from one side of the bridge to the other so that he could see along the length of each deck, had forgotten he was still there. To his relief, he heard the captain shout, "Quartermaster, save yourself." As Johnston hastily tied on a life jacket, he saw Bill Turner's lonely figure climb the ladder to the top bridge. Johnston "didn't have to do any jumping." Within moments he was "washed right across the ship" and carried wherever the tide took him. He struggled to keep his head up.

Other members of the crew were also abandoning ship. Senior Third Officer John Lewis was trying to make his way through the rising water and across to the port side to dive off when the ship went down under him. He had no life jacket. Third Engineer Robert Duncan "walked down the port side in nearly an upright position" into the water with Chief Engineer Archibald Bryce by his side. He never saw Bryce again. Chief Steward Jones "jumped into the water when the ship was sinking." Engineer Andrew Cockburn jumped from the rail in the final minute of the ship's life. First-Class Steward Robert Barnes slid down the deck to the rail as the *Lusitania*'s stern rose in the air. He leaped into the water with the sound of shouting and screaming ringing in his ears.

Bellboy Ben Holton had tried to help launch the lifeboats but gave up in despair. Looking toward the bridge, he saw a wretched-looking Captain Turner "watching the ship go down." Afraid to dive from the starboard side in case the funnels broke off, the boy slipped through a mass of "pushing and struggling" people, hopped on the rail under the bridge on the port side, and took a header into the Atlantic Ocean. It was "very, very cold." He put his head down and swam as fast as he could.

Third Officer Albert Bestic, still at his post on the port side, was "dragged down with the ship" but managed to grab hold of one of the collapsible lifeboats. So did Able Seaman Frank Hennessy, who hauled himself onto another collapsible boat floating upside down, only to find some twenty-five people on it so that "every time you got on to the bottom the boat would keep turning over all the time." Chief Third-Class Steward John Griffith was also washed off the Boat Deck into the sea to join the despairing white-faced human detritus "all bouncing around in the water."

Ship's Carpenter Neil Robertson was plunged into the sea to find "there were three collapsible boats, one on top of the other, and with the help of another man we pinched off the top boat." They broke off an oar in their efforts and damaged the boat, but it was still something to cling to.

Elderly Boatswain John Davies went down with the ship. He found himself thrashing helplessly in the water but was fortunate to be able to scramble onto an upturned collapsible boat. Later, with the help of two firemen, he climbed into another that was "right side up."

Some crewmen were determined to stay with the ship. An elderly bedroom steward named McLeod was grimly clinging on to the rail on the port side and refusing to budge. He told bellboy Clark, "She's been my home and now she will be my grave." The frightened boy had seen people killed and maimed by wreckage, including, he thought, Elbert Hubbard, "the great American author." The writer was "pretty well smashed up."

Able Seaman Thomas O'Mahoney saw "six or seven passengers try-ing to get down on to the deck from the awning spars" above the Veran-dah Café. One called to him for help, and the seaman told him to climb on his shoulders. At that moment the spars collapsed, and all the men came tumbling down on top of him. He scrambled up winded and bruised and saw that the ship was sinking rapidly. He decided to climb over the stern into the sea. He threw a rope over the side and swarmed down, only to discover he was suspended "over the propellers, which were still revolving slowly." In a panic, he heaved himself back up the rope onto the deck, now some sixty feet in the air, and jumped from far-ther forward, landing painfully in a tangle of wreckage.

George Wynne, still wearing his galley clothes of white undershirt, check trousers, and slippers, was amazed by the chaos: "Chairs was being thrown over, bodies was jumping over." Knowing his son could not swim, Joseph Wynne had rushed in search of a life jacket for him. Meanwhile another man pushed the cook toward the rail, telling him it was no use waiting for anyone—time had run out. The distraught young man, still shuddering at the memory of his colleagues trapped in the elevators and screaming for help, hesitated, then jumped overboard. Trimmers and

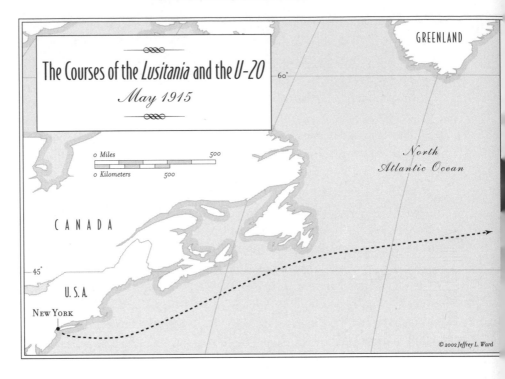

firemen ripped off their heavy stokehold boots and jumped with him as the ship began her dive under the waves.

Captain Schwieger's war diary described the death of the *Lusitania* in some detail:

> *2.10 p.m.* Great confusion on board; boats are cleared away and some are lowered into the water. Apparently considerable panic; several boats, fully laden, are hurriedly lowered, bow or stern first and are swamped at once. Because of the list fewer boats can be cleared away on the port side. . . . The ship blows off steam; the name *Lusitania* is visible in gold letters on the bows. . . .

> *2.25 p.m.* Since it seems as if the steamer can only remain afloat a short while longer, dive to 24 meters and head out to sea. Also it would have been impossible for me to fire a second torpedo into this crushing crowd of humanity trying to save their lives.

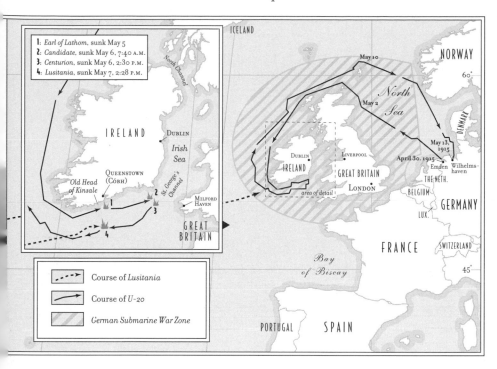

1: *Earl of Lathom*, sunk May 5
2: *Candidate*, sunk May 6, 7:40 A.M.
3: *Centurion*, sunk May 6, 2:30 P.M.
4: *Lusitania*, sunk May 7, 2:28 P.M.

- - - - ▶   Course of *Lusitania*

———▶   Course of *U-20*

▨▨▨   *German Submarine War Zone*

It was, as the *U-20*'s radio officer, Otto Rikowsky, described it, "not pretty," not even for seasoned U-boatmen. Schwieger later told his friend Max Valentiner: "The ship was sinking with unbelievable rapidity. There was a terrible panic on her deck. Overcrowded lifeboats, fairly torn from their positions, dropped into the water. Desperate men ran helplessly up and down the decks. Men and women jumped into the water and tried to swim to empty, overturned lifeboats. It was the most terrible sight I have ever seen. It was impossible for me to give any help. I could have saved only a handful. And then the cruiser that had passed us was not very far away. . . . She would shortly appear, I thought. The scene was too horrible to watch, and I gave orders to dive to twenty meters and away."

For those he was leaving behind, the struggle was far from over.

CHAPTER EIGHTEEN

A Long Lingering Moan

S THE *Lusitania* plowed into the sea, water rushed into her collapsing stacks. Margaret Gwyer was sucked deep inside the cavernous vent of a funnel. Moments later she was amazed to be shot out again in a huge column of ashes, soot, and oily black water. Most of her clothing had been torn off. Detective-Inspector William Pierpoint also was drawn down a stack, then ejected "as air rushed out with a terrible hissing sound." He began "swimming like ten men" he was so scared.

Some were caught by the funnel stays and dragged under. Others found themselves ensnared by the ship's falling wireless aerials, sharp enough to slice a collapsible boat "in two like so much paper." Charles Lauriat, splashing about in the water, felt one graze the top of his head, slip down to his shoulders, and push him under. Before he understood what was happening, it had turned him upside down. He kicked out hard to escape. James Brooks swam as fast as he could from the ship but was appalled to see wires descending right over him. He dodged the first, managed to fend off the second while it was still in the air, and pushed himself hastily back. The wire passed over his toes.

Professor Holbourn, struggling amid the debris in the water, found himself caught in a tangled web of ropes. He managed to free himself and continued to look around anxiously for Avis Dolphin. Glancing back, he saw the *Lusitania* about to take her final plunge. Like many others, he forgot his own plight for a moment, transfixed by the shocking, almost incredible sight. To Oliver Bernard it had "something of picturesque grandeur about it, even tho' we knew that many hundreds of help-less souls, caught like rats in a gilded trap, were in her." Lifeboats were still hanging lopsidedly and futilely from the davits. A man dangling from a rope over the ship's stern was heard to shriek as a still-revolving propeller sliced off his leg. The stern itself "was crowded with people who seemed to make for the last piece of the wreck left above water; while others, unsuccessful in their efforts to gain this temporary safe place, were falling over the side. All around were wreckage and human beings struggling for life." The sea was a mass of "waving hands and arms, belonging to struggling men and frantic women and children in agoniz-ing efforts to keep afloat."

Third Officer Albert Bestic hung on to an upturned collapsible lifeboat and shuddered at the awful sound, "like the despair, anguish and terror of hundreds of souls passing into eternity." Charles Lauriat heard "a long lingering moan"—"they who were lost seemed to be calling from the very depths." Leslie Morton, swimming on his back, watched as the stern reared yet higher in the air. "The propellers became visible and the rudder, and she went into a slow, almost stately dive by the head, at an angle of some forty-five or fifty degrees."

In those last seconds the ship's nose hit the seabed some 340 feet below and pivoted. Bellboy Ben Holton heard "a roar like thunder inside

Oliver Bernard's sketch of the Lusitania's *funnels just before they disappeared under the sea.*

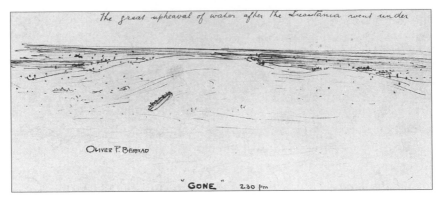

The great upheaval of water after the Lusitania went under

Oliver P. Bernad

"GONE" 2.30 pm

Oliver Bernard recorded the upheaval of water after the Lusitania *went under.*

the ship as if the vital parts had broken loose." To James Brooks, it sounded like "the collapse of a great building during a fire." As the *Lusitania* slid down into the water, some onlookers thought she nearly righted herself. Then the "mighty crescendo of screams and cries of fear ... died away to a whisper" as the ship turned slowly onto her starboard side "and went under the water." At 2:28, a mere eighteen minutes after the *U-20* had attacked, the *Lusitania* had disappeared.

Within moments Steward Barnes and Seaman Thomas O'Mahoney felt a "violent underwater explosion." Holton saw "clouds of steam and surging water" over the spot where the ship had gone down. The ocean seethed. To Oliver Bernard, it was "a boiling wilderness that rose up as if a volcanic disturbance had occurred beneath a placid sea." The mound of foaming water sent "swimmers, corpses, deckchairs, oars, and ... wreckage churning upwards to the surface." Harold Boulton instinctively shielded his head with his hands as a tidal wave of debris surged toward him.

As the waters gradually stilled, they left a pathetic residue, "a circle of people and wreckage about half a mile across." In places the wreckage was so thickly clotted that it formed "an undulating horrible mattress of deckchairs, oars, boxes and human heads." Many bodies had been "mangled or disfigured in the surge and grinding of the wreckage so as to stain the ocean with blood."

Those in the water—some with life jackets, some without—fought for survival. Flor Sullivan, torn away from Julia and clinging to a box with nine others, saw a woman in the water nearby hold up her bag and shout,

"This is my purse. It contains nothing but money and I will give it to any-one who saves me." A man answered, "I will." She threw him the purse, but as he grabbed for it he upturned the box so that everyone holding on to it went under. Flor Sullivan was the only one to resurface. To actress Josephine Brandell, "the cries for mercy, the people drowning and com-ing up again . . . were too terrible." As she clung to an oar, people gasping in the water beside her asked hysterically whether she had seen their loved ones. Those with sufficient presence of mind looked toward land in the hope of seeing rescue ships steaming out from Queenstown. There was nothing. They could only cling to wreckage and hope to be picked up by one of the wooden lifeboats or collapsibles that had got away from the *Lusitania*.

In some cases they had most to fear from each other. Steward Barnes came to the surface after leaping from the rail, only to be grabbed by two desperate men seeking something to hang on to. Fear-ing they would drown him, he dived to free himself. Matt Freeman, the boxing champion, had gashed his head open when he dived into the sea, then struggled with five other men for a hold on a barrel that clearly could not support them all. In desperation he let go but managed to grab the keel of an upturned lifeboat. Theodate Pope also had an unnerving experience. Having jumped into the water, she found she could not reach the surface because she was "being washed and whirled up against wood." Opening her eyes, she saw through the green water that she was being dashed against the keel of a lifeboat. Something hit her hard on the head, but she was saved from serious injury by her hair and "stiff straw hat." Half stunned, she surfaced at last to find she was being jos-tled by "hundreds of frantic, screaming, shouting humans in this grey and watery inferno."

"People all around me in the water were fighting, striking and strug-gling," she later recalled. Then a man "insane with fright" made "a sud-den jump and landed clean on my shoulders, believing I could support him." He had no life jacket, and his weight was pushing her back under. Somehow she found the strength to say "Oh, please don't" before the waters closed over her again. Feeling her sink, the man let go. Theodate surfaced to find herself floating on her back. She looked around for Edwin Friend. Instead she saw close by her an elderly man, another man with a bloody gash in his forehead, and a third clasping a small tin tank as a float. Seeing an oar floating nearby, she pushed one end toward the old man and took hold of the other. She decided it was all "too horrible to be true" and that she was dreaming. Moments later she lost consciousness.

Margaret Mackworth also felt threatened by others. Sucked from the deck into the sea, she found herself "deep down under the water." It was "very dark, nearly black." She fought to come up, but her wrist was trapped by a rope. She managed to jerk free, though the rope burns left a scar she would carry all her life. Trying not to swallow any more water, she floated up toward the light. Something was impeding her movements, and she realized it was the life jacket she had been holding for her father. As she reached the surface, she managed to grab a piece of board. It was thin—just a few inches wide and some two or three feet long. She hoped it would keep her afloat.

Feeling "slightly stupefied," she looked around her to find that she was now "part of a large, round, floating island composed of people and debris of all sorts, lying so close together that at first there was not very much water noticeable in between." She saw "people, boats, hencoops, chairs, rafts, boards and goodness knows what besides, all floating cheek by jowl." Then a man with "a white face and yellow moustache" grabbed hold of one end of her board. She feared it could not hold them both but felt she could not object. Then he began edging around toward her. Instinct told her "he wanted to hold on to me." She summoned the courage to ask him to go back to his own end, which he did. Later she noticed he had disappeared and wondered whether he had gone off to "a hencoop which was floating near by."

In the fear and confusion people took any chance they could. Fireman O'Connell, clinging to a plank, was attacked by three men who tried to grab it from him. Archie Donald saw the macabre sight of "a grand lady" who had been thrown into the sea but had found "something to hold on to." That "something" was "a dead man. She straddled her legs over him and they rose to the top." Others too clung doggedly to corpses. Doris Lawlor saw "a person who had died in the water and another person sitting on top of that person trying to survive." A passenger who could not swim was supporting himself by clinging to "a life jacket with a dead woman in it."

Dead and drowning people were "dotting the sea like seagulls." Many bodies were floating upside down because people had put their life jackets on the wrong way up. Others had put the jackets on back to front, so that their heads were pushed under the water. One man, clinging to a waterlogged boat, watched with horror "the drowning struggles of a group composed of a woman and infant and a gray-bearded, feeble old man" right beside him, unable to do anything to help.

Alice Middleton, a children's nurse from Seattle, was one of the women Vanderbilt had helped. Sinking under the water, she got her head jammed in a half-open porthole. The pressure was so intense she thought her eardrums had burst. Somehow she managed to get free and rise to the surface. The first thing she saw was a screaming woman in the process of giving birth. It seemed to Alice a final irony that, as she did so, the waters around her were full of dead children floating like drowned dolls.

Michael Byrne was also horrified by "the bodies of infants laid in life jackets, and floating around with their dead innocent faces looking towards the sky." As he swam he had to push them aside "like lily pads on a pond."

Parents tried desperately to hold their children out of the water. Bellboy Ben Holton, clinging to an upturned dog kennel, watched a man pathetically pushing a dying child along on a folded life jacket "trying to do his best."

Others had already lost their children. Mabel Henshaw had been clutching her baby, Constance, as she fell into the sea. Mabel was a good swimmer, but as the *Lusitania* sank she found herself pulled "down and down and down." The force of the water "sucked the baby" right out of her arms. Just before this had happened, according to Mabel: "[I] looked at her and I knew she was dead. . . . I guess I almost smothered her, I held her so tight." Despite her anguish, at least she knew—or thought she knew—that her child had died peacefully.

Charlotte Pye, whom Vanderbilt had also helped, had lost her little baby, Marjorie. Clutching the infant, Charlotte fell from a lifeboat, and the next thing she knew she was in the water. "My baby gave a terrible scream and we both sank. When I came up the baby was gone and I was dragged under a second time." When Charlotte finally surfaced, all she could see were dead bodies "and those that were living were screaming and shouting, wanting to be saved." She drifted on with the tide, washing up against an upturned boat. A man was sitting on top of it with a dead woman sprawled beside him. A collapsible boat rowed toward them. Charlotte dimly heard someone shout, "Take the lady on, for God's sake, she's almost gone." For a moment the occupants debated whether to help her. Then she was pulled on board. Covered in grease and soot from the water, she could do nothing but sit there "crying and wanting my baby" and knowing she would never see her again. The child had met "such a terrible end." She tormented herself that "she could have taken better care of her." Her will to live was gone, and she took no interest in efforts to row the boat in the direction of Queenstown.

Another mother fought a losing battle to keep her three young children afloat. By the time she was pulled into a boat, two were already dead. Realizing that space in the boat was needed for the living, she "gave the bodies to the sea herself," saying, "They are mine to bury as they were mine to keep." Her third child died moments later.

One woman was in the water with her baby for two hours before being pulled aboard a lifeboat. As another later recalled: "Just as we got her to the raft . . . her baby girl closed its tiny eyes in her arms. Almost overcome with exhaustion the mother caught hold of the side of our boat, the lifeless mite still close to her heart, and when we got her into the boat she could hardly speak. For a few moments her eyes were centred on her baby. Then, lifting the little one in her arms, she turned to those in the boat, and, in a tearful voice simply said, 'Let me bury my baby.' Within a few seconds the almost naked body of the child floated peacefully on the sea."

Canadian Percy Rogers saw one young child wearing a life jacket and crying for her mother. He could not reach her and had to watch her die. Soren Sorenson, the poker player who had been so reluctant to leave his game when the ship was hit, watched a mother trying to save a child of about one year by putting it on some wreckage, but it died and she "let it go." The small bundle drifted away. An Irish couple, Walter and Nettie Moore, were gripping an upturned lifeboat. Walter was trying to hold their baby son out of the water, but as time passed the child's skin turned a dark, bruised color and froth appeared on his lips. They realized he was dead. By now Walter was losing consciousness. Whispering "I can't hold on any more, Nettie," he slid under the water still clasping his son's lifeless body.

Margaret Cox was more fortunate. After throwing her baby son, Desmond, into a lifeboat from the *Lusitania*'s deck, she had been pushed after him. The boat was successfully lowered, but at first she had a struggle to get her son back. Desmond was "yelling his head off." When she tried to pick him up, hysterical people shouted, "We don't know if it's your baby or not." Margaret insisted. Sitting in the lifeboat, clutching Desmond to her, she tried not to look at "the people that swam up . . . and begged to be taken in." The boat was bursting, with people "packed one on top of the other." She knew it was impossible to help, but the "horror of a scene like that" was overwhelming and she felt herself go "a little mad." A man in the boat was repeating over and over that there were some very important papers he must have. She heard herself shout angrily, "Put him overboard papers and all!"

Norah Bretherton and her son, Paul, were also lucky to be in a lifeboat commanded by "a splendid seaman" which pulled away safely. However, she had no idea what had happened to her daughter, Betty, in the confusion.

Some children had been tied onto chairs or placed on pieces of wreckage. Others were struggling in the waves. Isaac Lehmann, washed overboard after his attempt to get a lifeboat lowered at gunpoint, found a little baby beside him in the water. He and another man managed to lift it on to one of the steamer chairs bobbing past. They kept it alive for an hour and a half, but as they watched, "it died from exposure." Nine-year-old Edith Williams, separated from her mother and five siblings, was saved by a young woman who saw her being swept away and managed to grab hold of her skirt. Against all odds, Avis Dolphin had managed to surface, choking and spluttering. She owed her life to the fact that Professor Holbourn had tied on her life jacket correctly. Looking around, she saw no sign of the two nurses or of anyone else who had been in the lifeboat with her. Eventually she was picked up by a lone man in a collapsible boat.

As time passed, the tight-packed mass of people and wreckage began to drift apart with the current. People were becoming paralyzed with cold—the water temperature was only about 52° F (11° C)—and their hands were losing their grip on pieces of wreckage as their blood vessels constricted. Many were losing consciousness as their bodies' core temperature dropped below 95° F (35° C). The first symptom of hypothermia is an intense feeling of cold. The body responds by shivering, constricting the flow of blood to arms and legs and releasing catabolic hormones like adrenaline to convert stored sugars into energy and heat. But as time passes, this ceases to have any effect, and body temperature drops further. Below 89.6° F (32° C) the brain function is impaired. One begins to feel disoriented and have delusions. The metabolism slows so that one burns less glucose and therefore produces less heat. Heart rate also slows to one beat every few seconds. When the core temperature falls below

86° F (3o° C), death is not far off, probably from ventricular fibrillation, when the heart muscle merely twitches instead of beating. Those most at risk from hypothermia are the old, whose thermoregulatory mechanisms are poor, small people, and the very young.

The *Lusitania* survivors in the water who were still conscious could only hope that a lifeboat would soon come to their rescue. But many boats were now full to capacity, and their traumatized occupants were terrified of taking on more people and capsizing. The occupants of other boats, which were still relatively empty, worried that if they approached the knots of people struggling in the water they would be swamped.

Professor Holbourn made for the nearest lifeboat he could see, trying to help a man floating nearby by pushing him along. Reaching the boat, he was shocked to find his companion was dead. Even worse, the people inside the boat refused to take Holbourn aboard. In desperation, teeth chattering with cold, he tossed his manuscripts in, hoping that they at least would be saved. Then he took hold of a line trailing from the stern of the boat and grimly hung on.

Spotting an empty boat floating some yards away, the occupants of the first boat rowed toward it. But progress was agonizingly slow. Holbourn felt he could not last much longer. He asked repeatedly how near it was. Each time, he was told to hang on for another five minutes. After what seemed "an interminable age," the exhausted man begged someone in the boat to hold his hand. It was futile: "So deadening . . . is the sight of wholesale horror that they actually refused to do so as it was 'uncomfortable.'" At last he was dragged into the second boat but climbed determinedly back into the first one to retrieve the sodden remains of his precious papers. The inhumanity of what he had suffered, coupled with "the sight and sound of the people drowning all around," was too much. He tried to shut his eyes and ears.

Mabel Henshaw, desolate after the loss of her baby, also met with callous indifference. She had been floating around in a state of shock and with most of her clothes torn off. Coming to her senses a little, she managed to find an oar. Then, seeing some men on an overturned boat, she swam over to them. She offered them the oar if they would help her, but they refused. Shocked at their reaction, she swam away, taking her oar with her. Someone nearby was singing "Abide with Me." It comforted her a little, but she found she could think of nothing but "the loss of the baby." Before long she blacked out.

Charles Hill was also dismayed by the determined selfishness of his fellow passengers. He had been repeatedly dumped into the sea because his lifeboat had no plugs and had kept filling with water and capsizing. The ship's barber, Lott Gadd, who had helped to lower the boat, swam away to find another one. As Hill thrashed in the water and began to go under again, he had the irrelevant thought that "I hadn't paid the barber for my week's shaves." He almost laughed. But moments later, as he tried to swim to the surface, he felt he was "dragging something heavy." When he came up he found that "a woman with a child in her arms was hanging on to my right leg and an old man was clutching me round the left ankle which made me lose my left shoe." Rising to the surface, he heard one of the men in the boat say, "Don't pull them in, they are nearly dead anyway and we must lighten the boat." To Hill's relief, one of the stokers, a mere boy of eighteen, "insisted on saving us and pulled us into the boat."

In another boat, when a male passenger suggested to the other occupants that they should try to pick up survivors, they refused. He decided that "it was as much as his life was worth to suggest it again." When an exhausted Michael Byrne put his head over the side of a collapsible boat, the people inside shouted, "This boat is full." He tried again fifteen minutes later and was lucky to be spotted by a steward who exclaimed, "Oh, Mr. Byrne, I am glad to see you." The shivering Byrne gasped, "If you are, please pull me in," which the steward did.

Lucy Taylor was distressed by the inhumanity she witnessed. Convinced her husband, Harold, was dead, she was sitting numb and miserable in her lifeboat when some people foundering in the water tried to clamber in. She watched appalled as her fellow passengers set about "rapping their knuckles" to make them drop off. She reflected that "everyone was for themselves . . . but it seemed terrible to me to do that."

Mrs. Henry Adams, washed overboard and separated from the husband she had tried so hard to protect, was dragged onto a floating raft only at the insistence of the one woman on it. The men had wanted to leave her.

But many passengers and crew did do their best to help one another. Charles Lauriat, Fred Gauntlett, and James Brooks climbed onto a collapsible lifeboat. Getting out their penknives, they "went at a kind of can-opening operation" to try and raise the boat's canvas sides and lash them in place. But it was difficult. Terrified, half-drowning people were hanging to the rail to which the canvas was attached. It was impossible to lift it into place. Lauriat tried to persuade them to let go and hold on to the life ropes instead. But they were convinced he meant to "push them off." Lauriat later wrote that he had never heard "a more distressing cry of despair" than when he appealed to them to relinquish the rail for a few moments.

At last they managed to raise the sides but Lauriat noted they "were unable to make them stay in position until we picked up some pieces of wreckage and placed it under the seats." The boat's collapsible seats were supposed to help hold up the sides, but the tackle for raising them was rusted and broken. Also, there were no oars. They "had to go overboard and get the oars out of the ocean and swim around till we found them." They were fortunate to find five. One was broken, but the resourceful Lauriat used it as a rudder. By this time there were fifteen people in the precarious craft, some of whom had fallen and injured themselves among the half-erected seats.

They picked up more people, loading the boat "until it sunk flush with the water." They took "those whom we could help," but Lauriat realized that there were "many, many past human assistance." One woman impressed him with her courage. When there were "about as many in our boat as we ought to take," Lauriat heard her say, "in just as natural a tone of voice as you would ask for another slice of bread and butter, 'Won't you take me next? You know I can't swim.'" He peered into the debris around the boat to see "a woman's head, with a piece of wreckage under her chin and with her hair streaming out. . . . She was so jammed in she couldn't even get her arms out, and with it all she had a half smile on her face and was placidly chewing gum." Lauriat told her "that if she'd keep cool," he'd come for her. She replied that "it was not at all necessary, just hand her an oar and she'd hang on." He managed to maneuver around to her and pull her in.

They started to row for the shore, making for the lighthouse on the Old Head of Kinsale, helped by two redheaded stokers whose language was "something to remember." After about a quarter of a mile Lauriat was astonished to see a lone man floating around by himself who yelled when he saw them. Although the boat, with some thirty-two crammed in, was full, Lauriat felt "you couldn't go off and leave that one more soul floating around." He picked him up.

Elizabeth Duckworth was resolutely determined to save lives. At the last moment she had found a place in a lifeboat that got away safely. At first she was so overcome by all the terrible sights that she began to recite the Twenty-third Psalm. Then, rousing herself, she saw a man "struggling in the water right near our boat and I said to the mate: 'Can't we help him?' He said 'No.' I said, 'Yes, we can.'" After "a very hard struggle," they succeeded in pulling him in.

Archie Donald and another passenger managed to force up the canvas sides of a collapsible lifeboat. They "started to take those who had come to the surface"—finding it "a most terrible thing to see the people struggling for their lives"—but it seemed a monumental task. Looking back to where the ship had gone down, Donald could see that "the water was black with people; every available piece of wreckage seemed to be covered, and still there were hundreds in the water." He did not dare go too close but managed to rescue thirty-four. These included a woman dressed only in a thin petticoat and blouse, with a two-inch gash to her head and cuts on her back, all bleeding profusely. Despite her injuries, she at once began working to save others, "giving artificial respiration to two people."

Charles Bowring reached a lifeboat together with one of the ship's officers. It was half full of water, and the two men baled out frantically with their hands. Then they spent the next few hours "diving in and out of the water, rescuing as many as we could." Although they managed to pull about twenty in safely, "most of the people we got hold of were already dead."

Oliver Bernard was also at work. He had managed to clamber into a badly waterlogged boat, helped to bale it out, and begun rowing hard, sharing an oar with a steward. Even in these desperate moments Bernard's artist's eye took in the surrounding scene. He watched, fascinated, as, "like a famous picture of Ophelia, a woman's face came floating just level with and green as the sea." Bernard and the steward hauled her in over the gunwale and propped her up against Bernard's knees. There was "a frothy mucous on her lips," and "she remained peering blindly as if at some enigma of this world or that which she discerned beyond."

Belle Naish, who had given so much generous help to others, was lucky to be picked up by a lifeboat. After being thrown from the ship, she had found herself lying on her back in the water, resting on the pillow of her life jacket. She was thinking "how wondrously beautiful the sunlight and the water were from under the surface" when something bumped her head. Putting up her hand, she caught the bumper of a lifeboat. She was pulled in shivering with cold and "with chattering teeth." She could hear a man playing a harmonica. Then someone said they would be unable to hear the cries for help, and he stopped.

Amy Pearl, separated from the rest of her family and hanging on to a piece of board, dazedly heard a voice call out, "Somebody save that woman." A man perched on an upturned lifeboat managed to pull her up beside him. Her husband, Surgeon Major Warren Pearl, who had been pulled down "five or six times by suction," was in the water for over three hours clinging to first a plank, then a deck chair, then a box, and finally a tin can before being helped into a collapsible boat.

Many owed their lives to crew members. First Officer Arthur Jones managed to transfer some of the passengers from his heavily loaded lifeboat into another boat and ordered both back to pick up more survivors. He dragged the heavy, over 200-pound Isaac Lehmann into a boat after four hours in the water. Able Seaman Thomas O'Mahoney managed to climb on a collapsible boat. With the help of another seaman, he succeeded in freeing it from the surrounding debris and began to pull other exhausted survivors aboard. Josephine Brandell was hauled onto a boat by Assistant Purser Harkless, who at first thought she was dead. Ship's Carpenter Neil Robertson saved a drowning Texan by helping him into a damaged collapsible. The grateful man later wrote a heartfelt letter thanking him for acting "as a good seaman and a brave man." Leslie Morton would be commended for his dedication in searching for survivors. Leo Thompson, who had managed to scramble back into the boat from which he had fallen when it became momentarily trapped under the Marconi wires, also did his best to gather up survivors.

But it was distressing work. Crewman Brennan had dived overboard, then surfaced minus his overalls and underpants. Now he was naked from the waist down, wearing just an undershirt and waistcoat. Nevertheless, he helped pull people onto an upturned boat only to watch many die of exposure. As the minutes turned to hours, they began "just driftin' away, water was cold, see. They were lettin' go, we couldn't do nothin' for them . . . you couldn't hold on to them." He was particularly distressed by the dead and dying children. At 1 P.M. he had been "turnin' a skipping rope for them" on deck. Now they bobbed past him facedown and lifeless.

Captain Turner was also saved by a crewman. As the waters had risen around him on the *Lusitania*'s bridge, he had felt his way along the mast and jumped, managing to clear the Marconi wires and swim to the surface. He clung first to an oar, then a chair. But as the hours passed, he found himself "constantly fighting off attacks by seagulls." He later described how the birds "swooped down on the dazed and benumbed people floating helplessly on the surface and pecked their eyes out." Weakening through cold and exposure, he "flung up a gold-braided arm" to attract attention. Jack Roper, a crewman, saw him and helped support him in the water until a rescue craft picked him up. Turner apparently remarked, "What bad luck. . . . What have I done to deserve this?"

Some of those rescued had been horribly injured by explosions or by debris. A trimmer balanced on a collapsible boat reached into the water to help a man, grabbing him by the arm. The next thing he saw was the man's other arm almost completely severed except for "a little skin." Joseph Myers was finally pulled onto a collapsible boat with a broken leg and smashed ribs. Ogden Hammond was dazed with pain from the hand he had skinned and broken grabbing the rope falls of the lifeboat he and his wife had tumbled from. He was eventually pulled into a boat, and a steward lent him a coat. Another passenger later recognized the trauma-tized man as the millionaire American by his "fashionable yellow boots and spats."

Floating in the water or perched on pieces of wreckage, those still conscious wondered when it would be their turn for rescue and whether they could survive that long. "We were all choking for a drink of water, our tongues were swollen," recalled one survivor. The "really blinding" sunshine seemed an additional torment.

Margaret Mackworth was dimly aware of people "praying aloud in a curious, unemotional monotone" and shouting for help "in the same slow, impersonal way, calling 'Bo-at . . . bo-at . . . bo-at.'" Her legs were becoming bitterly cold. She tried to swim to a boat but gave up after a few stokes, reluctant to abandon the board that she was still holding. She felt dazed and stupid, unable to collect her thoughts. She wondered vaguely whether the whole thing was a nightmare. Then, gazing at the pale blue sky and the calm, sparkling sea, she wondered "half-laughing" whether she was already dead and in heaven. But the motion of the water was making her feel seasick, and she realized she was still wretchedly alive, if only just.

The Reverend Simpson, perched on an upturned boat, "tied a pair of trousers to an oar and hoisted it as a signal of distress." The Welsh singer Parry Jones was clinging to a raft. Dr. Howard Fisher was floating on an upturned lifeboat with Lady Allan, who had a broken collarbone as well as an injured arm. There was no sign of her pretty young daughters, Anna and Gwen.

Quartermaster Hugh Johnston had managed to reach an upturned boat, where he was eventually joined by six other men. They shadow-boxed to keep warm. Meanwhile, Albert Bestic, carried away by the current, was feeling abandoned and alone as he struggled to remain afloat. For a time he had heard children wailing eerily, but gradually the cries had ceased.

Acting Senior Third Officer John Lewis was holding grimly to a piece of a boat chock. Sometimes he was on top of the chock, then it swung around so he was underneath. This motion was exhausting, and he was glad to exchange the chock after a while for a collapsible boat "floating stem up," which he was able to cling to.

James Leary was huddling with some twenty others on a collapsible boat. They had been unable to cut off the canvas cover. Every so often they were washed off by the waves and had to struggle back on again. Not everyone was strong enough. "Every once in a while we would miss one or two, bodies would float around, and we would push them away when they were dead."

George Wynne was adrift in the water but still living. At first he had been pulled into a boat just as the *Lusitania* was sinking and sat shuddering at the sight of "bodies swimming in the water" and "people trying to get into the boat." He could see no sign of his father's thin, spare figure in his scullion's clothing. When the boat began filling with water, Wynne baled out frantically with his slippers, but it was no use. The waterlogged boat capsized. Now, as the exhausted man drifted into unconsciousness in the cold water, he realized that someone must have tied him to some wreckage and that, miraculously, he was still afloat.

Rita Jolivet, torn from her friends by the force of the water, had sunk twice. There was no time to think about her little revolver as she struggled for breath. Coming up for the second time, she had managed to grab hold of an upturned lifeboat. It seemed very precarious. "A great many other people were clinging on to it, we were sinking." To her relief, a collapsible boat floated out from under it and "carried away the extra people."

Elizabeth Lassetter had found herself "in swirling water near the wash of the propeller" when suddenly she heard her son, Fred, call out. The two of them clung to some wreckage. Then they saw Harold Boulton floating on "a square box about 4 feet 6 inches," probably one of those used to store life jackets on deck. He helped his friend Fred get Elizabeth onto the box. Although she was knocked over several times by the swell, they at last managed to position her in the center and linked arms to hold the fainting woman up.

Bellboy Clark survived by clinging for four hours to bits of wreckage, including deck chairs. At last the exhausted boy was picked up by a collapsible boat but was almost instantly ordered out again to make space for women. Chilled and frightened, he was allowed to hang on to the side of the boat. He wondered whether he would be able to last.

Radio Officer Bob Leith, who had leaped into one lifeboat from another to escape the ship's falling stacks, gazed toward the land that seemed so ludicrously close. Where were the ships that should have been responding to his SOS call? To his horrified surprise, he could see nothing.

———

At 3:15 P.M., just over an hour after attacking the *Lusitania*, Walther Schwieger took one last look through his periscope. His war diary described the scene: "Astern, in the distance, a number of lifeboats are drifting; the *Lusitania* is no more to be seen." Five minutes later, he spotted another Cunard vessel. She was a two-masted freighter. Schwieger raced to get ahead of her and ordered a stern shot. This time, though, the torpedo missed. Oblivious to her own recent danger, or to the tragedy still unfolding barely a mile away on that lovely afternoon, the freighter continued on her way.

CHAPTER NINETEEN

Rescues and Recoveries

U.S. CONSUL WESLEY FROST was working quietly in his office above O'Reilly's bar in Queenstown when his agitated vice consul came running up the stairs. Lewis Thompson told Frost that there was "a wildfire rumor about town that the *Lusitania* had been attacked." Moving quickly to the window, the two men saw "a very unusual stir in the harbor." As they continued to stare, "the harbor's 'mosquito fleet' of tugs, tenders and trawlers, some two dozen in all, began to steam past the town toward the harbor-mouth." Frost immediately rang the Cunard office, which "admitted . . . that it appeared probable that the vessel was sunk or sinking." Now thoroughly alarmed, Frost telephoned Admiralty House, Vice Admiral Coke's headquarters. Lieutenant Norcocks, Coke's secretary, told him somberly, "It's true. . . . We fear she has gone."

Bob Leith's frantic SOS messages had been picked up by stations along the Irish coast, which had at once relayed the news to Coke at the Naval Centre in Queenstown. At 2:20 P.M. he had received the *Lusitania*'s direct cry for help: "COME AT ONCE—BIG LIST." Almost simultaneously came another forwarded message: "*LUSITANIA* TEN MILES SOUTH EAST APPARENTLY SINKING." At 2:41 P.M. a terse message from the signal station at Kinsale confirmed the worst. It said simply: "*LUSITANIA* SUNK."

Frost listened mechanically to the meager information Norcocks was able to give him. Replacing the receiver, he needed a few moments to recover from the "unforgettable mental shock." Collecting himself, he told Thompson to cable the news to the U.S. consul general Skinner in

London. He himself dashed to the Munster and Leinster Bank to withdraw all the gold in the consulate's deposit account and borrow an additional £200 in gold in case he needed it to help American survivors. He then dispatched Thompson by car to Kinsale, some eighteen miles away, with £100 to help any U.S. passengers who were landed there. Next, and with a heavy heart, he cabled Secretary of State William Bryan in Washington: "*LUSITANIA* SUNK 2.30 TODAY PROBABLY MANY SURVIVORS RESCUE WORK ENERGETICALLY PROCEEDING SHALL I CABLE LIST OF SURVIVORS?" The worst thing now would be the waiting since none of the small rescue craft had wireless. Frost noted gloomily that "no news could be had until they returned."

Throughout the town came the cry "the *Lusy*'s gone." Some persons along the coast had heard explosions and seen clouds of black smoke on the horizon. Fishermen, coastguardsmen, and schoolchildren, gathered on the Kinsale headland, had actually witnessed the ship's final moments. Fifteen-year-old John Murphy heard "a sort of heavy rumble like a distant foghorn" as the torpedo detonated. In Kinsale itself, the town dentist, Ernest Wolfe, received a phone call from the lighthouse on the Old Head of Kinsale to say that the liner had been struck. He closed up his practice and took his little daughter, Constance, high up on the town ramparts and watched a stream of little boats heading out of the harbor.

In Queenstown, shocked local Cunard agent Jerome Murphy was alerting the Royal Hospital, the volunteer first-aid corps, and the mortuaries. He also toured the town's hotels, putting them on standby to take in survivors. The town's leading hotel was the Queen's Hotel, owned for twenty years by a naturalized German, Otto Humbert. It faced the harbor, and an electric beacon shone from its roof as a welcoming guide to passengers arriving by sea after dark. Now its guests prepared to welcome survivors. Amy Biddulph, who was convalescing there, set to work with other women to make up fifty beds. Just as they were finishing, they were told "to prepare one hundred more."

Murphy also sent a series of messages to Cunard's headquarters in Liverpool, informing the staff there that the ship had been sunk and giving the approximate time and position. He also told them: "NO INTELLIGENCE AS TO CREW OR PASSENGERS." The first telegram, sent at 3:25 P.M., did not reach Liverpool until 5 P.M. because the Admiralty censor delayed it. But by early evening, rumors were spreading throughout the city, and anxious crowds were converging on Cunard's offices. In London Lloyd's posted a bulletin announcing the disaster shortly before 5 P.M. At 5:15 the foreign office issued a statement.

Admiral Fisher and Rear Admiral Oliver learned of the sinking from Coke shortly before 3 P.M. He told them he was sending all available tugs and small craft to the stricken liner's assistance. Churchill, in France at Sir John French's headquarters and preoccupied with news of a full-scale battle in the Dardanelles, was not told of the disaster until later that day. In New York, Cunard manager Charles Sumner received the news by cable during the course of the morning. According to one newspaper-man, he started trembling so badly he seemed likely to collapse: "She's gone," he said with a gasp. "What in God's name am I to do now?"

Meanwhile, Coke's small force of converted fishing trawlers, armed naval patrol craft, and elderly torpedo boats was steaming to the scene of the wreck some twenty-five miles from Queenstown. The steamer *Katrina*, several local fishing craft outside the harbor, and some auxiliary vessels joined the rescue. After conferring rapidly with Vice Admiral Hood, Coke had also ordered the elderly cruiser *Juno* to the *Lusitania*'s aid. The *Juno* had only just moored in the harbor, and it took her some thirty minutes to get up enough steam. She reached Roche's Point, at the entrance to the harbor, approximately twenty miles from where the *Lusitania* had gone down, at around 3 P.M.; Coke then changed his mind and ordered her back to port. The definitive news that the *Lusitania* had sunk had decided him that the *Juno* was not needed and should not be risked. He feared that, like her sisters the *Hogue* and the *Cressy*, which were destroyed when they went to the aid of the torpedoed *Aboukir*, she would be a tempting target for any lurking U-boat as she went about her rescue duties. The smaller boats would be adequate to pick up the survivors, even though the *Juno*, with her top speed of eighteen knots, could have been at the scene just after 4 P.M., considerably earlier than the other, slower craft.

From elsewhere along the coast, a motley collection of craft from lifeboats to fishing smacks was also going to the scene. They included the Courtmacsherry lifeboat, which set out at 3 P.M. with twelve men at the oars. The coxswain, on watch on Barry Point, had seen the *Lusitania* go down. He rushed to the lifeboat station, "fired the signal," and within minutes the crew were aboard. But without an engine it would take them some three hours to reach the scene. They prayed as they rowed "as hard as men could pray, a prayer with every stroke. 'O God, keep them alive until we're there.'"

The waiting seemed incomprehensible to those struggling to stay afloat and alive or huddled in lifeboats. Steward Robert Barnes, sharing an upturned collapsible lifeboat with ten others, including a dead woman, could not understand the delay since they were "in sight of Queenstown all the time." He was afraid that his frail craft was drifting out to sea.

⚬⚬⚬

The fishing smack *Peel 12* was among the first to reach the scene. Her crew of seven had just landed a catch of 800 mackerel when they saw the *Lusitania* sinking by the bows some three miles southeast of them. They met the first lifeboats some 400 yards from where the ship had gone down. A determined Elizabeth Duckworth was rowing hard in one of them. The fishermen helped the battered, exhausted survivors aboard. As she climbed in, Elizabeth was surprised to spot another lifeboat "tossing about in the water" with only three aboard. As soon as the boat was within hailing distance, a man stood up and shouted that he and his two companions were the only survivors out of the entire boatload. He begged for help to row back and rescue "some of the drowning." The captain of the fishing smack refused, saying he could not spare the men. Elizabeth was disgusted. Before anyone could stop her, the wiry, fifty-two-year-old Lancashire woman leaped the gap between the *Peel 12* and the lifeboat and seized an oar.

Elizabeth and her three male companions rescued "about forty of those struggling in the water" and brought them back to the *Peel 12*. The fishermen cheered her as they helped her back on board. While rowing about, she had been heartened by the sight of two steamers on the horizon. These were the British freighters *City of Exeter* and *Etonian*, westward bound for the United States. But, as she watched, the two ships vanished over the horizon. She decided grimly that they could "know nothing of our predicament." She was not entirely correct. The two vessels, together with a third in the vicinity, the Standard Oil Company's tanker *Narragansett*, had indeed heard the *Lusitania*'s distress calls, which had been picked up by ships' wirelesses as far afield as Land's End.

All three ships altered course to go to her aid, but a lookout on the *Narragansett* thought he saw a torpedo flash past through the water within ten yards of her. The *Narragansett* at once alerted the *City of Exeter* that U-boats were in the area. All three ships beat a retreat, deciding that assisting the *Lusitania* was a task for the Royal Navy. The captain of the *Narragansett* even suspected that the *Lusitania*'s SOS might not have been genuine but a German ruse to lure British shipping into the path of U-boats. The captain of the *City of Exeter* did not learn of the Lusitania's fate until 2 A.M. the next day, when he concluded that the Germans had deliberately stationed U-boats off the Old Head of Kinsale "for the express purpose of preventing any assistance being given to the passengers of the *Lusitania*."

Meanwhile Charles Lauriat, Fred Gauntlett, and James Brooks, in their lifeboat laden with moaning, groaning people, had struggled to propel the craft toward the sanctuary of the *Peel 12*. Looking around, Lauriat saw two other lifeboats also making for the smack. They were far from full, and he wondered why their occupants had not tried harder to pick up survivors. As they approached, he also noticed that the occupants were dry whereas his sodden passengers had all been fished out of the ocean. Margaret Gwyer, still thoroughly coated in oil and soot, was one of them. As the lifeboat approached the smack, she was ecstatic to see the tall figure of her husband standing at the rail with "a perfectly blank expression on his face." She was in such a terrible state and he in such shock that he did not recognize her until he seemed to pull himself together, leaned over the side, and looked her squarely in the face.

Lauriat landed his catch of thirty-three survivors on the *Peel 12* with enormous relief. Although "it was positively slippery with fish scales and the usual dirt of fishermen . . . the deck of that boat, under our feet, felt as good as the front hall of our own homes," he later wrote. The old fishermen were horrified by the survivors' condition. One bedraggled survivor recalled, "We looked like a bunch of sparrows." Many had been mangled and disfigured. Some were naked, and their teeth chattered. Some were bleeding. Others clutched limbs distorted by fractures. In the worst cases broken bones poked through torn flesh. The crew rushed to provide the shivering, stricken people with what help they could. They improvised bandages and pulled woolen blankets from their bunks. But it was very crowded, people were in shock, and the crew could not succor everyone. Lauriat gave his sweater to a near-naked young man and his jacket to a woman clad only in a nightgown. The crew brewed hot tea. When the tea ran out, they passed around mugs of boiling water. Sips from the boat's one bottle of whiskey were rationed out to those most in need.

Professor Holbourn was sitting huddled and dripping wet in the tiny hold, which still smelled strongly of fish. Next to him lay a man with a broken leg and an expectant mother with her ribs crushed. Another woman who had lost her child in the water was crying brokenly, "My baby, my little baby!" Ogden Hammond was thinking sadly of his wife, whom he had seen fall sixty feet headlong into the sea from a wildly tilting lifeboat. Others too were wondering anxiously about their loved ones and straining eyes and ears in the hope that they would spy them in the water or hear their voices from one of the lifeboats. Lauriat was glad to see a one-year-old baby pulled on board with his grateful mother and father. He noted that "the little chap was one of the few babies who were saved."

The *Peel 12* took on some 160 survivors. She was so crowded that James Brooks was forced to dangle his legs over the side. But he was thankful he was no longer rowing inexpertly, trying to avoid with his oar "the dead and the living among the debris." Realizing that his own ship was now in some danger of sinking, the *Peel 12*'s captain took two more boats in tow and set out for Queenstown. Those hunched on her deck kept watch for the arrival of more rescue ships. To a grieving woman whose toddler had been dragged from her arms in the water, it seemed that "everybody was more or less insane" by now. It was around 6 P.M., three and a half hours after the sinking, when the rescue fleet began to arrive in earnest. Oliver Bernard watched as "gradually smoke appeared on the horizon, east and west," and "all kinds of steamers heaved in sight. . . . A woman moaned, 'Why didn't they come before?'"

After about an hour, the venerable old tender *Flying Fish* met the fishing smack. The paddle steamer was nicknamed the *Galloping Goose* and had ferried passengers ashore in the days when the great ocean liners stopped at Queenstown. In the calm sea she was able to come right alongside the *Peel 12* to take on survivors. Even so, the process of transferring the miserable, suffering human cargo over the rails was difficult. Lauriat later wrote, "We carried our cripples across in our arms."

Oliver Bernard was also on the *Flying Fish*, sitting cheek by jowl with David Thomas. They were both chilled to the bone. Bernard tried pacing the deck for warmth and remarked, "An exciting day!" This prompted an infuriated diatribe from Thomas about the inefficiency of the *Lusitania*'s crew. He told Bernard that it had been "outrageous, simply outrageous."

Belle Naish, looking anxiously around in her lifeboat, felt overwhelmed to see the rescue force finally appear: "Smoke, then, in several places ahead on the horizon, finally the smokestacks, and then the bows of the vessels seemed suddenly to come to view. . . . the wonder we all felt when we realized that the sea was so smooth we could see the spray on the bows and swells behind each boat coming to our rescue." To another thankful survivor, suddenly "the whole sea seemed full of tugs and torpedo boats."

Belle Naish was taken on board the *Julia*. The sailors revived her with tea and gave her a hot brick while they ransacked their cabins for woolen socks and slippers for her and other survivors. One man passed around a box of cakes his wife had made for him. Meanwhile, Belle was trying to comfort a despairing seven-year-old boy, Robert Kay, who not only had lost his mother but was feverishly in the throes of measles. Suddenly she saw an unconscious Theodate Pope pulled in from the sea with boat hooks and laid among the dead "like a sack of cement." Victims of severe hypothermia often appear to be dead; their pulse can be so weak as to be undetectable, and they have no reflexes. At the same time people may survive drowning in cold water by up to forty-five minutes because of the lowering of the metabolic rate in the brain. Luckily for Theodate, Belle left Robert and went over to the stack of bodies. She hesitantly touched Theodate to find her body stiff; Theodate's face was swollen and discolored by bruising.

Nevertheless, Belle refused to believe that she was quite dead and pleaded with the sailors to give her artificial respiration. They hacked off her fashionable clothing with a carving knife brought up from the galley and went to work for what seemed like hours. To their amazement, she came around. Gazing confusedly around her, Theodate gradually realized she was lying on the floor wrapped in a blanket and staring into a small open-grate fire. She then saw a "pair of grey-trowsered legs." Painfully, she turned her head and saw a man watching her closely. She tried to speak but was so chilled and trembling so much that she could not make the words come. The sympathetic sailors placed hot bricks at her feet and against her back.

Leslie Morton was at last taken aboard the auxiliary patrol trawler *Indian Empire* after helping to pick up survivors and ferry them to rescue

Theodate Pope

vessels. Bellboy Ben Holton was also aboard the *Indian Empire*. He had passed out with the cold as he floated on some wreckage to which an unknown benefactor had tied him. He woke to find himself laid out on the ship's hatch among a pile of dead bodies "with the blue sky overhead and vibrations of engines below." He managed to sit up, causing an astonished sailor to say, "Good gracious, are you alive? We put you amongst the dead ones." He helped Holton cut off his sodden life jacket and gave him a cup of strong coffee. A near-dead George Wynne was also hauled aboard. Sailors thumped his chest and worked his arms to pump the water from his lungs. Then they gave him sugared tea. Cold and in shock, he was shivering violently in his thin, torn undershirt and checked kitchen trousers, so they put a blanket around him. Charles Hill, too, was picked up by the *Indian Empire*, together with Senior Second Engineer Andrew Cockburn. Both were unnerved to hear the vessel's captain suddenly yell, "There's a periscope!" It was a false alarm. Nevertheless, some of the 170 survivors crammed on her decks were convinced that submarines were still hovering to pick off the rescue craft and refused to take off their life jackets.

Fireman John O'Connell helped the injured Lady Allan onto the steamer *Katrina*. She managed a weak smile and said, "I like you. What for I don't know." There was still no sign of her daughters, Gwen and Anna, but her two maids were on board, together with Howard Fisher, Rita

Lady Allan and her two daughters

Jolivet, and Surgeon Major Warren Pearl. The Lassetters and Harold Boulton, plucked at last from their precarious wooden box, were also there. Boulton had been mightily relieved to spot the *Katrina* "coming hell for leather," thinking, "Thank God, we're going to be saved." The *Katrina* had been flying a Greek flag, but the surprised survivors quickly realized that they were aboard a British ship. Despite the name painted on her sides, she was in reality the SS *Westborough* commanded by Captain E. L. Taylor and sailing under neutral Greek colors as "a measure for safety."

The survivors were given the suitably British sustenance of mugs of strong black tea and slabs of jam tart. Some began to feel human again. But for others there were still grim scenes and wide-awake nightmares as they stared at close quarters, despite themselves, at the many people who were badly wounded and mutilated. O'Connell watched someone perform an emergency operation without anesthetic on the man with the partially severed arm whom he had helped to pull into a lifeboat: He "got a little bit of string and severed the rest of his arm . . . and threw it over the side." A wet, cold Joseph Myers was in agony from his broken leg and ribs. The crew stripped him as quickly and gently as they could of his sodden, clinging clothes, wrapped him in a rough blanket, and laid him across a warm grating in the engine room.

Mabel Henshaw, having given herself up for lost, was spotted floating on her back and taken aboard the fishing boat *Bluebell*. Like Ben

Holton, she was at first taken for dead and laid out on the deck. After a while, though, Mabel opened her eyes and looked up at the stars. Her first confused thoughts were "Where's this?" and "Gee whiz, it's cold." Someone shouted, "Oh quick, there's life here." She was carried down to a warm cabin, shivering with early symptoms of pneumonia and pleurisy. Although the sailors were "rough diamonds," the grateful woman thought they treated her like "a queen," holding up a blanket so she could take off her wet clothes.

Captain Turner was also aboard the *Bluebell*. The trawler's skipper wrapped a blanket around him and took him down to the mess room, where he sat by the stove "with his head in his arms." George Kessler was there, bruised legs wrapped in bandages. He had been taken from a boat in the bottom of which nine corpses were lying in the bilge water. The *Bluebell* also picked up the unconscious Margaret Mackworth. Charles Bowring spotted her as the water swept her by in the twilight on a wicker chair that had floated up under her unconscious body. Reviving, she found herself "lying naked between blankets on a deck in the dark." A fisherman was peering at her. With a muttered "That's better," he fetched her a cup of lukewarm tea.

The disoriented woman drank it while imagining she was still on the *Lusitania*. She wondered with vague annoyance why her stewardess had not brought the tea. Then her whole body began to shake violently. Her teeth chattered "like castanets." The fisherman offered to help her to go below, confiding that it had taken three men to get her prone body aboard. He also told her that they had left her on deck because "we thought you were dead and it did not seem worth while cumbering up the cabin with you." Supported now by a man on either side and with a third holding back her long, dripping hair, Margaret was helped downstairs and put in the captain's bunk. The sudden warmth made her feel "almost delirious." As she looked around her, she could see others "a little drunk" both with the heat and "the light and the joy" of knowing they were alive. Everyone was talking at the tops of their voices and laughing, even a woman who confessed that she was "almost sure her husband was drowned." Although he was all she had in the world, she was seemingly "full of cheerfulness and laughter."

There were two exceptions to this "merry hysteria." The first was Captain Turner, still sitting hunched and silent. Junior Third Officer Albert Bestic, who had been rescued from a drifting lifeboat that he had managed to keep afloat by plugging it with scraps of wood and cork, tried to offer his captain a few consoling words but was rebuffed. The second was a woman who "in a low rather monotonous voice" began to describe the loss of her baby. She told Turner that her child's death had been unnecessary, blaming the "lack of organisation and discipline on board." A sailor whispered to Margaret Mackworth that the woman was hysterical; Margaret thought the reverse: The poor bereft mother appeared to her "to be the one person on board who was not."

Doris Lawlor, along with her father, was rescued by a fishing smack. She was put into a bunk, and two fishermen fed her hot rum from a little enamel dish. Gradually she began to revive. The fishermen bound her chilled feet in pieces of newspapers to make shoes for her, tying them around each ankle with string.

Avis Dolphin had also been picked up. Wrapped in a rug and with a hot drink in her hands, the young girl was huddling near the stove where "there was a good fire burning." She had taken off her clothes to dry them. She was touched to see a little boy suddenly reunited with his parents. They had already lost their baby and had feared that their son, too, had been drowned.

Able Seaman Thomas O'Mahoney, who had narrowly missed being sliced in pieces by the *Lusitania*'s propellers, was picked up by a naval patrol boat.

Quartermaster Hugh Johnston, who had tried to steer the *Lusitania* in her dying moments, had nearly lost hope of rescue. He had watched smoke spiraling from six different vessels as they nudged their way through the debris and lifeless bodies looking for survivors, but was eventually spotted and brought in late at night into Queenstown.

Margaret Cox, still clutching baby Desmond, was transferred from her lifeboat to a trawler feeling "so ragged and tired and wet." A demented woman suddenly seized hold of her and began hitting her frenziedly with her fists until she was pulled away. Margaret forgave her when she understood the cause: "She was just crazy, she'd lost her child."

Steward Barnes, rescued by another boat, felt childishly delighted to be given corned beef and sailors' biscuits, which seemed "one of the nicest meals" he had ever had. But others were dismayed to find that although their tongues were swollen and their throats raw from swallowing seawater, some of the rescue boats "had no water" left to give them.

Parry Jones was in the water for eight hours before being rescued. He was one of the six Royal Gwent Singers to survive. Poker-loving Soren Sorenson was also picked out of the water and lay groaning on the deck of his rescue craft, his hands "black, blue and swollen." One survivor who encountered his bedroom steward on a trawler was so disoriented he mechanically gave him a tip. A husband and wife reunited on a rescue craft, each having believed the other dead, fell to their knees in prayer.

Mrs. Henry Adams, struggling in the water after the raft on which she had tried to float finally sank, was saved by one of the torpedo boats sent out by Coke. William Howard, a seaman aboard the torpedo boat 055, was told by his captain to forget about the dead and pick up the ones who were still alive. Some, though, had only a precarious hold on life; of the twenty-three rescued by the 055, two were dead before the boat reached Queenstown.

Ernest Hey, a young engineer on board another torpedo boat, the 050, rescued three semiconscious stewards he found slumped on the canvas cover of a collapsible. One of them still had a dinner napkin tied around his neck. He had had his last meal, dying on the way to Queenstown. Altogether, the 050 picked up twenty-seven survivors—including James Leary, who had survived four and a half hours of clinging to an upturned collapsible and watching fourteen of the original group hanging on to it slip under the water. His leg was badly gashed and bleeding, and he was groaning in agony from the stinging pain. One chilled survivor aboard the 050 was so desperate to get warm that he burned his flesh badly in the attempt as he clambered over the hot metal of the ship's engines.

The experience was traumatic for the rescuers. Even though they were hardened to the sea, it was macabre, often heartbreaking work. One crew was attracted by an intermittent flashing light and rowed hopefully toward it. Instead of a survivor, they found "a circular lifebuoy clasped by the hand of a drowned lady whose body depended entirely beneath the surface. But on one of the two or three unsubmerged fingers a great diamond was flashing in the sunlight." Boatswain John Maloney of the Courtmacsherry lifeboat looked through his binoculars to see corpses floating in the sea "as thick as grass." Although they had strained at the oars for three and a half hours "until our hearts were well-nigh broken," his men were "only in time to pick up dead bodies." Other rescuers were shocked by the many "mothers with their babies still clasped in their arms in death." The sailors also knew how distressing it was to survivors to see the lifeless forms floating stiffly and blindly by. One trawler captain, reproached for not staying longer at the scene on the chance of rescuing more people, answered his critic fiercely: "There were many left in the water, but they were all dead and many so horribly mangled I thought better to bring ashore my boatload of suffering women as they could not have stood much more."

There were practical as well as emotional problems for some of the rescuers. Two fishing vessels, the *Daniel O'Connell* and the *Elizabeth*, were trying to ferry survivors quickly ashore, intending to return later to look for more survivors. Making for their home port of Kinsale, they were stopped by the government tug *Stormcock*, a vessel which earlier in her career had towed the liner *Great Eastern* when she had been reduced to cable laying. The *Stormcock* had just rescued the *Lusitania*'s Third Electrician W. E. G. Jones and a lady, who were bobbing about in a large wooden coffinlike locker used to store life jackets. Now her captain, Commander Shee, haughtily insisted that the survivors aboard the *Elizabeth* and *Daniel O'Connell* be transferred to his vessel so he could take them to Queenstown.

Edward White of the *Elizabeth* and Jimmy Hagan of the *Daniel O'Connell* protested angrily. They argued that Kinsale was closer and that some of the women survivors were "very weak." The exchange quickly became heated. According to fisherman John Forde, Shee said he would have run down the *Elizabeth* if she had no passengers on board and that he would report White to Vice Admiral Coke. The situation became yet more fraught when some passengers refused to transfer, convinced that the larger vessel would be a more likely target for any U-boats. Eventually the transfer was completed, and the *Stormcock* was the first rescue vessel to enter Queenstown Harbor, sailing in past the Royal Dock Yard and the Royal Yacht Club, just after 8 P.M.

Consul Frost was waiting anxiously at the Cunard wharf. Police had put a makeshift barrier around it to keep sightseers away. Unfortunately, there was only space for one ship at a time to unload on the gaslit quayside. Lieutenant Norcocks with a surgeon and staff from the Royal Naval Hospital was also waiting. Behind him stood rows of policemen, soldiers, and sailors ready with blankets and stretchers. As boat after boat began to come in out of the darkness, the scene took on a nightmarish quality. Frost watched "the ghastly procession of the rescue ships as they landed the living and the dead that night under the flaring gas torches."

He saw "bruised and shuddering women, crippled and half-clothed men, and a few wide-eyed little children" helped or carried up the gangplank. Many were shoeless and wrapped in blankets.

Women grabbed at the sleeves of officials, begging desperately for word of their husbands. Frost saw men "with choking efforts at matter-of-factness move ceaselessly from group to group, seeking a lost daughter or sister or even bride. . . . Every voice in that great mixed assemblage was pitched in unconscious undertones, broken now and then by painful coughing fits of suppressed hysteria." Archie Donald found the sights on arrival at Queenstown nearly too much to bear, with "husbands looking for their wives and fathers for their children." One woman with a baby in her arms and a blanket given her by a sailor around her shoulders refused to leave the quayside "but waited until the last survivor had passed, searching each face as it went by, in the vain hope of finding her husband, from whom she had been separated in the last terrible scene on the liner's deck."

The *Flying Fish* reached Queenstown around 9:30 P.M. As the craft entered the harbor, a patrol boat halted her and a voice rang out, "What ship is that?" The reply came back: "The ship *Flying Fish* with survivors of the *Lusitania*." But the ordeal was not yet over. According to Lauriat, "there came very near being a real fight." As the flaming torches on the quayside came into view, the *Flying Fish*'s captain told the incredulous survivors that they could not go ashore until he had formally reported to the harbor authorities. Lauriat argued in "language that was decidedly to the point" that the people were in urgent need of hot food and drink and shelter. The captain refused to listen and went in search of a harbor inspector, leaving orders that the gangplank was not to be lowered.

As soon as he was gone Lauriat and others put the gangplank over the side. When a man on the dockside tried to stop them, Lauriat told him bluntly that he had three seconds to get out of the way. The man ran off. The furious bookseller and other able-bodied men then helped the weaker onto the quayside and went to summon ambulances and stretchers. As she staggered gratefully ashore, Elizabeth Duckworth broke down for the first but not the last time. She was treated for exposure and taken to the Westbourne Hotel. Oliver Bernard stumbled ashore to be helped by a sailor from HMS *Venus* who thrust a cigarette between his chilled lips. "Picture a bull-dog in blue helping a sooty rat along the main street of Queenstown lined by crowds of natives," he later wrote.

After seeing the injured taken care of, Lauriat bought himself some pajamas of the thickest wool he had ever put on, had a drink in the Imperial Hotel bar, and found himself a bed. At last he passed into "a dead, dreamless sleep."

The *Bluebell* reached Queenstown at about 11 P.M. Margaret Mackworth shuffled ashore in a khaki army greatcoat borrowed from a soldier over a blanket tucked around her waist and with the captain's carpet slippers on her feet. She was too weak to step up onto the gangway and crawled onto it on her hands and knees. At the other end she was overjoyed to find her father waiting for her. After leaving the *Flying Fish*, David Thomas had been looked after by a kindly Catholic priest who had taken him off to dinner and plied him with brandy, ignoring Thomas's protests that he had not drunk alcohol for fifteen years. Afterward he had waited light-headed and anxious on the quayside for news of his daughter.

Amy Biddulph, still making up beds at the Queen's Hotel, saw survivors come "dripping, pale, exhausted, some unconscious, others on stretchers—injured in every possible way, the children crying for their mothers—husbands looking with anxious eyes for their wives and families—wives looking for their husbands who they would probably never see again." She and her mother tore or cut their clothing from them, rolled them in blankets, dosed them with brandy, then put them to bed "with hot-water jars."

Charles Bowring, hobbling ashore in his sodden Norfolk jacket, put his hand in his pocket to retrieve his glasses. He found that "they were all twisted in a piece of paper but it was all pulp." Putting on his mangled spectacles and inspecting it more closely, he saw that the scrap of paper was the German warning that had appeared in the New York papers the day the *Lusitania* sailed. He reflected wryly that he had at least one souvenir of the day's events.

Captain Turner disembarked last from the *Bluebell*. One observer thought he looked "terribly broken down." He apparently remarked with quiet irony, "Well, it is the fortune of war."

The *Katrina* came in at around midnight. Harold Boulton, though not a drinking man, tossed down six whiskeys and soda that a soldier held out to him on a tray as he disembarked. He was convinced they saved his life.

Theodate Pope was carried ashore from her vessel by two sailors who made a chair with their hands and lifted her up, calling, "Way, way!" She was so weak she nearly fell when they set her gently on her feet, but a doctor caught her by the shoulders. She was taken by car to a hotel that, even in her desperate condition, she could see was "third-rate." She again tried to stand but immediately crumpled in a heap. The men carried her into a lounge, which was "full of men in all sorts of strange garments." The proprietress rushed to fetch her some brandy. Theodate recognized the young Englishman who had been so anxious to have enough time to finish his ice cream before any submarine attack. He was sitting limply in a pink dressing gown. He saw her and came over, and she asked anxiously after Edwin Friend. The young man "shook his head without answering."

Theodate was helped upstairs to share a room with other survivors but could not sleep. All night long she kept expecting Edwin Friend to appear, looking for her. A stream of other men kept coming into the room, "snapping on the lights, bringing children for us to identify, taking telegrams, getting our names for the list of survivors." Each time she scanned their faces, and each time she was disappointed. All she could think of was her "frightful anxiety" for the man she hoped "would be saved to carry on the work we had so much at heart." Seeing her distress, another passenger set out to check the hotels, hospitals, and private houses where survivors were sheltering. He returned every two or three hours, but each time with no news. That night Theodate found, like some other survivors, that her hair was beginning to fall out from the effects of shock.

Those survivors who were strong enough were ushered into the rear rooms of the brightly lit Cunard offices to register their names on the list of survivors that flustered company staff were trying to compile. Frost had received a cable from Secretary of State Bryan stating: "COMPANY REPORTS ALL PASSENGERS SAVED. IF REPORT UNTRUE CABLE NAMES OF AMERICANS LOST OR NOT ACCOUNTED FOR." He therefore asked that all survivors' nationalities be recorded and that American survivors be directed to him, but the Cunard officials were too distracted to pay much heed at first. Frost found disoriented Americans wandering about "wholly unmarshalled."

In London a grim-faced Ambassador Page was waiting for Frost's latest updates. During the afternoon Sir Edward Grey had called him to the foreign office to tell him that the *Lusitania* "had been torpedoed and sunk by German submarines off the Irish coast." The Pages were preparing to host a farewell dinner that night for Colonel and Mrs. House at their house in Grosvenor Square. Page decided that, as the reports from Cunard suggested there were no casualties, he need not abandon the dinner, but by the time he returned home he had learned that the first reports had been wrong. There had been massive loss of life. It was too late to cancel the party, which went ahead in a subdued mood punctuated by frequent bulletins from Frost and the Admiralty. Page read them aloud to his appalled guests. Colonel House, who had had a long day beginning with his visit to Kew Gardens with Grey, followed by his interview with the king, was among the most outspoken. "We shall be at war with Germany within a month," he predicted.

Meanwhile survivors were being taken into the back of the Queenstown post office on the harbor front to wire their families that they were alive. George Wynne, deeply anxious about his father, sent a telegram to his mother in Liverpool. He did not want to worry her and so wrote that they were both safe. His hand was "shaking very bad," and another cook had to guide it for him. Leslie Morton rushed in to send a cable to his father, confirming that he was safe but that he was looking for his brother. Margaret Cox, whose son, Desmond, was "almost in convulsions with crying," sent a wire to her husband. She was tormented by the thought that if she had taken her steward's advice and gone to the first sitting of lunch, she would have been two decks below in her cabin. She and Desmond would probably have been drowned.

Gradually survivors were dispersed to whatever accommodation could be found. Margaret Mackworth and her father went to the Queen's Hotel, which, despite the efforts of Amy Biddulph and fellow guests, seemed to her "by far the dirtiest place" she had ever seen. The staff could only provide biscuits and lemonade. A disgusted Margaret climbed into bed. A little later, a hysterical and traumatized Elizabeth Lassetter was brought in and placed in the second bed. She was so agitated that it was 3 A.M. before Margaret could persuade her to sleep. But they were more fortunate than some survivors. Seaman Duncan, who had been in the water until 8 P.M., staggered ashore in a terrible condition. Soldiers gave him some tea with whiskey in it, but it made him sick.

He was taken to a room slung with "wire cages for going to sleep like hammocks." He woke in the middle of the night unable to open his eyes because they were so sore and clogged with mucus from the salt water. For a while he believed he had gone blind. Some had to sleep three in a bed. Poker-playing Soren Sorenson was taken to a sailors' home that provided whiskey but no bedclothes.

Bellboy Clark, exhausted, wet, and with his fingers sticking painfully together where "the flesh was taken off," did not care where he was. Taken to a room in the Imperial Hotel, he at once fell into a deep sleep.

But many found it hard to rest, let alone sleep that night, despite their exhaustion. Mabel Henshaw was taken to the Royal Hotel but lay awake grieving and hoping for news that her baby's body had been found. Exhausted as he was, Professor Holbourn could not rest until he had news of Avis Dolphin. At last, at 2 A.M. in his hotel, "news was brought to him that she was safe." All Charlotte Pye wanted was to go and look for her baby. A doctor insisted she go to bed, but during the night she began to feel so ill that she said to a woman sharing her room: "Will you ring the bell? I'm dying." No one came. She eventually got out of bed and walked around a little, but it seemed to her "I'd never be able to live again without the child I'd loved so dearly."

As the night wore on, it became clear that many vessels were carrying greater numbers of dead than of living. Two trawlers and a steamship returned with over 100 corpses, mostly women. A tug brought 16 dead, including 3 babies. Wesley Frost saw how "piles of corpses like cordwood began to appear among the paint-kegs and coils of rope on the shadowy old wharves." Survivors searched frantically among them. Surgeon Major Warren Pearl steeled himself to check for members of his family. He was appalled to find "a father, mother and three daughters, all dead, clasped in each others' arms." Archie Donald stayed up until 4 A.M. "examining the dead bodies as they came in" while he searched for his friends. He was joined by Oliver Bernard, who was looking for Lesley Mason. Bernard met "only what were carried ashore, stiff already, mute fellow-beings." He decided that "in the flickering lamps and glow of furnace fires aboard tugs and trawlers, lying on open decks, the harvest was something that merited the imagination of a Gustave Doré."

Adult corpses were placed on stretchers and carried to the temporary morgues set up in a shed on the Cunard quay and then, as the numbers of dead rose, in the large town hall and in a disused ship's chandlery.

Curious onlookers outside the town hall used as a morgue.

The sailors carried the dead babies in their arms. Crewman Brennan went to the morgues to help with the task of identification. He broke down at the sight of all the stiff tiny bodies laid out in rows "and more still being carried in."

The human cost could not have been more horrible.

CHAPTER TWENTY

The Town of the Dead

$\mathcal{E}$VEN A MAN as cynical and detached as Oliver Bernard found the sights in the three makeshift morgues hard to stomach. He had risen again at sunrise, still driven by the sense of duty that one of his first tasks should be to resume his search for Lesley Mason. When he entered the first morgue, "a heap of what looked like battered, bruised, broken dolls laid aside as factory refuse" confronted his eye. As he peered more closely, he saw they were "nude, semi-nude innocents . . . babies so discoloured that it was difficult to believe that these effigies had ever lived. Mothers, wives and daughters lay in a row all round the shed, in sodden garments, not believably human persons of the day before."

He found the second morgue even worse. Sunlight filtering through its grimy windows fell on the "bloated features" of Staff Captain Anderson, "smeared with bloody mucous." Bernard could see that he had not died "without a hard struggle." In the third morgue the air was unpleasantly clammy with moisture evaporating from the piles of soaked corpses. The only one Bernard recognized was Charles Frohman, whose body, unlike most others, was not disfigured. He could discover no sign among the silent rows of William Lindsey's "little girl." As he walked back to his hotel, a depressed Bernard thought that "the streets of Queenstown reeked of death."

Charles Lauriat woke up at 6 A.M. in the room he shared with three other men at the Imperial Hotel. The elderly proprietress, a "dear old lady" who the previous night had fed him whiskey distilled by her grandfather, had dried out his clothes in her kitchen. He was grateful that his

Survivors in Queenstown.

wardrobe was complete—he had not even removed his shoes when he went overboard. Now he hurried out to see what he could do for those survivors he knew were near destitute. He presented a "still half-soaked" banker's draft for forty pounds at the bank. At first the cashier refused to honor it, saying he had no idea who Lauriat was. The exasperated man produced his sodden passport and told him he had "about 12 half-starved, half-naked Americans that had to be fed and clothed." The man relented. Lauriat doled out the proceeds to as many as he could. He then steeled himself to view the dead bodies and was thankful to see no one whom he recognized. Down by the Cunard wharf he noticed six of the *Lusitania*'s lifeboats drawn up by the quayside.

As the morning wore on, dazed survivors began wandering the town, some limping, some bandaged, many oddly dressed in borrowed garments or often ill-fitting new ones. Some, like Lauriat and Harold Boulton, who had managed to exchange four "very soggy" five-pound notes for some clean money, had funds. Most, however, had nothing. Cunard opened accounts with Queenstown's outfitters and clothes shops so that

Shocked surviving crewmen in Queenstown.

survivors could equip themselves, but there was confusion in some cases about the amount of credit allowed. French passenger Joseph Marichal was unable to secure a coat for his wife. She was left to travel shivering and ill to Dublin in a "wet silk blouse." Captain Turner, in the now shrunken uniform he had been wearing when the ship sank, went into a shop to try and buy a hat. A young female survivor recognized him and loudly berated him for being concerned over something so trivial when so many had lost everything.

Some survivors were bemused by comments from bystanders who "could not understand why the *Lusitania* came on when they had warned her from Queenstown that they [submarines] were waiting for her." "She'd been waiting for ye for days," said one old man to Oliver Bernard. Most, however, were completely preoccupied with trying to trace loved ones. The town seethed with rumors about "total people lost, total people saved, although nobody knew at that time exactly what the figure was."

Norah Bretherton was hoping against hope that her baby, Betty, had been saved. She begged a lady who had befriended her to place a notice in the shop windows: "*Lusitania*—missing baby: missing, a baby girl, 15 months old. Very fair curly hair and rosy complexion. In white woollen jersey and white woollen leggings. Tries to walk and talk. Name Betty Bretherton. Please send any information to Miss Browne, Queen's House, Queenstown."

There was no sign either of Ailsa Booth-Jones, the little girl who had proudly shown Professor Holbourn the prizes she had won, or of her parents and brother. An anxious relation placed an advertisement for Ailsa and her brother, Percival, in the *Cork Examiner*: "Wanted: any information regarding a girl of eight years, light-golden hair, blue eyes, nice complexion, very pretty. . . . Also a boy, aged five, short black hair, rather thin face." A wretched Mabel Henshaw described to a Cunard official the little bracelet on the wrist of her lost baby, hoping this would help identify her if she had been saved. A distraught father who had lost two of his four children was wandering distractedly and in shock between the morgues muttering, "Fifty percent! That is not too bad. Some fathers lost their whole families."

Some were lucky. Lucy Taylor was coming disconsolately down the steps of a hotel where she had been searching for her husband, Harold, when "a sailor ran up to me and it was my husband in sailor's uniform." George Hook and his daughter, Elsie, scoured the mortuaries but finally found eleven-year-old Frank Hook in Queenstown Hospital, where he had been lying, miserably certain that his father and sister were dead. Leslie Morton, still dressed in his sailor's jersey and blue serge trousers, went anxiously to a mortuary to start looking for his brother, John. He saw that "laid out in rows all the way down on both sides were sheeted and shrouded bodies, and a large number of people in varying states of sorrow and distress were going from body to body, turning back the sheets to see if they could identify loved ones." Leslie hesitantly put out his hand to twitch the sheet off a corpse when, "by the most amazing coincidence I shall ever know, a hand on the other side went to turn the sheet back and I looked up and there was my brother." John Morton had come ashore in nothing but a shirt and blanket but had equipped himself at Cunard's expense with "the loudest check suit, check tie, cap and horrible yellow shoes" his brother had ever seen. The happy pair went and celebrated with their first taste of Guinness.

The Sullivans were also fortunate. Julia Sullivan awoke in the white-washed ward of a hospital in Kinsale. The naval patrol boat *Heron*, flying

Survivor on a Queenstown street still wearing his lifejacket.

an "urgent signal" and with her flag at half-mast, had brought her ashore the previous night. The *Heron* was transporting five bodies and eleven survivors, including Ship's Bugler Vernon Livermore and Steward Cornelius Horrigan, whom Livermore had saved. Julia was looking so ill that the captain had not wanted to risk the longer journey to Queenstown. Later that day, a priest told her that her husband, Flor, was safe. She had more good luck. The valuables that Flor had urged her to stash in her bodice, including a gold ring, cash, and drafts amounting to £324 10s. 0d., had been recovered with her and were later returned.

Milliner Gerda Nielson and engineer John Welsh, who had fallen in love on the ship, had also survived. John had supported Gerda in the water until she was picked up by a lifeboat. She had had to plead with her rescuers, who claimed there was no more room in the boat, to pull him in as well.

Radio Officer Bob Leith too was safe. His brother Alex, who was serving in the Royal Navy, first heard of the sinking on his twenty-first birthday and was desperately worried. However, several days later another ship on the Admiralty's instructions broke radio silence to signal the good news that his brother had survived.

For many others, there was disappointment, heartbreak, and, sometimes, cruel confusion. Ogden Hammond was told that his wife had been rescued. Relieved and delighted, he "arose immediately" and despite his damaged knee rushed for a reunion. He found only a steerage passenger of the same name. She had lost her husband and was "absolutely without funds." Hammond gave her money to enable her to get home and limped painfully and sadly away. Of the six Williams children and their mother, Annie, only Edith and her seven-year-old brother had survived. They were being cared for on the magnificent Leahy estate in Cork. Journalist Ernest Cowper, who had saved six-year-old Helen Smith, took the little girl around the town in search of her parents unaware that they had in fact both drowned. As the child looked round expectantly for them, she chattered "gaily about submarines, declaring that she had often seen them in moving pictures." A local family gave her a doll, which the child gripped cheerfully in her arms.

George Wynne searched the morgues in vain for his father. The young cook also had to have two extractions that morning because "the salt had got into our teeth." The thought of the well-meaning telegram he had sent the night before, "both saved home later," must have been weighing on his conscience.

Surgeon Major Warren Pearl was hugely relieved to discover that his wife, Amy, was alive and had been taken in by Vice Admiral Coke's family at Admiralty House, but there was no news as yet of their four children and two nurses. Word came of a nurse answering Alice Lines's description. The anxious father rushed to the house to find Alice safe with baby Audrey and little Stuart. But nurse Greta Lorenson and his two other daughters, Amy and Susan, were missing. Surgeon Major Pearl and Alice Lines inspected the bodies in the morgues and went repeatedly to the railway station in case they might have been rescued elsewhere along the coast and sent on to Queenstown, but there was nothing.

Rita Jolivet, who had tended the injured Lady Allan during the night

Helen Smith holding dolls given to her in Queenstown.

at Queen's Hotel, was anxious for news of the Allan girls and her missing brother-in-law, George Vernon. All had, in fact, perished.

⸺⸺

The Cunard office in Queenstown was struggling to compile lists of the living and the dead. The task proved nearly impossible, with hundreds still unaccounted for and piles of dead to be identified. Details were also trickling in from elsewhere: New bodies were discovered on Garretston Strand and the mudflats of Courtmacsherry Bay where they had washed ashore during the night. Survivors besieging the Cunard office for news added to the highly charged atmosphere.

By now crowds of friends and relations were also massing at Cunard's premises in London and Liverpool. Officials were anxiously scrutinizing reports from Queenstown with "weeping women imploring [them] for word as to their dear ones and men far back in the crowd calling the names of friends and relatives in the hope that some of the office staff could hear and reply." As additional names were added to the survivors' lists, there were hysterical scenes as men and women fought their way to the counters. As they shouted the names and heard the ominous reply "Not received yet," they begged the clerks to go through the lists again. "It must be there. Have you got the spelling right?" they pleaded. Some fainted in the crush, falling beneath the feet of those surging up behind them.

There was similar frenzied anxiety in the United States. In New York, Alfred Vanderbilt's wife, Margaret, had locked herself in her suite on the top floor of the magnificent Vanderbilt Hotel, where flags were flying at half-mast. His mother, Alice, prostrate in her Italian Renaissance bedroom in her mansion on Fifty-seventh Street, was also praying he was still alive and in some remote port in Ireland. The Vanderbilts' London attorney, Walter Webb-Ware, was on his way to superintend the search and offer a reward of £1,000 ($5,000) for the recovery of the body, a handsome sum compared with Cunard's more modest offer of £5 ($25) per body.

Elbert Hubbard's artistic colony at East Aurora was in shock and waiting anxiously for any scrap of news. Scraps were all they got: In addition to bellboy Clark's possible sighting of Hubbard looking "pretty well smashed up," one American survivor thought he had seen Hubbard alone in the water. He had been repeatedly attempting to scramble onto a cylindrical drum, which, as he tried to throw his weight across it, "revolved slowly in the water and plunged him off the other side."

By the morning of Saturday, 8 May, an exhausted Wesley Frost had compiled a fairly accurate list of the identified American bodies and began wiring relatives. Perhaps unsurprisingly, he had to coax, even bully, traumatized survivors into visiting the morgues. "I think hardly a dozen Americans could be got to give their services toward aiding in identifications," he wrote angrily, "and in several cases we had to accompany these people bodily to see that they did not shirk this duty." James Brooks was willing to help the consul and identified the body of playwright Charles Klein by his clubfoot. There was no sign yet of younger writer Justus Miles Forman. The bodies of Charles and Mary Plamondon had, however, been recovered. Mary Plamondon's dress was stained with soot, and her characteristic pince-nez was gone. Succeeding where Bernard had failed, Frost discovered Lesley Mason's body lying at the back of the Cunard office "like a statue typifying assassinated innocence." The body of her husband, Stewart, washed up farther along the coast.

Frost was beginning to gather statements from twenty-one American survivors to send to the State Department. He also found himself inventing policy on the spot. He decided that no American victims should be buried in Ireland, unless relatives explicitly wished for this, but should instead be shipped home to the United States. In addition, he decided that the bodies of prominent and wealthy Americans like Frohman and other first-class passengers should be embalmed, since their relations would be likely to reimburse the cost. To his dismay, the local undertakers denied knowledge of the embalming process. It was not until early on Sunday, 9 May, that Frost found a surgeon at University College in Cork to take on the task at a fee of twenty pounds per body.

Frost also decided that other American bodies should be sealed in lead caskets. This could be done, he recorded, "at a cost of £16 per body, which would be reduced to £15 if there were more than 10."

As he toured the morgues checking his lists, Frost was struck by the "curious effacement of social or mental distinction by death." Dead stokers looked as distinguished to him as Charles Frohman. The commonest expression was of "reassured tranquility" mingled with puzzlement or aggrievement, "as though some trusted friend had played a practical joke which the victim did not yet understand." But the visits to the mortuaries also depressed him. The once-beautiful image of the *Lusitania* had become a travesty: "Scores and hundreds of corpses of men and women and little folks—some rotting in pools of blood in unnamed deal coffins, some staring wearily up past me from the damp floor of the old Town Hall, and some lying with vile disfigurements in shreds of clothing soaking with the salt ocean. But always corpses."

The arrival on 9 May of Captain A. M. Miller and Captain W. A. Castle, dispatched by the American embassy in London to help Frost with his gruesome task, was some relief. He briefed the two officers, then took them to call on Vice Admiral Coke, who read them the wireless dispatches sent to the *Lusitania*. According to Miller, Coke also suggested that "warnings were not properly obeyed; that the ship kept too close to the shore and that she should have been kept at a high speed within the danger zone, instead of at from 15 to 18 knots, which was the speed attributed to her when she was struck." Frost described the messages as "bare facts only. No instruction or interpretation. It is true that Turner should have kept further out; but to my mind it seemed that the Admiralty had by no means done their full duty by him."

As officials struggled with their emotionally and physically demanding tasks, many victims lay in bed recovering. Dorothy Conner visited Margaret Mackworth at the Queen's Hotel. The American was still dressed in the neat fawn tweed suit she had been wearing when she tumbled into the sea. Modesty had prevented her from loosening all the hooks and dispensing with her skirt as Margaret had done. She told Margaret that her brother-in-law, Howard Fisher, was also safe. He had swum to a lifeboat, where he had watched a man operate with a penknife on the leg of a crewmen badly injured by an explosion on the *Lusitania*. Later that morning, as Margaret lay naked under her blankets, a young woman staying in the hotel asked her what she needed. At Margaret's dictation, she made a list—everything from hairpins, underclothes, and stockings to blouse, coat, and skirt—and set off to Cork to buy them. Meanwhile, Margaret tried to wash off the "black-brown dirt" she was covered in. Many marks were not dirt after all, but bruises.

Isaac Lehmann was also staying at the Queen's Hotel, whose German proprietor, Otto Humbert, had reputedly spent the night hiding in the wine cellar because he was frightened of reprisals. The obstreperous and highly strung Lehmann, who had shared a room with three other men and been given nothing to eat, was complaining angrily and vociferously about his treatment.

Professor Holbourn was by now confined to bed in the same hotel, recovering from the hours he had spent in the chilly water clinging to a boat. Avis Dolphin, her hair still clotted with oil and grease, but otherwise remarkably well, came to see him.

Theodate Pope lay bruised and battered. She had convinced herself that Edwin Friend was alive but delirious or in a state of amnesia somewhere. When acquaintances took her to convalesce in Cork, she insisted that they insert notices in two newspapers for a week. But nothing came of it.

Elizabeth Duckworth had spent the night feeling ill in the Westbourne Hotel. She might have been amused to know that when a shopkeeper in Taftville, Connecticut, the town where she had worked as a weaver, told her son-in-law that the *Lusitania* had sunk, he had replied, "Well, she was told not to sail but you know how it is, some people have to learn the hard way."

As news of the disaster spread, relations everywhere set out for Queenstown to bring loved ones home or discover their fate. Major General Lassetter immediately left for Ireland to collect his wife and son.

Louisa Hadfield, who helped her mother run a village post office in the north of England, received news that her sister was missing but that her sister's eight-month-old son had been found alive. Reeling from the news, she and her brother hurried to Queenstown to claim the child. As soon as they arrived, they went to the Cunard office, but the scenes there unnerved her. She had "never seen such sadness before." She watched in shock a man who had lost both wife and children "in dreadful distress, burying his head in his hands."

On the Isle of Foula, Professor Holbourn's wife, Marion, was preparing to travel to meet her husband. She had not learned of the sinking until 8 P.M. on 7 May. Her neighbors had kept it from her until "one impetuous but quite well-meaning lady" called out: "Have you heard the news? The *Lusitania*'s down!" Mrs. Holbourn felt blackness surge toward her and clutched the doorjamb for support. The neighbor rushed to get Mrs. Holbourn a brandy, while someone else guided her to a chair. She began to recover, thinking back to her premonition the previous night. She recalled that she had seen a youth in uniform of about seventeen who said reassuringly: "Oh, he's all right. I think he got away in one of the boats." But at 3 A.M. on 8 May, she rose to buy an early edition of that morning's *Scotsman*. Her heart sank at the headline: "Very Few Survivors."

Soon after 8 A.M. came a telegram confirming that her husband was indeed safe. She told her two eldest sons what had happened. They ran joyfully about, shouting: "The whole world is in an uproar! The *Lusitania*'s down and my Daddie's saved!" A further telegram informed her that Professor Holbourn was taking "child Dolphin" to her relations near Worcester and suggested that she join him at Birmingham. The practical woman, realizing her husband must have lost everything, began her preparations at once, packing clothes and other necessities. She wondered what to bring for "child Dolphin," of whose age she had no idea.

The parents of newlywed Mrs. Shineman also read of the disaster in the Scottish papers but were at first unaware that it affected them. Then they discovered that their daughter had been on board, planning to pay them a surprise visit with her new husband. Mrs. Shineman was buried in Kinsale. Her husband, James, was not found until six weeks later and was then identifiable only by his gold watch.

In Chicago the family of William Mounsey, who had sailed with his daughter and son-in-law, Sarah and Charles Lund, in the hope that a woman in a Liverpool asylum might be his wife, now learned that although Sarah was safe, the two men were missing. Their anguish was soon compounded by the knowledge that they had died on a wild-goose chase. Sarah Lund had decided to complete the mission alone. She traveled to Liverpool but found the mystery woman "to be nothing at all like her mother. The quest had been futile from the start."

Survivors began leaving Queenstown the day after the disaster. Many wanted to get away from this "town of the dead" as soon as possible. Surviving crew members who were strong enough to travel, including Able Seaman Thomas O'Mahoney and Steward Barnes, crossed the Irish Channel that night. The ferry carrying the first crewmen reached Holyhead early on 9 May; from there, they caught the train to Liverpool. Crowds had been keeping vigil outside the Cunard offices as bulletins were posted with the latest news. Sometimes as a new name appeared on the list of survivors, "a piercing cry was heard, 'He's saved,' and three or four women would rush away frantically exclaiming 'Saved! Saved! Saved!'" Now hysterical crowds surged over the platforms of Liverpool's Lime Street Station as the carriage doors opened and weary processions of men filed off the trains. Some were bandaged; some were limping. A reporter from the *Liverpool Daily Post* noticed that "not all of them had recovered from their daze and stupor. One man . . . was clad from head to foot in a light-coloured dressing garment and looking singularly strange. He carried his life jacket and although friends were anxious to relieve him of his interesting relic he declined explicitly to let it out of his personal keeping." Other observers noted a strange contrast between the blank faces of the survivors and the anxious, fear-strained faces of the throng of women and girls by whom they were immediately surrounded.

Fireman John O'Connell arrived at the station, dodged through the crowds, and then walked the three miles to his home in Bootle. He felt self-conscious in the suit he had bought in Queenstown with Cunard's money. His grandmother, who had taken him in after both his parents died and he was faced with the workhouse, pawned it the next day. His uncle greeted him with nothing more emotional than "So there you are."

George Wynne had had a nerve-shredding journey across the Irish Sea. He and the other passengers were told to put on their life jackets because "subs was knocking about." Now, wearing a new suit a size too large for him, he shuffled miserably through the throng at Lime Street and made his way to his home on London Road. Unknown to him, his mother, holding her youngest child in her arms, was waiting anxiously at

Survivors at the railroad station.

the station to be reunited with both her husband and her son. When she finally returned to the tiny terraced house, George could not bring himself to tell her what had happened. It was only later when a church minister called wanting "to know the truth" that George at last admitted that his father was missing.

Charles Lauriat was among the first passengers to leave Queenstown. He caught an Irish mail packet across the Irish Sea on 8 May but found he could not sleep. He went to the saloon where "a weird sight" met his eyes. "Every man who had been a passenger on the *Lusitania* was sitting by a table, or reclining on a couch, with a life jacket strapped around him." Many were still wearing their original *Lusitania* jackets.

Lauriat reached Euston station at 6:30 on Sunday morning, 9 May, on the first train bringing survivors to London. He was "almost mobbed" by reporters and refused to be interviewed. A "poor old woman . . . with tears in her eyes" asked whether he knew of one "Johnny Keene." He deduced from her worn clothes that he had probably been a stoker or steerage passenger. He answered as gently as he could that he had not seen him, but comforted her that there were still many other survivors about to disembark from the train.

Other anxious relatives immediately surrounded him. A woman in black moved from group to group trying to find out whether anyone knew what had happened to art expert and connoisseur Sir Hugh Lane. He could not give "any cheerful answers" and realized his nerves were near the breaking point. He was relieved when a young man pushed his way through, introduced himself as Ambassador Page's secretary, and asked what he could do to help. The young man took him over to meet the ambassador. Refusing offers of accommodation at the embassy, Lauriat went to the home of a business contact in the suburbs, where he retired gratefully to bed with "a big-fat-hot-water-bottle."

Oliver Bernard, oddly dressed "thanks to local clothiers in Queenstown," found that, unlike Lauriat, he was in "that mental condition which induces reckless garrulity." He wanted to talk to somebody, anybody, to relieve the stress of pent-up emotions. On the train taking him to catch the boat over to England, he had shared a table in the dining car with a tight-lipped Anglo-Irish couple "of that type which goes by the term 'country gentry.'" The usually reserved theatrical designer could barely wait for the soup before asking the man how the war was affecting Ireland. His dinner companion fixed his eyes on the hat rack above Bernard's head before replying with studied detachment, "The war is not seriously disturbing people in this country as a whole, but every man who is a gentleman is, of course, in uniform." This prompted Bernard to blurt out, "It's a gentleman's war, is it?" Conversation languished.

Now that he had arrived at Euston, Bernard still felt a compulsion for human contact. He was accosted by a journalist who was eager to pump him about his experiences, and went happily to breakfast with him on Fleet Street. He enjoyed the meal of ham and eggs—it was the first proper food he had had since his last lunch on the *Lusitania*—and was flattered by the interest shown in him. Later that day, a man from the *Illustrated London News* tracked him down and asked the designer to make a few pencil sketches of the sinking to be worked up by the journal's own artist. Bernard duly obliged. As his pencil moved deftly over the page, he found himself reliving the scene. He told his eager listener how the *Lusitania* "was swallowed in a gorgeous sea . . . the colour of Damascus steel, the kind of smooth, treacherous sea that—that I never want to look at again." He titled his last sketch simply "Gone." The next day, Bernard called at the offices of the *Illustrated London News*. The editor plied him with champagne and told the gratified young man that he would print his sketches just as they were.

Bernard's attitude was unusual. Most of the survivors now reaching London wanted nothing more than to forget their experiences and to avoid the press. Many looked listless and bedraggled, with torn, unkempt clothes. Observers noticed that their faces were blank, their eyes dazed, and that they moved with an uncertain, bewildered gait. Very few could be induced to speak about their ordeal to the avid journalists, pencils and pads at the ready, clustered around the station's ticket barriers. One reporter described how many were "simply dumb with horror, and even the strongest of those who could talk had a tremor in their voices and fear in their faces." Cunard officials met orphaned children and shepherded them off to the company offices, where attempts were being made to contact their relations. Little Helen Smith, still uncomprehending, told people: "Everybody is sorry for me because my mummy and daddy have gone. They're coming on another boat."

Avis Dolphin's case was happier. Marion Holbourn, waiting at the Birmingham railway station, was overjoyed to be reunited with her husband. He introduced her to Avis, who, as "a well-grown young lady of twelve years," was not the infant she had imagined "child Dolphin" to be.

Oliver Bernard

The professor was carrying a pair of wet trousers over his arm. Mrs. Holbourn went to find her trunk to pack them away, explaining to a puzzled porter, "I've been meeting my husband—he was on the *Lusitania*." "O-oh," the man replied. "Was 'ee drowneded then?" The Holbourns took Avis to her grandparents near Worcester. Her grandfather, a man with large serious eyes and a long white beard like that of an Old Testament Patriarch, confessed to Mrs. Holbourn that he had had an almost identical premonition to hers the night before the sinking. He had seen a ship go down and a little girl rise to the surface and said to his wife, "Depend upon it, that's our Avis!" The young girl had recovered remarkably quickly. She had already written a long letter home, which began: "My dearest Mother, I hope you are well. I am just splendid. I will tell you everything from the time we got on the boat until now."

Many others were suffering the serious aftereffects of their experiences. Margaret Mackworth had begun to feel feverish and ill. When she did snatch a few minutes' sleep, it was only to dream of shipwrecks. She felt sure she was going to die. She begged her father to move her from "that filthy hotel" as she felt she could not bear to breathe her last there. He procured medical advice and as a result moved the almost delirious Margaret by train to Dublin two days after the sinking. They were met by an ambulance and taken to the Shelburne Hotel, where Margaret, by now in the throes of serious bronchial pneumonia, spent three weeks in bed. Her angry father made a long statement to the *Morning Post*: "Why were we not protected[?] . . . Other ships have been, why were not we? Then, also, why were we going so slowly?" He accused the crew of only being concerned for themselves: "There was absolute panic, and they crowded into the boats."

Both Lucy and Harold Taylor had also taken ill. They just managed to reach Harold's parents in Salford, giving their last half-crown to an aggressive cabdriver, before they collapsed.

Elizabeth Duckworth remained in Queenstown long enough to identify her dead friend Alice Scott and arrange for Alice's ten-year-old son, Arthur, to be taken back to his relations in Nelson in England. She remained in a state of shock for some time.

Many of the *Lusitania*'s survivors were never to make a complete recovery. They would be dogged by the mental and physical effects of the sinking for the rest of their lives.

CHAPTER TWENTY-ONE

A Sad and Horrible Task

*M*EANWHILE, in Ireland, officials were struggling to deal with the aftermath of the sinking. On Saturday, 8 May, in Kinsale, county coroner John J. Horgan had opened an inquest into the deaths of two males and three females, whose corpses were brought in with Julia Sullivan on the *Heron*. The dead included Canadian officer Robert Matthews, still wearing a jaunty checked cap. In the pocket of his well-made tweed Norfolk suit was the badge of the *Lusitania* awarded to Annie. It was attached to a slip of paper marked "Second Prize. Potato Race Ladies. Mrs Matthews."

Horgan swore in a jury of local shopkeepers and fishermen, all "good and lawful men," and called the *Lusitania*'s bugler, Vernon Livermore, and Steward Cornelius Horrigan to give evidence. He also summoned the skipper of the *Elizabeth*, who commented angrily on the behavior of Commander Shee of the *Stormcock* in subjecting survivors to a journey of several hours to Queenstown instead of a shorter one to Kinsale.

The key witness was, of course, Captain Turner. Horgan personally served notice on him to attend. On Monday, 10 May, the tired, strained-looking captain arrived at the Old Market House in the center of Kinsale to take his place in the witness box. In response to Horgan's questions he confirmed that he had been aware of the German warning, that the *Lusitania* had been unarmed, and that on entering the danger zone he had taken such precautions as ordering the lifeboats to be swung out and the watertight bulkhead doors to be closed. He told Horgan that although he had not been informed of the sinking of the *Earl of Lathom* on 5 May, he had been in radio contact "all the way across" and had received messages that submarines were off the Irish coast. Turner also readily answered questions about the weather conditions and the ship's speed. It soon became clear, though, that there were areas that the captain was not prepared to discuss in open court. He told the coroner that he had "received special instructions" and had carried them out, but that he was not "at liberty to say what they were."

Horgan turned to the sinking itself. Turner told him that the *Lusitania* had been hit by one torpedo, that there had been one explosion followed immediately by another, that he had ordered boats lowered to the rails but had not been able to slow the ship, that the *Lusitania* had been struck between the third and fourth funnels, and that she was not zigzagging at the time of the attack. In response to further questions about the ship's last moments, Turner said that his orders had been promptly obeyed, that there had been "very little panic," and that "all the passengers were served with life jackets." A juryman asked him whether he had made any special application to the Admiralty for an escort in view of the German warning. Turner said he had not: "I leave that to them. It is their business."

Finally, Horgan asked whether the submarine had given any warning before launching its attack. Turner replied: "None whatever, sir. It was straight and done with, and the whole lot went up in the air." The coroner responded: "We all sympathise with you . . . in the terrible crime which has been committed against your vessel. We express our appreciation of the high courage you have shown, which is worthy of the high traditions of the service to which you belong, and we realise the deep feeling you must have in this matter." Turner, who was sitting with bowed head, burst into racking sobs. Horgan thanked him for assisting the inquiry. Turner slowly stood up. "I was glad to come and help in any way," he said, and left the witness box.

Addressing the jury, Horgan ruled that the dead had perished from "prolonged immersion and exhaustion." He also told them that the sinking of the noncombatant, unarmed *Lusitania* had been a criminal act. He directed the jury to return a verdict placing the burden of guilt squarely on the Germans. "We find that this appalling crime was contrary to international law and the conventions of all civilised nations, and we therefore charge the officers of the said submarine, and the Emperor and Government of Germany, under whose orders they acted, with the crime of wilful and wholesale murder."

Half an hour later, just as Horgan was on the point of leaving the Old Market House, his friend Harry Wynne, crown solicitor for Cork, asked urgently to see him. Wynne told the astonished Horgan that the Admiralty had instructed him to stop the inquest and were particularly concerned that no statement should be made "as to instructions issued by Naval Authorities for guidance of merchant vessels in avoiding submarines." Captain Turner was not to be called to give evidence but was to remain silent until called before a formal Board of Trade inquiry into the loss of the *Lusitania*. Since Ireland was at the time part of the United Kingdom, Horgan would have had to comply. But, as he told Wynne, it was too late. Even while they were speaking, the verdict was being wired to the world's press. He later wrote that the Admiralty was "as belated on this occasion as [it] had been in protecting the *Lusitania* against attack."

——————

That same day, horse-drawn hearses, supplemented by wagons and carts brought from all over County Cork, were rumbling over the cobblestones of Queenstown. They carried load after load of wooden coffins—some shaped caskets with handles, others just plain pine boxes—draped with the Union Jack and chalked with numbers. The local undertakers had run out of coffins, and more had had to be brought by train from Dublin and Kildare. Cunard had employed local photographers like Mr. O'Keefe, "Photographer, Cycle and Antiques Dealer," to photograph the bodies of unidentified victims inside them in the hope that this would later help to identify at least some. The coffins had been left open until just before the funeral procession began so that people could take one last look. Small groups of people in twos and threes walked mutely past the caskets. An observer described the scene: "Packed in their tiny brown boxes like dolls, lay the babies and children killed in the disaster. Their faces held none of the terror which was stamped on those of the other dead. Mothers of Queenstown had piled the little coffins high with flowers."

When the coffins had finally been closed, the funeral procession wound its slow way up Harbour Hill, past the great granite and limestone edifice of St. Colman's Cathedral, where a requiem mass was being held, to the Old Church cemetery two miles outside Queenstown. A military band played the somber strains of Chopin's "Funeral March." The townspeople closed their shutters as a mark of respect and stood silent and

The funeral procession.

bareheaded along the streets. Flags on buildings and ships in the harbor were all at half-mast. Soldiers of the Fourth Royal Irish Regiment, Connaught Rangers, and Royal Dublin Fusiliers lined the route of the cortege. Men of the Royal Navy and Royal Garrison Artillery marched behind the hearses, followed by a stream of mourners on foot or in carriages and cars.

As the mourners sang "Abide with Me," the bodies of more than 140 unidentified victims were lowered into three cavernous common graves designated simply A, B, and C. Dug by soldiers the previous day, they measured twenty by thirty feet. In one lay sixty-five coffins but sixty-seven bodies (two contained infants buried with their mothers). A firing party loosed a volley of shots, and twenty buglers sounded "The Last Post."

Other bodies were buried in Kinsale. Little Constance Wolfe, whose dentist father had taken her up on the town walls when news came the *Lusitania* was sinking, watched while her mother and other women lined the graves with moss and flowers.

The atmosphere in Queenstown was almost too much for some distraught relatives who had arrived to search for their loved ones. Mostyn Prichard, brother of missing medical student Dick Prichard, wrote in anguish, "The place is alive with miserable creatures like ourselves." He had combed the hospitals and morgues without success and felt helpless. "It is bewildering to know what to do," he added, although he felt comforted by "the universal sympathy of the entire town."

The day after the funeral in Queenstown, Wesley Frost sent a detailed dispatch to Secretary of State Bryan in Washington, D.C. He reported the details of the sinking, including his view that the ship had been struck by a single torpedo, writing: "Second torpedo dubious: probably boiler explosion." He also reported that hundreds of people were still missing and that he was worried that the search for bodies was being "wretchedly managed." An Admiralty tug had cruised to the scene of the wreck on the night of 7 May but returned "with neither news nor bodies." The next vessel was a Cunard tug, which set out on the night of 8 May but returned after several hours. No other vessel went out until 4 P.M. on Monday, 10 June. Frost had threatened Cunard with diplomatic intervention if mat-

One of the mass burials for the Lusitania's *dead.*

ters did not improve. In response, the company agreed to charter a Dutch tug.

Frost also reported to Bryan his belief that "the Cunard people and the Admiralty each appear willing to shift responsibility to the other. . . . The Admiralty protests that all their vessels are busy on regular patrols. . . . Cunard claim that the Admiralty has direction of all available vessels." Frost's concern to recover and identify bodies was so strong that, a month later, he even wrote to Bryan forwarding his vice consul's suggestion that "explosives might be dropped on to the wreck of the *Lusitania* in such a manner as to burst the hull . . . and allow corpses and wreckage to rise to the surface."

Frost knew it was important to move quickly since it would become harder to identify corpses with every passing day. Indeed, as early as 22 May Cunard's Queenstown office was reporting "bodies coming in now not recognisable except through papers, clothing or identification marks." In many cases flesh had already been eaten away, making the task of both Cunard officials and the American consulate more difficult and more distressing. At the same time, relations and officials, far removed from the scene of the tragedy and unaware of the difficulties, pressed unceasingly for news.

Nevertheless, it was possible to identify the bodies of Dr. Fred Pearson (the eminent engineer) and his wife, Chief Purser McCubbin, Dr. McDermott (the ship's doctor), and three of the six Crompton children (although there was no sign of the remaining children or of their parents). The corpse of Commander Stackhouse was found and buried in a little Quaker graveyard in Cork. The contents of the explorer's pockets were returned to his widow and included a slip of paper on which he had written, perhaps just before the ship went down, "Let mercy be our boast, and shame our only fear."

The remains of Ailsa Booth-Jones were also found. Still on the body were her green velvet dress and lace-up boots. Pinned to her blue jersey was the imitation gold brooch of the *Lusitania* which she had won during deck games and which she had proudly shown to Professor Holbourn and Avis. She was interred in a private grave in Queenstown.

The body of Charlotte Pye's baby, Marjorie, was finally recovered. Charlotte, lying wretchedly in her hotel bed, had been persuaded to go and stay with a wealthy and kind woman in the town. At first she had resisted, saying, "all I wanted to do was to go and look for my baby." She later relented, spending each day hoping for news. Eventually and reluctantly, Charlotte had left Queenstown for England, but the very next day received a wire that "my baby had been found" about 100 miles from where the *Lusitania* had sunk. The tiny corpse had been identified by her underclothing. Cunard officials added the child to their lists in brief, clinical terms: "No. 239 Female child about 2 years, identified as Miss Pye by Archdeacon Daunt from clothing. No property." Charlotte sent instructions for the burial, and her benefactress ordered a tiny white coffin and attended the service.

The body of Norah Bretherton's baby girl, Betty, eventually washed up on the shore and was buried in a Cork convent.

The corpse of one of Lady Allan's daughters, Gwen, was found and sent to London for burial, but her sister's was lost forever. So was the body of Sir Hugh Lane. Father Basil Maturin's corpse washed up on the stony beaches of Ballycotton Bay, where two elderly fishermen found it. His pince-nez, fountain pen, silver watch, and bankers' drafts for over £2,000 were still on the body. His remains were shipped to England for a funeral ceremony at London's fashionable Brompton Oratory. Marie de Page's corpse was identified, embalmed, and taken to Belgium by her grief-stricken husband, while that of Belle Naish's husband, Theodore, was found and shipped home to Kansas City. The remains of Annie Matthews were also recovered.

The body of Alfred Vanderbilt was never found, despite the many people who, eager for the reward, combed the coves and inlets. Chief Electrician George Hutchinson claimed to have seen him in the water wearing a life jacket the wrong way around. He had tried to adjust it for him, but the two men had drifted apart.

In later weeks a number of corpses washed up on the beaches and mudflats along the western coast of Ireland. Many were in an advanced state of decomposition, often limbless, sometimes headless. A female corpse with no legs or arms, and with "nothing but the skull to indicate features," was found still clad in black skirt and black silk blouse with white linen collar. It was identified by name tags on the clothing. Other finds included a male body—now "almost a skeleton and unrecogniseable" but wearing "new tennis boots"—and a badly decomposed female corpse clad in just a corset, part of a chemise, and some ragged scraps of dress. These remains were quickly buried in a workhouse graveyard. A Cunard official informed company headquarters that "hot

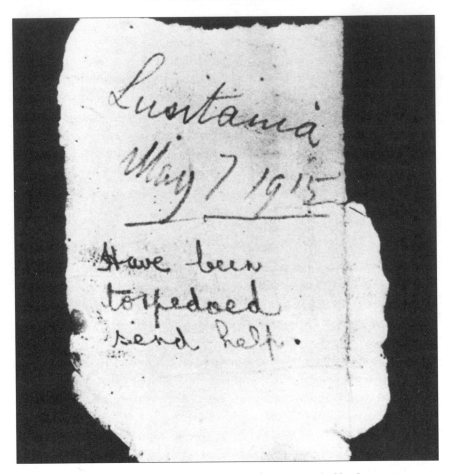

*This note, thought to be a hoax, was found in a corked bottle
that washed up on the English coast.*

weather having set in . . . is adding to the difficulty of keeping any bodies
for any length of time."

Officials tried to match the awful objects being fished from the sea
to photographs and the sometimes vague and disjointed descriptions
furnished by relatives. One such pen-portrait telegraphed to Queenstown by the Liverpool office read: "MARY LAMBIE SECOND CABIN AGE 27
FAIR BLUE EYES HAIR LIGHT BROWN 5 FEET 9 INCHES SLIGHT BUILT THREE
FALSE UPPER FRONT TEETH BRIDGE ENAMEL FRONTS GOLD BACK MOLE
BACK SHOULDERS FOUR RINGS STOP DAUGHTERS ELIZABETH AGE 10 MARY

AGE 3 BOTH FAIR CURLY HAIR BROWN EYES ENDS." The wife of a missing crewman sent details of tattoos on his arm—"Maggie, a Rose, a Five-Pointed Star"—in the hope that this would help locate him.

The officials, in turn, recorded every detail of every corpse and its attire. One report read: "Description of No. 241, male unidentified, about 50 . . . face much eaten away on left side, fair complexion, blue eyes. Fair hair turning grey. . . . Wore blue trousers and vest with stripe, white flannel drawers and white flannel undershirt and white linen shirt with blue stripe, turned down collar and turned up cuffs, laced toe-capped boots and stockings and a pair of suspenders." Sometimes they snipped a small scrap of fabric from a jacket or pair of trousers in case it might help identify a victim. A fragment of dark, speckled tweed still remains in the Cunard archives.

The Queenstown office also had to document property in scrupulous detail before sending it on. In the case of one female, this included such small items as "eyeglasses rimless with gold hairpin holder and chain, engraved silver pencil case, small circular purse mirror, folding button hook, 1 black handbag." Despite their efforts, property could not always be returned—a magnificent diamond ring found on the quayside remained unclaimed—and sometimes it went mysteriously astray. The American relations of a drowned woman took receipt of her body on 3 June expecting her "modest looking but beautiful" diamond necklace still to be on the corpse, together with some $2,500 which they believed she would have "tucked within her corsets." However, the undertakers reported "that her corsets were unfastened when she arrived." An especially unsavory task for the already harassed employees was the shipping of a noxious trunk belonging to a deceased man. His relatives demanded it, and the railway was refusing to transport it. The Liverpool office wrote impatiently to Queenstown: "We think you might endeavour by some means or other to forward all the effects possible. . . . probably by placing them in a wood box and sprinkled with a little sanitary liquid might help same being passed over the various railroads."

The Cunard officials in Queenstown had other macabre problems. For example, they had overinvested in coffins, at some four pounds apiece, because they had never anticipated that such a large number of bodies—over 900—would never be recovered. They wrote to their colleagues in Liverpool, "To get rid of our surplus stock we must be prepared to make great sacrifices . . . in case they are left as a drag on our hands." The situation was further complicated because some of the coffins had for a short while held corpses which were later transferred elsewhere. The coffins were therefore unappealing to the undertakers of Cork and Queenstown as a job lot. Only one made an offer, but the Liverpool office dismissed his bid of £325 as derisory. It asked its Queenstown office whether it could not dispose of the caskets individually. This was the final straw. The Queenstown officials responded firmly that "even the very poorest people in this country are particularly sensitive regarding such matters, and would not accept one of these coffins for their dead even if offered for nothing."

The Cunard headquarters was also concerned about "the very large cost" of twenty pounds for embalming some of the bodies and about the charge of ten pounds per casket being made by the Cork Steam Packet Company for shipping bodies back to Liverpool. Surely, the Liverpool staff suggested, "in view of the fact that there have been such a large number of caskets, they could see their way to make some modification in the rate of freight." They further pointed out that the White Star Line was transporting American cadavers home for free. They were also annoyed to discover that the company had inadvertently paid for the burial of the American victim of the steamer *Falaba*, sunk by the *U-28* in March. The body of Leon Thresher washed up on the shore of County Kerry on 12 July, and his corpse had at first automatically been assumed to be from the *Lusitania*.

Against this background, the Queenstown office tried to keep meticulous lists of deceased and where they were buried. Mistakes, of course, were inevitable. One child recorded as dead was discovered some weeks later to have survived. Cunard also found that a number of bodies had "apparently been buried without proper record." Others had been wrongly identified. Body number twenty-three was at first recognized by one of the *Lusitania*'s crew as being that of a steward named Glancy, but later "it was identified as that of Mr. Abercomby by his brother and sister." In other cases contradictory information was sent to relations about the location of graves. One man wrote complaining that he had been told his dead brother had been buried in "Grave C, 2nd Row, Lower Tier," while another family member had been informed that the body was in "Grave A, 3rd Row, Lower Tier." Harrowed and harassed company officials like manager Jerome Murphy, tormented by guilt and unable to sleep, could, however, be glad that by the middle of July the last hospital cases in Queenstown had been discharged so that they could concentrate fully on the dead rather than the living.

It fell to Wesley Frost to examine any bodies that might be American. He found the task "revolting." Unlike those corpses washed ashore in the immediate aftermath, which had for him an "unearthly aura of personality lent them by the rigor mortis," these monstrous, flaccid forms were devoid of humanity: "The rigidity relaxed into an inebriate flabbiness and the features broke down into a preposterously animal-like repulsiveness." In his capacity as official witness he had to attend an autopsy performed on one body seventy-two days dead. The sight and smell sickened him, "but other corpses equalled it in the ravages they displayed. The faces registered every shading of the grotesque and hideous. The lips and noses were eaten away by seabirds, and the eyes gouged into staring pools of blood. It was almost a relief when the faces became indistinguishable as such. Towards the last the flesh was wholly gone from the grinning skulls, the trunks were bloated and distended with gases, and the limbs were partially eaten away or bitten clean off by sea-creatures so that stumps of raw bone were left projecting."

Frost, like the Cunard officials, was under great stress. Although he won the admiration of Ambassador Page and his staff for his coolness and sound judgment, he was privately tormented by his experiences. "One night at my home," he later recalled, "I went into a bedroom with a lighted match and came unexpectedly upon the sleeping form of my own little daughter." It put him instantly in mind of "the poor livid little midget-corpses" of the children drowned on the *Lusitania*. "I give you my word I recoiled as though I had found a serpent." He was glad when the sad and horrible task of accounting for the *Lusitania*'s dead finally ended.

⟞∞⟝

The final toll was 1,198 dead (1,201 including the three anonymous stowaways). Of the 1,257 registered passengers, 785, including 128 Americans, had died, as had 413 members of the 702-strong crew. Of the 129 children on board, 94 had been killed, including 35 of the 39 babies. Compared with daily casualty figures at the Front, the *Lusitania* fatalities were tiny. But world reaction to what had occurred off the Irish coast on Friday 7 May 1915 was enormous.

PART FOUR

"Remember the *Lusitania!*"

CHAPTER TWENTY-TWO

The Hun's Most Ghastly Crime

*A*T 8:15 P.M. ON 7 MAY, Admiral Pohl, commander in chief of the German High Seas Fleet, had received a brief wireless message. Based on a British radio signal intercepted by the battleship *Posen*, it told him that the *Lusitania* had been torpedoed. On 8 May the German Admiralty's daily top-secret intelligence report opened with a brief statement that the *Lusitania* had been torpedoed and sunk off the Old Head of Kinsale but made no comment. The next day Crown Prince Wilhelm, who had determinedly supported Tirpitz's campaign for all-out U-boat warfare, sent the kaiser an exultant telegram from his headquarters at Stenay in northern France. There was, he told his father, "great joy" at the news. He added that the more single-mindedly the U-boat war was prosecuted, the faster the war would end.

The German press at once applauded the attack as an "extraordinary success." While regretting the loss of life, they praised the action as an example of Germany's seamanship and technical prowess. They presented it as a justified attack on a ship that had been armed and carrying both munitions and Canadian troops and which had been warned before she sailed. They placed the blame firmly on British pride and indifference, accusing Cunard of wanton irresponsibility in carrying passengers on board a Royal Navy Auxiliary vessel—in other words, a warship. One paper declared that "hundreds of non-participant passengers were victims, victims of the haughty greed of English shipping lines." Another accused Britain of cynically using "citizens from neutral nations as a shield." The *Kölnische Volkszeitung* went farther, claiming the sinking as "a success of moral significance" and a just response to British attempts to starve the German people to death through her blockade.

In the early hours of 12 May the Germans—and the British—finally learned for certain which U-boat was responsible for the attack. Some 200 miles from Heligoland and now back in radio contact, Walther Schwieger instructed his radio officer, Otto Rikowsky, to signal German wireless stations with news of his triumph: "HAVE SUNK ONE SAILING VES-SEL TWO STEAMERS AND LUSITANIA." In a further signal he stated that he had sunk the Cunard liner with one torpedo. Room 40 intercepted both messages and immediately recognized their significance. Sir Alfred Ewing, head of Room 40, had them checked with each of ten different lis-tening posts and asked for certified copies to be sent to him. He gathered these copies in a special file, as well as including them in the normal daily list of intercepts, circulated, among others, to Churchill (first lord of the Admiralty), Admiral Fisher (first sea lord), Rear Admiral Oliver (chief of war staff), and Captain Reginald Hall (director of the Intelligence Divi-sion). Each now knew that whatever had caused the second explosion reported by so many survivors, it was not a second torpedo.

The Room 40 team also decoded the congratulations sent within hours by Pohl to the *U-20*: "MY HIGHEST APPRECIATION OF COMMANDER AND CREW FOR SUCCESS ACHIEVED OF WHICH THE HIGH SEAS FLEET IS PROUD AND MY CONGRATULATIONS ON THEIR RETURN."

On 13 May, Schwieger was ordered to sail not to Emden, the German naval base on the North Sea, but on to Wilhelmshaven. This presented no problems—he still had about one-third of his fuel left. As the *U-20* arrived at the end of her journey of 3,006 nautical miles, 250 of them under water, jubilant sailors assembled on the decks of the nearby war-ships gave three cheers.

The reaction in the British press, meanwhile, was bitter, virulent, and predictable. The papers raged about the "Latest Achievements of German Frightfulness at Sea" and "The Hun's Most Ghastly Crime." Editorials sug-gested that the act was a further example of a new and unprincipled form of warfare: "Sowing of illegal mines, submarining of merchantmen, butch-ery of fishermen, the *Falaba* case, the *Lusitania* case—it is a long and terri-ble list. On land the sacking of towns, the massacres of non-combatants, the use of explosive bullets and asphyxiating gas."

Images of confused, pale-faced orphans, bereaved women, and dead

Winston Churchill and "Jackie" Fisher

babies stared out from the pages. Survivors' accounts depicted the liner's last moments with grim pathos. They conjured traumatic hours spent clinging to wreckage among a harvest of dead bodies. The *Daily Mirror* played on readers' emotions with a tale of how a two-year-old boy was tossed into a lifeboat at the last moment. An elderly woman tried to comfort this "Little Unknown," but he "pressed his chubbie fists into his eyes and sobbed, 'Mummie, mummie.'" The only person able to quiet him was "a burly stoker" streaked with coal dust who said soothingly, "Don't cry, sonny. We shall soon be all right."

Several accounts told of submarines circling around, and gloating U-boatmen leaning from their conning towers to taunt their victims. Some even told of submariners machine-gunning people in the water. The *Times* insisted that the countries of the world "must join in branding . . . the renegade among the nations." The *Daily Express* hoped that President Wilson, "good man that he is," would be stirred to do "something more than protest." The papers also reported that, according to the sources that had predicted the destruction of the *Lusitania*, another Cunard liner, the *Transylvania*, would be next. Recruitment posters depicting a blazing, sinking ship with victims struggling helplessly in the water urged men to join up to "avenge the *Lusitania*." Recruitment offices reported a surge in applicants.

Anti-German rioting broke out at once in many British cities. In London, German-owned businesses or those whose owners had German-sounding names were systematically looted from the East End to Kentish Town. One bakery lost everything down to its baking tins. Newspapers reported "widespread havoc," "pillage and fire." The disturbances were particularly violent in Liverpool. Two Americans who had just arrived on the liner *New York* joined in. One of them later told the *New York Times* what happened when the mob attacked a cutlery shop: "The crowd was muttering and growling and the shop was dark but there were people upstairs. So I just picked up a brick and heaved it through the window. . . . Then everyone took to shying them, and in a few minutes the place was a wreck. Then everyone broke into the place and soon all the furniture, carpets and everything else were thrown out of the windows into the street. There were several policemen at the corner . . . and they only grinned. The crowd then went on down the street and wrecked four German pork shops and carried away some of the meat. I saw one young fellow going off with half a hog and an old woman was dancing in the middle of the street with strings of sausages all over her and flying in the wind." In some places the mobs were 2,000 or 3,000 strong, and by 13 May £40,000 worth of property had been destroyed in Liverpool alone. In desperation the authorities closed the city's pubs early. They advised German and Austrian nationals to quit the city and head inland for their own safety.

In Leeds the Corn Exchange passed a resolution demanding the immediate departure of anyone of Austrian or German extraction. A small group hastily left, watched by 600 members roaring out "Rule Britannia." In London the Stock Exchange asked naturalized members of German and Austrian birth not to attend and to present their papers for vetting. On 13 May, Prime Minister Asquith announced the internment of all enemy aliens of military age. The following day, the kaiser's banner was unceremoniously hauled down in the Chapel Royal at Windsor Castle to mark his expulsion from the British Order of the

Garter, bestowed on him thirty-eight years earlier by his adored grand-mother, Queen Victoria.

There was also serious anti-German rioting in British dominions overseas. In Canada, the capital of British Columbia, Victoria, was placed under martial law. The mayor was forced to read the Riot Act and deploy 800 soldiers on the city streets. He also provided the German-born wife of the lieutenant governor with special protection.

The French joined their British ally in declaring the sinking an act of unprecedented barbarity. One paper declared that "the Germans' divorce from civilization is complete." Another reported a supposed prediction by an official of the North German Lloyd Line just four days before the attack: "As for the *Lusitania* we'll get her for certain." All predicted hopefully that neutral countries would now join the war on the side of the Allies.

Neutral countries indeed condemned the attack. The Norwegian *Morgenblad* wrote that "the news of the sinking of the *Lusitania* puts . . . all other events in the background and arouses the whole world to a feeling of horror. The Germans have meant to terrify. They have ter-rified their friends and terror breeds hate." The Dutch *Telegraaf* declared, "Criminal is too mild a word to be applied to this outrage; it is devilish."

In Germany there was surprise at the world's reaction. Officials carefully analyzed the reporting of the *Lusitania* incident in neutral countries, and Foreign Secretary Jagow moved quickly to brief Ger-many's embassies so they could counter press criticism. The kaiser was shocked by the extent to which he was being demonized. He was particu-larly affronted by the references to "Hunnish" barbarity, although he was, to some extent, to blame. In a notorious speech to German troops departing for China in 1900, he had urged them to "give no quarter! Take no prisoners!" but to kill. "Even as, a thousand years ago, the Huns under their leader Attila gained such a name for themselves as still resounds in terror . . . so may the name of Germany resound!" The "Hun" imagery immediately caught the attention of the world press and never faded, although, in reality, there was no racial kinship between the Germans and the Huns.

The German government was, of course, most concerned about opinion in the neutral United States. The immediate public reaction in America was shock. The press condemned the act as barbaric in an almost unanimous chorus of horror. Editors broke the news using the banner headlines reserved for only the most dramatic stories, set in the enormous typeface they irreverently called "Second Coming type." The *Minneapolis Journal* declared: "Germany intends to become the outlaw of nations. Perhaps we are yet to witness savagery carried to its ultimate perfection."

As the news ricocheted around Manhattan on 7 May, the day of the sinking, word spread that the German ambassador, Count Bernstorff, was staying at New York's Ritz-Carlton Hotel. Besieged by the press, he decided to stay in his suite. He asked the German naval attaché, Captain Karl Boy-Ed, to attend in his stead a charity concert that evening at the Metropolitan Opera House, a fund-raiser for the German Red Cross. The Opera House's management feared trouble and stationed plain-clothesmen all over the theater. They banned the flying of German flags and also the singing of "Deutschland über Alles." Madam Gadski, wife of the Krupps' representative in America and one of the star performers, substituted "the triumphant cry of the Valkyrie" for Germany's national anthem. Nevertheless, Boy-Ed and Franz von Papen, the German military attaché who attended with him, were booed and hissed. Afterward, people complained that the private box of the missing Alfred Vanderbilt had been sold for a performance in aid of a German cause.

Count Bernstorff tried to slip out of New York at 5:30 the next morning, but even at that early hour eager newsmen were outside the hotel to jostle and hustle him as he got into a taxi. He shouted that he would not make a statement, and when the driver showed no sign of moving yelled, "Go on, damn you, go on!" The shaken diplomat was pursued all the way to Pennsylvania Station, down to the platform, and onto the train home to Washington. Persistent reporters asked him for reactions to claims that he had provoked the attack on the *Lusitania* by placing the warning in the papers, even that he was a murderer. Bernstorff responded angrily that he was indifferent to anything the papers might allege. This was not strictly true. When German propagandist Bernhard Dernburg insisted to reporters that Germany had an absolute right to sink without warning any ship carrying contraband "without regard to nationality or neutrality" and that the Americans on board the *Lusitania* had committed suicide, Bernstorff reacted to his gaffe by packing him straight back to Germany.

In Berlin, Foreign Secretary Jagow initially took a bullying line with

U.S. ambassador James Gerard, asserting to him that America "will do nothing in this case." On another occasion, according to Gerard, Jagow struck his desk with his fist as he declared that Germany had "500,000 German reservists in America who will rise in arms against your Government if your Government should dare to take any action against Germany." Gerard responded that there were "501,000 lamp-posts in America, and that was where the German reservists would find themselves [hanging] if they tried any uprising."

But there was real anxiety behind the German rhetoric. The kaiser asked for details of the *Lusitania* incident as early as possible. Schwieger was therefore ordered to report as soon as he landed. On 14 May Admiral Gustav Bachmann, the naval chief of staff, sent a telegram direct to the kaiser relaying Schwieger's story. Bachmann added in a postscript that British claims that the *U-20* had fired two torpedoes were unfounded, and that the second explosion was most likely caused by munitions on board.

In the highly charged atmosphere, with accusations and counter-accusations flying thickly, the German government was determined to establish the true cause of the second explosion beyond doubt. German experts carefully scrutinized a report in the *New York Times* suggesting that the *Lusitania* had been carrying 250,000 pounds of tetrachloride for the French government for use in fabricating gas bombs. The German government decided to commission its torpedo laboratory at Kiel to undertake a full forensic analysis in the utmost secrecy. Laboratory scientists looked closely at the construction of the *Lusitania*, Schwieger's report of what had happened, and even press reports of Captain Turner's comments. The scientists concluded that the torpedo hit the forward section of the number-one boiler room, that a boiler explosion could not "easily be discounted," but that this could not account for the immediate outbreak of fire observed by Schwieger. The cause of the second explosion was probably munitions, but they did not rule out a coal-dust explosion, which they knew could be triggered when "coalbunkers are hit by shells."

An official version of Schwieger's war diary was produced. The standard procedure was for each U-boat commander to deliver his handwritten war diary, completed en route, to the bureau of his flotilla in whichever port he arrived. It would then be typed, each day's report personally signed off by the commander, and the original manuscript returned to him. Significantly, the only surviving version shows that Schwieger, on this occasion, signed for every day except 7 May.

Schwieger meanwhile was ordered to report to Berlin, where, as Tirpitz later recalled, he was "treated very ungraciously." His reception reflected a growing realization that the sinking of the *Lusitania* had done Germany far more harm than good.

CHAPTER TWENTY-THREE

Fool or Traitor?

THE BRITISH GOVERNMENT soon recognized that the sinking of the *Lusitania* could be a powerful weapon in the propaganda war and were anxious that no blame for it could be laid at their door. The Royal Navy and Admiralty moved quickly to fend off any criticism of their actions, collective or individual.

Vice Admiral Coke in Queenstown was particularly swift to guard his own back. At 6:25 P.M. on the day of the sinking, well before the first survivors had reached land, he had signaled the Admiralty in London that the *Lusitania* had been "SPECIALLY WARNED [OF] SUBMARINES ON SOUTHERN COAST AND TO KEEP MID-CHANNEL COURSE AVOIDING HEADLANDS. ALSO POSITION OF SUBMARINE SIGHTED OFF CAPE CLEAR 10.00 A.M. TODAY WAS COMMUNICATED BY W/T TO HER." Captain Richard Webb, director of the Trade Division of the Admiralty and responsible for providing guidance to merchant shipping, dashed off a message to Coke asking him to confirm that he was continuing to warn merchant ships of U-boat movements. Coke confirmed tersely that he was.

Admiral Jackie Fisher ordered all reports of U-boat movements and sightings to be collated. He remained under great strain. In early May, Clementine Churchill had been sufficiently concerned about him to suggest to her husband that he, Churchill, should not go to France as planned to discuss Italy's entry into the war. She tried to support Fisher in Churchill's absence and invited him to lunch. Although he seemed "as nervous as a kitten," all appeared to go well. Fisher left the room in a cheerful mood, but when Clementine followed a moment later, she encountered him lurking in the corridor. He suddenly burst out: "You are a foolish woman. All the time you think Winston's with Sir John French he is in Paris with his mistress." She interpreted his spiteful remark as a sure sign his mind was becoming unbalanced.

Churchill cannot have been pleased, on returning to London on 10 May, to learn of Fisher's unfounded accusations. Clementine would have been a remarkably trusting wife had she not told him. As well as being worried about Fisher's mental state, Churchill faced that day a barrage of key questions about the *Lusitania* in the House of Commons from, among others, his old bête noire Lord Charles Beresford. What was the ship's speed when she was sunk? What were the captain's instructions? Where were the naval patrols? Why had she not been escorted when submarines were known to be in the area? What action had been taken in response to the newspaper warning in America?

Churchill's performance in the Commons was not among his best. He was, he noted, inhibited by the requirement not to disclose classified information. As announced that morning, the Board of Trade had set up an independent inquiry into the sinking of the *Lusitania*. It would be chaired by Lord Mersey, a senior judge and Britain's commissioner for wrecks, with "the assistance of skilled assessors." While confirming that the *Lusitania* had received instructions and at least two warnings from the Admiralty, Churchill said that he could not discuss them since "it might appear I was trying to throw blame on the Captain of the *Lusitania* in regard to an affair which will be the subject of full investigation."

This was a mere hint of the "blame Turner" attitude within the Admiralty, the spin the government was giving the story in the early days after the sinking. Vice Admiral Coke's detailed report of 9 May on his own activities included a gratuitous dig at Turner: "From reports received, the *Lusitania* was 8 to 10 miles from the land, which in view of the warning given her was dangerous." Captain Webb built extensively on this theme in a memorandum he was now composing. The key paragraphs read:

> In taking the course he did, the Master of the Lusitania acted directly contrary to the written general instructions received from the Admiralty and completely disregarded the telegraphic warnings received from Queenstown during the hours immediately preceding the attack. On the facts at present disclosed, the Master

appears to have displayed an almost inconceivable negligence, and one is forced to conclude that he is either utterly incompetent or that he has been got at by the Germans. In considering this latter possibility it is not necessary to suppose that he had any conception of the loss of life which actually occurred and he might well have thought that being close to the shore there would be ample time to run his ship into a place of security before she foundered.

Supposing however that no suspicion of treachery attaches to the Master, it is conceivable that in conversation with his fellow officials he may have expressed his intention of following his usual track regardless of the submarine menace. In this case, having regard to the nationalities and sympathies of the high officials of the Cunard Company in New York, it is very possible that his intention may have been communicated to the German Embassy, and in this case it is not difficult to explain the confident prophesies spread abroad in New York.

Lord Mersey is escorted to the official inquiry.

Webb attached to his memorandum a telegram from Sir Cecil Spring-Rice reporting Consul General Bennett's comments about the Germanic antecedents of many of Cunard's New York staff and questioning their loyalty. He sent both items to Rear Admiral Oliver on 12 May. Oliver forwarded Webb's communication to Churchill and Fisher. He included a cover letter supporting the director of the Admiralty Trade Division's views and suggesting action be taken over the staffing of the overseas offices of British shipping companies.

For his part, Fisher had little doubt whom should be blamed for the *Lusitania*, scribbling "Fully concur" in his characteristic green ink against Webb's comment that Turner was either utterly incompetent or had been got at. Fisher added: "As the Cunard Company would not have employed an incompetent man, the certainty is absolute that Captain Turner is not a fool but a knave. I hope that Captain Turner will be arrested immediately after the enquiry whatever the verdict." He then noted on Oliver's submission, "Ought not Lord Mersey to get a hint" and "I feel absolutely certain that Captain Turner of the *Lusitania* is a scoundrel and [had] been bribed." He concluded, "No seaman in his senses could have acted as he did."

Churchill was only slightly more circumspect. He wrote in red ink: "Fully concur with DTD [Webb]. I consider the Admiralty case against the Captain should be pressed before Lord Mersey by a skilful counsel and that Captain Webb should attend as witness if not employed as assessor. We should pursue the captain without check." Having communicated this very clear government policy guidance for what should have been an independent and impartial inquiry, Churchill and Fisher now left the detail to their staffs. They turned instead to a topic that both considered more important than the *Lusitania* but over which they disagreed—the Dardanelles.

A final confrontation between the two men was not long delayed. Bolstered by intercepts from Room 40 indicating that more German submarines were on their way to the Mediterranean, Fisher insisted on 12 May that the navy's newest battleship, the *Queen Elizabeth*, be withdrawn back to the Home Fleet. He reluctantly agreed to Churchill's demand that she be replaced in the Dardanelles by older vessels. On Friday, 14 May,

Churchill pressed for further additions to the Dardanelles force. That evening the two met. At the end of the meeting Fisher believed that they had agreed to limit further reinforcements to a level acceptable to him. He retired to bed early as usual but on rising before dawn discovered that, in the small hours, Churchill had written him a memo requiring reinforcements "greatly in excess" of the number they had agreed on. Around 5 A.M. Fisher wrote his letter of resignation, concluding, "I am off to Scotland at once so as to avoid all questionings."

At first neither Prime Minister Asquith nor Churchill took his resignation seriously. The volatile old man had, after all, threatened to resign on at least nine previous occasions since the beginning of 1915. However, they became alarmed at his continued absence from his post. Both tried to persuade him to relent, but he would not.

At the same time, Asquith and his administration were themselves under great pressure following an article in the *Times* of Friday, 14 May alleging a "scandalous shortage of shells on the Western Front." The author was a *Times* correspondent named Colonel Repington. It was rumored that Churchill had leaked him the story during his visit to France to further his own political ambitions. If so, the affair backfired on him badly. To avoid an onslaught from the Conservative opposition, Asquith decided on Monday, 17 May to seek a coalition government of national unity with the Conservatives. Churchill had crossed the floor of the House of Commons, deserting the Conservatives in favor of Asquith's Liberals. Also, his conduct of the Dardanelles operation and other naval matters, including the *Lusitania* disaster, was under severe criticism by Conservatives such as Beresford. Part of the Conservatives' price would therefore be the removal of Churchill.

Fisher saw an opportunity for himself to ride back to power. On 19 May he wrote to Asquith a most ill-judged note. He graciously agreed to return and "guarantee the successful termination of the War and the total abolition of the submarine menace" on six conditions, among them that "Mr Winston Churchill is not in the Cabinet to be always circumventing me," that he should have "absolutely untrammelled sole command of all the sea forces whatsoever," and that he have an equally free hand in all appointments. He had clearly overstepped the mark. This "extraordinary ultimatum" angered Asquith, who told the king that it "indicated signs of mental aberration." Fisher's resignation was, to his chagrin, accepted.

Churchill did not long survive him. Under the new coalition government he was moved on 26 May to be chancellor of the duchy of Lancaster, a less important position with few and ill-defined duties. He resigned from the government entirely on 12 November to become a battalion commander on the Western Front. His successor as first lord of the Admiralty was the cool, languid, self-contained former prime minister Arthur Balfour. Thus, by the time the inquiry into the sinking of the *Lusitania* opened on 15 June, two key figures had disappeared from the Admiralty scene.

One of Captain Webb's first tasks in preparing the Admiralty's deposition for the inquiry was to ensure that nothing was said that might undermine national security. He therefore had deleted from the list of questions proposed by the Board of Trade (the government department responsible for setting up the inquiry), and which had to be answered in the published report, the simple question: What were Captain Turner's instructions from the owners or the Admiralty? He did, however, allow two questions to stand. Had the captain received instructions? If so, had he carried them out? Both were susceptible to single-word answers—"yes" or "no."

The nature of the instructions would, however, be discussed in closed sessions. Captain Webb therefore had to decide which ones had been received by Turner. In a carefully constructed schedule, he listed the detailed note of 10 February 1915 with its instructions to avoid headlands, to steer a midchannel course, to operate at full speed off harbors, to post extra lookouts, and to ram any attacking submarine. He added four further instructions, including some that had been issued earlier and that related mainly to avoiding attacks by surface vessels. His sixth and final choice was an instruction dated 16 April advising captains that "fast steamers can considerably reduce the chance of successful surprise attack by zig-zagging."

Webb was not on firm ground here. He knew that a more comprehensive version of the zigzagging note, this one including an illustrative diagram, had not in fact been issued by the Admiralty until 13 May. However, he thought it possible that an initial three-paragraph note had gone out on 16 April. If so, and if Turner could be claimed to have received and ignored it, it would be further proof of his incompetence. Webb put inquiries in hand with Cunard to establish whether the company had received and issued it. The answer was inconclusive. Cunard's marine superintendent believed that Captain Turner either had received a copy or had read it. A manuscript note in the Admiralty file, added as an after-thought, carefully distanced the Admiralty from this information. It qualified the statement that the instruction had been received with the phrase: "It is understood that . . ." These four "weasel words" remain a standard formula in the British civil service to imply doubt and indicate that the information is not directly known to the writer, who cannot vouch for it.

Captain Webb also had to decide what should be said to the inquiry by the admiralty about signals sent to the *Lusitania* during her final voyage. He asked the various wireless stations to provide details of all messages and then produced a list. The list included only general messages to all ships in the area, such as the one sent out nightly and based on the February guidance about avoiding headlands and steering a midchannel course. It did not include messages sent to the *Lusitania* alone during the two days before the sinking. It did not, for example, list the "QUESTOR"/ "WESTRONA" exchange, which established which code the *Lusitania* was using, or seemingly personal messages, such as the one from May Barwell to Alfred Vanderbilt.

It appears probable—from gaps in the telegram sequence in Admiralty files, and from informal statements made by the Ministry of Defence to previous historians—that there were further official messages sent only to the *Lusitania*. Their nature has been a matter of much speculation. If they indeed existed, they were certainly not included in any draft of Captain Webb's note. What he did include, albeit in more statesmanlike language than in his internal memorandum, was criticism of Turner for failing to follow instructions. He had failed to zigzag; he had not kept a midchannel course; he had tarried at reduced speed in a danger zone. Webb's concluding sentence read: "He thus kept his valuable vessel for an unnecessary length of time in the area where she was most liable to attack, inviting disaster."

The sensitivities were such that Webb produced at least two drafts of his note. The major change in the later version was to spell out the trouble taken by the Admiralty to ensure that Captain Turner received the messages sent, and to give further details of some of them. All the drafts of Webb's note and the final version are dated 8 May—the day immediately after the disaster and a Saturday. This must have been an error. The information could never have been collected, collated, checked, and reviewed on that single hectic day.

Webb was being pulled in many directions. On Saturday, 8 May the United Kingdom's wartime censor had stopped a report from the *Daily Mirror*'s New York office to its London headquarters reading: "Cunard guaranteed passengers *Lusitania* would be conveyed by destroyers, big guns. White Star captains never see destroyers." However, on Monday, 10 May the harassed Webb still had to draft a reply to an urgent letter from the chairman of the White Star Line asking whether, in view of the sinking, the Admiralty still considered vessels "of good speed" as "almost immune from the consequences of torpedo fire from submarines." The reply did not go out until the following Friday, 14 May. It read: "No special protection which it is in the power of the Admiralty to afford would be of service in protecting fast liners from the danger of a surprise torpedo attack which is the only form of attack to which these ships are liable." Rather curiously, perhaps, it did not mention the benefits of zigzagging.

Webb's note, on behalf of the Admiralty, and a mass of other information were put before Lord Mersey and his four assessors. These comprised Admiral Sir Frederick Inglefield; another serving naval officer, Lieutenant Commander H. J. Hearn, who was a submariner; and two merchant navy captains. Admiral Inglefield clearly believed it was his duty to ensure that the inquiry took government views on board and that its findings were not contrary to government expectations.

Lord Mersey himself was not only an intelligent man but also a patriot with a clear understanding of the national interest. At the time of the inquiry the wrecks commissioner was seventy-four years old and highly experienced in marine investigations. He had led the inquiry into the loss of the *Titanic* and was currently pondering his report on the sinking of the *Falaba*. Out of court he was a mild man with a love of good food and wine. In court he could be impatient and brusque with both witnesses and counsel who failed to follow his thinking.

Appearing for the British government were the attorney general, Sir

The New York Times, *May 8, 1915.*

Edward Carson, and the Solicitor General, Sir Frederick E. Smith, usually known as "F. E." Carson had successfully defended the criminal libel
suit brought by Oscar Wilde against the marquis of Queensberry, which
had led to Wilde's imprisonment in Reading Gaol for homosexual acts.
Smith was devastating in cross-examination, with a strong line in witty
put-downs. Tall and vain, he habitually wore a red flower in his buttonhole and smoked large cigars. Butler Aspinall, another distinguished

lawyer, represented Cunard. Only the government and Cunard lawyers would attend the two closed sessions, which discussed the classified information, but passengers, crewmen's unions, and the Canadian government were all represented in the open sessions, to which the public was admitted.

In addition to Webb's material, statements had been collected from every surviving member of the crew. All were recorded in an identical hand on partially preprinted forms, but each was signed by the witness. In cases where witnesses were illiterate—like Able Seaman Frank Hennessy, who had been on lookout in the crow's nest when the torpedo was sighted—each man marked his form with a cross. In almost identical wording they stated that the ship was in good order, that she was unarmed, and that boat drills had been carried out before the vessel left New York.

Hugh Johnston, the quartermaster who had been at the wheel until told by Captain Turner to save himself, later recalled the pressure from Cunard to be loyal to the company. More surprisingly, perhaps, witnesses were also encouraged to testify that there had been two torpedo strikes. According to Johnston, "I was asked in Liverpool getting ready to go to London how many torpedoes struck the ship. I said one. Well I was told two would help the case. I said there was only one."

A careful sift was made of passengers' statements. Five passengers were initially invited to give evidence, and a few more volunteered to do so during the course of the inquiry and were accepted. Oliver Bernard's repeated offers were, however, ignored despite the prominence given to his statements and drawings in the press. He wrote to the grieving mother of Dick Prichard, "I have been prepared and am still ready to declare under oath that we were struck by only ONE torpedo . . . abaft the bridge."

The inquiry was held at Central Hall, Westminster, where Lord Mersey and his assessors took evidence from 15 to 18 June. Sir Edward Carson opened proceedings for the government. He was clear that the first torpedo had hit between funnels three and four. Then, contrary to the information known to the Admiralty through Room 40's decoded messages, he stated that "there was a second and perhaps third torpedo." He said that the ship was just eight to ten miles from land when hit. She was capable of traveling at twenty-one knots at the time of the sinking but was in fact doing only eighteen. He suggested that the court would need to consider whether the captain was right in traveling at this speed. He added that the captain had received "specific instructions and directions." Again the court would need to consider how far the captain had acted upon them.

Predictably, after such a prologue, most interest centered on how Captain Turner would defend himself. He gave evidence at both the open and closed sessions. The inquiry was taking place barely a month after the sinking. There were whispers that he should have gone down with his ship and claims that he had ordered survivors off an upturned lifeboat while continuing to cling to it himself. A well-dressed woman gave him a white feather as he entered the building. He may well have been suffering from post-traumatic shock. Indeed, just before the Inquiry opened he wrote to a well-wisher that he still could not bear "to think or speak" about the disaster. However, he now had to do so in the witness box.

He would not have been encouraged to know that the Admiralty had been thoroughly investigating his background. On 18 May Captain Webb had announced the results: "As regards Captain Turner I have ascertained that he was born at Liverpool in 1856 and that he has been in the service of the Company off and on since 1877. He joined as a Boy before the mast and worked his way up by sheer merit." He noted that Turner had an English wife and concluded that there was no evidence to suggest that Turner had German connections or sympathies.

At his first appearance in open session, Captain Turner surprised those present by his answer to a question probing whether the *Lusitania*'s crew had been proficient in handling lifeboats. He replied simply, "No, they were not." He later explained that they lacked practice and experience. Later still, in response to prompting by Cunard's counsel, he confessed that he was "an old-fashioned sailor man" who did not believe that present standards matched up to those of his youth. Also surprisingly, he denied that he had ever given instructions for women and children to be removed from the lifeboats. Furthermore, contrary to his evidence at the Kinsale inquest, he now seemed convinced that there had been two torpedoes, not one, and that the first had struck between the third and fourth funnels.

The matter of the Admiralty's instructions to Captain Turner was discussed at two closed sessions. Sir Edward Carson cross-examined him very precisely and aggressively. He described all the instructions Turner had received (including those relating to avoiding enemy surface vessels, which in the end could be reduced to two: stick to the coast and "remember the enemy will never operate in sight of land if he can possibly avoid it.") These, of course, directly contradicted advice on how to avoid submarines—that is, stay out of sight of land. Carson was very careful to quote the date of each instruction and on each occasion to ask Turner, "Did you get that?" However, when it came to the guidance on zigzagging, Carson read out all three paragraphs of the note of 16 April flagged by Webb but did not give a date for it. He simply asked Turner, "Did you *read* that?" Perhaps bemused, Turner replied, "I did." Carson then hopped back to another note dated 22 March 1915 about steering a midchannel course. Reverting to his previous style of questioning, he quoted the specific date and asked, "Did you get this?"

His cross-examination probed further into why Turner had been so near to land. Carson suggested that land was eight to ten miles distant. Turner thought he had been some fifteen miles from the Irish coast. He insisted that he had closed in to take a four-point bearing to find out precisely where he was. Carson contended that he must already have known his approximate location. Turner replied that while he had, he was in part relying on guesswork. In response to further pressure, he for once showed some animation, snapping back: "I wanted to get my proper position off the land—I do not do my navigation by guesswork." Turner went on to say that he had been doing only eighteen knots to allow him to time his arrival at the Mersey Bar so that he could cross it, as advised, without delaying in known dangerous waters outside the harbor. Pressed on why he was not zigzagging at the time his ship was struck, Captain Turner said that he thought he needed to do so only when he saw a submarine. In any case the words about zigzagging that had been read to him seemed different from those he recalled.

Throughout his appearances, Turner's answers tended to the monosyllabic. He seemed anxious and, on occasion, confused. Butler Aspinall guided him as best he could, on one occasion telling him, "Pull yourself together and think before you answer." Aspinall also interpolated extra information helpful to Turner and thus to Cunard's case. Before the final closed session on 18 June, he apologized to Lord Mersey for Turner's being "a bad witness" in the sense that "he was confused." Lord Mersey replied, "In my opinion at present, he may have been a bad Master during that voyage, but I think he was telling the truth."

The lawyers then discussed evidence substantiating Turner's view that it would have been hazardous to tarry outside Liverpool Harbor. In the process Lord Mersey discovered that Captain Webb and the Admiralty had supplied him with a less full memorandum, in particular with regard to signals sent to the *Lusitania*, than had been given to the solicitor general. Both were, however, dated the same day. They were probably the different versions of Webb's memorandum of 8 May. Lord Mersey was plainly annoyed. He agreed with the solicitor general that because of the confusion and possible uncertainty over which version Turner had thought they were referring to during cross-examination, they would find it difficult to use much of the information contained in them formally against him.

The day after Captain Turner's appearance, Lord Mersey took evidence from Commander Anderson, the only member of naval or Admiralty staff to be called. He testified to the benefits of zigzagging and of sailing at top speed to avoid submarines. Surprisingly, he was not questioned about the Admiralty's own deliberations on how best to warn and protect the *Lusitania*, and its consequent action or inaction.

The remainder of the open sessions included evidence on the number of torpedoes. Most witnesses, including Leslie Morton, said there had been two, but two crewmen, both British naval reservists, said that in addition a third torpedo had been fired, perhaps by a second submarine from the port side. Lord Mersey very pointedly and firmly deflected the seamen's union representative, Clem Edwards, from discussing the nature of the alleged torpedo strikes, their points of impact, and the consequences for the watertight compartments of the ship—this despite Edwards's pleading that both he and Lord Mersey had found bulkheads a fruitful avenue of exploration at the *Titanic* inquiry. Thus any discussion of the effect of the torpedo on the vulnerable longitudinal bulkheads was ruled out.

Nor was there any substantive discussion of the nature of the cargo at the main sessions of the inquiry. Five days before the inquiry had begun, on 10 June, a broadening of the Defence of the Realm Act had made it an offense "to collect, record, publish, or communicate or attempt to elicit information" on the nature, carriage, and use of His Majesty's "war materials" for any purpose. Previously the act had only prohibited the collection, recording, et cetera, of such information if intended for communication to the enemy. Thus, in compliance with the act, there was no detailed discussion of the *Lusitania*'s cargo. Sir Edward Carson merely read out the U.S. government's note to Germany refuting German allegations about the cargo. This he backed up with a confirmatory note from the collector of customs, Dudley Field Malone, to the Cunard general manager, Charles Sumner, that the cargo was not in violation of U.S. law on what could be transported on passenger steamers.

However, Lord Mersey did decide, after reflection, to hold an additional session on 1 July at the Westminster Palace Hotel. The purpose was to hear evidence from passenger Joseph Marichal, who was claiming that ammunition had exploded on the *Lusitania*. Marichal was a French-born lecturer in Romance languages at a Canadian university. He was a former officer in the French army and had been traveling to England with his pregnant English wife and three children for a holiday. The entire family survived, but Madame Marichal had miscarried as a result of the trauma. Marichal had written to Cunard threatening legal action unless he received substantial compensation. Lord Mersey probably feared that if he did not call Marichal, and if the Frenchman subsequently publicized his claims, the German government and others might be able to cast doubt on the breadth of evidence taken by the inquiry.

Lord Mersey and the government and Cunard legal teams handled Marichal roughly, and he did not have his own counsel to protect him. The thrust of his evidence was that he considered the second explosion on the *Lusitania* to have sounded "similar to the rattling of a machine gun." He thought that it might have occurred beneath the second-class dining room at the aft of the ship where he was sitting. He claimed that it shook the whole floor, but he could not identify the location clearly. He went on to complain about the poor treatment of the survivors by Cunard, the low speed of the ship, the incompetence of the *Lusitania*'s captain, and the fact that some crew members had neglected passengers in order to save themselves. He even took the opportunity to disparage the cooking of the second-class chef.

Under cross-examination Marichal denied, on the basis of his experience in the French army, that the sounds he heard could have been caused by the fracturing of steam lines rather than by ammunition. He admitted that he had written to Cunard stating that, unless he received immediate payment, he would "produce publicly evidence which will certainly not be to the credit either of your company or of the Admiralty." He denied that this meant that if he had been paid he would have said nothing—in other words, he was not a blackmailer. He concluded by complaining to Lord Mersey about the shameful way witnesses had been treated by the inquiry.

After Marichal's evidence, a plan showing where the cargo had been stowed was admitted as an exhibit. Captain Turner was asked to confirm its accuracy—that is, state that the cargo was some distance from where the torpedoes had exploded—and this he did.

The British government was, however, sufficiently perturbed by Monsieur Marichal to make inquiries into his background. On 9 July the French government replied that twelve years earlier he had been found guilty by court-martial of brawling and concealing his identity. A fortnight later he had been sentenced to two months in prison for desertion. He was then cashiered from the army and in 1904 had been convicted of fraud. In 1915, after his return on the *Lusitania*, he had applied for reinstatement in the army, only to be refused on 26 June. This information was immediately leaked to the British press to discredit Marichal and was exaggerated in the telling.

The only other witness to question the behavior of the crew was David Thomas, Margaret Mackworth's father, whose character, unlike Marichal's, could not be impugned. As he had previously done in his indignant statement to the *Morning Post*, Thomas suggested that organization was lacking on the sinking ship, that there was some panic, that the boats were badly launched and that the order "women and children first" had not always been obeyed. The solicitor general did, however, suggest that much of his evidence was hearsay and drew from him the admission that, in the case of the only lifeboat he knew about directly, the one in which he had got away, everyone had behaved correctly.

On 1 July, their inquiry complete, Lord Mersey and his assessors retired to contemplate their verdict. It was clearly Mersey's original intention to blame Captain Turner. He inquired through Admiral Inglefield whether the government would consider it expedient that "blame should be very prominently laid upon the Captain" for disregarding Admiralty instructions. Lord Mersey was apparently concerned that if he did so, the Ger-

mans "might use it as another pretext for defending their action in sinking the vessel." Both the new first lord of the Admiralty, Arthur Balfour,
and the foreign office were consulted. The Admiralty's reply, direct to
Lord Mersey, was that neither Balfour nor the foreign office would object
to a verdict "that the Master received suitable written instructions which
he omitted to follow and that he was also fully informed of the presence
of hostile submarines. . . . If you should still have any doubts on the subject, Mr Balfour would be glad to see you."

Whether Lord Mersey took up the invitation is unknown. However,
he decided not to place the blame on Captain Turner. His concise, two-
paragraph report was published on 17 July. It placed responsibility for
the disaster fairly and squarely on the captain and crew of the German
submarine that carried out the attack and their superiors in Berlin.
The second paragraph gave the unsubstantiated view that "in the opinion of the Court the act was done not merely with the intention of sinking the ship, but also with the intention of destroying the lives of the
people on board."

In a ten-page addendum, Lord Mersey stated that both Captain
Turner and Staff Captain Anderson were "competent men and . . . did
their duty." He went on: "No doubt there were mishaps in handling the
ropes of the boats and in other such matters but there was, in my opinion,
no incompetence or neglect and I am satisfied that the crew behaved well
throughout and worked with skill and judgement." Like the masters and
officers, "they did their best in difficult and perilous circumstances and
their best was good." The passengers generally behaved well, although
some did "more harm than good" in attempting to assist in launching the
boats. The German warning was evidence that the attack was premeditated and planned before the *Lusitania* sailed.

Lord Mersey concluded firmly that there were two torpedo strikes,
the first hitting the starboard side between funnels three and four. He
concluded that the same U-boat fired the second torpedo, although he
gave some credence to the evidence of a second submarine firing from
the port side. Lord Mersey dismissed Marichal with the damning sentence "I did not believe this gentleman." He went on: "In my opinion
there was no explosion of any part of the cargo." He said that the Admiralty had devoted the most anxious care and thought "to the questions
arising out of the submarine peril" and that the officials concerned
deserved "the highest praise." The advice given to Captain Turner was

not meant "to deprive him of the right to exercise his skilled judgement. . . . His omission to follow the advice in all respects cannot fairly be attributed either to negligence or incompetence. He exercised judgement for the best. . . . The whole blame for the cruel destruction of life in this catastrophe must rest solely with those who plotted and with those who committed the crime."

With this judgment the *Lusitania* disappeared from the front pages of the British press, submerged by news of further massive loss of life in battles that failed to break the stalemate on the Western Front.

CHAPTER TWENTY-FOUR

No Longer Neutral Spectators

*I*N THE UNITED STATES it was a very different matter—
the *Lusitania* incident would remain a live issue until her own
entry into the war and beyond. The news of the *Lusitania*'s
sinking reached President Wilson shortly after the end of a cabinet
meeting. At his first meeting with his private secretary, Joe Tumulty,
there were "tears in his eyes." Wilson told him that if he pondered over
the personal tragedies reported in the newspapers, he would "see red in
everything. . . . I am afraid that when I am called upon to act with reference to this situation I could not be just to anyone. I dare not act unjustly
and cannot indulge my passionate feelings." After a pause, he added, "In
God's name how could any nation calling itself civilized propose so horrible a thing?"

On Wall Street, industrial stocks plunged on news of the sinking.
Bethlehem Steel went from 159 to 130, Amalgamated Copper from $74\frac{3}{4}$ to
63, and National Lead from $65\frac{1}{2}$ to 56. News of these sudden falls was followed by a message from Colonel House in London arguing that "America has come to the parting of the ways when she must determine
whether she stands for civilized or uncivilized warfare. . . . We can no
longer remain neutral spectators." A telegram from Ambassador Page
warned that "THE UNITED STATES MUST DECLARE WAR OR FORFEIT EURO-
PEAN RESPECT."

Faced with this challenge and with continuing angry American press
reaction, Wilson told Tumulty that he was bound to consider his first
step carefully and cautiously "because once having taken it I cannot

withdraw from it." He took his time, pondering the public mood. British ambassador Sir Cecil Spring-Rice gauged correctly that, although there was widespread indignation and hostility to Germany in the United States, there was no real appetite for war. Wilson's secretary of state, William Jennings Bryan, was leading the call for moderation, arguing that the Allies could not rely upon neutral passengers to protect ships carrying contraband from attack. "It would be like putting women and children in front of an Army," he wrote to Wilson.

Spring-Rice noted that the "German Embassy is openly provocative and it is probable that war would not be unwelcome as it would mean prohibition of exports of [U.S.] arms." He was equally worried about the aggressive tone in the British press. On 9 May he telegraphed London, "AS OUR MAIN INTEREST IS TO PRESERVE U.S. AS A BASE OF SUPPLIES I HOPE LANGUAGE OF OUR PRESS WILL BE VERY GUARDED." The British press was indeed watching with growing impatience. The *Glasgow Herald* cautioned that if America held back, "there [would] not be enough of American dignity and honour left to cover the coffins in which American rights [were] enclosed."

The tenth of May was a busy day for Wilson. He had fallen passionately in love with Edith Bolling Galt, a handsome, buxom southern widow sixteen years his junior. On 4 May she had refused his proposal of marriage on the grounds that she had not known him long enough and that it was less than a year since his wife had died, but she had encouraged him to continue their relationship. On 10 May he found time to meet her at least once as well as to write to her: "When I know that I am going to see you and am all a-quiver with the thought how can I use this stupid *pen* to tell you that I love you? . . . the greatest and the most delightful thing in the world [is] that I am permitted to *love you*." This was all before heading for Philadelphia, where he had determined to test public opinion on the *Lusitania*. He addressed an audience of 15,000, including 4,000 newly naturalized citizens, in the convention hall. He dwelt on America's unique character and told the crowd that "the example of America must be the example not merely of peace because it will not fight but of peace because peace is the healing and elevating influence of the world and strife is not. There is such a thing as a man being too proud to fight. There is such a thing as a nation being so right that it does not need to convince others by force that it is right."

Wilson had, for once, misjudged the mood badly. While the American public did not want war, neither did they want intellectual theorizing that seemed close to cowardice. The backlash was immediate, not only from hawks like Theodore Roosevelt, who was calling for "immediate decision and vigor," but also from the moderate press. Wilson recognized his misjudgment and called a press conference the next day. He explained to the journalists that he had been "expressing a personal attitude," that he had had no specific thing in mind, and that he had not been giving "any intimation of policy on any special matter." He confessed to Edith Galt that "I do not know just what I said in Philadelphia. My heart was in such a whirl.

Spring-Rice telegraphed London: "IMPRESSION IS THAT PRESIDENT'S SPEECH WAS A FEELER AND RESPONSE TO IT FROM COUNTRY SHOWED HIM THAT A STRONGER LINE WAS ADVISABLE." Nevertheless, the sound bite "too proud to fight" would dog Wilson for the rest of his career.

⚬⚬⚬

On the same day as Wilson's speech, Count Bernstorff submitted a note from his government addressed to all neutral countries affected by the sinking. It took special pains to express "deepest sympathy at the loss of American lives" but placed all responsibility on the British government. The sinking was one of the retaliatory measures to which the British hunger blockade had forced Germany; British merchant ships were usually armed and had "repeatedly tried to ram submarines," thus preventing the use of "visit and search" procedures; the *Lusitania* was carrying contraband. The German government regretted that the American passengers had relied on British promises rather than heeding German warnings.

Although Germany appeared to be presenting a tough and united front, the *Lusitania* incident had deepened the long-existing divisions between the imperial navy hawks and more moderate civil and military voices. The kaiser was at the castle of Pless in Upper Silesia, a magnificent white palace of 300 rooms and marble staircases. Among his accompanying entourage were Admiral Georg Alexander von Müller, chief of the naval cabinet, and Carl Georg von Treutler, the foreign affairs liaison official at imperial headquarters. Both shared Chancellor Bethmann Hollweg's misgivings about the unrestricted U-boat campaign. On 9 May, as Müller was settling into his "splendid quarters" overlooking Pless's famous lawns, Treutler came to see him. Müller told him of dispatches received that day from Admirals Tirpitz and Bachmann arguing for a hard line with the United States over the *Lusitania*. Bachmann was insisting that "shackling U-boat commanders beyond their current orders is utterly impossible" and that any attempts to impose limits would anger the public, "especially now when the effectiveness of submarine warfare is evident as a result of the *Lusitania* case."

A deeply alarmed Treutler fired off a telegram to the chancellor: "I AM OUTRAGED ABOUT THE TORPEDOING OF THE LUSITANIA AND ITS INCAL-CULABLE CONSEQUENCES." Bethmann Hollweg telegraphed back that the torpedoing of the *Lusitania* was justified but it would not be advisable to "DESTROY ANOTHER PASSENGER SHIP IN THE NEAR FUTURE." Bethmann Hollweg was by now aware of a report from Kriege, director of the foreign office's legal department, that although the British had intended the *Lusitania* for possible operation as an armed auxiliary cruiser in war, she had not actually been taken into the navy for this purpose. He did not pass this information—marked secret on the file—on to Treutler.

Müller, meanwhile, tackled the kaiser about the political risks of attacking neutral shipping. He found it hard going. He wrote gloomily that "His Majesty has no understanding of the seriousness of the situation." All he won was "a halfway concession" that Bachmann should be told to respect the chancellor's views.

———

When the U.S. cabinet met on Tuesday, 11 May to consider its response to the German note, the general feeling was that the reply must be tough while neither severing diplomatic relations nor being likely to precipitate an immediate break by Germany. During a three-hour discussion the cabinet worked through a draft response based on material prepared by Robert Lansing, counselor to the State Department. Later that day, the president redrafted it himself. The note, which was cabled under Bryan's signature on 13 May, reminded Germany of the principle of "strict accountability" and that the United States had warned Germany not to destroy the lives of American citizens on the high seas. Employing submarines humanely against merchant shipping was a "practical impossibility." Referring to the German newspaper warning, Wilson made clear that "no warning that an unlawful and inhumane act will be committed can possibly be accepted as an excuse or palliation for that act" or abate "the responsibility for its commission." The note looked forward to the German government disavowing the action, offering reparation, and taking immediate steps to prevent its reoccurrence.

Bryan had fought for a simultaneous protest to Britain about her blockade of Germany. He had also revived his previous suggestion that the U.S. government should warn its citizens of the danger of sailing on the ships of combatant nations. Wilson rejected both proposals, the latter after consultation with Lansing, still Bryan's subordinate, on the grounds that his "strict accountability" statement of the previous February could be seen as giving support to U.S. citizens traveling on belligerent ships. To change policy now might cause the public mind to reflect on the wisdom of the administration's previous judgment. Bryan also argued in vain for a more friendly tone in the final paragraph of the note to Germany, including the insertion of references looking forward to the continuation of the friendship between the two nations.

Bryan believed he had had greater success in persuading Wilson to agree that publication of the note to Germany should be accompanied by a press statement suggesting that a cooling-off period might permit a peaceful settlement. This proposal was not at all to the taste of either Lansing or the secretary of war, Lindley Garrison. Garrison alerted Tumulty, who was likewise appalled. He immediately went in to see the president and used all his persuasive skills. He said that the American people would be outraged and accuse Wilson of double-dealing; the Germans would conclude that the United States would not fight for her rights and, in this belief, ignore the forceful formal note. At first Wilson argued that Bryan was a sound politician and a competent judge of public opinion, but Tumulty persisted. Finally, the president gave in. Tumulty emerged "white as a ghost" to join Garrison for lunch. "I have just had the worst half-hour of my life," he explained, but Garrison, learning of his success, told him that he should "receive a medal for this day's work."

———— ∞∞∞ ————

The more hawkish members of Wilson's cabinet and entourage were now clearly in the ascendancy—not least because Wilson's private and deepest sympathies chimed with theirs. Nevertheless, Wilson did not admit this bias to himself, committed as he was to the principle of evenhandedness.

In any event, the administration's firm note to the German government struck the right chord with most American opinion and with opinion elsewhere. The *Baltimore Sun* thought it contained "all the red blood that a red-blooded nation can ask." The *New York Times* stated that the president had "the united support of the American people." In London the *Times* declared that "both in substance and expression [it] recalls the best traditions of American diplomacy." America's fellow neutrals approved as well. *La Prensa* in Buenos Aires considered that "if the principles laid down in the Note don't prevail, there will be an end to all neutrality and universal war will come."

American opinion against Germany grew even stronger with the publication of a British government report by a highly respected former British ambassador to Washington, Lord Bryce. Compiled with the help of thirty attorneys who had sifted through all the evidence, this account of German atrocities in Belgium carried great weight. In addition to such confirmed atrocities as the burning of Dinant and Louvain and some indiscriminate shooting of civilians, it contained allegations of rape and baby-murder that later were found to be groundless. Nevertheless, Bryce's prestige, and the outrage at the sinking of the *Lusitania*, ensured that they were readily believed when the report was released in May 1915. The *Washington Herald* remarked that the Germans who were guilty of the "frightfulness against Belgium" were the same "who sank the *Lusitania* and murdered 115 [sic] Americans because England interfered with her commerce."

On 15 May in London, the *Times* published a horrific story that had been circulating widely among troops at the Front for some time. It described how counterattacking Allied troops discovered the body of a Canadian sergeant crucified on a Belgian barn door, hands and neck pierced by German bayonets. No firm evidence was ever produced and the story is almost certainly untrue, but again it was immediately believed, relayed around the world, and grew in the telling. It provided a further spur to the revulsion felt by American public opinion against Germany and made it ever more difficult for Bryan to soften the president's approach.

Nor was Bryan's case helped by what he adamantly claimed was a misrepresentation by the Austro-Hungarian ambassador to the United States, Constantin Dumba, of a conversation between them on 17 May. Immediately afterward Dumba had cabled Vienna to report that, accord-

William Jennings Bryan and Robert Lansing

ing to Bryan, "the United States desires no war. Her Notes, however strongly worded, meant no harm, but had to be written in order to pacify public opinion."

A copy of Dumba's cable was passed to Arthur Zimmermann, the deputy German foreign secretary. Zimmermann was still highly irritated by the "blunt and abrupt manner" of the Anglophile American ambassador in Berlin, James Gerard, when he had presented the American protest note. Gerard had further annoyed Zimmermann by personally and ostentatiously going to the train reservations office in Berlin to book "places for himself and his family, as if a break of diplomatic relations between Germany and the United States were imminent." Zimmermann decided to get even. When Gerard next called, Zimmermann read him the text of the Austro-Hungarian envoy's telegram, remarking sardonically, "You see from Dumba's telegram that the State Department's Note is not meant to be taken very seriously but only as a sop to public opinion."

An alarmed and highly annoyed Gerard at once wired Bryan, reporting the conversation. Bryan contacted Dumba, who wrote pacifyingly that he agreed with Bryan's recollection of the conversation. Although Bryan had said that the United States had no desire for war, he had not suggested her warning note to Germany was for home consumption only.

Dumba insinuated that the German foreign office must have been trying to bluff Gerard.

Bryan reported all this to Wilson, who formally accepted Bryan's version. Privately, however, he probably agreed with Robert Lansing, now his most trusted State Department adviser, that Bryan was "indiscreet" and that "it is impossible to avoid the conclusion that he said something which conveyed to Dr. Dumba an intimation such as the latter sent to his Government."

It is certainly true that Bryan was suggesting to foreign diplomats that he, at least, was doing his best to ensure peace. Bernstorff reported to Berlin: "Bryan spoke to me very seriously about the *Lusitania* incident. His influence will be exerted in a peaceful direction. This influence is large, since Wilson depends on Bryan for his re-election."

Meanwhile in Germany the American note of 13 May had been angrily received. It encouraged an incensed kaiser to pay yet greater heed to Tirpitz's views and to speak of "the necessity of intensified submarine warfare, even against neutrals." Germany's uncompromising reply reached Washington on 31 May. It simply said that her general note to neutral countries had already expressed "deep regret" for the deaths of neutral citizens and suggested the U.S. government should order a "careful examination" of events surrounding the sinking. Despite the report from the foreign office's legal director, it repeated Germany's claims that the *Lusitania* was an armed auxiliary cruiser. The British government allowed its ships to hide behind American flags, British merchantmen had orders to ram submarines, and the *Lusitania* had been carrying Canadian troops and munitions of war whose explosion had caused the sinking.

Chancellor Bethmann Hollweg, anxiously awaiting American reactions, appreciated just how much depended on no further incidents. He warned his colleagues that if the U-boat campaign continued as at present, it would provoke the United States to declare war. He also asked the kaiser to convene a Crown council of military and civil leaders.

The kaiser agreed and summoned the chancellor, General Falkenhayn, chief of the army general staff, and Admirals Tirpitz and Bachmann; Treutler was to represent Jagow. Tirpitz and Bachmann arrived on the evening of 30 May to find the kaiser playing skat, one of his favorite card games, and unwilling to be disturbed. They were served sandwiches in their rooms and waited. Müller dropped in on Tirpitz and was irritated to find him "on his high horse again." Tirpitz claimed that members of the Reichstag were warning that any attempt to restrict the U-boat war could result in serious public disturbances. The next day, 31 May, the council convened.

The mood was tense. Falkenhayn stated that Germany's military position on land would be prejudiced if "more neutral powers joined our enemies as a result of the U-boat war." Tirpitz and Bachmann clung passionately to their argument that the safety of neutral ships could only be guaranteed by suspending the U-boat war, a course that they would not support. The kaiser agreed with them, adding that the chancellor would have to bear the responsibility for stopping submarine warfare, a decision "which would be very unpopular among the people." Müller recommended a compromise. It should be possible to issue orders to U-boat commanders about attacking neutral ships "which would take the political situation into account." To his relief, the kaiser agreed. Orders were duly issued on 1 June. They instructed U-boatmen that, when in doubt, it was preferable to allow an enemy ship to escape than to sink a neutral.

However, frictions continued. On 5 June the chancellor complained that Bachmann would not agree to his further request that, for political and diplomatic reasons, U-boats should be ordered not to torpedo passenger liners, even enemy ones. An exasperated kaiser ruled that the chancellor's wishes must be met during the negotiations with America about the *Lusitania*. The orders of 1 June must be amended to forbid attacks on any large passenger liners whatever their nationality.

As the weather grew hotter, so did tempers. Tirpitz and Bachmann sent coded telegrams for the kaiser's attention, inveighing against the chancellor, refusing to accept responsibility for the amended orders, and arguing that by restricting the U-boat war Germany was giving up her ultimate weapon against Britain. The kaiser stood by his decision, insisting that the new orders remain secret, and hence undisclosed to the United States, to prevent Tirpitz, Bachmann, and their allies from whipping up public anger in Germany. On 7 June the two of them offered their resignations, which were rejected.

While the German high command bickered and sniped at one another, the American press strongly condemned Germany's latest note. "Impudently trifling in spirit and flagrantly dishonest in matter," wrote the *Philadelphia North American*. The *New York World* called it "the answer of an outlaw who assumes no obligation to Society." George Viereck's mouthpiece for the German propaganda bureau, the *Fatherland*, was virtually alone in praising it as "sweetly reasonable."

President Wilson immediately began to bash out a draft response on his Hammond typewriter. It took him several hours. Its tone was firm. He put it to a cabinet meeting the next morning, 1 June. Bryan seemed to another cabinet member to be "under great strain" during the meeting, sitting back in his chair most of the time "with his eyes half closed." When Bryan's renewed suggestion of a simultaneous protest to Britain about her blockade was rejected, he burst out, "You people are not neutral—you are taking sides." President Wilson turned on him with a "steely glitter" in his eyes and said, "Mr. Bryan, you are not warranted in making such an assertion. There are none of us who can justly be accused of being unfair." Bryan apologized but after the meeting continued to insist to Wilson that "arbitration was the proper remedy."

Wilson's next draft of the response asserted that American customs officials had done their duty in verifying that the *Lusitania* was not a naval vessel, was not armed, was not serving as a troop transport, and that her cargo was in compliance with the laws of the United States. If the Germans had evidence to the contrary, they should produce it. In any case, questions of carrying contraband and of any contribution to the sinking from exploding munitions did not justify attacking the *Lusitania* without warning. Only her resistance or refusal to allow "visit and search" could justify the submarine commander hazarding the ship.

Deeply worried by the latest draft's persistently uncompromising tone, Bryan argued that there was no hurry for a reply and, as usual, that a period of reflection or cooling off would be beneficial. But he could see that his efforts were futile and that he was losing all influence. On the afternoon of Saturday, 5 June, he briefly discussed the latest version of the reply with Lansing, who was about to leave to watch a baseball game. He then visited William McAdoo, the secretary of the treasury, who was not only an old friend but also President Wilson's son-in-law. A "visibly nervous" Bryan told him that he feared this second note, as drafted, "would surely lead to war with Germany." He believed that "his usefulness as Secretary of State was over" and proposed to resign.

McAdoo tried to dissuade him, arguing that his resignation would create the impression that the cabinet was divided. Bryan replied that it was a matter of conscience. Later that day, McAdoo called on Bryan's wife, Mary. She told him that Bryan had spent many sleepless nights. He thought that Colonel House and Lansing had more influence with the president, who, in any case, produced most of the policy drafts himself. Bryan was unhappy to remain a mere figurehead. Both Bryans "looked jaded." McAdoo persuaded them to go to the country for the weekend to think it over but was under no illusions that Bryan would change his mind. McAdoo then went to the White House to warn the president. Wilson showed no surprise, remarking that Bryan had been "growing more and more out of sympathy with the Administration in the controversy with Germany." Wilson had been even more blunt in his private correspondence with Edith Galt remarking that Bryan "is a traitor, though I can say so as yet only to you."

Bryan spent a restless, troubled weekend. His wife had to summon a doctor to prescribe him sleeping pills, but his views remained unchanged. On 8 June, Bryan called on Wilson and tried for an hour to make him change his policy but realized it was hopeless. He commented bleakly that "Colonel House has been Secretary of State and I have never had your full confidence." Then he went back to his office and wrote out his resignation.

Lansing was immediately installed as acting secretary of state. His first act, on 9 June, was to dispatch the final version of the United States's second protest to the German government. It remained firm, concluding with the curt request to the German government to accept the right of American citizens "bound on lawful errands" to travel as passengers on merchant ships of belligerent nationality and that the lives of noncombatants "cannot lawfully or rightfully be put in jeopardy by the capture or destruction of an unresisting merchantman." The German government was requested to adopt the "measures necessary to put these principles into practice in respect of the safeguarding of American lives and American ships."

Bryan had fully expected to be vilified by the press and by his oppo-

Cartoon in the New York World *in which the kaiser applauds*
William Jennings Bryan's reasons for resigning.

nents following his resignation. He was not wrong. A sarcastic *New York Times* called his resignation the wisest action of his political career. The *New York Telegraph* said that his "idea of an ultimatum seems to be that it should be addressed to the President of his own country." To the *Springfield Republican*, he had suffered a "'Mad Mullah' outbreak" and was "a statesman destroyed by an interior explosion." The *New York World* declared his resignation to be "unspeakable treachery, not only to the President, but to the nation." The statement he issued "to the American People" on 11 June, justifying his actions "as a humble follower of the Prince of Peace," found little favor.

Even many fellow Democrats rejoiced. Ambassador Page sent delighted congratulations to Wilson on being a fine "executioner." He also wrote: "One American newspaper says truly: 'There always was a

yellow streak in [Bryan], and now in this crisis he shows a white liver.'
. . . Conscience he has about little things—grape juice, cigarettes, peace
treaties, etc.—but about a big situation, such as embarrassing a President, he is fundamentally immoral. Well, cranks always do you a bad
turn, sooner or later. Avoid 'em, son, avoid 'em!"

CHAPTER TWENTY-FIVE

⌦

German Agents Are Everywhere

HE POLITICAL DRAMA of Bryan's resignation had been played out against a backdrop of tales of espionage and conspiracy that would continue all summer. Washington and New York hummed with rumors. Robert Lansing received a letter from a man claiming that, while standing in an elevator at around 10 A.M. on 7 May, he overheard a messenger from the German embassy say, "This is the day we are going to blow up the *Lusitania*." On 2 June a gentleman named C. C. Speiden, who claimed to be known to State Department officials, sent a telegram to the president insisting that he had "firsthand dependable information from one of the submarine captains that for six weeks prior to sinking of *Lusitania* they had special instructions to get her going either direction, East or West, that is regardless nature of cargo; avowedly for the moral effect expected thereby in enemy country. This can be substantiated." The German warning in the newspapers, and the bombarding of newspaper editors' offices with questions on the eve of the sinking, seemed further evidence of premeditation and foreknowledge. Sir Cecil Spring-Rice alerted London, "I hear from [U.S.] Secret Service that warning was issued by instructions from Berlin, and that exact manner of attack was known in Washington at 8.30 A.M. on May 7."

A worried President Wilson became so concerned about the possible involvement of German and Austrian embassy staff in the sabotage of shipping and in arms dealing that on 14 May he ordered William Flynn, head of the Secret Service, to put a special watch on them. This included tapping their telephones. Among the first clandestine activities to be revealed were Bernstorff's amorous calls to various Washington ladies, during which they likened the athletic, fashionably dressed blond diplomat to the hero of a popular play titled *The Great Lover.* Each evening Flynn received and reviewed the stenographer's notes of all conversations—"dull, interesting, spicy, naughty, and—occasionally—important." Every word was passed to the State Department.

The constant reports of alleged German sabotage attempts at American munitions factories and at the docks prompted the U.S. government to tighten security. Spring-Rice reported to London that "extraordinary measures of precaution have now become necessary in all the arms factories, at the docks, and on board vessels, even vessels of the United States Navy." He added, "It is probable that German agents are everywhere and excellently organised under the leadership of Boy-Ed, the German naval attaché."

Spring-Rice had good reason to suspect the complicity of Boy-Ed and his colleague von Papen in espionage activities. From the day of the sinking they had set their own network of agents to search out firm evidence that the *Lusitania* had been carrying explosives or volatile materials, knowing such evidence would be of great value in the propaganda battle. Unfortunately, Steward Neal Leach, to whose arrival in the United States the German embassy in Washington had attached such importance, had drowned. So had the three German stowaways. The British press had been quick to report the fate of the "three alleged German spies who were arrested in the *Lusitania* during her voyage and put into irons." Although Detective-Inspector William Pierpoint steadfastly refused to speak publicly of his interrogation of the three stowaways, it was widely reported that they "all went down with the *Lusitania*."

Nevertheless, the agents tried to piece together what evidence they could about the ship and her possible armaments and cargo from among their surviving espionage contacts. At their instigation, spymaster Paul König sent agent Harold Thorsten to see Herbert Kienzle of the Kienzle Clock Company at 41 Park Avenue. His mission was to ascertain whether Kienzle "knew what was the nature of a bronze powder said to have been shipped on the *Lusitania*, and also, if possible, the name of the shipper." The *Lusitania*'s last manifest had become known to the press and clearly listed fifty barrels of bronze powder.

König also at once set about obtaining a sworn affidavit from a "witness" prepared to swear that he had seen guns aboard the *Lusitania* the night before she sailed. This witness was the German reservist and associate of Neal Leach, the slightly built, twenty-seven-year-old named Gustav Stahl, whom König had employed previously to spy for him for three dollars a day.

On 1 June, the same day that Bryan confronted Wilson at the cabinet meeting, Count Bernstorff submitted Stahl's sworn affidavit to the secretary of state. Stahl claimed that "on the day prior to the sailing of the S.S. *Lusitania*, April 30th, 1915, I was asked by my friend, A. Lietch [*sic*], who was employed as first cabin steward to help him bring his trunk on board." On deck toward the stern he saw "two guns, of 12 to 15 centimeter," one on the port side and one on the starboard. "They were covered with leather, but the barrel was distinctly to be seen. To satisfy my curiosity I unfastened the buckles to ascertain the caliber of the guns." He claimed there were two similar guns on the foredeck. Bernstorff also submitted four more affidavits supporting Stahl's story.

Lansing at once sought and received written confirmation from Dudley Field Malone that his customs officials had made proper checks of the cargo and for armaments. The U.S. Department of Justice began carefully evaluating Gustav Stahl's claims, together with the supporting affidavits. Josephine Weir, proprietress of the boardinghouse at 132 West Sixteenth Street where Neal Leach had lodged until the night before the sailing, claimed that she had asked Leach about the dangers of sailing on the *Lusitania* "under the present conditions." Leach told her that there was no cause for alarm, since, "to protect herself, the *Lusitania* carried four brightly polished copper-colored cannons on board." A witness to this conversation, one John Greve, repeated Leach's comment. According to Greve, Leach also said, "We are not afraid, because we have four guns on board the ship for our protection."

The third affidavit came from a thirty-two-year-old Lutheran pastor and superintendent for the Society for the Care of German Seamen in the Port of New York, a German citizen named Brückner. He claimed that he had sailed past the *Lusitania* on a ferry while she was lying at her pier and had noticed "the pipe of a light gun" between two shields that were painted white to match the color of the superstructure. The fourth affidavit was from Josephine Weir's daughter Gertrude, who stated that she had heard Leach say that the *Lusitania* was carrying cannons on board and that "you may just as well call it a warship."

Stahl's affidavit, published almost immediately in full in the *New York Times*, aroused huge interest. The inquiry into the evidence was therefore conducted amid avid press and public speculation. Some survivors of the *Lusitania* became involved. Michael Byrne wrote to then Secretary of State Bryan on 6 June offering to make a formal affidavit that the ship had not carried any guns.

Austro-Hungarian ambassador Constantin Dumba also weighed in, forwarding to Lansing an affidavit signed by a naturalized former Austro-Hungarian chemist from Cleveland named Ritter von Rettegh. Rettegh insisted that the British naval attaché, Captain Guy Gaunt, had summoned him to Washington on 26 April to provide technical advice because of "my experience and skill." Gaunt had asked him what would happen if seawater were to come into contact with the explosive pyroxiline, commonly known as gun cotton. When Rettegh asked why he wanted to know, Gaunt replied, "We are required to send by one of our fastest steamers in the next day or so about six hundred tons of gun cotton, which we have purchased from the Du Pont Powder Company."

Rettegh told him that a certain type of gun cotton could explode if it came into contact with seawater. The chemist then claimed that, after the *Lusitania* incident, he told the Austro-Hungarian consul in Cleveland, Ernest Ludwig, about his conversation with Gaunt. Ludwig, apparently puzzled why the *Lusitania* had sunk so quickly, wondered whether exploding gun cotton could have been the cause. He asked Rettegh to investigate whether Du Pont had supplied gun cotton to the British. In his affidavit Rettegh claimed to have uncovered evidence that some 600 tons had indeed been shipped to New York in late April addressed to Cunard for loading on the *Lusitania*.

In his letter to Lansing, Dumba described Rettegh as a clever chemist but "highly nervous" and insisted that he took no responsibility for the veracity of his account. He merely wished to place at the disposal of the State Department "information which seems interesting." In a further note to the State Department, Dumba, who was perhaps himself nervous about being drawn into another potentially embarrassing situation, suggested that Rettegh was "possibly not quite normal." The State Department took the hint and did not pursue the matter.

The State Department was, however, interested when, on 17 June, Cecil Spring-Rice wrote to Lansing reporting that one Morris Spiers, proprietor of Spiers Theatre Realty, was offering to sell the British consul general in Philadelphia "a moving-picture film" of the *Lusitania* leaving New York on her last voyage. Spiers had been approached by "a German or Austrian who wished to purchase the negative," and figured that the British, too, would want to get their hands on it. The U.S. Department of Justice appointed a special agent to investigate. He reported on 27 June that he had viewed the film twice and that "I could not see the slightest evidence on any of the decks of a gun, either exposed or hidden."

The investigators took additional evidence from Neal Leach's uncle and cousin. They testified that they had seen him the night before he sailed and that he had said nothing about guns. Daniel Genny, who had known Neal Leach, also said that he never heard him mention guns, adding that "Stahl lied awfully," was very hard up, and probably "thought he could make a couple of dollars by saying he saw guns." Leach's friend Heinz Hardenberg, who had lodged at the same roominghouse, gave damning evidence that Stahl had said, "Come on, Heinz, I have got a fine thing, we will make plenty of money, we will go together to the Consul, tell him there were four guns on the *Lusitania*; that we were together with Leach on the *Lusitania* the day before she sailed; that he took his trunk on board; that we would get $10,000." Even the lawyer who had taken Stahl's original statement told the Department of Justice that he had seemed to be untruthful, unwilling, and only acting under Paul König's direction.

Pastor Brückner's claim to have seen guns on the *Lusitania* from the decks of a passing ferry was discounted when it became clear that the ferry in question passed a mile and a half away from where the *Lusitania* had been berthed. In addition, investigators concluded that, given the ferry's speed, the *Lusitania* would have been visible to him for only thirty seconds. They also decided that Josephine Weir, her daughter Gertrude, and John Greve had taken seriously remarks made by Leach "in a joking way" while they were dancing to his accordion in the kitchen.

Stahl's story soon fell apart in the face of the evidence. Perhaps anticipating this, Stahl vanished from New York City and fled upstate to Albany. He returned only when ordered to do so by Paul König, who, knowing that he was the star witness on whom the German case depended, had promised "to produce Stahl" for examination. A nervous, furtive-looking Stahl confirmed to the investigators that he was a German reservist who had served in the army from 1909 to 1911. He said he had known Leach in Germany three or four years earlier as a traveling salesman. He then reiterated his claims about what he had seen when he helped Leach carry his trunk on board the *Lusitania*. The investigation concluded that he was "a man of bad reputation, untruthful," and that "he had been employed by the German Secret Agents." At the time he claimed to have been with Leach there was conclusive proof that both he and Leach had been elsewhere. There was also proof that Leach's trunk had never been near the *Lusitania*. The large leather trunk was discovered to be still at the boardinghouse. Josephine Weir testified that Leach had left the boardinghouse alone and carrying only some hand baggage.

Stahl was asked to appear before the grand jury in the hope that he might break down. Wearing his finest clothes—a dark suit, new straw hat, green tie with a stickpin bearing a porcelain dog's head, polished tan shoes, and lavender socks with scarlet-embroidered flowers—he repeated his story under oath and through an interpreter for two and a half hours. He was immediately arrested and charged with perjury. The American press reported Stahl's subsequent trial with gusto. He pleaded guilty and was sentenced to eighteen months' imprisonment and a fine of one dollar.

The climate of suspicion was further heightened by acts of violence. On 2 July a bomb exploded in the Senate wing of the Capitol. The very next day brought an attack on the financier J. P. "Jack" Morgan Jr., head of J. P. Morgan and Company, the British government's commercial agents in the United States. Cecil Spring-Rice was a witness to it; he was a guest of Morgan and his wife at their house on Long Island at the time. The three were breakfasting when the butler suddenly shouted for Morgan to go upstairs at once. All three dashed up believing fire had broken out. They found nothing but, as they turned to go down again, were horrified to see the butler backing up the broad staircase before a gaunt-faced man brandishing a revolver in each hand.

Seeing the banker, the man raised his pistols with the cry "So you are Mr. Morgan!" Before he could fire, Mrs. Morgan sprang at him, but her husband pushed her aside. He wrestled his would-be assassin to the ground but was shot twice, in the stomach and thigh. Luckily the wounds were slight. The assailant was arrested and gave his name as Frank Holt, though he was later identified as the German Erich Münter. He was already known to the police. He had taught German at Harvard but had vanished a few years earlier after being questioned about the death of his wife from arsenic poisoning. He now confessed to the bombing of the Capitol and refused all food and drink.

Just two days after this murder attempt, Spring-Rice reported, "What may possibly have been an attempt on me occurred at night." He was being driven from the Morgans' house after his visit when a large car without lights and carrying five men passed him and stopped. The men got out, lined up across the road, and signaled to Spring-Rice's driver to pull up. Luckily, the chauffeur had the presence of mind to drive straight through them.

When Erich Münter was found dead in prison under mysterious circumstances, Spring-Rice was convinced he had been killed because he had offered to make a full confession that would have exposed the extent of the German spy rings. As the news of Münter's death broke in the press, further sensation was provided by a message from Münter's new wife in Texas. She claimed that he had confessed to her that he had planted time bombs on eastbound liners. Within days there was a violent explosion on a ship en route to England with munitions.

———— ∞ ————

The British had become sufficiently concerned about the risks to British shipping in America to take steps themselves. While Captain Webb had been carefully preparing the Admiralty's evidence for the Mersey inquiry into the sinking of the *Lusitania*, urgent investigations had been launched into Consul General Bennett's accusations that staff with German sympathies or origins working in Cunard's New York offices had passed information about the *Lusitania* to the Germans. Bennett, of course, had long believed Cunard's general manager Charles Sumner to be "rabidly anti-British." Now he also accused Herman Winter, the assistant manager and a "pure German," of being a probable traitor. Bennett cited as proof the fact that he had asked a friend to ring the Cunard office, as a test, to warn of a plot to waylay and possibly murder the consul general. The caller was put through to Winter, who replied that the matter was no business of his and that "the Consul-General should protect himself." The pompous Bennett was outraged to have received no communication from Cunard on the matter, "although common decency would have required some action to be taken, even if the message concerned merely an Italian Boot Black."

Bennett listed a number of other suspect employees, concluding, "I do not go so far as to say that the *Lusitania* met her fate through informa-

"Remember the *Lusitania*!"

Sir Alfred Booth, chairman of Cunard

tion supplied by the Cunard Office in New York as to her movements, but there is at least more than a little reason to suspect that, if the knowledge of the movements of the *Lusitania* were in the possession of certain persons in the New York Office, such knowledge might have conceivably been conveyed to German agents." He added, "The Cunard New York Office should be overhauled, cleaned and made reliable, and every single German, male and female, dismissed, or we will have still more trouble."

In London Cunard chairman Sir Alfred Booth was summoned to a meeting with the president of the Board of Trade, Walter Runciman. Booth did his best to defend his New York staff from what was threatening to become a witch hunt. At the same time, he tried to reassure Charles Sumner by writing to him: "I assured Mr. Runciman, that while your manner might sometimes be exasperating, I was convinced of your loyalty. . . . You might be inclined to growl, but nevertheless you delivered the goods." Runciman accepted Booth's assurances. And yet, the British embassy "practically insisted" that Cunard place an Englishman in the New York office to act as Sumner's assistant. Booth appointed Captain J. T. W. Charles of Cunard to transact all personal business between the company in New York and the British embassy and consulate.

Booth wrote soothingly to Sumner that this was no personal reflection on him. Sumner nevertheless felt threatened. He protested his loyalty and pointed out that although he was an American citizen, he had unbroken English ancestry going back to one Roger Sumner of Bicester in 1575. He added: "I am willing to do almost anything to save you trouble or embarrassment that does not tend to reflect upon me or prejudice my position before the public. Rather than that you can have my resignation upon request. No human being in this country has done more to forward government requirements than myself."

⁂

Meanwhile, the heightened security in the aftermath of the sinking of the *Lusitania* had proved deeply frustrating to Captain Franz von Rintelen, who had been forced to place his own schemes, including the use of Walther Scheele's cunningly contrived cigar-shaped firebombs, on hold. He hoped for a while that the United States might decide to embargo shipments of arms to the allies. When this failed to happen, he decided: "We simply *had* to carry on!" He resumed his attacks and claimed that his first success was the SS *Phoebus*, which caught fire at sea. But a telegram from Berlin addressed to the naval attaché Boy-Ed put a stop to further activities. It read: "CAPTAIN RINTELEN IS TO BE INFORMED UNOBTRUSIVELY THAT HE IS UNDER INSTRUCTIONS TO RETURN TO GERMANY."

Rintelen suspected that his recall was the handiwork of his enemies Boy-Ed and von Papen. Certainly, both were fearful of being embarrassed by the antics of the maverick agent and must have rejoiced at the prospect of his removal. Also, the intriguing of all three with Victoriano Huerta to set up a pro-German government in Mexico had been exposed. Guy Gaunt's Czech agent Emmanuel Viktor Voska had succeeded in bugging the rooms of the New York hotel where Huerta was secretly conducting his negotiations with the Germans. Huerta was arrested by a federal marshal before he could cross the border at El Paso, Texas. Boy-Ed and von Papen could hide at least for a while behind diplomatic immunity. Rintelen, on the other hand, was in some danger of arrest. He sailed from New York on 3 August aboard the neutral SS *Noordam*, once again under the identity of the Swiss citizen Emile Victor Gaché. But ten days later, when the ship was off Ramsgate, he was arrested by the British, who had been waiting for him.

Yet another absurd twist to this complex tale of spying and subterfuge that summer was the affair of the German commercial councillor Heinrich Albert's briefcase. On 24 July, in a moment's absentmindedness, he left it on the elevated railway. An American secret agent, who had been trailing him, quickly made off with it. The briefcase was delivered that night to William McAdoo, who was on vacation in Maine. The contents painted such a damningly comprehensive picture of German espionage activities in the United States that House advised Wilson to give them the widest possible exposure. They gave Albert's papers to the *New York World*, which published them complete. Bernstorff hurried off to the Adirondacks, where, the State Department was informed by the Department of Justice's agent, "he has been buried for the last ten days with his inamorata." Albert was less adept at avoiding unpleasantness. He found himself lampooned mercilessly for his lost briefcase as the "Minister without Portfolio."

Next, one of Voska's agents tracked down a newspaperman, John J. Archibald, who was acting as a courier for the Germans and Austrians under his neutral American passport. Captain Gaunt alerted Captain Hall, and Archibald was arrested immediately on reaching England. The documents seized included a report by Count Dumba describing strikes that his agents had provoked among Hungarian munitions workers; details of payments to agents and saboteurs; progress reports from Boy-Ed and Von Papen about sabotage; and, less sinister but almost as damaging, a letter from von Papen to his wife referring to "these idiotic Yankees." Boy-Ed's and Von Papen's role in the Huerta affair was also conclusively proved.

Captain Hall presented the findings with considerable glee to Ambassador Page in London. An exasperated President Wilson demanded Constantin Dumba's recall. He did not yet seek to expel Boy-Ed and Von Papen—"the obnoxious underlings," as House called them. They would not leave until the U.S. administration finally requested their departure in December 1915 after further revelations of their "undiplomatic" activities.

Yet this series of incidents, from the Rintelen affair to Albert's briefcase to these latest disclosures, exacerbated the tensions caused by the sinking of the *Lusitania* and its aftermath. Colonel House wrote to Wilson in mid-September that a break with Germany would come before he got the letter. However, as with his previous predictions of war, he was wrong.

∽∽∽

CHAPTER TWENTY-SIX

The Kaiser's Business Only

*I*N BERLIN, American outrage over Germany's espionage activities was noted with dismay. The arrival of the second American protest, the uncompromising tone of which had prompted Bryan's resignation, also exacerbated the tensions. Hard on its heels came unequivocal evidence that Fregattenkapitän Hermann Bauer, leader of Schwieger's U-boat Half-Flotilla, had deliberately failed to forward at least some of the flood of restraining orders to his U-boat men. These orders were issued earlier in the year—on 18 April, after a submarine attack on the neutral Dutch ship *Katwijk*—and called for special care to be taken with Dutch shipping. Bauer's attitude seemed to the kaiser to demonstrate arrogance of the highest degree. On the kaiser's instructions, Admiral Müller wrote to Admiral Pohl calling for Bauer's dismissal and seeking advice on a suitable replacement.

In the end, the naval high command rallied to defend Bauer. Bachmann and Pohl argued that Bauer had not recognized the orders to be orders because of ambiguity in the way they were transmitted to him. They also claimed that a relevant and damning section of Bauer's log expressing his view that "such an instruction would only complicate matters further" had been wrongly transcribed. Bauer kept his job, but the incident was worrying evidence of a spirit of determined independence, even rebellion, within the navy.

On 23 June the chancellor and the foreign secretary arrived at Pless "in a very depressed mood." There was increasing agitation in Berlin in the Reichstag and in the newspapers against Bethmann Hollweg while "pro-Tirpitz sentiment was growing." They predicted a violent reaction in the press if the second American note were not vigorously rejected. The next day Müller sat down with the chancellor to try and draft a response that would satisfy German public opinion but also ward off a hostile U.S. reaction. But they knew that the real stumbling block would be Admiral Tirpitz.

They had underestimated their wily and determined adversary. Tirpitz and Bachmann had been busily producing their own draft, which they presented at a meeting on 25 June. The chancellor and his confederates were dismayed by Tirpitz's text "because there was no agreement to the positive points of Wilson's note." Later that day, they all gathered to report to the kaiser. The discussion soon reached stalemate. The meeting lamely agreed that the naval staff should confer further with the chancellor in Berlin to seek a compromise. Tirpitz and Bachmann left that evening "deeply disturbed and agitated."

It was not until 8 July that the German reply was sent. It was as unsatisfactory to the American administration as the previous German note had been. It affirmed that Germany agreed completely with America's belief in "the principles of humanity" and the freedom of the seas for peaceable trade but evaded the issue of sinking enemy ships without warning. The note asserted that Britain had violated the freedom of the sea by her illegal blockade and her mining of the North Sea; that Britain was flouting America's principles of humanity by attempting to starve the German population; that Germany had been obliged to resort to submarine warfare to defend "her national existence." The note offered to guarantee the safety of American ships and lives, not by abandoning submarine warfare but by introducing a safe-conduct scheme. Designated American ships, flying the Stars and Stripes, appropriately painted and carrying no contraband, would be given safe conduct through the submarine zone provided reasonable advance notice was given.

The German note misjudged the American mood. Wilson had no intention of abandoning his quest to see Germany give up her inhuman weapon of "self-defense." Nor was he disposed to give up any American rights. The American press backed him. The German suggestion that American ships should be painted with red, white, and blue stripes like barber's poles was insulting. The papers made quips about "barber ships" instead of "barber shops." Nevertheless, Americans still had no appetite to go to war. The press and the public were, like Wilson, content to continue to press the nation's case through diplomatic exchanges.

The United States was far quicker to respond in the battle of words than was Germany. Her third protest note was dispatched less than two weeks later, on 21 July. Largely the handiwork of Lansing, it was in many ways the firmest statement yet. The note declared that by offering special privileges to American ships Germany was setting international law aside; that by proclaiming that her submarine blockade was an act of reprisal she was admitting her use of illegal tactics (reprisals being by their nature illegal); that what was at issue was the "grave and unjustifiable violations of the rights of American citizens." Even if Britain were acting illegally, this was a matter for Berlin and London. Germany had no right to retaliate with a weapon and in a way that endangered neutral lives. Any further violation of American rights would be regarded "as deliberately unfriendly."

If Britain was gratified by this final American note, Germany was not. The kaiser wrote furious comments in the margin: "Immeasurably impertinent," "You don't say!" "Unheard of!" and "i.e., war." At the bottom he scrawled angrily that in bearing and tone it was "about the most impudent note which I have ever read. . . . It ends with a direct threat!" Meanwhile the internal sparring was continuing. Bachmann and Tirpitz believed that the position for the U-boat service had become intolerable: "Order, Counter order, Disorder!" as Tirpitz later wrote.

On 19 August 1915, the *U-24* sank an unarmed British White Star passenger ship, the *Arabic*, fifty miles off the Old Head of Kinsale. Forty-four people, including two Americans, were killed. The U-boat commander, Schneider, claimed to have mistaken her for a freighter but had clearly contravened the orders issued in June.

The chancellor induced the kaiser to impose yet further limitations on U-boat deployment. Germany now openly promised Washington that no unresisting passenger liners would be sunk without warning or without ensuring the safety of those aboard. Bachmann wrote to the kaiser complaining that the definition of a "passenger ship" was unclear and would cause confusion. A furious Tirpitz insisted that it was impossible to follow these instructions without gravely endangering the U-boats.

His arguments were underlined by the fact that on the same day that the *U-24* sank the *Arabic*, the German U-boat service learned in brutal fashion of the existence of British "Q," or decoy, ships. Originally the brainchild of Churchill and Fisher, these ships were disguised to resemble ordinary tramp steamers but carried guns hidden behind collapsible screens. Their role was to entice U-boats to surface and approach, sometimes by pretending to be foundering, sometimes even by launching lifeboats crammed with apparently panic-stricken crewmen. Then, at the last moment, they would hoist the White Ensign of the Royal Navy and attack. Their holds were filled with timber to make them more buoyant in case their hulls were ruptured.

Among the "Q" ships was HMS *Baralong*. On 19 August she approached the *U-27*, the submarine which earlier that year had lain in wait for the *Lusitania* and which was now attacking a British freighter. The *Baralong* suddenly revealed her guns and opened fire. The U-boat began to sink, and her crew abandoned her. The *Baralong*'s crew shot some of the submariners while they were in the water, then hunted down, killed, and threw overboard those who had sought refuge on the freighter. The British action was reported by horrified American muleteers on board the freighter.

Ambassador Bernstorff protested to Secretary of State Lansing that the *Baralong* had been flying the U.S. flag until just before revealing her guns, when she hoisted the British one. But Lansing did not protest to the British about either the use of the American flag or the merciless killing of the U-boat survivors, which the British tried lamely to defend on the grounds that they had believed the men to be armed.

Once again Tirpitz submitted his resignation. Once again the kaiser refused to accept it. He wrote to Tirpitz trying to convince him that it was absolutely vital to prevent America from entering the war since she could provide "unlimited money for our foes." He also asserted his absolute right as "Supreme Warlord" to dictate policy: "First *the war must be won*, and that end necessitates absolute protection against a new enemy; how that is to be achieved . . . is *My business*. What I do with My navy is *My business only*."

The kaiser did, however, dismiss the vociferous Bachmann.

———⚬⚬⚬———

In the weeks that followed, the kaiser must have wondered what more he needed to do to bring the U-boat service to heel. On the evening of 4 September as dusk was falling, Walther Schwieger in the *U-20* sighted a ship some eighty-five miles southwest of Fastnet Rock. He noted in his war diary that she was outside the usual shipping channels; she was also zig-zagging and had dimmed her lights. It was not dark enough, in his view, for a surface attack, so he submerged and fired a torpedo. He scored a direct hit and did not remain in the vicinity to watch the ship sink. His victim was the 10,920-ton British passenger liner *Hesperian*. She had gone down in the waters through which the *Lusitania* had passed just two hours before her own sinking. By a strange quirk of fate, she had been carrying the corpse of a *Lusitania* victim recently retrieved from the sea.

Schwieger was summoned to Berlin and asked why he had attacked a passenger ship against orders. His explanation that he had believed the *Hesperian* to be an auxiliary cruiser received short shrift. He was even asked whether he was suffering from a guilty conscience, which he angrily denied. Schwieger was then ordered to acquiesce in the fiction, already put about by the authorities, that the *Hesperian* had not been torpedoed but had hit a mine. He was told to order his men to keep quiet. He was also told, "Hereafter follow your instructions exactly."

His hostile reception took Schwieger by surprise, and he wrote a bitter letter to Hermann Bauer. His flowing black script covers six pages of thick, now yellowing paper and is one of the very few documents in his hand to survive. He ended the letter with a complaint that it was impossible to expect U-boat men to distinguish between auxiliary cruisers, troop transports, and ordinary shipping, particularly at night. Bauer was sympathetic. He believed that the German government should have had the courage to claim the sinking of the *Lusitania* as a victory and to follow it up by attacking further such targets.

The Germans suffered another self-inflicted propaganda setback in October 1915. To the horror of the world press, they executed nurse Edith Cavell, whom Marie de Page had so wanted to work with, for hiding British and Belgian soldiers and helping them to escape.

Then, on 7 November, the *U-38* sank the Italian passenger liner *Ancona* bound for New York. The tally of over 100 dead included over 20 Americans. At Lansing's prompting, Wilson allowed his secretary of state to use the *Ancona* incident to press for a reply to the last American note. The Germans had been hoping, as Ambassador Gerard wrote from Berlin, "to keep the *Lusitania* matter 'jollied along' until the American papers get excited about baseball or a new scandal and forget."

Lansing turned up the heat on Germany even more while the president, who had married Edith Galt on 18 December, was away honey-mooning at Hot Springs, Virginia. Bethmann Hollweg believed that the stark choice confronting Germany was either to admit the illegality of the sinking of the *Lusitania* or face war with America. But in early 1916, President Wilson suddenly reined Lansing in. He had discovered to his surprise, while on a tour of midwestern states, that the public was rather less concerned about the *Lusitania* than Lansing had led him to believe. Encouraged in turn by Lansing's apparent mellowing, Germany presented a draft of her reply informally on 4 February to test the reaction of the United States.

It said that, in deference to American concern, Germany had already limited the scope of U-boat warfare. It also expressed "profound regret" for the American dead of the *Lusitania*, assumed liability for them, and offered to pay "a suitable indemnity." The note did not specifically acknowledge any illegality in Germany's act. In submitting it, Bernstorff told Lansing that the wording was as far as his government was prepared to go given the state of public opinion in Germany. Lansing, conscious that he had little support from Wilson in forcing a breach, told the president that although the word *illegality* was not used, America could interpret Germany's concessions as an indirect admission of wrongdoing. The preliminary note of 4 February, with some minor changes, became the formal and final German note of 16 February.

German public opinion was less tractable. Feeling in support of unrestricted submarine warfare was continuing to run high. So was anti-American sentiment. Gerard was convinced that the United States, not Britain, had now become the true focus of popular hatred. The American defense attaché in Berlin had previously reported to Washington that "every German feels and believes that America has been unneutral and that America is aiding in a great measure the Allies. They feel that by sinking the *Lusitania* they have 'got back' at us in a small way for what we are doing."

Nevertheless, having defused the American situation, the chancellor continued to have his way in holding back the submarine lobby. In March 1916 Bethmann Hollweg even induced the kaiser to remove some of Tirpitz's ministerial powers. This was the final straw for the naval secretary, who for the third time offered his resignation. This time it was accepted.

Despite the war, Admiral Fisher, who perhaps saw some parallels with his own exit, quickly dispatched Tirpitz a frank and consoling letter. It began "Dear Old Tirps" and ended "Cheer up, old chap! Say 'Resurgam'! You're the one German sailor who understands War! Kill your enemy without being killed yourself. I don't blame you for the submarine business, I'd have done the same myself. . . . Yours till hell freezes."

Within days of Tirpitz's resignation, a U-boat torpedoed the small, slow, French cross-Channel steamer *Sussex* without warning on 24 March 1916, demolishing a portion of her bows. Although the ship did not sink and was towed into Boulogne, some eighty persons, including a number of women and children, had been killed. The wounded included four Americans. The attack once again violated Germany's promise, given just seven months earlier at the time of the *Arabic*'s sinking, not to attack unresisting passenger ships without warning. At first Germany denied any responsibility, as she had done in the case of the *Hesperian*, but in the face of overwhelming evidence changed tack and declared that the U-boat captain had taken her for a warship. The *New York World* carried a cartoon showing the kaiser clutching a wreath labeled "*Lusitania*" while behind him the stricken *Sussex* exploded. The caption read: "Of course I didn't do it—Didn't I promise I wouldn't?"

President Wilson issued an ultimatum that "unless the Imperial Government should now immediately declare and effect an abandonment of its present methods of submarine warfare against passenger and freight-carrying vessels, the Government of the United States can have no choice but to sever diplomatic relations."

The kaiser had by now come to the conclusion that "there was no longer any international law," but on 4 May he yielded and ordered that no more unresisting merchant ships and passenger liners were to be sunk without prior warning. Tirpitz called this "a decisive turning point of the war, the beginning of our capitulation."

Later that year, Germany was embarrassed by reports in the foreign press of a German medal celebrating the sinking of the *Lusitania*. Investigations revealed that a Munich metalworker, Karl Götz, had cast about 100 such medals. One side carried a German inscription reading "No Contraband" at the top. Beneath it was a depiction of the *Lusitania*'s decks so crammed with airplanes and weaponry that there was barely space for passengers. The ship was sinking by the stern, rather than the prow, which reared up, looking viciously sharp—as if it could slice a U-boat in two. The inscription at the bottom read, "The liner *Lusitania*

The Karl Götz medal.

sunk by a German submarine. May 5, 1915." On the other side was the inscription "Business Above All." A line of male passengers was shown waiting in line to buy tickets from a Cunard agent, depicted as a skeleton representing Death. One passenger was reading a newspaper warning of the submarine risk. A bearded German official in a top hat was trying to warn another passenger not to sail.

The British press decried the medal as another example of German "frightfulness" and the Hun's heartless gloating over death and destruction. They also pointed to the date—two days before the actual sinking— as evidence of a German conspiracy to sink the ship.

A discomfited German government launched an inquiry. Götz explained that he was a satirist and that the medals, which he had cast for the first time in August 1915, were intended to be allegorical. He was not celebrating the sinking but condemning the cynicism of Cunard in enticing innocent people on board an armed ship carrying contraband. He attributed the mistaken date to an error that he had later corrected.

Since the medals were so obviously open to misinterpretation, Jagow asked the Bavarian government to prevent their distribution. The Germans discovered only later that British propagandists, having learned of the Götz medal, had cheerfully commissioned Gordon Selfridge, owner of the famous department store on London's Oxford Street, to strike another quarter of a million copies. They were distributed worldwide to help win sympathy for the Allied cause and to raise money for the British Red Cross.

Meanwhile, the German position was changing and hardening. The naval battle of Jutland in May 1916 had failed to dent the British blockade, and the German High Seas Fleet had retreated back to its base, never to reemerge. As the year drew on, the kaiser faced increasing pressure to unleash the U-boats. Members of the pro-submarine lobby told him that Germany now had even greater numbers of submarines of improved design. They produced table after table illustrating the effectiveness of the U-boats while they had been allowed to operate without restriction and showing that a relentless campaign of only five or six months would be enough to push Britain out of the war. Even if such action brought the United States into the conflict, it would not matter; U-boats would sink much of the Allies' transatlantic shipping before America was ready to send troops. When U.S. forces did finally embark, U-boats would prevent them from reaching Europe.

An additional factor in German thinking was that Wilson had in November 1916 been reelected president. Although he won by only a very narrow margin, his victory suggested to many Germans that Americans preferred a "writing" to a "fighting" president and that his campaign slogan, "He Kept Us Out of War," remained potent. Ambassador Gerard was convinced that Germany now believed that "America could be insulted, flouted, and humiliated with impunity."

In January 1917 the kaiser called a meeting at Pless at which Bethmann Hollweg, vainly arguing against a new unrestricted submarine campaign, found himself completely isolated and yielded to the will of the majority. In despair he told a court official that this was "finis Germaniae"—the end of Germany. The kaiser signed the document, which stated: "I order that unrestricted submarine warfare be launched with the utmost vigor on the first of February . . . Wilhelm I. R." All ships enemy and neutral, armed and unarmed, would be attacked. The decision was to be kept secret and not announced to neutral countries until the evening of 31 January, within hours of the first potential torpedo attacks. The United States was offered a small concession: One specially marked merchant vessel a week would be allowed to enter and leave the English port of Falmouth on designated days.

Washington's response was instant and emphatic: On 3 February it severed all diplomatic relations with Germany. Captain Guy Gaunt, the British naval attaché, sent a jubilant telegram to Captain Reginald Hall: "BERNSTORFF GOES HOME. I GET DRUNK TONIGHT."

President Wilson determined to wait and see whether the Germans meant what they said before he took the final step of going to war. Hall, however, had in his safe a document of such potency that it would place an irresistible pressure on the president.

The German government had foreseen that their declaration of unrestricted submarine warfare would be likely to bring the United States into the war. They had therefore made plans to keep America busy at home. As usual, these plans involved Mexico. On 16 January 1917 Arthur Zimmermann, who had replaced Jagow as foreign secretary, sent a telegram to Bernstorff for onward transmission to the German embassy in Mexico. It baldly proposed an alliance between Germany and Mexico: "MAKE WAR TOGETHER, MAKE PEACE TOGETHER, GENEROUS FINANCIAL SUPPORT, AND AN UNDERSTANDING ON OUR PART THAT MEXICO IS TO RE-CONQUER THE LOST TERRITORY IN TEXAS, NEW MEXICO, AND

ARIZONA." It also proposed that Japan should be invited to switch sides and declare war against the United States.

Room 40 had decoded this extraordinary telegram and passed it to Hall, who pondered, in his usual cool, detached fashion, how best to use it. He waited until the middle of February, by which time it was clear that the German announcement of an unrestricted submarine campaign was not going to push Wilson into an immediate declaration of war. Hall then showed it to Edward Bell, intelligence officer at the American embassy and his close, long-term associate, whom he used to get messages quickly and accurately across the Atlantic to Washington.

Bell, in turn, showed Zimmermann's telegram to Ambassador Page. Together the three men devised a way of presenting it to the rest of the U.S. administration that, while emphasizing its veracity, would not betray its source and thus expose to Germany the success of the Room 40 team. The message was forwarded to Wilson on Saturday 24 February. Wilson and Lansing decided to release it to the press. "Profound sensation" was how Lansing described its reception.

Then, in mid-March, U-boats sank five unarmed American freighters with the loss of thirty-six lives.

Wilson summoned Congress. On 6 April, the event that Bethmann Hollweg had feared for so long, and in particular since the sinking of the *Lusitania*, finally happened: America went to war. Just three months later, in July 1917, hounded by German army chiefs Paul von Hindenburg and Erich von Ludendorff and a large part of the Reichstag, Bethmann Hollweg resigned. The kaiser—who had lacked the strength, albeit not the will, to save his chancellor—remarked, "Now I may as well abdicate."

In America recruitment posters appeared, headlined "Remember the *Lusitania!*" One depicted a drowning woman, hair streaming like seaweed in the blue-green water and a baby clasped tightly in her arms. A single bloodred word was superimposed over the image: "ENLIST." It would be said that the *Lusitania* had failed to deliver 198 American passengers to Britain but finally delivered 2 million American soldiers to the Western Front.

CHAPTER TWENTY-SEVEN

"That Story Is Forever Disposed Of"

A S AMERICAN TROOPS went into battle shouting "*Lusitania!*" the aftermath of the sinking rumbled on back home. Sixty-seven lawsuits had been filed against Cunard, claiming compensation for injury and loss of life and property. These were consolidated and heard in New York by Judge Julius Mayer in 1918. By agreement between the plaintiffs and the defendant, the fifty-two-year-old judge heard the case alone without a jury. Mayer, a staunch Republican with a strong sense of the national interest, was once described as "more a Czar than a judge." His obituary recalled that "one of his most famous remarks to attorneys was to come to the point and be brief. His methods did not please all by any means." He had ruled in favor of the White Star Line in the similar *Titanic* case, during which Captain Turner had given evidence before embarking on the *Lusitania* for the last time.

Significantly, during preliminary discussions between the two sides' lawyers, the plaintiffs agreed to drop allegations that the ship had been armed and carrying clandestine ammunition and Canadian troops, all of which, if proven, would have considerably aided their case. Judge Mayer said simply, "That story is forever disposed of so far as we are concerned."

A formidable array of evidence was assembled. In June, thirty-three British witnesses gave evidence under oath and were cross-examined before Commissioner R. V. Wynne in London mainly because of the difficulty of bringing serving seamen to New York in wartime. Judge Mayer also reviewed the evidence given in open court to the Mersey inquiry. However, the British Admiralty refused on grounds of national security to disclose either its communications with Captain Turner or the evidence given to Mersey in closed session. The extended British Defence of the Realm Act was cited as the reason that witnesses could not answer questions on these topics. Judge Mayer also took evidence in New York from American and other witnesses. Curiously, though, neither the witness statements collected by the American consul in Queenstown, Wesley Frost, nor his own reports from the scene were volunteered by the U.S. government.

The key witness giving evidence in London was Captain Turner, again supported by Cunard's counsel, Butler Aspinall. His evidence on zigzagging differed from what he had told the Mersey inquiry. He now argued that his experience until May 1915 had suggested that there was no need to zigzag in a ship as fast as the *Lusitania*. (He also pointed out tartly that in between his respective appearances before Lord Mersey and Commissioner Wynne, his new command, the troopship *Ivernia*, had been torpedoed and sunk while he was zigzagging.) He said that he had been drawing closer to the coast to avoid what he believed to be the location of the submarine off Coningbeg, to which he had been alerted. Questioned about his orders, he replied wearily, "It would be a task to tell you what instructions I have had from the Admiralty and everyone else; I could paper the walls with them." The experience of giving evidence was clearly stressful. At one point he confessed to Commissioner Wynne that he was still haunted by the events of 7 May 1915: "It is two years ago and I have been trying to forget the thing and I cannot."

Other British captains were questioned about whether merchant ships routinely zigzagged before the sinking of the *Lusitania*. Fifty-eight-year-old Thomas Taylor insisted that prior to the incident no one zigzagged. "We would not have done it. We never thought of it up to that time." Edwin Fear, master of the Canadian Northern Steamship Company's *Uranium*, said, "No, I never heard of any [such] practice, it was more of a joke than anything."

However, at least one of Turner's fellow master merchant mariners was less than sympathetic about his insistence on taking a four-point bearing on the Old Head of Kinsale to determine his precise position.

James Durie asserted that a two-point cross-bearing should have been sufficient. An accurate cross-bearing could be taken between Galley Head and the Old Head of Kinsale in "only three minutes." It could even have been done while the ship was zigzagging, since a single straight leg of a zigzag took more than the three minutes required to take the bearing.

Officials from Cunard's New York office, examined before Judge Mayer, claimed not to have known that one boiler room was shut down and that they could not therefore have told passengers. They did, however, confirm that they knew that the *Lusitania*'s crossings were slower than before the war. Therefore they had given passengers an "indication" that the ship would arrive on the "sixth day" rather than at a precise time.

Passenger after passenger confirmed that many portholes had been open on the day of the attack. Fred Gauntlett testified that "nearly all were open" in the dining room. James Brooks said that passengers had never been told to close the portholes "during the voyage." Expert witness Professor Hovgaard, a prominent marine architect from the Massachusetts Institute of Technology, stated unequivocally that if an open porthole with an eighteen-inch diameter were submerged to a depth of three feet in the conditions of the *Lusitania*'s sinking, it would let in 3.75 tons of water a minute. Twenty-four such portholes would let in 360 tons of water in four minutes.

Judge Mayer took much evidence on the total number and location of the torpedo strikes. The number of torpedoes that people claimed to have seen or heard ranged from one to three, while the locations varied from between the first and second funnels to between the third and fourth.

Judge Mayer also focused on the *Lusitania*'s cargo as detailed in her manifest. Armaments specialists from the Winchester Repeating Company and the Remington Arms Company stated that the small-arms ammunition in the *Lusitania*'s cargo would not have exploded through shock from the torpedo impact. One testified: "We have dropped cases of those cartridges on a cement floor. We have dropped them about 60 feet without exploding them." Another said that he had seen a rifle fired into the cartridges without causing them to explode. They were equally unanimous about the effects of fire. William Thomas of Remington waved a report that showed "that you could not explode the cases of cartridges by setting them afire in mass or in bulk." Irving Lippincott agreed: "We have made what we call a fire test, putting in full cases of cartridges and starting with a hot fire. They went off like a lot of fire-crackers. . . . There was no explosion in mass, the individual cartridges went off as the primer was heated to the flashing point." He added that these flying pieces were insufficient to penetrate any substantial piece of metal.

William Struble, superintendent of the Bethlehem Steel Company's Reddington Plant, was asked whether the shrapnel shells supplied by his company had powder in them. He replied, "None whatever." He added that they could not have been filled elsewhere and furthermore that the contract with Britain had specifically provided for them not to be filled. He also stated that the separate consignment of fuses did not contain any explosives.

Unsurprisingly, Cunard seems to have continued to encourage its staff to be supportive of the company when giving their evidence. Crewman Jack Roper, who had rescued Captain Turner, wrote to the Cunard chairman in 1919, claiming expenses and payment. He insisted he had been promised them for following the line "on going to court that I was a Cunard Line servant and whatever evidence I had to give was to be in favour of the C.S.S. Co. [Cunard Steamship Company]."

Judge Mayer's opinion, published on 23 August 1918, absolved Cunard and Turner from blame. He ruled that "the cause of the sinking of the *Lusitania* was the illegal act of the Imperial German Government, acting through its instrument, the submarine commander, and violating a cherished and humane rule observed, until this war, by even the bitterest antagonists." But he also remarked wisely that "throughout the case it must always be remembered that the disaster occurred in May 1915 and the whole subject must be approached with the knowledge and mental attitude of that time."

Judge Mayer also ruled that no materials had been carried which "could be exploded by setting them on fire in mass or in bulk nor by subjecting them to impact." He agreed with Lord Mersey that there were two torpedoes, declaring that "the weight of the testimony (too voluminous to analyze) is in favour of the two torpedo contention" and that "as there were no explosives on board, it is difficult to account for the second explosion except on the theory that it was caused by a second torpedo."

On Captain Turner's actions, Mayer concluded that "the fundamental principle in navigating a merchantman whether in times of peace or of war is that the commanding officer must be left free to exercise his judgement. Safe navigation denies the proposition that the judgement and sound discretion of the Captain of a vessel must be confined in a mental straitjacket." He dismissed the possibility of "open portholes being a contributory factor" to the sinking and praised the "calm heroism" of the passengers who showed "marked consideration for women and children." There was "no panic but, naturally, . . . a considerable amount of excitement." In his view, the number of boat drills and other emergency arrangements were fully satisfactory by the standards of 1915. Judge Mayer suggested in conclusion that American claimants should apply to the German government for compensation under the promised indemnity.

This was to prove a lengthy process. The last awards were not made until December 1925 by a commission set up in 1922. Survivors and relatives of the deceased claimed nearly $15.5 million. The total sum— awarded for personal injury and for loss of personal possessions—was just over $2.5 million.

For some, like champagne magnate George Kessler, who had died in 1920 from an enlargement of the liver, the awards came too late. His estate received $35,000 to compensate for the four hours Kessler had spent in the water, for contusions, and for shock. Charles Frohman's and Alfred Vanderbilt's families received no compensation. The principles drawn up by the commission were based on a calculation of the benefits claimants could have expected to receive from the deceased had they lived. As such, they favored rich passengers over poor. However, Frohman's and Vanderbilt's heirs were excepted because the commission judged that they had suffered "no pecuniary loss." Their wills left the beneficiaries financially better off than they had been during the dead men's lifetimes.

The awarding of compensation closed a chapter in the *Lusitania* story. But for survivors and those who had lost loved ones, the process of trying to forget would take a very long time and money would be poor compensation.

CHAPTER TWENTY-EIGHT

—⊶⊷—

Diving into the Wreck

*T*H E *Lusitania* had lain at the bottom of the Irish Sea for less than three years when the first newspaper reports of salvage or recovery operations appeared. The *Sunday Examiner* of 7 April 1918 described the plans of Carl Lundquist, a marine engineer, to raise the ship. Lundquist and his investors claimed to be motivated not by money but by the "sentimental interest of the American public" roused by the tragedy and heightened by America's entry into the war. Nevertheless, they estimated the value of the cargo, jewelry, precious metals, and bonds on board to be around $12 million.

Lundquist proposed to construct a special salvage ship. Its hull would be capable of extension to the seabed to reach the wreck. Hydraulic jets would then be used to shift the sand and create a trough beneath the vessel to allow lines to be placed beneath her. Next, four huge, hollow, cylindrical steel pontoons would be sunk and attached to the wreck. Once these were emptied of water, the *Lusitania* would rise with them to the surface.

Nothing came of this theoretically elegant scheme, nor of the plan, put forth in 1920, to slice the *Lusitania* into five sections underwater "as though by a giant saw held by a giant hand" and raise each separately by large pontoons. A newspaper ghoulishly reviewed how the bodies might look, telling its readers that drowned bodies were usually found in the same position as medieval crusaders "represented in sepulcher sculptures—arms folded and legs crossed." The paper suggested that, if raised, the contents of the ship should be inspected by a neutral commission to silence continuing German claims that the ship had been an armed ammunition carrier.

Interest in the wreck remained high, prompting further proposals for salvaging the ship or diving on her. In 1922 the German ambassador to London was sufficiently concerned about press reports that an American company was attempting to raise the *Lusitania* to make informal inquiries. An American embassy official in London reported his comments that Germany was "naturally much concerned and anxious that there be no possibility of misrepresentation of conditions found to have existed when [the] ship was sunk" and that the exact truth should be "certified beyond question by unprejudiced observers." The plans were, however, soon abandoned.

As time passed, estimates of the value of the salvage increased while ever more novel recovery techniques were put forward. One scheme proposed extending air-filled tubes down to the ship through which divers would descend to an air lock near the wreck, from where they could move into the water. It was even suggested that there should be a viewing platform for spectators at the end of the tube. Although a modified version of the tube concept was used elsewhere, nothing came of the proposed scheme.

The site of the wreck was not formally pinpointed until 1935, when a Glasgow-based consortium located the *Lusitania* lying on the bottom of the Irish Sea at a depth of 312 feet, with the highest point of the wreck some 84 feet higher. The consortium secured the necessary permissions to dive on the wreck, including from the British Admiralty.

In Germany, the *Lusitania* was still an issue of great national sensitivity. On 7 May 1935 an article by Karl Scherb, the *U-20*'s officer of the watch at the time of the sinking, was published in the Nazi *Völkischer Beobachter* to mark the twentieth anniversary of the attack. Scherb repeated all the claims that the *Lusitania* had been an armed vessel carrying munitions.

The consortium began its exploration of the wreck. Jim Jarratt, a British diver, donned one of the exceedingly heavy diving suits of the period and was lowered to the *Lusitania*. He established her identity partly by checking the size of the ship's large rivets, which still protruded from the plates. She was indeed the *Lusitania*, and these were the rivets, which had so lacerated the port-side lifeboats during the frantic attempts to lower them. In the murky light and with his vision impaired by his cumbersome suit, Jarratt wrongly thought that the ship was lying on her port side. After this single dive, bad weather forced the postponement of any further activity for the winter. The consortium began to plan its next expedition, intending to use novel, more flexible diving suits and better equipment and lighting. As it turned out, no further dives could be made before the Second World War broke out.

After the end of the war there were persistent rumors that the Royal Navy was sending diving expeditions to the wreck to remove any armaments or evidence of large amounts of ammunition. The Royal Navy refused to comment, and the alleged key participants, naval and civilian, denied any involvement. The Royal Navy also allegedly depth-charged the wreck to destroy evidence. The latter seems particularly unlikely since the force of depth charges is mainly directed upward rather than downward and charges are known to be of little use for removing obstacles on the seabed. If the navy did depth-charge the wreck, it was likely to have been during the Second World War either as an exercise or because naval radar operators aboard destroyers mistook the *Lusitania*'s image on their green flickering screens for that of an enemy submarine.

———— ∞ ————

The *Lusitania* lay in peace until the 1960s, when a former U.S. Navy diver, John Light, arrived in Kinsale to explore and film the wreck on behalf of American and British TV interests. The possible presence of arms and ammunition was a key preoccupation of all concerned. Light and his team made a total of forty-two dives to the wreck over a period of two years. They were diving with compressed-air equipment to depths beyond recognized safety limits. In consequence they suffered badly from the mental and physical effects of a condition known as "nitrogen narcosis." Divers call it "the Martini effect," in which every additional ten yards' depth beyond the limit has as much effect on the brain as a double Martini. They also found the water intensely cold. Light reported that the ship was lying on her starboard side and that the bow had been almost severed on the visible port side by what must have been an internal explosion, probably of a cargo of ammunition. One of Light's companions saw what he believed to be a gun barrel, but he was at the limit of his time on the wreck and had no opportunity to make a detailed exploration. The black-and-white film they shot in the murk shows very little.

The next few years brought rapid improvements to diving equipment and methods, stimulated by the demands of underwater oil exploration and production. Meanwhile, John Light had never lost his interest in the *Lusitania* wreck and its mysteries and had begun to work hard seeking information from British government and Cunard archives. In 1967, with financial backing from an American publishing house, he bought the wreck—but not the cargo—for £1,000 from the insurers, the British War Risks Association. After securing further financial support from private investors and TV companies, he set to work to convert a trawler into a sophisticated diving facility. The novelty and technical complexity of his equipment caused time and cost overruns. At the end of 1969 the project was abandoned with a reputed $500,000 spent and without a single dive having been made.

John Light continued his work in the archives, where he unearthed a considerable amount of material. Financial pressures led him to collaborate with *Sunday Times* journalist Colin Simpson on a book about the *Lusitania*. They soon quarreled, then parted. In Simpson's own book, published in 1972, he claimed to have found evidence that the *Lusitania* was armed and carrying large quantities of ammunition and gun cotton. He also implied that the British authorities had deliberately exposed her to the risk of being sunk by a submarine to embroil the United States in the war. John Light disputed his use of the evidence and most of the conclusions drawn from it, as did academic researchers.

The next diving expedition to the *Lusitania* was made in 1982 by the major international underwater contractor Oceaneering International backed by ABC Television and the British Broadcasting Corporation. The British Ministry of Defence warned Oceaneering International that "it would be imprudent not to point out the obvious but real danger if explosives did happen to be present," but added that "the Ministry does not know of any evidence whatever that might substantiate rumours of other explosives than the ammunition in the manifest."

Initial surveys used a remotely operated submarine vehicle to pho-

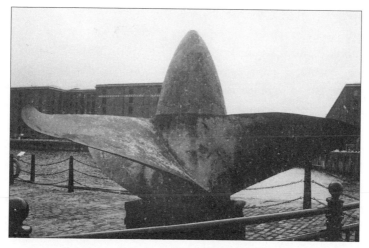

Propeller from the Lusitania, *on the docks at Liverpool.*

tograph the wreck. The next stage was a diving expedition using new saturation diving methods. The expedition's main success was the retrieval of artifacts. These included three of the four sixteen-ton bronze propellers, two of the ship's anchors, the ship's whistle, one reel of a 1915 film, *The Carpet from Bagdad*, which an American distributor had been bringing to England, crockery bearing the Cunard crest, and personal possessions of all kinds. From a historian's perspective, the most significant finds were brass fuses. Examination showed that they conformed exactly to the fuses listed on the ship's manifest and could not have been the source of any explosion.

The expedition was less successful in exploring the strong room and locating the purser's safe, where the gold of wealthy passengers like Theodore and Belle Naish presumably still sits. The team members burned and blasted the door to the strong room but found no precious metals, although they did locate some brass boxes containing valuable chronometers. Perhaps surprisingly, when the recovered items were auctioned at Sotheby's, the prices they fetched were much lower than expected. Indeed, many failed to reach their reserve. One of the propellers was melted down by an American company and turned into 3,500 sets of golf clubs priced at $9,000 a set. Another is now exhibited on the Liverpool dockside.

—∞∞∞—

In 1993 Bob Ballard, fresh from his explorations of the *Titanic* and the *Bismarck*, mounted a large expedition backed by the National Geographic Society to explore the wreck using much improved remotely operated vehicles and modern video and lighting equipment. Like John Light, he expected to find evidence of explosions caused by ammunition. He and his team produced the first really clear pictures of the *Lusitania*. They showed the liner lying on her starboard side, her bow unsevered from the rest of the wreckage. Ballard described how, because it had bent upward when the ship hit the bottom, the bow was one of the few areas of the ship where it was possible to see the starboard side. One of his key conclusions was that team members "were able to inspect the entire exposed area of the magazine and it was clearly undamaged. If it held munitions, they were not the cause of the secondary explosion that sank the ship. The distance between the torpedo's impact and the magazine was too great." He decided that the most likely cause of the second explosion was one of those suggested by the Kiel torpedo-laboratory study—a coal-dust explosion in the longitudinal bunkers.

—∞∞∞—

In 1994 another team of divers went down to the *Lusitania*. They used modern mixed-gas diving techniques and could thus move around the wreck relatively unencumbered. They were led by an Englishwoman, Polly Tapson, and the leading team members included a well-known American wreck diver, Gary Gentile. In his book on the dive, Gentile gives the latitude of the wreck as 51°24.727′ N and the longitude as 8°32.866′ W. The nearest land was Brow Head—eleven and a half miles away—with the Old Head of Kinsale eleven and three-quarter miles away. The *Lusitania*'s bow was pointing northeast. The highest point of the wreck was now 270 feet beneath the surface. The wreck had thus collapsed in on itself considerably since the explorations in 1935, which had shown a minimum depth of 228 feet, and John Light's dive, which had shown a depth of 240 feet.

Among Gentile's finds on the bridge was the annunciator, which registered communications with the engine room. It showed the engine to be still in forward drive. If Captain Turner had ordered the engines to

The Lusitania*'s stern docking telegraph.*

be reversed, as stated in evidence, the order had apparently been neither acknowledged nor carried out. More sensationally, Polly Tapson claimed to have identified the lead containers that housed the lost works of art, possibly including pictures by Monet and Rubens, which Sir Hugh Lane had been transporting to Ireland. The containers seemed to be intact, raising the prospect that the canvases had survived. The Irish arts minister shortly afterward placed a Heritage Protection Order on the wreck and its contents.

This was the first such order on a ship less than 100 years old. Divers now require governmental permission to explore the *Lusitania*. A team supported by the wreck's current owner, Gregg Bemis, was licensed to dive in 1999, 2000, and 2001. They report that the wreck is collapsing ever more rapidly. One of the divers, Mark Jones, describes the *Lusitania* as "smashed to pieces and very tricky," but still he rates her as "the best wreck in the world."

The liner's triple chime whistle.

Cutlery, plates, and fruit bowls litter the seabed, but the fate of Sir Hugh Lane's case of oil paintings remains a mystery. Some argue that the canvases were unlikely to have been particularly valuable or significant. The British art market was in serious recession, and prices had dropped by some 50 percent since the start of the war. Commercially there would therefore have been little point in shipping them to Europe. On the other hand, Lane was an art connoisseur with passionate feelings about art. He might have had other motives for bringing certain works with him. It will take more dives and much luck to provide a final answer.

⸎

The remains of the *U-20* also lie under the sea. In November 1916 she ran aground off the coast of Denmark in thick fog. Walther Schwieger's attempts to refloat her were unsuccessful. Rather than allow her to fall into Allied hands as the notorious submarine that had sunk the *Lusitania*, he blew her up by detonating two torpedoes in her tubes. Walther Schwieger was subsequently given command of the better-armed, larger, and more powerful *U-88*. In July 1917 he was awarded the prestigious Pour le Mérite, the highest honor a German naval officer could receive, in recognition of the 190,000 tons of Allied shipping he had sunk. The citation praised him for seizing "every opportunity" but did not specifically mention the *Lusitania*. Two months later, the *U-88*, Schwieger, and her crew were lost at sea, probably after sailing into a British mine cordon.

The two wrecks of the *Lusitania* and the *U-20* symbolize a conflict between opposing nations. They also represent a battle between two technologies.

When the *Lusitania* left New York on her final voyage, she was the apogee of technological sophistication. No one on the thronging quayside could have realized that the great liners would soon be in decline. They would serve in future wars as troop carriers, but their ultimate destiny would be as cruise ships, hopping from port to port, not as "ocean greyhounds" competing to shave time off the transatlantic run.

Conversely, the submarine had entered the First World War as an untried, somewhat crude, and widely underestimated weapon. By 1918 it was on the way to becoming the supreme naval vessel whose strategic importance would outstrip battleships. Today it is the submarine that carries the weapon of total war—the guided nuclear missile.

PART FIVE

Willful
Murder?

CHAPTER TWENTY-NINE

~∞∞~

A Legitimate Target?

HE FIRST OFFICIAL accusation of guilt for the loss of
the *Lusitania* came within seventy-two hours of the sinking.
Coroner John J. Horgan's verdict of "wilful and wholesale
murder" against the kaiser and the German government was unequivocal. So were the conclusions of Lord Mersey's inquiry a few weeks later
and the hearings by Judge Julius Mayer in 1918. The statements put out by
the German government, denying any guilt, were equally clear-cut. But
it was wartime. The loss of the Cunarder had far-reaching political and
propaganda implications. Each government, British, American, and
German, immediately recognized this and sought to distance itself from
blame. But was a charge of "wilful murder" correct and, if so, against
whom? Was any party guilty of lesser charges?

In assessing the evidence from today's perspective, one does well to
recall the words of Judge Mayer's that "the disaster occurred in May 1915
and the whole subject must be approached with the knowledge and mental attitude of that time." Also, in assessing statements by eyewitnesses,
one should remember that people may have a distorted picture of what is
happening, particularly when events are occurring quickly. Afterward
their recollections may be conditioned by the expectations of the public
and the press.

In the case of the *Lusitania* many people, including Harold Boulton
and Rita Jolivet, later recalled that the German submarine had surfaced
after the attack, even that heartless U-boatmen taunted those struggling
for their lives in the water. According to other evidence, neither event

seems likely. Yet these stories of "frightfulness" matched British and American public perception of how the barbarous "Hun" would behave. They were also helpful to propagandists.

Also, people quickly forget. They cannot accurately recall the sequence of events or the passage of time. Speech and gesture are particularly difficult to remember and susceptible to involuntary elaboration, the so-called trick of memory. In the case of the *Lusitania*, problems are further compounded by the difficulty of gaining access to all the written evidence. When the former secretary of the Admiralty Sir Graham Greene asked in 1924 for a reminder of the position on arms and ammunition carried by the *Lusitania* following some press comment, Sir Oswyn Murray of the Admiralty confessed, "Curiously enough I had some difficulty in laying my hand on any document containing the exact facts." Murray concluded, "It is better to let sleeping dogs lie!!"

The British government is still unwilling to disclose all its information about the *Lusitania* case and the associated machinations of its espionage and counterespionage activities in the United States. Even evidence that apparently was once available has disappeared. For example, the present Lord Mersey has no knowledge of the papers belonging to his forebear which author Colin Simpson states that he examined at the family home in the early 1970s. Nor are they in any national collection. Many of the Cunard Company's *Lusitania* files disappeared under mysterious circumstances. Some but not all of them have resurfaced and been purchased by the Cunard archives. Official files in Britain, the United States, and Germany give tantalizing leads that then disappear. Blank sheets inserted to preserve pagination sequences suggest that certain documents, like telegrams sent to and from the ship during her final voyage, have been removed. The authenticity of certain "official" documents or alleged statements is open to question.

On the other hand, the passage of time has made access possible to new documents, particularly in the German archives, that help illumine the complex and extraordinary circumstances surrounding the attack on the *Lusitania*. These documents go some way toward answering the charges of conspiracy that still dog the events of May 1915. Britain, Germany, and the United States continue to be suspected of activities of varying malignity, scale, and probability, both before and after the sinking.

Of course, conspiracy is always more interesting than error or negligence, though rarer in practice than in the minds of conspiracy theorists. Conspiracy has been alleged since ancient times. Did Alexander the Great's generals conspire to poison him? Did Harold promise the English throne to William of Normandy? Was Richard III really the crook-backed murderer of the princes in the Tower? Did James II smuggle a baby in a warming pan into his wife's birthing chamber to secure the succession? Was the identity of Jack the Ripper concealed because he was heir to the British throne? Was Yuri Gagarin the first man in space, or did the USSR cover up an earlier flight by Vladimir Ilyushin? Who killed President John F. Kennedy? Some conspiracy theories have been laid to rest by political change and the arrival of new scientific techniques like DNA testing, but many persist because they are so fascinating.

Assessments of the evidence in the *Lusitania* case will inevitably be influenced by perceptions of the character of alleged conspirators as revealed by their actions elsewhere and of the climate in which they operated. But there is sufficient evidence from sufficient sources to deduce a realistic picture of what really happened and why. It reveals conspiracy on all fronts. But it also shows a significant and related element of simple human error and negligence. These are more pervasive and frequently even more damaging than conspiracy. Examples of devastating mistakes through history are legion. A recent Mars space probe failed simply because NASA scientists confused metric and imperial measurements. Thousands of lives were lost because the British failed to grasp that their first day's landings at Gallipoli were not heavily opposed and so did not occupy the high ground. The stupidly magnificent Charge of the Light Brigade down the wrong valley and into the teeth of the Russian guns was the result of a basic error in communication. The *Lusitania* incident, too, was influenced by errors and complacency as well as by deeper, more disturbing, and deliberate factors.

───※───

In the angry exchange of words following the sinking of the *Lusitania*, the German government made a series of specific allegations. Replying to the first American protest note on 31 May, it insisted that the *Lusitania* not only had been constructed with government funds as an auxiliary cruiser but was "expressly included in the Navy List published by the British Admiralty." Therefore, under international law, Germany had been entitled to attack her without warning. But the Germans already knew that the *Lusitania* was not a ship of the Royal Navy when they sent their note. The director of the German foreign office's legal department, Kriege, had told Chancellor Bethmann Hollweg quite explicitly that, although the British had originally intended the *Lusitania* to operate as an armed auxiliary cruiser in wartime, she had not been taken into the navy for this purpose at the beginning of the war.

He was correct. The *Lusitania* was listed in *Jane's Fighting Ships* for 1914, along with all British and German liners capable of eighteen knots and over, but for identification purposes only. In *Brassey's Naval Annual 1914*, she was described as "a Royal Naval Reserved Merchant Cruiser." The designation "Reserved" reflected the fact that, under the terms of the agreement between Cunard and the British government, the *Lusitania* could be called into naval service during a crisis or war. But this had never happened. When war broke out, the British government considered whether to use the ship as an auxiliary cruiser. But after a month's consideration, it decided the cost of fueling the *Lusitania* was excessive compared to her utility as a naval vessel and released her back to Cunard for commercial service. The *Lusitania* was therefore undertaking her normal transatlantic run at the time of her destruction as evidenced by the advertisement of her service and departure dates in the press on both sides of the Atlantic and duly noted in Berlin. The departure of naval vessels was, of course, not advertised.

Another key German claim was that the *Lusitania* was armed. There are two sources of evidence for this. The first is the statements made by Gustav Stahl, at the instigation of Paul König, to the American authorities just after the sinking. The U.S. Department of Justice investigated them and found them false. Stahl was duly convicted and imprisoned for perjury. The second is the reported sighting of a gun by one of John Light's diving companions when they visited the wreck in the 1960s. However, the divers were at the limit of their dive time and could not search further. They were also working beyond the limits of their diving and lighting equipment and the technology of the time. According to modern dive experts, they must have been suffering from nitrogen narcosis, which, in addition to its physical effects, numbs the mind and blurs perception. John Light himself did not regard the identification as definitive, and his own films and photographs reveal nothing—the water was murky and visibility low. No subsequent expeditions with the benefit of improved technology have seen any sign of guns. What the diver might have glimpsed was a spar or rail protruding at an angle.

There is no evidence in surviving records that guns were ever mounted. The only preparations made for the use of the *Lusitania* as an auxiliary cruiser were the emplacement in the deck of four six-inch gun rings in 1913. These are visible in some photographs of the ship after that date. Yet no one saw guns mounted on them or elsewhere on the ship despite many careful inspections, including those by Dudley Field Malone's U.S. customs staff before departure and by some of the *Lusitania*'s curious passengers during the final voyage.

After the sinking, the U.S. consul in Queenstown, Wesley Frost, specifically asked all American survivors whether they had seen guns. None had. Those questioned included Michael Byrne, who, after Stahl's evidence was published, wrote to the U.S. administration stating that he had made a thorough search and found nothing. Equally, the movie film of the ship leaving New York for the last time, which was viewed by both U.S. and British officials, showed nothing. In June 1915 the British consul general in Philadelphia wired the foreign office: "HAVE SEEN PICTURES IN COMPANY WITH NAVAL ATTACHE. THERE ARE NO GUNS. SPLENDID VIEW OF DECKS." The same is true of still photographs taken as the *Lusitania* departed.

Some writers have suggested that guns were stored secretly, to be mounted if the need arose. If so, they were neither reported by officials, passengers, or crew nor seen on the wreck by divers. More significant, it would have taken at least twenty minutes, perhaps more, to have retrieved and mounted them at sea in an emergency. By that time any raider would have disappeared, or the *Lusitania* would have been sunk.

At any rate, it would have served little purpose to mount guns on the *Lusitania* in the spring of 1915. All Germany's surface raiders were accounted for, and the *Lusitania*'s best defense against submarines was her speed. Even with only three boiler rooms in operation, she had an advantage of some six knots over a submarine on the surface, even more over one that was submerged. If a periscope were sighted, the *Lusitania*'s most sensible course was to speed away rather than waste time taking potshots.

One may question the veracity of statements made by U.S. and British government officials after the sinking. One may question even the reassurances by Alfred Booth to Charles Sumner that he was safe in testifying that the ship carried no armament. However, when British consul general Courtenay Bennett writes in a letter dated eight months before the sinking that "the Lusitania has no guns," his words carry conviction. So do the words of the German naval attaché, Captain Karl Boy-Ed, that, in his personal opinion, regardless of the affidavits, the Lusitania was "certainly not carrying guns on deck or concealed below." So does the agreement of the claimants in the case heard by Judge Mayer to rule out discussion of armaments. Had they been able to establish that the Lusitania was armed, their case would have benefited substantially. Most conclusively of all, if the Lusitania was armed, why did no survivors report attempts to man or mount the guns when the U-20 attacked? The evidence that the Lusitania was not armed is therefore overwhelming.

Another charge made by the German government was that the Lusitania was carrying Canadian troops on her last voyage. If the troops were "organized and armed," their presence would, under international law, have made her into a troopship, which could legitimately be sunk without warning. Yet the survivors' accounts show no evidence of any organized body of troops. No one saw anyone in uniform, carrying rifles, or drilling. Certainly a few men such as Oliver Bernard and Harold Boulton were traveling with the intention of enlisting, but they were not yet soldiers. Dudley Field Malone and other U.S. customs officials testified on 4 June 1915 that "the Lusitania did not have Canadian troops or troops of any nationality on board" when she left on her last voyage. Malone added that since the beginning of the war the Lusitania had "never carried . . . Canadian troops or troops of any other nationality."

In 1973 the Canadian Ministry of Defence checked whether any unaccompanied male passengers of British nationality (there was no separate Canadian nationality until 1947) whose journeys began in Canada and who died in the disaster were listed in the Canadian Book of Remembrance for 7 May 1915 as servicemen dying on duty. There were none. Nor was there any evidence elsewhere in the ministry's records of the presence of Canadian troops on the Lusitania.

German suspicions that the Lusitania was transporting Canadian soldiers may have been aroused by the fact that Canadian lieutenant Robert Matthews was among the five dead named at the public inquest at Kinsale. His presence on board has certainly been cited as evidence by previous writers. However, far from leading a body of troops, he was traveling alone with his mistress, Annie, who also drowned. Matthews had had a commission in the Sixtieth Rifles of Canada, a local militia regiment, but had missed all the drills in the winter of 1914–15 when he left his wife and moved with Annie from Moose Jaw to a farm in northern Manitoba. He had subsequently applied for a commission in the Forty-sixth Battalion of the Canadian Expeditionary Force but had been rejected. It is not clear why he was traveling to England. Perhaps it was to enlist. Perhaps it was simply to make a new life with Annie. The lapel badge found on Matthews's corpse was Annie's prize for coming in second in the women's egg-and-spoon race, not a regimental badge as one writer has suggested. His presence on the *Lusitania* was not evidence that Canadian troops were aboard. Nor is there evidence that there were troops of any other nationality.

The German accusation that the *Lusitania* was carrying ammunition and other "contraband" was, on the other hand, entirely correct. Her supplementary cargo manifest, given out at the New York Custom House after the sinking, specifically states that the *Lusitania* was carrying 4,200 cases of rifle bullets, with approximately 1,000 cartridges per case. It also lists 1,250 cases of 3.3-inch shrapnel shells—afterward said not yet to be filled with their explosive—and 18 cases of percussion fuses—said to have only steel and brass parts and, once again, no explosive content.

Percussion fuse made by the Bethlehem Steel Corporation,
recovered from the Lusitania.

The rest of the cargo was, by the admission of both British and American governments and officials, "nearly all contraband"—material for uniforms, leather belts, and so forth.

Nevertheless, the issue of contraband was largely irrelevant in the circumstances of the sinking. The presence of contraband would undoubtedly have justified a German vessel stopping and searching the *Lusitania* under the Cruiser Rules, impounding her cargo, and seizing the vessel as a prize or destroying her after making proper provision for the safety of the crew and passengers. It did not justify a "sink on sight" policy.

Yet from the immediate aftermath of the sinking to the present day, two aspects of the *Lusitania*'s cargo have been hotly debated. First, were the munitions on board precisely as described in the manifest and at subsequent inquiries, or were the shrapnel shells, in reality, filled and did the fuses contain explosives? The suppliers denied both charges at the Mayer hearing, at which a cutaway example of the shell was produced. Most important, a recent researcher has shown conclusively that the individual shell weight of eighteen pounds, derived from the manifest and other shipping documents, is, indeed, that of an unfilled shell—a filled one would have weighed twenty-two pounds. Also, examples of the fuses, which were stowed at the stern (and not forward of the boiler rooms with the other cargo), have been retrieved by divers and shown to conform to their specification. There therefore is no basis for this charge.

Second, was the *Lusitania* carrying additional munitions to those on her manifest, either undeclared or listed as something else to disguise them? There have been numerous attempts to confirm this theory, but none have succeeded. Some have shown that explosives were handled in the New York docks near to where the *Lusitania* was berthed alongside cargo ships, but have been unable to prove that extra material was taken on board the *Lusitania* rather than the cargo ships. One of the main items suspected of concealing clandestine ammunitions was a large consignment of furs, but there is plenty of evidence that these were, indeed, furs. After the sinking, many were washed up on the Irish coast, dried, and resold.

Any attempts to load clandestine munitions and explosives would have meant deceiving or suborning Malone's customs officials. Neither was impossible, but, still, the Germans were never able to prove that such materials had been smuggled on board. They had been keeping a careful eye on the *Lusitania* through their network of agents. Captain Boy-Ed commented to Berlin on 27 April 1915 on the understaffing of the ship and the poor morale of the dwindling crew members after her last eastbound crossing. He cannot have heard of any impending arms shipments on the *Lusitania*, or he would have mentioned them to Berlin as he did in his report on the SS *Trinidad*, also on 27 April 1915, which he noted was "loaded with powder and munitions."

Nor could Paul König come up with any conclusive evidence from his investigations. In the spring of 1914 he had sent his American agent William McCulley to Britain. According to the U.S. Department of Justice, his mission was to telegraph information on British marine activity for submarine targeting purposes. König had in addition since 1914 regularly been paying Germans such as a man named Franz von Brun, and of course Gustav Stahl, three dollars a day for searching along the New York docks and among dockworkers for information about which ships were carrying arms and ammunition.

It seems likely that the Germans were relying on Steward Neal Leach to report on the *Lusitania* and her cargo. He was almost certainly a German agent. He may have agreed to help their activities in New York as a condition of his release from internment in Germany; he may have been acting under duress or blackmail; he may simply have wanted the money. He was frequently in debt and not entirely trustworthy. His check in payment for his New York room bounced in his absence. He had left his trunk in New York, and it seems likely, therefore, that he was planning to return at the end of his mission. Leach's value to the Germans is shown by the newly found and unique notification from Berlin to its Washington embassy of his departure from Germany in February 1915. This message was intercepted by the British and, because of the code it was in, may not have been decoded immediately. But his name would have been suspect by the time the *Lusitania* sailed and passed to Liverpool Detective-Inspector William Pierpoint.

The inspector had clearly been assigned to counterespionage activities on the *Lusitania* to thwart attempts at sabotage and spying, as had some Scotland Yard detectives to other ships at that time. He was traveling in a first-class cabin, which he could never have afforded on his salary. According to his evidence to Commissioner Wynne, he was assigned a boat station, clearly marking him as a member of staff and not a passenger. Crew were assigned boat stations; passengers were not. His testimony to both Lord Mersey and Wynne adhered closely to the government line, and his silence on the stowaways is eloquent.

We cannot now be certain as to Leach's mission, but it was likely to have been carried out in association with the three German stowaways arrested by Pierpoint near a steward's cabin, probably Leach's. It was probably to find out information on any fixed guns and on the nature of the cargo. (Some reports claim that the stowaways had a camera with them when they were caught.) It could have been sabotage, using Rintelen's cigar-bombs, although the latter makes no mention of this in his memoirs. The usefulness of the three stowaways—anonymously and clandestinely aboard—ceased with their deaths. Leach was, however, useful dead as well as alive. Once he knew that Leach had not survived, Paul König used his name to give credence to Gustav Stahl's affidavit, although he had to look elsewhere for better evidence to substantiate the German claim that the *Lusitania* was carrying clandestine munitions. His attention was caught by the reference in the supplementary manifest to "bronze powder," and, as shown in a newly discovered Department of Justice document, he sent one of his agents to try to find out what it really was.

Clearly, neither these nor König's other activities can have revealed anything or the German embassy would have used it immediately to discredit the British and the Americans. The fact that it could not produce any proof—despite their wide-ranging and numerous contacts on the docks and in arms factories where, according to the papers taken from John J. Archibald and Heinrich Albert, their agents were fomenting strikes—is one of the strongest pieces of evidence that there was no additional ammunition on board. So, too, is the dropping of claims related to concealed ammunition by the Mayer claimants. Also, on a practical level, the *Lusitania*'s cargo capacity was small—one tenth of that of a cargo ship of the time. She was hardly the best of ships on which to transport large quantities of war matériel.

Yet accusations about whether the *Lusitania* was armed and carrying troops and munitions were only part of the picture. In the weeks and months following the sinking came other, deeper allegations. Germany charged that the British had allowed the *Lusitania* to be sunk for political ends, even that they had used the ship to spring a trap to lure America into the war. She also accused the United States of conspiring against the laws of neutrality to favor one belligerent against another through the supply of arms. The British, in turn, claimed that the Germans had deliberately plotted to sink the *Lusitania* in contravention of international law.

The truth was that no government, British, German, or American, was entirely free of blame for the situation leading up to the attack. Nor, in its wake, was any government hesitant to twist the facts, or use the disaster, to its own political ends.

—∞∞∞—

CHAPTER THIRTY

Harm's Way

*T*HE BRITISH ADMIRALTY had known from the first of the sailing of the *U-20* and her sister boats through intercepted radio messages. Indeed, Captain Reginald Hall and British naval intelligence had deliberately provoked the U-boats' departure by feeding false information to the Germans about likely troop sailings from Britain in a ruse to discourage the German high command from diverting forces to the Dardanelles. The Admiralty also knew from decoded messages that the Germans considered the *Lusitania* a target. The Admiralty was additionally aware that the German embassy in Washington had openly inserted a newspaper advertisement warning passengers not to sail on British ships and that this had appeared next to Cunard's timetable on the day the *Lusitania* sailed. Also, as the *Lusitania* sailed eastward, the Admiralty learned of the sinkings of the *Earl of Lathom*, *Centurion*, and *Candidate* in the waters she would soon be entering.

British inaction toward merchant shipping in May 1915 contrasted sharply with the Admiralty's determined albeit abortive attempts to protect the *Lusitania* in March, another time of U-boat danger, when two destroyers were assigned to escort her. Despite all its foreknowledge, this time the Admiralty sent no specific warnings and instituted no special measures to protect the *Lusitania*. It only issued general warnings to all commercial shipping in the area, notwithstanding the liner's well-understood importance as a symbol of national prestige and the political sensitivity of the fact that she was carrying important neutral Americans. The Admiralty did not even tell the relevant naval bases in Liverpool and Queenstown of the *U*-20's departure, although it knew from a decode that the submarine was to operate in their area. Conversely, the Admiralty took precautions to protect battleships and other naval vessels that were due to sail through the waters concerned. These ships were held in port, given destroyer escort, or diverted to safer routes.

Those few messages sent by the Admiralty to merchant shipping were vague. Included in the list submitted to the Mersey inquiry was one that advised captains to avoid headlands, pass harbors at full speed, and steer a midchannel course. This warning was routinely issued every night in code to all relevant shipping. The Room 40 staff knew that it had been picked up previously by the Germans and decoded, thus seriously invalidating its utility. For all they knew, U-boats might by now have sensibly decided to wait in midchannel for their prey. Yet despite knowing their merchant vessel code had been broken, the British continued to use it. On the night of 6 May they simply added to the usual message the additional caution: "SUBMARINES OFF FASTNET."

Some writers have cited Churchill's comments of 12 February 1915 to Walter Runciman, president of the Board of Trade, that "it is most important to attract neutral shipping to our shores in the hope especially of embroiling the U.S.A. with Germany." They link these words with the oddly limited efforts made to warn or protect the *Lusitania* to suggest that Churchill deliberately conspired to expose the *Lusitania* to bring America into the war. In some moods the kaiser, too, subscribed to this theory. Nearly a year after the sinking he told Ambassador Gerard in Berlin that "England was really responsible as the English had made the *Lusitania* go slowly in English waters so that the Germans could torpedo it and so bring on trouble."

There is, however, no evidence that the Admiralty deliberately ordered the *Lusitania* into the path of a submarine. The real issue is whether it deliberately did little to keep the liner out of harm's way. Any credible conspiracy would be through acts of omission rather than commission.

If there was, indeed, a conspiracy to expose the *Lusitania*, the motive must have been to bring the United States into the war. Yet this was by no means Britain's desire at the time. The British were aware that if America joined in the war, she would also wish to join in dictating the peace. More important, many on both sides of the Atlantic believed—as did

Robert Lansing, who produced a detailed analysis to this effect—that it was in Britain's interest to maintain the United States as a friendly neutral supplier of arms. That was why on 9 May 1915 Sir Cecil Spring-Rice sent his hasty telegram to London, cautioning: "AS OUR MAIN INTEREST IS TO PRESERVE U.S. AS A BASE OF SUPPLIES, I HOPE LANGUAGE OF OUR PRESS WILL BE VERY GUARDED." He believed there might be an initial advantage to Germany if the United States joined the Allies because America would keep her munitions for herself, giving Germany a window of opportunity to defeat France and Britain. He even suspected that Germany might have sunk the *Lusitania* deliberately to provoke war with the United States for this reason.

Churchill and Fisher were ruthless enough to be credible conspirators. Fisher had stated over and again that war was hell and that it was futile to attempt to humanize it. He had suggested shooting German prisoners in reprisal for air raids. Although Churchill brusquely rejected the idea, he was nevertheless one of the first British ministers to advocate bombing military targets inside towns. He contemplated violating Dutch and Danish neutrality to invade Germany. He advocated the use of poison gas against the Turks at Gallipoli. He was prepared to make secret alliances to facilitate his war aims. In the First World War he at one point considered allowing neutral Spain to annex Britain's oldest ally, Portugal, as her reward for joining the Allies. In the Second World War he was prepared to conclude covert deals with Stalin that sacrificed the interests of eastern European nations and China. He has also been accused of withholding information from President Roosevelt about the likely attack on Pearl Harbor because he hoped it would bring the United States into the war.

Also, Churchill's and Fisher's joint antisubmarine policy with its advice to ram and the defensive arming of merchantmen was, by Churchill's own admission, designed to force submarines below the surface. This reduced the risk to British shipping, particularly if Cruiser Rules were observed, but increased the likelihood of neutral shipping being attacked in error or of U-boat captains feeling compelled to fire without warning. The use of "decoy," or "Q," ships, not seen in action by the Germans until the summer of 1915, but developed during Churchill's reign at the Admiralty, was also designed, as Churchill later said, to keep submarines beneath the surface.

These factors, coupled with Churchill's clear belief that the *Lusitania* sinking redounded to Britain's benefit, make a plausible circumstantial case. So does the curious absence of any surviving correspondence from either Fisher or Churchill over the period of the sinking. So does the extent of other missing documentation and the continuing secrecy of the authorities. However, it is also likely that Churchill and Fisher were simply distracted by other matters. Churchill played a part in the maneuver to bring a new ally—Italy—into the field. That is why he went to Paris on 5 May, two days before the sinking. He was also intriguing with General Sir John French against Lord Kitchener, which is why he remained in France after the sinking. Above all, Churchill and Fisher were arguing bitterly and constantly about the Dardanelles—Churchill's "quick fix" to win the war.

The initial landings had not gone well. The two men disputed the priorities for the use of the Royal Navy. Churchill knew his political ambitions depended on success in the Dardanelles. Fisher knew that his past reputation would be eclipsed by disgrace if he allowed the British Home Fleet to be so weakened that it lost an engagement with the German High Seas Fleet. Both were preoccupied with matters far removed from the *Lusitania* and her fate.

Fisher, as he later admitted, was in a state of high agitation and close to a nervous breakdown. In such a condition he could not have initiated a conspiracy. Nor would he have been likely to have kept silent if Churchill had done so.

There was, however, another credible conspirator: Captain Reginald Hall. He was neither out of the country nor ill. He knew that Churchill and Fisher were distracted. Above all, he was aware, from the Room 40 decodes, that the *Lusitania* was a German target and the subject of keen espionage activity in New York. He also knew that a submarine pack had been sent out, in response to his own misinformation, to look for large troop transports off Liverpool—the *Lusitania*'s home port. He had access to all the relevant decodes and to material about sightings of submarines off Ireland. He had the right temperament. Hall clearly believed that ends justified the means, and he was a capable, ruthless operator. His close contact and confidant, American attaché Edward Bell, said of him that "no man could fill his place—a perfectly marvellous person but the coldest-blooded proposition that ever was—he'd eat a man's heart and hand it back to him." Hall is alleged to have sacrificed the agent who stole a German code to prevent the German authorities from discovering it had been taken. He is also alleged to have had a hand in the use of the so-called Black Diaries, detailing homosexual behavior, to discredit

Captain William Reginald Hall

Irish nationalist Sir Roger Casement and to stifle protests against his hanging for treason in April 1916. In addition, he seems to have advocated torture of captured enemies to secure information.

Hall's cool, independent approach to big issues is shown by his keeping secret for some days the momentous Zimmermann telegram before disclosing it even to his naval colleagues and British ministers. His love of conspiracy is evident from his attempt in early 1915 to render the Dardanelles campaign unnecessary by bribing the Turks to break with the Germans and to allow the British fleet free passage through the Dardanelles. Using the chief rabbi of Turkey as an intermediary, he personally guaranteed a bribe of £4 million. He claimed only to have told Fisher and Churchill of his entirely unauthorized actions two months later when their own plans were about to frustrate his continuing efforts.

If anyone conspired by omission to allow the *Lusitania* to be attacked, it was probably Hall, sitting calmly behind his desk, recognizing the threat, and failing to raise the telephone. He knew that if the sinking reflected badly on anybody, it would be on the head of Room 40, Sir Alfred Ewing, and Chief of War Staff Rear Admiral Henry Oliver, with neither of whom he was on particularly good terms. But the greater like-lihood is that everyone shared the sentiment of Cunard chairman Sir Alfred Booth that there was "no reason to believe that the ship was in any serious danger of being sunk."

But even if the key figures were preoccupied, this does not explain the apparent complacency and inactivity of other Admiralty staff toward the *Lusitania*. Part of the problem was that Churchill and Fisher had gathered the reins of power to themselves. They controlled information carefully and did not share it widely. This was justified in the case of the Room 40 decodes, which had to be restricted for security reasons, but was much less valid in the case of day-to-day operational material. Churchill and Fisher also discouraged initiative, preferring issues to be referred back to them. Hall called Churchill a "one-man show" and believed "it was not in his nature to allow anybody except himself to be the executive authority when any action of importance had to be taken." When they were not accessible, their subordinates felt it wiser if in doubt to do nothing. As the *Lusitania* steamed across the Atlantic and into the possible path of a U-boat, no one at the operational level was either sufficiently well informed or prepared to take responsibility for actions likely to attract public or parliamentary criticism.

The Admiralty certainly failed to supply the *Lusitania* with an escort vessel. In its defense, the view in 1915—as it remained during the Second World War—was that the main protection for ships like the *Lusitania* was their own speed, not naval escort. It was highly unusual in the first year of World War I to provide a naval escort. The loss of the *Lusitania* did not alter this opinion. Immediately after the sinking, the Admiralty confirmed to the anxious chairman of the White Star Line that it still thought speed the best defense. The well-intentioned but farcical March 1915 attempt to escort the *Lusitania* showed the difficulty of providing an escort that actually meets the ship without forcing her to slow down or break radio silence. There was also the compelling point that, under the international law of the time, a merchant ship that allowed herself to be protected by naval ships forfeited her right to "stop and search" and exposed herself to sinking without warning.

But was the Admiralty remiss in not doing more to warn the *Lusita-*

nia specifically? The fact that Admiralty staff knew that their code had been breached probably made them circumspect in the messages that they did send. Perhaps they feared that if the Germans decoded them, they would, in turn, discover that the German codes had been broken. Such games of deceit and the desire to protect intelligence sources have often led to field commanders receiving vague information and hence to suspicions that their headquarters were starving them of information for their own purposes. A friend of Admiral Husband Kimmel, commander in chief at Pearl Harbor, wrote that "Kimmel maintained to his last breath that the routine type of warnings sent to him were by no means adequate considering the far more specific knowledge Washington had as to Japanese intentions."

There was also a suspicion in the Admiralty that the Germans were making use of their knowledge of British practices and codes to lure ships to their destruction. There is clear evidence of this in Admiralty files, not only in the fears of the captain of the *Narragansett* that the *Lusitania*'s distress calls were a hoax, but also in the Admiralty's frantic but vain efforts, only days after the sinking, to check the claim by the master of the British SS *Demerara* that he had received a message at sea ordering all ships to divert around the north of Ireland because of a submarine threat to the south. (Nothing was found, but traces of such stories appeared in sensationalist books published later in the war, including one with a preface by Theodore Roosevelt maintaining that the *Lusitania* had been summoned to her doom by false wireless messages.)

There is insufficient surviving evidence that Captain Turner had further secret orders relating to this particular voyage beyond the general orders provided to all merchant ships, including those about avoiding headlands and about ramming which the Admiralty was legitimately eager to protect from enemy eyes and ears. The Admiralty could, of course, have ordered the *Lusitania* to go around the north of Ireland through the North Channel to Liverpool, or Captain Turner could have made a request to do so that was refused. However, the North Channel had only just been declared mine-free, and there was a possibility that mines were still in the area. Also, in going around the north of Ireland, the *Lusitania* would have had to cross the U-boats' known outward and return routings.

Diversion to Queenstown or Fishguard was possible, although one of the main reasons against it would have been inconvenience for passengers. Some suggest that a telegram now missing from the files indeed instructed the *Lusitania* to come into Queenstown. The latter seems unlikely since the ship's last turn before the torpedoing was away from the port. Also, nothing had been said to passengers, and nothing had been said in Queenstown, where preparations would have had to be made for an imminent arrival. U.S. consul Wesley Frost would surely have been alerted to it, but he made no mention of it in his reports. Above all, what was there to gain from concealing such an instruction?

The overriding evidence is that, whatever the merits of sending an escort, specifically warning the *Lusitania*, and diverting her out of harm's way, none of these actions was ever systematically considered. The reason why the tragedy was allowed to happen was that the Admiralty at senior levels was preoccupied with bigger issues and in particular the Dardanelles. Its first lord, Winston Churchill, was overseas. Admiral Fisher was close to a nervous breakdown. Junior officials preferred not to act without instructions. All believed that the Germans probably could not sink the *Lusitania* and that, even if they could, they would not. Far from being the subject of conspiracy, the *Lusitania*, in her last days and hours, was the victim of complacency and neglect. While neither a verdict of willful murder nor even one of manslaughter is sustainable on the basis of surviving evidence, a claim of contributory negligence certainly is.

After the sinking, it was a different matter. There is unequivocal evidence of conspiracy to deflect criticism from the British government and in particular to divert attention from the cause of the second explosion on board the *Lusitania*. The British government was clearly very nervous about the *Lusitania*'s cargo. Its concern may have been that some other material had been loaded hurriedly at the docks without proper clearance in the anxiety to meet the demands of an expanding army suffering from a shell shortage. More probably, the nervousness was simply a nagging doubt that, despite all the tests and the opinions of the experts, the cartridges had, in fact, exploded. (After all, a quick calculation would have shown that the 4.2 million cartridges in her cargo contained a total of some ten tons of explosive powder.) If it could have been proved that the Admiralty had acted incompetently or that munitions had exploded on board the *Lusitania*, it would have damaged Britain's claim to be an entirely innocent party in the disaster. British prestige and her ability to exploit the huge propaganda benefit of the sinking would have suffered. The personal reputations of Churchill, Fisher, and of Admiralty officers and staff would have suffered too.

The fears of the Admiralty led not only to the use of the official censor to suppress inconvenient press reports like dispatches from New York claiming that the *Lusitania* had been guaranteed a destroyer escort, but also to the deliberate manipulation by the government of Lord Mersey's "independent inquiry." Admiral Sir Frederick Inglefield, one of the assessors, was the main channel for this collusion. However, Arthur Balfour, the former prime minister and Churchill's replacement as the new first lord, thought it sufficiently important to volunteer to see Lord Mersey personally "at some convenient time" to offer guidance and clarification. In 1972 the then Lord Mersey told the BBC that his forebear had considered the whole episode discreditable.

Of course, the senior staff of the Admiralty had known unambiguously from Room 40 decodes on 12 May that the *U-20* had sunk the *Lusitania* with only one torpedo. But it was quickly realized that a single torpedo left the second explosion unexplained and raised potentially damaging questions. If it was not a torpedo, what was it? It would be better if it were a second torpedo. The crew's statements were written up for them in standardized words and expressions, and those chosen to give evidence were carefully selected. Quartermaster Hugh Johnston's comments show how the *Lusitania*'s crew members were pressured to testify to the Mersey inquiry that she had been hit by two torpedoes, rather than one, on the grounds that such evidence would be "helpful." When Johnston refused to cooperate, he was still allowed to appear as a witness—as the ship's helmsman, he could hardly have been omitted. But he was questioned only briefly and, unlike other crewmen, was not asked to comment on the number of torpedoes. Captain Turner himself now referred clearly to two torpedoes, whereas he had described only a single torpedo strike but also a possible internal explosion to Coroner Horgan at the Kinsale inquest. Interestingly, in his only public interview after the war, given in 1933 to the *Daily Mail*, Turner reverted to there having been only one torpedo.

Particular prominence was given at the inquiry to two men with Royal Navy experience who claimed that three torpedoes were fired. This was possibly to make a subsequent verdict that there had been two torpedoes appear moderate. Indeed, before evidence was even taken, Sir

Edward Carson in his opening statement on behalf of the British government asserted that there were two torpedoes, perhaps even three.

Statements claiming that the torpedoes struck aft, well away from where the ammunition was stored, also found favor. Captain Turner placed the first torpedo strike between the third and fourth funnels, which was entirely inconsistent with the ship sinking by the bow. There was also a clear logical inconsistency in Lord Mersey's report. It described how the first torpedo hit between the third and fourth funnels but blew the No. 5 lifeboat, some 200 feet farther forward, to pieces. The blast would of course have been carried backward, not forward, by the ship's speed.

Careful attention was paid to the choice of passengers invited to give evidence. For example, Oliver Bernard, despite his prominence in the aftermath of the sinking, was not allowed to testify that there had been only one torpedo and that it had hit near the bridge.

Also, even though pressed strongly to do so by the representative from the seamen's union, Lord Mersey admitted no discussion of the ship's compartmentalization and construction, or of the damage inflicted by the U-boat and its location, which might have led to discussions of a second explosion from whatever cause. Although Monsieur Marichal was called as a witness to describe the cartridgelike explosions he said he had heard, this was only so that his potentially damaging claims could be dismissed in favorable conditions rather than heard in a civil court or read in the press. His background was investigated, and his misdemeanors were exaggerated and leaked to the press to discredit him in the public mind.

There is also clear evidence of a plot to discredit Captain Turner. Turner was a useful scapegoat. Fisher went so far as to suggest that, whatever the verdict of the Mersey inquiry, Turner should be imprisoned. The thoroughness of this aspect of the conspiracy is shown by Churchill's implied criticism of Turner in Parliament on 10 May 1915; by Webb's distorted memoranda to the inquiry; by the relentless way Sir Edward Carson tried to confuse a traumatized Turner on the witness stand at the inquiry, aggressively quoting instructions to him, some of which were irrelevant and at least one of which, relating to zigzagging, it was very doubtful that Turner had ever received; and by Lord Mersey's decision to call only one naval witness, Commander Anderson, who was not questioned on the Admiralty's own actions but simply used to underline the benefits of zigzagging and steaming at high speed, areas in which it was implied that Turner had been deficient.

Willful Murder?

In the end, Lord Mersey chose not to blame Captain Turner explicitly, despite carefully obtaining confirmation through Admiral Inglefield that the government would be happy for him to do so. All blame was placed on the two-torpedo-firing German submarine and the "barbarous" German government. Perhaps it was simply that the sinking of the *Lusitania* was proving to be of such immense propaganda value that it was judged better to focus solely on German culpability rather than to diffuse blame by referring to possible contributory factors such as the actions of the captain and the crew. Perhaps, and less cynically, Lord Mersey was an inherently fair man. He preferred not to blame individuals who were victims of circumstance and whose actions were constrained by the expectations and instructions of others. In his earlier inquiry into the *Titanic* disaster, he had not convicted the ship's master, Captain Edward J. Smith, of negligence for steaming at twenty-two and a half knots at night in poor visibility in an area where he had been warned repeatedly of the presence of ice.

───── ∞ ─────

The plot to discredit Captain Turner does not, however, imply that he was entirely blameless for the loss of his ship. How well did he perform on the *Lusitania*'s last voyage judged against the standards and culture of 1915?

Turner was, by his own admission, "an old-fashioned sailorman" who believed that modern ships lacked the skilled seamen of his youth. He had been doing his best to run his ship efficiently despite the loss of experienced hands caused by the call-up of naval reservists. Some of the remaining crew members had jumped ship on arrival in New York, so he had to make do with last-minute replacements recruited on the dockside. Sometimes he was lucky, as with the Morton brothers. Sometimes he was not.

Like the senior merchant captains called to give evidence to the Mayer hearings, Turner was scornful of new ideas and resistant to direction. Nevertheless, he was an excellent peacetime master who, like many others in May 1915, had not understood the power of the submarine weapon or the ruthless way in which it would be used against his ship. He was, however, aware of the newspaper warnings and had taken more notice of the "instructions" issued to him and other merchant captains at various times by the Admiralty than Carson alleged.

As Lord Mersey confirmed in his report, these instructions were, in fact, not "instructions" but advice "meant for his most serious and careful consideration" and "not intended to deprive him of the right to exercise his skilled judgement." Judge Mayer echoed this view. Nevertheless, the captain had to take care where he departed from the advice. If he deviated irresponsibly, the War Risks Insurance, which was paid in the case of the *Lusitania*, would be void.

Captain Turner certainly did not receive the definitive government advice on zigzagging which Carson alleged he had. If he received any such advice, it was brief and probably oral. Like other masters who testified to Judge Mayer, he probably regarded zigzagging as more of a joke than anything else. He would also have been concerned about the effects of sudden sharp changes of course on his passengers. But he followed much of the other guidance. He kept radio silence within 100 miles of land and doubled the lookouts. He maintained his lifeboats ready, provisioned, and swung-out when entering the danger zone. His greatest concern was to follow guidance not to linger outside ports like Liverpool, acknowledged to be dangerous, but to arrive when the tide would allow immediate entry to the docks.

Turner's desire to avoid waiting at the Mersey Bar was the reason that the *Lusitania* was going "so slowly" when she was torpedoed. It led him to drop his speed to eighteen knots rather than the twenty-one knots of which the *Lusitania* was capable with only three boiler rooms active. (He did, however, order these three boiler rooms to be able to provide extra steam as soon as required.) To reduce speed other than in fog, which he had sensibly done, was contrary to Cunard's own wartime instructions to travel at "maximum speed." In mitigation, only nine other ships in the U.K. merchant fleet were capable of doing more then eighteen knots, and, as Cunard's chairman Alfred Booth later testified, no ship doing more than fourteen knots had previously been torpedoed. But with hindsight Turner was probably wrong to reduce speed, rather than to have used up the time by taking a circuitous route.

Proud of his precise navigation, which was a major safety factor in these days before radar, Turner was in the process of taking a four-point bearing when the *Lusitania* was hit. This was the reason that the ship was sailing in a dead straight line. Yet according to the consensus among maritime experts, a cross-bearing would have sufficed. The latter would have taken three minutes, whereas his four-point bearing required forty minutes straight steaming.

Turner's critics claim the taking of the bearing also brought him closer to land than the Admiralty would have advised near headlands, where the Admiralty warned that U-boats lurked. However, Turner did not go in as close to land as eight miles, as wrongly claimed by both Carson and Webb, without supporting evidence, in their attempts to discredit him. He was about twelve or thirteen miles out to sea when he was torpedoed. This was seven miles farther out than the farthest Captain David Dow had taken the *Lusitania* on any of the five wartime sailings he had commanded. Naval patrol boats reported vessels to the Admiralty for ignoring the guidance only when they came within five miles of the headlands. In peacetime liners usually passed about two miles from the Old Head of Kinsale.

Captain Turner has also been criticized for not taking a midchannel course as advised by the Admiralty, which would have taken him seventy or so miles out. First, it is doubtful whether, when framing its guidance, the Admiralty had this part of the Irish Sea in mind. Cunard told the Mayer hearings that "there is no part of those waters that can properly be considered a channel." The Admiralty probably intended its guidance to refer principally to the English Channel, the St. George's Channel, some eighty sea miles ahead of where the *Lusitania* was sunk, and the North Channel between southwest Scotland and Ireland. Second, on the basis of the limited and hours-old information that submarines were "last heard of 20 miles south of Coningbeg Lightship," Captain Turner believed he would be safer near the coast. He made this point in detail at the Mayer hearings, though only as an afterthought at the Mersey inquiry at the prompting of Cunard's counsel. His statement has something of the flavor of rationalization after the event. But so do most of the charges made against him.

In recent books some commentators suggest that Turner should have undertaken many more drills, including instituting passenger drills, even that he should have had passengers in life jackets on deck during his entire passage through the danger zone. They forget the culture of the liners of that time. Turner would not have wished unduly to alarm or inconvenience his pampered passengers. Many would have been reluctant to attend drills. One candidly gave evidence that "passengers would not have stood for it at the time." American passenger James

Brooks even admitted that although "instructions on how to put on life jackets were in a conspicuous place," he had paid no attention to them. Nevertheless, had there been even the most rudimentary drills, many fewer passengers would have died. They would have known how to put on their life jackets, many of which were of a new design, instead of wearing them upside down or tying them wrongly or too loosely. Charles Lauriat estimated that over half the passengers he had seen wearing life jackets had not put them on correctly.

Captain Turner ensured the appropriate level of blackout on 6 May. He ordered those watertight bulkheads not required to be open for operational reasons to be closed on approaching the danger zone. This appears to have been done, although some bulkheads may not have been closed fully. His instructions to close portholes seem only to have been by word of mouth and not through any notice pushed under cabin doors. The ship had just rudimentary air-conditioning, and many passengers, particularly in the stuffy, more cramped third-class accommodation lower down in the bows, must have opened portholes in their cabins, some only three feet above the waterline, to let in the spring air. Stewards were prevented by Cunard Line rules from invading the privacy of occupied cabins to check on such matters, and Turner does not seem to have insisted on his order being followed in some of the public areas like the dining rooms.

What of Turner's actions and those of his crew after the attack? They faced a difficult task. Unlike today, there was no public-address system, no loudspeakers placed strategically inside the ship or on deck. All orders had to be shouted over a pandemonium of noise—screams of the injured, the crying of children, and the noise of attempts to launch lifeboats. Many of the able-bodied seamen were trapped below in the mail and baggage rooms, and few were left to lower the boats. Also, given the ship's rapid list to starboard, launching the boats was nearly impossible in the time available. With hindsight, Cunard officials would have done well to heed more of the advice of the *Titanic* inquiry. For example, they should have spent the money to fit the recommended davits, which allowed the lifeboats to be swung out more easily; they should have replaced the rudimentary block and tackle with more sophisticated geared lowering systems to compensate for a list and for a ship being down by the head; they should have assigned passengers, as well as crew, to particular lifeboats as done today. This could have mitigated the chaos.

Also, one effect of Cunard's preoccupation with appearance was that some of the collapsibles were stuck by paint to the deck and could not be released in time.

Despite the problems, many crew members showed real heroism and devotion to duty, from Staff Captain Anderson, struggling in his shirtsleeves to lower the lifeboats, to quartermaster Hugh Johnston, clinging grimly to the wheel as the water rose, to Bob Leith, tapping out his SOS messages until the last possible moment. Many of the crew on deck or acting as stairway guides seem to have performed well. A number of stewards and stewardesses gave away their own life jackets and stayed to help passengers before trying to save themselves.

Because electrical power and the ability to reverse engines or to steer were quickly lost after the torpedo strike, Captain Turner and his crew had few options for remedial action. However, they did make some mistakes. Although Turner's initial decision not to lower the boats while the vessel still had considerable forward momentum was correct, there came a point where this had to be risked, and there was obvious confusion about his orders. Also, Turner should have detailed more men to release the collapsible lifeboats in the event of an emergency. But neither he, nor his crew, nor most of the passengers, believed that the *Lusitania* would be attacked without warning or that she would sink within eighteen minutes.

CHAPTER THIRTY-ONE

Anglo-Saxon Attitudes

*I*N 1900 ONE WRITER described the British and Americans—the "Anglo-Saxon race"—as preeminent because they are "in perfect accord with the characteristic conditions of modern life." The Anglo Saxon triumphs in world markets because "he has supreme gifts as an inventor of material things." He drives self-interest and ethical standards "in double-harness" in a way that marks him out from other races, but is "supremely unconscious of this duality in his nature. There is a psychological difference between English-speaking men and others which makes that which would be hypocrisy in others not hypocrisy in them. They are sentimentalists, and, as sentimentalists, not the best analysts of their motives."

The Germans charged the British with hypocrisy early in the war. They alleged that in declaring war, the British had cloaked their commercial and imperial motives with a falsely high-minded moral stand for Belgian neutrality. As the war progressed, this charge of hypocrisy was directed even more intensely against the United States. Germany accused America of promoting supposedly ethical standards like mediation and condemning German infractions of international law in hypocritical double-harness with commercial self-interest. She alleged that America was supplying the Allies with war matériel while downplaying the Allies' own infringements of the law. Germany also charged that the sentimental attachment of members of the American administration to the English language and culture prejudiced their judgment.

There is some validity in this charge of hypocrisy based on commercial self-interest and, sometimes, unacknowledged personal sentiment. It is apparent in the attitude of that most complex of characters, Woodrow Wilson. He set out high moral principles to justify his actions. He did his conscious best to be fair. He may even have held a secret meeting with Ambassador Bernstorff during the *Lusitania* crisis to emphasize his commitment to peace and mediation. Yet throughout he was, at least unconsciously, influenced by his partiality for Britain, her culture, and her parliamentary system of government. Others, in particular Lansing, House, Page, and Gerard but also McAdoo and Garrison, acknowledged their partiality to themselves more clearly, as their private writings and diaries show. Yet they too cloaked their external actions with a legalistic evenhandedness. Bryan was perhaps the only influential American closely involved in the *Lusitania* affair to be genuinely impartial.

Wilson's and Lansing's assertion in 1915 that Americans had the right to travel unmolested on the ships of belligerent countries showed that they were prepared to go beyond the recognized international law of the day. Previously, the United States had accepted that the flag (or nationality) of a ship applied to all its passengers. In the Civil War the Union had released two Confederate commissioners captured in 1861 on the neutral British ship *Trent* because it agreed that on a British ship the British flag protected them. Taken to the extreme, Wilson's position was that American lives were sacrosanct and thus Americans traveling on Allied ships were indeed human shields, just as the Germans claimed. The more evenhanded stance would have been for the U.S. administration to do as Bryan suggested—formally alert U.S. citizens to the dangers of traveling on the ships of belligerents.

Another example of hypocrisy is Lansing's use of a tortuous legal justification to permit the issue of credits to the Allies when, at Bryan's insistence, loans had been prohibited because "money was the worst of contrabands." Also, upon the outbreak of war in 1914, German liners were interned in New York on the grounds that, if released, they would immediately be converted into commerce-raiding auxiliary cruisers. Similarly unarmed British ships, with equally destructive potential, were allowed to enter and depart from U.S. ports at will.

The notorious *Baralong* incident, in August 1915, was a further and very specific incidence of partiality toward Britain. Ambassador Bernstorff protested to Secretary of State Robert Lansing that the "Q" ship *Baralong* had been flying the American flag just before she revealed her guns and attacked the *U-27*. Lansing did not protest to the British either about the use of the American flag or about the merciless killing of the U-boat survivors that the British sought lamely to defend on the grounds that they had believed the men to be armed. The *Baralong*'s fate must have made U-boatmen even more reluctant to follow Cruiser Rules. It certainly hardened German perceptions of America's lack of evenhand-edness between the two combatants.

Also, the United States was much less forceful in denouncing Bri-tain's hunger blockade of Germany than in protesting Germany's cam-paign of unrestricted submarine warfare. In part this was due to Britain's thin arguments of legality for her blockade, whereas Germany admitted she was acting in reprisal and reprisals are always illegal. But President Wilson reflected the attitudes of many of his fellow countrymen when he wrote on 2 June 1915 that "England's violation of neutral rights is differ-ent from Germany's violation of the rights of humanity."

There was also a sentimental reaction to the images of dead women and babies, Americans among them, from the *Lusitania*, whereas the devastating effect of the munitions sold to the Allies was not apparent. Similarly, the deaths on the *Lusitania* were irreversible, whereas the gradual starvation through the British hunger blockade was not. The British also had the unquestionable advantage of a shared language in which to chill and outrage American audiences with accounts of German gas attacks, atrocities in Belgium, the crucified Canadian sergeant, and so forth—all occurring within two months of the sinking.

With an American public increasingly emotionally attached to the Allied cause (albeit not to participation in the war), a strong commercial interest in the sale of munitions, including previous decisions on cred-its, and the doctrine of strict accountability, the administration could not afford a change of policy once the *Lusitania* had sunk. A U-turn at the behest of a U-boat would not be a vote winner. Nor would it accord with the personal preferences of those involved.

The rush to justification in the United States was therefore as marked as in the United Kingdom. Dudley Field Malone, collector of customs in New York and himself a Democratic political appointee, was pushed to confirm denials of German claims about troops and ammunition. The campaign to identify German espionage activities was intensified and included telephone tapping, which violated German diplomatic privileges. Cooperation between the U.S. Department of Justice and British officials increased, as did the exchange of confidences between Captain Guy Gaunt, British naval attaché in Washington, and Robert Lansing. There are many references in dispatches from the British embassy to information directly attributed to Robert Lansing or which could only have come from him. Cooperation grew, too, between Reginald Hall and Edward Bell, American intelligence attaché in London. Thus it was to Bell that, in the summer of 1915, Hall disclosed the contents of Ambassador Dumba's papers seized from the American journalist Archibald, acting as a courier for the Austro-Hungarian ambassador, in the sure knowledge that they would receive the desired publicity.

These activities bore fruit. German agents were arrested and tried. The revelations of very undiplomatic German espionage and sabotage activities on American soil gave credence in American minds to British allegations, and cooperation strengthened yet further. The manipulation by Hall, Bell, and Page of the release of the Zimmermann telegram decoded by Room 40 was the crowning achievement. Once the United States was at war, declared unity of purpose drew America and Britain closer. The relationship became so symbiotic that Bell could claim to have been decisive in the decision by the British Admiralty to adopt the convoy system for merchant shipping to protect against the U-boat menace.

Thus, when the *Lusitania* case came before Judge Mayer in 1918, the U.S. administration had every motive for acquiescing in the Mersey findings. An admission that there was only one torpedo (which must have been known to Bell through Hall) would have exposed the United States to the charge of being an accessory to the deaths of her own citizens, for she had allowed explosive munitions responsible for a second explosion to leave New York on a belligerent ship carrying American passengers. It would also have invalidated previous government statements. As in the case of Britain, any acknowledgment of mitigating circumstances would have handed Germany a propaganda advantage.

The U.S. government did not volunteer Wesley Frost's report labeling claims about a second torpedo as "dubious" or the statements he had collected immediately after the disaster from American survivors, many of which were critical of Captain Turner and at variance with the two-torpedoes theory. Nor did it volunteer the details about the content of the warning messages sent to the *Lusitania*, which were confided by Vice Admiral Coke to Frost and the two American attachés Captain Castle and Captain Miller immediately after the sinking. Instead the U.S. authorities were content for the wording of the communications with the *Lusitania* to remain classified and for questions relating to them to be ruled out by reference to Britain's Defence of the Realm Act. It is also revealing that the copy of the *Lusitania*'s manifest submitted to the Mayer hearings omits the barrels of bronze powder. The Department of Justice had, by then, discovered that Paul König was seeking information about the powder, and this seems have prompted the authorities to seek to avoid further questions on the subject.

Justice Mayer, an "old guard Republican and Establishment man," may not have needed the hints so conspicuously dropped to Lord Mersey to ensure he did his patriotic duty. Perhaps the clearest surviving indication of his partiality is the way in which, in his judgment, he dealt with the question concerning the number of torpedoes: "The weight of the testimony (too voluminous to analyse) is in favour of the two-torpedo contention. . . . As there were no explosives on board it is difficult to account for the second explosion except on the theory that it was caused by a second torpedo." First, Mayer avoided any discussion of the weight of evidence about the number of torpedoes. Second, Mayer implicitly discounted any other cause of explosion, despite the fact that both boiler and coal-dust explosions were by then known to result from torpedo strikes. He also prevented any serious exploration of the effects of structural damage on the speed with which the ship sank.

The worst judgment that can be handed down against the American administration is that, before the *Lusitania* sinking, it was not neutral but partial to the Allied cause, and that it masked its partiality by the stretching of legality. Afterward, it was as committed as the British to justifying its previous actions, to preventing unwanted questions, and to obtaining evidence of German wrongdoing. Had Wilson not been perceived by the Germans as hypocritical in his attitudes, his mediation attempts might have found more favor with Germany and her suspicious, sensitive, and occasionally paranoid kaiser.

CHAPTER THIRTY-TWO

The U-Boat Diary

*I*N RESPONSE to the United States's protests and the international press outcry, the German authorities claimed that the *Lusitania* had not been a target and that her identity had only become clear to the *U-20* as she sank. The kaiser in particular said that he would not have authorized the sinking with the consequent death of so many women and children had he known in advance. However, the German government continued to justify the act on the grounds of the *Lusitania*'s alleged armament, carriage of Canadian troops, and cargo of munitions. It did not recognize the logical discrepancy that if Schwieger had not known what ship he was attacking, he could hardly have known the nature of her armament, cargo, or passenger list, thereby making any justification based on them invalid.

The reality is that the *Lusitania* was an acknowledged target for the German U-boat service. This is evident from the targeting information sent out regularly by the naval commander in chief to submarines, for example: "FAST STEAMER LUSITANIA COMING FROM NEW YORK EXPECTED AT LIVERPOOL 4TH OR 5TH MARCH." The purpose of the information is clear especially when compared with the following communication also sent to U-boats: "AMERICAN S.S. PHILADELPHIA AND WEST HAVERFORD WILL PROBABLY ARRIVE IN THE IRISH SEA BOUND FOR LIVERPOOL. BOTH STEAMERS ARE TO BE SPARED." By definition, others were not.

In fact, the *Lusitania*'s name crops up the most frequently of all the merchant shipping targets identified in the telegrams decoded by Room 40. U-boat commander Wegener was certainly in no doubt that the liner was an authorized target when he lay in wait for her in the *U-27* in Liverpool bay in March 1915. He recorded his actions carefully in his war diary, including the fact that he was following guidance from his half-flotilla commander, Hermann Bauer. He signed off his war diary for each day of the cruise, and it was circulated as normal. There is no evidence whatever that he was rebuked or told that he was in error to target the *Lusitania*. Indeed, the submarine command continued to put out details of her movements.

Against this background, it is more than coincidence that the German authorities chose to make certain that their delayed warning was published just before the *Lusitania* sailed and placed next to Cunard's advertisement. Her sinking was obviously considered a real and desired possibility. Count Bernstorff himself told a well-known American newspaper editor within forty-eight hours of the attack that the notice had been sent by Berlin "two months previously" (that is, around the time that the *U-27* had waited for the *Lusitania* off Liverpool). However, "thinking it a great mistake," he threw it into his desk drawer and "hoped Berlin would forget about it." He had authorized publication only after receiving instructions from Berlin to do so at once. This account confirms information given to Cecil Spring-Rice by the U.S. Secret Service that the warning had originated in Berlin.

What, then, of the orders and actions of Kapitänleutnant Walther Schwieger in the *U-20*? His only surviving written orders were "large English troop transports expected starting from Liverpool, Bristol Channel, Dartmouth. . . . Get to stations on fastest possible route around Scotland. Hold as long as supplies permit. Submarines to attack transport ships, merchant ships and war ships." In the interwar years the German naval historian Admiral Arno Spindler confirmed the evidence in the *U-20*'s war diary that Schwieger received additional oral orders that his particular target area was the waters around Liverpool. The issuing of oral orders was apparently routine.

We do not know what other oral orders Hermann Bauer passed to Walter Schwieger. These may or may not have included a reminder about the *Lusitania*'s movements. What we do know is that Bauer clearly believed that his U-boat commanders needed flexibility in their operational instructions both to safeguard their crews and to maximize their impact on the enemy. On occasion he filtered out some of the restraining guidance issued by the high command in response to the concerns of the civil

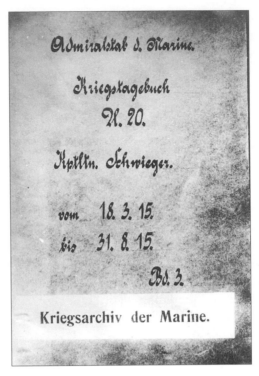

Cover of Walther Schwieger's U-20 war diary.

authorities. Correspondence in the German archives proves that the kaiser wanted him dismissed for such actions.

The first use Schwieger made of his discretion was not to take the "fastest possible route" to his Liverpool station, which would have been through the North Channel. Instead he chose to go around the west coast of Ireland presumably for safety reasons. He then sank the *Earl of Lathom*, *Candidate*, and *Centurion*. According to his war diary, he made the momentous decision not to go on to Liverpool because of the weather, poor visibility, danger of patrols, limited number of torpedoes, and level of fuel consumption. Instead, as he recorded, he decided to remain in the southern Irish Sea. Here, of course, he met the *Lusitania* on 7 May and sank her.

There is good reason to suspect that the *U-20*'s war diary was doctored after Schwieger returned to port and does not present a true picture of what was going on in Schwieger's mind that day. On completing a mission, U-boat commanders brought their war diaries on shore hand-written in pencil. They were subsequently and invariably typed up, usually on a purpose-designed form using both sides of the paper. Sometimes a form was not used, although both sides of the paper were still covered. Invariably, too, the U-boat commander signed off on each day's report. When copies were made, the position of his signature was faithfully recorded. The copy of the *U-20*'s war diary preserved at the German Military Archive at Freiburg does not follow the normal format. It is not on a printed form. It is not double-sided. Some of it is in a discursive style quite uncharacteristic of the war diaries for Schwieger's other voyages. Most significant, Schwieger's signature is recorded for every day of the cruise with one notable exception—7 May, the day that he sank the *Lusitania*. The copy also shows many signs of cutting, pasting, and rebinding compared to other war diaries. Entries are typed more closely together and ignore usual practice on lining up paragraphs.

The war diary's content is equally dubious. The first doubtful item is Schwieger's reasoning about whether to continue to Liverpool. Some of it relates to the practical dangers that an operational submarine commander might expect to face. The most questionable, however, relates to the shortage of fuel. When the *U-20* arrived back at Wilhelmshaven, according to Schwieger's war diary, she still had over 27 percent of her fuel left. This was a more than adequate safety margin to have allowed the *U-20* to reach Liverpool without running low, particularly if she had taken the shorter, though admittedly more dangerous, North Channel route home or gone between the Orkney and Shetland Islands as on her outward journey, rather than sailing north of them both. Perhaps all along Schwieger intended to wait for the *Lusitania*, which he knew was still following the Fastnet–Head of Kinsale route. The postwar verdict of British naval intelligence was that, although there was no direct evidence, prisoner statements made clear that "in German naval circles a view prevailed that Schwieger had definitely been ordered to lie in wait with a view to torpedoing her."

We can be more certain that elements of the unsigned entry for the day of the sinking are either inaccurate or later additions. There is a catalog of inconsistencies. According to Schwieger's war diary, when the *U-20* first sighted the target, she was dead ahead—*recht voraus*—and yet her four funnels were immediately visible. In practice they would have been hard, indeed impossible, to distinguish if the ship were approaching head-on from the horizon. The war diary also states that the *Lusitania* made the fatal, final turn that brought her into range of the *U-20* toward Queenstown. In fact she turned away from the port.

Then there is the late identification of the *Lusitania* by the name on her bow in gold letters as she sank. Yet there is ample evidence from impartial testimony that the ship's name had been carefully painted over in black. Curiously, earlier in his war diary Schwieger also named the *Candidate* as one of the ships he had sunk, although her name, too, was painted out in accordance with Admiralty guidance. More important, a competent, well-briefed U-boat commander like Schwieger, assisted by an experienced merchant mariner like Pilot Lanz, would have known from the start which ship he was attacking. There were only five British liners with four funnels, and the position of each was well known to the German authorities. Only the *Lusitania* could possibly have been inbound at the time. Schwieger's claim that he identified her only as she sank does not fit with his high praise later in his war diary of Lanz, "who [knew] all English ships by their build."

Schwieger's diary goes on to reflect in detail on what happened to the ship. What was the nature of the second explosion—"boiler or coal or powder?" He states that "the ship stops immediately." She did not. She was still moving when she sank eighteen minutes later. He incorrectly states that the bridge was torn asunder. Neither Quartermaster Hugh Johnston at the wheel nor Captain Turner mentioned any damage to the bridge. Johnston, who resisted pressure to toe the company line about the number of torpedoes, described how Turner went from one side of the bridge to the other to view what was happening along the decks.

Most striking of all are Schwieger's personal comments that "it would have been impossible for me to fire a second torpedo into this crushing crowd of humanity trying to save their lives." Such a remark is out of character and out of place. Personal remarks of any kind are not usually found in war diaries. Nor are such discursive observations as the following: "It is surprising that just today there is so much traffic here, although yesterday two big steamers have been sunk south of the St. George's Channel. Also that the *Lusitania* was not sent through the North Channel remains a mystery."

All these disingenuous remarks bear the hallmark of "institutional afterthoughts," comments added to the official record to display German conscience and to suggest British incompetence. The war diary was no doubt "beautified" after the original had been telegraphed to Berlin and following Schwieger's subsequent "ungracious" reception in Berlin. Some of the additions and changes may have been made as late as 1918 when a worried kaiser inquired about the possibility of war crimes charges. Schwieger was by then dead and could not have signed off on a revised entry for 7 May 1915.

Such misrepresentation of the facts of a sinking was not unknown. Bauer, Schwieger, and his crew were involved in another such case—the sinking without warning of the liner *Hesperian* by the *U-20* in September 1915—as one of the few surviving letters in Walter Schwieger's handwriting relates. On this occasion the German Admiralty chief of staff told him to maintain the fiction that the liner had been sunk by a mine. He was ordered to tell his crew that they had sunk an auxiliary cruiser (which the Germans knew the *Hesperian* was not) and to order them not to discuss the sinking with anyone outside the crew. Schwieger and his men dutifully obeyed.

None of the justifications given by the German authorities for sinking the *Lusitania* without warning was valid under the international law of the time—the Cruiser Rules—which insisted upon "stop and search." The *U-20* would have been perfectly within its rights to stop the ship, order passengers and crew to disembark in lifeboats, and to sink her because she was undoubtedly carrying war matériel.

There are mitigating factors for the sinking. Schwieger would have known that fast liners like the *Lusitania* were rumored to be gunrunners and that they had undoubted potential for use as troop transports or for conversion into armed merchant cruisers. He would also have known of the British Admiralty's advice to merchantmen "to steer toward" attacking submarines—in other words, to ram them. He would have been aware, too, that after Germany's declaration of unrestricted submarine warfare, Britain started segregating captured U-boatmen from other prisoners of war for possible trial as war criminals. Schwieger believed his duty above all was to protect his crew, and they loved him for it. He took longer but safer routes. Because he put his own men's lives above those of his enemies, he was prepared to remain submerged when attacking vessels even if they turned out to be passenger or hospital ships or neutral vessels.

Schwieger cannot be condemned for the subsequent cover-up to present the sinking in the most favorable light and placate and influence international opinion. The conspiracy was the result of the shock within some parts of the German hierarchy at the bitterness of worldwide reaction. In this climate, with the kaiser taking a close personal interest in the *Lusitania* incident, calling for Schwieger's war diary, and reeling under personal attack in the world's press, it is not surprising that the facts of the sinking were "massaged."

However, by firing without warning, Schwieger and those who dispatched him were guilty by the standards of 1915 of "willful murder." The act was premeditated both by Schwieger, who knew his target when he fired the torpedo, and by the naval authorities, who considered the *Lusitania* a target and had been so briefing their submarine commanders for some months. The urgency with which Germany's nervous civil administration had the warning advertisement published in the United States confirms that it, too, clearly recognized the potential for the *Lusitania* to be sunk on her May crossing.

Yet not even in Germany could anyone predict the damage that the *Lusitania* incident would inflict on her ability to win the war—or to achieve even a "draw."

CHAPTER THIRTY-THREE

A New Barbarism

*P*UBLIC OPINION and its manipulation were more important in the First World War than in any previous conflict, particularly in regard to neutral countries. The sinking of the *Lusitania* brought to Britain a propaganda victory that eclipsed her loss in lives and war matériel. Churchill was right, if hard-hearted, when he wrote in 1937: "In spite of all its horror, we must regard the sinking of the *Lusitania* as an event most important and favourable to the Allies. . . . the poor babies who perished in the ocean struck a blow at German power more deadly than could have been achieved by the sacrifice of a hundred thousand fighting men." To many neutral countries, the enormity of the incident confirmed everything Britain had been arguing about the illegality and barbarity of German behavior since the start of the war. The United States became an ever more sympathetic neutral— and, because of her own losses, ever more prepared to overlook Britain's own infringements of international law and to function as an arsenal for the Allies.

Indeed, the *Lusitania* affair came to have an even greater and more enduring resonance in the United States than in Britain. Once America was in the war, "Remember the *Lusitania!*" became a talismanic reminder of what the nation was fighting for. Images of the sinking ship and of drowning women, hair streaming behind them in the surf, were used on recruitment posters and to sell war bonds. Americans quickly forgot that nearly two years had elapsed between the sinking and their declaration of war. The myth grew, which still persists today, that the United States entered the war as an immediate consequence of the sinking of the *Lusitania*.

Although initially celebrated by her government and her people as a great naval victory, Germany was unequivocally the loser in the *Lusitania* incident. Not only was the sinking a propaganda disaster, but, in the weeks and months that followed, it disrupted and distracted the German high command and government at a critical stage of the war. It became a flash point for the already brittle and combative relations between the civil and military wings of the government, with a vacillating and increasingly neurotic kaiser caught in between. As the crevasses in Germany's leadership structure deepened, so the decision-making process suffered. It took ever longer to agree to responses to the successive American protest notes. The "constant battle" over U-boat deployment, as Schwieger's commanding officer Hermann Bauer bitterly described it, also resulted in disjointed, sometimes contradictory, orders to the U-boat service.

This indecision and bickering contrasted with Germany's single-mindedness in the early stages of the war. Germany's attack on Belgium had been prosecuted with a directness and, in some cases, a calculated brutality which Karl von Clausewitz, the Prussian military theorist, would have admired. When the war in the west became bogged down, Tirpitz had secured agreement to an equally single-minded and ruthless policy of unrestricted submarine warfare. Tirpitz and the German government were fully aware that, like the attack on Belgium, this new policy was illegal. Not only did it contravene the Cruiser Rules, but the U-boat blockade itself was formally illegal because it could not be deemed "effective." Indeed, the German government conceded the illegality of the blockade in an intercepted telegram from Berlin to its Buenos Aires embassy. Admittedly, the kaiser had only given permission for the U-boat campaign nervously and had immediately begun to impose all sorts of restrictions at the behest of his equally nervous civilian ministers. Nevertheless, despite this internal debate, the U-boat service had embraced the new policy wholeheartedly.

Germany's naval strategists led by Tirpitz had been quick to grasp that the new weapon of the submarine could not be humanized or regulated by outdated rules. Germany had been the first to use the new technology in an illegal way, just as she had ignored Belgian neutrality and been the first to use poison gas. Perhaps the undemocratic German government did not fully appreciate the impact such actions would have on public opinion in both neutral and belligerent nations. The kaiser's civilian ministers understood better than their naval and military colleagues the power of the press and the way that public opinion influenced policy in Britain and the United States. However, before the *Lusitania* affair, even they failed to appreciate its importance and the extent to which they should actively court popular opinion in neutral countries.

The most important neutral was, of course, America, and in the period before the sinking of the *Lusitania* Germany had failed dismally to win her over. Part of the problem was that in framing their Eurocentric policies German ministers had only half appreciated the latent military and commercial power of the United States. Hence they had taken little trouble to woo that nation. British ministers like Sir Edward Grey were prepared to welcome Wilson's emissaries, to debate British policies, and to provide moral and legal rationales for them even if the latter often stretched the bounds of the law. They were prepared to spend time discussing proposals for mediation with House and Page and to agree to give them careful consideration. In the end they conceded little to Wilson but acted in a way that preserved the relationship and converted the U.S. emissaries to the British cause. The behavior of the German government and its officials toward the United States was, with a few exceptions like Ambassador Bernstorff, more direct, blunt, even bullying. Germany seems at an early stage to have viewed the United States as a lost cause.

Because the Germans were wrapped up in a sense of grievance, few were prepared to empathize with American officials or to anticipate American reaction to the sinking of the *Lusitania*. Germany's attachés in Washington took little trouble to conceal their contempt for their hosts. A factor here, as elsewhere, was a feeling shared by Germans of all backgrounds of "race treachery" on the part of Britain and America. A sense of betrayal quickly combined with a pervasive inferiority complex to produce the unremitting petulant anger of the spurned suitor. Initial angry recriminations had focused mainly on the British but had soon moved with equal venom against the Americans and their uneven-handed arms sale policy. Von Papen, for example, remarked that the Americans only began walking on two legs instead of four when someone suggested that there was more profit to be made that way.

Willful Murder?

The sinking of the *Lusitania*, and Germany's response to the world's outrage, hardened American attitudes and exacerbated the tensions between the two countries. So did evidence that in direct contravention of both American national law and international diplomatic usage the Germans had ham-fistedly plotted bombings and sabotage, fomented strikes, and intrigued on American soil to bring back Victoriano Huerta to Mexico to make trouble for the United States.

However, Germany's great mistake, having sunk the *Lusitania*, was to edge slowly away from unrestricted submarine warfare. The personality of the kaiser is key here. His nervous, mercurial temperament combined paranoia, an inferiority complex, and a yearning to be loved with an intense pride and sense of his own and his nation's position in the world and what was owed them by others.

Anxious for approval and acceptance, he was acutely sensitive to the wave of criticism directed against Germany and in particular to his personal vilification in cartoons and elsewhere as a barbarous, murderous "Hun." At times he even seems to have been close to a nervous breakdown. Yet he was the unelected, irremovable head of a government and the ultimate arbiter of German policy. In the aftermath of the sinking, his ministers and commanders had to compete to exploit his changing moods and feelings. For a while, Chancellor Bethmann Hollweg and his allies managed to win the kaiser's ear and eventually to secure his agreement to a suspension of unrestricted U-boat warfare. Conversely, Tirpitz argued that Germany should have persisted. By calling a halt, she was losing her best chance of winning the war.

He was probably right. Fisher's extraordinary midwar letter of consolation to Tirpitz on his resignation underlines that naval strategists recognized an inevitability in the unrestricted use of the submarine weapon. A quarter century later, all nations practiced unrestricted submarine warfare in the Second World War. It had been a mistake to launch the U-boat campaign in February 1915 before Germany had sufficient boats to maintain a concentrated and concerted attack, just as the British should have waited until they had more, and more reliable, tanks before introducing them on the Western Front. Yet by continuing her campaign, once launched, Germany would have had her best chance of arriving at a mediated peace. The United States would have been unlikely to enter the war before the 1916 presidential election, particularly if the U-boats had avoided sinking passenger ships. German war

"Humanity Demands a Stronger Net," cartoon in the Cleveland Leader.

production could have concentrated on the U-boat. British imports would have diminished. After the high casualties on both sides from the battles of Verdun and the Somme which ended in stalemate, there might have been a chance of peace. Instead, the abandonment of unrestricted submarine warfare meant that Britain and France benefited from the easy transport of war matériel from the United States. By the time Germany resumed unfettered U-boat warfare in 1917, it was too late to help her achieve either victory or even a brokered settlement.

Not only did the *Lusitania* incident significantly influence the conduct of the war; it was also one of a series of events in the spring and early summer of 1915 that altered the very nature of warfare. On the evening of 22 April, German soldiers had opened the taps of 4,000 cylinders of chlorine and released 168 tons of the gas onto the French and Canadian trenches in the world's first poison-gas attack. On 1 June 1915, a solitary German zeppelin launched the first air raid on London to bring war to the civilian population of the world's largest city. The Bryce Report on

Belgian atrocities was published in May 1915. Together with the destruction of the *Lusitania*, these acts provoked an unparalleled outcry. They seemed to symbolize a sea change in the conduct of warfare back to the barbarity of the Middle Ages. No longer could commanders claim to operate under a chivalric code of honor protecting civilians, the wounded, and those willing to surrender.

The concept of a clean, "no hard feelings" war—which had prompted the fraternization and games of football between opposing troops on the Western Front, mainly at the instigation of German soldiers singing "Silent Night," at Christmas 1914—was banished. Instead, the events of early summer 1915, including the destruction of the *Lusitania*, were signposts on the path to Guernica, Hiroshima, and beyond. They heralded a time when best-available technology would be unleashed without warning on the enemy's population regardless of age, sex, and whether or not they were combatants, to secure victory at the lowest cost to the attacker. Despite their protestations as to the moral superiority of their cause, each major power would feel compelled to follow down that path. The new barbarism of total war had begun.

Epilogue

*T*HE RESEARCH for this book began on a chilly November day in Liverpool, former home of the Cunard Company and birthplace of Captain Will Turner. The starting point was one of the *Lusitania*'s bronze propellers, salvaged by Oceaneering International in 1982. It sits on the quayside outside the Merseyside Maritime Museum. Stark and huge as a dinosaur bone, it still conveys the size and the power of the vessel it once helped propel through rough Atlantic waters. Within the museum itself, fragments of letters and a deck chair and a silver teaspoon salvaged from the wreck conjure something of what happened on 7 May 1915.

So do the Cunard Company archives at the nearby University of Liverpool. Yellowing, cracking photographs of the dead lie in cardboard boxes. The pictures of the children are the hardest to look at, even after all these years. Some are curled fetuslike in their plain, wooden boxes. Some look like sleeping dolls, tiny faces framed by ruffled bonnets. Some are named, others mere numbers. I found fragments of faded material, cut from the clothing of victims to help the process of identification, tucked into now-brittle envelopes. I read letters between anxious Cunard officials about articles lying unclaimed in the company safe: wedding rings, diamond rings, signet rings, brooches, necklaces. I found file after file of letters and telegrams conveying the scale of the task faced by Cunard staff and by American consul Wesley Frost in Queenstown as they attempted to match bodies and possessions to names on endless lists.

The Cunard files, and other *Lusitania* archives in Britain and the United States, reveal much of the human aftermath of the *Lusitania*'s sinking: the public expressions of grief, the private trauma, and the struggle of survivors as they tried to come to terms with what had happened to them. They describe how some 3,000 people attended Elbert Hubbard's memorial service at East Aurora. His distraught disciples were convinced the kaiser had ordered the *Lusitania* sunk precisely because the outspoken Hubbard was aboard. Old newspapers describe how Charles Frohman's embalmed body lay in state in Manhattan's Temple Emanu-El. His corpse had been brought back on the American liner *New York*, which also carried thirty survivors home. Admission to his funeral was by ticket only. A simple bunch of violets from actress Maude Adams adorned the coffin. Although she denied to reporters that they had ever married, she gave up her stage career on Frohman's death.

Letters and memoirs show how nightmares of being trapped in a sinking ship troubled many survivors for years. They woke night after night drenched in sweat and screaming with fear. It was particularly hard for the many young children who had lost parents, brothers, and sisters. Nine-year-old Edith Williams's mother and four of her five siblings had all been killed. Edith remained haunted by the ghostly sensation of her dead little sister's hand slipping through hers as they were dragged apart in the panic. Margaret Mackworth also suffered recurring bad dreams. But at the same time, the realization that she had found the strength to survive gave her a new self-confidence. She lost her fear both of water and of dying. Within weeks of the sinking she was giving glowing testimonials in the press to the effectiveness of her Boddy's Patent Life Jacket.

The *Lusitania* brought romance to some. Gerda Nielson and John Welsh had fallen in love on the ship. The disaster bound them yet closer, and they married a week after the sinking. One female survivor later wed a sailor from the rescue vessel that saved her.

For others, the terrifying events of 7 May 1915 became the prelude to deep, lifelong friendships. Nurse Alice Lines kept in close touch with Audrey Pearl, the tiny baby she had wrapped in her shawl and saved. In 1994, aged nearly one hundred, she told the *National Geographic* that Audrey was still "her baby." Audrey herself is "weary" of talking of the event that claimed her two sisters. Instead, she recently turned her energies to working with the Royal National Lifeboat Institute to raise funds for a lifeboat on the southern Irish coast. The lives of Professor

Holbourn, laird of Foula, and Avis Dolphin became similarly inter-linked. As he had promised when she once complained that books for girls were so dull, he wrote her the adventure story *The Child of the Moat*. They remained close until his death in 1933, seven years after Avis's marriage to journalist Thomas Foley.

But for others, their experiences on the *Lusitania* were the prelude to further danger or sorrow. Margaret Cox, who had managed to fight her way onto the decks and into a lifeboat with her baby son, Desmond, was very nearly killed the following year when she became unwittingly trapped during fighting in the Irish Nationalist Easter Rising. A man trying to help her was mown down by machine-gun fire in front of her. Sir Montague and Lady Allan, still grieving for the loss of their two pretty young daughters on the *Lusitania*, lost their only son two years later when he was shot down flying over the German lines. Julia and Flor Sullivan, who had settled on the Sullivan family farm in Kerry, lost their only daughter, a nurse, when she was killed in an early bombing raid on London during the Second World War.

The psychological burden was especially hard for the relatives of victims whose bodies were never found. Papers in the Cunard archives describe how groups of relations were invited to Cunard's offices to gather in silence around a table. Laid out neatly in rows were those same photographs of unknown victims of the *Lusitania*, now shut away in their boxes and casually inspected by impersonal researchers. Leaning over them, friends and relations of the missing blanched at images of little children still clutching teddy bears and dolls and of mothers cradling drowned babies.

For many, there was disappointment. Their friends and loved ones were not among the stark, stiff forms in the photographs. Papers recently bought at auction by the Imperial War Museum show the lengths to which some anguished relatives went. They chart the pathetically persistent but fruitless efforts of Mrs. Prichard to contact any surviving passenger or crew member who might have seen her medical-student son, Dick. It seems she was tormented by the thought that he might have died trapped belowdecks in the darkness, and she even published a poster showing what Dick looked like to jog people's memories. Theodate Pope, Oliver Bernard, Belle Naish, Elizabeth Duckworth, and Margaret Mackworth were among the many who wrote consolingly but could provide no insight into his fate. All Mrs. Prichard learned was that her

LUSITANIA DISASTER.

Information Wanted.

Reward for **Recovery** of the **Body.**

Reward for **Recovery** of the **Body.**

Wanted any information regarding

Richard Preston Prichard,

Lusitania Passenger, 2nd Cabin D 90.

Aged 29 years.   Height, 5 ft. 10 in.   Dark brown hair, with high forehead, blue eyes, and prominent features.   Very deep dimple in chin. (Probably wearing gold ring on tie, with red and white lava heads inset.)

Any information regarding him on the voyage, or that will lead to his discovery, will be most thankfully received, by wire or otherwise, by

MOSTYN PRICHARD, 7, Brockenhurst Road, Ramsgate.

normally carefree, cheerful son had taken the precaution, before he sailed, of putting his papers in order and of telling a fellow student at McGill University, Montreal, where to find his will in case anything should happen to him. It feels strange to read this correspondence and then to see the off-white, salt-stained Boddy's life jacket from the *Lusitania* displayed in the museum. Whom, if anyone, did it save? Did Dick Prichard ever manage to find himself a jacket?

Even when bodies were recovered, the stress was sometimes too much for family and friends. Rita Jolivet's sister Inez was so distressed at the loss of her husband, George Vernon, that in the summer of 1915 she dressed herself carefully in a black evening gown, put on her jewels, sat down at her dressing table, took a revolver from the drawer, and shot herself through the head.

Of course, some survivors, like Oliver Bernard, James Brooks, and Charles Lauriat, managed to pick up their lives again. Several wrote accounts of what had happened to them, perhaps as a form of catharsis. The year after the sinking, Rita Jolivet married Count Giuseppe de Cippicio. Two years later, they made the film *Lest We Forget* in memory of her mentor, Charles Frohman. Elizabeth Duckworth, though still weak from her ordeal, summoned up the grit to report for war work at the Royal Arsenal ammunition factory in Blackburn. She later returned to the United States and, after a worrying five-hour wait on Ellis Island, was readmitted. She died in 1955 at the age of ninety-two, one of the real though unsung heroines of 7 May 1915.

Theodate Pope also made a good recovery. Within a year of the sinking she had married former U.S. ambassador to Russia John Wallace Riddle. Her convalescence had been helped by reports from the American Society for Psychical Research of visitations from Edwin Friend. His face was apparently "flushed" as he thundered against the "dastardly deed" that had cost him his life, while his impressive oratory was interrupted by the witty asides of Elbert Hubbard. Theodate died in 1946.

The *Lusitania*'s crew met a variety of fates. After being torpedoed a second time, as he had wearily described to Judge Mayer, Captain William Turner finally retired in November 1919 at the age of sixty-three. He had given forty-one years' service. His marriage over, he at first tried to find seclusion with Mabel Every in a quiet village near Dartmoor in Devon. Curious journalists, however, tracked him down and badgered him with questions. In disgust he returned to Liverpool, where he succeeded in leading a quiet, almost reclusive, life. His most flamboyant gesture was to fly the Union Jack from a tall flagstaff in his garden on important occasions. He died in 1933, at age seventy-six, having rarely talked about the events of 7 May 1915 to anyone except a few close friends and to Mabel

Every, who had remained as his housekeeper. According to Albert Bestic, who visited Turner a few months before the latter's death, his former captain told him that he had never received Admiralty instructions to zigzag. He insisted that he had not been given "a fair deal." His grave overlooks the Mersey estuary.

Several other crew members were also torpedoed again. First Officer Arthur Jones, one of the three deck officers to survive the *Lusitania* sinking, was drowned when his ship was torpedoed not long after the Mersey inquiry. Able Seaman Leo Thompson was more fortunate. Although torpedoed on two further occasions—in 1916 on a westbound banana boat and in 1917 on a small steamer—he survived to sail again. In fact, many *Lusitania* crewmen chose to remain at sea. Able Seaman Leslie Morton became a master mariner. Bellboy Robert Clark went on to serve in the Royal Navy, although he later became a clergyman.

But for many, the memories of 7 May 1915 were hard to erase. Sixteen-year-old cook George Wynne never recovered from the trauma of being unable to save his father. On his bedside table in the Liverpool sailors' home where he spent his final years, he kept a photograph of Joseph Wynne and another of himself wearing a black armband the day after his return to Liverpool from Queenstown.

Inevitably, myths about the *Lusitania*'s crew and passengers grew. Many newspapers reported the story of the indestructible stoker Frank Tower, who, it was claimed, had survived the sinking of the *Titanic* in 1912, the loss of the *Empress of Ireland* two years later in the St. Lawrence River, and then the torpedoing of the *Lusitania*. However, the records of all three ships reveal that such a man never existed.

The German Military Archives in Freiburg give some clues to the thoughts, feelings, and fates of some of the *U-20*'s crew. Many files still bear the labels stuck on them when they were seized by advancing Allied troops in the last weeks of the Second World War. They suggest that, although he did not allow it to affect the single-minded way he carried out what he believed to be his duty, the *Lusitania* affair had a profound effect on Walther Schwieger. A rare surviving letter in his handwriting in the Freiburg archive reveals a softer, more reflective side. At Christmas 1916, some nine months before his death, he wrote to a submarine comrade of his hope that "this very sad time" would soon end.

A postwar newspaper interview with his fiancée, the daughter of a Berlin physician, also hints at a sense of melancholy and guilt. The "very frail . . . prematurely old young woman" recounted how Schwieger had visited her after the sinking. He was "so haggard and so silent and so different" that she knew immediately that something was wrong. With deep emotion he described the attack and how he had prevented his comrades looking through the periscope at the stricken liner. He also told her that he did not believe that the second explosion was due to exploding munitions because too long a time elapsed between the first and second explosions. He thought it might have been a steam plant explosion.

A number of *U-20* crewmen who were with Schwieger the day of the attack survived the First World War, which claimed the lives of over 5,000 U-boatmen out of the 13,000 engaged. Surviving letters and records of interviews show how they remained loyal to Schwieger's memory and vigorous in defense of his actions. Karl Scherb, the officer who claimed he was the first officer who sighted the *Lusitania*, asserted that he was not guilty of "willful murder" but had merely performed "his onerous duty." Raimund Weisbach, the torpedo officer on board the *U-20*, agreed. By 1916 he was commander of the *U-19*, which landed Irish nationalist Sir Roger Casement on the Irish coast just before the Easter Rising. The *U-20* had been scheduled to carry Casement but had had to be withdrawn for repairs. Weisbach was later himself captured by the British and interned as a prisoner of war. His widow, with whom I corresponded about this book, still believes, as her husband did, that, however terrible, the sinking was a justified attack against "an armed ship" carrying munitions.

The *U-20*'s radio officer, Otto Rikowsky, survived both world wars. In the 1960s he gave an interview to the Canadian Broadcasting Corporation in which he defended Schwieger's actions.

The last surviving crew member on board the *U-20* the day the *Lusitania* was sunk was Hermann Lepper, who was on watch at the time of the attack. He died in his nineties having steadfastly defended his commander's actions in newspaper interviews.

A question mark still hangs over the fate of Charles Voegele, the young Alsatian electrician who reputedly mutinied on board the *U-20* on the day of the attack, was sentenced to three years at his court-martial in May 1915, and was imprisoned at Kiel. He died in 1926, and his grave can be seen in Strasbourg. But the details of what really happened remain tantalizingly obscure. None of the surviving crew members of the *U-20* seems ever to have referred to the incident. There is no trace of his court-martial papers. Perhaps the details of his case were removed from the files because of potential embarrassment. But in Strasbourg he is still remembered as a hero, and local historians plan to include him in a forthcoming book about Alsatian patriots.

Toward the end of my research I learned that the *U-20*'s conning tower, deck gun, and propeller had recently gone on display in Denmark in the Strandingsmuseum, Thorsminde, West Jutland. These parts of the submarine were retrieved from the sea after she hit sand banks in 1916 and Walther Schwieger and his men abandoned her. The chance to see, even touch, parts of the *U-20* seemed extraordinary. Her propellers are so much smaller and more delicate than the *Lusitania*'s. The museum's curator invited my husband and me to climb inside the conning tower, which stands just outside the main building. It felt very cramped, con-

U-20 conning tower at the Strandingsmuseum, West Jutland.

Danish women and children standing on the hull of the stranded U-20.

veying the oppressive claustrophia that the U-boatmen must have experienced. Only two, at most three, could have stood here at one time. Marks show where the metal ladder they once climbed ran up the side of the tower. It was eerie standing where Walther Schwieger watched the *Lusitania* through his periscope and where he gave the order to fire.

The curator drove us along the windswept, silvery dunes for which this coastline is so famous and on which so many vessels have foundered. As a watery afternoon sun emerged from behind clouds to glint on the water, he pointed out the spot at which the *U 20* ran aground several hundred yards offshore and where part of the hull still sits. Photographs in the Strandingsmuseum archives show smiling local people who, hearing a U-boat had stranded, eagerly charted trains from neighboring towns to come and see the sight. When Schwieger gave the order for the submarine to be blown up, he and his crew shouted to people to get clear. Curiosity proved stronger than fear. Many only ran into the grassy dunes for sanctuary as pieces of hot metal showered around them. Remarkably, no one was hurt. As photographs show, the wrecked *U-20* remained a local attraction for years for local families who brought picnics to the beach.

⸺⸺

Of all the places my husband and I visited, Cobh, formerly Queenstown, in County Cork, was easily the most evocative. The town looks almost uncannily as it did a century ago. The stucco-fronted buildings are sprucer, some now painted in ice-cream colors, but they are all still there. We stayed at the Queen's Hotel, now renamed the Commodore, from whose roof a welcoming light once shone to show disembarking travelers the way, and whose German owner hid in the cellar the night that dripping and exhausted *Lusitania* survivors were helped inside. Our bedroom, with its deep window seats, overlooked a small esplanade with an ornate bandstand. Beyond was the wide sweep of the harbor. Buoys marked the channel leading out to Roche's Point, from where HMS *Juno* was recalled from her rescue mission to the stricken *Lusitania*. Along the waterfront, the old White Star Line offices, where the *Titanic*'s last passengers waited to be taken out to board her, are now a restaurant. A little farther along are the old Cunard offices. Behind them we found the remains of the wooden pier where the rescue vessels arrived and where the bodies were piled up.

We walked Cobh's unchanged streets with their old gas lampposts past narrow-fronted shops where Norah Bretherton advertised for news of her baby girl, Betty. We climbed the steep Harbour Hill up past St. Colman's Cathedral, whose bells once tolled for the *Lusitania* victims. We followed the exact route of the funeral cortege of Monday, 10 May 1915, out through the town to the old cemetery in the damp, green countryside beyond. The three mass graves, each marked with a slab of stone, are at the far end, next to open country. Birdsong is the only sound. Here and there around the cemetery lie individual graves like that of the young ship's doctor, McDermott.

The pretty nearby town of Kinsale is also little changed, except that many of the fishermen's cottages are now smart restaurants. The slate-hung, open-arched seventeenth-century Court House on Market Square looks much as it did when Coroner Horgan convened his inquest there on 8 May, summoning a traumatized Turner from Queenstown. Out beyond the town, on the steep, ruin-strewn cliffs of the Old Head of Kinsale,

*The memorial to the dead of the Lusitania in Cobh
(formerly Queenstown).*

the lighthouse still flashes its sliver of light over a restless sea. A small, round memorial erected in 1995, on the eightieth anniversary of the tragedy, is inscribed "In memory of the 1198 civilian lives lost on the LUSITANIA." A carving shows a sinking ship and a woman with long, flowing hair, clasping a baby in her arms as she tries to grip a lifeboat. Beside the memorial a tiny shrine containing a white-robed, blue-cloaked Madonna faces out to sea.

From Kinsale, we followed the coastal road south through villages and around numerous bays and inlets. Swans bobbed on the gentle, incoming tide, which once washed corpses ashore. Skirting an estuary, we came to the stone-built lifeboat station of Courtmacsherry. It was from here that the brave and determined crew set out on their marathon journey to row in search of survivors. Today, a high-tech orange-and-blue Trent Class lifeboat lies permanently moored and ready in the estuary. The end point of our journey was Galley Head, the wild green finger of land that was one of Captain Turner's landmarks. Waves were crashing on the beach below with such force that, tens of feet above, the air was filled with flecks of foam, whirling like snowflakes.

Driving back toward Cobh along a more sheltered stretch of coast, we stopped and walked along sand soft as mud. We wanted to understand just a little of what people experienced on 7 May 1915. What would it really have been like to be in the sea for so many hours? It was the same time of year as when the ship went down. The sun was shining just as it had shone that day. The sea looked the same brilliant blue that *Lusitania* survivors recalled. I waded into the water up to my knees. In a very short time, no more than one or two minutes, the numbing coldness became painful. I retreated. It seemed incredible that people like Ian Holbourn, clinging to the side of a lifeboat whose occupants refused to pull him in, managed to survive for so long.

That night, back in Cobh, with the sun setting and the harbor lights beginning to shine across the darkening water, we stood at the feet of the town's memorial to the dead of the *Lusitania*. It was built just a stone's throw from what was once Wesley Frost's office and from where, on the afternoon of 7 May 1915, he had suddenly become aware of frantic activity in the harbor. An angel with tranquil face stands with hands stretched out toward the Irish Sea. An inscription reads *Siochain in Ainm Dé*—"Peace in God's name."

───⊗⊗⊗───

The *Lusitania*
in Facts and Figures

BUILDER: John Brown and Company, Clydebank, Scotland

LAUNCHED: 7 June 1906

MAIDEN VOYAGE: September 1907

LENGTH BETWEEN PERPENDICULARS: 760 feet

LENGTH OVERALL: 785 feet

BEAM (WIDTH): 88 feet

DRAFT: 34 feet

DEPTH: 60 feet

GROSS TONNAGE: 30,395 tons

NET TONNAGE: 12,611 tons

RIG: fore and aft

BOILERS: 25 cylindrical Scotch (23 double-ended, 2 single-ended) in 4 boiler rooms

FURNACES: 192 with total heating surface of 158,350 square feet

STEAM PRESSURE: 195 pounds per square inch

AVERAGE COAL CONSUMPTION: just under 1,000 tons a day

MACHINERY: 4 propeller shafts driven by Parsons steam turbines with a total power output of 68,000 horsepower (the propellers were 3-bladed until 1909, thereafter 4-bladed).

ELECTRICITY GENERATION: 4 generator sets, each of which had a 375-kilowatt capacity and a voltage of 110 to 120

DESIGNED SPEED: 25 knots

HIGHEST SPEED ATTAINED: 25.88 knots

LIFEBOATS: As designed, 16 standard boats
In May 1915, 22 standard and 26 collapsibles

DESIGNED PASSENGER ACCOMMODATION: 1st class 540
2nd class 460
3rd class 1,200
Total 2,200

DESIGNED CREW ACCOMMODATION: 850 (max)

MISCELLANEOUS

LARGEST ROOM: the double-tiered first-class dining room at 85 feet long and 81 feet wide

WEIGHT OF RUDDER: 56 tons with an area of 420 square feet

GALLEY CAPACITY: 10,000 meals a day

NUMBER OF RIVETS USED IN CONSTRUCTION: over 4 million

COOLING WATER CONSUMPTION: 65,000 gallons of water per minute

~∞~

A Technical Account of the Sinking

The British, American, and German conspiracies that followed the destruction of the *Lusitania* had one thing in common. No one in any of the three countries was sure what had caused the second explosion; no one understood why the ship had sunk so quickly. The British and Americans feared a connection with munitions. The Germans insisted that there was one and even commissioned their own forensic analysis as their laboratory report reveals. But no one knew for certain. Succeeding years have brought all kinds of theories—some more plausible than others, some highly technical, some sensation-seeking—but none entirely convincing. They have concentrated on the causes of the second explosion, rather than considering the full sequence of events and, in particular, the devastating effect of Walther Schwieger's single torpedo on a ship ill designed to resist such a weapon.

Having observed the *Lusitania*'s approach from the horizon, Schwieger submerged and maneuvered the *U-20* into an optimal attack position at right angles to the almost 800-feet-long *Lusitania*. The *U-20* then launched one G-6-type torpedo at a distance of 2,300 feet with a shallow setting so that it would travel at a depth of ten feet beneath the surface of the water. The submarine torpedo was twenty-one inches in diameter, twenty feet long, weighed over 3,000 pounds, and contained 350 pounds of a TNT-like explosive. The speed setting for such torpedoes was thirty-eight knots, and so, relative to the liner steaming at eighteen knots, the minimum approach speed of the torpedo toward the *Lusitania* was forty-two knots (or nearly fifty miles per hour). Thus the *U-20* had launched a torpedo longer and heavier than an automobile, with a diameter similar to that of a steering wheel, at a distance of just under three times the length of the *Lusitania*.

Schwieger made some errors in his firing calculations, including overestimating the *Lusitania*'s speed by four knots. However, the torpedo hit her starboard side 160 to 180 feet aft of the bow, roughly below or just after the bridge. The torpedo's twin-detonator system had armed itself during the approach by using the passage through the water to unscrew a propellerlike safety cap on its nose. The run time of the torpedo from launch to impact was just over thirty-five seconds, and in that time the *Lusitania* would have traveled nearly one and a half times her own length. If Schwieger had launched the torpedo either five seconds earlier or twenty seconds later, he would have missed his target altogether.

Witnesses on the deck of the *Lusitania* saw the bubble wake produced by the steam exhaust from the torpedo's propulsion system approach the ship diagonally, an illusion created by the weapon traveling toward the liner at right angles to her forward motion. When the torpedo hit, there was a heavy muffled explosion and extensive vibration. A plume of seawater rose above the height of the ship's bridge, some sixty feet above the waterline. The plume and the associated blast were so powerful that they damaged weak parts of the superstructure, showered the decks with debris, and blew one of the thirty-foot lifeboats, No. 5, the third from the bows on the starboard side, from its davits into the sea.

The size of the plume confirms the shallowness of the torpedo's run since much of the energy of its explosion was dissipated into the air. Despite this waste of energy, the damage inflicted by the explosion was considerable because the surrounding water concentrated the majority of the energy generated in the direction of the relatively pliant hull of the ship. Based on damage observed on other ships, a conservative estimate of the size of the hole punched into the side of the *Lusitania* would be at least twenty feet long and ten feet high. In addition, the damage would have penetrated at least ten feet into the structure of the ship.

The consequences would not have been confined to the puncture area alone. The hull of the *Lusitania* had been laid down using a series of overlapping plates, usually one inch thick by five feet wide and thirty-two feet long, which were riveted together. The explosion would have loosened or popped rivets surrounding the hole over an area more than fifteen times greater than that of the blast hole. Thus the total area that the torpedo opened up immediately, either completely or partially, to the surrounding seawater was over 5,000 square feet.

Many witnesses described how, when the *Lusitania* was hit, she trembled violently. The *Lusitania* had always suffered vibration. Her second-class accommodation had had to be gutted after her sea trials to allow stiffening of her structure. In 1909 she suffered further vibration damage. This was so severe that she had to be dry-docked for repairs. Although attempts were again made to improve her resistance to vibration, she remained prone to such problems. Therefore it is not surprising that when she was hit by the torpedo and yawed abruptly to starboard, the whole ship shuddered violently. This violent shuddering was structural vibration, which led to substantial further weakening and popping of the riveted plate hull around the area originally damaged by the torpedo. It is difficult to quantify the extent of the hull damage caused by the vibration. However, it was probably equivalent to that produced by the initial explosion, so that up to 10,000 square feet of the starboard side of the ship had been exposed to seawater to some degree.

The most important factor in the damage a torpedo causes is the point at which it hits. At the forward end of boiler room one, at or just in front of the point of impact inside the hull, was a major transverse bulkhead. This bulkhead was a vertical wall of steel plate, designed to be watertight, which braced the two sides of the ship with the keel to a height of about ten feet above the low-waterline. A similar bulkhead, nearly thirty-five feet farther forward, created a cross-bunker where coal destined for boiler room one was stored.

Forward of the bulkhead beyond the cross-bunker were storage areas for baggage and cargo. Above the cross-bunker, inboard of the Orlop Deck access way, was a refrigeration plant used to chill perishables. Access to all these cargo areas was via the number-two cargo hatch located on the Main Deck, some thirty feet in front of the bridge.

Immediately behind the bulkhead that separated the cross-bunker from boiler room one were two single-ended Scotch boilers followed twenty feet farther aft by two double boilers. Stokers used the gangway between these facing pairs of boilers to fuel them. Two vertical vents above the stoking gangway against either side of the ship rose from boiler level through all the decks to exhaust above the Navigation Deck on top of the ship. These pairs of boilers were positioned symmetrically about the centerline of the ship, as were those in the other boiler rooms running back to the stern.

Between the boiler rooms and the hull, along the length of the ship ran the longitudinal coal bunkers, which were similar to those in the British cruisers *Aboukir*, *Hogue*, and *Cressy* sunk by the *U-9* in September 1914.

Significantly, there was another longitudinal access way—the Lower Orlop Deck—below the Orlop Deck. This ran along the outer hull and over the longitudinal wing bunkers on both sides of the boiler and engine rooms for most of the length of the ship. The floor between the Orlop and Lower Orlop Decks was approximately ten feet below the waterline, hence on a level with the strike of the torpedo. Thus the water would have immediately gained access not only to the longitudinal and cross-bunkers but also to both Orlop Decks.

The conclusions of a British Institution of Naval Architects committee, created during the First World War to investigate the structures of merchant ships subjected to torpedo and sea-mine explosions, are highly relevant when visualizing the effects of the impact and detonation of the torpedo. Having examined the voluminous evidence, the committee concluded in early 1918 that, in comparison with large cargo vessels, the hatchways in large passenger ships were small and so did not permit "instantaneous relief" from any air and gas pressure created by an explosion. Therefore the bulkheads near any explosion were more likely to be damaged in passenger liners than in cargo ships. Watertight doors in these bulkheads could not be relied upon to close, and hence seal, after an explosion due to both the resultant bulkhead distortion and collateral damage to the bridge-activated electrical and hydraulic systems that operated the doors.

In essence, the safety features in passenger liners, designed to prevent water reaching undamaged parts of the ship after a collision, did not work after a major explosion. Hence large passenger ships suffered considerably more damage from the impact of the same amount of explosive in similar circumstances than cargo ships. The committee's conclusion is borne out by the speed of sinking of such ships. The White Star liner *Arabic* of some 16,000 tons went down in nine minutes when torpedoed off the Irish coast just three months after the *Lusitania* was sunk. Because she was outward-bound for the United States from Liverpool, she would not have been carrying any explosives.

The speed of sinking of the cruiser *Aboukir*, which capsized and sank only twenty-five minutes after being hit by a single torpedo, demonstrates that ships with longitudinal bulkheads were also particularly vulnerable. Vice Admiral Coke recognized this shortcoming when recalling the cruiser's sister ship the *Juno* from her rescue mission to the *Lusitania* on 7 May.

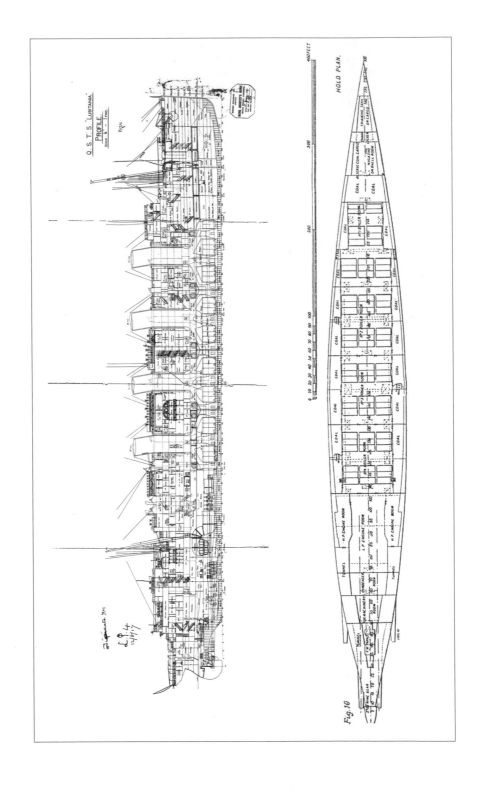

Q.S.T.S. "LUSITANIA"
PROFILE
Scale ½ = 1 Foot

HOLD PLAN.

Fig. 10

Stokers feeding coal into the Lusitania's *massive boilers.*

In the case of the *Lusitania*, the inability to seal off damaged sections of the ship, allied to the huge area of the hull, which had lost its structural integrity, meant that nothing prevented the free flow of seawater between and around the damaged compartments. Many of these abutted on open, capacious sections of the ship (such as longitudinal bunkers, access ways, and boiler rooms). The forced flooding of some, if not all, of these sections immediately after the explosion—created by the pressure generated by the ship's passage through the water at eighteen knots—explains the rapid list reported by all eyewitnesses. The speed with which water entered is illustrated by the fact that only one crew member in boiler room number two survived—he escaped through a ventilator shaft—and that the most forward bulkhead of this boiler room was some 80 to 100 feet from the torpedo impact. While making his escape from boiler room number two, the crewman saw water pouring into that boiler room from the starboard longitudinal bunker. This suggests strongly that the Orlop and Lower Orlop Decks immediately above were also flooding by that time.

As the committee's report suggested, the general layout of the *Lusitania* inboard of the impact position did not allow explosive pressure to be relieved rapidly. Accordingly, the pressure wave generated by the torpedo detonation would have torn into the ship, creating the major structural damage and distortions that disabled the safety features. In doing so, the pressure wave would have taken "the path of least resistance" in order to disperse its energy.

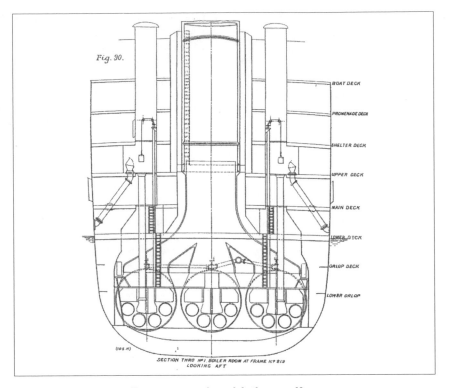

Transverse view through boiler room No. 1.

After the blast had caused extensive damage in and around the two Orlop Decks, the bulkhead of the number-one boiler room, and surrounding equipment, the confines of the ship's hull channeled the blast upward through the decks immediately above, outward throughout the closely packed nearby companionways and central stairwells, and also through weaker structures such as partitions and vent walls.

The electrical power failure, which plunged much of the ship into darkness almost immediately after the torpedo exploded, and the loss of hydraulic power exacerbated difficulties in coping with the flooding and with disabled safety systems. For example, the longitudinal, or wing, coal bunkers should have been isolated from the boiler rooms by sliding watertight doors. However, these hatches could have proved difficult, if not impossible, to close manually in the dark. In any case, such was the speed of the flooding that the stokers had no time to act before being overwhelmed or fleeing for their lives.

The *Lusitania*'s hull, with its one-inch-thick riveted steel plates, was designed to be strong enough to withstand only the pressure of the outside water, just as an aircraft fuselage is designed to confine internal air pressure, and not internal explosions. The liner's overall rigidity and resistance to bending was provided by the internal honeycomb of decks, stringers, and the main bulkheads that defined the major compartments of the vessel.

Appendix B

The relative weakness of the hull meant that the damage from the torpedo impact significantly changed the overall structural loadings on the hull and bulkheads, thus compounding the damage. In addition to the damage to the plates of the hull caused by structural vibration, the entry of seawater into the liner had its own effect on the structure. On the very conservative assumption that the flow rate of seawater into the ship through the hole created by the torpedo explosion was only 10 percent of the potential, the liner would have been shipping well over 800 tons of seawater per minute when traveling at a speed of eighteen knots. Some researchers have suggested that the parent steel from which the *Lusitania*'s plates were manufactured could have been gradually embrittled and thus become less shock- or impact-resistant over time. If so, then any damage from the torpedo explosion and consequent events would have propagated throughout the hull even more rapidly and hastened her sinking by increasing the rate of water flow.

Additionally, there is clear evidence from witnesses that, contrary to Captain Turner's orders, many portholes were open, some close to the waterline. According to expert evidence at the Mayer hearings, each open eighteen-inch diameter porthole submerged to a depth of three feet would let in three and three-quarter tons of water a minute. This is also a very conservative estimate. There were 500 portholes on each side of the ship. Assuming that only 20 percent were open, by the time half of those open were submerged the ship would have been letting in 375 tons of water per minute from this source, or about 1,200 tons per minute in total. Also, because of the list, the open portholes on the starboard side would have gone below the water more quickly than those on the port side, increasing the water flow on the starboard side and hence the list.

As the *Lusitania* sank, water levels against bulkheads would have built up and so would the hydrostatic pressure created by the seawater's own weight. Distortion and then buckling of these bulkheads under such strain would produce characteristic sounds of groaning, creaking, and cracking. Final catastrophic failure would sound like an explosion. If a large amount of pressure and hence water volume were released, the explosive failure would be accompanied by a rumbling sound similar to a large waterfall. Oliver Bernard's recollection of "a sullen rumble in the bowels of the liner" was very likely the sound of such a failure.

Water entering the ship toward the bow changed the balance of the *Lusitania*. A starboard list allied to the bow-down position altered her buoyancy-loading in such a way that the stern of the ship attempted to lift and rotate, as described by Margaret Mackworth and by Wesley Frost in his book based on survivors' accounts. Twisting and bending pressures increased the rate of failure of the plate joints and the popping of rivets. (Bob Ballard and his team proved that a major section of the stern of the *Titanic* split from the main hull in a comparable manner as she sank nose first.) Such a gradual reduction in the overall stiffness of the vessel's hull transferred further loading to the internal structures such as bulkheads and so hastened their failures.

Whether on the surface, or during the reported pivoting of the liner's prow on the seabed immediately prior to her sinking, the *Lusitania*'s hull was subjected to forces that far exceeded her strength. Using the hole created by the torpedo explosion as a precursor, the mechanisms for hull failure discussed here probably tore open a major section of the starboard side of the ship toward the bow. This allowed both water in and coal and cargo out. It would go some way toward explaining why significant amounts of coal were found on the seabed and much of the liner's consignment of furs was washed ashore.

In short, the *Lusitania* sank because, as fate would have it, a single torpedo found her most vulnerable spot. An explosion at or near the main bulkhead between boiler room number one and its cross-bunker storage area, at a level that allowed seawater access to the Orlop and Lower Orlop Decks and the longitudinal coal bunkers, was one of the very few events that could have damaged the *Lusitania*'s structural integrity so severely. Secondary effects from both the explosion and structural vibration substantially increased damage to the plates of the hull and the area open to seawater. Loss of electrical power and light, and of steam for hydraulic power and propulsion, severely reduced the chances of remedial or delaying action. The ship could not be steered. Nor could her engines be reversed to slow her forward momentum through the water. The collateral damage caused by the explosion to the ship's safety systems prevented the closure of watertight doors and thus allowed additional large volumes of seawater to pass rapidly into and through major sections of the liner, impelled by both hydrostatic pressure and the velocity of the liner through the sea.

Regardless of whether a second explosion occurred, the catastrophic level of hull damage was clearly the principal cause of the rapid sinking of the *Lusitania*. Even without a second explosion, the ship could not have remained afloat more than a minute or two longer than she did.

Yet it is the second explosion that has so fascinated and preoccupied researchers. Undoubtedly there was one; there were probably several more. The varied evidence of its location, timing, and nature is the seed from which many controversial theories have grown. One of the most frequently advanced is that some of the munitions declared on the supplementary manifest exploded. Among these were some 1,250 boxes, each containing four 3.3-inch shrapnel shells. When fully assembled, these antipersonnel weapons had two separate sections comparable to a bullet. The front section comprised the shrapnel, the airburst delivery charge, and the timing fuse. The second stage was the propellant cartridge, which would detonate and then accelerate the shrapnel stage along and out of the gun barrel.

According to the Mayer evidence, the shells carried by the *Lusitania* contained no powder, propellant charge, or fuse. These would have been fitted later in Britain. As shown earlier, these shells were almost certainly as specified in the manifest. However, even if they had contained their powder and propellant charge, they would have remained inert since shells were never fused during transport for obvious safety reasons. Also, the shells' robust design allowed them to withstand the enormous shock loadings associated with being fired from a gun barrel. Thus the combination of shock, explosion, and flame from the torpedo impact is highly unlikely to have caused filled but unfused shells to explode.

The consignment of arms included over 4 million complete live rounds of .303 rifle ammunition; these contained powdered charge in the propellant cartridge section. In theory they had the potential to cause fire or explosion, but safe transport of this and similar ammunition was routine over many decades. Therefore the question of safety had been investigated through extensive practical testing by both the manufacturers and the military. These comprehensive tests, as reported to the Mayer hearings, included exposure to severe shock and direct flame or fire. The results showed to the satisfaction of the U.S. authorities that these types of live rounds would not explode en masse but would smolder or burn harmlessly. This led the U.S. authorities in 1911 to clear such ammunition for transport on passenger liners as "nonexplosive in bulk."

More recent U.S. military experience suggests that heat applied to an unboxed and exposed pile of similar ammunition would only cause it to "cook off"—in other words, the cartridge case would rupture with little or no expulsion of the projectile. Cartridges adjacent to the ruptured one would not explode sympathetically but would instead be tossed aside by the burst. An opinion given by the U.S. military in 1973 was that any explosion would be similar to that of Chinese firecrackers. Another anecdote from a senior U.S. Navy munitions officer in 1972 provides further evidence: "A [railway] boxcar full of 7.62-millimeter open round (0.3 inch) ammunition caught fire and was about half-consumed. Much of the ammo cooked off but none of the bullets penetrated the metal boxes in which they were packed. Each box when opened afterwards contained nothing but scrap. The boxes weren't even bulged."

The only types of explosive that would detonate sympathetically (for example, through concussive effects) would be unstable substances such as nitroglycerine and, perhaps, gun cotton. Despite rumors, these have never been shown to be aboard. Had they been present in any quantity, the explosion would have been immense and obvious, probably blowing off the bows of the ship, as suggested by the *Scientific American* some three weeks after the loss of the *Lusitania*. The journal dismissed as "absurd" the exploding-munitions theory and suggested that structural damage from the torpedo explosion was the primary cause of sinking. The conclusive evidence against exploding munitions is that provided by Bob Ballard's thorough survey of the wreck. This survey showed no evidence of any damage to either side of the hull caused by an explosion in the areas in the bows where the munitions were stored.

⸎

It has also been suggested that aluminum powder might account for the second explosion. The *Lusitania*'s supplementary manifest included significant quantities of aluminum powder destined for the explosives manufacturing section of the Woolwich Arsenal on the River Thames near London. Aluminum powder is highly volatile and can ignite spontaneously in air. It burns fiercely when exposed to moisture, producing highly flammable hydrogen gas. When distributed in air to create a uniform cloud, aluminum powder can be ignited by static electricity, a friction spark, or a naked flame to produce a violent explosion.

Although we have no details of the barrels and cases in which the aluminum powder was stored, the latent danger of this material was well-known in 1915. Thus the robustness of their transport containers would have matched the danger. Storage containers could only have been breached by a sharp point being driven into them with great force. Although several compartments separated the area where they were stowed from the point where the torpedo hit, it is conceivable that debris like shrapnel did, indeed, damage some containers, allowing powder to escape or air or water to enter.

Normally, burning hydrogen alone, such as that released from a chemical reaction between water and aluminum powder, is not visible. Aluminum powder itself burns so brightly, rapidly, and hence so fiercely that it is used in filmmaking as a special effect to simulate lightning. Thus a fierce and lightning-bright flame is the signature of burning aluminum powder. The only way these flames can show another color is through a "parasitic" effect from the glow of other flames—from, say, a burning wooden transport box—when they would seem bright orange. However, witnesses reported no intense flames of any color.

Particulate explosions, such as in aluminum powder and coal, require a roughly uniform distribution of the powder in the air, akin to an aerosol. This allows an explosive reaction or "flame-front" to propagate efficiently throughout a volume of powder and air. If the mixture is too dense or too lean, it will not explode. The likelihood that these ideal conditions were present aboard the *Lusitania* is very remote. Also, despite its location directly in front and in full view of the wheelhouse and main forward passenger observation room, no one reported the explosive destruction of the number-two cargo hatch, which any significant blast would have caused. This, plus the Ballard evidence that the bow is relatively undamaged in the cargo areas, means that a significant aluminum powder explosion or fire is unlikely. The fact that only a few men, including Boatswain's Mate Sikking and Able Seaman Frederick O'Neil, escaped from the baggage room is explained not by the explosion but by the fact that the only access to it was by the elevator that was quickly disabled by power failure. Had there been an immediate explosion in the cargo area, none would have survived.

—∞∞∞—

Another theory is that there was a coal-dust explosion. The fuel used to generate heat and hence steam for the *Lusitania*'s turbines was, of course, coal. Her fuel consumption averaged a little less than 1,000 tons a day. The coal was stored in the longitudinal and cross-bunkers, allowing easy access from the main boiler rooms. These bunkers held a total of about 6,000 tons of coal, but well into the final day of her voyage only some 1,000 tons would have remained, spread proportionately through each of the bunkers so as to preserve the balance of loading and hence the ship's "trim." The trim aimed to ensure the most fuel-efficient and stable passage through the water possible. With proportionate usage of coal from each bunker, the bunkers around boiler room number one would have contained at least 80 percent air. The loading of the coal and the subsequent shoveling of it would have generated coal dust and fine debris.

When the torpedo hit close to the corner of the cross-bunker and the wing bunker of boiler room one, the shock from the torpedo's detonation and the whip response from the ship could, theoretically, have shaken the dust and debris into the air. Coal, like many types of dust, including not only aluminum powder but also other everyday substances like flour and sawdust, can ignite if subjected to a spark or flame while in a uniform mixture with air. The torpedo impact and explosion would have created the necessary ignition sources.

However, "ideal conditions" for an explosion were unlikely. The bunkers were not insulated and were separated from the cold sea by only the hull plating. Seepage of seawater into the hull of any vessel was an inherent problem. Moisture migrated to the lowest parts of the ship to produce pools of bilge water. Also, all air contains some water. The moist air from the *Lusitania*'s boiler rooms would have penetrated the very much cooler bunkers and condensed against the cold hull to produce a film of condensation, if not further pools of water, in those compartments. Even if we ignore the almost instantaneous spray of seawater that accompanied the rapid flooding of the bunkers after the torpedo detonated, the coal dust would almost certainly not have ignited. The dampness of the compartments would have prevented the dust from being shaken uniformly into the air to create an explosive aerosol.

⸎

Reliable witness reports of dense, moist steam accompanying the second explosion and enveloping the decks suggest strongly that some part of the liner's power plant was involved. None of the other postulated causes produces steam. Similarly, the second explosion was reported as loudest by those on the decks, supporting the theory that it occurred in a boiler room where sound could be carried to the decks via the funnels and vents.

The torpedo struck the hull toward the forward end of the number-one boiler room, which contained five double- and two single-ended fire-tube boilers. Each single boiler had a diameter of over seventeen feet and a length of eleven feet, while the double-ended boilers were twenty-two feet long. Within the lower half of each single boiler were four furnaces, which extended through the length of the boiler and were each about two feet in diameter. Stokers shoveled in coal through furnace doors at the front of the boiler. The hot gases generated in the furnaces by the burning coal passed to the back into a combustion chamber. Thence the gases were distributed through several hundred fire tubes running the length of the boiler above the furnaces. Finally, they were exhausted through boiler uptakes to the funnel. The complete boiler structure was held together by rivets, and the pressure integrity was achieved by caulking and machining of joints to tight tolerances.

The heat of the gas produced in the furnaces was well over 2,000° F (1,100° C). Only the pressurized water in the boiler surrounding the furnaces and tubes prevented them from melting. The boiler was designed to operate at a pressure of around 200 pounds per square inch and at about 400° F (200° C). Pressurized water at 400° F (200° C) has the capability to cool the steel tubes and furnaces sufficiently. However, since steam has far less capacity than water to absorb and transport heat energy, if the water changed to steam at a similar temperature, the cooling effect would reduce dramatically and the tubes would quickly overheat. The tubes would then melt and burst inward, allowing pressurized steam and water to reduce to atmospheric pressure within the furnace and fire tubes. In this process the high-pressure, high-temperature water would expand almost instantaneously and explosively to about 1,500 times its initial volume and escape by blowing off the end of the boilers.

During the nineteenth century this type of boiler explosion in coal-fired, fire-tube boilers was very common. Loss of water level was nearly always the cause. Any rapid drop led to an explosion since it was physically impossible to prevent the hot gases from passing through the furnaces and fire tubes. Only shutting down the furnaces' forced-draft ventilation fans and then raking out the burning coals from the furnaces by hand could halt the production of combustion gases. Such raking could not easily be done rapidly, especially in an emergency.

Appendix B

The *Lusitania*'s number-one boiler room suffered structural damage when the torpedo exploded. If this damage extended to the feedwater system or to a boiler, one or more boilers would have suffered rapid water loss and exploded. (In modern naval engineering, all primary systems—like boiler feedwater—are fitted well clear of the hull of the ship to avoid their being damaged by a torpedo exploding against the hull.)

If one of the single-ended boilers had exploded as a result of water loss, the amount of energy released to create physical damage would have been equivalent to around 480 pounds of high explosive such as TNT. (A double-ended boiler could release twice this energy.) The steam generated in a boiler explosion had on land been known to blow boilers almost 100 feet, or through brick walls, such was its latent energy. When the steam was released into an enclosed space such as a ship's boiler room, there was the added danger of pressurizing the space. Even a small rise in pressure would have caused substantial damage to an area not designed to withstand it, resulting in buckled plates and decks. Therefore, any energy generated by boiler explosions would have added considerably to the damage caused to the liner's hull.

The steam released explosively would also attempt to escape the confining space. In the boiler room the escape routes were restricted to the funnel, the forced draft fans, and the air vents. The boiler would almost certainly shear its connection to the funnel, leaving a route to the atmosphere, but the damage caused to the funnel would probably restrict flow through it. Similarly the forced-draft connection to the furnace would be likely to be sheared and badly damaged. The only other route the steam could take would be through the standard ventilation shafts from the boiler room. These vents were not connected to the boiler and would suffer less or little immediate damage from an explosion, thus offering a relatively direct route for the steam to escape.

The consequences of a boiler explosion would have been massive shocks throughout the liner, with steam and smoke blown through the vents and funnels. Smoke would have been carried with the steam due to the furnace coals being ejected as the boiler exploded. Hence the air on deck would have been filled with a dense vapor mixture, which would have made it difficult for any passenger to breathe. This chimes well with many witness reports. However, the main argument against boiler failure as the cause of the second explosion is that there were survivors from both boiler rooms number one (Madden and Davis) and number two (McDermott). This outcome would have been unlikely if there had been immediate boiler explosions. Certainly the survivors reported none before they escaped. If a boiler was the cause of the second explosion, the explosion could not have taken place until at least a minute or two after the torpedo hit. As the ship sank, there were undoubtedly boiler explosions, which accounted for the expulsion from the funnels of survivors such as Margaret Gwyer after they had been sucked in as the ship went under.

⸺⸺

The final theory as to the cause of the second explosion is the failure of the steam lines, which carried high-pressure superheated steam from the boilers to the turbines. The steam generated by each boiler was transferred by branch piping to a main steam line at roof level of the boiler room. (The steam lines were at the level of the boiler room nearest to the torpedo explosion.) The main steam line then carried the steam from each boiler room along much of the length of the ship through the bulkheads to the distribution manifold in the turbine room. From this manifold steam was supplied directly to the high-pressure turbines and thereafter reduced in pressure to the low-pressure turbine system.

The steam line and its branches were made up of sections of pipe connected by flanges welded to their ends. At each bulkhead specialized couplings allowed for expansion or contraction of the pipes between the ship's ambient temperature and 400° F (200° C) during operation. Because of these differences in temperature, the pipes could expand over the length of boiler room number one alone by nearly two inches. This may appear insignificant. However, these twelve-inch or larger pipes were confining forces approaching 400 tons. Their couplings could only withstand the mechanical loadings associated with normal operation such as changes in temperature and flexing caused by steam-pump vibration.

A survivor from boiler room number one stated that "the bang seemed to come from the after end on the starboard side of the number one boiler." The first potential cause of a steam explosion is the shock vibrations created when the torpedo detonated close to this boiler. They would have severely shaken both boiler and steam line. The shock would certainly have damaged some, if not all, of the steam line connections in that area. The failures probably resulted in the explosive release of high-pressure, superheated steam produced by boiler number one and considerable back-pressure steam from other boilers in that boiler room and beyond. Almost on top of boiler number one was the vertical vent to the upper decks, probably already punctured or otherwise damaged, and so this is the likely path whereby steam reached passengers on various decks and also became a cloud visible over the top of the liner.

Alternatively, if cold seawater sprayed into the area, drenching an exposed steam line, the thermal shock produced would have caused the pipe to contract almost immediately, causing joint and connection failures and the explosive release of steam.

Some researchers have proposed a third mode of steam line failure: thermal shock allied to a catastrophic condensation of the steam back into water. If steam is cooled suddenly, its volume collapses by a ratio of more than 1,000 as it changes back to water. This reduction in volume would have created a near vacuum in the feed pipe. More important, it would have created a "slug" or "slugs" of water in the pipe traveling at high speed. The enormous energy of these slugs would again have caused the pipework to fail catastrophically, producing the effects described previously.

However caused, steam-line explosions are easily the most likely source of the second explosion. Captain Turner certainly believed one occurred. In his evidence to the Mayer hearings he said, "The torpedo burst the steampipe and put the engines out of commission."

Nevertheless, both the diverse eyewitness reports from different positions on the ship about the timing, location, nature, and sound of the second explosion and the technical analysis of potential structural and steam-plant failures mean that there was probably more than one "second explosion." The *Lusitania* experienced a series of structural shocks: hull breach, torpedo detonation, collateral structural damage, shock and motion-induced vibration, secondary hull-plate and joint failures, and steam-line explosions, culminating in boiler explosions as she sank. Each produced noises of different types.

But the truth is that the *Lusitania* sank so quickly because she was not designed to withstand a torpedo hitting her in such a vital spot as did that fired by the *U-20*. On 7 May 1915, her captain, Walther Schwieger, had mounted the perfect attack.

ACKNOWLEDGMENTS

The story of the *Lusitania* is one of many people of many nationalities caught in a sweep of extraordinary events. I am grateful to my husband, Michael, my partner in writing as in life, for the idea of telling that story and for his work on all aspects of the project. Not least he suggested that, as part of the research, I stand, for just a few minutes, in a numbingly cold May sea near Cobh to experience what it must have been like for the *Lusitania*'s passengers and crew on 7 May 1915.

I am indebted to several individuals and organizations in the United Kingdom for their help and expertise, in particular Dr. Mike Wood for his analysis of the causes and effects of the explosions on board the *Lusitania*; Donald Wallace, F.R.C.S., and Dr. Ingrid Wallace for advice on the physiological effects of hypothermia; Peter Allmond of the Bodleian Library, who traced a number of rare books; and Adrian Allan of Liverpool University, who helped us find our way through the Cunard archives and guided us to other sources of information. I am also grateful to the staff and archivists of the British Library, the London Library, Churchill College, Cambridge, the National Maritime Museum, the Merseyside Maritime Museum, the Public Record Office, and the BBC Written Archives Centre. I must also thank Iain MacKenzie of the Historian's Office of the Ministry of Defence for help with declassification of official files and access to new documents; Simon Baker of the British Film Institute for information about *The Carpet from Bagdad*; Mark Jones, who recently dived on the wreck; and Audrey Lawson-Johnson, survivor of the *Lusitania*.

In the United States I am grateful to Ronald Bulatoff of the Hoover Institution, Stanford University, for guiding us through the extensive Bailey-Ryan archive; to Mary Hoehling, who generously pointed me to the material that she and her husband had deposited with the Mariners' Museum, Newport News, Virginia, whose archivist, Heather Friedle, was extremely helpful; to Lily Bardi-Ullmann, who tracked down out-of-print books, researched unstintingly through archives in New York, and translated key German documents; and to Professor John Hattendorf of the Naval War College, Newport, Rhode Island, for his help in tracing documents.

In Germany I would like to thank Frau Zandeck of the Militärarchiv, Freiburg, for helping uncover new material in the German naval files and Frau Annelott Weisbach-Zerning, widow of the *U-20*'s torpedo officer, Raimund Weisbach, for her recollections. I am particularly grateful to Holger Nehring of Tübingen and Oxford Universities for his extensive research in the German archives and into the history of Charles Voegele in Strasbourg, and to the Traditionsarchiv Unterseeboote, Cuxhaven, for making material available to him.

In Canada I must thank the CBC, and, in particular, Ken Puley for allowing me access to its taped interviews with *Lusitania* survivors and with *U-20* radio officer Otto Rikowsky. I am also grateful to *Lusitania* survivor Desmond Cox for his insights into the experiences of his mother, Margaret Cox.

In Ireland the generous help of Dr. John de Courcy Ireland, Paddy O'Sullivan, Dr. Alicia St. Leger, Dr. Philip Smyly of the National Maritime Museum, and Heather Bird of the Cobh Museum made our research enjoyable as well as interesting. Kathryn Ward of the Department of Arts, Heritage, Gaeltacht, and the Islands in Dublin was very helpful in explaining the Irish government's current position on the status of the *Lusitania* wreck. Guy Westbrook of the Irish Marine Institute kindly supplied data on sea temperatures in May 1915.

In Denmark I must thank Morten Sylvester, curator of the Strandingsmuseum, Thorsminde, for showing us the surviving portions of the *U-20* and for taking us to the dunes where, in 1916, she ran aground.

Friends and family have, as always, been generous. In particular I want to thank St. John Brown, Clinton Leeks, Kim Lewison, Neil Munro, and Robert Scoble for comments on the text and for historical insights, Eric Hollis for the loan of books, Fred Prior for help at the planning stage, and my mother and parents-in-law for their encouragement.

The help and advice of my agent, Bill Hamilton, have been invaluable. I am very grateful to George Gibson and his team at Walker & Company, New York, especially my editor Chris Carduff, and in the United Kingdom, to my editors Alison Tulett and Sarah Westcott and the team at Transworld.

Archive material on events surrounding the *Lusitania* incident is prolific. It may therefore be helpful to indicate briefly those sources that provided new information and fresh insights.

The mass of material in German archives, which has not previously been comprehensively trawled, was particularly valuable. For example, the war diaries of U-boats other than the *U 20*, which show that additional submarines were hunting the *Lusitania*; the forensic analysis of the causes of the *Lusitania*'s rapid sinking commissioned by the German authorities; the evidence of friction and disregard of orders within the U-boat service; the German government's private recognition that the *Lusitania* was not an auxiliary cruiser and that she was unarmed.

In the United States, previously unconsulted files in the National Archives and Records Administration provide a comprehensive picture of the German spy network in America. They show the extent of the penetration of New York's docks and the efforts made by German agents after the sinking to discover whether the *Lusitania* had been carrying hazardous substances like bronze powder which could have hastened her sinking.

In the United Kingdom, the surviving archives of Room 40 are revealing. They enable comparison to be made between the information culled by the British authorities from intercepted German messages and their actions and statements. For example, they prove that the British government knew that Neal Leach was a German agent and, shortly after the sinking, that the *Lusitania* had been hit by only one torpedo despite its public claims that the ship had been hit by two or perhaps more. New information about the experiences of passengers on board the liner was also helpful. For example, the Prichard collection recently purchased by the Imperial War Museum shows how Oliver Bernard was prevented from giving "inconvenient" evidence to Lord Mersey.

I was also fortunate that some previous writers had generously placed their material in archives, for example, the Bailey-Ryan collection in the Hoover Institution, Stanford University, and the Hoehling collection at the Mariners' Museum, Newport News, or, in the case of Paddy O'Sullivan, kindly made some of their recent research available to me.

Less helpful was the response of the British Secret Service, which I approached for information about the work of British intelligence in penetrating German spy rings in 1915. It declined to offer any details on the grounds that "despite the passage of time" its methods of operation were "still extant."

Notes and Sources

To help simplify the notes, I used the following abbreviations and designations to identify some of the main sources:

Archives

- **BBC.** Interview transcripts in the production files for two programs—"Fifty Fathoms Deep" and "Who Sank the Lusitania?"—which contain much unused material, and a file about salvage operations between 1932 and 1937, The British Broadcasting Corporation's Written Archives Centre, Caversham Park, U.K.

- **CBC.** Lengthy taped interviews (around eight hours in total) with *Lusitania* survivors and a member of the *U-20*'s crew recorded by the Canadian Broadcasting Corporation for its program "Rendezvous with Death," broadcast in 1965.

- **Cunard archives.** The archives of the Cunard Steamship Company, Liverpool University, Liverpool, U.K.

- **German Military Archive, Freiburg.** The Bundesarchiv-Militärarchiv, Freiburg, Germany, which holds the German naval files for the period.

- **Hoover Institution.** The Hoover Institution on War, Revolution, and Peace, Stanford University, Stanford, Calif., U.S., which houses the extensive papers collected by Thomas A. Bailey and Paul B. Ryan for their analysis *The Lusitania Disaster*.

- **Imperial War Museum.** The archives of the Imperial War Museum in London, whose holdings on the *Lusitania* include a large collection of correspondence with survivors (the Prichard collection) recently acquired at auction and transcripts of the Kinsale inquest (Special Miscellaneous Collection V5).

- **Mariners' Museum, Newport News.** The Mariners' Museum, Newport News, Va., U.S., which holds a collection of letters from *Lusitania* survivors and their relations collected in the 1950s by A. A. Hoehling and M. Hoehling for their book *The Last Voyage of the Lusitania*.

- **NARA.** National Archives and Records Administration, Maryland and New York, U.S., which holds many of the key political documents for the period, papers describing the German spy rings in America and the statements of American survivors given to Consul Frost. Unless otherwise specified, material quoted is from microfilms M 580 197, M 580 198, and M 973 187.

- **PRO.** The Public Record Office, Kew, U.K. Individual file numbers are given in each case. The prefixes *ADM*, *FO*, and *DT* denote respectively the Admiralty, foreign office, and Department of Trade.

Specific Documents

- **Mayer (O).** Opinion of Judge Mayer
- **Mayer (T).** Transcript of Mayer Limit of Liability Hearings
- **Mersey (R).** Report of Mersey inquiry
- **Mersey (TO).** Transcripts of open sessions of Mersey inquiry
- **Mersey (TC).** Transcripts of closed sessions of Mersey inquiry

- **Wynne (T).** Transcripts of evidence given before Commissioner Wynne in London for the Mayer Limit of Liability Hearings in New York
- **War Diary of the *U-20*.** The daily diary kept by Walther Schwieger, commander of the *U-20*. All quotes for the voyage of April–May 1915 are from the version on file in the German Military Archive, Freiburg. My English translation is based on that in the Hoover Institution, with some modifications.

———

Because this book is for the general reader, I have not given sources for each individual quote from passengers and crew of the *Lusitania* and others except where it is unclear who is speaking or where the quote is significant for understanding what happened. However, the main sources for those whose words are not always referenced are given below. Full details of the sources are in the bibliography.

Sources for Quotes from Passengers

Mr. and Mrs. Henry Adams: NARA
William M. Adams: NARA
Oliver Bernard: Account in his book *Cocksparrow*; articles in the *Royal Magazine*, September 1915 and *Current Opinion*; correspondence in the Imperial War Museum
Harold Boulton: BBC and CBC interviews
Charles Bowring: Mayer (T)
Josephine Brandell: NARA
Norah Bretherton: NARA
James Brooks: Mayer (T); Mariners' Museum, Newport News; NARA
Michael Byrne: NARA
Margaret Cox: CBC interview
Harold Day: CBC interview
Avis Dolphin (married name Foley): BBC; Mariners' Museum, Newport News
Archie Donald: Mariners' Museum, Newport News
Elizabeth Duckworth: Imperial War Museum; Mariners' Museum, Newport News (personal account and letters from son-in-law)
Charles Frohman: Isaac F. Marcosson and D. Frohman, *Charles Frohman: Manager and Man*
Fred Gauntlett: Mayer (T); NARA
Oscar Grab: Mayer (T)
Ogden Hammond: Mayer (T); NARA
Charles Hardwick: Mayer (T)
Mabel Henshaw: CBC interview
C. T. Hill: NARA
Ian Holbourn: Mariners' Museum, Newport News (letter from wife) and account in his book *The Isle of Foula*
Rita Jolivet: Imperial War Museum; Mayer (T)
Parry Jones: BBC; Mariners' Museum, Newport News
Elizabeth Lassetter: Mersey (TO); Harold Boulton's BBC and CBC interviews

Charles Lauriat: Account in his book *The "Lusitania's" Last Voyage*; Mayer (T)
Doris Lawlor: CBC interview
James Leary: Mayer (T); NARA
Isaac Lehmann: Mayer (T); NARA
Ethel Lines: Mariners' Museum, Newport News
Basil Maturin: M. Ward, *Father Maturin*
J. W. McConnel: Wynne (T)
J. McFarquhar: NARA
Joseph Myers: Mayer (T); NARA
Belle Naish: NARA
Florence Padley: Mariners' Museum, Newport News
Amy Pearl: NARA
Major Warren Pearl: NARA
Theodate Pope: Mariners' Museum, Newport News
Charlotte Pye: CBC interview.
Viscountess Rhondda (Lady Mackworth): Mariners' Museum, Newport News; her
    article in the *Spectator*, 5 May 1923; account in her book *This Was My World*
Soren Sorenson: CBC interview
Julia Sullivan: Cunard archives; D. Hickey and G. Smith, *Seven Days to Disaster*
Lucy Taylor: CBC interview

Sources for Quotes from Crew Members

Albert Bestic: BBC interview; Mariners' Museum, Newport News; Mersey (T); PRO;
    Wynne (T)
William Burrows: BBC interview
R. Clark: BBC interview
Ben Holton: BBC interview
Leslie Morton: BBC interview; Mariners' Museum, Newport News; Mersey (T);
    account in his book *The Long Wake*
George Wynne: BBC

Prologue

1 "ghastly procession of rescue ships": W. Frost, *German Submarine Warfare*, p. 211.

1 Queenstown was originally called Cove but was renamed in honor of Queen Victoria's visit in 1849. When Ireland regained her independence, the town reverted to its former name but using the Gaelic spelling of Cobh.

1 "like cordwood . . . shadowy old wharves": Frost, *German Submarine Warfare*, p. 212.

1–2 "until the last . . . liner's deck": F. D. Ellis, *The Tragedy of the Lusitania*, p. 29.

2 The German newspaper warning appeared on 1 May 1915 in over half a dozen New York papers, including the *New York Times* and *New York World*. It was also published in a number of other cities, including Boston. Some copy editors failed to spot that *Britain* was misspelled as *Britian* and printed the text with this mistake.

2 "the United States . . . European respect": R. Gregory, *Walter Hines Page*, p. 96.

2 "great joy": Telegram of 9 May 1915, RM 5/2981, German Military Archive, Freiburg.

3 "wilful and wholesale murder" and "the Emperor . . . they acted": "Proceedings of Coroner John J. Horgan's Inquisition into the Death of Captain R. Matthews as a Result of the Sinking of R.M.S. *Lusitania*," May 1915, Imperial War Museum.

3 "the latest . . . at sea": *Daily Chronicle*, 8 May 1915.

3 "scientific torture": L. Marshall, *Horrors and Atrocities of the Great War*, p. 288.

4 "no gentleman . . . children": J. W. Gerard, *My Four Years in Germany*, p. 179.

5 "Remember the *Lusitania*": *New York Times*, 6 July 1918.

5 "In spite of all its horror . . . fighting men": *News of the World*, 6 June 1937.

5 "in a sweat of terror": Viscountess Rhondda, *This Was My World*, p. 261.

1. A Scrap of Paper

9 "already in Belgium" and "Our invasion . . . military goal has been reached": The full text is in R. H. Lutz, *Fall of the German Empire, Documents 1914–18*, vol. 1.

9–12 The next day . . . keep its solemn compact: The sources for this paragraph are T. Bethmann Hollweg, *Reflections on the World War*, p. 159, and the Blue Book of British Goverment, no. 160, Goschen to Grey. Bethmann Hollweg also described the encounter in his *Reflections*: "On my refusing [a different answer to the ultimatum] the Ambassador asked whether we could not have a private and personal conversation as to the awful situation in which the world found itself. I at once agreed and asked the Ambassador to dinner. . . . It appears to me an unusual diplomatic proceeding to exploit a private conversation officially. But in doing it Sir E. Goschen might at least have been thorough and since my emotion struck him so much, he might have reported that in taking leave of me he burst into tears and begged me to allow him to wait a little in my anteroom because he did not feel himself fit to appear before the clerks in the chancery."

12 It was still . . . "to the taxi cabs": The sources for this paragraph are Sir H. Rumbold, *The War Crisis in Berlin, July–August 1914*, p. 323 and M. Gilbert, *The First World War*, p. 33.

13 "My blood boiled . . . into the war": Bethmann Hollweg, *Reflections*, p. 159.

14 "very mediocre" and "it might mean . . . take up the idea": A. von Tirpitz, *My Memoirs*, vol. 1, p. 1.

14 "I worked . . . own hands": Ibid., p. 36.

15 "high-minded man . . . to be followed": Ibid., p. 46.

15 "for Germany . . . as great a number as possible": The full memorandum is quoted in J. Steinberg, *Yesterday's Deterrent—Tirpitz and the Birth of the German Battle Fleet*, pp. 209–21.

16 "tabooed": A. J. Marder, ed., *Fear God and Dread Nought* (Fisher correspondence), vol. 1, p. 199.

16 "The Germans . . . with France and Russia": Ibid., p. 218.

16 "penniless, friendless and forlorn": J. A. Fisher, *Records*, p. 25.

16 "I wrote out . . . glass of sherry": Marder, *Fear God and Dread Nought*, vol. 1, p. 19.

16 "I believe . . . waltz with you": Quoted in R. K. Massie, *Dreadnought—Britain, Germany, and the Coming of the Great War*, p. 404.

17 "Would you . . . in my face": J. A. Fisher, *Memoirs*, p. 40. In later years Edward VII was teasing Fisher about sailors having a wife in every port. Fisher responded by asking the king whether he would not have liked to be a sailor. Others around the table fell silent, and the king frowned for a moment but then burst out laughing.

17 "Yours till hell freezes" and "Yours till charcoal sprouts": Marder, *Fear God and Dread Nought*, vol. 2, p. 18.

17 "deepened his faith in Providence . . . as a nation": A. J. Marder, *From the Dreadnought to Scapa Flow*, vol. 1, p. 17.

17 "danced down . . . in the ballroom": A. J. Marder, *Anatomy of British Sea Power*, p. 346.

18 "The humanising of war . . . keep clear of you": Admiral Sir R. Bacon, *The Life of Lord Fisher of Kilverstone*, vol. 1, p. 121.

18 "Suppose that . . . affect me still less": *Review of Reviews*, February 1910.

18 "these invisible demons" and "Death . . . unavoidable!": Fisher, *Records*, pp. 177–78.

19 Lord Charles Beresford was able to serve as a member of Parliament since his title was only a "courtesy" one denoting him as a nobleman's son. It did not entitle him to sit in the House of Lords.

20 Winston Churchill's own son wrote of his father's childhood that "the neglect and lack of interest in him shown by his parents were remarkable, even judged by the standards of late Victorian and Edwardian days": R. Churchill, *Winston S. Churchill's Youth, 1874–1900*, p. 43.

21 "Restless . . . and some originality": Quoted in Massie, *Dreadnought*, p. 766.

21 "the sea-officers . . . 'Lower Deck'" and "Thus, even in England . . . don't get along!": Captain Erich von Muller to Tirpitz, 3 December 1913, German Military Archive, Freiburg.

23 The kaiser . . . "of Prussia about him": The source for this paragraph is *Empress Frederick Letters*, pp. 24 and 119.

24 "Considering the unripeness . . . with foreign affairs": O. von Bismarck, *New Chapters of Autobiography*, p. 815.

24 "The position . . . Full steam ahead!": Quoted in Massie, *Dreadnought*, p. 99.

24 "I could never . . . like a kaleidoscope": Tirpitz, *My Memoirs*, vol. 1, p. 99.

24 "as Kaiser . . . his generals": C. Clark, *Kaiser Wilhelm II*, p. 226.

25 King George V had little sympathy for how the kaiser conducted himself. When Colonel House asked him in 1915 why he did not address the British nation "in the forceful manner in which he had talked to him regarding the war and war measures," the king replied that he did not do so for the reason that "his distinguished cousin, the Kaiser, had talked so much and had made such a fool of himself that he had a distaste for that kind of publicity. Then, too, he added, this was a different sort of monarchy and he did not desire to intrude himself in such matters." Quoted in C. Seymour, ed., *The Intimate Diaries of Colonel House*, p. 386.

25 "I have . . . good enough for me": Quoted in Gilbert, *The First World War*, p. 25.

25 "George . . . never have allowed it": Quoted in M. Balfour, *The Kaiser and His Times*, p. 355 from *Die Grosse Politik der Europaischen Kabinett* 34, document 8193.

25 "I have had all through my life . . . liked by us": Quoted in Massie, *Dreadnought*, p. 167.

25 "the English . . . like Portugal": Tirpitz, *My Memoirs*, vol. 1, p. 235.

25 "All is then lost": Quoted in Gilbert, *The First World War*, p. 32.

25–26 "The army . . . dictator of the world": Gerard, *My Four Years in Germany*, p. 64.

26 "assailed . . . Teutonic throats": Ibid., p. 93.

26 "against the armies . . . to use them": C. Tansill, *America Goes to War*, p. 18.

26–27 "the invasion . . . of fear or of law": Ibid., p. 24.

27 "to reap a permanent glory": Remarks to a press conference, quoted in full in A. S. Link, ed., *The Papers of Woodrow Wilson*, vol. 30, p. 332.

28 "I found . . . use it wisely": Mary Bryan quoted in M. R. Werner, *Bryan*, p. 21.

29 "republic . . . in disputes": J. Dos Passos, *Mr. Wilson's War*, p. 12.

30 "take up the white man's burden": R. Kipling's poem "The White Man's Burden."

31 "I can think of . . . is suffering": Dos Passos, *Mr. Wilson's War*, p. 98.

31 "stood ready": Remarks to a press conference, quoted in full in Link, *The Papers of Woodrow Wilson*, vol. 30, p. 332.

31 "neutral . . . action . . . speak . . . play the impartial mediator": These remarks are from President Wilson's address to the American people, ibid., p. 394.

2. The Weapon of the Weaker Nation

Unless shown below, the sources for the quotes in this chapter are P. R. Compton-Hall's *Submarine Boats*, H. C. Fyfe's *Submarine Warfare*, and D. Van der Vat's *Stealth at Sea*, which all give very interesting insights into submarine development.

32 In 1625 Ben Jonson amused his audiences with topical references to Dutchman Cornelius Van Drebbel's quirky invention of an underwater vessel based largely on Bourne's design. A character in *The Staple of News* comments wonderingly:

> *they write here one Cornelius' son*
> *hath made the Hollanders an invisible eel*
> *to swim the tavel at Dunkirk and sink all*
> *the shipping there.*

Another replies:

> *I'll shew you, sir,*
> *It is an automa, runs under water*
> *With a snug nose, and has a nimble tail*
> *Made like an auger with which tail she wiggles*
> *Betwixt the costs [sides] of a ship and sinks it straight.*

While such devices caused mirth in the playhouse pit, scientists and men of letters took notice. On 14 March 1662 Samuel Pepys recorded thoughtfully in his diary: "This afternoon came the German Doctor Kuffler [Drebbel's son-in-law] to discourse with us about his engine to blow-up ships. We doubted not the matter of fact, it being tried in Cromwell's time." In 1648 Cromwell's brother-in-law John Wilkins, later bishop of Chester and a founder of the Royal Society, had written a remarkable article titled "An

Ark for Submarine Navigation: The Difficulties and Consequences of Such a Contrivance." The clergyman predicted that one day submarines would travel the ocean floors undetected and untroubled by tide, tempest, or pirates. Practical as well as visionary, Wilkins grappled with the problems of sanitation. Voyages would be both dangerous and uncomfortable unless "noisome and offensive things" could be thrust outside. He therefore recommended a cunning contrivance of interlocking and open-ended leather bags through which sewage could be released while keeping the vessel watertight.

32 "effort of genius": Letter from George Washington to Thomas Jefferson, 26 September 1787.

38 "submarines . . . defensive" and "we know all about them": Response to parliamentary question asked on 6 April 1900 by Captain Norton, M.P. (Hansard). Lord Goschen was the eldest brother of Sir Edward Goschen, British ambassador to Berlin on the eve of the First World War.

38 "the immense impending . . . weapons of war": Letter from Fisher to Admiral May, 24 April 1904, in Marder, *Fear God and Dread Nought*, vol. 1, p. 308.

39 "we must . . . neglect it ourselves": *Times*, April 1902.

39 "by no means certain . . . exhalations!": Admiral Sir R. Bacon, *From 1900 Onward*, p. 56.

39 Bacon did not actually invent the periscope. It had been used on land and by surface vessels during the American Civil War. When Bacon tried to patent the idea, he was told that a similar device already existed for examining patients' bladders.

40–41 Estimates of the numbers and type of Germany's U-boats vary slightly. These figures are taken from material in the German Traditionsarchiv Unterseeboote, Cuxhaven.

41 "because they . . . accidents had occurred": Account by Johannes Spiess, watch officer in the *U-9* from 1912 to 1914, quoted in Compton-Hall, *Submarine Boats*, p. 175.

41 "suffocate its crew": H. G. Wells, *Anticipations of the Reactions of Mechanical and Scientific Progress upon Human Life and Thought*, pp. 200–201. He wrote further: "It must involve physical inconvenience of the most demoralising sort simply to be in one for any length of time . . . while for your submarine to be 'got' is certain death. You may, of course, throw out a torpedo or so, with as much chance of hitting vitally as you would have if you were blindfolded, turned round three times, and told to fire revolver shots at a charging elephant. . . . At the utmost the submarine will be used in narrow waters, in rivers, or to fluster or destroy ships in harbour, or with poor-spirited crews—that is to say, it will simply be an added power in the hands of the nation that is predominant at sea."

41 In the years before the First World War Germany, the United States, France, Italy, and the United Kingdom all tried to develop effective methods of escape. The British fitted salvage-lifting eyes to their submersibles and designed various cumbersome types of escape apparatus. The Italians experimented with detachable conning towers that could float to the surface. The Americans tried firing two dogs through the torpedo tube of USS *Shark*. They were later found paddling about happily in the water. Despite all these creative efforts, the fact remained that submarines were hazardous in peacetime and yet more so in war. The recent Kursk tragedy shows that problems of escaping from a stricken submarine have still not been solved.

42 "would play . . . in future wars . . . sudden destruction": Quoted in R. Hough, *First Sea Lord*, p. 5.

43 "submarines . . . revolutionised naval warfare": Letter from Sir Percy Scott sent to the *Times* on 15 December 1913 and again on 31 May 1914.

43 "Will feelings of humanity . . . using it?": Letter from Sir Percy Scott sent to the *Times* on 9 July 1914.

43 "England has often been stupid . . . saviour always": Extract from *Danger!* an article published in the *Strand Magazine* in July 1914.

44 Yet many members . . . "from the sea": All quotes in this paragraph are from a letter from Lord Charles Beresford to the kaiser, 28 July 1914, file RM2/157, German Military Archive, Freiburg.

3. More Beautiful than Solomon's Temple

Unless shown separately, sources for quotations in this chapter are the Cunard archive, J. M. Brinnin's *The Sway of the Grand Saloon*, T. Coleman's *The Liners*, and J. Maxtone-Graham's *The North Atlantic Run*. The quotes by Charles Dickens are from his *American Notes* (chap. 2, "The Passage Out"), to be found, inter alia, on the Internet at www. people.virginia.edu (edited by J. L. Griffith, University of Virginia).

45 "a skyscraper adrift": *New York Times*, 14 September 1907.

45 "No one . . . this ship": Ibid.

45 "that have made . . . of Columbus": *New York American*, 14 September 1907.

45 "Gorgeous in Apartments": *New York Telegraph*, 14 September 1907.

45 "A Marvel of Speed and Luxury": *New York American*, 14 September 1907.

46 "the thrill . . . his achievements": Ibid.

46–47 In Britain, *Engineering* . . . Milton Abbey: The quotes in this paragraph are from *Engineering*, 19 July 1907.

48–49 "the vessel . . . in a merchant ship": Ibid., 12 July 1907.

51 The figurehead was a dog, in recognition of the fact that "Sirius" is "the dog star." The *Sirius* later ran aground off Cork Harbor with the loss of twenty lives. The ship was damaged beyond repair, but her main shaft was salvaged and used for over a century to power a spade mill. It is now on display in Passage, southern Ireland, the birthplace of Captain Roberts, who took the *Sirius* on her pioneering voyage of 1838.

The United States had, however, made a great contribution to transatlantic navigation and safety during this period. In 1855 U.S. naval lieutenant Matthew Maury defined a series of high-speed lanes for use by the new breed of liners. While slightly longer than the traditional routes, Maury's lanes significantly reduced the risk of collision.

55 The *Great Eastern* was originally intended to carry cargo on the long run to Sri Lanka and perhaps on to Sidney. She needed to be able to carry enough coal because of a lack of coaling stations en route. Sadly, the vision was greater than the reality. Her owners went bankrupt, and Brunel himself died while she was still undergoing sea trials. Although he had cautioned against her use in Atlantic conditions, her new owners ignored the advice. Brunel was proved right when her paddle wheels broke up and her single screw proved too weak to push her through rough seas. Brunel had intended the ship to have steam-powered steering, but, due to penny pinching by her builders, this feature was omitted. In heavy seas it took more than ten men to steer her. Jules Verne sailed on *The Great Eastern* in 1867 when she took American visitors to the Paris Exhibition. Lying in his deck chair, he watched children scamper over the vast decks and later described his experiences in *A Floating City*. Although her sheer size was in it own way a marvel, it was also an inconvenience. She was far too long for orders to be shouted along her decks, and her crew had to use semaphore.

55–56 Another of Cunard's competitors, although it was a small company, was the Guion Line, which had its roots in the emigrant trade and had adopted steamers in the late 1850s. In 1879 its ship *Arizona* hit an iceberg at fifteen knots. Some twenty-five feet of her bow was stoved in, but she did not sink. This contributed to a growing and complacent belief—not finally debunked until the 1912 *Titanic* disaster—that modern technology could produce ships that were virtually unsinkable. (The *Arizona* also had the distinction of being the ship that bore Oscar Wilde to New York, where he famously informed startled customs officials that he had nothing to declare but his genius.) The company took the Blue Riband when the *Alaska* became the first ship to cross from Ireland to New York in less than seven days but eventually failed financially.

56 Crossing the Atlantic . . . "deep lies between": The quotes in this paragraph are from K. Ledoux, *Ocean Notes for Ladies*.

60 "a licence . . . earth": S. Jackson, *J. P. Morgan, the Rise and Fall of a Banker*, p. 232.

61 "Great will be . . . Riband of the Atlantic": *Daily Mail*, 23 June 1904.

62 "First 4-Day Liner": *New York Evening Sun*, 11 October 1907.

62 "He attacked . . . ship's hospital": *Philadelphia Record*, 12 October 1907.

62 The *Mauretania* was such a byword for up-to-date luxury that she was featured in the U.K. Law Reports in 1911 (Lurcott v. Wakely) as an example of the highest possible standard of condition.

63–64 "a marvelous ship . . . just as they do on shore": Gerard, *My Four Years in Germany*, p. 1.

64 "as unsinkable as a ship can be": *New York Shipping Illustrated*, 14 September 1907.

4. *Gott Strafe England!*

65 "at the summit . . . wins a great battle": W. S. Churchill, *World Crisis*, p. 298.

66 "entirely unexpected . . . had not been anticipated": Quoted in L. Thomas, *Raiders of the Deep*, p. 34.

67 "as England completely . . . within a short time": Quoted in R. H. Gibson, *The German Submarine War, 1914–1918*, p. 26 as an extract from a memorandum from the leaders of the fleet to Admiral Pohl, chief of the naval staff in November 1914.

68 "would be destroyed . . . neutral ships": Quoted in full in R. H. Gibson, *The German Submarine War*, p. 27. Hermann Bauer interpreted the announcement in unequivocal terms, writing to his submarine commanders on 22 February 1915 that henceforth "all English ships and any which in spite of neutral flags and markings could be taken for such" were to be annihilated (RM 86/224, Freiburg Military Archive).

68 "neutral vessels . . . dangerous complications": Message from Berlin to German embassy in Washington, decoded by the British, PRO file ADM 137/3962.

68 "could not be . . . to dispense with these": Quoted in Thomas, *Raiders of the Deep*, p. 35.

68 "We are . . . blockade": K. Neureuther and C. Bergen, eds., *U-Boat Stories*, p. 28.

68 The description of the German medal is from Gerard, *My Four Years in Germany*, p. 154.

68 "most effective weapon": Tirpitz, *My Memoirs*, vol. 2, p. 391.

69 "fought, with . . . U-boat warfare": F. von Rintelen, *The Dark Invader*, p. 48.

69 "a truly terrible threat . . . commerce": Fisher, Records, p. 184.

69 "he is a German . . . his present position": Quoted in M. Gilbert, *Winston S. Churchill, 1914–16*, companion vol. 3, p. 148.

69 "Lord Fisher . . . Turkish rug": Quoted in J. Morris, *Fisher's Face*, p. 202.

69 "I'm *exceeding* . . . stirring up accordingly": Letter from Fisher to Lord Remant, 5 November 1914, Fisher Collection, Churchill College, Cambridge.

70 "nearly jumped . . . their boats": Johann Spiess's diary quoted in Thomas, *Raiders of the Deep*, p. 39.

70 "the well-known . . . the enemy": Churchill, *World Crisis*, p. 725.

71 The faint, handwritten letter is in file RM2/1982, Military Archive, Freiburg.

71 "impracticable . . . God-given": Quoted in Dos Passos, *Mr. Wilson's War*, p. 59.

71 "My dear friend . . . one another always": Quoted in Seymour, *The Intimate Diaries of Colonel House*, p. 45.

71 "very wealthy . . . a partisan": *Daily Mirror*, 10 May 1915. House once said, "My ambition has been so great it has never seemed to me worthwhile trying to satisfy it!" (*Intimate Papers*).

71–72 As the liner . . . "save the passengers": The quotes in this paragraph are from Colonel House's diary for 5 and 6 February 1915.

72 "Every newspaper . . . this incident": Ibid., 6 February 1915.

72 "utmost to escape" and "utmost speed": PRO file ADM 137/2958.

73 "merchant ships . . . to search them": Memorandum of 15 February 1915, RM2/1982, German Military Archive, Freiburg.

73 "if the British ships . . . ammunition": *Hansard*, 26 March 1913, Cols. 1776/1777. In March 1914 he told Parliament specifically that forty merchant ships had been equipped with two 4.7-inch guns apiece and that by 31 March 1915, seventy merchant ships would be so armed.

73 "pure piracy": *Review of Reviews*, March 1915.

73 A specific instruction to interrogating officers of one batch of prisoners suggested that "it is desirable that the prisoners be interrogated before they have had their dinner" (memo to Commander in Chief Chatham from War Room of 6 March 1915, PRO file ADM137/3950).

74 "picking . . . Great Britain": Gerard, *My Four Years in Germany*, p. 115.

74 "strict accountability": *Foreign Relations of the U.S., 1915 Supplement*, pp. 98–100.

74 "I do not see . . . from entering Germany": Telegram from Page to Bryan, 20 February 1915, in ibid.

74 "I did not tell him . . . anything else": Diary of Colonel House, 26 March 1913.

75 "a quality that is invincible . . . race and blood": Quoted in Gregory, *Walter Hines Page*, p. 56.

75 Baron Forstner's description of the sinking is contained in his war diary for the voyage of the *U-28*, file RM2/1962, German Military Archive, Freiburg.

76 "most important . . . better still": Gilbert, *Winston S. Churchill*, companion vol. 3, 501.

76 "The *Lusitania* . . . attacking her": War diary of *U-27*, file RM/97–680, German Military Archive, Freiburg.

76–77 The information about the abortive attempt to escort the *Lusitania* is in PRO file ADM 137/1057.

5. The American Armory

78 "the worst . . . other things": Letter from Bryan to Wilson, 10 August 1914, Bryan Correspondence.

78 "inconsistent . . . neutrality": Ibid.

78 "A greater lot . . . first class country": Letter from J. P. Morgan to H. White, 5 June 1914, White Correspondence.

79 "meticulous, metallic and mousy": J. Daniels, *The Wilson Era*, vol. 1, *The Years of Peace, 1910-1917*, p. 441.

79 "an arrangement . . . loan of money": "A Memorandum Written by R. Lansing at 9.30 p.m., October 23, 1914 of a Conversation with President Wilson At 8.30 p.m. That Evening," Lansing Papers and Link, *The Papers of Woodrow Wilson*, vol. 31, p. 219.

80 "I have nothing . . . enemies of Germany": J. Gerard, *My Four Years in Germany*, p. 155.

80 "quite seriously . . . Germany . . . exchange professors": Ibid., p. 43.

80 "in reality . . . Germany as well": Ibid., p. 166.

81 "heavy artillery . . . American ammunition": Ibid., p. 159.

81 "The sabotage . . . suitable people for sabotage": Quoted in R. Doerries's foreword to Rintelen, *The Dark Invader*, p. xv.

82 The information about the gun cotton is in NARA.

82 "might . . . what I can't": Rintelen, *The Dark Invader*, p. 74.

82 "I cannot . . . see me": Ibid., p. 82.

82 "good horses . . . amenities": Ibid., p. 90.

82 "What is . . . America": Ibid., p. 84.

82 "rather decadent poet": Ibid.

83 "a nation . . . morality": N. M. Johnson, *George Sylvester Viereck*, p. 32.

83 "the story . . . exposed": *Times*, 1 May 1915.

83 "each received . . . crimes": Count J. von Bernstorff, *My Three Years in America*, p. 108.

83 "Stegler . . . Passport Case": RM2/1127, German Military Archive, Freiburg.

83 "idiotic Yankees": *UK Command Paper 8012*.

83 "financed . . . dynamiting a bridge": NARA.

83–84 Details of the attachés' activities are given in a report by the German naval attaché on 27 April 1915, German foreign office documents archive, St. Anthony's College, Oxford.

85 "the excessive stupidity . . . its source": Letter from Gaunt to Dow, 26 February 1916, Cunard archives.

85 "There is no doubt . . . tied up": PRO file FO 115/1943.

86 The information about Pinkerton's is in PRO file FO 115/1979.

86 "the question of enemy . . . on board British ships": Cunard memorandum of 18 December 1914, Cunard archives.

86 Bennett's warning about bombs on board is in PRO file FO 115/1809.

86 "undoubtedly hostile . . . British Government": Letter from Gaunt to Dow, 26 February 1916, Cunard archives.

86 "how far . . . existed before": Ibid.

86 Meanwhile . . . "those allied to her": All quotes in this paragraph are taken from Rintelen, *The Dark Invader*, pp. 84, 88, and 92.

87 "as big as a cigar": Ibid., p. 95.

87 "great dark ship" and "ghostly activity": Ibid., p.107.

87–88 Evidence about the infiltration of the New York Police Department and about Paul Konig and his spies is in NARA M 1085 264 OG 119. The file names Otto Mottola and Albert Ackerly as two of the policemen on Konig's payroll.

88 "high-power naval rifles . . . passenger ships": *New York Tribune*, 19 June 1913.

88 "Sooner or later . . . hell to pay": G. S. Viereck, *Spreading Germs of Hate*, p. 64.

6. The Warning

92 The account by the newspaper editor O. G. Villard of his discussion with Count Bernstorff is given in Villard's *Fighting Years*, pp. 268–69, and also in an article titled "The True Story of the 'Lusitania,'" published in the *American Mercury* XXXVC (May 1935), pp. 41–45.

92 "Above notice . . . 'patriotically' 1776": Quoted by British embassy, Washington, in telegram of 1 May 1915 in PRO file FO 115/1196.

93 "The Germans . . . can get near her": *New York World*, 2 May 1915.

93 "mighty good care . . . nothing to fear": *New York Times*, 2 May 1915.

93 "Well . . . your picture": O. Bernard, *Cocksparrow*, p. 146.

93 "Last voyage . . . *Lusitania*": Letter from O. Hanson to A. A. Hoehling, 13 June 1955, Mariners' Museum, Newport News.

93 "no officer . . . about my baggage": M. Byrne's letter of 8 June 1915 to Secretary of State W. Bryan, NARA.

94 "were all about the ship . . . smuggled aboard": Ellis, *The Tragedy of the Lusitania*, p. 175.

94 "suspicious characters": Sworn statement of C. T. Hill to W. Frost, 10 May 1915, NARA.

97 "to worry about trifles": Marshall, *Horrors and Atrocities of the Great War*, p. 14.

98 "'Bill Kaiser' . . . compared with the kaiser": Ellis, *The Tragedy of the Lusitania*, p. 103.

98 "the crazy kaiser": Ibid., p. 106.

98 The offending joke read: "The bride of a year entered a drugstore. The clerk approached. 'Do you exchange goods?', she asked. 'Oh, Certainly! If anything you buy here is not satisfactory we will exchange it.' 'Well,' was the reply; 'here is one of those whirling-spray [contraceptive] affairs I bought of you, and if you please, I want you to take it back and give me a bottle of Mellin's [baby] Food, instead.' And outside the storm raged piteously, and across the moor a jay-bird called to his mate, 'Cuckoo, cuckoo!' "

98 Now, standing on deck . . . "the bottom": The quote in this paragraph is from Ellis, *The Tragedy of the Lusitania*, p. 107.

99 "tall and divinely fair": Quoted in D. Hickey and G. Smith, *Seven Days to Disaster*, p. 27.

100 "mysterious inquest": *New York Tribune*, 9 May 1915.

100 "inevitable pink carnation": Article by J. Lawrence, *Coronet*, March 1950.

100 "THE *LUSITANIA* . . . DO NOT SAIL ON HER": Ibid.

100 "somebody . . . fun at my expense": Ibid.

102 Sir Hugh Lane's commission was honored after his death. The sitter eventually chosen was President Wilson, who sat for Sargent in 1917. The portrait was widely exhibited and is now in the collection of the Irish National Gallery.

102 "too absurd for discussion": Quoted in D. B. Chidsey, *The Day They Sank the Lusitania*, p. 13.

103–4 The information about Lieutenant Robert Matthews comes from an article by P. Chaplin, senior research officer, Department of National Defence, Ottawa, titled "The Lusitania, Lieutenant Matthews, and the Draft That Never Was," June 1974, Hoover Institution.

104 "men were needed for war work": Taped interview given by G. Smith to CBC.

105 "Flor" Sullivan's first name was short for "Florence," a male as well as a female name at that time, especially in Ireland. The *Lusitania*'s boatswain's mate was called Florence Sikking.

106 The story about the Mounseys appeared in the *New York Times* of 8 May 1915 and *Chicago Tribune* of 16 October 1915. There are also several poignant pieces of correspondence in the Cunard archives.

7. Leaving Harbor

107 Details of the coal taken on in New York are given in a letter from Cunard's New York office of 5 June 1915 in the Cunard archives.

107 "giving pamphlets . . . kind of business": Interview given by trimmer Mr. Kennedy to BBC.

108 "We had no idea . . . catch us": Interview given by H. Johnston to BBC.

108 "Quite a lot of passengers . . . a bit jittery": Interview given by B. Holton to BBC.

108 "they daren't sink her": Ibid.

108 "It's the best joke . . . torpedoing the *Lusitania*": Ellis, *The Tragedy of the Lusitania*, p. 168.

108 "up to a point": Letter from A. Bestic to A. A. Hoehling, 10 June 1955, Mariners' Museum, Newport News.

108 "ordinary type . . . Sunday best": Bernard, *Cocksparrow*, p. 146.

108 "bloody monkeys": Letter from A. Bestic to A. A. Hoehling, 10 June 1955, Mariners' Museum, Newport News.

108 "respectable": Letter from N. Turner (Captain Turner's son) to A. Hoehling, 18 September 1955, Mariners' Museum, Newport News.

110 "tired and really ill": A. Booth's evidence to Mersey (TO).

110 "very big . . . fight": Letter from N. Turner (Captain Turner's son) to A. Hoehling, 18 September 1955, Mariners' Museum, Newport News.

110 "mixed up . . . brick wall": Ibid.

110 "with a preference . . . cooking": Ibid.

110 "I don't bother . . . I get out": *New York Times*, 14 May 1915.

110 "it will happen again": Ibid.

111 "entirely impractical . . . outgoing ship": Article in the *Nation*, 23 January 1923.

111 "the crew . . . adequately": A report by the German naval attaché on 27 April 1915, German foreign office documents archive, St. Anthony's College, Oxford.

111 "the old-fashioned sailor": Evidence of Captain W. Turner to Mersey (TO).

112 Another new crew member . . . a combatant: The information about Neal Leach is from a report to the attorney general from A. B. Bielaski, chief of Division of Investigation, Department of Justice, June 1915 and from D. Genny's affidavit of 6 June 1915, NARA.

112–13 "PLEASE INFORM DERNBURG . . . FOR AMERICA": PRO file ADM 137/3962.

114 "regarded as confidential": Evidence of A. Booth to Commissioner Wynne.

116 "armed with teeth": Bernard, *Cocksparrow*, p. 148.

117 1 May . . . around 8 May: This secret intelligence report dated 26 April 1915 is in file RM2/1962, Germany Military Archive, Freiburg.

8. The Ostrich Club

118 "looked about . . . any incident": Letter from O. Hanson to A. A. Hoehling, 13 June 1955, Mariners' Museum, Newport News.

118 "the origin . . . the present war": The Victoria League leaflet is in the Cunard archives.

118 "wherever possible . . . nationality": Instruction of 19 September 1914, Cunard archives.

118 "epidemic . . . fever": Note to surgeons of *Lusitania* and other Cunard ships from health officer of Port of New York, 26 April 1915, Cunard archives.

118 "not calculated to cause offence": Instruction of 26 June 1914, Cunard archives.

119 "as little as possible . . . no messages": Evidence of A. Booth to Wynne.

119 "GOD BLESS YOU DEAR FRIEND": PRO file ADM 116/1416.

121 "quite a number . . . sheets for the beds": E. Sauder and K. Marschall, *R.M.S. Lusitania, Triumph of the Edwardian Age*, p. 36.

122 "we joked . . . fairly well": Account of the sinking (undated) by A. D. Donald, Mariners' Museum, Newport News.

122 "the personality . . . sail in": Letter from Mrs. K. Simpson (daughter of Steward R. Barnes) to M. Hoehling, 14 July 1955, Mariners' Museum, Newport News.

123 "Madam . . . a lady?": Letter from G. Ball, lifelong friend of Captain Turner, to A. A. Hoehling, 22 July 1955, Maritime Museum, Newport News.

127 "a wild lot": Account (undated) by A. D. Donald, Maritime Museum, Newport News.

128 "as far as . . . their job": Interview given by H. Johnston to BBC.

128 "It was Turner's idea of humour" and the anecdote about the Turk's head knot are in a letter from Third Officer A. Bestic to A. Hoehling, 10 June 1955, Mariners' Museum, Newport News.

128 "It was a record . . . *Lusitania*": *New York Times*, 8 June 1915.

129 "advisedly simpler": *Engineering*, 19 July 1907.

129 "many mothers . . . somebody else's child won": Taped interview given by Mabel Henshaw to CBC.

130 "angry with the captain . . . panic or worry": Letter from A. Foley (née Dolphin) to A. Hoehling, 25 August 1955, Mariners' Museum, Newport News.

130 "We should not . . . at that time": Evidence of J. McConnel to Wynne.

131 "impracticable": *New York Tribune*, 10 May 1915.

131 "climbed up . . . launched": Bernard, *Cocksparrow*, p. 149.

131 "pitiable": Survivor statement, NARA.

131 "unless . . . wear the boat out": Evidence of C. Hardwick to Mayer (T).

131 "Would you like . . . torpedoed": Evidence of J. Leary to Mayer (T).

132 "give your name . . . the lot": Interview given by J. O'Connell to BBC.

132 "no idea . . . any damn thing": Ibid.

132 "a padded football . . . the shoulders": C. E. Lauriat, *The "Lusitania's" Last Voyage*, p. 21.

132 "sounding the boat": Evidence of Ship's Carpenter N. Robertson to Mersey (TO).

133 Michael Byrne's account of his search for guns is in his letter of 8 June 1915 to Secretary of State W. Bryan, NARA.

134 "We got some electric . . . pastime": Interview given by bellboy R. Clark to BBC.

134 A copy of the manifest and "Supplemental Manifest" are in the Franklin D. Roosevelt Presidential Library in New York.

134 "Practically all . . . some kind": Letter from A. J. Peters, Treasury Department, to R. Lansing, 8 May 1915, NARA.

134 "a new phase": *New York Times*, 9 May 1915.

134 "a very barbarous form . . . gases": *Times*, 1 May 1915.

134 "by means of poisonous gases": *Review of Reviews*, June 1915.

135 "a more serious breach . . . consequences": Colonel House to President Wilson, 5 May 1915, quoted in Seymour, *The Intimate Diaries of Colonel House*, p. 432.

135 "make good . . . 'strict accountability' ": *Westminster Gazette*, quoted in the *New York Herald*, 6 May 1915.

135 "the ship . . . sunk": Evidence of A. Booth to Wynne.

135 The quote from the *Times* about the warning is from the edition of 3 May 1915.

136 "The reference . . . and fast as the *Lusitania*": Frost, *German Submarine Warfare*, p. 186.

136 The rumor that the stowaways were German spies is included in the sworn statement of C.T. Hill made in Queenstown to Frost on 10 May 1915, NARA.

9. Fellow Passengers

137 "double-stuffed settees . . . easy chairs": *Engineering*, p. 69.

141 "Austrian claret . . . mineral water": Cunard instruction of 19 September 1914, Cunard archives.

141 The message about Fred Davies is contained in PRO file ADM 116/1416.

142 "as far apart . . . planets": C. Vanderbilt, *The Vanderbilt Feud*, p. 224.

142 The day the *Lusitania* sailed, Columbia announced "the first ever opera ever completely recorded." It was *Aida*, and the seventeen records cost seventy-five cents each.

143 "if Teddy Roosevelt . . . couple of days": Interview given by bellboy R. Clark to BBC.

144 Elbert Hubbard's *A Message to Garcia* is fourth in the list of the world's leading copyrighted best-sellers. Its sales were surpassed only by the *Guinness Book of Records*, first published in 1955, the *World Almanac and Book of Facts*, first published in 1868, and Dr. Benjamin Spock's *The Common Sense Book of Baby and Child Care*. Runners-up sharing position number five were Margaret Mitchell's *Gone With the Wind*, Harper Lee's *To Kill a Mockingbird*, and Jacqueline Susann's *Valley of the Dolls* (N. McWhirter, *Book of Millennium Records*: Virgin Publishing, 1999).

144 "Great men . . . commonplace women": F. Champney, *Art and Glory—the Story of Elbert Hubbard*, p. 76.

145 "I can't . . . the Channel": Undated note by Viscountess Rhondda (Lady Mackworth), Mariners' Museum, Newport News.

10. Inside the *U-20*

All times quoted for the voyage of the *U-20* are GMT, that is, one hour earlier than the times noted in Walther Schwieger's war diary.

148 "Large English . . . warships": War diary of H. Bauer, German Military Archive, Freiburg. The orders given to the U-30 were decoded by the British and are in PRO file ADM 137/3956.

149 "The commander . . . his hands": Journal of submarine commander Forstner, p. 15.

149 "The submarine commanders . . . activities": Letter from Admiral A. Spindler to Professor T. A. Bailey, 14 January 1935, Hoover Institution.

149 "yet harsher measures": Note to kaiser from Admiral Bachmann 18 April 1915, RM2/1982, German Military Archive, Freiburg.

151 "all English ships . . . usually run": Schwieger's war diary, RM97/578, German Military Archive, Freiburg.

151 "good-humored, solid seamen": Interview of Lieutenant Zentner with L. Thomas, Hoover Institution.

151–52 "the poor living conditions. . . . In order . . . one's feet": J. Spiess, quoted in Compton-Hall, *Submarine Boats*, p. 175.

152 "gleaming . . . 'eels' ": Neureuther and Bergen, *U-Boat Stories*, p. 16.

152 "I had . . . 'Dutch wife' ": J. Spiess quoted in Thomas, *Raiders of the Deep*, p. 89.

152 "enough to give you a headache . . . over": J. Spiess quoted in ibid., p. 29.

153 "the moisture . . . sleeper": J. Spiess quoted in Compton-Hall, *Submarine Boats*, p. 176.

153 "it was really . . . damp cellar": Ibid.

153 "with considerable mucus . . . 'oil-head' ": Ibid.

153 "the real pirates of old days": Neureuther and Bergen, *U-Boat Stories*, p. 17.

153 Some of the crew . . . "underseas": All quotes in this paragraph are from Commander von Forstner, *Journal*, p. 12.

153 "this iron tube . . . scrambling men": Neureuther and Bergen, *U-Boat Stories*, p. 11.

154 "In the dim glow . . . the commander": Ibid., p. 12.

154 "foaming masses . . . more calm": Ibid., p. 13.

154 "the magical green light": Ibid.

154 "greased and glittering": Ibid.

154 "come and stare . . . in the turret": Forstner, *Journal*, p. 16.

154 Later . . . on the surface: The quotations in this paragraph come from Neureuther and Bergen, *U-Boat Stories*, p. 13.

154 "peculiar thrill and nervous sensation": Thomas, *Raiders of the Deep*, p. 12.

154 "a gigantic mouse-trap": Neureuther and Bergen, *U-Boat Stories*, p. 55.

155 "A burst . . . witness": Ibid., p. 145.

155 "death . . . conjure": J. Spiess quoted in Thomas, *Raiders of the Deep*, p. 11.

155 Schwieger . . . "our trail": All quotes in this paragraph are from ibid., pp. 87–88.

155 "Light objects . . . the entire horizon": Forstner, *Journal*, p. 14.

155–56 "The periscopes . . . the U-boat": Ibid., pp. 14 and 15.

156 "It is their highest ambition . . . small favor": Ibid., p. 16.

156 "found a snug resting place . . . North Sea": Thomas, *Raiders of the Deep*, p. 83.

156 The tiny mess room . . . Dröscher: The quotes in this paragraph come from ibid., pp. 83–84.

156–57 "The commander . . . the waters": Forstner, *Journal*, pp. 18 and 19.

158 "in view . . . safety of the ship": Order from H. Bauer to U-boat commanders, 29 April 1915, RM8/525, German Military Archive, Freiburg.

158 "Signals good at both ends": War diary of *U-20*, RM97/578, German Military Archive, Freiburg.

11. "The Miraculous Draught of Fishes"

160 "priceless sea-stained documents": Churchill quoted in P. Beesly, *Room 40*, p. 5.

160 The PRO file containing the *Magdeburg* (SKM) codebook is ADM 137/4156.

163 "square holes . . . boot-heels": Neureuther and Bergen, *U-Boat Stories*, p. 6.

163 *"Gott strafe England!"*: Quoted in A. A. Hoeling and M. Hoehling, *The Last Voyage of the Lusitania*, p. 51.

164 "in the service of the enemy": Article by Captain Friedrich Schlosser, "Germany's Submarine Campaign," *Living Age* 327 (31 October 1925).

164 "We are . . . good catch": Neureuther and Bergen, *U-Boat Stories*, p. 27.

164 However . . . poor weather: The description of the *U-20*'s activities and the quotations in this paragraph and the subsequent seven paragraphs come from the *U-20*'s war diary, RM97/578, German Military Archive, Freiburg. The German intelligence report about the use of Danish flags is in RM2/1962 and details about failed torpedo launches are in RM 86/98.

166 Vice Admiral Coke describes sending the messages in a report of 1915, in PRO file ADM 137/113.

12. Into the War Zone

167 "any other men . . . raise": Mayer (T), Acting Senior Third Officer John Lewis.

167 "they did not . . . three": A. Donald, undated report, Mariners' Museum, Newport News.

168 "a blotter . . . the light": Statement of J. Leary, NARA.

168 "that the attempt . . . last night": Lady Mackworth, Maritime Museum, Newport News.

169 "without regard . . . neutral flags": Memorandum from Bachmann to the kaiser, 3 May 1915, RM8/525, German Military Archive, Freiburg.

169 Bethmann Hollweg . . . would be final: The quotations in this paragraph are from Gerard, *My Four Years in Germany*, pp. 161–62.

169 Untroubled . . . Milford Haven: The description of the *U-20*'s activities in this paragraph and the subsequent four paragraphs comes from the *U-20*'s war diary, RM97/578, German Military Archive, Freiburg.

170 The timing of the receipt of information about the sinking of the *Candidate* is in PRO file ADM 137/1058, as are the signals sent to the *Lusitania*.

171 "I fooled them that time": Quoted in T. A. Bailey and P. B. Ryan, *The Lusitania Disaster*, p. 140.

172 May Barwell's message is in PRO file ADM 137/1058.

172 "on entering the war zone . . . Royal Navy": NARA.

172 "of course . . . alarm": Quoted in Hickey and Smith, *Seven Days to Disaster*, p. 155.

173 Smoking was still considered very much a male pleasure. It was only seven years since the O'Sullivan Ordinance had forbidden women in New York City to smoke in public.

13. "Suppose They Should Sink the *Lusitania*?"

176 "That wretched foghorn . . . away": Quoted in Hickey and Smith, *Seven Days to Disaster*, p. 160.

176 "in view . . . on board": Letter from R. J. Mecredy to the *New Statesman*, 23 March 1957.

176 "a confirmed Cunarder": Ellis, *The Tragedy of the Lusitania*, p. 42.

176 "the loom . . . the haze": Able Seaman Leo Thompson, Mayer (T).

178 "You could hear . . . 'told us[?]' ": Statement of M. Byrne, NARA.

178 "curiously cautious . . . escort": Bernard, *Cocksparrow*, p. 150.

178–79 The QUESTOR/WESTRONA exchange and the other messages are in PRO file ADM 137/1058.

179 The description of the precautions taken by Captain Turner are to be found in his evidence to Lord Mersey in 1915 and to Commissioner Wynne in 1917.

180 "in the event . . . exceptional speed": Evidence of Senior Third Engineer George Little to Wynne.

180 "everybody was tense" and "You could catch . . . submarines around": Interview given by Quartermaster Hugh Johnston to BBC.

180 "watching . . . the water": Evidence of Neil Robertson to Wynne.

180 The description of Sir Alfred Booth's thoughts and actions comes from his evidence to Commissioner Wynne.

180–81 U.S. consul . . . limited time: The quotes in these three paragraphs are from Frost, *German Submarine Warfare*, pp. 1, 174, and 175.

182 "In his place . . . breaking-point would come": Unfinished autobiography of Reginald Hall, Hall Papers, Churchill College, Cambridge.

182–83 However . . . "passengers aboard": The description of Colonel House's activities on the morning of 7 May 1915 comes from his diary, Yale University, New Haven, Conn.

183 "We can see . . . safe journey": Letter from A. Loynd, Cunard archives.

183 The Cunard *Daily Bulletin* is in the Cunard archives.

183 "Please, God . . . away": I. Holbourn, *The Isle of Foula*, p. 227.

184 "SUBMARINES . . . AT TEN A.M.": PRO file ADM 137/1058.

184 "very quickly": Taped interview with Doris Lawlor, CBC.

185 The principles of the four-point bearing are well explained in a footnote to an article by P. B. Ryan in the *American Neptune* (vol. 35, 1975). He states that a "point" equals 11¼ degrees. A navigator can obtain his position by the four-point, or "bow and beam," method. When a particular landmark is four points (or forty-five degrees) on the bow, a navigator takes a bearing and plots it on his chart. The ship must then maintain a steady course and speed until the landmark is broad on the beam (eight points or ninety degrees). A second bearing is then taken and plotted, effectively forming an isosceles triangle. The ship's distance to the landmark is equal to the distance traveled by the ship between observations.

14. "My God, We Are Lost"

190 "very beautiful weather": From the *U-20*'s war diary, RM97/578, German Military Archive, Freiburg.

190 Hermann Lepper, on watch that day, described what happened in an interview with the *Bochumer Anzeiger* on 21 February 1985.

190 "a forest of masts and stacks . . . over the horizon": Schwieger quoted in Thomas, *Raiders of the Deep*, p. 97.

190 "When the steamer . . . we waited": Ibid.

192 "laughing and joking": Letter from Grace Hope French to Mostyn Prichard, 19 September 1915, Imperial War Museum.

192–93 Meanwhile . . . only a buoy: The quotations in this paragraph are from a note from T. O'Mahoney (undated), Mariners' Museum, Newport News.

193 "Here's a torpedo coming, Frank": Evidence from Able Seaman F. Hennessy to Wynne.

193 "This is the approach of death": Quoted in Hickey and Smith, *Seven Days to Disaster*, p. 184.

193 "There's a torpedo": Evidence of Turner to Wynne.

193 "like the banging . . . day": Ibid.

193 "a kind of a rumble": Ibid.

194 "we couldn't see . . . straight over": Interview given by Quartermaster Hugh Johnson to BBC.

196 "the awful crash . . . life and ambition": Letter from Grace Hope French to Mostyn Prichard, 10 September 1915, Imperial War Museum.

199 "what looked like . . . port hole": Letter from Irene Paynter to M. Hoehling, 8 October 1955, Mariners' Museum, Newport News.

199 "just like . . . clap of thunder": Evidence of Acting Senior Third Officer John Lewis, Mayer (T).

199 "give such a shudder": Evidence of Senior Third Engineer Robert Duncan, Mayer (T).

199 "this terrific explosion . . . put it back again": Interview given by bellboy R. Clark to BBC.

200 Fireman . . . "what happened": All quotes in this paragraph are from an interview with John O'Connell in the BBC archives.

200 "hard-a-starboard the helm": Evidence of Hugh Johnston, Mersey (TO).

200 "keep her head into Kinsale": Deposition of Hugh Johnston, 12 May 1915, PRO file ADM 137/1058.

200 "hard-a-starboard": Evidence of Hugh Johnston, Mersey (TO).

15. "Come at Once!"

201 The *Lusitania* . . . "My God": The quotes in this paragraph are from a letter from Hugh Johnston to A. A. Hoehling of 25 September 1955, Mariners' Museum, Newport News, and his interview with the BBC.

201 "to be lowered to the rail": Evidence of Captain Turner, Mersey (TO).

201 "all women . . . first": Ibid.

201 "COME . . . OLD KINSALE": Evidence of Radio Officer R. Leith, Mersey (TO).

202 On deck . . . "exercise": All quotes in this paragraph are from Ben Holton's interview with the BBC.

202 "crowded with passengers . . . what was the matter": Quoted in Ellis, *The Tragedy of the Lusitania*, p. 75.

202 "a large flowerpot . . . and fell": Evidence of J. W. McConnell to Wynne.

202 "die game anyway": *New York Tribune*, 10 May 1915.

203 "as if . . . top of us": Taped interview of Margaret Cox with CBC.

203 "that everything . . . hurrying": Account of sinking (undated) by A. D. Donald, Mariners' Museum, Newport News.

203–4 "I had taken hold . . . heavy explosion": Letter from K. Simpson on behalf of her father, R. Barnes, to M. Hoehling, 14 July 1955, Mariners' Museum, Newport News.

204 "in a rocking motion . . . heavily to starboard . . . over and over and over": Evidence of Mr. Duncan, Senior Third Engineer, Mayer (T).

204 "Keep the Boat Deck clear . . . had no control": Letter from Michael Byrne to Secretary of State W. Bryan, 8 June 1915, NARA.

204 "She felt . . . children": Avis Foley (née Dolphin's) interview with the BBC.

205 "What is to be, is to be": Letter from Ethel Lines to A. A. Hoehling, 11 October 1955, Mariners' Museum, Newport News.

206 "One thing's sure . . . is indecent": Quoted in Ellis, *The Tragedy of the Lusitania*, p. 110.

206 "neat little signs": Lauriat, *The "Lusitania's" Last Voyage*, p. 60.

207 "noxious fumes . . . many passengers": BBC.

208 "Don't worry . . . into the sea": Quoted in the *New York Tribune*, 10 May 1915.

208 "the first time . . . forgot them": Viscountess Rhondda, *This Was My World*, p. 253.

209 "doubtless . . . ashore": Bernard, *Cocksparrow*, p. 156.

209 "Well . . . right": Quoted in the *New York Times*, 8 June 1915.

211 "nothing . . . gone": Evidence of Senior Second Engineer A. Cockburn, Mersey (TO).

211 "You can . . . yourself": Evidence of Senior Third Engineer R. Duncan, Mayer (T).

211 "a loud bang" . . . "objects blowing about": Evidence of Trimmer F. Davis, Mersey (TO) and Mayer (T).

211 "a rush of water . . . ventilation shaft": Evidence of Trimmer I. McDermott, Mersey (TO) and Mayer (T).

211 "filled with dust": Quoted in PRO file ADM 137/1058.

211 "wounded and bleeding": BBC.

213 "to save her": Ibid., p. 181.

213 "telling everybody . . . come on deck": Evidence of Chief Steward J. Jones to Wynne.

213 "to keep . . . not one person was left": Evidence of Stewardess M. Bird to Wynne.

213 "like a bunch of wild mice": H. Day's interview with CBC.

213–14 John Griffith . . . were now afloat: All quotations in this paragraph are from Chief Third-Class Steward J. Griffith's evidence to Mayer (T) with the exception of "silver . . . dishes," which is from A. D. Donald's account of the sinking (undated), Mariners' Museum, Newport News.

215 "they . . . the list": W. Pierpoint's evidence to Wynne.

215 "Don't lower the boats . . . upper deck": Quoted by H. Boulton in BBC interview.

216 "what do you wish . . . engine room, Madam": Quoted in Lauriat, *The "Lusitania's" Last Voyage*, p. 11.

216–17 Walther Schwieger . . . "by the bow": The quotations in this paragraph are taken from the *U-20*'s war diary, RM 97/578, German Military Archive, Freiburg.

217 "He put . . . 'Lusitania!'": Quoted in Thomas, *Raiders of the Deep*, p. 97.

217 "ghastly drama": Otto Rikowsky's interview with CBC.

16. A Bizarre Orchestra of Death

218 "all swinging . . . ship's side": L. Morton, *The Long Wake*, p. 104.

218 "just like . . . 15 degree list": Evidence of N. Robertson to Wynne.

219 "to the ship's side . . . into the boat": Evidence of Acting Senior Third Officer John Lewis to Wynne.

219 "had been . . . twisted around his leg": Evidence of C. Bowring to Mayer (T).

219 "not generally acted upon": Quoted in Marshall, *Horrors and Atrocities of the Great War*, p. 51.

220 "to go to . . . it was impossible": Evidence of Third Officer A. Bestic to Wynne.

222 "Don't you drop . . . the water": Testimony of C. Hardwick, Mayer (T).

222–23 First Officer . . . "point blank": All quotations in this paragraph are from the testimony of Acting Senior Third Officer J. Lewis to Wynne and to Mayer (T).

224 "rolled . . . the deck": Evidence of E. Wild, Mersey (TO).

224 "we had to sort of rush down . . . seamen": Evidence of M. K. Leigh Royd, Mersey (TO).

226 "The bows . . . boat deck": Evidence of Boatswain's Mate F. Sikking to Wynne.

227 "For God's sake . . . Queenstown": Evidence of Senior Third Officer J. Lewis to Mayer (T).

227 "Row for your lives . . . too terrible to see": Statement of J. MacFarquhar, May 1915, NARA.

227 Able Seaman Leo Thompson . . . and capsized: The quotations from Thompson in this and the subsequent paragraph are from his evidence to Mayer (T).

227 "full of people": Ibid.

227–28 David Thomas . . . then followed: The quotations in this paragraph are from Thomas's evidence to Mersey (TO).

228 "One . . . into the water": Evidence of Detective-Inspector William Pierpoint to Wynne.

229 Now there was . . . down on them: Quotes in this paragraph are from the evidence of the Reverend Clark to Mersey (TO).

229 "the last boat . . . leaving": Evidence of Stewardess M. Bird to Wynne.

229 "which . . . rail": Evidence of Stewardess F. Morecroft to Wynne.

229–30 "trying to . . . too heavy": Evidence of J. Lehmann to Mayer (T).

230 "tied . . . do it": Evidence of C. Hardwick to Mayer (T).

17. Wave upon Wave

231 "shoved . . . her feet": Taped interview given by G. Smith to CBC.

231 "Passengers . . . will not sink": Letter from Anne Richardson, archives of Merseyside Maritime Museum, Liverpool.

231–32 The story of Mr. and Mrs. Stroud is told by A. D. Donald in his undated account of the sinking and related manuscript notes, Mariners' Museum, Newport News.

232 "skirt . . . dropped": Also described in ibid.

232 "Find its mother": M. Ward, *Father Maturin*, p. 60.

233 "snuggled . . . deck house": Ellis, *The Tragedy of the Lusitania*, p. 36.

233 "trying . . . children everywhere": Quoted by J. Lawrence in an article in the *Coronet*, March 1950.

233 "Find all the kiddies . . . boy": A. Hurd, *Murder at Sea*, p. 10.

234 "into a boat . . . water": Evidence of Radio Operator R. Leith to Mersey (TO).

236 "a pleasant smile . . . face": *New York Tribune*, 11 May 1915.

236 "There Is a Green Hill Not Far Away": Quoted in Hoehling and Hoehling, *The Last Voyage of the Lusitania*, p. 143.

237 "standing . . . boat deck": Letter from F. Bailey (widow of Commander Stackhouse) to M. Hoehling, 21 August 1955, Mariners' Museum, Newport News.

237 "Why . . . gives us": Quoted in Ellis, *The Tragedy of the Lusitania*, pp. 38–39.

237 "a mighty . . . debris": Isaac F. Marcosson and D. Frohman, *Manager and Man*, p. 4.

238 Up in the wheelhouse . . . keep his head up: All the quotes in this paragraph are from Quartermaster H. Johnston's interview with the BBC and from a letter from him to A. A. Hoehling of 25 September 1955.

238 "walked . . . position": Evidence of Third Engineer R. Duncan to Mersey (TO).

238 "jumped . . . sinking": Evidence of Chief Steward J. Jones to Mersey (TO).

238–239 "every time . . . time": Evidence of Able Seaman F. Hennessy to Wynne.

239 "all bouncing . . . water": Taped interview given by D. Lawlor to CBC.

239 "there were three . . . top boat": Evidence of Ship's Carpenter N. Robertson to Wynne.

239 "right side up": Evidence of Boatswain J. Davies to Wynne.

239 Able seaman . . . tangle of wreckage: All quotations in this paragraph are from T. O'Mahoney's note (no date), Mariners' Museum, Newport News.

241 "not pretty": Taped interview given by Otto Rikowski to CBC.

241 The account Schwieger gave to Valentiner is quoted in Thomas, *Raiders of the Deep*, p. 97.

18. A Long Lingering Moan

242 "as air" . . . so scared: *New York Times*, 21 November 1915.

242 "in two . . . paper": Frost, *German Submarine Warfare*, p. 201.

243 "was crowded . . . life": J. McFarquhar, NARA.

243 "waving hands and arms . . . afloat": Bernard, *Current Opinion*.

244 "mighty crescendo . . . under the water": Interview given by bellboy Ben Holton to BBC.

244 "violent underwater explosion": Note by O'Mahoney (undated), Mariners' Museum, Newport News.

244 "swimmers . . . the surface": Frost, *German Submarine Warfare*, p. 200.

244 "a circle . . . across": Letter from K. Simpson, on behalf of R. Barnes, to M. Hoehling, 14 July 1955, Mariners' Museum, Newport News.

244 "mangled . . . with blood": Frost, *German Submarine Warfare*, p. 203.

245 "This is my purse . . . who saves me": Flor Sullivan's account of this incident is in the *Cork Examiner*, 10 May 1915.

246 "a life jacket . . . woman in it": Taped interview given by H. Day to CBC.

246 "dotting . . . seagulls": Ellis, *The Tragedy of the Lusitania*, p. 136.

247 "the drowning struggles . . . man": Frost, *German Submarine Warfare*, p. 203.

248 "gave the bodies . . . to keep": Marshall, *Horrors and Atrocities of the Great War*, p. 28.

248 "Just as . . . sea": *Daily Mirror*, 10 May 1915.

248 "I can't . . . Nettie": This incident is described in an account by Nettie Moore's granddaughter, Colleen Frew, in "A Lusitania Memory," *Familia* 16 (2000).

249 The information about seawater temperature on 7 May 1915 comes from the Irish Marine Institute.

251 "it was . . . again": Account of the sinking (undated) by A. D. Donald.

254 "Somebody save that woman": Quoted in BBC interview.

254 "as a good seaman . . . brave man": Letter from R. J. Timmis to N. Robertson, 21 June 1915, Merseyside Maritime Museum.

254 But it was distressing . . . lifeless: All quotations in this paragraph are from crewman Brennan's interview with the BBC.

255 "constantly . . . seagulls . . . swooped . . . out": Letter from N. Turner, Captain Turner's son to A.A. Hoehling, 9 July 1955, Mariners' Museum, Newport News.

255 "flung . . . arm": *New York Tribune*, 9 May 1915.

255 "What bad luck . . . deserve this": P. Masson, *Les Naufrageurs du "Lusitania" et la Guerre de L'Ombre*, p. 122.

255 "a little skin": Interview given by trimmer Kennedy to BBC.

255 "fashionable . . . spats": *Daily Mirror*, 10 May 1915.

255 "We were . . . really blinding": Interview given by crewman Duncan to BBC.

255 "tied . . . distress": *New York Tribune*, 9 May 1915.

256 "floating stem up": Evidence of Acting Senior Third Officer J. Lewis to Mayer (T).

257 "Astern . . . seen": War diary of *U-20*, RM 97/578, German Military Archive, Freiburg.

19. Rescues and Recoveries

258 U.S. consul . . . "gone": The quotations in this paragraph are from Frost, *German Submarine Warfare*, p. 187 and from his report to the U.S. State Department, 11 May 1915, NARA.

258 Bob Leith's frantic SOS messages . . . "SUNK": The three messages quoted in this paragraph are all in PRO file ADM 137/1058.

258 "unforgettable mental shock": Frost, *German Submarine Warfare*, p. 188.

259 "LUSITANIA . . . SURVIVORS": Telegram from W. Frost to the U.S. State Department, 7 May 1915, NARA.

259 "no news . . . returned": Report by W. Frost to the U.S. State Department, 11 May 1915, NARA.

259 "the *Lusy*'s gone": Interview given by T. McCarthy to BBC.

259 "a sort . . . foghorn": Quoted in Hoehling and Hoehling, *The Last Voyage of the Lusitania*, p. 122.

259 Queenstown (Cobh) had many associations with the great transatlantic liners. The town was the *Titanic*'s last port of call on her maiden voyage in 1912. She anchored outside Roche's Point, and two tenders carried 123 passengers and 1,400 sacks of mail out to her.

259 "to prepare one hundred more": Letter from A. Biddulph, 7 May 1915, National Maritime Museum of Ireland, Dun Laoghaire.

259 "NO INTELLIGENCE . . . PASSENGERS": Cunard archives.

260 "She's gone . . . now": J. Lawrence's article in the *Coronet*, March 1950.

260 Vice Admiral Coke's report to the Admiralty of 9 May 1915, in PRO file ADM 137/1058, describes his decision to recall the *Juno*.

260 "fired the signal": *Cork Examiner*, 18 May 1915.

260–261 "as hard . . . 'we're there'": Ibid.

261 "in sight . . . all the time": Letter from K. Simpson, on behalf of R. Barnes, to M. Hoehling, 14 July 1955, Mariners' Museum, Newport News.

261–62 The story of the *Narragansett* and of the *City of Exeter* is in PRO file ADM 137/113.

262 "for . . . *Lusitania*": Marshall, *Horrors and Atrocities of the Great War*, p. 58.

262 "a perfectly blank expression . . . face": Lauriat, *The "Lusitania's" Last Voyage*, p. 34.

262 "We looked . . . sparrows": Taped interview of G. Smith with CBC.

263 "everybody . . . insane": Letter from L. Pye to Mrs. Prichard, 26 November 1915, Imperial War Museum.

263 "Why . . . before": Bernard, *Cocksparrow*, p. 162.

264 "the whole sea . . . boats": Statement by W. M. Adams, NARA.

265 "There's a periscope": Evidence of Second Engineer A. Cockburn to Mayer (T).

265 "I like you . . . don't know": Interview given by Fireman J. O'Connell to BBC.

266 "a measure for safety": Cunard archives.

266 "got a little bit of string . . . the side": Interview given by trimmer Kennedy to BBC.

267 "with his head in his arms": Interview given by Crewman Brennan to BBC.

267–68 There were . . . "who was not": The quotations in this paragraph are from Viscountess Rhondda, *This Was My World*, pp. 249–50.

268 "had no water": Interview given by Crewman Duncan to BBC.

269 "a circular lifebuoy . . . the sunlight": Frost, *German Submarine Warfare*, p. 205.

269 "as thick as grass": Quoted Hickey and Smith, *Seven Days to Disaster*, p. 248.

269 "until our hearts . . . broken": *Cork Examiner*, 18 May 1915.

269 "only in time . . . dead bodies": report, Cobh Heritage Centre.

269 "mothers . . . death": Ellis, *The Tragedy of the Lusitania*, p. 185.

270 "There were many left . . . much more": Ibid., p. 30.

270 "very weak": Evidence of E. White to Kinsale inquest, Imperial War Museum.

270 "the ghastly . . . gas torches": Frost, *German Submarine Warfare*, p. 211.

271 "bruised . . . children": Ibid., p. 212.

271 "with choking efforts . . . hysteria": Ibid., p. 212.

271 "but waited . . . deck": Ellis, *The Tragedy of the Lusitania*, p. 29.

271 "What ship . . . *Lusitania*": Lauriat, *The "Lusitania's" Last Voyage*, p. 38.

271 "language . . . point": Bernard, *Cocksparrow*, p. 165.

272 "dripping, pale . . . never see again": Letter from A. Biddulph, 7 May 1915, National Maritime Museum of Ireland, Dun Laoghaire.

272 "with hot-water jars": Ibid.

272 "terribly broken down . . . fortune of war": *New York Times*, 9 May 1915.

273 "company . . . not accounted for": Note from U.S. State Department to W. Frost, NARA.

273 "wholly unmarshalled": Report of W. Frost to Secretary of State, 11 May 1915, NARA.

274 "had been torpedoed . . . Irish coast": Report from C. Carver to Ambassador Page, 12 May 1915, NARA.

274 "We shall be at war . . . within a month": B. J. Hendrick, *The Life and Letters of Walter Pope*, vol. 2, p. 2.

275 "wire cages . . . hammocks": Interview given by Duncan to BBC.

275 "piles . . . wharves": Frost, *German Submarine Warfare*, p. 212.

275 "a father . . . arms": Quoted in Ellis, *The Tragedy of the Lusitania*, p. 178.

276 "and more . . . carried in": Interview with BBC.

20. The Town of the Dead

279 "wet silk blouse": Evidence of J. Marichal to Mersey (TO).

279 "could not understand . . . waiting for her": Letter from Irene Paynter to A. Hoehling, 24 July 1955, Mariners' Museum, Newport News.

279 "total people . . . figure was": Morton, *The Long Wake*, p. 112.

280 "Fifty percent . . . families": Quoted in D. A. Butler, *The Lusitania*, p. 175.

282 "arose immediately . . . without funds": *New York Tribune*, 11 May 1915.

282 "gaily . . . moving pictures": Ellis, *The Tragedy of the Lusitania*, p. 181.

283 "weeping women . . . reply": Ibid., p. 45.

284 "Not received . . . spelling right": Ibid., p. 51.

284 "revolved . . . other side": Frost, *German Submarine Warfare*, p. 204.

284 "I think . . . this duty": Ibid., p. 227.

284 "like a statue . . . innocence": Hoehling and Hoehling, *The Last Voyage of the Lusitania*, p. 218.

285 "at a cost . . . more than 10": Report of Captain Castle to Ambassador Page, 14 May 1915, NARA.

285 "curious effacement . . . yet understand": Frost, *German Submarine Warfare*, p. 228.

285 "Scores . . . always corpses": Ibid., p. 236.

285 "warnings . . . was struck": Report of Captain Miller of 12 May 1915, NARA.

285 "bare facts . . . by him": W. Frost, Report to Secretary of State of 11 May 1915, NARA.

286 "Well . . . hard way": Letter from W. Smith to A. Hoehling, 27 June 1955, Mariners' Museum, Newport News.

287 "never seen . . . head in his hands": Taped interview given by L. Hadfield to CBC.

287–88 The information about the Mounseys comes from the *Chicago Tribune* of 16 October 1915.

288 "a piercing cry . . . 'Saved'": *Times*, 10 May 1915.

288 "not all . . . personal keeping": *Liverpool Daily Post*, 10 May 1915.

288 "So there you are": Quoted in Hickey and Smith, *Seven Days to Disaster*, p. 274.

290 Sir Hugh Lane's body was never recovered. The terms of his will led to a cele-brated, still-running dispute between the National Gallery in London and the Dublin Municipal Gallery over thirty-nine of his paintings. He had originally bequeathed these pictures to the London gallery, but in February 1915 he changed his mind. He wrote a codicil leaving the pictures to Dublin, but the codicil was not witnessed. Both galleries duly claimed the works of art, London arguing that it had the legal right to them and Dublin that it had the moral right. Over the years a series of temporary com-promises was reached. Under the current agreement, due to expire in 2005, the paint-ings are being loaned in rotation by London to Dublin. But the fundamental question of ownership is still unresolved and is likely to remain so.

291 "simply dumb . . . faces": *New York Tribune*, 10 May 1915.

291 "Everybody . . . another boat": Quoted in Hickey and Smith, *Seven Days to Dis-aster*, p. 274.

292 "Why were we . . . into the boats": *Morning Post*, 10 May 1915. Within weeks Margaret Mackworth was giving public testimonials to the "Boddy Belt" life jacket. The company's advertisement in the *Journal of Commerce* of 18 June 1915 quoted her com-ment: "Without your belt I could not possibly have survived."

21. A Sad and Horrible Task

293–95 The account of the Kinsale inquest is taken from the transcript of the "Proceedings of Coroner John J. Horgan's Inquisition into the Death of Captain R. Matthews as a Result of the Sinking of R.M.S. Lusitania," May 1915, in the Imperial War Museum, supplemented by reports in the *Times* weekly edition of 14 May 1915 and in the *Cork Examiner* of 10 May 1915. Coroner Horgan later joined the Coast Patrol Service to help in "bringing the criminals to justice" for the sinking of the *Lusitania*.

295 The telegram requesting the stopping of the inquest was sent by Captain Webb and is in PRO file ADM 137/113.

295 "as belated . . . against attack": J. J. Horgan, *Parnell to Pearce*, p. 275.

295 "Packed . . . flowers": *New York Tribune*, 11 May 1915.

296–97 The atmosphere . . . "the entire town": All quotations in this paragraph are from M. Prichard's letter of 10 May 1915, Imperial War Museum.

297–98 "Second torpedo . . . all available vessels": Report of W. Frost to State Department, 11 May 1915, NARA.

298 Sadly, one of the fishing boats that had brought in bodies, the *Antoinette*, col-lided with one of the *Lusitania*'s rafts and sank.

298 "explosives . . . surface": Report from W. Frost to Secretary of State, 17 June 1915, NARA.

298 "bodies . . . marks": Telegram from Cunard, Queenstown, to Cunard, Liver-pool, 22 May 1915, Cunard archives.

298 "Let mercy . . . only fear": Letter from F. Bailey (widow of Commander Stack-house) to M. Hoehling, 21 August 1955, Mariners' Museum, Newport News.

299 "No. 239 . . . No property": Letter from Cunard, Queenstown, to Cunard, Liv-erpool, 27 May 1915, Cunard archives.

299 "nothing . . . features": Report on unidentified remains, Cunard archives.

299 "almost . . . tennis boots": Ibid.

299–300 "hot weather . . . length of time": Letter from Cunard, Queenstown, to Cunard, Liverpool, 27 May 1915, Cunard archives.

300–01 "MARY . . . ENDS": Telegram from Cunard, Liverpool, to Cunard, Queenstown, 22 May 1915.

301 "Maggie . . . Star": Letter, Cunard archives.

301 "Description . . . suspenders": Report on unidentified remains, Cunard archives.

301 "eyeglasses . . . handbag": Cunard, Queenstown, to Cunard, Liverpool, 27 May 1915, Cunard archives.

301 "modest looking . . . when she arrived": Letter from M. H. Justice to Cunard, 3 June 1915, Cunard archives.

301 "We . . . railroads": Letter from Cunard, Liverpool, to Cunard, Queenstown, Cunard archives.

301–02 "To get rid . . . our hands": Letter from Cunard, Queenstown, to Cunard, Liverpool, Cunard archives.

302 "even . . . for nothing": Cunard, Queenstown, to Cunard, Liverpool, Cunard archives.

302 "the very large cost": Cunard, Liverpool, to Cunard, Queenstown, Cunard archives.

302 "in view . . . freight": Letter from Cunard, Liverpool, to Cunard, Queenstown, 22 May 1915, Cunard archives.

302 "apparently . . . record": Letter from Cunard, Queenstown, to Cunard, Liverpool, 6 July 1915, Cunard archives.

302 "it was . . . sister": Letter from Cunard, Queenstown, to Cunard, Liverpool, 10 July 1915, Cunard archives.

302 "Grave C . . . Lower Tier": Letter to Cunard from P. Lancaster, 18 September, 1915.

303 It fell to . . . finally ended: The quotations in both these paragraphs are from Frost, *German Submarine Warfare*, pp. 228, 235, and 326.

303 On 7 June 1915 the *St. Louis* and the *Cameronia* brought seven survivors, including Charles Bowring and Oscar Grab, to New York. As the *St. Louis* passed over the spot where the *Lusitania* rested, a female survivor who had lost her husband tossed a large fragrant wreath of lilies and roses overboard. (*New York Times*, 8 June, 1915)

22. The Hun's Most Ghastly Crime

307 "great joy": Telegram of 9 May 1915, RM 5/2981, German Military Archive, Freiburg.

307 "extraordinary success": *Frankfurter Zeitung*.

307 "hundreds . . . lines": *Neue Preussische Zeitung*, 10 May 1915.

307–08 "citizens . . . shield": *Kölnische Volkszeitung*, 8 May 1915.

308 "a success of moral significance": *Kölnische Volkszeitung*.

308 The decoded translations of the German signals are in PRO file ADM 137/4353 and ADM 137/1359.

308 "MY HIGHEST APPRECIATION . . . RETURN": The decoded translation is in PRO file ADM 137/4353.

308 "Latest Achievements . . . at Sea": *Daily Chronicle*, 8 May 1915.

308 "The Hun's . . . Crime": Ibid.

308 "Sowing . . . gas": *Daily Chronicle*, 8 May 1915.

309 The story of "the Little Unknown" is from the *Daily Mirror*, 10 May 1915.

309–10 Several accounts . . . next: The quotations from the *Times* and the *Daily Express* are from their 8 May 1915 issues.

310 "widespread . . . fire": *Daily Telegraph*, 13 May 1915.

310 The story of the two Americans joining in the rioting in Liverpool is told in the *New York Times*, 25 May 1915.

311 "the German's divorce . . . complete": *Chatillonais et Auxois*, 13 May 1915.

311 "As . . . certain": (Paris) *Journal*, 10 May 1915.

311 "the news . . . hate": *Morgenblad*, 8 May 1915, quoted in the *Times* of 10 May 1915.

311 "Criminal . . . devilish": *Telegraaf*, quoted in the *Observer*, 9 May 1915.

312 "Germany intends . . . perfection": *Minneapolis Journal*, quoted in Marshall, *Horrors and Atrocities of the Great War*, p. 76.

312 "the triumphant cry of the Valkyrie": Viereck, *Spreading Germs of Hate*, p. 69.

312 "without . . . neutrality": *New York Times*, 10 May 1915.

312 committed suicide: *New York Tribune*, 10 May 1915.

313 "501,000 . . . any uprising": Gerard, *My Four Years in Germany*, p. 167.

313 Bachmann's telegram of 14 May 1915 to Berlin is in RM 2/162, German Military Archive, Freiburg.

313 The torpedo laboratory's forensic report of 21 July 1915 is in RM 5/2981, German Military Archive, Freiburg.

314 "treated very ungraciously": Tirpitz, *My Memoirs*, vol. 2, p. 415.

314 The extent of the anxiety and mutual recriminations can be seen in the fact that Hermann Bauer felt it necessary on 8 May 1915 to reassure his U-boat commanders that although they might be asked to report on their missions urgently by radio, this was only to enable false reports in the enemy and neutral press to be countered. It did not imply any intention on the part of the naval authorities to pass judgments on their activities. (RM 86/224, German Military Archive, Freiburg)

23. Fool or Traitor?

315 "SPECIALLY . . . TO HER": Telegram from Vice Admiral Coke to Admiralty, 7 May 1915, PRO ADM 137/113.

315–16 Admiral Jacky Fisher . . . unbalanced: The quotations in this paragraph are from Gilbert, *Winston S. Churchill, 1914–16*, vol. 3, p. 419.

316 The full text of the House of Commons debate is given in *Hansard*, 10 May 1915, columns 1359–63.

316 "From reports received . . . dangerous": PRO file ADM 137/1058.

316–18 Captain Webb's memorandum of 12 May 1915, together with the telegram from Spring-Rice reporting Bennett's comments about Cunard staff in New York, Oliver's memorandum, and Fisher's and Churchill's comments, is in PRO file ADM 137/1058.

319 "greatly in excess": Quoted in Hough, *First Sea Lord*, p. 336.

Notes and Sources

319 "I am off . . . questionings": Fisher to Churchill, 15 May 1915, in Marder, *Fear God and Dread Nought*, vol. 3, p. 228.

319 "guarantee . . . sea forces whatsoever": Fisher to Asquith, 19 May 1915, ibid., p. 241.

319 "extraordinary ultimatum . . . mental aberration": Quoted in Marder, *From the Dreadnought to Scapa Flow*, vol. 2, p. 285.

319 Admiral "Jackie" Fisher's life continued to run along its eccentric groove. After his resignation, rather than live with his wife, he had moved in with the duchess of Hamilton, to whom he was close, and her husband. He spent his remaining years writing peppery and disjointed memoirs, dying in 1920.

320–21 The nature . . . vouch for it: The documents and quotations in these two paragraphs are all in PRO file ADM 116/1416.

321 Among the informal statements from the Ministry of Defence is one to P. Beesly, Imperial War Museum archives.

321 "He thus . . . inviting disaster": The various versions of Webb's memorandum are in PRO file ADM 116/1416.

322 "Cunard . . . destroyers": PRO file ADM 137/113.

322 The correspondence between the Admiralty and the White Star Line is in PRO file ADM 137/1058.

323 F. E. Smith later became lord chancellor and viceroy of India. He is said to have once received a large set of legal papers on which to advise, to have sat up all night reading them and drinking champagne, and to have written an opinion that read (in full): "Sue and the damages will be enormous."

324 In addition to . . . "only one": The few sworn crew statements that survive are in PRO file ADM 137/1058. The quotation from H. Johnston is from his BBC interview.

324 "I have . . . abaft the bridge": Letter from O. Bernard to Mrs. Prichard, 15 August 1915, Imperial War Museum.

324–25 The inquiry . . . acted upon them: The quotations in this paragraph come from Mersey (TO).

325 "to think or speak": Letter from Captain Turner to Miss Bryant, 10 June 1915, Cunard archives.

325 "As regards . . . sheer merit": Note by Webb, 18 May 1915, PRO file ADM 137/1058.

325–27 At his first appearance . . . longitudinal bulkheads was ruled out: All quotations in these seven paragraphs are from Mersey (TO) and Mersey (TC).

327 "to collect . . . information": The Defence of the Realm Act Regulation concerned was number eighteen.

328–29 However . . . correctly: All quotations in these five paragraphs are from Mersey (TO).

329 The French government reply about Marichal's background is in PRO file MT/9/1326/M 1984.

329–30 On 1 July . . . "glad to see you": All quotations in this paragraph come from PRO file ADM 116/1416. The Admiralty reply to Lord Mersey making the offer of a meeting with Balfour is dated 30 June 1915.

330–31 Whether Lord Mersey . . . "committed the crime: All quotations in these three paragraphs are from Mersey (R).

24. No Longer Neutral Spectators

332 "tears in his eyes": J. P. Tumulty, *Woodrow Wilson as I Knew Him*, p. 232.

332 "see red . . . horrible a thing": Ibid.

332 "America . . . spectators": Colonel House to President Wilson, 9 May 1915, in Link, *The Papers of Woodrow Wilson*, vol. 33, p. 134.

332 "THE UNITED STATES . . . EUROPEAN RESPECT": Gregory, *Walter Hines Page*, p. 96.

332–33 "because . . . withdraw from it": Tumulty, *Woodrow Wilson as I Knew Him*, p. 233.

333 "It would be . . . in front of an army": W. Bryan to President Wilson, 9 May 1915, Bryan Correspondence, Library of Congress.

333 "German Embassy . . . arms": Private note by C. Spring-Rice in PRO file FO 115/1998.

333 "AS OUR MAIN INTEREST . . . GUARDED": Telegram from C. Spring-Rice to foreign office, 9 May 1915, in PRO file FO 115/1998.

333 "there . . . enclosed": *Glasgow Herald*, 10 May 1915.

333 "When . . . *love you*": President Wilson to Edith Bolling Galt, in Link, *The Papers of Woodrow Wilson*, vol. 33, pp. 146–47.

334 The quotation from President Wilson's Philadelphia speech is in ibid., vol. 33, p. 149.

334 "immediate . . . vigor": *Literary Digest*, 22 May 1915.

334 "expressing . . . special matter": Link, *The Papers of Woodrow Wilson*, vol. 133, p. 154.

334 "IMPRESSION . . . ADVISABLE": C. Spring-Rice to foreign office, 13 May 1915, PRO file FO 115/1998.

334 "deepest sympathy . . . ram submarines": The text of the German note is in *Foreign Relations of the U.S., 1915 Supplement*, part 2, p. 389.

334 "splendid quarters": Müller's diary for 9 May 1915, quoted in his book *Regierte der Kaiser?*

335 "shackling U-boat . . . *Lusitania* case": Bachmann to Bethmann Hollweg, 10 May 1915, RM8/525, German Military Archive, Freiburg.

335 "I . . . INCALCULABLE CONSEQUENCES": Treutler to Bethmann Hollweg, 9 May 1915, German foreign office documents archive, St. Anthony's College, Oxford.

335 "DESTROY . . . FUTURE": Telegram from Bethmann Hollweg to Treutler, 10 May 1915, ibid. The pencil notation by Kriege was added as a "secret note" on a copy of this telegram, probably for the eyes of the chancellor and foreign secretary.

335 "His Majesty . . . situation": Müller's diary for 9 May 1915, quoted in his book *Regierte der Kaiser?*

335 "a halfway concession": Ibid.

336 Bryan . . . "day's work": The quotations in this paragraph are from a letter from L. Garrison to J. Tumulty, 18 November 1928, quoted in J. M. Blum, *Tumulty and the Wilson Era*, p. 160.

337 The text of the first American note to Germany is in *Foreign Relations of the U.S., 1915 Supplement*, part 2, pp. 393–96.

337 "all the red blood . . . ask": *Baltimore Sun*, 15 May 1915.

337 "the united . . . people": *New York Times*, 13 May 1915.

337 "both . . . diplomacy": *Times*.

337 "if the principles . . . will come": *La Prensa*, Buenos Aires.

337 "frightfulness . . . her commerce": *Washington Herald*.

338 "the United States . . . public opinion": Quoted in Tansill, *America Goes to War*, p. 315.

338 "blunt . . . manner": Bernstorff, *Memoirs*, p. 156.

338 "places . . . imminent": C. Dumba, *Memoirs of a Diplomat*, p. 234.

338 "You see . . . public opinion": Ibid.

339 "indiscreet . . . to his Government": R. Lansing, *War Memoirs*, pp. 30–31.

339 "Bryan . . . re-election": Bernstorff to Berlin, 11 May 1915. The British decoded this message when it was transmitted, and the decode is in PRO file ADM 137/3963.

339 "the necessity . . . neutrals": Müller's diary for 27 May 1915, quoted in his book *Regierte der Kaiser?*

339 The text of Germany's response, which was dated 28 May 1915 and arrived in Washington on 31 May, is given in *Foreign Relations of the U.S., 1915 Supplement*, part 2, pp. 419–21.

340 "on his high horse again": Müller's diary for 30 May 1915, quoted in his book *Regierte der Kaiser?*

340 "more neutral powers . . . war": Official report of 31 May 1915, cited in Admiral A. Spindler's *Der Handelskrieg mit U-Booten*, vol. 2, p. 101.

340 "which would be   people": Ibid.

340 "which would take . . . account": Ibid.

340 The text of the orders is in RM 2/1982, German Military Archive, Freiburg, D/21/b/3, with an excellent translation in A. S. Link's *Wilson—the Struggle for Neutrality*, p. 408.

340 The text of the order amending the orders of 1 June is given in a telegram from Müller, 5 June 1915, RM 8/525, German Military Archive, Freiburg.

341 While the German . . . "sweetly reasonable": The press quotes are taken from the *Literary Digest*, 12 June 1915.

341–42 President Wilson . . . wrote out his resignation: The quotations in these five paragraphs about the cabinet meeting and subsequent events are from Seymour, *The Intimate Diaries of Colonel House*, vol. 2, pp. 5–6 and from W. G. McAdoo's *Crowded Years*, pp. 330–36.

342 Lansing . . . "American ships": The text of the second American note to Germany is in *Foreign Relations of the U.S., 1915 Supplement*, part 2, pp. 436–38.

343–44 "executioner avoid 'em!": Quoted in Gregory, *Walter Hines Page*, pp. 102–3. Sir Cecil Spring-Rice was pleased too—he had considered Bryan a "jelly fish . . . incapable of forming a settled judgement on anything outside party politics" (C. Spring-Rice to foreign office, 25 August 1914, quoted in ibid., p. 101).

He might have been less pleased had he known that Bryan's successor, Lansing, regarded him with contempt for looking and acting like "a foreign office clerk" and suspected he was in cahoots with Roosevelt and the Republicans (quoted in Dos Passos, *Mr. Wilson's War*, p. 134).

25. German Agents Are Everywhere

345 "This is . . . blow up the *Lusitania*": W. J. Kavanagh to R. Lansing, 8 May 1915, NARA.

345 "first hand . . . substantiated": Telegram from C. C. Speiden to President Wilson, 2 June 1915, NARA.

345 "I hear . . . May 7": Telegram from Spring-Rice to foreign office, 9 May 1915, PRO file FO 115/1998.

346 "dull . . . important": Article by W. J. Flynn, "Tapped Wires," *Liberty*, 2 June 1928.

346 The constant reports . . . "naval attaché": The quotations in this paragraph are from Spring-Rice's report to the foreign office of 21 July 1915, Spring-Rice Collection, Churchill College, Cambridge.

346 "three alleged German spies . . . down with the *Lusitania*": Daily Mirror, 10 May 1915.

346–47 The account of König's activities and Thorsten's visit to Kienzle are in NARA M 1085 264 09 119.

347 On 1 June . . . supporting Stahl's story: The quotes in this paragraph and in the subsequent eight paragraphs, including the text of Stahl's affidavit and of the four supporting affidavits, together with the details of the investigation by the Department of Justice, are contained in NARA. So too is the correspondence between Lansing and Dumba about the unstable Rittegh.

349–50 Stahl's story . . . fine of one dollar: All quotations in these two paragraphs are from NARA with the exception of the description of Stahl, which comes from the *New York Times*, 11 June 1915.

350 The climate of suspicion . . . food and drink: Among other sources, the story of the attack on Morgan is well described in a letter from Spring-Rice to Mrs. Henry Cabot Lodge, 5 July 1915, Spring-Rice papers, Churchill College, Cambridge.

351 "What . . . night": Letter from C. Spring-Rice to Sir E. Grey, 21 July 1915, in ibid.

351–52 The British had . . . "more trouble": C. Bennett's accusations in these two paragraphs are in his note to C. Spring-Rice, 10 May 1915, in PRO file FO 115/1943.

352 "I assured . . . the goods": Letter from A. Booth to C. Sumner, Cunard archives.

352 "practically insisted": Letter from A. Booth to Mearns, 11 June 1915, Cunard archives.

353 "I am willing . . . than myself": Telegram from C. Sumner to A. Booth, 13 June 1915, Cunard archives. Captain Charles turned out to be at best ineffectual, at worst incompetent. British naval attaché Captain Guy Gaunt wrote with contempt that "honestly if Charles had any brains he successfully concealed the fact" (G. Gaunt to Captain Dow, 26 February 1916, Cunard archive). Sumner was left to get on with his job.

353–54 As a sop to British government concerns, Booth forbade Cunard employees to eat at a New York restaurant run by a former German employee of the company, though he wrote kindly to him, "I never doubted your loyalty to the Cunard Company as long as you were in our service." He also tactfully deployed Herman Winter to other duties in California and agreed to Sumner's suggestion that Winter call on Spring-Rice in Washington to assure him of his loyalty. (A. Booth to Farnham, 12 July 1915, PRO file FO 115/1998)

353 Meanwhile . . . "RETURN TO GERMANY": Quotations in this paragraph are from Rintelen, *The Dark Invader*, pp. 119–21.

353 Rintelen's indiscreet behavior may also have contributed to his recall. Anne L. Seward, niece of a former secretary of state, was so alarmed by the tenor of her conversation with him that she wrote to the president warning that he must be "a secret but intimate emissary from the Kaiser" whose "utterances are distinctly offensive and his threats alarming" (letter of 2 July 1915, box 209, Records of the Office of Counsellor, RG 59, NA).

353 After his arrest by the British, Rintelen was interrogated by Reginald Hall. There were strong rumors in British Intelligence circles that the telegram recalling the German had come not from Berlin but from Hall. Rather than face a firing squad as a spy, Rintelen eventually admitted that he was a German naval officer. After eighteen months in a British prisoner-of-war camp, he was extradited to the United States, charged with other German agents with firebombing merchant ships, and sentenced to four years' penal servitude in an Atlanta penitentiary.

In 1920 President Wilson commuted his sentence, and he returned to Germany, where he was awarded the Iron Cross. In later years Reginald Hall, now an admiral and knighted for his services, contacted Rintelen to question him further about German espionage activities in America during the First World War. The two former opponents now became such close friends that Rintelen attended the wedding of Hall's daughter and his own daughter was a bridesmaid.

In the 1930s Rintelen and his views became non grata with the Nazi authorities. He settled in England, and the Nazis placed him on their blacklist of those to be murdered when they invaded Britain. He collapsed with a heart attack outside the South Kensington tube station and died in 1949.

353 "he has . . . inamorata": Diary of Chandler P. Anderson, quoted in B. Tuchman, *The Zimmermann Telegram*, p. 86.

353–54 The full story of the famous briefcase affair is that commercial councillor Henrich Albert and propagandist George Viereck left Albert's office at 45 Broadway, the headquarters of the Hamburg-Amerika steamship line. Unknown to them, they were being tailed by American secret agent Frank Burke. Burke noticed that Viereck, whom he knew by sight, seemed to be treating his companion with great deference and respect. He was uncertain at first who this second man was but, noting that he was about fifty years old, tall, and with dueling scars on his cheek, identified him correctly as Albert. He also noted that he was carrying a bulging briefcase.

Viereck and Albert caught the elevated railway, or "El," along Sixth Avenue. Viereck got out at Twenty-third Street, leaving Albert—who dozed off. He woke up in a panic as the El reached the Fiftieth Street station and hurriedly jumped out, forgetting his briefcase. Burke grabbed it and stepped out onto the platform. Albert at once realized that he had lost his case and began peering wildly around. Burke flattened himself against the wall and pretended to light a cigar. Albert ran down to the street while Burke took another staircase and managed to jump on a moving trolley. At that moment, Albert saw him and ran shrieking after him. Burke told the surprised conductor that Albert was "crazy—stark raving mad," some kind of a "nut."

In desperation Albert placed an advertisement in the *New York Evening Telegram*: "LOST—on Saturday, on 3.30 Harlem elevated train, at 50th St. station, brown leather bag, containing documents . . . $20 reward." It was no use.

354 "these idiotic Yankees": British government white paper, *Command 8012*. The British published the most startling of the documents in this parliamentary white paper in August 1915 to ensure that they were not brushed under the carpet.

354 Von Papen had his baggage searched with disastrous consequences when the ship taking him home to Germany in 1915 called at Falmouth and was boarded by British officials. They confiscated his checkbook stubs, which confirmed the extensive spy ring he had been funding in the United States. As a diplomat, von Papen was immune from arrest and continued his journey home. The kaiser awarded him the Iron Cross and the Order of the Red Eagle. Von Papen became chancellor of Germany in 1932 and Hitler's vice chancellor in 1933. He was tried at Nuremberg for war crimes but was acquitted.

Spymaster Paul König was never tried on major spying and sabotage charges, not even for the infamous explosion at the munitions depot on Black Tom Island in New Jersey in which he was plainly implicated. He was deported at the end of the war, having steadfastly refused to divulge anything about his activities and contacts.

26. The Kaiser's Business Only

355 The story of Bauer's insubordination and the kaiser's irritation is in RM 8/526, German Military Archive, Freiburg.

355 "such an instruction . . . further": RM 2/1982, German Military Archive, Freiburg.

355 "in a very depressed mood": Müller's diary for 23 June 1915 in *Regierte der Kaiser?* p. 110.

356 "pro-Tirpitz sentiment was growing": Ibid.

356 They had underestimated . . . "and agitated": The sources in this paragraph are Müller's diary for 25 June, pp. 110–11.

356 The text of the second German note is in PRO file FO/115 1998 and is given in *Foreign Relations of the U.S., 1915 Supplement*, part 2, pp. 480–82.

357 The text of the third American note is in PRO file FO/115 1998 and is given in *Foreign Relations of the U.S., 1915 Supplement*, part 2, pp. 480–82.

357 The kaiser's furious notes are quoted in Link, *Woodrow Wilson—the Struggle for Neutrality*, p. 449.

357 "Order . . . Disorder": Tirpitz, *My Memoirs*, vol. 2, p. 416.

357 Bachmann's inquiry about the definition of a passenger ship is in his note of 3 September to the kaiser, RM 2/1992, German Military Archive, Freiburg.

357 Tirpitz's complaint about instructions is in his telegram of 2 September 1915, RM 2/1992, German Military Archive, Freiburg.

357–58 The "Q" ships had enjoyed their first successes in June 1915, working not alone but with a British submarine towed behind them. However, because there were no nonnaval witnesses and the German survivors were made prisoners of war, the existence of the ships was not yet revealed to the world.

358 "unlimited money . . . *My business only*": Quoted in Clark, *Kaiser Wilhelm II*, p. 232.

359 The copy of the war diary of the *U-20* for the patrol of 29 August to 15 September 1915, held in the German Military Archive, Freiburg, records the sinking of the *Hesperian*.

359 "Hereafter . . . instructions exactly": Schwieger's letter to Bauer, dated 21 September 1915, is in RM 97/384, German Military Archive, Freiburg.

359 Bauer's bitter comments about Germany's handling of the *Lusitania* affair are from his book *Reichsleitung und U-Bootseinsatz, 1914 bis 1918*, p. 39.

359 Edith Cavell's last words should have been better remembered by the war's eventual victors: "Patriotism is not enough. I must have no bitterness towards anyone."

359 "to keep . . . forget": J. Gerard quoted in Bailey and Ryan, *The Lusitania Disaster*, p. 267.

359–60 Wilson, although seeming so "buttoned up" in public, was, in private, a passionate man. At the time of his engagement the following joke made the rounds in Washington: "What happened when Woodrow Wilson proposed to Edith Bolling Galt?"—Pause—"She fell out of bed!"

360 The third and final German note is contained in C. Savage, *Policy of the United States toward Maritime Commerce in War*, vol. 1, pp. 458–59.

360 The defense attaché's report is dated 18 May 1915, archives of the U.S. Naval War College, Newport, Rhode Island.

360–61 Fisher's letter of consolation to Tirpitz was written on 29 March 1916 and is contained in Fisher's *Memories*, p. 31.

361 "unless . . . relations": Lansing's note is dated 18 April 1916 and is given in *Foreign Relations of the U.S., 1916 Supplement*, pp. 232–34.

361 "there was . . . international law": Gerard, *My Four Years in Germany*, p. 246.

361 "a decisive . . . capitulation": Tirpitz, *My Memoirs*, vol. 2, p. 423.

362 Jagow's note reporting that he had asked the Bavarian government to prevent the distribution of the medals is dated 16 November 1916, RM 5/2981, German Military Archive, Freiburg.

363 "finis Germaniae": Tuchman, *The Zimmermann Telegram*, p. 141.

363 "I order . . . Wilhelm I. R.": *Official German Documents Relating to the World War*, vol. 2, p. 1210.

363 "BERNSTORFF . . . DRUNK TONIGHT": Tuchman, *The Zimmermann Telegram*, p. 151.

364 The text of the Zimmermann telegram is in *Official German Documents*, vol. 22, p. 1337.

365 "Profound sensation": Quoted in Tuchman, *The Zimmermann Telegram*, pp. 168 and 175. Americans were outraged that Germany should plot a war on the American continent and offer parts of U.S. territory to another power if she would join in. This "Prussian Invasion Plot," as the papers called it, seemed an even more direct threat to U.S. interests than was unrestricted submarine warfare to her commerce.

365 "Now I may as well abdicate": Clark, *Kaiser Wilhelm II*, p. 238.

27. "That Story Is Forever Disposed Of"

366 "Lusitania": *New York Times*, 6 July 1918.

366 "one . . . means": Ibid., 1 December, 1925.

366 "That story . . . concerned": Mayer (T).

367 "It is . . . I cannot": Turner's evidence to Wynne.

367–68 The statements from Captains Taylor, Fear, and Durie are in Mayer (T), and so is the evidence from Cunard's New York office, Fred Gauntlett, James Brooks, Professor Hovgaard, and the respective arms experts.

369 "on going . . . C.S.S. Co.": J. Roper's letter of 16 July 1919 is quoted in a letter from D. O'Connor, NBC, to P. Bailey of 22 February 1974, Hoover Institution.

369–70 Judge Mayer's opinion . . . promised indemnity: All quotations in these three paragraphs are from Mayer (O).

370 This was . . . lifetimes: Details in these two paragraphs are from Awards by Mixed Claims Commission—U.S. and Germany Decisions and Opinions, May 1925.

28. Diving into the Wreck

371–72 Nothing . . . ammunition carrier: All quotations in this paragraph are from documents in the Cunard archives.

372 "naturally . . . unprejudiced observers": Telegram from U.S. embassy, London, to State Department, 24 June 1922, NARA.

374 Among the academic researchers, T. A. Bailey and P. B. Ryan stated that Simpson's book "mingles history with historical fiction in a thoroughly misleading fashion" (Bailey and Ryan, *The Lusitania Disaster*, p. 341).

374 "it would be . . . manifest": R. D. Ballard, *Exploring the Lusitania*, p. 194.

376 The information about the location of the wreck is given in G. Gentile, *The Lusitania Controversies*, vol. 2, p. 301.

29. A Legitimate Target?

383 "the disaster . . . of that time": Mayer (O).

384 "Curiously . . . exact facts": Letter from Sir O. Murray to Sir G. Greene, 10 March 1924, National Maritime Museum archives.

384 Lord Mersey's letter of 22 September 2000 to the author confirms the statement about his forebear's papers.

386 Kriege's pencil note, marked "secret," about the status of the *Lusitania* is a pencil notation on a telegram from Bethmann Hollweg to Treutler, 10 May 1915, German foreign office documents archive, St. Anthony's College, Oxford.

387 Michael Byrne's comments about his search of the ship are in his letter of 8 June 1915 to Secretary of State Bryan, NARA.

387 "HAVE SEEN PICTURES . . . VIEW OF DECKS": British consul general in Philadelphia to foreign office, 21 June 1915, PRO file FO 115/1943.

387–88 The reassurances from Alfred Booth to Charles Sumner are in a telegram of 3 June 1915, Cunard archives.

388 "the *Lusitania* has no guns": C. Bennett to Sir C. Spring-Rice, 6 September 1914, PRO file FO 115/1805.

388 "certainly not . . . concealed below": Boy-Ed's note of 2 June 1915, RM 3/460, German Military Archive, Freiburg.

388–89 The information about Canadian troops and about Robert Matthews is in a letter from P.A.O. Chaplin, Senior Research Officer, Directorate of History, Canadian Ministry of Defence to P. B. Ryan, 10 June 1974, Hoover Institution, supplemented by the author's own researches in the Cunard archives.

388 Dudley Field Malone's testimony is given in Savage, *Policy of the United States*, vol. 2, pp. 333–34.

389–90 The supplementary cargo manifest was given out at the New York Custom House and reported in the *New York Times*, 3 June 1915, although some have claimed it was kept secret for many years.

390 The calculations about shell weight are by P. O'Sullivan and are given in his book *The Lusitania, Unravelling the Mysteries*, p. 100.

391 Boy-Ed's comments to Berlin of 27 April 1915 about the *Trinidad* are in the Hoover Institution archives.

391 The activities of König, McCulley, Brun, and Stahl are documented in NARA M.1085/264 oG 119.

391 The telegram about Leach from Berlin to the German embassy, Washington, dated 24 February 1915, is in PRO file ADM 137/3962.

391–92 Pierpoint's evidence to Wynne refers to him going to his "proper station," which was "starboard side near to the bridge . . . A deck." Pierpoint became governor of one of Liverpool's main prisons, retiring in 1929. He died in 1950.

30. Harm's Way

394 The intercepted radio messages about the *U-20* and her sister submarines are in PRO file ADM 137/3956.

395 The evidence that the Germans were aware of the Admiralty advice about headlands is in PRO file ADM 137/1428.

395 "it is most important . . . U.S.A. with Germany": Churchill to Runciman, 12 February 1915, Runciman papers and Gilbert, *Churchill*, companion volume 3, p. 501.

395 "England . . . bring on trouble": The kaiser's comments are reported in Ambassador Gerard's telegram to the State Department, 6 May 1916, *Foreign Relations of the U.S., 1916 Supplement*, p. 260.

396 Robert Lansing's analysis is given in Foreign Relations of the U.S., the Lansing Papers, vol. 1, p. 367.

396 "AS OUR . . . GUARDED": Telegram from C. Spring-Rice to foreign office, 9 May 1915, PRO file FO 115/1998.

396 Spring-Rice's suspicions that Germany might be trying to provoke the United States into joining the war are in a private note which is in PRO file FO 115/1998.

396 Fisher's suggestion of shooting prisoners was rejected by Churchill in his letter to Fisher of 4 January 1915, Churchill Collection, Churchill College archives.

396 Evidence of Churchill's willingness to contemplate extreme measures during the First World War is given in a letter from his biographer, Martin Gilbert, to the *Times* of 4 January 1973.

396 Churchill describes his policy of keeping submarines below the surface in *World Crisis*, p. 725.

397 Fisher's admission that he was close to a nervous breakdown is documented in Gilbert, *Churchill*, vol. 3, p. 507.

397 "no man . . . back to him": Note by Edward Bell on Admiralty staff, undated, Hall Collection, Churchill College archives.

399 "one-man show . . . had to be taken": Draft of Hall's autobiography, ibid.

400 "Kimmel . . . Japanese intentions": Letter from E. Beach to P. Ryan, 2 April 1975, Hoover Institution.

400 The captain of the *Narragansett*'s fears about a hoax are in PRO file ADM 137/113. The checking of the *Demerara*'s claim is in PRO file ADM 137/3960.

402 Admiral Inglefield's correspondence with the Admiralty and the letter in which Lord Mersey is told that First Lord Balfour would be willing to see him are in PRO file ADM 116/1416.

402 The then Lord Mersey's views are quoted in the BBC archives. The certified copies of the decodes etc. are in PRO file ADM 137/4353.

402 Hugh Johnston's statements are in the BBC archives.

403 Oliver Bernard's unhappiness at not being allowed to give evidence is recorded in his letter to Mrs. Prichard of 15 August 1915, Imperial War Museum.

404 "an old-fashioned sailorman": Mersey (TO).

405 Cunard's wartime instructions about "maximum speed" are in A. Booth's evidence to Wynne.

406 The information about the distances from the coast is contained in Cunard evidence submitted to Judge Mayer and is quoted in Bailey and Ryan, *The Lusitania Disaster*, p. 280.

406 "there is . . . a channel": *Brief on the Facts for the Petitioner*, Mayer hearing, p. 75.

406 "passengers . . . at the time": Evidence of J. W. McConnell to Wynne.

407 "instructions . . . place": Evidence of J. Brooks, Mayer (T).

407 The statements about the portholes and Cunard's policy preventing stewards entering occupied cabins come from Mayer (T).

31. Anglo-Saxon Attitudes

409 The comments on the characteristics of the Anglo-Saxon race are from an article in the *Review of Reviews (Anglo-Saxons and Others)*, reviewing a book by A. Gorren in July 1900.

410 "money . . . of contrabands": W. Bryan to President Wilson, 10 August 1914, Bryan correspondence, Library of Congress.

411 "England's violation . . . humanity": President Wilson to W. Bryan, 2 June 1915, quoted in Tansill, *America Goes to War*, p. 328.

411–12 Dudley Field Malone, New York's harassed collector of customs, resigned from his post in 1917 in protest at Wilson's failure to support female suffrage strongly enough. In 1943, because of his startling resemblance to Winston Churchill, he was chosen to play the role of the British prime minister in the famous pro-Russia propaganda film *Mission to Moscow*.

413 "old guard . . . man": Quoted in Bailey and Ryan, *The Lusitania Disaster*, p. 273.

413 "The weight . . . second torpedo": Mayer (O).

413 The transcript of Hovgaard's evidence to Judge Mayer shows Mayer's determined efforts to prevent discussion of the *Lusitania*'s design and the structural damage caused to her.

413 In 1919, President Wilson traveled some 8,000 miles across America in three weeks trying to drum up support for Senate ratification of his proposals for the League of Nations. After his fortieth speech he collapsed with a cerebral thrombosis. Wilson was taken back to the White House seriously ill and partially paralyzed. His wife, Edith, controlled access to his bedroom and became a powerful political force, selecting who could see the president. Those she disliked, such as Colonel House, were excluded.

On Capitol Hill, it was Republican Senate majority leader Henry Cabot Lodge who was chief opponent of Wilson's proposals for the League of Nations and prevented their approval. The personal antipathy between the two men derived in no small part from Lodge's claims that during the 1916 presidential election Wilson had shown weakness in handling the *Lusitania* sinking. Late in the campaign Senator Henry Cabot Lodge from Massachusetts had accused Wilson of adding a postscript to the second *Lusitania* protest note to Germany to the effect that the Germans should ignore the severe language and that he, Wilson, would consider putting the dispute to arbitration. Lodge suggested that the postscript had been withdrawn only following violent pressure by the cabinet. The accusation, of course, referred to Bryan's proposal and not to the president's, but the implication stuck.

America now retreated into isolation. Her absence severely weakened the League of Nations. Wilson himself died in February 1924.

Wilson sacked Robert Lansing as secretary of state in 1920. By 1925, former secretary of state William Jennings Bryan, an ardent fundamentalist Christian, was leading a campaign against the teaching of evolution in schools. In July of that year, he appeared for the prosecution as an expert on the Bible in the so-called Monkey Trial of a schoolmaster accused of teaching evolution. In the 100° F heat of a Dayton, Tennessee, courtroom, Bryan propounded his beliefs against skilled and skeptical cross-examination. The press lampooned him as a simpleton. Distressed and exhausted, he died during his postlunch nap only five days later, at the age of sixty-five.

32. The U-Boat Diary

414 "FAST STEAMER . . . MARCH": PRO file ADM 137/4177.

414 "AMERICAN S.S. PHILADELPHIA . . . TO BE SPARED": Decoded telegram to U-boat commanders of 19 February 1915 is in PRO file ADM 137/3958. Another copy is in ADM 137/1428. Reports of the timings of the *Lusitania*'s sailings, including the one quoted, are in both these files.

415 The signed version of the *U-27*'s war diary for March 1915 is in RM 97/680, German Military Archive, Freiburg.

415 "two months . . . forget about it": Newspaper editor O. G. Villard's account of his discussion with Count Bernstorff is given in Villard's *Fighting Years*, pp. 268–69 and also in the article "The True Story of the 'Lusitania,'" published in the *American Mercury* (May 1935), pp. 41–45.

415 Schwieger's orders are in the war diary of Fregattenkapitän Hermann Bauer, reproduced in the *Journal of Modern History* 8 (1936), pp. 323–25.

415–16 Bauer's refusal to pass on orders is documented in RM 2/1982 and RM 8/526, German Military Archive, Freiburg.

417 "in German naval circles . . . torpedoing her": Quoted in Beesly, *Room 40*, pp. 108–9.

419 Schwieger's letter complaining about his treatment over the *Hesperian*, dated 21 September 1915, is in RM 97/384, German Military Archive, Freiburg.

33. A New Barbarism

421 "In spite of . . . fighting men": *News of the World*, 6 June 1937.

422 "constant battle": Bauer, *Reichsleitung und U-Bootseinsatz*, p. 39.

423 "race treachery": Sir H. Rumbold, *The War Crisis in Berlin, July to August 1914*, p. 323.

423 Tirpitz's comment that by calling a halt to unrestricted U-boat warfare Germany was losing her best chance of winning the war is in his book *My Memoirs*, vol. 2, pp. 424 and 439.

424 In the final stages of the war, as it became clear that Germany had no chance of winning and civil unrest grew, the kaiser's position became increasingly untenable. He toyed with various proposals from going to the front to die with his troops to abdicating as kaiser but remaining as king of Prussia. He was still considering the advantages of the latter when news came, on 9 November 1918, that his chancellor, Prince Max von Baden, had already announced his abdication of both thrones. The kaiser boarded the royal train and on 10 November 1918 crossed the border into Holland, never to return. In the immediate aftermath of the war, he remained worried that the Allies might try him as a war criminal, but they did not.

The kaiser watched the rise of national socialism with mixed emotions, hoping initially that it might lead to his restoration but realizing eventually that there was no hope that Hitler would restore the monarchy. When France fell in 1940, he nevertheless rejoiced, regarding it as revenge for the events of 1918. He died in Holland in 1941 at the age of eighty. Hitler wished him to be buried in Potsdam, but Wilhelm had instructed that his body was not to leave Holland until Germany was once again a monarchy. He was buried in a quiet service at Doorn, which was only briefly disrupted by a British air raid.

Admiral Tirpitz became a nationalist deputy in the Reichstag from 1924 to 1928 and died in 1930. Former chancellor Bethmann Hollweg died in 1921. Ambassador Bernstorff became ambassador to Turkey after leaving Washington. He then entered politics both as a Liberal deputy in the Reichstag and as president of the League of Nations Union in Germany. When Hitler came to power in 1933, he went into self-imposed exile in Switzerland, where he died in 1939.

The *Lusitania* affair had some strange resonances on the British side. On the opening day of the Second World War, Winston Churchill, returned from the wilderness, was once again appointed first lord of the Admiralty. On the same day, a German submarine north of Ireland sank without warning the 13,500-ton British ship *Athenia*, sailing from Glasgow via Liverpool to Canada with some 1,400 on board. This was despite Germany's signature in 1936 of a protocol outlawing unrestricted submarine warfare. Over 100 people were killed, including 28 Americans. Hitler's propaganda minister, Joseph Goebbels, at once accused Churchill of having planted a bomb that could be detonated by wireless signal and of sending British destroyers to the scene to complete the sinking because he wished to create "a new *Lusitania*" for his own political advantage.

The very next day Churchill convened an Admiralty conference, at which it was agreed that "merchant skippers must be made to obey" Admiralty instructions. The meeting also agreed on special procedures to ensure that merchant captains were thoroughly briefed on what the Admiralty expected so that there could be no doubt or confusion. Churchill, shortly to go on to greater things, had clearly not forgotten some of the lessons of the *Lusitania*.

In later years many noted that the date of the *Lusitania*'s sinking achieved an ominous significance in German history. On 7 May 1919 at the Trianon Palace, the draft terms of the Treaty of Versailles were handed to Germany. On 7 May 1945 near Reims, Field Marshal Alfred Jodl surrendered Germany's armies in the west to General Eisenhower.

Epilogue

433 "this very sad time": Note from Schwieger of 14 December 1916, in file SM U20, German Military Archive, Freiburg.

433 "very frail . . . so different": Article by Hayden Talbot, 8 November 1919 contained in PRO file ADM 137/1058.

433 "his onerous duty": Interview in Nazi *Völkischer Beobachter*, May 1935.

433 Frau Weisbach-Zerning's comments are from a letter to the author of 28 January 2000.

433 Hermann Bauer, Schwieger's commanding officer, survived both world wars and in 1956 published an acid account of the confrontation between the civil and naval leadership during the First World War. Although forty years had passed, he was still bitterly critical of Bethmann Hollweg's lobbying against unrestricted U-boat activity, the kaiser's vacillations, and the flood of contradictory orders he had unilaterally sometimes decided to ignore.

Appendix B. A Technical Account of the Sinking

441–54 This analysis is based on a technical review of the evidence by consulting engineer Mike Wood, commissioned by the author for this book, supplemented by the author's own researches.

A number of theories and suggestions have been advanced over the years to explain the explosions on the *Lusitania*:

- A coal-dust explosion is suggested in Schwieger's log, in the forensic analysis undertaken by the German torpedo laboratory at Kiel in 1915, and is proposed as the most likely candidate by R. D. Ballard in his book *Exploring the Lusitania*.
- Munitions explosions were also suggested in Schwieger's log and the German forensic analysis as well as in Colin Simpson's and Butler's books, both titled *The Lusitania*. In the latter three cases they are considered the most likely cause.
- Boiler explosions are suggested in Schwieger's log, in the German forensic analysis, and are reviewed in most other works on the sinking.
- An aluminium powder fire or explosion is suggested by Patrick O'Sullivan in his book *The Lusitania. Unravelling the Mysteries*.
- The technical article "The 'Titanic' and 'Lusitania': A Final Forensic Analysis" by W. H. Garzke Jr. and colleagues reviews in detail boiler explosions and introduces both the effect of steel plate embrittlement on the hull and a detailed analysis of boiler feedpipe failure.
- Daniel Butler suggests in his book that the dense white steam observed by witnesses came from a failure of valves during an attempt to reverse the turbines, but that the main secondary explosion came from exploding ammunition. His theory as to the reversed turbine failure seems unlikely to be true given the relatively small amount of energy available, the tolerances likely to be designed into the system to cope with such a foreseeable event, and the improbability of an exhaust valve being closed mistakenly during the reversing process by experienced engineering officers.

442 Many witnesses described . . . to some degree: This paragraph describes structural vibration. All structures have inherent natural frequencies, and so, when subjected to either shock or harmonic excitation, those frequencies will manifest themselves as vibrations. For example, hitting a tuning fork on a tabletop results in audible vibrations in the form of a note of specific pitch. The closer an excitation is to a structure's natural frequency, the larger and hence more violent are the structural responses. In such cases sympathetic responses can be seen with the naked eye. One extreme example occurred in 1970 at the Tacoma Narrows Bridge in the United States; a steady forty-two-miles-per-hour wind across the bridge deck coincided with one of its natural frequencies, producing violent swaying in the roadway prior to the bridge's catastrophic disintegration.

443 "instantaneous relief": "Effect of Torpedo Explosions on the Structure of Merchant Ships," *Engineering* 105 (22 March 1918), p. 312.

449 More recent U.S. military experience . . . "even bulged": This experience is documented in a letter from D. Birdsell, U.S. Department of the Army to P. B. Ryan, 5 February 1973 (Hoover Institution); a letter from Captain W. D. Surface, Department of the Navy Ammunition Depot, San Francisco, to P. B. Ryan of 11 December 1972 (Hoover Institution); and a letter from E. S. Brem, Naval Ammunition Department, Oahu, Hawaii, to Birdsell of 12 December 1972 (Hoover Institution).

449 "absurd": *Scientific American*, 29 May 1915.

Notes and Sources

The new research commissioned for this book suggests the following order of likelihood of the various events as the cause of the second explosion (10 is the most likely, 1 is the least):

Steam-line explosion	9
Boiler explosion	7
Aluminum powder (fire or explosion)	4
Coal dust (fire or explosion)	3
Declared or undeclared munitions	1

BIBLIOGRAPHY

Books, Dissertations, and Government Publications

Bacon, Admiral Sir R. *From 1900 Onward*. London: Hutchinson, 1940.
———. *The Life of Lord Fisher of Kilverstone*. Vols. 1 and 2, London: Hodder and Stoughton, 1929.
Bailey, T. A., and Ryan, P. B. *The Lusitania Disaster*. New York: The Free Press, 1975.
Balfour, M. *The Kaiser and His Times*. London: The Cresset Press, 1964.
Ballard, R. D. *Exploring the Lusitania*. New York: Warner/Madison Press, 1995.
Bauer, H. *Reichsleitung und U-Bootseinsatz 1914 bis 1918*. Lippoldsberg: Klosterhaus-Verlag, 1956.
Beesly, P. *Room 40*. London: Hamish Hamilton, 1982.
Beresford, Lord C. *Memoirs*. Vols. 1 and 2. Boston: Little, Brown, 1914.
Berghahn, V. R. *Germany and the Approach to War in 1914*. London: Macmillan, 1993.
Bernard, O. *Cocksparrow*. London: Jonathan Cape, 1936.
Bernstorff, Count J. von. *Memoirs*. London: William Heinemann, 1936.
———. *My Three Years in America*. New York: Charles Scribner's Sons, 1920.
Bethmann Hollweg, T. von. *Reflections on the World War*. London: Thornton Butterworth, 1920.
Bismarck, O. *Autobiography*. London: Smith Elder, 1898.
———. *New Chapters of Autobiography*. London: Hodder and Stoughton, 1920.
Blood-Ryan, H. W. *Franz von Papen*. London: Rich and Cowan, 1940.
Blum, J. M. "Tumulty and the Wilson Era." Ph.D. diss., Harvard University, 1949.
Botting, D. *The U Boats*. New York: Time Life Books, 1979.
"Blue Book" of U.K. government. London: HMSO, 1914–16.
Brinnin, J. M. *The Sway of the Grand Saloon*. London: Macmillan, 1972.
Bryan, W. J., and Bryan, M. B. *The Memoirs of William Jennings Bryan*. Chicago and Philadelphia: John C. Winston, 1925.
Burton, D. H. *Cecil Spring-Rice, a Diplomat's Life*. London and Toronto: Fairleigh Dickinson, University Press, 1960.
Busch, F. O. *U-Boots—Taten*. Berlin: Reimar Hobbing Verlag, 1934.
———. *U-Bootsfahrten*. Berlin: Franz Schneider Verlag, 1938.
Butler, D. A. *The Lusitania*. Mechanicsburg: Stackpole Books, 2000.
Calhoun, F. S. *Power and Principle*. Kent: Kent State University Press, 1986.

Champney, F. *Art and Glory—the Story of Elbert Hubbard*. Kent: Kent State University Press, 1983.

Cherny. R. W. *A Righteous Cause*. Boston: Little, Brown and Company, 1985.

Chidsey, D. B. *The Day They Sank the Lusitania*. New York: Award Books, 1967.

Churchill, R. *Winston S. Churchill's Youth, 1874—1900*. Boston: Houghton Mifflin, 1966.

Churchill, W. S. *World Crisis*. Revised edition. London: Thornton Butterworth, 1931.

Clark, C. *Kaiser Wilhelm II*. London: Longman, 2000.

Coleman, T. *The Liners*. London: Allen Lane, 1976.

Command 8012, Austrian and German Papers Found in the Possession of Mr. James F. Archibald, Falmouth, August 30 1915. London: HMSO, 1915.

Compton-Hall, P. R. *Submarine Boats*. London: Conway Maritime Press, 1983.

Craig, J. D. *Danger Is My Business*. New York: Simon and Schuster, 1938.

Daniels, J. *The Wilson Era*. Vol. 1, *The Years of Peace, 1910—1917*. Chapel Hill: University of North Carolina Press, 1944—46.

Dickens, C. *American Notes*. Ed. J. L. Griffith (University of Virginia). wwwpeople. virginia.edu.

Dos Passos, J. *Mr. Wilson's War*. London: Hamish Hamilton, 1963.

Dumba, C. *Memoirs of a Diplomat*. Boston: Little, Brown, and Company, 1932.

Ellacott, S. E. *Ships Under the Sea*. London: Hutchinson, 1961.

Ellis, F. D. *The Tragedy of the Lusitania*. Philadelphia: National Publishing Company, 1915.

Esposito, D. M. *The Legacy of Woodrow Wilson*. Westport, Conn.: Praeger, 1996.

Evans, H. *The American Century*. London: Jonathan Cape, 1998.

Fischer, F. *From Kaiserreich to Third Reich*. London: Allen and Unwin, 1986.

———. *Germany's Aims in the First World War*. London: Chatto and Windus, 1967.

Fisher, Admiral Lord J. A. *Memories*. London: Hodder and Stoughton, 1919.

———. *Records*. London: Hodder and Stoughton, 1919.

Foreign Relations of the U.S., the Lansing Papers. Vols. 1 and 2. Washington, 1939.

Foreign Relations of the U.S., 1915 and 1916 Supplements. Washington.

Forstner, Commander von. *Journal*. Trans. Mrs. Russell Codman. Boston: Houghton Mifflin, 1917.

Frederick, Empress. *Letters*. London: Macmillan, 1929.

Frost, W. *German Submarine Warfare*. London: D. Appleton, 1918.

Fyfe, H. C. *Submarine Warfare, Past, Present, and Future*. London: Grant Richards, 1902.

Garrett, R. *Submarines*. London: Weidenfeld and Nicholson, 1977.

Caycr, Admiral von. *Die deutschen U-Boote in ihrer Kriegfuhrung, 1914—1918*. Vol. 2, Berlin: E. S. Mittler, 1930.

Gentile, G. *The Lusitania Controversies*. Vols. 1 and 2. Philadelphia: Gary Gentile Productions, 1988 and 1989.

Gerard, J. W. *My Four Years in Germany*. London and New York: Hodder and Stoughton, 1927.

Gibson, R. H. *The German Submarine War, 1914—1918*. London: Constable, 1931.

Gilbert, M. *The First World War*. London: HarperCollins, 1995.

———. *A History of the Twentieth Century*. Vol. 1, 1900—1933. London: HarperCollins, 1997.

———. *Winston S. Churchill, 1914—16*. Vol. 3. London: Heinemann, 1971.

———. *Winston S. Churchill, 1914—16*. Companion vol. 3. London: Heinemann, 1973.

Gray, E. *The Devil's Device*. London: Purnell Book Services, 1975.

Gregory, R. *Walter Hines Page*. Lexington: University Press of Kentucky, 1970.

Groner, E. *Die deutschen Kriegsschiffe, 1815–1945*. Koblenz: Bernard and Graefe Verlag, 1985.

Groos, D. *Der Krieg in der Nordsee*, Vol. 4. Berlin: E. G. Mittler, 1924.

Gwynn, S. *The Letters and Friendship of Sir Cecil Spring-Rice*. Boston: Houghton Mifflin, 1929.

Hendrick, B. J. *The Life and Letters of Walter Page*. Vols. 2 and 3. New York: Doubleday, Page, 1926.

Henshel, A. E. *The Lusitania Case by Historicus Junior*. New York: Masterson, 1915.

Herzog, B., and Schonmaekers, G. *Ritter der Tiefe—Graue Wolfe*. Munich: Verlag Welsermuhl, 1965.

Hickey, D., and Smith, G. *Seven Days to Disaster*. London: Collins, 1981.

Hoehling, A. A., and Hoehling, M. *The Last Voyage of the Lusitania*. Lanham, Md.: Madison Books, 1996.

Holbourn, Professor I. B. S. *The Isle of Foula*. Lerwick: Johnson and Greig, 1938.

Horgan, J. J. *Parnell to Pearce, Some Reflections*. Dublin: Browne and Nolan, 1948.

Horne, C., and Austen, W. F. *Source Records of the Great War*. 7 vols. Indianapolis: National Alumni Press, 1923.

Hough, R. *First Sea Lord*. London: Allen and Unwin, 1969.

Houldermann, B. *Albert Ballin*. London: Cassell, 1922.

Hurd, A. *Murder at Sea*. London: T. Fisher Unwin, 1915.

Inglis, B. *Roger Casement*. London: Hodder and Stoughton, 1973.

Ireland, Dr. J. de Courcy. *The Sea and the Easter Rising*. County Dublin: Maritime Insitute of Ireland, 1996.

Jackson, S. *J. P. Morgan, the Rise and Fall of a Banker*. London: Heinemann, 1984.

James, Admiral Sir William. *The Code Breakers of Room 40*. New York: St. Martin's Press, 1956.

Johnson, N. M. *George Sylvester Viereck*. Champaign, Ill.: University of Illinois Press, 1972.

Jones, J. P. *America Entangled*. New York: A. C. Laut, 1917.

Keegan, J. *The First World War*. London: Pimlico, 1999.

Kirchhoff, Vice Admiral H. von, and Sanders-Bremen, F. *Der Weltkrieg zur See*. Berlin: Askanischer Verlag, 1916.

König, P. *Die Fahrt der "Deutschland."* Berlin: Ullstein, 1916.

———. *Fahrten der U "Deutschland" im Weltkrieg*. Berlin: Ullstein, 1937.

Lansing, R. *War Memoirs*. London: Rich and Cowan, 1935.

Latham, R. and Matthews, W., eds. *The Diary of Samuel Pepys*. London: G. Bell, 1970.

Lauriat, C. E. *The "Lusitania's" Last Voyage*. Boston: Houghton Mifflin, 1915.

Ledoux, K. *Ocean Notes and Foreign Travel for Ladies*. New York: Cook, Son and Jenkins, 1878.

Link, A. S. *Woodrow Wilson—Revolution, War, and Peace*. Arlington Heights, Ill.: AHM Publishing, 1979.

———. *Woodrow Wilson—the Struggle for Neutrality*. Princeton: Princeton University Press, 1960.

———. *The Papers of Woodrow Wilson*. Vols. 30, 31, 32, and 33. Princeton: Princeton University Press, 1980.

Bibliography

Lord, Walter. *A Night to Remember*. London: Penguin, 1976.

Luetzow, F. *Der "Lusitania" Fall*. Leipzig and Munich: Sueddeutsche Monatshefte, 1921.

Lutz, R. H. *Fall of the German Empire, Documents, 1914–18*. Vol. 1. Stanford, Calif.: 1932.

MacDonogh G. *The Last Kaiser*. London: Weidenfeld and Nicholson, 2000.

MacKay R. *Fisher of Kilverstone*. Oxford: Oxford University Press, 1973.

Marcosson, I. F. and Frohman, D. *Charles Frohman: Manager and Man*. London: John Lane/The Bodley Head, 1916.

Marder, A. J. *Anatomy of British Sea Power*. New York: Octagon Books, 1976.

———. *From the Dreadnought to Scapa Flow*. Vols. 1–4. Oxford: Oxford University Press, 1961–66.

———, ed. *Fear God and Dread Nought, the Correspondence of Admiral of the Fleet, Lord Fisher*. Vols. 1, 2, and 3. London: Jonathan Cape, 1952–59.

Marshall, L., ed. *Horrors and Atrocities of the Great War Including the Tragic Destruction of the* Lusitania. New York: L. T. Myers, 1915.

Massie, R. K. *Dreadnought—Britain, Germany, and the Coming of the Great War*. London: Jonathan Cape, 1992.

Masson, P. *Les Naufrageurs du Lusitania et la Guerre de L'Ombre*. Paris: Albin Michel, 1915.

Maxtone-Graham, J. *The North Atlantic Run*. London: Cassell, 1972.

Mayer Hearings, United States District Court, Southern District of New York, Steamship Lusitania Petition of Cunard for Limitation of Liability Before Hon. J. M. Mayer (all in Federal Archives, New York):

   a. *Opinion*
   b. *Transcript of Oral Hearings*
   c. *Evidence Taken Before Commissioner R. V. Wynne in London*
   d. *Brief on the Facts for the Petitioner*

McAdoo, W. G. *Crowded Years*. Boston: Houghton Mifflin, 1931.

McWhirter, N. *Book of Millennium Records*. London: Virgin Publishing, 1999.

Mielke, O. *Der Fall "Lusitania."* Schicksale Deutscher Schiffe No. 78. Munich: Arthur Moewig Verlag, 1955.

Mixed Claims Commission—(U.S. and Germany) Administrative Decisions and Opinions of a General Nature and Opinions in Individual Lusitania Claims and Other Cases to June 30 1925. Washington, D.C., 1925.

Morgan, T. *Churchill, Young Man in a Hurry*. New York: Simon and Schuster, 1982.

Morris, J. *Fisher's Face*. London: Viking, 1995.

Morton, L. *The Long Wake*. London: Routledge, 1968.

Muller, Admiral G. A. von. *Regierte der Kaiser?* Ed. W. Gorlitz. Berlin: Musterschmidt-Verlag, 1959.

Neureuther, K., and Bergen, C., eds. *U-Boat Stories*. London: Constable, 1931.

O'Byrne, R. *Hugh Lane*. Dublin: Lilliput Press, 2000.

Official German Documents Relating to the World War. 2 vols. New York: Oxford University Press, 1923.

O'Sullivan, P. *The Lusitania, Unravelling the Mysteries*. Cork: Collins Press, 1998.

Papen, F. von. *Memoirs*. London: Andre Deutsch, 1952.

Peeke, M., and Walsh-Johnson, K. *"Lusitania" and Beyond*. Wirral: Avid Publications, 2001.

Bibliography

Pelling, H. *Winston Churchill*. London: Macmillan, 1974.

Petzold, J. *Franz von Papen*. Buchverlag Union, 1995.

Ponsonby, A. *Falsehood in War-Time*. London: Allen and Unwin, 1940.

Preston, A. *Submarines*. London: Octopus, 1975.

Rappaport, A. *The British Press and Wilsonian Neutrality*. Gloucester, Mass.: Peter Smith (Stanford University Publications University Series), 1965.

Rhondda, Viscountess (Lady Mackworth). *This Was My World*. London: Macmillan, 1933.

Rintelen, Franz von (foreword by R. Doerries). *The Dark Invader*. London: Frank Cass Publishers, 1997.

Ritchie, C. *Q-Ships*. Lavenham, U.K.: Terence Dalton, 1985.

Royce, J. *The Hope of the Great Community*. New York: Books for Libraries Press, 1916. (First published in *Hibbert Journal*, October 1915)

Rumbold, Sir H. *The War Crisis in Berlin, July to August 1914*. London: Constable, 1940.

Sauder, E., and Marschall, K. *R.M.S. "Lusitania," Triumph of the Edwardian Age*. Blandford Forum, U.K.: Waterfront Publications, 1993.

Savage, C. *Policy of the United States Toward Maritime Commerce in War*. 2 vols. Washington, D.C., 1936.

Scott, Admiral Sir P. *Fifty Years in the Royal Navy*. New York: George H. Doran, 1919.

Seymour, C., ed. *The Intimate Diaries of Colonel House*. 2 vols. Boston: Houghton Mifflin, 1930.

Shipping Casualties (Loss of the Steamship "Lusitania"), Proceedings in Camera at the Formal Investigation into the Circumstances Attending the Foundering of the British Steamship "Lusitania," Command 381. London: HMSO, 1919. (Known as *The Mersey in Camera Proceedings*)

Shipping Casualties (Loss of the Steamship "Lusitania"), Proceedings on a Formal Investigation into Loss of the Steamship "Lusitania." London: HMSO, 1915. (Known as *The Mersey Proceedings*)

Shipping Casualties (Loss of the Steamship "Lusitania"), Report of a Formal Investigation into the Circumstances Attending the Foundering of the British Steamship "Lusitania," Command 8022. London: HMSO, 1915. (Known as *The Mersey Report*)

Simpson, C. *The Lusitania*. New York: Little, Brown, 1972.

Smith, D. M. *Robert Lansing and American Neutrality, 1914–1917*. New York: Da Capo Press, 1972.

Snyder, L. *The Military History of the "Lusitania."* New York: Franklin Watts, Inc., 1965.

Soames, M. *Speaking for Themselves, the Personal Letters of Winston and Clementine Churchill*. London: Doubleday, 1998.

Spindler, Admiral A. *Der Handelskrieg mit U-Booten*. Vols. 1 and 2. Berlin: E. S. Mittler, 1932 and 1933.

Sproule, A. *Port Out, Starboard Home*. Poole: Blandford Press, 1978.

Steinberg, J. *Yesterday's Deterrent—Tirpitz and the Birth of the German Battle Fleet*. New York: Macmillan, 1965.

Strother, F. *Fighting Germany's Spies*. New York: Doubleday, 1918.

Stumpf, R. *War, Mutiny, and Revolution in the German Navy*. New Brunswick, N.J.: Rutgers University Press, 1967.

Tansill, C. *America Goes to War*. Boston: Little, Brown, 1938.

Bibliography

Tantum W., and Droste C. L. *The "Lusitania" Case*. Riverside, Conn.: 7C's Press, 1972.

Terraine, J. *Business in Great Waters*. London: Leo Cooper, 1989.

Thomas, L. *Raiders of the Deep*. London: William Heinemann, 1929.

Tirpitz, Grand Admiral A. von. *My Memoirs*. Vols. 1 and 2. London: Hurst and Blackett, 1919.

Tuchman, B. *August 1914*. London: Papermac, 1980.

——. *The Proud Tower*. London: Papermac, 1980.

——. *The Zimmermann Telegram*. New York: Viking Press, 1958.

Tumulty, J. P. *Woodrow Wilson as I Know Him*. New York: Doubleday, 1921.

United States Senate Documents, 66th Congress, 1st Session, No. 62, Brewing and Liquor Interests and German and Bolshevik Propaganda. Washington, D.C., 1919.

Vanderbilt, C. *The Vanderbilt Feud*. London: Hutchinson, 1957.

Van der Vat, D. *Stealth at Sea*. London: Weidenfeld and Nicolson, 1994.

Viereck, G. S. *Spreading Germs of Hate*. London: Duckworth, 1931.

Villard, O. G. *Fighting Years*. New York: Harcourt Brace and Co., 1939.

Voska, E. V., and Irwin W. *Spy and Counterspy*. New York: Doubleday, 1940.

Wall, R. *Ocean Liners*. London: Collins, 1978.

Ward, M. *Father Maturin*. London: Longmans, 1920.

Warren, M. D. *The Cunard Turbine-Driven Quadruple-Screw Atlantic Liner "Lusitania."* Wellingborough (UK): Patrick Stephens, 1986.

Washington, G. *Letters*. 26 September 1787.

Wells, H. G. *Anticipations of the Reaction of Mechanical and Scientific Progress upon Human Life and Thought*. London: Chapman and Hall, 1902.

Werner, M. R. *Bryan*. New York: Harcourt Brace, 1929.

Whittle, T. *The Last Kaiser*. London: Heinemann, 1977

Winton, J. *The Submariners—Life in British Submarines, 1901–1999*. London: Constable, 1999.

Wynne, R. V. *Evidence Taken Before Commissioner R. V. Wynne in London*. See *Mayer Hearings*

Journals and Magazines

Where no specific dates are given, the issues appeared during the First World War.

American Historical Review (October 1935–July 1936)

American Mercury (May 1935)

American Neptune (1975)

Coronet (March 1950)

Current Events

Current Opinion

Engineering (July 1907 and March 1918)

Familia (2000)

Hansard (1913–18)

Journal of Modern History (1936)

Liberty (2 June 1928 [W. J. Flynn, "Tapped Wires"])

Listener (1972)

Literary Digest
Living Age (1925)
Marine Rundschaue (1973)
Marine Technology (October 1996 [W. H. Garzke Jr., D. K. Brown, A. D. Sandiford, J. Woodward, and P. K. Hsu, "The 'Titanic' and 'Lusitania'—a Final Forensic Analysis"])
Nation (1923)
National Geographic Magazine (April 1994)
New Statesman (1957)
New York Shipping Illustrated (1907)
Review of Reviews
Scientific American (29 May 1915)
Sports Illustrated (1962)
Strand Magazine (July, 1914)

Newspapers (Main Sources)

UNITED KINGDOM

Daily Chronicle
Daily Despatch
Daily Express
Daily Mail
Daily Mirror
Daily Telegraph
Journal of Commerce
Liverpool Daily Post and Mercury
Liverpool Echo
News of the World
Observer (1967)
Times

UNITED STATES

Boston Globe
Boston Herald
Chicago Tribune
New York American
New York Evening Sun
New York Herald
New York Sun
New York Telegraph
New York Times
New York Times Book Review (September 1999)
New York Tribune
New York World
Philadelphia Record
Providence Journal

Bibliography

Richmond Times Despatch
Washington Post

GERMANY

Berliner Tagesblatt
Bochumer Anzeiger (February 1985)
Frankfurter Zeitung
Kölnische Volkszeitung
Neue Preussische Zeitung
Norddeutscher Allgemeine Zeitung
Der Spiegel
Völkischer Beobachter (May 1935)
Vorwaerts
Vorwarts
Die Welt

IRELAND

Cork Examiner
Sunday Press (1995)

FRANCE

Chatillonais et Auxois
Le Monde (3 November 1972)

Specific Collections Consulted

Bailey, Thomas A., and Ryan, Paul B. Archive. Hoover Institution on War, Revolution, and Peace, Stanford University, Stanford, Calif., U.S.

Beesley, Patrick. Collection. Churchill College Archives, Cambridge University, Cambridge, U.K.

Bundesarchiv-Militärarchiv. Freiburg, Germany. Collection of key German naval files for the period (in particular RM2/ 127, 157, 1962, 1982, 1992; RM5/ 2981, 2982, 2983; RM8/525; RM97/578; and the Press Bureau files in the RM3 series [9771/10312]).

Bryan, William Jennings. Correspondence. Library of Congress, Washington, D.C., U.S.

Churchill, Winston. Collection. Churchill College Archives, Cambridge University, U.K.

Cunard archives, Liverpool University, U.K.

Fisher, Admiral John. Collection. Churchill College Archives, Cambridge University, U.K.

Garrison, Lindley. Papers. Seeley G. Mudd Manuscript Library, Princeton University Library, Princeton, N.J. U.S.

Hall, Reginald. Papers. Churchill College Archives, Cambridge University, Cambridge, U.K.

Hoehling, A. A. and Mary. Archive. Mariners' Museum, Newport News, Va., U.S.

Hobson, Richard. Papers. Library of Congress, Washington, D.C., U.S.

House, Colonel Edward. Diary. Yale University Library, New Haven, Conn., U.S.

Lansing, Robert. Papers. Library of Congress, Washington, D.C., U.S.

Public Record Office, London, U.K. The main files are: Admiralty series (all prefixed by letters *ADM*) 137/47, 137/113, 137/1057, 137/1058, 137/1428, 137/2958, 137/3883, 137/3912, 137/3923, 137/3956, 137/3957, 137/3958, 137/3959, 137/3960, 137/3962, 137/3963, 137/4101, 137/4152, 137/4156, 137/4161, 137/4162, 137/4168, 137/4177, 137/4353, 116/1416, and foreign office series (all prefixed by letters *FO*) 115/1805, 115/1806, 115/1808, 115/1809, 115/1843, 115/1847, 115/1936, 115/1938, 115/1943, 115/1962, 115/1979, 115/1998, 371/2587. In the Ministry of Trade series (prefixed *MT*) there is one major relevant file, MT 9/1326. This slightly scruffy file contains a number of folders, key among which are: M 1984, M 12666, M 15233, M 17227, M 198845.

Root, Elihu. Papers. Library of Congress, Washington, D.C., U.S.

Runciman, Walter. Papers. University of Newcastle, U.K.

Spring-Rice, Sir Cecil. Collection. Churchill College Archives, Cambridge University, U.K.

White, Henry. Correspondence. Library of Congress, Washington, D.C., U.S.

Wilson, Woodrow. Papers. Library of Congress, Washington, D.C., U.S.

Other Archives Consulted

Amis du Vieux Strasbourg

BBC Written Archives Centre, Caversham, Berkshire, U.K.

Bundesarchiv, Zentralnachweisstelle, Aachen, Germany

Canadian Broadcasting Company radio archives, Ontario, Canada

Cobh Heritage Centre, Cobh, Ireland

Cobh Museum, Cobh, Ireland

Deutsche Dienststelle (WASt), Berlin, Germany

Franklin D. Roosevelt Library, New York City, U.S.

Imperial War Museum document archive, London, U.K.

Library of Lincoln's Inn, London, U.K.

Merseyside Maritime Museum, Liverpool, U.K.

Merseyside Police, Liverpool

MOD Naval Historian's Department, London

National Maritime Museum, Greenwich, London, U.K.

National Maritime Museum of Ireland, Dun Laoghaire, Ireland

Naval War College, Newport, R.I., U.S.

Strasbourg Municipal Archives

U-Boat Museum Archives, Cuxhaven, Germany

U.S. Federal Archives, New York City, U.S.

U.S. Government Records, National Archives and Records Administration (NARA), Maryland and New York, U.S.

ART CREDITS

———⊶⊷⊶———

The images on the pages noted have been reproduced from the following sources.